COMMUNIST CHINA

&

ASIA

Challenge to American Policy

COMMUNIST CHINA & ASIA

Challenge to American Policy

A. DOAK BARNETT

Vintage Books
A DIVISION OF RANDOM HOUSE
New York

The Council on Foreign Relations is a non-profit institution devoted to study of the international aspects of American political, economic, and strategic problems. It takes no stand, expressed or implied, on American policy.

The authors of books published under the auspices of the Council are responsible for their statements of fact and expressions of opinion. The Council is responsible only for determining that they should be presented to the public.

Copyright, ©1960, by Council on Foreign Relations, Inc.

All rights reserved, including the right to reproduce this book or any portion thereof in any form

For information, address Council on Foreign Relations, 58 East 68th Street, New York 21

Published as a Vintage Book by arrangement with the Council on Foreign Relations

VINTAGE BOOKS
are published by ALFRED A. KNOPF, INC.
and RANDOM HOUSE, INC.

First Vintage Edition, January, 1961
Second Printing, October, 1961

Manufactured in the United States of America

COUNCIL ON FOREIGN RELATIONS

OFFICERS AND DIRECTORS

JOHN J. MCCLOY
Chairman of the Board

HENRY M. WRISTON
President

FRANK ALTSCHUL *Vice-President & Secretary*	DAVID ROCKEFELLER *Vice-President*
ELLIOTT V. BELL *Treasurer*	GEORGE S. FRANKLIN, JR. *Executive Director*
WILLIAM HENDERSON *Associate Executive Director*	FRANK D. CARUTHERS, JR. *Assistant Treasurer*

HAMILTON FISH ARMSTRONG	GRAYSON L. KIRK
WILLIAM A. M. BURDEN	R. C. LEFFINGWELL
ARTHUR H. DEAN	WALTER H. MALLORY
LEWIS W. DOUGLAS	PHILIP D. REED
ALLEN W. DULLES	WHITNEY H. SHEPARDSON
THOMAS K. FINLETTER	CHARLES M. SPOFFORD
WILLIAM C. FOSTER	ADLAI E. STEVENSON
JOSEPH E. JOHNSON	JOHN H. WILLIAMS

COMMITTEE ON STUDIES

HENRY M. WRISTON
Chairman

HAMILTON FISH ARMSTRONG	JOSEPH E. JOHNSON
ARTHUR H. DEAN	GRAYSON L. KIRK
BYRON DEXTER	AUGUST MAFFRY
CARYL P. HASKINS	WILLARD L. THORP

JOHN H. WILLIAMS

STUDIES PROGRAM

PHILIP E. MOSELY
Director of Studies

WILLIAM DIEBOLD, JR. *Director of Economic Studies*	JOHN C. CAMPBELL *Director of Political Studies*

To My Parents
EUGENE E. and BERTHA S. BARNETT

PREFACE

THIS IS a study of Communist China's growing impact on Asia and the problems it poses for the United States. It attempts to appraise the Chinese Communist challenge throughout Asia and to examine its political and economic as well as its military facets. My emphasis in the study is on the present rather than the past, and my purpose has been to stimulate serious thought on policy alternatives for the future.

I started work on the book early in 1958, when the Council on Foreign Relations organized a Study Group on Communist China and United States Policy in Asia. At a series of meetings held throughout the winter of 1958-1959, this group discussed a series of background papers in which I dealt with most of the problems which are presented in the book. Despite the controversial nature of many of the issues, our discussions were full and free.

I have profited immensely from the knowledge and insights which the members of the study group contributed, both collectively in our regular meetings, and individually in conversations with me. I am sure that the members of the group join me in expressing particular gratitude to our chairman, Joseph E. Johnson, President of the Carnegie Endowment for International Peace, for the skill with which he conducted our meetings. Every member of the group made a substantial contribution to our discussions, and I take pleasure in expressing my deep appreciation to each of them. The members were: Hamilton Fish Armstrong; M. Searle Bates; Whitman Bassow; Howard L. Boorman; Robert R. Bowie; Major General Paul W. Caraway, USA; O. Edmund Clubb; Arthur H. Dean; William Diebold, Jr.; Russell H. Fifield; James C. Graham; William Henderson; Warren S. Hunsberger; Harold R. Isaacs; Lt. Colonel Amos A. Jordan, USA; Henry R. Lieberman; John M. H. Lindbeck; Paul M. A. Linebarger; William W. Lockwood; LaRue R. Lutkins; George W. Mallory; Edwin W. Martin; George A. Morgan; Philip E. Mosely; J. Morden Murphy; C. Hoyt Price; Dean Rusk; Phillips Talbot; Richard L. Walker; C. Martin Wilbur; Kenneth T. Young, Jr.

On several occasions, guests joined our meetings and contributed their knowledge and insights on particular problems; among them were Richard Moorsteen, G. William Skinner, and Allen S. Whiting. I should like to express my special gratitude to those members and guests who served as discussion leaders at our meetings: Robert R. Bowie; John C. Campbell; Major General Paul W. Caraway; James C. Graham; William W. Hollister; John M. H. Lindbeck; Paul M. A. Linebarger; August Maffry; James W. Morley; Dean Rusk; Phillips Talbot; Richard L. Walker; C. Martin Wilbur. I am also much indebted to Arthur H. Dean, Joseph E. Johnson, and Henry M. Wriston, for reading the entire manuscript in its final stage. David J. Padwa served ably as rapporteur.

Having expressed my debt to all those named, I should like to emphasize that the statements of fact and opinion in this book are entirely my own. No attempt was made in our discussions to reach unanimous conclusions, and on most issues there were wide differences of opinion. The members of the group bear no responsibility, therefore, for what I have written.

In addition to those who participated in the Council study group, there are many others I should also like to thank. I owe a great debt of gratitude to Walter S. Rogers, Director of the Institute of Current World Affairs, who made it possible for me to study and write in China during 1947-1949, the period in which the Communists came to power. I began serious research on Communist China at that time. I should also like to express my special appreciation to Phillips Talbot and the American Universities Field Staff; they have allowed me to draw freely from numerous reports on Communist China which I wrote for them during 1952-1956. Chapters 3 and 9 are based in large part on a more detailed study which I have written for the National Planning Association, entitled *Communist Economic Strategy: The Rise of Mainland China* (Washington, D.C., 1959); I should like to acknowledge gratefully the permission granted me to use material drawn from that study, as well as the helpful advice of Henry G. Aubrey, Director of the National Planning Association Project on the Economics of Competitive Coexistence. I also offer my sincere thanks to Mrs. Alice Hsieh of The RAND Corporation; her advice and criticism assisted me greatly in preparing Chapter 10.

I am deeply indebted to the staff of the Council on Foreign Relations, which made possible the preparation of this book. In particular Philip E. Mosely, who first encouraged me to undertake this study, has made many contributions at every stage, from my initial planning to the final editing. Miss Ruth Savord, Donald Wasson, and the entire library staff have been unfailingly helpful in filling my requests for needed materials. John Kotselas, Wesley F. Strombeck, and Miss Lorna Brennan have assisted greatly in the preparation of my manuscript for the press, and Mrs. Marguerite Hatcher, Aaron Cohen, Miss Barbara Sue Stein, and Miss Sandra Collison have been tireless, faithful, and skillful in typing.

Finally, I am grateful to my wife, Jeanne. For more than a year, her patience has been severely tested, yet her encouragement and support have been unfailing.

A. D. B.

September 30, 1959
New York

CONTENTS

1.	THE CHALLENGE OF COMMUNIST CHINA	1
2.	COMMUNIST CHINA, A TOTALITARIAN POLITICAL POWER	10
3.	ECONOMIC DEVELOPMENT	38
4.	THE ROOTS OF MAO'S STRATEGY	65
5.	EVOLVING TACTICS IN FOREIGN POLICY	87
6.	MILITARY STRENGTH AND THE BALANCE OF POWER	110
7.	COMMUNIST SUBVERSION AND THE POLITICAL STRUGGLE	147
8.	THE OVERSEAS CHINESE	172
9.	TRADE, AID, AND ECONOMIC COMPETITION	211
10.	COMMUNIST CHINA'S FOREIGN POLICY: JAPAN AND KOREA	255
11.	COMMUNIST CHINA AND SOUTH AND SOUTHEAST ASIA	291
12.	THE SINO-SOVIET ALLIANCE	337
13.	TAIWAN AND THE CHINESE NATIONALIST REGIME	384
14.	THE POLICY OF NONRECOGNITION	430
15.	THE CHOICES BEFORE THE UNITED STATES	459
	APPENDIX: PEKING AND THE COMMUNIST PARTIES OF ASIA	476
	NOTES	502
	BIBLIOGRAPHIC NOTE	549
	INDEX	561

COMMUNIST
CHINA
&
ASIA

Challenge to American Policy

Chapter 1

THE CHALLENGE OF COMMUNIST CHINA

A DECADE HAS PASSED since the rise to power of a Communist regime on the China mainland. During these ten years Communist China has emerged as one of the most dynamic, disrupting, and disturbing influences on the world scene. This has probably been the most important political and strategic change in the international situation since World War II.

The coming to power of the Chinese Communists in 1949 was a major defeat for American policy in Asia. For almost half a century before 1949 the United States had viewed China as the key to American interests in that part of the world, and during the 1930s and 1940s it had supported the Chinese Nationalist regime in the hope that it could build China into a strong, unified, democratic nation, allied with the United States and exercising a stabilizing influence upon Asia. In the decade since 1949, while the Nationalists with American support have maintained a precarious existence on Taiwan, mainland China under Communist rule has become a strong, unified, and totalitarian nation, allied with the Soviet Union, intensely hostile to the United States, and posing a serious threat to the future of Asia.

Although it is clear that the establishment of the People's Republic of China was a serious blow to American interests and purposes in Asia, the question of whether or not the United States might have prevented it cannot be answered easily. The Chinese Communists did not suddenly appear out of nowhere in 1949; their victory in China came after a century of revolutionary upheaval. And although the Chinese revolution of the past century was caused, in a fundamental sense, by the impact of the West upon China, it has been too vast a force to be subject to over-all direction or control by any outside power.

From the middle of the nineteenth century onward, over-population, agrarian crises, the decline of effective government and administration—and many other domestic problems—tended to undermine China's internal stability, at a time when China was also subject to increasing pressure from the West and Japan. During the early years of the twentieth century the momentum of revolution increased greatly, and the Chinese people groped for some new basis for national reintegration. The Kuomintang, or Nationalist party, emerged first as the focus of hope for regeneration, and for many years it symbolized the driving force of the Chinese desire to modernize, to reform, and to achieve national power. But ultimately the Nationalists proved unable either to satisfy existing urges for change among the Chinese people or to provide China with a new basis for unity and stability at home and prestige abroad.

The causes of Nationalist failure were numerous and complex. The Nationalist party suffered from many internal weaknesses, and the long drawn-out war with Japan had devastating consequences in China, setting in motion forces of political and economic disintegration which Nationalist leaders were unable to control or contain. In the face of the Japanese invasion, the Nationalists failed in their attempts to overcome provincial warlordism, to cope with runaway inflation, and to maintain public morale, and the forces set loose by the war provided the Communists with their opportunity to build a successful, competing revolutionary movement.

Inspired by the Russian revolution, and especially by its slogans of anti-imperialism, a small group of Chinese Communists had embarked upon a struggle for power in the early 1920s. Then, during the 1930s and 1940s, they took full advantage of the Nationalists' weaknesses and failures, appealing to both the discontent of the peasants in China and the nationalism of Chinese intellectuals, and evolved a strategy of revolutionary guerrilla warfare which was skillfully adapted to exploit the unrest of an agrarian society in turmoil.

During the war with Japan the Chinese Communists steadily built up their military forces and extended their administrative control over wide areas of rural China, thereby consolidating a strong position which was to enable them ultimately to challenge Nationalist rule. Then, after the postwar American effort to encourage the formation of a coalition government in China broke down, the smoldering Nationalist-Communist conflict burst into full-scale civil war. Both the United States and the Soviet Union had a large stake in the ensuing struggle, but neither played the decisive role in determining its outcome. The United States supported the Nationalists, but it was unwilling to become fully entangled in the conflict. The Soviet Union gave indirect assistance to the Communists in Manchuria, but officially it adopted an aloof posture, and it avoided open intervention. The outcome of the struggle was determined, therefore, within China itself by the millions of Nationalist and Communist foot soldiers who fought the civil war to its bitter end in remote areas of the Chinese countryside.

While these revolutionary developments were taking place, most Americans were only vaguely aware of the forces at work in China. Few Americans genuinely understood the Chinese revolution, and most were not greatly concerned by it. Then, when the Chinese Communists suddenly exploded onto the international scene, the American people, realizing that the Communist victory in China was a disaster to United States interests and hopes, began asking what had gone wrong. Ever since 1949 many Americans have demanded a simple answer to the question "Who lost China?" In doing so they have tended not only to obscure and confuse the past, but also to divert attention from the pressing problems of the present and the future.

There is certainly a need to reexamine the past, in order to gain a better understanding both of the origins of the Communist victory in China and of its impact on Asia today. Too often, however, this reexamination has been concentrated upon a search for scapegoats, or it has assumed that the outcome of the Communist-Nationalist struggle was due to a few policy mistakes made by a few individuals in the United States government. This approach to a complex historical problem is not likely to be fruitful. The question which needs careful examination now is whether during the long years when the Chinese revolution was gaining momentum the United States could have developed on a broad front more effective policies which might have helped China to cope with its fundamental problems, thereby assisting the non-Communist forces in China to control and shape the future of their country. If American policy toward China in the years prior to 1949 is examined in this perspective, much can be learned which should be directly relevant to the problems the United States now faces in dealing with many other countries, particularly those in Asia and Africa, as they struggle with their multiple problems of political, social, and economic change.

The most urgent need today, however, is not to look toward the past but to grasp the present and future challenge which Communist China poses to the United States and the non-Communist nations of Asia. To the Communists, the achievement of political power on the China mainland was merely the beginning, not the culmination, of their revolution, and since 1949 the leaders of the Peking regime have relentlessly pursued ambitious domestic and international goals. Within China they have engineered one of the most tremendous and startling revolutions in history. They have mobilized the Chinese people to take part in what may well constitute the most impressive outburst of disciplined human activity ever witnessed, and they have transformed China from a weak, fragmented nation into a monolithic totalitarian state. At the same time, they have projected Communist China's influence far beyond its borders. Their military power has grown steadily, and this has had a profound impact upon the world-wide balance of contending forces. In Asia today, Peking's power and dynamism create some of the most complex and perplexing problems facing the United States and the other nations of the non-Communist world.

Under any conditions, the advent to power of a totalitarian

The Challenge of Communist China

regime in China was bound to have a significant impact upon world affairs in general and upon Asia in particular. The impact of Communist China since 1949 has been greatly magnified by the fluid state of Asian and world affairs during the past two decades. In 1949 the Chinese Communists emerged into a world characterized by an uncertain and uneasy balance of power, revolution and instability throughout Asia, and world-wide "cold war" between the Soviet Union and the United States.

World War II shattered the prewar pattern of relationships and balance of forces in Asia. Imperialist Japan was reduced to impotence, and the foundations of European colonialism in the region were undermined. At the end of the war Russian power intruded into Asia more vigorously than it had at any time since the Russo-Japanese War of 1904-1905, and the United States found itself in an unprecedented position of power, influence, and responsibility throughout the region. A new balance appeared to be emerging, but its outlines were far from clear.

During and after the war, independence movements and nationalist revolutions swept almost all of Asia. In one country after another, new or reconstituted states were established, and most of these new states were weak and unstable.

Soon after the war the pressures of Soviet ambitions and the developing rivalry between Russia and the West dissipated the wartime hopes for Soviet-American cooperation. By the time the Chinese Communists had established their new regime in Peking and had aligned mainland China with the Communist bloc in world politics, the "cold war" was already well under way, and the focus of immediate conflict already appeared to be shifting from Europe, where a rough sort of balance had emerged, to Asia, where the situation was volatile and the stakes were immense.

Since 1949 the clashes of Chinese Communist and American interests all along China's periphery have been bitter and violent. For almost half of the past decade, in fact, the United States and Communist China have been either engaged in military struggle or poised on the brink of conflict. The war in Korea from 1950 to 1953, and subsequent crises over Indo-China and the offshore islands, have intensified the deep hostility and suspicion with which the two nations view each other.

The conflict of Chinese Communist and American purposes in Asia is clearly based upon fundamental issues. Peking's leaders constantly stress their determination to "liberate" Taiwan and complete their unification of China, to force the West to accept their country as a Great Power, and to work steadily to promote the spread of communism. They regard the United States as a hostile power intervening in their domestic affairs, as the symbol of hated "capitalism" and "imperialism," and as the basic obstacle to achieving their major foreign policy objectives. The United States is making great efforts to deter Communist aggression and block the expansion of Communist influence; it is attempting to prevent the domination of Asia by any single state, to support the principles of independence and self-determination in the area, and to encourage the political and economic growth of democratic, non-Communist Asian states. From the United States' viewpoint, Communist China is the principal threat to these basic American aims and interests in Asia.

The problem of how to check the advance of Chinese Communist influence and power has dominated American policy toward Asia during the past decade, but the specific policies which the United States has evolved have not obtained general international support. They have, in fact, been subjected to continuing and fairly widespread criticism in many of the non-Communist nations allied with the United States as well as in most of the nonaligned countries.

Within the United States there has been relatively little public debate about China policy during recent years. Immediately after 1949 China policy was, it is true, an important issue in American politics, but much of the public debate at that time consisted primarily of recriminations over the past and it was notably lacking in sober, responsible analysis of the problems of the present and the future. The bitterness and emotionalism of the debate at that time inhibited serious public discussion of American policy toward China for some years thereafter. More recently, particularly since

1957, a few individuals in the United States have raised questions about China policy or proposed certain modifications of it. But undoubtedly it is still true that there is less responsible public discussion in the United States of China policy than of any other foreign policy question of comparable importance.

The first requirement for responsible examination of American policy toward China is a wider understanding of the profound and growing challenge which Communist China poses to the United States throughout Asia. The American public now lacks this understanding, mainly because the reporting, research, and writing required to create it are largely lacking. For almost a decade the United States has not had any regular newspaper correspondents in Communist China, and although a few American scholars have attempted to study the Chinese Communists' domestic and foreign policies, there is not a single important research center in the United States, outside the government, which is now concentrating its main effort on the study of Communist China. The lack of adequate basic research as well as of current news reporting makes it difficult even for the specialist, to say nothing of the American public as a whole, to try to understand Communist China and what it means for Asia and the United States. Yet it is essential that the American public understand the challenge which Communist China poses.

The starting point for any analysis of this challenge must be the realization that the United States and other non-Communist nations are engaged in a long-term struggle with Communist China throughout Asia. This contest is now taking place, and will continue to take place, on many different levels and in many different fields—ideological, political, and economic, as well as military. Communist China's strength and its influence throughout Asia are growing steadily, and the United States must face up to this fact. It must recognize that a heavy commitment of American resources—intellectual and moral as well as material—will be required to check the expansion of Communist China's influence and to support the growth of viable, non-Communist Asian states able to preserve their independence, resist Chinese Communist pressures, and generate their own political and economic dynamism.

During recent years American policy toward Communist China has been shaped in large part by the military and strategic problems along China's immediate periphery, and especially by the direct conflict of Chinese Communist and American interests over Taiwan. While these problems are of great importance, preoccupation with them has led many Americans to look upon the struggle between the United States and Communist China primarily in military terms, instead of viewing the military problems merely as one aspect of a much broader, long-term contest.

Any examination of the many-sided challenge of Communist China must deal with a wide range of questions and problems. It should logically start with a realistic appraisal of the strength and weakness of Communist China's domestic base, the stability of its rule at home, and the prospects for its economic development. To understand how Peking's leaders look on world politics, it is necessary to assess carefully their basic motivation and philosophy and to grasp both their short-term foreign policy tactics and their long-range strategy. A close look should be taken at how Peking utilizes its major instruments of foreign policy—diplomacy, military power, Communist subversion, Overseas Chinese minority groups, trade and aid. Communist China's relations with the Communist bloc as a whole and its policies toward the countries along its periphery should be examined in some detail. The present position and prospects for the future of the Chinese Nationalist regime on Taiwan require careful appraisal. And the many problems which Communist China's ambitions and tactics create for American policy—including the question of recognition or nonrecognition of the Peking regime—must be analyzed in the context of the broad, long-term problem of meeting the Chinese Communist challenge throughout Asia.

There is certainly no panacea which can produce quick and easy "solutions" to the problems which Communist China poses. And there are bound to be honest differences of opinion in evaluating both the problems and the relative effectiveness of alternative policies designed to meet them. What is beyond dispute, however, is the pressing need for greater understanding of the problems, since it is only on the basis of such understanding that the American people can intelligently evaluate the various policy alternatives which are open to the United States.

Chapter 2

COMMUNIST CHINA, A TOTALITARIAN POLITICAL POWER

During the past decade one of the most far-reaching political revolutions in history has taken place in China. In a few short years the Chinese Communists have established a strong, monolithic, totalitarian regime which has brought the most populous nation in the world under tight political, social, and psychological control. They have demonstrated with frightening efficiency how the dynamism of a totalitarian state and the power of its "organizational weapon" can be applied even in a nation of roughly 650 million people with deep-rooted traditions which clash with totalitarian discipline. Today Communist China is a huge mass in motion under strict control. Virtually the entire population of the country has been organized, regimented, and mobilized in support of the revolutionary goals set by Peking's new leaders.

There is, it is true, considerable evidence of disaffection within Communist China. Widespread currents of popular dissatisfaction have come to light to a greater extent since 1956-1957 than at any time since the Peking regime was established. Although the expression of this dissatisfaction has been suppressed by rigorous controls, its sources have certainly not been removed. In some regions of mainland China, furthermore, there have continued to be clear signs of political unrest and of dissatisfaction with the policies and demands of the Communist regime. In Tibet, in particular, there has been open revolt. But this evidence of internal unrest and dissatisfaction in Communist China must be weighed together with other evidence which indicates that the Peking regime undoubtedly has the ability to control the mass of the Chinese people and to press forward toward its basic goals.

The fact that totalitarian rule and revolutionary upheaval have produced disaffection in China is less surprising than the fact that Peking has established an awesome degree of control over China's huge population. The Chinese Communist regime has undoubtedly exercised its power more effectively during the first decade of its rule than the Soviet regime did during a corresponding period, and in all probability Mao Tse-tung's government now exercises more extensive and thorough control over the Chinese people than any previous regime in China's history.

The speed with which the Chinese Communists consolidated their political power after 1949 was in itself remarkable. Within a very few years they had achieved several of their basic political aims. They had restored centralized Chinese rule over a large part of the traditional Chinese empire, including important borderland areas—Manchuria, Inner Mongolia, Sinkiang (Chinese Turkestan), and Tibet— which had not been effectively controlled by the central government for many years. They had destroyed the political and military roots of warlordism and provincial regionalism, which had plagued and weakened every Chinese national government between 1911 and 1949. They had established an effective central government, capable of making clear-cut decisions and formulating national policies and possessing both the will and the organizational apparatus to implement its policies. And they had built up a totalitarian party-government-army structure which carried central authority and control down to the village level in a way unprecedented in Chinese history.

There are several facts which help to explain the rapid success of the Chinese Communists in establishing their control. By 1949 the mass of Chinese people, exhausted by years of war and civil strife, had lost all enthusiasm about the Nationalists and were prepared to accept almost any rulers who could reestablish peace. Knowing almost nothing of political democracy, and accustomed to authoritarian control, they had little basis for judging what Communist rule might mean. The Nationalist regime collapsed, leaving a vacuum, and the leadership as well as the military, ideological, and organizational framework for mobilizing effective resistance on the China mainland disappeared. The Communists moved into this vacuum and rapidly achieved a monopoly of control over the real centers and instruments of power. They then proceeded to impose a new totalitarian pattern of organization upon the Chinese people.

The organizational skill which the Chinese Communists quickly demonstrated after 1949 can only be understood if two further important facts are remembered. First, by 1949 the Chinese Communist party had over 28 years of revolutionary struggle behind it. For many years it had controlled large areas of rural China, ruling millions of people, and in the process it had acquired valuable administrative experience. Second, the Chinese Communists could and did draw upon the Soviet regime's four decades of experience. They borrowed, adapted, and refined many Soviet techniques of political control and—equally important—they avoided many of the Russians' mistakes. In 1949 the Chinese Communists assumed power with a much greater sense of assurance and self-confidence than the Bolsheviks had felt in 1917.

Military Control

The initial take-over of power by the Communists in China was accomplished by the People's Liberation Army. It was military force, therefore, which first impressed upon the mass of Chinese people the power of the new regime, and Peking's huge armies, under close Communist party control, still provide the ultimate guarantee of the party's monopoly of political power.

From the start the Chinese Communists systematically and ruthlessly crushed all signs of armed or open resistance. Direct military control of the country was exercised for some years by military and administrative committees, headed in most cases by generals. Fairly widespread guerrilla opposition persisted until about 1952—although it generally lacked unified purpose or organization. But since then, even though there have been a number of isolated local uprisings, and a major revolt in Tibet, no group in China has been able successfully to challenge Peking's will.

Since their initial assumption of power the Chinese Communists have generally attempted to keep their military forces in the background of their domestic controls, but they nonetheless maintain an effective military system of "public security" and militia forces which, in effect, occupy and garrison the whole country. During recent years there have been perhaps as many as a half million "public security" troops located at key centers throughout the nation, numerous "people's armed police" in the *hsien* or counties, and millions of militiamen in the villages. Furthermore, in a few areas of the country, most notably in China's border regions, the army also fulfills broad economic and political functions and continues to play a very direct part in enforcing Chinese Communist rule; in Tibet Peking has had to revert to open military rule since the revolt of early 1959.

The Chinese Communists' military forces are much more effectively organized, trained, and controlled than were comparable forces in China in the past. A high percentage of the military are members of the Communist party, and all members of the armed forces are subjected to intensive indoctrination. From time to time, the leadership detaches military personnel from army duties and assigns them to important functions in implementing Peking's economic and political policies. During the 1958 communization campaign, for example, many soldiers were sent to help organize the new communes. The army has also been used fairly widely in certain economic development projects, particularly for public works which require a fairly high degree of discipline or skill.

The duty of the public security forces and militia in China is to enforce order and guarantee the control of the Communist party. Since the initiation of Peking's communization program, the political role of military and semimilitary organizations appears to have become even more important than previously. During 1958 tens of millions of peasants were brought into the expanded militia, and thousands of demobilized servicemen were assigned to organize and train them. It is not wholly clear how far the expanded militia has been developed since then, but the communes, even as modified since late 1958, seem to have introduced many military features into rural China, and the military forces appear to have assumed a new importance at the level of the villages.

Despite the importance of direct military power in the establishment and consolidation of Communist rule in China, however, the role of the army in domestic affairs today should not be exaggerated. The army is not an independent source of power; it is an instrument of the Communist party and is clearly subordinated to the party. It is merely one of many instruments through which the Communists rule the country.

One-Party Rule

The Communist party is the ultimate political authority and the source of all important decision-making on the mainland of China today. It directs and controls the army, the government, the mass political organizations and, in fact, every element in the extraordinarily extensive political apparatus of the Peking regime. It is a Leninist organization, based upon the principles of "democratic centralism," and is controlled by a hierarchy which effectively wields authority from the top—from the 7 members of the Politburo Standing Committee, the 20 members of the Politburo, and the 193 regular and alternate members of the Central Committee—down to the tens of thousands of local party branches. By late 1957 the party contained 12.7 million members—and was the largest Communist party in the world—while its auxiliary, the Young Communist League, had 23 million members. Together, the members of these two organizations, amounting to about 5 per cent of China's population, effectively control and direct roughly 650 million people.

The membership of the Chinese Communist party blankets the country and infiltrates every important locality and activity. At every level there is a complex and effective system of interlocking directorates, which link the party with the army, government, and all other important organizations. The

A Totalitarian Political Power

party has maintained a degree of unity and discipline which is remarkable, particularly when viewed in the context of China's past. Historically, the Chinese have not been noted for giving priority to political loyalties or for exhibiting organizational discipline.

There is no easy explanation for the Chinese Communists' success in uniting their party's members and in getting the party's adherents to adopt new values and a new way of life which in many respects seem "un-Chinese." Several factors, however, are clearly important. One is the positive nationalistic and ideological appeal which the Chinese Communists exert. In a country where traditional values have decayed and alternative modern ideologies have been discredited, Marxism-Leninism has exerted a definite appeal to many, because its basic philosophy purports to explain man, society, and history and to predict the future. Many have been attracted by the Maoist application of Marxist principles to China, which defines a clear course of social and political action, and by the nationalism inherent in the Communists' vision of a modernized and powerful China. In a situation of revolutionary upheaval and change, the party has attracted people, particularly younger men and women, who were dissatisfied with the past. And, since achieving a virtually total monopoly of power, it has controlled all the channels through which people who wish to acquire status, prestige, and influence can achieve their ambitions.

The party's organizational system helps to explain the effectiveness of party discipline. It combines careful selection, indoctrination, training, and testing of new members with built-in procedures for mutual surveillance and checks on individual behavior. Another factor of great importance is the stress placed by party leaders in China upon constant "inner party struggle" to keep the membership on its toes. By comparison with the Soviet Communist party, the Chinese party has carried out few bloody purges among its own membership, but it has conducted an almost constant process of relatively nonviolent purging. One "inner party struggle" has followed another since the first "rectification" movement of 1942-1943, the latest being the "rectification" campaign initiated in early 1957. Often these campaigns of selective tightening up within the party have been combined with efforts to indoctrinate broader segments of the population, and party leaders have stated that this process will continue in the future. In November 1957 Mao Tse-tung declared: "In the future we aim to conduct a rectification campaign every year or every other year—a very short campaign—as one of the main methods of resolving various social contradictions in our country during the whole period of transition [to socialism and communism]."[1]

The Communist Leadership

One of the greatest sources of organizational strength of the Chinese Communist party has been the unity and continuity of its top leadership. By comparison with most Communist parties, the Chinese party has experienced very few factional struggles which have reached the point of threatening the cohesion of the organization. In striking contrast with the Russian Communist party, it has accepted the top authority of a single man for more than 20 years; since 1935 Mao's personality and strong leadership have been a major unifying force within the party. During the past few years the only serious challenge to party unity at the top was the alleged attempt during 1954-1955 of two Politburo members, Kao Kang and Jao Shu-shih, to achieve positions second only to that of Mao himself. Their efforts were unsuccessful, and they were purged; after a subsequent tightening up of its organization, the party's strength appeared to be unimpaired.

There has been considerable speculation outside China about the possible existence of cliques among top-level Chinese Communist leaders—such as a nationalist clique and an internationalist clique (the latter ostensibly linked more closely with Moscow). Clearly, there have been important differences of opinion among top leaders over some major policies, but available evidence does not confirm the speculation about significant clique divisions. The members of the Chinese Communist Central Committee and Politburo—

most of whom have played leading roles in the party since the early days of its struggle for power—have kept nearly all of their private disagreements from public view and have successfully maintained an impressive degree of unity. A comparison of the party Central Committee elected at the Eighth Party Congress of 1956 with the previous Central Committee elected by the Seventh Party Congress of 1945 reveals few significant changes in leadership.[2] Despite the many internal tensions in China since 1956, no major purges of top party leaders had taken place by the early autumn of 1959; however, certain signs of increased tensions within the leadership had appeared, and conceivably these might lead to purges in the future.

Government and Administration

The present structure of governmental administration in China, modeled in general upon that of the Soviet Union, and, like that of the Communist party, based upon the principles of "democratic centralism," is completely the creature of the party. Communist party members occupy the strategic positions in government at all levels. This has been the case in large measure ever since the "People's Republic" was first established in 1949 under a provisional constitutional document, the Common Program, and it has been even more true since the promulgation of a formal constitution in 1954.

The government still employs many non-Communist civil servants, and it even continues to maintain the façade of a "united front," with representation from several minor "parties." But the Communists are frank in stating that policy decisions on key problems are first made by the party's Central Committee, and many major statements of policy in China are actually issued either jointly by the party's Central Committee and the State Council, or Cabinet, or by the Central Committee alone.

The huge size of China's government, and the extreme concentration of decision-making authority, make for cumbersome bureaucratism and inefficiency, but at the local level there is little questioning of the authority which emanates from the top. One of the most significant differences between present and past governments in China is the fact that decisions made at the top are now actually translated into implementing action throughout the country, whereas formerly there was an enormous gap between the formulation of policy and its implementation. Suppression of graft and corruption has been an important element of the Communists' efforts to make government administration an effective instrument of their rule. Although corruption has an almost inevitable tendency to reappear, the Communists have largely stamped it out through their vigorous anticorruption campaign of 1951-1952 and continuous measures taken since then.

Although the mass of ordinary Chinese do not take part in political decision-making under Communist rule and, furthermore, have less real control over their own lives now than in the past, virtually everyone in China is at present involved in political organizations and processes of various sorts, as well as in ritualistic elections and other political activities. The Chinese Communists' philosophy of government and political rule, based upon their so-called "mass line," calls for maximum participation by the people in strictly controlled political activities. As a result, practically the entire Chinese population is being politicized and made conscious of national affairs in an unprecedented way. The effect of this has been to increase greatly Peking's ability to mobilize the mass of people for purposes which it chooses.

The Chinese Communist regime still tolerates a number of minor political "parties," but these parties are merely small political associations of organized fellow travelers. They have no independent power and no distinctive programs differing from those of the Communists, and since the antirightist campaign of 1957 their impotence has been made steadily more apparent. The Chinese Communists have found them to be useful appendages, however, and apparently intend to go on utilizing them for a period of time, as devices for manipulating and controlling important groups such as non-Communist intellectuals, businessmen, and civil servants. Until recently maintenance of the façade of a "coalition" government has probably been an asset to Communist China in its external relations, too; it seemed to convince some Asians that Communist China was more "democratic" than the other totalitarian regimes. However, recent political trends in China—including the organization of communes—appear to have led an increasing number of Asians to look more carefully and critically at the harsh realities of Chinese Communist rule.

Control of the Population

The most revolutionary political innovation in China under Communist control has been the totalitarian regimentation of the entire population, which has extended centralized political control down to the level of the village and the individual.[3] Peking's instruments of persuasion have effectively mobilized the energy and enthusiasm of millions of potential supporters, and its instruments of repression have forced almost everyone else to conform and submit with a kind of collectivized docility. Practically every distinguishable occupational, economic, or social group in China has been organized, and virtually everyone has been brought into some type of party-controlled organization. The Chinese Communists have complete control not only over the educational system, but also over all media of communication. An effective police force, organized on a national basis and with both uniformed and secret branches, is ubiquitous and effective. The courts are partisan organs used to enforce the party's will. The entire urban population is organized into small residents' units under police supervision. The rural population was organized first into various types of collective groups, and then in 1958 it was herded into the new communes. An effective system of mutual surveillance and anonymous denunciation encompasses virtually everyone in Communist China, and the all-pervasive web of political organization creates an atmosphere in which ordinary people feel themselves to be under constant scrutiny by the political authorities.

One of the most remarkable features of Peking's techniques

of political control is the extraordinary attention which the Chinese Communists devote to what people think as well as what they do. Quite clearly they regard ideology as the cement which holds together and activates their political apparatus, and they give a high priority to the continuous propagation of "the faith" within the party and among its supporters. Going beyond this, the Chinese Communists are also attempting to indoctrinate the entire Chinese population in the new ideology, to change its basic patterns of behavior and human relations.[4] They are trying to root out traditional Chinese thought and modern Western ideas alike in order to implant new Marxist ideas and values in their stead. There is a revivalist flavor to much that they do, and they show the determination of zealots in demanding not only passive acquiescence to their control but also positive conversion to their beliefs. Their fundamental approach to dissidents and opponents is to attempt to "remold" their thinking and attitudes.

One of the Chinese Communists' major instruments for this "remolding" or "thought reform"—called "brain-washing" in the West—is the *hsüeh hsi* group, or study group.[5] A large part of the population, especially in urban areas, has been organized into small study groups in which they learn by rote the new orthodoxy and are put under great pressure to confess and denounce their past errors.

It is difficult to judge what the real effect of all of this intensive indoctrination is. Undoubtedly many of the older generation and some of the youth retain dissident views in private, even though publicly they may submit to authority. The impact upon the values and attitudes of a large proportion of the younger generation has been unquestionably very great, however. A new generation is being nurtured on Marxist concepts about the nature of man, society, and history.

Through both organization and indoctrination, the Chinese Communists have demonstrated a startling power to control enormous masses of people—a power which seems almost to add a new dimension to traditional concepts of political power. They have mobilized the manpower, resources, and skills of the nation for military purposes, for economic development, and for planned and engineered social revolution. The degree of mobilization has been of a type which non-Communist countries do not even attempt—except during periods of war.

Social Revolution

The Communists have also been carrying out the greatest social and economic revolution in Chinese history. Their aim has been not only to develop a modernized, industrialized, and socialized economy, but also to alter fundamentally the social institutions, habits of thought, and patterns of human behavior in China. Through a succession of mass campaigns led by the party they have attacked the foundations of traditional Chinese society and have tried to "remold" the entire country. Their major campaigns have periodically convulsed the nation, keeping the Chinese people off balance, and have moved China steadily along the road toward the kind of society, under total state control, which Peking's leaders have accepted as their goal. These campaigns have greatly weakened the fabric of traditional Chinese society, depriving one group after another of its previous basis for independent influence or action.

The agrarian reform campaign, involving nation-wide redistribution of landlords' holdings as a preliminary step toward collectivization, destroyed the traditionally dominant landowning class in rural China and basically altered Chinese social structure at the village level. Several millions of landlords and their families were killed in the process. The campaign against "counterrevolutionaries," first conducted in 1951-1952 and renewed in 1955, instituted a violent reign of terror in which hundreds of thousands of people accused of activities hostile to the regime were publicly executed. The "Resist-America Aid-Korea" campaign, by exploiting Peking's allegation that the United States planned to invade and conquer China, aroused intense nationalistic feelings; it also was an important step in the Communists' continuing effort to stamp out "bourgeois" and pro-Western attitudes. The "Three Anti" and "Five Anti" campaigns, particularly the latter, undermined the business class, charging industrialists and merchants with numerous types of illegal and subversive activities, and reduced them to submissiveness. The collectivization campaign in the villages, which after a relatively gradual beginning was pushed at a spectacular pace in the winter of 1955-1956, was without doubt one of the most remarkable examples of planned social engineering in history. In a society which for almost two millennia had been based primarily upon small-scale individual farming, almost a half-billion people were herded together within a few short months and with a minimum of effective opposition into collective farming units which altered the whole pattern of their traditional life. During the same brief period, in 1955-1956, the remaining private entrepreneurs in China, a group long renowned throughout Asia for aggressive commercialism, were organized into state or semisocialized economic units, and they created a remarkable spectacle by participating in public "celebrations" to mark their acceptance of socialization. All these changes pale, however, before the program of communization on which the Chinese embarked in 1958.

The Communes

The first model of the new communes, called "Sputnik," was formed in China in April 1958. Then in late August the Chinese Communist Central Committee issued a directive calling for nation-wide communization, and by the end of 1958 virtually all the collective farms in China, over 700,000 in all, had been merged into over 26,000 huge communes. In the space of a few months a radically new form of organization had been imposed upon China's rural population.[6]

Since late 1958, it is true, the Chinese Communists have backed away from some of the ultimate goals outlined in the Central Committee's resolution of August 1958,[7] but they have nonetheless proceeded with their attempts to consolidate these new rural units.

The communes are tremendous organizations. Each one usually includes all the people in a *hsiang* or township, and the average membership is 5,000 families. They have generally been formed by merging all existing collectives within a single *hsiang,* and they have taken over the local government functions of the *hsiang.* Under each commune administration various commissions and departments have been established to handle every activity in the area—agriculture, commerce, finance, education, and military affairs. The membership of each commune is organized "along military lines" into production brigades and teams for work in agriculture and industry, as well as for other functions.

At first the communes moved rapidly toward absorbing most of the vestiges of private property remaining in rural China, and although they have subsequently retreated somewhat from this goal, it appears that in time the rural population is expected to be paid on a "wage-plus-supply" basis, according to which the communes will ration and distribute some commodities "free" to members and, in addition, will pay certain wages in kind or money.

After the initial wave of communization, the Chinese Communists called for a slowdown and for a period of consolidation at the end of 1958.[8] In rural areas, where the first steps toward communization were already completed by late 1958, on paper at least, the Central Committee cautioned against too great haste in introducing some of the more radical innovations of the program. In urban and industrial areas, where the Communists had just begun experimenting with the organizing of communes, they postponed the whole program. The Central Committee also retreated ideologically, significantly qualifying the tone of its earlier statements which had implied that China was moving rapidly from the "transition to socialism" toward the stage of communism. Since then, there has been considerable evidence that in many areas the most extreme features of the communes have been modified, and in late 1959 the communes in some areas seemed to represent a transitional stage of organization between the previous collectives and the ultimate goals as announced in August 1958. There is no indication to date, however, that the party intends to relax its efforts to push steadily toward the basic goals of the program. Whether, in the process of taking two steps forward and one step back, the Chinese Communists will find it necessary to alter some of their goals remains to be seen.

The communes have portentous implications for China's future. Economically, they represent an audacious attempt to organize and mobilize the entire rural population behind a regimented, intensive campaign to develop both agriculture and rural industry. They have greatly expanded the size of the labor force which the regime can control and have increased Peking's ability to mobilize rural capital. In terms of military organization they may enable the Chinese Communists to develop relatively self-contained local units with strong militia forces. And in the ideological sphere the communes symbolize a spurt ahead toward the ultimate goal of a communist society. In its resolution of August 1958 the Chinese Communist party called the communes "the best form of organization for the attainment of socialism and gradual transition to communism" and asserted that they "will develop into the basic social units in communist society." Following Peking's partial retreat in December 1958, the Chinese Communists toned down their claims, but we do not know whether they changed their real opinions.

Perhaps the most startling features of the communes have been their social innovations. If carried through to their logical conclusion, these will give Peking a degree of political control over the Chinese population which is almost Orwellian. The aim of the communes, as expressed in 1958, is to organize the population for communal living as well as for collective labor.[9] Meals are to be eaten in communal mess halls rather than in the home. Children are to be put into communal nurseries, which ultimately are to become full-time boarding institutions. Old people are to be placed in special homes for the aged. The many functions which women have traditionally performed at home—sewing and weaving as well as child care and cooking—are to be taken over by the commune, so that women can be released from household work to participate fully, along with men, in the labors of the commune. Where practicable, the rural population is to be rehoused either in new villages or in special barracks-like buildings, and old houses are to be torn down to provide necessary building materials.

These are the most revolutionary goals of the communes—and for this reason they have already encountered the most resistance. However, the development of communal mess halls, daytime nurseries, homes for the aged, and other institutions which are designed to "liberate" women from their homes appears to have proceeded fairly rapidly, even though in some communes participation in them is currently "voluntary," and all of these measures are undermining the traditional role of the Chinese family.

The decision to embark upon the communization program is perhaps the Chinese Communists' biggest gamble to date. In treating the Chinese people callously, impersonally, and ruthlessly, as raw material to be organized and manipulated by the state for its own purposes, they may be going too far, even for a totalitarian regime. However, although Peking did backtrack somewhat in 1959, there has been no really effective resistance as yet to the communes by the Chinese people, and if the program proves successful, even in part, it will greatly augment Peking's already enormous political power over its people.

It is not possible at present to predict the long-run reactions of the Chinese people to the communes. Nor can we know how the leaders of Communist China may react to pressures from the people. Conceivably, however, growing pressures from below could force the regime to modify its program in some basic respects and to abandon those features which conflict most radically with traditional Chinese social practices. The Chinese Communists have shown considerable flexibility and adaptability in the past and have modified their policies when it was necessary to take into account political realities. If such pressures were to continue growing and Peking were to ignore them, then the foundations of the regime might well be threatened. For the present it seems probable, however, that there is less possibility for the development of effective popular protest or opposition than there was before communization.

Some Political Problems

Despite the Communists' success in imposing their totalitarian rule upon China, they have encountered many serious political problems. Some of these have traditionally plagued Chinese rulers in the past. Others are the consequences of revolutionary, totalitarian rule and of the political repression and social upheaval which it imposes.

The problem of the interplay between central and regional authority has deep roots in Chinese history. Centralization of power has been a consistent purpose of strong Chinese governments over the past two thousand years, and centrifugal forces in the direction of provincial or regional autonomy have represented a persistent counterreaction to it. On first coming into power the Communists divided China into several large regions for purposes of military control and administration and granted these regions a substantial degree of localized authority. Basically, however, any division of authority ran counter to Communist thinking, and from 1952 onward Peking took a number of steps to increase central control. Regionalism was an issue of crucial importance in the purge of Kao Kang and Jao Shu-shih, who were accused of developing their local power in defiance of central authority. At about the time of their purge, and probably as a result of it, Peking moved to dissolve regional bodies and tightened central control. The balance then swung so far in the direction of centralization, however, that it was clearly stifling local party initiative, and by 1956 the regime felt compelled to beat a partial retreat by assigning greater responsibilities to its provincial leaders.

The communization program in its early stages appeared to represent a major move toward the further decentralization of many administrative functions. In announcing the drive to communize the villages Peking's leaders played up the traditional Marxist concept of the "withering away of the state." Eventually "the function of the state will be limited to protecting the country from external aggression," they proclaimed in August 1958, "but will play no role internally." In actual practice, however, the Chinese Communists appear to have steadily increased the degree of centralized control exercised by the party, and their talk of the eventual withering away of the state during a period in which Peking has been greatly expanding its control over the villages has a completely unreal ring to it.

The relationship of military and civilian power has also raised some problems for the Peking regime. During the Communists' struggle for power in China the distinction between military and political affairs was often obscure, but a clearer demarcation between them has emerged since 1949. Until 1954 the chain of military command in China came directly under Mao and by-passed the Cabinet. The constitution of 1954, however, established a Ministry of Defense responsible to the Cabinet, and at about that time the large military districts were dissolved, the majority of well-known military leaders were assigned to posts nearer the center of power and deprived of their previous regional authority and responsibility, and a more regularized system of military organization, seemingly under closer civil control, took shape.

The Chinese Communists also face many complicated colonial problems. China is, in practice, a colonial power, even though its subject peoples are on the Asian continent rather than overseas, and the relations between the Han majority, of Chinese language and culture, and the minority non-Han peoples have been a recurrent problem throughout its history. China now has over 35 million people of minority races, classified into more than 50 groups; although they constitute only 6 per cent of China's population, they occupy over one-half of its territory. They are important politically because they are concentrated in the arc of borderlands stretching from Manchuria through Inner Mongolia and Sinkiang to Tibet, an area of great strategic importance to the Chinese, and in South China, where both they and the Han Chinese have often resisted control from political centers in the north. The minorities have tried throughout history, with varying degrees of success, to oppose Chinese political control and cultural influence, and there is considerable evidence now of dissatisfaction in the minority-inhabited borderlands.

Following in the footsteps of the conquerors of the Ch'in, Han, T'ang, Yüan, Ming, and Manchu dynasties, the Chinese Communists have attempted to strengthen their control over minority areas. They have stationed large garrison forces in these areas and have promoted the migration of Han Chinese into them. Peking has also applied new methods, modeling its policies toward minorities upon those of the Soviet Union. By combining increased political penetration, through local personnel indoctrinated by the party, with the granting of a certain measure of cultural and linguistic autonomy, it appears to have increased its control over most of its borderland regions.

In many minority areas, however, serious unrest has continued, and increased agitation for autonomy on the part of both non-Han Communist cadres and the non-Communist rank and file has been evident ever since 1956, infecting not only the Tibetans but also the Uighurs, Mongols, and other minority groups.[10]

The Tibetans have posed the greatest challenge to Peking. In mid-1957 the Communists beat a temporary tactical retreat in Tibet and responded to local pressures by withdrawing many of their Han cadres and promising not to introduce "democratic reforms" until after 1962. But Tibetan resentments against Chinese overlordship steadily built up and finally exploded in the revolt of March 1959 which forced the Dalai Lama to flee to India, where he condemned the Chinese Communists in scathing terms. But the Tibetans' attempt to challenge Peking's power was abortive,[11] and the Chinese quickly broke the back of the rebellion. Following the revolt, the Chinese Communists abandoned all pretense of respecting Tibet's autonomy, ruthlessly crushed every sign of opposition, took violent steps to increase Chinese control and to step up the process of social revolution, and exerted strong pressures on the Indian border to seal off Tibet from the outside world.

"Local nationalism" among China's minorities will undoubtedly continue to create many problems for the Communists, and in Tibet specifically continued resistance might well create major problems for Peking for a long time to come. There seems little doubt, however, that with its overwhelming power Peking can impose its will on its minority peoples under existing conditions.

Relaxation and Dissatisfaction

Throughout China widespread currents of popular discontent came to the surface in 1956 and 1957 more than at any time since 1949. Open expressions of dissatisfaction revealed tensions and grievances which had been built up during the previous six years, but they were triggered by, and would not have been possible without, a deliberate decision by top Chinese Communist leaders to loosen their controls. Following the post-Stalin relaxation in the Soviet Union and Khrushchev's attack on Stalin in February 1956, Mao Tse-tung, apparently hoping to stimulate greater initiative and responsiveness among China's intellectuals, proclaimed in May 1956 the slogan "Let All Flowers Bloom Together, Let Diverse Schools of Thought Contend." [12] Chinese intellectuals at first reacted with caution, which was not surprising in the light of past repression, but some student and worker strikes took place in 1956, and rumblings of discontent increased among the minorities. Then in the fall of 1956 the Hungarian revolution took place. It had a great impact in China, and in the spring of 1957 Mao Tse-tung admitted: "Certain people in our country were delighted when the Hungarian events took place. They hoped that something similar would happen in China, that thousands of people would demonstrate in the streets against the people's government." [13]

After the Soviet military repression in Hungary, which Peking fully endorsed, the Chinese Communists reexamined the problem of dealing with their own internal stresses and tensions—they had just completed their collectivization and socialization drive—and decided to open the valve of free expression somewhat wider, perhaps in order to let people blow off steam, perhaps as a means of uncovering critics in order to repress them later. In his famous secret speech of February 1957 "On the Correct Handling of Contradictions among the People," Mao admitted that "contradictions"—that is, political, social, and economic conflicts and tensions—were to be expected even in a socialist society. He stressed the need for differentiating between dangerous counterrevolutionary ideas ("poisonous weeds"), which should be repressed, and "contradictions among the people," which should be handled by milder methods of discussion and persuasion. At the end of April the party launched a "rectification" movement within the party's ranks, and in May it invited nonparty intellectuals to express their opinions and criticisms.

The period of relatively free expression in Communist China lasted just one month, during May and June 1957. But the results of even that brief relaxation of thought control must have been startling and disturbing to Peking's leaders, even if, as they later implied, the aim from the start had been to uncover dangerous criticism in order to counter it.[14] With some of the key figures in the minor "parties" together with some of China's most respected non-Communist intellectuals taking the lead, a flood of blunt criticism was publicly expressed regarding almost every aspect of the Communist regime. Its targets included basic Marxist ideology, political dictatorship, suppression of freedom, current economic policies, and Sino-Soviet relations. Following the intellectuals' example, spokesmen of almost every stratum of society spoke up during the month the lid was off.

Control and Repression

Then "freedom" was turned off almost as abruptly and effectively as it had been turned on. The Communist party counterattacked in a massive, antirightist campaign against its critics, and the minor "party" leaders and intellectuals were brought effectively to heel.[15] Three prominent members of the non-Communist "parties" were expelled from their ministerial posts, and more than 50 were ousted from the National People's Congress. The "rectification" movement gained increasing momentum throughout the second half of 1957 and early 1958. A significant number of important second-rank party leaders was purged, including three alternate members of the Central Committee, a number of members of provincial party standing committees, several provincial governors, a vice-minister, a leading Communist writer, and others. Well over a million bureaucratic functionaries were transferred to working jobs in the villages. During the same period there was increased evidence that various forms of peasant obstructionism were delaying consolidation of newly formed collectives. And in many minority areas expression of dissatisfaction, "local nationalism," and demands for real political autonomy became stronger.

To cope with all these symptoms of dissatisfaction, Peking expanded and developed its "rectification" and antirightist campaigns into a massive effort to isolate and root out critics of the regime and to indoctrinate the entire population. These indoctrination campaigns helped to lay the groundwork for the radical innovations in policy adopted in 1958, when the Communists embarked upon their communization program and claimed a "great leap forward" in the country's economic development.

The Communists' counterattack against disaffected elements in 1957-1958 demonstrated once again the effectiveness of their totalitarian apparatus. Disaffection alone cannot create significant opposition. Organized opposition in China would require a conjunction of several basic elements: intellectual leadership capable of providing alternative ideological appeals and programs of action, organized mass support, and military power. Such a combination is difficult to foresee as long as the Communists' apparatus of power does not weaken from within.

Both the revolt in Hungary in 1956 and the Tibetan revolt of 1959 indicate, it is true, that even in a Communist state pressures can build up to an explosion point, and desperate people can lash out against an oppressive regime even when it is fortified by a totalitarian political apparatus. There is little basis, however, for drawing a parallel between Hungary and Communist China. The Hungarians revolted against a seriously divided and internally weakened regime, which had clearly been imposed upon the country from without and therefore represented an affront to the national pride of the entire Hungarian nation. The situation is hardly comparable in China.

Future Problems

The events of 1957-1958 in China suggest that a significant segment of non-Communist intellectuals may be much less cooperative with the Peking regime in the future than they were before the brief blooming of open criticism. Their resentment, even if denied outward expression, might create new problems for Peking's leaders. But these intellectuals do not constitute an organized political force; they lack any organized mass following or control of military power. Furthermore, despite the disaffection which came into the open in 1957, it is clear that many intellectuals in China, for reasons of nationalism and ideology, continue to give the regime strong backing in its basic aims.

Peasant dissatisfaction may well be fairly widespread in China, as a result of communization, and the peasantry can create many difficulties for the regime by various forms of passive resistance. However, the speed and effectiveness of Peking's initial communization indicate a high degree of control over the villages. If in the future economic conditions in the countryside should deteriorate seriously, localized peasant revolts might take place; China has a long history of peasant revolts occurring in situations of extreme distress. However, even if such revolts should take place, they would not necessarily constitute a threat to the survival or the strength of the regime unless they were widespread, organized, and effectively led.

Control of urban areas has always been easier for Chinese regimes than control of the countryside. Furthermore, even though there is evidence of some working class grievances, Peking has definitely given preferential treatment to urban labor, and former businessmen in China appear to be thoroughly cowed and controlled. There seems to be little basis today, therefore, for effective and organized opposition developing in the cities.

Some of the minority areas may well give Peking very serious trouble, as recent events in Tibet suggest, but the Chinese Communists are undoubtedly able to maintain at least the requisite minimum of top-level control in these areas, by military measures if necessary.

Chinese Communist control seems unshakable in the foreseeable future, therefore, as long as the party maintains the centralized unity and strength of its own party-army-government apparatus. This, despite its many internal problems, it seems capable of doing. Furthermore, the consequence of increased dissidence, if it were to develop, might well be either more ruthless repression at home or diversionary adventures abroad, instead of a basic weakening of the regime.

The Chinese Communist leaders appear confident at present that they can resolve or at least cope with their internal problems and maintain essential unity. Even the Kao-Jao affair—the only serious open threat to party unity since the 1930s—appeared to have had very little effect on the party organization. In the election of a new Central Committee and Politburo in 1956, after the purge of Kao and Jao, it became apparent that no other top leaders had been relegated to obscurity, as they would most certainly have been if they had been implicated in the activities of these two men.

At present it seems unlikely that fundamental divisions among the top Chinese Communist leaders will soon occur, or that if they do take place they will undermine the strength of Peking's political apparatus. Circumstantial evidence suggests, it is true, that since 1956 significant differences on domestic policy have existed within the Chinese Politburo.[16] There was a profound difference, for example, between the proposals for orderly and relatively gradual economic development, as expounded by Chou En-lai in late 1956, and the frantic, breakneck tempo of the "great leap forward," proclaimed by Liu Shao-ch'i in early 1958. But whatever struggles may have gone on at the top levels of the party between various factions, they were well hidden from the outside world, and to date they have not, apparently, seriously weakened the party's unity.

The question of the succession to Mao Tse-tung will in time introduce an element of uncertainty into China's political situation. In a totalitarian regime, transfers of power are never simple. However, the Chinese Communists apparently have attempted to lay the groundwork for an orderly transmission of power. In the years immediately following the adoption of a constitution in 1954, a kind of balance appeared to develop between the two ranking heirs to top authority—Liu Shao-ch'i and Chou En-lai. Mao relinquished many of the responsibilities of day-to-day administration which he had carried up to that time, while Liu and Chou, the second- and third-ranking members of the party, carried the principal operational burdens of government in their capacities, respectively, as head of the Standing Committee of the People's Congress and Premier of the State Council.

Then in late 1958 Mao announced that he would relinquish his chairmanship of the government, and Liu Shao-ch'i, who assumed this post in early 1959, seemed to emerge as Mao's first choice as his successor. Despite speculation in the West that Mao was being pushed aside or demoted, there has been little or no basis for believing this to be the case. Actually, Mao has continued as chairman of the party—the real locus of power in the regime—and his retirement from the chairmanship of the government was presumably due, as the Central Committee's explanation of the move suggested, to a desire to concentrate his attention upon "questions of the direction, policy, and line of the party and the state." [17] The creation by the party of the post of honorary chairman—which is still unfilled—suggests that at some future date Mao may withdraw still further from active affairs; perhaps he expects, from this honorary position, to use his influence to facilitate an orderly succession of power, either to a single political heir or to some sort of "collective leadership."

There is, of course, no certainty that the Chinese Communists will be successful in their attempts to arrange an orderly succession to power after Mao Tse-tung passes out of the picture. Conceivably, the top party leadership could be split in a struggle for power. If such a split were paralleled by a division of loyalty among military leaders, it could threaten the structure of the regime. The unity of the regime might also be subjected to severe strains if its major programs at home were a complete fiasco or if it became involved in a major war and China were subjected to large-scale destruction. However, any split in the top leadership appears to be considerably less likely in China than in the Soviet Union, on the evidence to date of the higher degree of party unity which the Chinese Communist party has maintained. And even in the Soviet Union, it should be noted, bitter factional and personal struggles among the leaders have not undermined the strength of the Communist regime.

Unless basic changes do occur in the internal situation in Communist China, the Peking regime must be viewed not only as a viable one, but also as one which enjoys a relatively strong domestic political position despite its many internal problems and tensions.

In approaching the numerous problems which Communist China poses, the United States would be well advised to base its policy upon the premise that Peking exercises effective control over the China mainland and that in the years immediately ahead there is little prospect either for the overthrow of the Chinese Communist regime from within or for a return to the mainland by the Nationalists. The United States must also realistically accept several other premises about Communist China. Because of the strength of its internal totalitarian control, the Peking regime can devote a large part of its energies and resources to building up its military power and its international prestige. It seems to view the external world with considerable and growing self-confidence, and it possesses a high degree of flexibility and maneuverability in advancing its foreign policy aims.

There is relatively little the United States can do to influence the internal political situation in Communist

China. In practice, furthermore, it is by no means clear whether increased pressures from outside would produce desirable or undesirable effects, either upon Peking's domestic rule or upon its foreign policies. The periods of greatest conflict or tension between Communist China and the United States have in fact been periods in which the Chinese Communists have tightened their totalitarian repression and control at home. In launching its violent anticounterrevolutionary campaign during the Korean War, for example, Peking conjured up the alleged dangers of an American invasion. Likewise, the communization program of 1958 coincided with the second Quemoy crisis. And its pressures on the Indian border and Laos in late 1959 followed a period of significant internal difficulties and tensions. Of course, totalitarian regimes often justify repression at home on the grounds of alleged threats from abroad, but in any case external dangers and pressures have undoubtedly made it easier for the Communists to appeal to Chinese nationalism in order to justify their totalitarian measures and to label any opposition as treason.

Nor is it by any means certain that even if external pressures could increase Communist China's domestic political problems, this would necessarily affect Peking's foreign policy in ways which would be desirable from the United States' point of view. Very possibly, if its internal political problems took a more serious turn, Peking might respond not by concentrating its efforts more upon domestic affairs but by seeking new gains abroad. Significantly, soon after the "hundred flowers" period, with its outpouring of internal dissatisfaction, was abruptly ended in China, Peking deemphasized its "peaceful coexistence" policy and adopted a more militant posture in world affairs. Instead of responding to the evidence of increased problems at home by cutting back its risks and commitments abroad, the Chinese Communists displayed greater belligerency and recklessness than they had for several years.

The strength of Communist China's totalitarian political regime at home is an important factor in Peking's growing influence abroad. China's Asian neighbors have few illusions about the Peking regime's political strength or viability. This is true of almost all Asian leaders whether they are repelled by the Chinese Communists' ruthless methods and fearful of Peking's intentions or are fascinated and attracted by Peking's dynamism and impressed by the success the Communists have achieved in establishing national unity and in infusing China with a sense of disciplined national purpose.

Peking's success in inducing other Asian nations to follow the totalitarian path which Communist China has chosen will depend on many complex factors. Above all, it will depend upon the success or failure of the non-Communist nations in solving their own pressing problems by alternative, non-Communist methods. Meanwhile, whether it applies force or persuasion to promote its own aims abroad, Communist China will loom large in Asia as a model of communism in action and as an example of one sort of political dynamism. In this role it has, and will continue to have, a disturbing effect upon all of Asia.

Chapter 3

ECONOMIC DEVELOPMENT

COMMUNIST CHINA IS now building up its economy at a rate as high as or higher than that of any other underdeveloped nation. Since its leaders regard heavy industry as the key to great-power status in the modern world, they are concentrating their efforts on expanding this sector of the economy at an unprecedented speed. With the Soviet Union's forced industrialization as their model, and with totalitarian political control as their tool, they have undertaken a program of economic development which, if it is successful, may profoundly change the face of Asia. What Mao's regime is attempting is to apply the Stalinist formula for economic development, with some important modifications and adaptations, to an overpopulated and underdeveloped Asian country. Despite the immense problems which it still faces, Peking has effectively mobilized the skills and resources of China to this end, and it has made impressive progress, even though the Chinese people have paid a high price for it. Under present trends, Communist China will probably outstrip India in its general economic development, and it may be able, within a relatively short time, to build a heavy industrial base stronger than that of Japan, which today is the only industrialized state in Asia.

When the Chinese Communists took power in 1949, they inherited an underdeveloped economy, which had been disrupted by several decades of foreign and civil war, inflation, and weak government. Despite the great impact of the West over the past century, China was still essentially a preindustrial, agricultural nation. Some modern factories had been built, largely by Western and Japanese capital, in a few coastal centers—Shanghai was the most important of them—

and during the 1930s a center of heavy industry had been constructed by the Japanese in Manchuria. By almost any standard, however, China was one of the least industrialized of the major nations. The Nationalist government had made many efforts to improve economic conditions, but these were largely nullified by the war with Japan, the Soviet removals of industrial equipment from Manchuria right after the war, and the civil conflict with the Communists. In 1949 both industry and agriculture were operating at levels far below the best prewar years.

Farming, which occupied some four-fifths of China's huge population, was intensive in methods, and the output per acre was fairly high, but modern techniques were almost unknown to the peasants. The basic problem created by a shortage of land had been intensified by the pressure of growing population and the concentration of land ownership in fewer and fewer hands. And the standard of living of the rural population, plagued by periodic floods, droughts, and famines, remained close to subsistence levels.

The First Phase: Economic Rehabilitation

Following their formula of "revolution by stages," the Chinese Communists at first moved rather cautiously in the field of economic policy. Initially, they talked in terms of a long period of coexistence between state and private enterprise. In agriculture they began by confiscating and redistributing the landlords' holdings and played down public discussion of collectivizing the land. It was only after they had consolidated their political power that they pressed forward rapidly toward their goals of socialization and collectivization, which revolutionized completely the economy and society of China. Even at this more advanced stage the Communists attempted to assimilate the remaining businessmen and rich peasants into the new economic structure in a way which impressed many people, the Russians included, by its novelty and shrewdness.[1] In essentials the Chinese Communists have adhered to the Stalinist economic pattern, but they have also made significant adaptations to fit it to China's specific situation.

Between 1949 and 1952 the Chinese Communists' principal aim was simply to rehabilitate the economy—to repair and restore existing production capacity and achieve economic and financial stability.[2] Despite the economic strains of the Korean War, they were largely successful in this. Inflation was first slowed down and then brought to a halt by stringent fiscal and financial measures. The establishment of unified political control, the repair of transportation, the rehabilitation of existing factories, the revival of domestic trade, and the initiation of a number of large-scale public works projects resulted in a steady rise of output toward prewar levels. By 1952 Peking claimed the output of 33 major industrial products had risen to 26 per cent above prewar peak levels—16 per cent in capital goods and 32 per cent in consumer goods. This claim somewhat exaggerated the regime's accomplishments, but by the end of 1952 the rehabilitation of the economy had advanced sufficiently for Peking to proclaim the end of the "period of reconstruction" and the beginning of a "period of construction" or economic development.

From 1949 to 1952 the Chinese Communists also carried out their program of agrarian reform, eliminating landlordism and redistributing agricultural land. Through a process of violent class warfare in the villages, this program did much to undermine the traditional structure of Chinese rural society and to consolidate the Communists' control over the peasantry. In the "Three Anti" and "Five Anti" campaigns of 1951-1952 (the latter was a bitter attack against "five evils," including tax evasion and corruption, attributed to the business class), they also undermined the position of private enterprise. These campaigns, designed to disrupt and destroy any real or potential sources of resistance to further changes, were accompanied by a steady growth of state controls. In this period the Communists laid the groundwork for their future drives toward collectivization and socialization.

Economic Planning

As early as 1950 Peking's leaders started to discuss the drawing up of a long-range development program, and in 1951 they began preliminary work on an economic plan. Then in

1952 the Chinese Communists formulated in clear terms their twin goals of "socialization (including collectivization) and industrialization" in a policy statement defining "the General Line of the State for the period of transition to socialism." [3] The first Five Year Plan was officially inaugurated at the start of 1953. Although Peking had not yet completed drawing up a detailed long-range plan, it went ahead with its development program on the basis of a series of year-by-year plans. Finally, in mid-1955—well after the conclusion of important economic agreements with the Soviet Union and the end of the fighting in Korea—it was able to publish a detailed first Five Year Plan for the years 1953-1957.[4] Even this plan underwent extensive revisions in late 1955 when the leadership decided to speed up collectivization and socialization and to set bolder economic targets. Despite this start-and-stop procedure, which resulted in the detailed Five Year Plan serving only a limited planning function, from 1953 on the Chinese Communists did, in fact, embark on a very ambitious program of planned development. The targets of the first Five Year Plan and the achievements claimed for it are the best available key, in broad terms, to the economic objectives and accomplishments of the regime through 1957.

Communist China's first Plan clearly reflected the image of its Soviet model in essentials. It called for a concentration of effort on rapid industrialization so as to enable China to catch up with the more advanced industrial nations, and it gave priority to the building of heavy industry, to provide an industrial base for national power and for future economic development. It held living standards at a low level in order to make possible a steadily rising level of state investment, primarily in industry and transportation.

The ambitious goals set by the Plan for plant expansion and increased production were regarded by the Chinese Communists as merely the first step in a process requiring many decades. In mid-1955 Communist leaders spoke of China requiring some 40 to 50 years to become "a powerful country with a high degree of socialist industrialization." In late 1956 preliminary targets for a second Plan were made public at the Eighth Congress of the Chinese Communist party, and the second Plan, with targets which had meanwhile been stepped up tremendously, got under way in 1958.

First Five Year Plan

The struggle to fulfill the Five Year Plans has been a central theme of Communist policy and propaganda ever since 1953. Peking has dramatized the development effort in every possible way, for its effect at home and abroad. When the first Plan period got under way, the Chinese Communists proclaimed that "the Soviet Union of today is the China of tomorrow!" As the second Plan period started, Peking, in announcing an "upsurge" and a "great leap forward," called upon the Chinese people to surpass within fifteen years the total output of Britain in steel and other key heavy industries. Even if this goal is achieved, China will, of course, still produce only a fraction of what British output is in per capita terms; but that fact does not deprive this and similar slogans of their pyschological impact.

The investment program set for the first Five Year Plan, as announced in mid-1955, offers one of the best indicators of the Chinese Communists' scale of priorities and their general approach to economic development. According to the plan, "capital construction," or government expenditures for fixed capital investments, was to total over U.S. 18 billion dollars, averaging 3 to 4 billion dollars a year, while all "economic construction expenditures" plus supporting cultural and educational outlays were to total over 32 billion dollars during the five years.[5] These are large figures for a poor country such as China. "Capital construction" investments were allocated as follows: 58.2 per cent to industry (88.8 per cent to heavy industry and 11.2 per cent to light industry); 19.2 per cent to transportation and communications; 7.6 per cent to agriculture, forestry, and water conservation; and the remaining 15 per cent to education, health, culture, municipal utilities, banking, trade, stockpiling, and other purposes. Over 7,600 specific construction projects were called for by the Plan, including 1,600 large "above-norm" projects. A very high percentage of these were in the field of industry. Indeed, the entire Plan was heavily weighted toward the industrial sector.

The first Plan called for roughly doubling the value of gross industrial output, increasing gross agricultural output by close to one-quarter, and increasing by about one-half the gross commodity output of agriculture and industry combined. The specific target figures were 98.3 per cent, 23.3 per cent, and 51.1 per cent. To achieve these goals, the Plan demanded average annual increases in production as follows: 14.7 per cent in industry, 4.3 per cent in agriculture, and 8.6 per cent in gross commodity output.

From 1953 to 1957 the Communists pressed the Chinese people hard to meet these goals, and one austerity program followed another, all in the name of such slogans as the "small betterment of today must be subordinated to the big betterment of tomorrow." By the end of the Plan period it appeared that many of the goals had been reached and that some had been exceeded.[6] Peking claimed that it had surpassed its investment target for the Plan period and had invested over 20 billion dollars, instead of the 18 billion planned, on "capital construction." It also asserted that over 800 "above-norm" industrial projects had been completed. The value of gross industrial output, it claimed, had increased by close to 120 per cent (over 200 per cent in capital goods and 85 per cent in consumer goods produced by modern machine industry); gross agricultural output by almost 25 per cent; and gross commodity output of industry and agriculture by more than 60 per cent. These official claims implied that under the first Plan the regime had exceeded all of its major over-all economic targets except the one for consumer goods.

Evaluating Peking's official claims poses difficult problems. The Communists admit frankly that they have encountered many difficulties in securing accurate statistics. Furthermore, their statistical standards and methods have undergone numerous changes, many of which distort the regime's accomplishments. There is also the problem of translating Peking's official figures into terms meaningful in the West, since, like the Soviet Union, Communist China bases many of its figures on concepts different from those currently used in the West. In addition, the Chinese Communists deliberately use statistics for propaganda purposes and are not averse to manipulating their figures. For all these reasons, Peking's specific economic claims must be treated with caution, and as more Western economists study the Chinese economy in detail it should be possible to adjust Peking's official figures realistically. Nonetheless, there is every reason to take the basic Communist claims for the period 1953-1957 seriously. It seems legitimate, in fact, to differentiate between three periods in examining Peking's statistics. Prior to late 1954 Peking presented most of its statistics in terms of percentage increases, which were often extremely misleading. And during 1958 and 1959 it published claims which were obviously greatly inflated, a fact which was publicly admitted in August 1959. However, the figures which Peking issued between 1954 and 1957, and especially the over-all year-end figures issued up through 1957, including statistics for earlier years, appear to be fairly consistent and credible. Although some of them probably exaggerate Communist China's accomplishments, they clearly have a basis in fact, and they reflect in general terms the very significant process of economic growth which the Chinese Communists were able to launch during their first Plan period.

Growth of National Income

One meaningful way to express an over-all rate of economic growth is to define it in terms of changes either in national income or in gross national product (GNP). In late 1957 and early 1958 the Chinese Communists published, for the first time, data on the growth of national income during the first Plan, and these data revealed a rapid pace of development.[7] According to Peking's figures, Communist China's national income, computed in terms of current prices, rose from perhaps 25.8 billion dollars in 1952 to 41.5 billion dollars in 1957. Expressed in terms of constant (1952) prices, it rose from 25.8 billion dollars in 1952 to 39.5 billion dollars in 1957. In short, Peking claimed that China's total national income had increased by over one-half during the first Five Year Plan. The claimed per capita increase in national income was, of course, lower, probably closer to 38 per cent, because of a population rise estimated at 11.6 per cent.

A number of economists in the United States have attempted to make their own independent calculations of China's rate of growth, based on Western methodology. William W. Hollister's estimates indicate that during the first Plan Communist China's GNP increased at an average annual rate of 11 per cent if computed in current prices, or 8.6 per cent if computed in constant (1952) prices.[8] Another economist, T. C. Liu, estimates that during the first Plan the average annual increase in net domestic product in Communist China, expressed in 1952 prices, amounted to 6.9 per cent.[9]

In view of the discrepancies among these and other estimates, it is difficult to accept any one figure with finality, but the available evidence suggests that Communist China's GNP rose during 1953-1957 by an average annual rate of at least 7 to 8 per cent. This represents an impressive rate of over-all economic growth, substantially above that of most underdeveloped countries. Significantly, it is close to double the rate of 4 per cent which India achieved between 1951 and 1956.[10]

Japan is the only important Asian country which has been developing at a rate comparable to that of Communist China. Japan's real national income is estimated to have increased by an average annual rate of 8.6 per cent during 1950-1956,[11] and the Japanese achieved this high rate despite the fact that rates of growth generally decline as a nation becomes more industrialized. The performance of the Japanese indicates that it is possible for a non-Communist Asian country to make rapid economic progress without resorting to totalitarian methods, but Japan is no longer an underdeveloped country, and it is in comparison with other underdeveloped nations in Asia that Communist China's rate of growth takes on a particular significance. At present, China's economy is growing at a rate considerably faster than that achieved by any of its underdeveloped, non-Communist neighbors. The potential significance of this fact should not be underestimated. Most leaders in underdeveloped areas feel a strong drive to develop their nations rapidly, and the world-wide competition between the Communist and non-Communist nations will undoubtedly be profoundly affected by the relative success of differing formulas for economic growth.

During 1956 and 1957, as the first Plan period drew to a close, the Chinese Communists drew up preliminary plans for the period 1958-1962.[12] The general pattern of this second Five Year Plan called for continuing high investment rates, rapid industrial growth, and consumer austerity. The preliminary targets involved raising total national income again by about 50 per cent and achieving an average annual increase of about 9 per cent. By comparison with the first Plan's targets for 1957, gross output of industry and agriculture combined was scheduled by 1962 to increase by 70 to 75 per cent, requiring another doubling of industrial output and a further increase of 35 per cent in agricultural production. To achieve these goals, Peking planned to collect roughly 30 per cent of national income as state revenue and to devote approximately 40 per cent of state expenditures to "capital construction."

These preliminary projections for the second Five Year Plan appeared fairly reasonable in terms of the results of the first Plan. Then, in early 1958, throwing caution to the winds, Peking adopted radically new policies, calling for a "great leap forward" in the economy. However, before attempting an appraisal of the new economic developments since early 1958, it is necessary to review in somewhat greater detail the major changes which had taken place through 1957, the end of the first Plan period.

Socialization and Collectivization

Although the "General Line of the State," formulated in 1952, had clearly defined socialization of the economy as one of Peking's central aims, until 1955-1956 the Communists made relatively gradual advances in that direction. By the beginning of the first Plan the state already owned about 50 per cent of modern industry in China, accounting for roughly 60 per cent of modern industrial output, and much of this had been taken over from the Nationalist regime. The remainder was to be taken over in a step-by-step process through several intermediary stages of so-called "state capitalism," with each stage increasing state control over the remaining private enterprises.[13] The program of collectivization in agriculture also called for a step-by-step approach, which involved organizing peasants first into mutual aid teams, then into agricultural producers' co-operatives, and finally into full-fledged collectives.[14] The Communists had experimented with all these forms of agricultural organization from 1951 onward, but when the first Plan started their goal was still a relatively modest one: they planned by 1957 to bring only about one-fifth of the peasants into producers' cooperatives.

Then, in response to numerous economic problems and pressures, including a serious grain shortage, Mao Tse-tung called in mid-1955 for a rapid speed-up of socialization and collectivization, and his apparatus promptly swung into a major drive to achieve these objectives. By the end of 1956 over 90 per cent of all industry not previously state-owned had been organized into state-controlled "joint state-private" enterprises, and over 96 per cent of China's peasants had been brought into producers' cooperatives, 88 per cent of which were "higher stage cooperatives" (that is, collectives). The regime encountered no opposition effective enough to impede this process, and within a year private business and farming had been largely eliminated. According to the Communists, "the great revolution in our social system" had thus been largely completed, at least on paper, by the end of the first Five Year Plan; the remaining task, they asserted, was to consolidate the new economic institutions into workable organizational units.[15] By 1958 Peking's "General Line" had changed from a policy for the "transition to socialism" to one for the "construction of socialism."

The Role of Soviet Assistance

Under the first Plan the industrialization of China, and particularly the development of new heavy industries, was geared to various types of Soviet assistance. However, Soviet aid took the form primarily of supplying technical advice and needed equipment and materials, rather than financial aid. Basically, the Chinese were paying their own way—which was one of the reasons for the heavy burdens which the Plan placed on the economy and the people of China. The published record reveals not a single financial grant from the Soviet Union to Communist China. Even the financial credits provided by the Russians were not large by comparison either with China's needs or with Soviet credits provided to other countries.

In other respects, however, the Soviet assistance was of tremendous importance. It is doubtful that the Chinese could have carried out their first Five Year Plan without the technical help and equipment which they received from Russia, or without the credits which the Soviet Union did give for economic development projects.

In a series of commitments made in 1950, 1953, 1954, and 1956 the Russians promised to help the Chinese Communists construct 211 major projects by selling them the necessary equipment and supplies and by providing the essential technical assistance. These promises involved commitments by the Soviet Union to provide equipment and supplies to the value of 2 billion dollars for the 211 projects—which the Chinese referred to as the "key Soviet aid projects" and which constituted the core of Peking's program of industrialization. Equally important, the Russians sent several thousand advisers and technicians to assist the Chinese in every aspect of industrialization, from planning and construction to the actual operation of new plants. Without this Soviet backing China's progress would have been far slower.

The Progress of Industrialization

One of Peking's stated goals is to "transform China from an agricultural into an industrial country," and by 1957 it had made a significant start in this direction. Actually, the rise in industrial output during 1953-1957 was considerably larger than the increase in operating plant capacity. This was accomplished by making more intensive use of existing plants. Peking also pressed forward with the construction of new plants, however, and many of these are now coming into production under the second Plan.

After 1953 Peking deliberately promoted industrialization in the interior, away from the older and more vulnerable coastal centers. Manchuria, the only important base of heavy industry inherited by the Communists, has continued to play a central role in the industrialization program, but much new construction has been undertaken in North, Northwest, and Southwest China, where there had been little or no modern industry. Of the "above-norm" industrial projects slated to be started during the first Plan period, over two-thirds were planned for locations outside the coastal provinces.

This industrial dispersion has been accompanied by a great deal of railway and communications development in the interior. During the first Plan, substantial progress was made on a new Northwest-Southwest China rail network, a new railway was built linking Inner Mongolia with Outer Mongolia and the Trans-Siberian Railway, and a railway connecting Northwest China with Soviet Central Asia across Sinkiang was partially completed. Clearly, strategic as well as economic factors motivated the Chinese Communists in their decision to develop China's interior regions and to build two new railway lines to Soviet territory.

In the industrial expansion under the first Five Year Plan, basic heavy industries such as iron and steel underwent the most rapid development. There were also impressive developments in minerals, fuels, and electric power, but at the end of the Plan these industries still created serious bottlenecks in the over-all development program. During 1953-1957 rapid progress was also made in the metallurgical and machine-building industries. By the end of 1957 the Chinese Communists were producing trucks on a limited scale, had begun building an aircraft industry, and had started construction of an atomic reactor, which was completed in 1958. The output of consumer goods lagged, however, and did not adequately meet domestic demands.

According to official claims, between 1952 and 1957 the production of key heavy industries in Communist China increased as follows:[16]

steel	1.35 to 5.35 million (metric) tons
pig iron	1.9 to 5.94 million tons
coal	63.53 to 130 million tons
electric power	7.26 to 19.3 billion kwh
cement	2.86 to 6.86 million tons
machine tools	13.7 to 28 thousand sets

Even if some of these figures must be discounted to a degree (the figures for coal, for example, probably represent unwashed, unprocessed coal), they suggest in general terms the rapidity with which the output of China's heavy industries grew in the first Plan period. In many basic industries production was more than doubled. However, a few key heavy industries, notably petroleum, fell seriously short of goals.[17]

Under the first Plan the development of consumer-goods industries was considerably less rapid than that of heavy industries, and output lagged behind the growing demand. According to official claims, during 1952-1957 the output of cotton yarn rose from 3.62 to 4.61 million bales, and cotton piece goods from 112 to 150 million bolts.[18] However, severe shortages and tight rationing in the domestic market provided clear proof of the gap between supply and demand. Consumer-goods production—of cotton textiles and many other products—depends directly on farm output, and it was in agricultural development that the Peking regime encountered some of its most serious problems during the first Plan.

The decision to emphasize heavy industry and give low priority to consumer goods has meant that, to date, the average Chinese consumer has benefited relatively little from the enormous efforts and sacrifices exacted by Peking's development program. Although official Chinese Communist statistics indicate an annual rise of about 4 per cent in per capita national consumption during the first Plan, this figure includes governmental as well as personal consumption; the figure for personal consumption alone would be much lower. Throughout the period of the Plan, and especially in its final year, 1957, there was widespread evidence of consumer-goods shortages and consumer discontent throughout China.[19]

Rationing of the most important basic consumer goods was started in 1953, and the number of commodities rationed was enlarged in 1957. Peking has stated officially that during the first Plan the value of consumer goods made available to the Chinese public increased on the average by only $1.69 per capita annually.[20]

The Chinese Communists claim that wage earners increased their monetary income considerably during 1953-1957, and it is possible that certain favored categories of urban workers may have improved their economic situation in some degree. At the same time, however, the status of millions of people was affected adversely by the economic leveling which took place, and the huge mass of Chinese peasants saw relatively little improvement in their welfare. Essentially, Peking's economic program demands of the Chinese people hard work and austerity in the present for the sake of impersonal national aims and promises of deferred economic rewards at some time in the future. It is a program, characteristic of totalitarian states, which focuses on national power rather than welfare. It stands in profound contrast to the programs of democratic countries, such as India, with their emphasis on raising the people's standard of living and preserving and strengthening democratic freedoms.

Agricultural Development

Although Peking's primary economic aim is industrialization, agriculture is still the foundation of the Chinese economy, and it must provide raw materials for industry and increased food for a rapidly growing population, as well as most of the exports needed to pay for essential imports of capital goods. It is also the mainstay for the financing of economic development. During the first Five Year Plan there was a direct correlation between varying annual rates of over-all economic growth and the year-by-year fluctuations in farm output.

Agriculture, far more than industry, is subject to factors difficult to control or predict—above all, to the weather. Despite the annual mobilization of literally millions of peasants to work on water conservation projects, China suffered serious natural disasters in 1953-1954, 1956, and 1957. In 1954 one-tenth of all agricultural land was affected by floods, and in 1956 the damage was even greater.

The shortage of arable land is a fundamental problem in China, and during the first Plan Peking carried out numerous projects, both to bring wasteland under cultivation and to increase irrigation and double-cropping of land already under cultivation. These efforts were significant, but by 1957 the Communists were still a long way from having solved the problem of raising agricultural output, which depends above all on securing an adequate increase in per acre output on the limited available land.

Planning and directing the economic activities of China's half-billion farm population is a tremendous task, but since 1949 the Communists have steadily tightened their controls over the rural economy. First, they eliminated the power and influence of landlords and rich peasants, established strong political control over the villages, and took into their hands the peasants' markets, sources of supplies, and credit. Then in 1953 they established nation-wide state control and rationing of all grain. From that time on they steadily collectivized the peasants, and by 1957, after the massive collectivization efforts of the previous two years, they had organized China's 125 million rural households into roughly 750,000 collective farms.

In the agricultural areas Peking focused its efforts during the first Plan on achieving maximum state control over the peasants, while putting a minimum of capital into agriculture and extracting the maximum from it. Peking did attempt, however, to improve farm output by antipest campaigns, by introducing simple new tools, by double-cropping, and by converting land to crops which are more productive per acre. After collectivization the state was forced to step up its investment in agriculture; by the end of the Plan period, in 1957, it had put about 10 per cent of its total investments into this field rather than the 7.6 per cent originally allocated.

During 1953-1957 the output of key agricultural products did rise, but the increases fell short of the original goals set by the planners, thus creating serious problems in the development program as a whole. Soon after the Plan started, Peking stated that in rough terms it hoped by 1957 to raise grain output by about 30 per cent; this involved an increase of about 50 million tons above the 1952 grain output figure of 164 million metric tons (a figure which includes soybeans and potatoes). This represented a vague hope rather than a carefully formulated target, however, and when in mid-1955 Peking announced definite goals for 1957 it set the grain target considerably lower, at a figure of 192.8 million tons, representing a five-year increase of 17.6 per cent.

For many reasons it is particularly difficult to evaluate Chinese Communist claims on grain production. One reason is that Peking has altered its definition of "grain." Early statistics included soybeans and potatoes, as well as grain, in this category, whereas later figures separate out soybeans, which is a fairly large item. More important, the coverage and efficiency of Peking's crop reporting have probably improved steadily, making it difficult to compare recent statistics with earlier ones.

Nonetheless, it seems clear that a rise in grain output did take place during the period of the first Plan, and in 1957 Peking claimed an output of 185 million tons of grain and 10 million tons of soybeans.[21] Despite this increase, however, grain shortages created continuing and fundamental stresses in the Communists' development program. Consumption levels had to be kept low, even though the rationing system apparently met the minimum subsistence requirements for most of the population, and starvation was kept to a minimum.

The production of other agricultural commodities also fell short of goals during much of the first Five Year Plan. Although the claimed output of cotton exceeded the Plan target in 1957, during several years of the Plan shortages forced textile plants to operate well below capacity, despite some imports of raw cotton. Output of pork and some other commodities did not even approach Plan targets. Furthermore, despite domestic shortages in these basic commodities, Peking continued to export a portion of its available supplies. This helped to pay for the capital-goods imports needed for industrialization, but it also intensified consumer dissatisfaction within China.

At the end of the first Plan the Communists claimed to have increased gross agricultural output by an annual average of over 4 per cent annually, but this figure undoubtedly was too high, and Peking showed increasing concern over the lag in agricultural production and its limiting effects upon China's future development.

China's Population Problem

In 1953 the Chinese Communists conducted their first nation-wide census and reported the population of mainland China to be 583 millions.[22] The announcement of this figure was received in the West with much skepticism at first, but it has found increasing acceptance as at least a general indication of China's population in 1953. Apparently it was accepted by Peking's leaders from the start, for, despite their continued insistence that a huge population is basically a national asset, after 1953 they in fact fundamentally altered their attitudes toward birth control and other population policies. Before the census they dismissed Western population theories as subversive "neo-Malthusianism." After it, Communist spokesmen endorsed and promoted various birth-control measures, even though this reversal raised serious ideological problems for them, for the standard Marxist view denies that there can be such a phenomenon as "overpopulation" under a socialist system. During 1957 and 1958, it is true, Peking appeared to be retreating somewhat toward the orthodox position. Leading Communists talked a great deal about labor shortages and reemphasized the view that a large and growing population is desirable.[23] But Peking has nonetheless continued to promote a birth-control program.

It is not merely the over-all size of China's population which poses serious problems for Peking; it is also the continued rapid rate of population growth, revealed by the census data.[24] Detailed studies of selected areas in 1953 showed an average annual birth rate of 37 per thousand and a death rate of only 17 per thousand, resulting in a net annual increase of 2 per cent.[25] Subsequently, Peking officially estimated the rate of annual increase to be 2.2 per cent, which meant that China's population was increasing during the period of the first Plan by about 13 million persons annually. Official data published by the Chinese Communists indicate that during 1952-1957 total population increased by over 11 per cent, or some 65 millions, from 569 millions in mid-1952 to 634 millions in mid-1957. In other words, the increase over five years was greater than the total population of all but a few major nations!

During the same period, the farming population rose from 482 millions to 530 millions and the total rural population from 503 to 548 millions, while the nonfarm population increased from 93 to 110 millions and the total urban population from 72 to 92 millions. Roughly 40 per cent of the urban increase—or 8 million people—was attributed to immigration from rural areas, due in large part to difficult economic conditions in the countryside.[26] Meanwhile, the total net increase in jobs in the government administration and in state-controlled enterprises (since 1956 these have included most nonagricultural jobs) probably did not exceed 5 or 6 million. As a result of these and other factors, the Communist regime has faced a fairly serious problem of urban unemployment, as evidenced by its continuous efforts to force surplus population to return to the villages and to restrict the unplanned migration into the cities.

Improved sanitation and health measures, as well as the establishment of public order, have contributed to declining death rates, while birth rates probably still continue close to the biological maximum. China seems, therefore, to be experiencing a "demographic explosion" similar to that which other countries have undergone during industrialization. If present trends continue, Communist China will have a population of one billion by some time in the 1980s.[27] Before that happens, of course, Peking may possibly decide to implement birth-control measures more vigorously than it has to date, and if it does so, it conceivably might achieve a greater success in population planning than is generally possible for democratic nations, because of its effective control over China's population. What is certain, however, is that for many years to come, a "Malthusian counterrevolution"[28] will be competing with the industrial revolution for new resources. In China's situation a large amount of economic growth, and of new investment to achieve that growth, will be required merely to meet the basic needs of the rapidly growing population at near-subsistence levels.

Military Costs and Other Problems

Peking's military programs also impose a heavy burden on China's economy. The Communists have been trying simultaneously to build China into a great military power and to transform it into a major industrial country. Of course, the new heavy industries can be used for or converted to military purposes, and to this extent military and industrial investments are complementary, rather than competitive. But Peking's direct military costs—for waging war or supporting military operations in Korea, Vietnam, and along the China coast, and for maintaining and modernizing its own large military forces—have been very great. Even since the Korean truce published expenditures for "national defense" have averaged 2 to 3 billion dollars a year—much larger than the entire national budgets of any past Chinese regimes. During the first Five Year Plan they totaled more than 12 billion dollars.[29] In the last two years of the Plan, however, the strains on the economy were reflected in a reduction in the military burget from 2.7 billion dollars in 1955 to 2.6 billions in 1956 and to 2.3 billions in 1957. The problem of allocating available resources, as between military purposes and economic development, is likely to pose difficult policy questions for the regime in the future.

By and large, the Chinese Communists have been successful in combating price inflation. Fully aware that the runaway inflation in the years before 1949 was a major cause of the political as well as economic disintegration of the Nationalist regime, Peking from the start attached a high priority to the control of inflation. Despite a temporary setback in its anti-inflationary efforts during the Korean War, it had, for all practical purposes, achieved price stability by 1952. Through strict control of finance and banking, heavy taxation, savings campaigns, bond issues, rationing, and similar measures it maintained this stability reasonably well during the first years of the Five Year Plan. From 1953 through 1955, despite rapidly growing budgets, current revenues exceeded current expenditures each year. In 1956, however, partly as a result of a big jump in capital investments, the budget showed a deficit of 775 million dollars, and the Chinese Communists were forced to increase their note issue and use up a sizable proportion of their reserves and stocks. The following year, 1957, was one of retrenchment and stringency. Peking drastically cut its major investment plans for 1957, and also scheduled a reduction in its over-all budget from 12.9 billion dollars in 1956 to 12.4 billions in 1957—the first cutback in its total budget since the start of the Plan. During 1957, also, the pressure of commodity shortages resulted in a certain amount of price inflation in the remaining small free market for nonrationed agricultural goods. At the same time the government raised the prices of rationed goods, and long queues of people waiting to buy available commodities gave ample evidence of repressed inflation.

Many other problems have also confronted Peking. At every level its program of industrialization has been hampered by shortages of technicians and skilled laborers. The Chinese Communists have made strenuous efforts to meet this problem, however. While drawing heavily on Soviet experts for top-level skills, they have also developed large-scale in-service training programs for workers and have reorganized their whole system of higher education to emphasize technical training.[30] Scientific research has been given the highest priority, and numerous research institutes, the most important ones guided by a national Academy of Sciences, have been set up. University enrollments more than doubled during the first Plan, rising to 440,000 in 1957. But the dimensions of the training problem are enormous, as illustrated by Chou En-lai's statement in 1957 that over 70 per cent of the total population was still illiterate, even though more than 22 million illiterates had been taught to read and write between 1949 and 1956.[31] Peking's training programs, modeled on those of the Soviet Union, will certainly accelerate the accumulation of skilled personnel, but mass training costs money and takes time.

During the first Plan, as the Chinese Communists have admitted, some very serious mistakes were made in economic planning, which helped to make the course of development quite erratic.[32] Peking asserts, for example, that after the crop failures of 1953 and 1954 it underestimated development possibilities in 1955; then in 1955 it exported certain basic commodities which were in surplus, only to face serious shortages in the same commodities during the next year.[33] In 1956 it pushed ahead too rapidly in industrial construction, with the result that in 1957 it had to cut back its program all along the line. The year 1957 was not only one of great austerity for the population—which certainly contributed to the rising political tensions in China—but was also a period of major retrenchment in the regime's basic program. In 1957, as compared with 1956, total national expenditures were cut by 4 per cent, national defense outlays by 10 per cent, "economic construction" by 9 per cent, and "capital construction" by 21 per cent.[34] The increase in industrial production scheduled for the year was relatively small.

The "Great Leap Forward" of 1958

By early 1957 it looked very much as if the process of economic development which the Chinese Communists had achieved during the first Plan was losing its momentum. Peking began to show an obvious concern about the need to retrench and to tailor its policies to its resources. It decided, for example, to devote more attention to agriculture and to the construction of decentralized, small-scale industries. China's basic economic problems appeared to be catching up with the Communists, and it was widely predicted that Peking's preliminary targets for its second Five Year Plan, which called for a rate of growth comparable to that achieved under the first Plan, might prove overoptimistic.

Then the Chinese Communists threw away the book, so to speak. Starting in late 1957, they began, on an unprecedented scale, to mobilize the Chinese people for intensive state-directed projects, and in early 1958 they announced their determination to take a "great leap forward" in economic development.[35] They scrapped the output targets previously set and during 1958 raised their goals repeatedly, projecting new rates of development unprecedented in China or anywhere else. They embarked upon a startling program to build small "factories" for the production of pig iron, steel, and many other commodities throughout rural China. Most startling of all, they set about communizing the peasants. In a brief span of months they pushed through the merging of over 700,000 collective farms into more than 26,000 communes. The frantic intensity with which the entire population was regimented and goaded to meet the regime's goals can be measured by Peking's official recommendation, in late 1958, that provision should be made for the peasants to have eight hours of sleep a night.

The course of events in China since the "great leap forward" started in 1958 make it virtually impossible to assess accurately the economic accomplishments Peking may have made during the past two years. Throughout 1958 Peking announced literally fantastic claims of production increases, and at the end of the year it asserted that the output of most major agricultural and industrial products had been doubled since 1957. Its claims were simply not believable, however, in the light of past experience anywhere else in the world. Then, after encountering increasing economic problems during 1959, the Chinese Communists suddenly announced a completely new set of much lower output figures for 1958 to the mystification of the rest of the world. Why the first inflated claims were made is still hard to explain. Perhaps Peking's pressures on local leaders forced the latter to pad their claims. Perhaps Peking itself deliberately falsified and manipulated figures to impress the world and to spur the Chinese people on to still greater efforts. Whatever explanations are given, however, it is difficult to account for the gross distortions which the following figures indicate.[36]

	Claimed 1957 Output	First Claims on 1958 Output	Revised Claims on 1958 Output
Steel (million metric tons)	5.35	11.08	8.00 *
Grain (million metric tons)	185.00	375.00	250.00
Cotton (million metric tons)	1.64	3.32	2.1

* In its revised figures Peking asserted that 3.08 million tons of locally made pig iron was unusable for modern industrial purposes.

The revised figures on 1958 production issued in August 1959 are very far below the original claims, and until further information is available even they are difficult to evaluate, yet the confusion which all of this has caused should not obscure the fact that since late 1957 the Chinese Communists have undoubtedly achieved a sizable spurt in over-all production, even though the exact dimensions of their "great leap" may remain in doubt for some time to come.

The primary idea behind the "great leap forward" was clearly that of mobilizing China's human resources to the maximum degree possible to develop both agriculture and industry. As a preliminary step, Peking had already marshaled tens of millions of peasants to build new irrigation works. According to official claims, between October 1957 and June 1958 over 100 million peasants were organized to build irrigation projects, bringing new water supplies to 80 million acres of land. This spurt allegedly increased the total irrigated land to almost 150 million acres and raised the percentage of all cultivated land under irrigation from 31 per cent in 1957 to 56 per cent in mid-1958.[37]

Since 1957 Peking has taken numerous other steps to intensify agricultural production. Deep-plowing, close planting, and other techniques designed to increase yields per acre have been energetically promoted, and as enormous amounts of labor have been applied in agriculture, Chinese farming has become more and more like gardening. Special efforts have been made to collect all forms of manure and fertilizers, and Peking claims that immense amounts of it have been applied to the fields since 1958. Both domestic production and imports of chemical fertilizer have been stepped up. In 1958 total investments by the government in agriculture rose by 40 per cent, compared with 1957. And in 1957-1958 over one million party, administrative, and other urban workers were transferred to work in agriculture.[38] All of these factors, plus favorable weather, certainly helped to raise farm production in 1958.

While continuing to push the development of large-scale modern industry,[39] since early 1958 Peking has also promoted extensively the development of both medium-size and miniature local industries.[40] The most publicized aspect of this program was the construction in 1958 of literally hundreds of thousands of tiny "blast furnaces" using local scrap or iron ore and coal to turn out low-grade pig iron and steel; this policy has proved to be a fiasco for the most part, and most of the blast furnaces have been abandoned. But in addition to promoting these and other semihandicraft types of industry, Peking has also promoted standardized, decentralized industrial plants of medium size to manufacture a wide range of products. Apparently, large numbers of these plants have been set up all over China, with local capital as well as local labor and other resources, and they will probably continue to be important, as a supplement to large-scale industry.

The nation-wide communization of the villages initiated in the fall of 1958 was started only after the "great leap forward" was well under way, but it fitted into and backed up Peking's other new economic policies. The communes are designed to increase vastly the state's ability to mobilize and allocate both population and resources. Clearly, the Chinese Communists have already expanded substantially the labor force available to the regime and increased their ability to harness the entire rural population, female and male, to many different types of labor-intensive projects, both agricultural and industrial. The communes also make possible a tighter control over consumption and a stricter mobilization of capital for investment. Some of the new communes, according to Peking's estimates, are now able to mobilize annually up to 20 or 30 per cent more capital for investment than the collectives which they absorbed.

The herculean efforts invested in these programs have undoubtedly produced substantial results, since the start of 1958, even though they have also created new dislocations and problems. If the Communists' claims, even as revised, are close to the truth, Peking may have laid the groundwork for more rapid future progress in increasing agricultural output, and the program of building decentralized industries may well have an important part in China's future development—despite the failure of the backyard blast furnaces—since the more effective utilization of local labor, capital, and other resources can add substantially to China's industrial capacity, by supplementing the output of large-scale modern factories. The communes raise some extremely complex questions, involving, as they do, immense human strains and administrative problems. But if they prove workable, even in modified form, they are bound to strengthen the Communists' network of totalitarian control over China's human resources and consequently may enhance Peking's ability to press forward its program of forced-draft development.

The evidence filtering out of China during 1959 suggests that Peking will find it difficult to sustain the pace of the "great leap forward," however. The economic dislocations caused by the spurt in 1958 have been serious, particularly in transportation.[41] Food shortages persist, despite Peking's claim that output increased greatly in 1958, and as a result of serious floods and droughts in mid-1959 the Chinese Communists have scaled down most of their targets for new production increases. As a result, the increases in output are likely to be much smaller in 1959 than in 1958. The production targets for the year which Peking announced in August 1959 were 12 million tons of steel, 335 million tons of grain, and 2.3 million tons of cotton. Nonetheless, it is clear that Peking is continuing to make extraordinary efforts to hasten China's economic growth, and it apparently is determined to bulldoze ahead despite all difficulties and regardless of the costs to the Chinese people.

Some Implications for the Future

On the basis of Peking's performance since 1949, it is only prudent, therefore, to assume that despite numerous and formidable problems, Communist China will continue to make important economic advances. In the years immediately ahead the Chinese Communists can be expected to sustain an impressive rate of growth; the rate will probably be comparable at least to that achieved during the first Five Year Plan, and conceivably it may be even faster. The prospect of Communist China's continued rapid growth in economic strength holds important implications for all of Asia and for United States policy.

China's economic development will steadily strengthen Peking's base for military power, thereby improving its entire power position in world affairs. The rapid build-up of heavy industry, the planned dispersal of industry, and the development of strategic transport and communications will unquestionably strengthen China militarily. China's increasing economic strength is likely also to bolster Peking's political and economic influence abroad. The already great gulf between Communist China's power and that of other Asian nations seems likely to widen if present trends continue. And if China's strength in heavy industries surpasses Japan's within a relatively short time, this can have serious effects upon the balance of power in Asia. There is little basis, therefore, for hoping that the security problems which Communist China now poses for the United States will become less serious or less urgent in the years immediately ahead.

Communist China's impressive rate of economic growth may also have a profound psychological impact in the rest of Asia and elsewhere among the peoples of underdeveloped countries. If the Chinese Communists continue building their economy at a rate surpassing that of other underdeveloped nations in Asia, this disparity may enhance the attraction of the Communist formula for economic development. It may also breed increasing fear of a newly dynamic China, followed by a resigned adjustment to Peking's growing strength. In any case, it seems likely to increase the feelings of frustration in nations whose economic progress is less rapid than China's. Peking's economic successes may also reinforce Communist movements elsewhere in Asia by holding out an impressive model of dynamic growth, wholly apart from Peking's ability to give increasing support to subversive activities.

There is nothing inevitable about these grim prospects, even though Peking propagates the idea that the force of its example helps make communism an irresistible force throughout Asia. The psychological effects of China's progress will very much depend on the degree to which non-Communist leaders in other Asian nations achieve success in developing their own economies without resorting to totalitarian methods. This means that the United States has every reason to concern itself more closely than it has so far with the economic prospects and needs of the non-Communist countries of Asia. Encouraging and assisting economic progress in India and Japan, in Thailand and Indonesia, and elsewhere in Asia is important for its own sake, regardless of Communist China's rate of progress, but this new and dynamic factor reinforces the compelling arguments in favor of assisting the non-Communist countries in Asia to step up the pace of their economic development.

If, instead of making new economic strides, the Chinese Communists should encounter increasingly serious economic crises and failures, would this drastically change or diminish the problems which Communist China poses for the rest of Asia and hence for the United States? In some respects it might. It would reduce China's psychological impact on Asia. It would also weaken the base for Communist China's economic and political power. Under certain circumstances, it might lead Peking's leaders to concentrate their attention more on domestic problems and to slacken their efforts to expand Communist China's influence abroad. Possibly, however, the effects of economic failure would be quite different. If economic conditions in China deteriorated seriously or the pressure of population became intolerable, Peking's leaders might then be tempted to solve their domestic problems through expansion abroad. Although, conceivably, they might turn their attention to the underdeveloped and underpopulated areas of Soviet Asia, they would more probably be tempted into foreign adventures to the south, in the relatively underpopulated areas of Southeast Asia, with their rich natural resources and food surpluses.

Chapter 4

THE ROOTS OF MAO'S STRATEGY

It is not easy to grasp the underlying motivations and outlook of the leaders of any major nation, and in seeking to define the purposes of the Chinese Communists the difficulties are compounded by many cultural, ideological, and historical barriers. Both as Asian nationalists and as Communist revolutionaries, Mao and his followers view the world in terms which are little understood in the West. It is essential, however, to formulate tenable assumptions about Peking's aims and basic approach to international affairs. Unless we learn in some fashion to relate the Communists' variable short-run tactics to their long-run goals and strategy, it is almost futile to attempt to trace the day-to-day shifts in their foreign policy.

Although there is considerable room for disagreement about many of Communist China's aims, one purpose stands out clearly. Peking's leaders consider their country to be one of the world's major powers, and they are determined that China shall play the role of a great power. About this they are explicit, and there can be no doubt of their determination to press for international acceptance as a world power. Chou En-lai has claimed that Communist China's views must be heard "in the settlement of any major international issue." [1] And the official Chinese Communist press has stated bluntly that "no solution of any international problem, any Asian problem in particular, is possible without the participation of the Chinese People's Republic." [2]

The Chinese Communists feel that they can and should play a special and leading role in Asian affairs. When they first came to power, they pressed their claim to primacy above all in terms of China's revolutionary leadership. They proclaimed their own revolution the "classic example" and the model for revolutions in other Asian and underdeveloped areas, exhorting the people in all "colonial and semicolonial" countries to follow "the path taken by the Chinese people." [3] In recent years their claim to leadership has generally been phrased in the more conventional terms of international politics. In effect, they have propagated a kind of Chinese "Monroe Doctrine" for Asia.[4] Asian nations should consult among themselves and solve their own problems, they say, and all non-Asian nations should keep "hands off." For obvious reasons they do not explicitly demand a paramount position for themselves, but they doubtless believe Communist China would have the dominant role in an Asia reserved for Asians.

The strength of the Chinese Communists' insistence on achieving both great-power status and a position of leadership in Asia cannot be explained merely in terms of China's size, population, and geographical position. The history of China, the traditional Chinese view of the world, and the force of modern nationalism all play a part in making this a driving force in Peking's policy.

Traditional Attitudes and Modern Nationalism

The Chinese Communists are heir to a great civilization with an impressive imperial past, and, although they are revolutionaries, they are very much aware of this heritage. Throughout most of the last two thousand years the rulers of China have exercised hegemony over large areas of the Far East, Central Asia, and Southeast Asia, and over the centuries Chinese imperialism and colonialism have ebbed and flowed. China has almost invariably been expansionist whenever it has had a strong government. In the past its expansionism has taken many forms: the spread of cultural influence, the inexorable pressure of population movements, and, in many periods, territorial conquest.

China's long history and imperial tradition have bred in its people a deep sense of cultural superiority and a belief in China's natural primacy in Asia. Until the modern period the Chinese regarded their country as the "central kingdom," the center of the civilized world, surrounded by states which either accepted a subordinate tributary relationship or were considered inferior nations outside the pale of the China-centered civilized world.[5] Although the old basis for this world view has faded, most Chinese, including the Communists, still harbor a feeling of superiority over their neighbors (a feeling not dissimilar to that which many Westerners have felt toward the non-Western world in the modern period). In many respects China's resurgence in recent years can be viewed as the latest of many periods over the centuries in which a strong authoritarian government has aroused and harnessed the energies of the Chinese people and reasserted China's power and influence in the entire region around China. Previous periods of dynamism have always been both creative and destructive, and they have invariably had a profound impact upon China's neighbors.

Nationalism has been one of the strongest and most fundamental forces shaping the course of events in modern China. In recent decades every important political group, including the Communists, has been inspired by a fierce anticolonialism, by a determination to wipe out the humiliations of past foreign encroachments, and by the desire to remake China into a unified, strong, modern, world power. The Communist party's victory within China was due in no small measure to its success in appealing to nationalist sentiment both during the war with Japan and afterward. The merging of revolutionary communism with nationalism was shrewd tactics, but it was more than that; it was also a reflection of the Communists' determination that China achieve self-respect, international prestige, and world power. "Our nation will never again be an insulted nation," Mao Tse-tung proclaimed in September 1949: "We have stood up." [6]

The Impact of Communist Ideology

Although nationalism is one of the driving forces behind the Chinese Communist actions, it is clearly the ideological convictions of Peking's leaders which shape their present view of the world, mold their strategy, and provide the rationale for both the ends and means of their policy. Like the Russians, the Chinese Communists are capable of clothing in ideological terms virtually every issue which concerns their national interests, but their ideological motivations are more than mere rationalizations. Peking's leaders do, in fact, think in terms of a world-wide revolutionary struggle. They have a strong sense of their mission to spread Marxism-Leninism, to speed up the course of an "inevitable" world revolution, and to expand the area of Communist political control. Chou En-lai has given profuse assurances to Asians, ever since 1954, that "revolution is not for export." Yet, Mao Tse-tung stated the basic Communist position categorically at Moscow in November 1957:

In the end, the socialist system will replace the capitalist system. This is an objective law independent of human will. No matter how hard the reactionaries try to prevent the advance of the wheel of history, revolution will take place sooner or later and will surely triumph.[7]

It is true that the Chinese Communists are pragmatic in interpreting their ideology to take advantage of concrete situations and are flexible in formulating their day-to-day tactics. But to underrate the importance of ideology as a determinant of Peking's long-range policy, or to argue that ideology is no more than a cloak for Chinese national interests, would be a serious mistake. The Chinese Communists are motivated by a genuine revolutionary zeal which is probably stronger than that of the present leaders in the Soviet Union. Ideology greatly influences their conceptions of China's national interests, and the Communist belief in world revolution definitely impels them to project their influence beyond China's borders.

Although Marx is little read in China, the Chinese Communists accept as articles of faith the basic Marxist concepts of dialectical and historical materialism, world-wide class struggle, and the inevitable overthrow of "decaying capitalism" by the "proletariat" of all countries. They accept Leninism (Lenin for present-day Communists is a more important prophet than Marx) and its key doctrines: the idea that imperialism is the final stage of capitalist decay; the stress upon the importance of "colonial" and "semicolonial" countries in the revolutionary struggle against capitalist countries; the importance of anti-imperialism in world revolution; the identification of the "proletariat" with a disciplined, elite, "democratic-centralist" party which must lead the revolution; the recognition of the potential revolutionary importance of the peasantry; and the idea that in less developed countries revolution may go through a "bourgeois-democratic" phase, predominantly anti-imperialist in character, before entering its socialist stage. The Chinese Communists also accept most of Stalinism and its doctrines on the totalitarian organization of state power, on state-directed economic development, and on other questions such as the problem of dealing with national minorities.

The Meaning of Maoism

In applying Marxist-Leninist doctrines to the Chinese scene, the Communists in China, and above all Mao Tse-tung, have developed ideological formulas which may legitimately be called "Maoism," although the Chinese themselves refer to them merely as "the thought of Mao Tse-tung." [8] The degree of actual originality in Maoism is arguable. Almost all of its individual elements can be traced to Lenin and Stalin, but they have been combined into new forms and adapted to new conditions. The Chinese themselves claim to have developed a unique pattern of revolution, a "new contribution to the treasury of Marxism-Leninism." [9] It should be noted that no other Communist party outside the Soviet Union has had any basis for making comparable claims, although the Yugoslavs are also responsible for some ideological innovations.

The Chinese formulas include several basic principles for revolution in "colonial" and "semicolonial" areas: the idea of a two-stage revolution leading from a "bourgeois-democratic" stage to a socialist stage; the concept of "new democracy" during a transitional period; the great emphasis placed upon the need for mass peasant support under Communist and "proletarian" leadership in a "worker-peasant alliance"; the necessity for the broadest type of anti-imperialist, four-class, united front including even "national capitalists" as well as the petty bourgeoisie and workers and peasants; and the need for building a revolutionary army with a territorial base to conduct armed struggle in the revolutionary process. Even some of these basic strategic principles have undergone important changes of emphasis, however. For example, since about 1952 Maoist ideas about the importance of united front tactics have gained wide acceptance outside China, while the central role of revolutionary armed struggle has generally been played down, at least temporarily, in Chinese doctrine and in the Communists' strategy in Asia.

It is not possible here to discuss all these doctrinal concepts, or to trace in detail the process of interpretation and adaptation to which they have been subjected in Communist China and elsewhere within the Communist bloc. It is essential, however, to point out a few of the basic ideological concepts which underlie Peking's strategy.

Revolutionary Change

Peking genuinely sees the world as engaged in a prolonged, continuous, and intense revolutionary struggle, and this simple fact has profound implications. The Chinese Communists think in terms of constant change and developing processes rather than static situations, and in terms of unlimited and world-wide revolutionary aspirations rather than limited national aims alone. In short, they view the world in terms of a dialectical revolutionary development of international forces.

Communist leaders visualize specific situations in a context very different from that generally accepted by leaders of *status quo* powers, or even by those leaders of national revolutions who think primarily in terms of national rather than world-wide aims. Peking's leaders are not fundamentally concerned with freezing the existing positions, "stabilizing" situations, or permanently "solving" problems. Instead, they are interested in promoting change, provided each change, however small in itself, enhances their power. If they agree to "settle" issues by compromise it is because they have come to believe that compromise is an unavoidable necessity, or because they are confident that the situation which has been temporarily stabilized will again shift in favor of their own revolutionary forces. In examining each new situation, Chinese Communist leaders ask themselves not only "What now?" but also "What next?" As they analyze a problem, they do not ask how an issue can be solved permanently, but how they can exploit the existing situation to lay the best possible groundwork for future advances.

The world-wide struggle which is now going on is regarded by the Chinese Communists as one in which great social, economic, and political forces—some identified with particular national states and others cutting across national lines—are contending for supremacy. This viewpoint also has far-reaching implications. International relations are not only, or in many situations not even primarily, a matter of conventional dealings between nation and nation or government and government. Official government policy and government-to-government relations are, it is true, important aspects of Peking's foreign policy. But the Chinese Communist approach to foreign policy demands the use of every possible instrument, formal and informal, overt and covert, to influence and shape the changing pattern of social, economic, and political forces outside China's borders. Even Peking's official policy is often conceived primarily in terms of influencing social trends, political opinions, and economic conditions within foreign countries, to exert an indirect influence on the policies of other governments and, in favorable situations, to promote revolutionary changes which might weaken or overthrow the existing governments. Its policy frequently attempts to by-pass intergovernmental channels, therefore, in order directly to influence or manipulate the people of foreign countries.

World-wide Alignment of Forces

The concept of the united front, which played an important part in the Communist victory within China, is often applied by Peking in its strategy abroad, both in its relations with other governments, and in its nonofficial, revolutionary campaigns to mobilize present or potential followers. Its aim is to achieve everywhere the broadest possible alignment of both national and class forces, to bring them under Communist influence or leadership, and to harness them to cooperate in struggling for common goals. Peking has been willing to accept major tactical compromises on short-term goals in order to achieve a broad alignment of forces which supports its long-range aims. The exact composition of the "united front" has been subject to frequent redefinition, depending on the Chinese Communists' views of current political needs and opportunities. Most recently, since about 1954, it has been defined in such broad terms as to encompass almost any nationalist, anticolonial, and anti-Western forces.

Peking's leaders inevitably classify all countries into certain groups or blocs, in accordance with their varying roles in the central struggle between communism and "imperialism" and their relationship to two clearly defined poles. At one pole is the Soviet Union, "the leader of the socialist camp." To this pole Communist China is attached by what the Communists label an "indestructible friendship," and, although within the Communist bloc Peking has risen to a position of associate leadership with Moscow, it still acknowledges the primacy of the Soviet Union. The Soviet-led bloc also embraces the "people's democracies," including both Russia's East European satellites and the smaller Communist states in Asia which stand in a special relationship to Communist China as well as to the Soviet Union.

At the other pole stands the United States, the strongest member of the "world imperialist camp." Attached to it are other "imperialist," "colonialist," "capitalist," and "reactionary" countries which are its allies and dependents. Whereas the "socialist camp" is viewed as a new "world system" which has developed a special type of unbreakable fraternal cooperation among "equals," the "imperialist camp" is described as one divided and weakened by fatal internal "contradictions," or conflicts of interest among its members, in particular between the United States and all its other members. However topsy-turvy this view of the world may seem to people outside the Communist bloc, it is rigidly upheld within the Communist orbit.

Two Poles and the Uncommitted World

Since 1949 a very significant change has taken place in Peking's view of the place of these two poles in world politics and their relationship to the rest of the world. In 1949 Mao's regime enthusiastically embraced the then current Soviet picture of a world sharply divided into only two hostile camps. Liu Shao-ch'i had written in 1948:

The world today has been divided into two mutually antagonistic camps: on the one hand, the world imperialist camp, composed of American imperialists and their accomplices, the reactionaries of all countries of the world; on the other hand, the world anti-imperialist camp, composed of the Soviet Union and the New Democracies of Eastern Europe, and the national liberation movements in China, Southeast Asia and Greece, plus the people's democratic forces of all countries of the world. American imperialism has become the bastion of all the reactionary forces in the world; while the Soviet Union has become the bastion of all progressive forces. . . . These two camps include all the peoples of the world—of all countries, classes, sections of the population, parties and groups.[10]

In this black-and-white, for-us-or-against-us view, the world which lay between the two poles was regarded as a political battleground on which all people were arrayed with either the revolutionaries or the reactionaries. The governments and leaders of those countries which refused to align themselves with the Communist bloc were classified by Peking and Moscow as "running dogs" and "hirelings" of the "imperialists." Peking looked forward to their early replacement by Communist-led forces and did everything in its power to hasten the day this would take place.

Since about 1952-1954 a somewhat more sophisticated and subtle classification of nations and governments has emerged in Soviet and Chinese Communist thinking. A new conception of the role of the countries standing between the two blocs—the uncommitted nations—has evolved. In 1948 Liu Shao-ch'i had stated bluntly, "to remain neutral or sitting on the fence is impossible," [11] and Mao Tse-tung underlined this view in 1949, declaring that "neutrality is merely a camouflage and a third road does not exist." [12] In November

1957, however, Liu asserted that the most important trends in the forty years since the October Revolution in Russia included not only "the decline of capitalism," the "rise of socialism," and the "upsurge of proletarian revolutionary movements," but also the development of "national independence and liberation movements" and the "extensive growth of the world peace movement." [13] "Mutual friendly relations in line with the five principles of peaceful coexistence [14] have been established and developed," he said, "between many nationally independent countries and socialist countries, which together form a broad zone of peace."

In effect, this new conception is one in which the world is divided into three main groupings, two of which—the Communist bloc and the newly independent uncommitted countries—Moscow and Peking seek to align together against the third, the "imperialist" bloc led by the United States. The Chinese Communists now draw more subtle distinctions than formerly within these three major groupings, and they are able to be even more flexible than before in formulating their policy.

Since the days of Lenin, Communists everywhere have been taught to regard the "colonial" and "semicolonial" areas—including most of the underdeveloped areas of Asia, the Middle East, Africa, and Latin America—as crucial to the worldwide revolutionary struggle. These areas, described by Lenin as "rear bases" essential to world imperialism, offer many opportunities for the Communists to launch flank attacks against the "citadels" of imperialism. As Asians, the Chinese Communists have long believed they should have a leading role in guiding the underdeveloped countries into the revolutionary path, and, on first coming to power, they openly incited violent revolutions throughout Asia. The shift since then in Peking's and Moscow's view of world politics has involved, not the abandonment of the long-run aim of encouraging Communist-led revolutions, but rather the decision to attach a higher immediate priority to promoting and supporting revolt by all underdeveloped areas against the dominant position of the West, while lowering somewhat the priority for instigating revolts against the existing regimes within these areas. The Chinese Communists feel that, as

Asians, they can and should play an especially important role in aligning anticolonialist and nationalist forces with the Communist bloc.

Philosophy of Power

As a result of their own successful revolutionary struggle, Mao Tse-tung and the other top Chinese Communist leaders have evolved a very sophisticated view of political power. It is a view which recognizes power as the product of many complex factors—military, political, economic, and psychological.

Chinese Communist leaders attach extraordinary importance to psychological factors. They appear to believe that if they can succeed in manipulating men's minds, they can then exercise control and direction over basic social forces. What Marx would have thought of this it is difficult to say, since he maintained that society molds men's thinking rather than the reverse, but the Chinese Communists' faith in the power of ideas has been reinforced by their successes in political action.

Communist China's leaders also attach very great importance to the intimate relationship between military and political power. As Mao Tse-tung stated bluntly in 1938, "Political power grows out of the barrel of a gun. . . . Anything can grow out of the barrel of a gun." [15] The Chinese Communists have no moral scruples or inhibitions about the use of force, whenever they consider it advantageous to their over-all strategy. At present, Peking's leaders apparently prefer to avoid a major war, partly because the risks would be so great, and partly because a "peace" policy currently seems to offer them many psychological and political advantages. But they regard force as a perfectly legitimate instrument of policy. As Mao wrote in 1936,

War is one of the highest forms of struggle for the settlement of contradictions between classes, nations, states, or political groups in a certain stage of development since the beginning of class society. . . . There are only two kinds of wars in history: revolutionary and counterrevolutionary. We support the former and oppose the latter. Only a revolutionary war is holy. We support holy national revolutionary wars and holy class revolutionary wars.[16]

In recent years the Chinese Communists have maintained that a new world war would result in "the utter destruction of the imperialist camp and the complete collapse of the entire capitalist system." [17] There are many reasons to believe, however, that in their broad strategy Peking's leaders do not think primarily in terms either of Chinese territorial conquest abroad or of exporting revolution by overt Chinese aggression. World conquest in traditional military terms and world revolution in Communist terms are very different concepts. Yet, Peking does attach high priority to the building up of its military strength, and in many ways it can attempt to use pressure and force while still trying to avoid a major war.

The Emphasis on Flexibility

The history of the entire Communist world movement has been characterized by tactical opportunism and adaptability, and Mao Tse-tung, during the long struggle for power in China, elaborated a doctrine of flexibility with a unique Chinese flavor. The Chinese Communists place special emphasis, therefore, on the need for flexibility in both domestic and foreign policy, and Mao maintains that the revolution must be viewed as a prolonged struggle, involving retreats as well as advances. He evolved a sixteen-word basic formula which originally applied to guerrilla warfare but also reflects his strategic thinking in general: "Enemy advances, we retreat; enemy entrenched, we harass; enemy exhausted, we attack; enemy retreating, we pursue." [18] "To defend in order to attack, to retreat in order to advance, to take a flanking position in order to take a frontal position, and to zigzag in order to go straight—these," Mao stated, "are the inevitable phenomena in the process of development of any event or matter." [19] Stressing the necessity, and even the desirability, of retreat under certain circumstances, he compared strategy to Chinese boxing: "All of us know that in a boxing contest the wise boxer usually yields a step, while his stupid opponent would display all his might and skill at the very first moment like an avalanche. The result is usually that the yielding one downs the avalanche." [20]

Peking's doctrine of flexibility suggests two important assumptions about Chinese Communist thinking. It suggests that Communist China's leaders can be induced to compromise if they can be convinced that the existing balance of political and military forces makes this desirable or necessary. On the other hand, it also suggests that any compromises Peking accepts must generally be regarded as tactical moves—"to retreat in order to advance"—rather than as the abandonment of any of its long-term aims. Certain types of *modus vivendi* with Communist China may be possible, therefore, but they are likely to be unstable and subject to change if and when the balance of risks and opportunities shifts.

National Interests and Revolutionary Aims

It is necessary, in evaluating Peking's aims and strategy, to attempt to differentiate between those aims which it regards as vital Chinese national interests and those which constitute its long-term revolutionary objectives. This attempt must be approached with caution, for aims of differing origins often tend to merge, but the effort is, nevertheless, of some importance. Peking is likely to be much more impatient, militant, and uncompromising on issues which it believes involve its vital national interests than on those which do not. And the time scale which it applies in striving to promote its long-range revolutionary goals is undoubtedly quite different from that which it applies in attempting to achieve specific Chinese national interests. In general, Peking seems much more likely at present to use all instruments of policy at its command, including military force, to achieve what it regards as vital national interests than to promote long-term revolutionary goals.

One of Peking's basic national aims is to complete the territorial unification of the country. The Chinese Communists have shown no inhibitions about invading Tibet and dominating it with overpowering force, despite strong opposition within Tibet and highly unfavorable reactions in the outside world, because they regard Tibet as Chinese territory. Similarly, if the risks of a major war could be removed, Peking would feel no hesitation in using force to gain control not only of the offshore islands, but also of

Taiwan and the Pescadores, which it also regards as indisputably part of China's territory. This is one reason why issues relating to the Taiwan area are particularly explosive.

It is difficult to predict what other territorial claims Communist China might attempt to assert by force. Peking claims the Spratly and Paracel Island groups, but these relatively minor islands seem unlikely to become a major international problem.[21] Several of China's frontiers remain to be finally and exactly demarcated, including portions of its frontiers with India, Burma, and Outer Mongolia, and since 1949 the Chinese Communists have exerted outward pressure at several points on China's periphery. On the Burmese border Peking has exerted localized military pressure, while also negotiating inconclusively over a settlement comprising Chinese and Burmese claims. And in the autumn of 1959 it created a crisis in Sino-Indian relations by exerting strong pressures along the border between Tibet and India. Macao and Hong Kong also remain in foreign hands, and although the Chinese Communists have yet not pressed for their direct retrocession, they have built up a record of complaints and accusations, especially against Hong Kong, and may step up the pressures on these foreign enclaves at some time in the future. Peking has not made any official claims to other territories which China has controlled or claimed at some time in the past, including parts of Vietnam and Korea, Outer Mongolia, and the Soviet Khabarovsk and Maritime provinces. It seems unlikely to do so now, but it might decide to put forth irredentist claims to some of these areas in the future.

National security is another basic national interest which underlies Peking's foreign policy. In long-range terms, the Chinese Communists' aim clearly is to eliminate Western power from Asia and to prevent any other Asian nation, such as Japan, from developing into a strong and competing military power. Peking's minimum and short-run aims are more difficult to determine, however. It undoubtedly now regards North Korea and North Vietnam as essential buffer areas, and it probably would go to very great lengths to forestall a serious military threat to China in or from either area. Apparently, a sense of direct threat was strongly felt by

Peking in 1950, when the United Nations forces in Korea drove northward across the 38th Parallel, and was an important factor in the Chinese decision to intervene in the Korean War.

It is less clear what degree of importance Peking attaches to other peripheral areas, but undoubtedly the Chinese Communists regard all adjacent areas as of some importance to their security. In the 1930s Mao Tse-tung, in decrying the fact that "the imperialist powers had taken away many Chinese dependent states and part of her territories," specifically mentioned Korea, Taiwan, the Ryukyu Islands (Okinawa), the Pescadores, Port Arthur, Burma, Bhutan, Nepal, Hong Kong, Annam (North Vietnam), and Macao.[22] In the 1930s he also told an American journalist that Outer Mongolia ought to be returned to Chinese control.[23] Historical tradition and security considerations have tended to impel all Chinese governments to take a special interest in areas adjacent to their country. The Chinese Nationalist regime, for example, despite its relative internal weakness, also claimed Tibet, Outer Mongolia, Taiwan, and certain territories on the borders of Burma and India, and it, too, attempted to exert its influence and develop special relationships, within the limits of its capabilities, in all the areas along China's periphery.

Attitudes toward the United States and Japan

To strengthen their security, expand Chinese influence, and promote the spread of communism, the Chinese Communists hope, in the long run, to force the withdrawal of the United States and other Western powers from all of Asia and to neutralize the non-Communist nations, particularly Japan, in that region. This aim was stated most succinctly, perhaps, by Chou En-lai at the Geneva Conference in 1954. "We . . . hold," he said, "that interference in the internal affairs of Asian nations should be stopped, all foreign military bases in Asia be removed, foreign armed forces stationed in Asian countries be withdrawn, the remilitarization of Japan be prevented, and all economic blockades and restrictions be abolished." [24]

Quite obviously, Peking regards the United States, currently the only non-Communist nation strong enough to counterbalance Communist China's power in Asia, as the major obstacle to both its short-range and its long-range aims and, therefore, as its paramount enemy. Do the Chinese Communists also view the United States as a dangerous threat to the security of their regime? At times during the past decade they undoubtedly have, and perhaps it would be desirable to draw a distinction between hostility due to the role of the United States in blocking the achievement of Peking's long-term aims and hostility based on fear of a direct military threat to the survival of the Peking regime. Such a distinction is often difficult to make in practice, however. In their propaganda the Chinese Communists constantly portray the United States as a direct threat to their security, but it is not easy to judge to what extent they now genuinely feel this to be the case.

In the Far East the Chinese Communists clearly regard Japan, which Peking denounces as a tool of American "imperialism," as the key nation in terms of regional strategy. In 1953 Liu Shao-ch'i declared:

It would be impossible for American imperialism or any other imperialist power to launch large-scale aggressive war in the Far East without Japan as a base.... It can be said that peace in the Far East is assured as long as it is possible to prevent the resumption of aggression and violation of peace on the part of Japan or any other state that may collaborate with Japan directly or indirectly in acts of aggression.[25]

Instruments of Policy

In thinking beyond its direct national interests, Peking apparently views its revolutionary goals in fairly long-range terms and seems less willing to take serious risks to pursue these aims than it does to achieve more limited national interests. Yet, the Chinese Communists will certainly continue to press toward their long-range revolutionary aims, not only for ideological reasons, but also because the spread of Communist regimes across Asia would promote the immediate interests of China as well as those of the world revolutionary movement. A successful Communist revolution in any Southeast Asian country—such as Laos, for example—could drastically change the entire strategic balance in Asia.

It would be unrealistic not to expect Peking to use all the instruments of policy available to it—including military pressure, political action, diplomacy, psychological warfare, economic competition, and subversion—to promote its long-term aims. Not all of these instruments, however, can be used with equal effectiveness at all times and in all countries. Peking's diplomatic wooings, for example, may fail in their purpose if the country wooed feels threatened by Chinese military pressure or by Chinese-supported subversion. The degree to which Peking relies on each of these instruments will vary, therefore, in accordance with its assessment of the current balance of forces, as well as with its varying definition of short-term goals.

In broad terms, important changes have taken place over the past decade in the Chinese Communists' use of these instruments of policy. In the first years after 1949 Peking placed its major reliance on military force and revolutionary subversion. More recently it has increasingly emphasized political action, diplomacy, psychological warfare, and economic competition; between 1955 and 1957 Peking made every attempt to minimize any outward show of military pressure and subversion. But since late 1957 its posture has once again become more militant, and now it seems increasingly prone to use pressures to achieve certain aims.

It should also be noted that although Peking's numerous aims, and varied instruments of policy, may generally be mutually reinforcing, this is not necessarily always the case. At times the Chinese Communists encounter situations which involve conflicts of aims and tactics, and these situations confront them with serious dilemmas in deciding which aims or tactics to pursue. China's concerns regarding its domestic situation, territorial claims, and national security interests, its interests as a member of the Communist bloc, and its desire to expand Chinese and Communist influence in Asia through tactics of "peaceful coexistence" do not always coincide. There is considerable evidence, for example, that they clashed, to a considerable degree, in the latter half of 1959. In that period Peking, seemingly motivated in large part by its desire to seal off Tibet from the outside world as well as to assert certain traditional Chinese territorial claims, brought strong pressures to bear on the Indian border. This action conflicted dramatically with the "peaceful coexistence" tactics which Peking, together with Moscow, had been developing toward the entire underdeveloped non-Communist world during the previous years. And when the Russians urged a compromise on the border issue, without giving Peking strong public backing, this seemed to indicate that China's actions also conflicted with the bloc's immediate interests as then viewed by Khrushchev who was on the verge of his visit to the United States, ostensibly to ease international tensions.

The Role of External Determinants

Peking's approach to world affairs cannot, in any case, be understood solely in terms of its own aims and motivations. Communist China does not operate in a vacuum. Its policy, like that of other nations, is shaped to a considerable degree by a process of action and interaction between itself and other major powers, and between its leaders' ambitions and the stubborn realities of the outside world.

The Chinese Communists' attitudes toward and relationships with the two strongest powers are fundamental factors shaping their policies. Since achieving power in China, the Communists have had to adapt their policy continuously to the requirements and limitations imposed by their alliance with Soviet Russia. Neither Soviet nor Chinese Communist policy can be fully understood except in terms of the interaction of these two powers; the relations between them, and their implications for the West will be examined in Chapter 12.

The basic power struggle between Communist China and the United States which has unfolded over the past decade has also imposed limitations upon Peking's broad policy, as well as upon that of the United States in Asia. Both these powers react to each other as well as act on their own initiative. Although it is possible to analyze the policies of each protagonist in terms of its own motivations and aims, it is also possible to view their development in a different perspective—in terms of the reactions and countermoves which each side has made in response to actions and moves made by the other.

Some Implications for United States Policy

Even if the Chinese Communists were concerned only with their own internal affairs, the dynamism of their regime would have a strong impact upon Asia. Clearly, however, their interests and ambitions are far broader. Their leaders are determined to expand China's influence, to shape the future of Asia, and to promote world communism. If the United States is to prevent this, it cannot avoid accepting the challenge of a long-term competition with Communist China, the outcome of which will be decisive for the future of Asia.

It is very difficult for any democratically ruled nation to think and plan ahead in long-range terms, but it is imperative for the United States to do so in tackling the problems presented by Communist China. Even if some of the issues which now accentuate the tension between the United States and Communist China can be resolved—and sincere efforts should be made to resolve them—there is little ground for hoping that a peaceful and stable *status quo* can be achieved in Asia in the foreseeable future.

For many years to come, Asia will be caught up in a process of profound change, and Communist China will exploit this turbulent process in every way it can in order to promote both its own national interests and those of world communism. Since any attempt to freeze the *status quo* throughout Asia will have little chance of success, the United States must learn to think of the competition with Communist China in terms of how best to cope with this process of change. This does not come easily to Americans. In a basic sense, despite its revolutionary background, the United States now tends to think and act as a *status quo* power, a "have" rather than a "have-not" nation, primarily concerned with preserving its present institutions and way of life. In competing with Communist China in Asia, however, the problem posed for the United States is, in a major sense, that of assisting and helping to guide the process of change into non-Communist channels, accepting and supporting changes in certain preferred directions, rather than opposing change of any sort.

The United States is unavoidably engaged in a basic power struggle with Communist China, and the Chinese Communists' attitude toward the use of military power makes it essential to build up the necessary military strength to counterbalance Peking's power. But the military element is by no means the only, or even the most important, factor in the struggle. In dealing with a revolutionary nation such as Communist China, Americans must recognize that the calculus of power has undergone great changes in recent years. It is the development of new social and political forces in the region around China—the primary arena in the contest between Chinese Communist and American influence—that will probably determine the ultimate outcome of the struggle. And in the long run, ideological attractions, cultural influences, economic support, and similar factors are likely to be as important in determining the outcome as traditional diplomacy or military power.

To prevent Peking from achieving its aim of splitting the nonaligned countries of Asia from the West, the United States must do all it can to enlarge and strengthen the community of interests between itself, its allies, and all the non-Communist nations — "committed" or nonaligned — throughout the region. In this the United States, as a non-Asian country, faces many obstacles, but, as a nation which genuinely subscribes to and supports the democratic national aspirations of these nations, it also has important advantages.

The problem of dealing with Communist China's flexibility of tactics will not be an easy one. It is not possible to define in advance and in detail policies which will remain valid without change over an extended period of time, since both the situation in Asia and Peking's tactics can be expected to undergo constant change. The United States, consequently, will find it necessary to subject its own policies to constant review and adaptation. In short, it, too, will find it necessary to be flexible. This is not to say that flexibility will always be desirable, in all matters. In opposing military aggression by Communist China, the United States must stand firm. But standing firm does not necessarily mean standing still, and American policy will have little chance of success in the long run if the United States fails to exercise a substantial degree of flexibility in adapting its policy to fit the changing needs and attitudes of the non-Communist nations of Asia.

If it is true that the United States must commit itself to a long-run contest against Communist China's ambitions, it seems equally true that in the long run the Chinese Communists cannot be denied the status of a large and strong power. Although the United States can and must exert every effort to prevent Peking from expanding its influence in ways which threaten the independence of other Asian nations, there is also little doubt that Communist China's influence in Asia will increase in many ways over the coming years. It must be recognized, also, that if war is to be avoided, Communist China's basic security interests cannot be ignored. Over the long run, it will be impossible even to consider ways of solving many of the crucial problems of Asia without dealing with Communist China.

The prospect of a prolonged struggle between the United States and Communist China is not a comforting one, especially for those Americans who seek quick "solutions" to all international problems. Yet, this is what the immediate future holds. The best that the United States can hope for is that this struggle can be waged primarily by nonmilitary means, and if the United States acts wisely and effectively, this seems to be at least possible.

If, in time, the Chinese Communists moderate their revolutionary zeal, the prospects for a gradual lessening of existing tensions, and for ultimately achieving a genuine *modus vivendi* in Asia, may improve. The United States should do whatever it can, without compromising basic American interests or weakening the security of the non-Communist nations in Asia, to work toward this end. Yet, so far there is little basis for hoping that the nature of Chinese Communist aims, or the character of the struggle, will change basically in the years immediately ahead. The prospect for the predictable future, therefore, is one of intense and unrelenting competition.

CHAPTER 5

EVOLVING TACTICS IN FOREIGN POLICY

WITHIN THE BROAD FRAMEWORK set by their long-range goals, the Chinese Communists have shown considerable flexibility in adapting their foreign policy tactics to the pursuit of short-term aims. Some of Peking's tactical shifts during the past decade have been striking. The contrast, for example, between the relatively flexible posture of "peaceful coexistence" which the Chinese Communists dramatized at the Bandung Conference in 1955 and the rigid militancy and belligerency which Peking showed both in earlier years and more recently is remarkable. The most important of Peking's policy shifts have been closely coordinated with parallel moves made by the Soviet Union and other members of the Communist bloc. But Peking's role has not been that of a mere Soviet satellite. The Chinese Communists have played a very important part in determining and developing the major policies by which the Communist powers have attempted to keep the non-Communist world on the defensive and off balance.

Major Stages in Tactics

Attempts to discover a consistent pattern of action in Communist China's foreign policy can lead one to oversimplify or distort the real facts; it is easy to outline patterns too neatly or to attribute conscious design to situations in which the Communists' purposes and actions have actually been confused or inconsistent. Certainly the Chinese Communists and the Russians—like everyone else—often act in ignorance, make serious miscalculations, and find themselves uncertain about how they should pursue their goals. Yet it is possible to discern definite patterns of action and to identify certain important shifts in approach which are important.

Communist China's foreign policy since 1949 has gone through several broad stages which are quite distinguishable, even though they have overlapped in many respects. A first and brief period, from the founding of the Peking regime in October 1949 until the start of the Korean War in mid-1950, was marked by revolutionary and nationalistic militancy. During this period Peking allied itself firmly with the Soviet bloc, openly proclaimed its revolutionary aims in Asia, pressed forward to complete the unification of China by force, and energetically pursued its goal of expelling Western influence from China. The Korean War, and Communist China's intervention in October 1950, initiated a new wartime period. Peking pressed an all-out defense of what it conceived to be its threatened rights and interests, and combined this with a vigorous offense to achieve its national goals through the use of military force. The third period, starting about 1952, was one of shifting and inconsistent policies. When changes in general tactics first began to take place throughout the Communist bloc, Peking's foreign policy still presented many contradictory elements. However, despite the prolongation of the Korean War into 1953, the sharpening of the crisis in Indo-China during 1953-1954, and the Taiwan crisis of 1954-1955, an extremely important modification was taking place during this period. The change was highlighted by the Korean truce of 1953, the Geneva Conference and Indo-China truce of 1954, and the Bandung Conference of 1955. By the time of the Bandung Conference the new tactics were clear, and in the name of the "five principles of peaceful coexistence" and "Asian solidarity," Peking now deemphasized the use of military force and overt incitement to revolution and initiated a major political and economic offensive.

Since 1955 "peaceful coexistence" has been Peking's main theme in its dealings with most of the underdeveloped countries, and until fairly recently it has been an extremely effective slogan. Particularly in the brief period between the Bandung Conference and the Hungarian revolt, its impact on Asia was tremendous. During the past two years, however, the slogan has been significantly tarnished. Following the Polish and Hungarian crises of 1956 and the Soviet advances in military technology during 1957, Peking, together with Moscow, once again adopted a more militant posture, and in a new period of shifting policies, since late 1957, Chinese Communist tactics have displayed many more contradictions and inconsistencies than during the brief heyday of the "Bandung spirit." While continuing to talk of long-term competitive coexistence, they have exerted new pressures not only against the United States but also against several Asian nations, and this has highlighted the fact that Peking's policy is never confined exclusively to either blandishments or pressures. Attraction, intimidation, and subversion are always mixed, in a varying recipe, even though for tactical reasons Peking may emphasize one or another of these various elements at any particular time. This is probably a good deal clearer now to many Asians than it was during 1955 and 1956 when the "Bandung spirit" was at its height.

Revolutionary and Nationalistic Militancy

The starting point of Peking's official foreign policy in 1949—and the cornerstone of its policy ever since—was the decision to align China closely with the Soviet Union. The Chinese Communist party had been oriented toward the U.S.S.R. since its founding, and in mid-1949, even before the Chinese Communist regime had been formally established, Mao Tse-tung proclaimed Peking's determination to "lean to one side" in the world-wide conflict. The new government immediately established diplomatic relations with the Soviet Union, and between December 1949 and February 1950 the Chinese and Russian leaders negotiated the Sino-Soviet Treaty of Friendship, Alliance, and Mutual Assistance, as well as important economic and other agreements, laying the cornerstone of their future cooperation.

In those first months of victory revolutionary aspirations and hopes dominated the Chinese Communists' attitude toward the non-Communist world. One of their first major moves was to convoke a Trade Union Conference of Asian and Australasian Countries, which was held at Peking in

November 1949 under the auspices of the World Federation of Trade Unions. This important gathering brought together Communist and left-wing labor leaders, rather than government representatives, from all over the region. Not long before the Conference met, Mao Tse-tung had said that "in an era when imperialism still exists, it is impossible for a genuine people's revolution in any country to win its own victory without different kinds of help from the international revolutionary forces."[1] At the Conference, Liu Shao-ch'i asserted that "our Trade Union Conference of Asian and Australasian Countries should support the wars of national liberation" throughout Asia and declared:

The war of national liberation in Vietnam has liberated 90 per cent of her territory; the war of national liberation in Burma and Indonesia is now developing; the partisan warfare against imperialism and its lackeys in Malaya and the Philippines has been carried on over a long period; and armed struggles for emancipation have also taken place in India. In Japan, the progressive labor movement and the progressive people's movement against the conversion of Japan into a colony by American imperialism are developing. The movement of the Korean people against Syngman Rhee, puppet of American imperialism, and for the establishment of a unified people's democratic republic of Korea cannot be halted. The labor movements and national liberation movements in Siam and the Near East countries as well as in Africa are also growing.[2]

He predicted that revolution could be developed in most of Asia through "armed struggle," following the "path of the Chinese people."

The fluid state of affairs in much of Asia had apparently convinced the Chinese Communists that, under the decisive impetus of the Communist victory in China, revolution was destined to sweep across the entire region. In 1948, on the eve of that victory, the world Communist movement had launched a militant drive in Asia. Following an important Communist gathering held at Calcutta, Communist-led rebellions had been started or intensified in Burma and India, Indonesia and Malaya, the Philippines and Indo-China. Once in power, Peking's leaders pledged their support to these uprisings. The Peking Conference in November 1949 established a Trade Union Liaison Bureau, so that "the working people in this part of the world shall not remain unguided and unaided in their struggle for rights" and so that there would be "a nerve center from where contacts will be permanently and constantly maintained." [3]

Elimination of Foreign Influence and Unification of China

Immediately after 1949, because the Chinese Communists considered their own revolution not yet completed, they frequently gave first priority to two primary goals: elimination of foreign influence in China and complete unification of the country.[4] The Common Program, Peking's provisional constitution adopted on September 29, 1949, directed the government to "abolish all prerogatives of imperialist countries in China" and to "undertake to wage the people's war of liberation to the very end, liberate all the territory of China, and accomplish the cause of unifying the country." [5]

One of Peking's first aims, therefore, was to eliminate "all prerogatives" which Westerners had previously held in China. This nationalistic, anti-imperialist goal was pursued within China through a systematic program to expel foreigners (other than those from the Soviet bloc who soon began to replace other Westerners in China).

The Common Program adopted in 1949 also repudiated all of China's pre-1949 agreements and commitments by specifying that the new government should "examine the treaties and agreements concluded between the Kuomintang and foreign governments, and recognize, or abrogate, or revise or renew them according to their respective contents." [6] While the government could "negotiate and establish diplomatic relations on the basis of equality, mutual benefit, and mutual respect for territory and sovereignty," this was to be done only with "foreign governments which sever relations with the Kuomintang reactionaries and adopt a friendly attitude toward the People's Republic of China." [7]

In actuality, Peking appeared to be in no great hurry to establish diplomatic relations with countries outside of the Soviet bloc, and the conditions which the Chinese Communists set for establishing formal relations were a significant factor in their failure to achieve rapid and general international acceptance. Although during late 1949 and 1950 a total of fourteen non-Communist governments recognized the Peking regime and indicated a willingness to establish diplomatic relations with it, the Chinese Communists established formal relations immediately with only six—Burma, India, Indonesia, Switzerland, Sweden, and Denmark.[8] With the other eight—Pakistan, Ceylon, Afghanistan, Norway, Finland, Great Britain, the Netherlands, and Israel—they procrastinated; in several cases, they attempted to use the establishment of diplomatic relations as an instrument of political pressure.

The Chinese Communists' initial attitude toward most Western diplomatic and consular representatives who remained in territory under their control combined indifference and contempt. Peking's violations of traditional diplomatic usages were particularly flagrant in several cases involving American diplomatic and consular personnel—most notably in that of Angus Ward, United States Consul in Mukden, who was severely mistreated and then arrested in late 1949. It was the seizure of property belonging to the American Consulate-General in Peking in January 1950 which precipitated the U.S. decision to withdraw all official personnel from Communist China.

In pursuit of their goal of "liberating" and unifying all the territory associated with China's traditional imperial domain, the Communists in late 1949 and early 1950 made active preparations to invade both Taiwan and Tibet; they mustered their forces along the East China coast and consolidated their control in Southwest China. In early 1950 they seemed confident that both these territories would be secured by military force within a short time.

Korean War and Invasion of Tibet

June 1950 marked a major turning point in the Far East. The sudden, open, and carefully planned aggression by Russia's North Korean satellite shocked much of the world into a realization of the military dimension of the Communist threat, rallied outside powers to the defense of South Korea, and paved the way for the United Nations to support the principle of collective security. It resulted in an immediate and major change in American policy toward China and stimulated the United States to exert great efforts to build up an anti-Communist defense system in the Far East. Peking's response was to embark upon a program of direct military action in Korea, Tibet, and elsewhere. The Chinese Communists clearly felt that these developments threatened vital Chinese national interests, and they chose to take the offensive, with little regard for the attitudes or conflicting interests of other states, rather than to seek compromises.

It seems highly probable that the Russians consulted the Chinese Communists, perhaps during the Stalin-Mao meetings of early 1950, prior to the launching of the attack in Korea. It is also probable that the Chinese approved the attack; if successful, it would have greatly weakened, and perhaps might have undermined, the United States' position in Japan as well as Korea. However, on the basis of available evidence, it appears that before June 1950 Peking had not been preparing to wage war itself in Korea.

The consequences of the North Korean attack, and the American response to it, immediately involved vital Chinese interests, however. Although in January 1950 the United States had disassociated itself from any military obligations to the Nationalist regime on Taiwan, on June 27 President Truman declared that a Communist attack on Taiwan would be a threat to American security. He instructed the Seventh Fleet to neutralize the Taiwan Strait by preventing either Communist or Nationalist attacks across it, and he reopened the whole question of Taiwan's legal status by asserting that this was a question still to be decided in a peace treaty with Japan or by the United Nations. Peking reacted with anger and dismay. In the next few months, in fact, it seemed more concerned over American policy toward Taiwan—which blocked the "liberation" of the island and challenged Communist China's territorial claims—than over the fighting in Korea. Chou En-lai promptly accused the United States of "armed aggression against the territory of China,"[9] and in late August he presented this charge, by cable, to the United Nations.

As the tide of battle turned, following the landing of the United Nations forces at Inchon, Peking showed increasing concern about Korea itself, particularly as fighting approached the 38th Parallel. On September 30 Chou En-lai gave a veiled public warning that "the Chinese people will not tolerate foreign aggression, nor will they supinely tolerate seeing their neighbors savagely invaded by imperialists,"[10] and later K. M. Panikkar, Indian Ambassador in Peking, relayed to the Western powers more specific warnings of possible Chinese intervention. In his report on his ambassadorship, Panikkar asserts that Chou told him on the night of October 2-3 that, if the Americans crossed the 38th Parallel, Communist China would be forced to intervene.[11] Whether or not the crossing of the parallel actually precipitated Peking's intervention, the first Chinese Communist troops did, in fact, arrive in Korea in the guise of "volunteers" in mid-October, a week after United Nations forces had moved north of the parallel, and in late October and November they entered in full force.

Numerous factors may have been involved in the Chinese Communists' decision to intervene. The Russians may have exerted pressure on them to step in and avert a serious Communist defeat, which would have had an adverse effect on the Communist movement throughout the world. Doubtless, Peking genuinely feared the consequences of complete control of the strategic Korean peninsula by unfriendly military forces. It may actually have feared a direct threat to China's own security, despite the repeated assurances offered by the United Nations and the United States. In November, when Wu Hsiu-ch'uan presented Peking's charges against the United States at the United Nations, he accused the United States of "systematically building up a military encirclement of the People's Republic of China, in preparation for further attack on the People's Republic of China," and claimed that the United States "follows the beaten path of the Japanese imperialist aggressors."[12] This path was based, he said, on the idea that "to conquer China, one must first conquer

Manchuria and Mongolia. To conquer Manchuria and Mongolia, one must first conquer Korea and Taiwan."

Although motives of self-defense may well have been an important element in Peking's decision to intervene in Korea, once it had intervened it defined its war aims in fairly broad terms and launched a vitriolic hate campaign against the United States.[13] It rejected United Nations proposals for a cease fire, insisting, as long as the fighting was going in its favor, that the conditions of peace in Korea must include the seating of Communist China in the United Nations, the end of the United States' support for Taiwan, and the removal of all foreign troops from Korea. However, after the conflict had settled into the pattern of a limited war with both sides possessing the use of inviolable sanctuaries as rear bases—and after it had become clear that neither side could win a quick or complete victory without risking a major war—the Chinese Communists gradually abandoned their broader aims, and both major Communist powers undertook a reevaluation of their militant foreign policy strategy. In June 1951 the Russians, obviously with Peking's approval and perhaps on its initiative, suggested the opening of negotiations for a cease fire, and actual negotiations were begun in July.

Communist China's invasion of Tibet took place simultaneously with the first stages of its intervention in Korea. In early October its troops began to move into Tibet, and on October 24 Radio Peking announced that the People's Liberation Army had been ordered to "liberate" the area. In Tibet, as in Korea, the Chinese Communists paid little attention to opinion in the non-Communist world.

Signs of a Major Shift in Tactics

Soon after the Korean truce talks started, the first signs of a slow shift in Communist-bloc tactics appeared. In 1951 a Communist-run World Peace Council meeting proposed that an International Economic Conference be held in Moscow in the following year; obviously, both Moscow and Peking were feeling the pinch of the restrictions on trade with them. The conference, held in April 1952, led to the signing of millions of dollars' worth of private trade "contracts"; although few of these were actually carried out, the conference marked the beginning of what eventually developed into a major drive to reopen trade with the non-Communist world.

During 1951 and 1952 the first significant indications of a shift by Asian Communist parties from a policy of armed insurrection to one of political action were discernible. In the spring of 1952 wide publicity was given to a statement by Stalin that world war was no closer than it had been two years previously and that "the peaceful coexistence of capitalism and communism is fully possible." [14] Stalin's treatise on "Economic Problems of Socialism in the U.S.S.R.," written in early 1952 and published in October 1952, on the eve of the 19th Congress of the Communist Party of the Soviet Union, set the keynote for the Congress and pointed to an important shift of Communist strategy. Emphasizing the growing economic strength of the "camp of socialism," and underlining the impact which it could have on the rest of the world, Stalin declared that the markets of the capitalist countries were bound to shrink and that this would hasten the development of crises and conflicts within the capitalist world, contributing greatly to the ultimate triumph of socialism over capitalism. He underscored, in short, the Communists' opportunities for competing against the West economically.

Following Stalin's death in March 1953, the trend toward a policy of competitive coexistence was accelerated, until it reached a climax with the 20th Congress of the Communist Party of the Soviet Union held in February 1956. Perhaps the most basic reason for this world-wide shift in the Communists' tactics was the fact that their earlier militant policies, first codified in the Cominform meeting of 1947, had essentially failed. They had, actually, stimulated the West to build up its defensive strength in both Europe and Asia, and the West had demonstrated its determination to resist Communist military aggression.

The Chinese Communists had their own special reasons for deciding on a major shift in policy. As the Korean War dragged on, Peking watched the steady development of

United States military strength in Asia. There were also compelling domestic reasons. The Korean War had been costly, and the strains on the Chinese economy were severe. At the same time, Peking was preparing to launch its first Five Year Plan with ambitious economic goals, at the start of 1953. In this conflict between internal aims and external commitments, a decision to push ahead with economic development at home almost inevitably demanded a more cautious foreign policy, so as to avoid an otherwise impossible strain on China's modest resources.

The shift in Chinese policy first became evident in the field of foreign trade. The Chinese Communists took an active part in the International Economic Conference at Moscow, and they followed this up in June 1952 by signing an unofficial "trade agreement" with some of the Japanese participants in the conference. Later in 1952 they concluded an important trade agreement, bartering rice for rubber, with the government of Ceylon. Thereafter, the promotion of trade with non-Communist areas was developed steadily into a major element in Peking's foreign policy.

"People's Diplomacy"

From 1949 until 1952 Peking's interest in Asian countries outside the Communist bloc had been centered principally upon the Communist parties, insurrectionary groups, and other active revolutionary forces. It had shown relatively little interest in actively cultivating relations even with those non-Communist nations, such as India, which were most disposed to take a favorable view of the new regime in China. The first important indications of a change appeared in 1952, when Peking began seriously to develop its "people's diplomacy."

In October 1952, at a well-attended Asian and Pacific Peace Conference held in Peking, the Chinese Communists proclaimed their new line of "peaceful coexistence." The strenuous campaign to mobilize widespread Asian support behind this conference gave dramatic evidence of their new tactical approach. The meeting differed greatly in composition and purpose from the Trade Union Conference of 1949.

Although the delegates were not government officials, neither were they all militant revolutionaries. And instead of talking primarily of violence and revolution and the necessity of backing the Soviet Union in the struggle between two camps, the 1952 conference talked of peace and coexistence. In a message to the United Nations it called, among other things, for measures to "end the fighting in Vietnam, Malaya, and other countries and bring about just and reasonable settlements through negotiations," and it declared that "countries with differing social systems and ways of life can coexist peacefully." [15] It also set up a permanent Liaison Bureau to promote increased cultural and other contacts.

The Asian and Pacific Peace Conference opened up new vistas for Communist China's foreign policy. It marked a partial retreat from rigid and militant revolutionary dogmatism and was a first step in Peking's bid for leadership in Asia on a broader and less doctrinaire basis. It stressed, above all, the idea of common Asian interests cutting across ideological lines. This harbinger of a new "soft" line was largely overshadowed at the time, however, by the continued fighting in Korea and then by Communist China's military threats against Indo-China and Taiwan.

Indo-China War and Geneva Conference

After the Korean truce was at last signed in June 1953 and a shaky stabilization of power had been restored to Northeast Asia, Chinese Communist and world attention shifted almost at once to Southeast Asia, in particular to Indo-China. During 1953 the Communist-led Vietminh stepped up their military efforts, the Chinese Communists began to supply substantial amounts of military equipment to them, and the French intensified their war effort with greatly increased U.S. aid. Late in 1953, however, both the Vietminh and the French showed signs of wanting to end the fighting and both appeared willing to negotiate a settlement. The Chinese Communists also had indicated that they would approve of a negotiated settlement. Yet the fighting became heavier and tension mounted, presenting a serious threat that the conflict might expand to involve the United States and Communist China. Then the Foreign Ministers of the Big Four agreed in early 1954 to convene a special conference to consider the problem of peace in Indo-China, as well as the issue of a permanent settlement in Korea.

When the conference convened at Geneva in April 1954, Communist China occupied the center of the international stage. At the first major conference officially attended by the Chinese Communists, Chou En-lai sat at the conference table as an equal of the Foreign Ministers of the great powers. At Geneva Chou played a leading role, and it was clear to all that Peking held a power of decision which could be crucial in leading either to an armistice or to a broadening of the conflict. The shadow of Communist China's military strength hung over both conference table and battlefield. Chinese military support enabled the Vietminh to step up their pressure and achieve a decisive psychological victory at Dienbienphu in May, while the Geneva Conference was in progress. This growing military pressure, backed by the threat of the vast Chinese armies, played a major role in bringing about a negotiated armistice in July.

At Geneva Chou En-lai was instrumental in negotiating an acceptable formula for the armistice. His proposals, and his private meetings with French Prime Minister Pierre Mendès-France, helped to break what at one point appeared to be an insoluble deadlock. Chinese Communist views on the importance of concluding an armistice, and on the acceptability of the formula finally agreed upon, appear to have prevailed in the end over differing views held by the Vietminh.[16] At the start, at least, the Vietminh had argued strongly for some kind of general settlement for all of Vietnam—rather than a territorial division of the area—since this would undoubtedly have facilitated their struggle to seize control throughout the country. The Chinese Communists, however, finally agreed to divide Vietnam at the 17th Parallel, as well as to accept separate settlements for Laos and Cambodia, and this became the basis of the final agreements. Apparently convinced by the American stand that it was wise to settle for half a loaf, Peking accepted a settlement which would give international sanction to a Communist regime in the north, stabilizing the military situation along a defined line and maintaining North Vietnam as a buffer state. Again, as in Korea, the agreement did achieve a shaky stabilization of power, but it left the political problems unresolved.

Active Diplomacy

The Geneva Conference marked a new and important stage in the development of Chinese Communist tactics. After Geneva, Peking's leaders seemed suddenly to have discovered the potentialities of an active, positive diplomacy, and the importance of government-to-government relations. Very quickly Chou En-lai launched a freewheeling drive to broaden and strengthen Communist China's influence, particularly among the nonaligned countries of South and Southeast Asia. Peking's first move was the signing in April 1954 of an agreement with India on Tibet. Acknowledging China's sovereignty over Tibet, this agreement also set forth the first statement of the so-called "five principles of peaceful coexistence." [17]

Shortly thereafter in June, in an interlude during the Geneva Conference, Chou En-lai stopped off in both New Delhi and Rangoon, en route back to China. The joint communiqués which he signed with Nehru and U Nu reiterated the five principles: "Mutual respect for each other's territorial integrity and sovereignty; nonaggression; noninterference in each other's internal affairs; equality and mutual benefit; and peaceful coexistence." Chou went to great lengths to give verbal assurances of Communist China's peaceful intentions. In New Delhi, he said:

All the nations in the world can peacefully coexist, no matter whether they are big or small, strong or weak, and no matter what kind of social system each of them has. The rights of the people of each nation to national independence and self-determination must be respected. The people of each nation have the right to choose their own state system, without interference from other nations. Revolution cannot be exported; at the same time, outside interference with the common will expressed by the people of any nation should not be permitted. If all the nations of the world put their mutual relations on the basis of these principles, intimidation and aggression by one nation against another would not happen and peaceful coexistence of all nations of the world would be turned from a possibility into a reality.[18]

This was a far cry from Peking's military clarion calls of 1949.

From June 1954 on the five principles became a primary theme in Peking's diplomacy. The West discounted the five principles as pure propaganda, but for several reasons they had a significant impact in Asia, particularly among the uncommitted nations. Through them the Chinese Communists attempted to appeal to deep and widespread currents of feeling prevalent in much of Asia: anticolonialism and anti-Westernism; the desire to be left alone to concentrate on urgent domestic problems; a sense of weakness; a sincere desire for peace; a conviction that military alliances and bases increase rather than decrease the chances of conflict; a feeling that Asians have common bonds which they do not share with the West; and a belief in the desirability of nonalignment and the possibility of avoiding involvement in struggles among the great powers.

There was a further reason why the five principles had a significant impact. By 1954 Communist China, partly as a result of the Korean War, already loomed as the colossus of the East in the eyes of many Asians. Fearful, or at least uneasy, about the Chinese Communists, many Asians felt increasingly the need for seeking an accommodation with Peking, and many of them welcomed any sign from Communist China that this might be feasible on reasonable and dignified terms. Peking's demonstrated power now convinced many Asians that neutralism and accommodation with Communist China were necessary and desirable; Peking's new "peaceful coexistence" line was designed to make this course seem not only possible but attractive.

From Communist China's point of view, the new policies, symbolized by the five principles, were directed toward aims which were more limited but also seemed more readily attainable than its world-shaking purposes of 1949. By fostering Asian solidarity and neutralism, Peking hoped to corrode the U.S.-supported anti-Communist alignment which had slowly developed in reaction to its own "hard" policies. It hoped to offset the pull of SEATO (Southeast Asia Treaty Organization) which was under active consideration at that very time. Its new line sought, in short, to mobilize Asian sympathies against Western-supported military alliances and bases and to divide Asians from the West, as well as to create a benign image of Communist China and reduce fear of the Communists. Above all, Peking hoped throughout Asia to create sympathetic attitudes toward Peking and the entire Communist bloc. The Chinese Communists set out to achieve what they called an "area of collective peace," which would exclude the West.

Following Geneva the Chinese Communists took the initiative in extending their diplomatic contacts in Asia and elsewhere. From the end of 1950 until 1953 Peking had agreed to exchange diplomatic representatives with only two countries, Finland and Pakistan, but after Geneva it was able to extend its formal contacts considerably. In 1954 it established diplomatic relations with the United Kingdom, Norway, and the Netherlands; in 1955 with Yugoslavia, Afghanistan, and Nepal; in 1956 with Egypt, Syria, and Yemen; with Ceylon in 1957; and with Cambodia, Iraq, Morocco, and Sudan in 1958. Since 1957 Peking has also recognized Malaya (which to date has not reciprocated), Ghana, and Guinea. Parallel with the expansion of its diplomatic contacts, Peking also developed even wider cultural and economic relations in many parts of the world.

Taiwan Crisis of 1954-1955

In late 1954 Taiwan remained the principal issue on which Peking still maintained a threatening and bellicose posture, and in his first major speech after Geneva, Chou En-lai indicated clearly that following the settlement in Indo-China, Communist China was turning its attention to Taiwan.[19] Then in September the Chinese Communists opened a heavy bombardment of the Nationalist-held offshore islands. Once again the Far East was gripped by a war scare. Peking's ominous actions seemed, in the eyes of the United States and much of the West, to make a mockery of Peking's assertions of peaceful intentions. This was not the universal reaction, however. Some nonaligned Asian countries, such as India, although urging Peking not to use force, accepted Communist China's territorial claims to the offshore islands and Taiwan and felt that Peking's action toward these islands could not be used as a basis for judging its general policy.

By its bombardment of the offshore islands, Peking made limited gains. Under pressure from the United States, the Nationalists in February 1956 evacuated the Tachen Island group, which had come to be regarded in Washington as a military liability. But the United States responded strongly to the broader Chinese Communist threat; Congress authorized President Eisenhower to defend Taiwan and the Pescadores and left it to his discretion whether or not to defend some of the offshore islands as well. In the face of this response, Peking decided to back down. In retrospect it seems probable that the Chinese Communists were not then prepared to attack Taiwan but were attempting to test what could be accomplished by the threat of force. When threats failed, they retreated temporarily and decided to rely for the time being on political rather than military tactics. By the spring of 1955, with the crisis over Taiwan subsiding, the change in the tactical framework of Peking's foreign policy was almost complete. This was made dramatically clear in two conferences held in April 1955: the Conference of Asian Countries at New Delhi, and the Conference of Asian and African Countries at Bandung.

The New Delhi Conference, composed of nonofficial representatives, mainly Communists and fellow travelers, proclaimed "Asian solidarity" as the new central theme of Communist-controlled or Communist-influenced "people's movements" throughout Asia. Serving as a prelude to Chou En-lai's performance at Bandung, it marked the start of a new campaign of "people's diplomacy" to develop a wide movement under the slogan of "Asian solidarity."

The Bandung Conference of 1955

The Asian-African Conference at Bandung was convened by five nations—India, Burma, Indonesia, Pakistan, and Ceylon—the so-called "Colombo powers" who in the spring of

1954 had established an informal grouping to cooperate in meeting common problems. It was described by many government leaders who attended it as a symbol of the "resurgence of Asia and Africa." There is no doubt that it was an historic and unprecedented gathering, bringing together as it did the principal leaders of 29 Asian and African countries in a meeting free from the influence of great Western powers.[20] It symbolized the increasing importance of the non-Western nations in world affairs.

The Bandung Conference gave Chou En-lai an unprecedented opportunity to use all of his diplomatic skill to win friends and influence people, to create the image of a conciliatory Chinese Communist regime, and to promote Peking's new foreign policy line. Together with Nehru, Chou played a dominant role at the meeting. Within the conference halls he adopted a patient demeanor, even when there were heated arguments on whether "Communist colonialism" should be condemned along with "Western colonialism." He even assumed the role of a pacifier. "The Chinese delegation has come here to seek unity and not to quarrel," he said. "We do not hide the fact that we believe in communism," but "there is no need at this conference to publicize one's ideology and the political system of one's country." The aim of Communist China, he declared, was "to seek common ground, not to create divergence." Common ground, he said, could be found in "doing away with the sufferings and calamities of colonialism." Communist China, he asserted, "is prepared to establish normal relations with all Asian and African countries, with all the countries of the world, and first of all with our neighboring countries."

Outside the conference halls Chou made well-timed peaceful or conciliatory gestures on two important issues. He signed a treaty with Indonesia concerning the status of Overseas Chinese, and he offered to negotiate with the United States on "relaxing tension in the Taiwan area." In addition, while at Bandung, Chou En-lai carried on the most active kind of extracurricular diplomacy and made friendly gestures to the delegates of numerous countries.

In the period following the conference Communist China energetically pursued its new foreign policy tactics, within the framework of its approach at Bandung. Both Peking and Moscow played up the theme of competitive coexistence, stressing in particular the willingness of the Communist bloc to enter into long-term economic competition with the West, the fostering of neutralism, and the development of "a zone of peace" uniting the uncommitted areas of the world with the Communist bloc.

The New Militancy

It is useful, as a kind of shorthand, to distinguish between "hard" and "soft" Communist tactics—between tactics which emphasize threats or pressure and those which emphasize conciliation or attraction. However, Communist China's policies cannot always be fitted into these simple categories. Its approach to any particular situation or problem often combines both pressure and attraction and is actually both "hard" and "soft" at the same time. Furthermore, its policies toward different areas can be strikingly different; Peking may be "soft" toward one area and "hard" toward another simultaneously.

In recent years the Chinese Communists have tended to divide the world rather schematically into three general groupings of nations: the Communist bloc, the Western bloc, and the nonaligned countries of the underdeveloped regions. Their relationships with the Communist bloc nations are very different in almost every respect from those which they maintain with the rest of the world. In addition, Peking is capable of pursuing quite different tactics toward each of the two main non-Communist groupings. Immediately after 1955 the Chinese Communists, as sponsors of the "Bandung spirit," and the Russians, as sponsors of the "Geneva spirit," attempted to emphasize, on a world-wide basis, their reasonableness, their willingness to negotiate on all outstanding problems, and their desire to "relax tensions." This lasted for only a brief period of time, however. By the end of 1957 the leaders of the Sino-Soviet bloc had reverted to a more militant posture in dealing with problems within the bloc and in their approach to the United States and other countries closely aligned with the West. Even in their policies toward Asian nations, they began to apply new pressures. Yet they did not, by any means, wholly abandon their attempts to attract the nonaligned nations of the Asian-African world; they continued wooing them under the banner of "competitive coexistence."

Some of the most important aspects of the hardening of Sino-Soviet policies since 1957 will be treated in later chapters.[21] In general terms, however, the shift may have been caused by several factors: the sudden release of pent-up tensions within the Communist bloc following Khrushchev's denunciation of Stalin at the 20th Congress of the Communist Party of the Soviet Union; the domestic strains encountered by both the Russian and Chinese Communists during 1956-1957; and a reassessment of the world balance of forces stimulated by Russia's success in launching an ICBM and earth satellite in late 1957.

Peking's relatively "soft" policy toward the nonaligned countries of Asia did not prevent it from giving full support to Moscow's "hard" policies on matters affecting the solidarity of the Communist bloc. The Chinese Communists promptly endorsed the Soviet military repression of the Hungarian revolt, and although for some months during 1956 and early 1957 Peking played a mediating role in relations between the U.S.S.R. and the East European satellites, by late 1957 the Chinese Communists had apparently concluded, along with Khrushchev, that the time had come to be tough toward all signs of "revisionism" within the bloc and to adopt a more militant posture toward the West.

This shift first became clearly apparent in November 1957. When representatives of Communist parties throughout the world gathered in Moscow to celebrate the fortieth anniversary of the Bolshevik revolution, Mao Tse-tung played a leading role in defining the bloc's new line. His speeches in Moscow strongly reemphasized the East-West struggle. "I consider that the present world situation has reached a new turning point," Mao declared on November 18.

There are now two winds in the world: the east wind and the west wind. There is a saying in China: "If the east wind does not prevail over the west wind, then the west wind will prevail over the east wind." I think the characteristic of the current situation is that the east wind prevails over the west wind; that is, the strength of socialism exceeds the strength of imperialism.[22]

The declarations issued at the close of the Moscow conference constituted a clarion call for strengthened discipline within the Communist bloc, renewed dedication to the world-wide Communist movement, and increased militancy toward the West. Subsequently, Mao's phrase—"the east wind prevails over the west wind"—was adopted by the Chinese Communists as a primary slogan in their new approach to East-West relations. It is difficult to know whether this was merely a propaganda slogan to divert attention from internal problems or whether it represented a genuine belief that world forces were shifting steadily in the Communists' favor. Evidence can be cited to support either view. The Chinese Communists undoubtedly were encouraged by "Sputnik" and other Russian technological developments, by the rapid rate of economic growth within the bloc, and by the growth of anti-Western nationalism and neutralism in the Asian-African world, but there is also no doubt that they were seriously disturbed by "revisionism" in Eastern Europe and by new tensions within China.

Events since November 1957 provide ample evidence in any case that Moscow and Peking have actively attempted to seize from the West the initiative in international action, and they have demonstrated once again that they are willing to use strong pressures and threats of force to pursue some of their basic goals. The Lebanon-Iraq crisis of early 1958, the offshore islands crisis of late 1958, the Berlin crisis of 1958-1959, and the Sino-Indian and Laotian crises of 1959 have followed in rapid succession.

Communist China's decision to precipitate the second major offshore islands crisis in the fall of 1958, on the heels of Khrushchev's dramatic and unannounced trip to Peking, has been the outstanding example of its new belligerency, but it is by no means the only one. In the spring of 1958 Peking assumed a bitterly hostile attitude toward Yugoslav "revisionism," adopting a line on this issue which was considerably harsher than that of the Russians.[23] In the summer of 1958, during the Lebanon-Iraq crisis, there was talk in Peking of sending "volunteers" to the Middle East. The Chinese Communists also intimated to the Indonesian government their willingness to come to Djakarta's support against the Indonesian rebels who were accused by both the Indonesians and the Chinese Communists of receiving encouragement and support from the West. During the same period, in order to obtain political concessions, Peking decided to bring strong pressure to bear against the Kishi government in Japan—which it accused of being a U.S. puppet—by cutting off all Sino-Japanese trade. Then the most startling deviation from the Chinese Communists' "peaceful coexistence" tactics occurred in the latter half of 1959 when Peking precipitated a border crisis with India and gave strong backing to renewed insurrection in Laos. These pressures on South and Southeast Asia, following Peking's brutal suppression of revolt in Tibet, opened the eyes of many Asians to the character of the Chinese Communist regime and had a tremendous impact on attitudes toward China.

The Implications of "Competitive Coexistence"

Do these recent developments mean that Peking has decided to abandon completely its tactics of "competitive coexistence"? Despite the hazards of attempting to predict the Communists' tactical shifts, it seems probable that the answer is no. One cannot, of course, rule out completely the possibility that Peking has made a major decision to place an increased reliance on military force to achieve its goals. However, as of the early autumn of 1959, there is little to indicate that the Chinese Communists have, in fact, decided to pursue a general policy of large-scale military aggression. The new pressures they have been exerting on China's neighbors have to date been limited pressures, and apparently Peking's aims both in regard to the Sino-Indian border and Laos have also been limited. In both of these situations, in fact, local factors rather than broad tactical considerations seem to provide the main explanation for Peking's recent actions, and it appears likely that after attempting to make local gains, Peking will probably try once again to reemphasize the carrot rather than the stick in its relations with South and Southeast Asia. Doubtless, it will then try to repair the damage to its broad policy of "competitive coexistence" which its recent actions have caused. This is not to say, however, that Peking will find this easy to do, even though people's memories tend to be short. It is now quite clear that the "five principles" and the "Bandung spirit" have been so badly tarnished, and public attitudes in India and many other Asian nations have been so profoundly affected by recent events, that even if Peking does become more conciliatory again, millions of Asians will have far more fear and suspicion of Peking in the years immediately ahead than they have felt in recent years.

Under any circumstances, the military factor in Communist China's policy cannot be ignored or underestimated. Peking's military power is an extremely important element in strengthening its prestige and influence throughout Asia, and particularly in those areas where it asserts territorial claims it displays a continuing reliance on force and threats to achieve its aims. Furthermore, if the world-wide balance of power should be altered significantly, Peking might well adopt a more aggressive general posture.

Assuming, however, that no drastic change is likely to upset the balance of power, it seems probable that in the next few years the Chinese Communists will continue, while rapidly building up their economic and military strength, to depend primarily on the use of political and economic rather than of military means to expand their influence abroad. They will probably continue attempting to exert attraction, as well as using political and economic influence, and in certain situations applying pressures, to achieve their foreign policy aims. Looking beyond the immediate future, Peking's leaders hope that in the long run internal revolutions will bring Communist regimes to power in most Asian countries, and they can be expected to work persistently toward this end. But in the short run Peking will probably place its first priority on exerting increased influence on the existing non-Communist governments in Asia, while standing ready to exploit revolutionary changes within any of these countries if and when they should occur.

Chapter 6

MILITARY STRENGTH AND THE BALANCE OF POWER

THE ESTABLISHMENT OF a strong Communist regime in China and its alliance with the Soviet Union have fundamentally altered the balance of power in Asia. The initial impact of these great changes was magnified because they came soon after the demilitarization of Japan and the withdrawal of almost all of Western Europe's military power from South and Southeast Asia. And since 1949 the Peking regime has transformed mainland China from a power vacuum into an important center of military strength.

Communist China's military development has created many new problems for all of those non-Communist countries, both Asian and Western, which are actively concerned either about their own defense or about the prevention of aggression in Asia. It has greatly complicated the task of guaranteeing United States security interests in that region. Whatever Communist China's military intentions may prove to be in the years ahead, the United States cannot avoid facing the basic problem of how to counterbalance Peking's new power.

The ground forces of Communist China are now second in size only to those of the Soviet Union, and they have been modernized into an effective fighting machine. Peking's air force has been built up with Soviet aid to substantial strength. Even though Communist China's naval and amphibious forces are still limited, it possesses greater naval strength than any of its Asian neighbors. As far as is known, Peking does not, to date, possess nuclear weapons or missiles, but in the event of a major conflict it might obtain them from the Soviet Union. Communist China's leaders have publicly declared that it is their intention eventually to possess these newest weapons.

Today Communist China is the only power of major military importance among the Asian states. The strength of its "People's Liberation Army" is probably greater, in fact, than that of the military establishments of all the non-Communist nations of the Far East, Southeast Asia, and South Asia combined. Its own military power is backed, furthermore, by that of the Soviet Union, which has supported Communist China with a continuing flow of military supplies and advice. Ever since 1950 the Sino-Soviet alliance has given Peking the assurance of Soviet support in the event of military conflict with Japan or a Japan-United States combination.[1] In September 1958 the Soviet Union appeared to extend its commitment even further when Khrushchev asserted that "an attack on the People's Republic of China, which is a great friend, ally, and neighbor of our country, is an attack on the Soviet Union"; he pledged that the Soviet Union would "do everything to defend, jointly with People's China, the security of both countries." [2] Communist China also has two close Asian allies of military importance, and it has given both of them military equipment and advice. North Vietnam now possesses the strongest military forces in Southeast Asia, and the military strength of North Korea is substantial.

Peking's Armed Forces

Communist China is first and foremost a land power, and the principal basis of its strength is its ground forces. At present its People's Liberation Army has a total of over two and one-half million men in active service in ground, naval, and air forces. The ground forces include over one hundred and fifty divisions of ten to twelve thousand men each, organized along lines similar to those of the Soviet army. In addition, the Chinese Communists have over half a million troops in public security units, which are responsible for frontier duties and internal security, plus a huge militia organization. In a fundamental sense, China under Communist rule has been militarized. Martial virtues and military men have been elevated to a position of new prestige in Chinese society, and the population of the country has been fully mobilized to support the military establishments.

Communist China's reserves of military manpower are tremendous. It is estimated that China has about 160 million men in the 15 to 49 age group and that, of these, roughly 80 million are physically fit for military service. The system of nation-wide conscription initiated in 1955, under which all men are liable for military service at eighteen, gives the Peking regime a broad base of military manpower.[3] Those not called up, as well as demobilized soldiers, are systematically organized into the reserves. The millions of partially trained local militiamen are also an important element in the reservoir of military manpower.

Greatly expanded during the offshore islands crisis in the fall of 1958 [4] the militia reportedly now totals several tens of millions, and the almost seven million regular army men demobilized [5] between 1949 and early 1958 play a key role in it. University and high school students in Communist China are also given rudimentary military training, and a nation-wide physical training program, under military supervision and in a military spirit, has been actively promoted.[6] Furthermore, in the communes which have been organized throughout China since 1958, virtually the entire rural population is disciplined and drilled along semimilitary lines.

Communist China's regular forces, reorganized and re-equipped since the start of the Korean War, constitute an effective, though still "conventional" and preatomic, military establishment. Specialization has been steadily developed, and today the forces include tank, artillery, parachute, antiaircraft, communications, and other specialized units. Some troops have received special training in amphibious operations. The system of logistics has been improved, as have communications and other supporting services. Firepower and modern equipment have been built up steadily, and standard weapons include 57-mm recoilless guns, heavy mortars, rocket launchers, 70-mm howitzers, and similar equipment. The army also has sizable numbers of Soviet tanks, heavy artillery pieces, heavy trucks, and armored personnel carriers. In short, Peking's ground forces have been converted from a large but fairly simple type of infantry force, which had grown out of earlier guerrilla and mobile units, into a complicated army with the numerous specialized units required for modern large-scale warfare.

Peking's air force, built entirely during the past decade, now consists of approximately 2,500 planes, of which 1,800 or more are jets. It is organized into about thirty air divisions. It includes numerous jet MIG-15s, and since 1958 it has acquired jet MIG-17s. Although essentially a tactical rather than a strategic air force, it has some IL-28 jet bombers, and it is believed to have a few TU long-range bombers. Jet air fields have been constructed in many parts of China, and there are now close to thirty bases concentrated near the East China coast opposite Taiwan.[7] Communist China's air force has never been completely tested in combat, and in 1958 its performance was not impressive in the limited encounters it had with Chinese Nationalist planes during the second Quemoy crisis—apparently because of deficiencies in the training of the pilots. Nevertheless, it constitutes an air force of major importance, one which is far stronger than that of any other Asian nation.

Although it is the weakest link in Communist China's forces, Peking's navy is the largest indigenous naval force in the Far East. It includes at least 1 light cruiser, 4 destroyers, 13 submarines, 15 frigates, 6 gunboats, 52 torpedo boats, and 150 other craft of various types. A heterogeneous collection of ships, it has considerable capabilities for coastal escort, patrol duties, mine laying, and amphibious assault, and the recent acquisition of submarines has substantially augmented its capabilities.[8] A number of important naval bases have been built along the China coast. In addition, the Chinese Communists possess thousands of junks, many of them motorized, which could be used in restricted amphibious operations —certainly against the nearby offshore islands along the China coast—and, if the United States fleet were to withdraw, possibly against Taiwan.

Other Military Factors

Since 1949, in addition to modernizing its armed forces, the Chinese Communist regime has made great efforts to strengthen its military position in other ways. It has substantially improved its internal communications system and has built numerous strategically important railroads and motor roads, including new rail lines on the Fukien coast opposite Taiwan and on the strategic Shantung and Liuchow peninsulas. It has also built or restored two railways connecting Communist China with North Vietnam. To supplement its Manchurian rail links with the Soviet Union it has built a new line connecting with the Siberian railway via Outer Mongolia; and a railway through Sinkiang, to connect with the Turk-Sib line in Soviet Central Asia, is scheduled for completion by 1960. In Southwest China it has built motor roads of major strategic significance, including two trunk highways to Tibet. A whole new railway system on a north-south axis, deep in the interior of China and far from the coast, is now under construction.

Communist China is now virtually self-sufficient in the production of small arms and ammunition. It has started producing trucks and small noncombat airplanes, and it claims to have produced jet aircraft—although it undoubtedly cannot yet manufacture all of the parts required. Much of the new heavy industry has been built in regions close to the Soviet Union and distant from the coastal areas—an obvious strategic advantage. And the recent trend toward industrial decentralization has great potential military significance. Despite their industrial advances, however, the Chinese Communists have not achieved self-sufficiency in military production; they are still dependent upon the Soviet Union for combat aircraft, tanks, heavy artillery, petroleum products, advanced communications equipment, and other important matériel.

Communist China's military leadership is competent and experienced. Until the Korean War its knowledge of advanced military technology and organization was limited, but it learned a great deal during the Korean War, and it has undoubtedly continued to learn from Soviet advisers. In the Korean War the Chinese Communists demonstrated that their troops could perform creditably against opponents armed with powerful, modern, conventional firepower and airpower. The morale of their troops held firm then, and there is every reason to believe that their morale is still dependable from the Communists' point of view. The party pays special attention to its political control over the armed forces. An estimated 75 per cent of Peking's troops are enrolled in either the Communist party or the Young Communist League. They are subjected to intensive and continuous indoctrination, with about 10 to 15 hours each week devoted to political instruction. Political officers are assigned to all units down to the company, and tight political control is exercised over the rank and file.[9] Military personnel also receive preferential treatment in many respects.

At the end of the Korean War 14,000 Chinese prisoners-of-war showed their opposition to the Peking regime by choosing not to return to Communist China. But while the fighting was still going on very few deserted or defected. In 1958, when the nation-wide "rectification" campaign in Communist China was implemented in the army, there was no evidence of extensive purges among the military; as far as is known, only one general officer was expelled at that time. One cannot rule out the possibility that if serious unrest were to spread through China the army might reflect discontent among the peasants—in particular among discharged veterans—but at present there are no signs of any significant loyalty problem in the army.

Atomic Weapons

Although Communist China must be ranked as a major military power in terms of "conventional" forces, it is not yet a first-rank military power because it still lacks nuclear weapons. It cannot be assumed, however, that the Chinese Communists will not obtain such weapons in the future, and the attitudes of Peking's leaders toward nuclear warfare must be weighed even now in evaluating Communist China's military potential.

In the years immediately following their coming to power Peking's leaders publicly depreciated the importance of nuclear weapons. The official propaganda line was reflected in numerous articles. For example, in an article published in November 1950, after Peking had intervened in Korea, the Chinese Communists argued that "the atomic bomb itself cannot be the decisive factor in a war," asserting that "the more extensive the opponent's territory is and the more scattered the opponent's population is, the less effective will the atom bomb be." [10]

Perhaps the real basis for the Chinese Communists' attitude in this period was reflected in a statement, in the same article, which expressed faith in the deterrent effect of the atomic strength of China's ally, the Soviet Union. "The atomic bomb . . . is now no longer monopolized by the U.S.," the article stated; "the Soviet Union has it too." Yet there were numerous indications in those years that Peking's leaders may in fact have believed that China's huge population and territory made their regime relatively invulnerable. Just prior to Communist China's entry into the Korean War, a top Chinese general said privately to the Indian Ambassador, K. M. Panikkar: "The Americans can bomb us, they can destroy our industries, but they cannot defeat us on land. . . . We have calculated all that. They may even drop atom bombs on us. What then? They may kill a few million people. Without a sacrifice a nation's independence cannot be upheld. . . . After all, China lives on the farms. What can atom bombs do there?" [11]

In recent years there have been indications of some change in the Chinese Communist view of nuclear warfare. Since about 1955, in its propaganda toward the Japanese, Peking had emphasized Japan's vulnerability to atomic warfare. And the idea of creating a nuclear-free zone in Asia through a regional agreement forbidding the use of nuclear weapons has become an increasingly important theme in its propaganda. These and other developments seem to suggest a shift of attitude. Perhaps this shift is the result of the Chinese Communists' learning more from the Soviet Union about the potentialities of nuclear warfare, or it may be due to the West having developed an increasingly effective arsenal of tactical atomic weapons. In any case, by 1958 Chinese Communist leaders began to talk of their determination to get possession of nuclear weapons. Early in the year Foreign Minister Ch'en Yi stated that Communist China would eventually acquire them, without specifying when.[12]

After Khrushchev's visit to Peking in July and August 1958

reports circulated in Eastern Europe that the Soviet Union had agreed to supply Communist China with both atomic weapons and missiles.[13] These rumors have not been definitely confirmed, but in the summer of 1959 Khrushchev reportedly claimed, in an interview with former New York Governor Averell Harriman, that Russia has shipped numerous rockets to China,[14] and in the early autumn of 1959 it was "reliably reported," according to the *New York Times* correspondent in Hong Kong, that Lin Piao, Peking's new Defense Minister, had obtained assistance from a Soviet military commission in working out a reorganization plan for China's forces which would involve changing existing units into pentomic divisions capable of using nuclear weapons. Actually, although Moscow appears to have been reluctant to arm even its most important ally with nuclear weapons, as Peking's bargaining power has grown, it has appeared increasingly possible, or even probable, that the Chinese Communists would gain access to atomic weapons if they should become involved in a major conflict in which Communist China was itself threatened with atomic attack.

Possibly, the Chinese Communists may still believe that, because of China's size and population, they are relatively invulnerable to atomic weapons. In 1958 Tito asserted that Peking's leaders felt they could afford to sacrifice 300 million people in an atomic war if it were necessary. Without accepting any such extreme statement as literally true, it must be recognized that Communist China's leaders have often displayed callousness to military casualties and other human losses, and it cannot be assumed, therefore, that they would be unwilling to risk a major conflict, even with atomic powers, over certain issues.

Sino-Soviet Military Relationship

Communist China is not a member of the Soviet-led Warsaw Pact; it has merely been an observer rather than a full participant at its meetings. Yet in 1955 P'eng Teh-huai, who was then Peking's Minister of Defense, proclaimed publicly in Warsaw:

I am authorized to state on behalf of the Government of the Chinese People's Republic that it will give unreserved support and cooperation to all resolutions adopted by the Warsaw Conference for Safeguarding Peace and Security in Europe by European Countries. . . . Peace is indivisible. If peace in Europe is undermined, if imperialist aggressors light the flames of war against the peaceful countries of Europe, then our Government and the 600 million heroic people of China will struggle against aggression jointly with the people and governments of our fraternal countries until final victory.[15]

Leading Chinese generals have publicly recognized that in a new world war "the major and decisive battlefield will be Europe"; [16] China seems pledged, however, to support the Soviet Union in any such war, possibly by taking coordinated action in Asia.

The Soviet pledges to Peking, which seemed considerably less sweeping until 1958, appear to have been broadened by Khrushchev's statement in September 1958 in which he promised Russia's full support to Peking in the event of any attack on Communist China, threatening to take retaliatory action elsewhere in Asia. An assessment of Communist China's military position in the event of a major war must take into account, therefore, the half-million men in Soviet forces maintained east of Lake Baikal, and the air and naval strength, particularly submarines, stationed in the Maritime Provinces. In a large-scale war involving both Communist China and the Soviet Union, Russia would immediately become the major Communist protagonist, with Communist China playing a supporting role.

The Chinese Communists' dependence upon the Russians is greater in respect to military supplies than in any other field, and the railway supply routes between the two countries are long and would be easy targets for assault by air. Despite Peking's program of industrial dispersal, China's industries are vulnerable too. In any large-scale war the Chinese might encounter serious supply problems, therefore, but this would not necessarily prevent them from employing their vast manpower in many ways, with the weapons and equipment already on hand.

North Korea and North Vietnam

On Communist China's northeastern frontier the North Korean regime has an army of over 350,000 men with good armor and artillery and an air force of over 700 jet aircraft, mainly fighters but including some bombers. Since the withdrawal in 1958 of some 300,000 Chinese troops from North Korea,[17] the North Korean regime has been definitely weaker in terms of military strength than the South Korean regime, which has nearly twice as many men under arms. The North Koreans have a stronger air force, however, and Chinese Communist troop reinforcements would undoubtedly be readily available in the event of renewed North-South conflict. In divided Vietnam the ratio of local troop strength is the reverse of that in Korea. Communist North Vietnam has close to 300,000 troops, roughly double the number in South Vietnam's forces.

Both Communist China and the Soviet Union have provided military equipment and advice to North Vietnam as well as to North Korea. Since external support is required for both to maintain their present levels of strength, Peking and Moscow will probably continue giving them military aid, and these two allies provide the Chinese Communists with useful strength on their two most sensitive flanks.

The Forces of Non-Communist Asian Nations

The military strength built up by Communist China and its allies has completely altered the balance of power among Asian nations. In this new situation substantial American forces, equipped with atomic weapons, have been required to create a counterbalance to Communist strength. In the Far East alone, from the Soviet Far East through Southeast Asia, the ratio of strength between Communist and non-Communist armed forces is roughly 1.8 to 1. The Communist nations have over 3.65 million men under arms in that area, while the non-Communist nations, including the United States, have only a few more than 2 million. The forces of Communist China and its allies have the advantages of relative concentration and interior lines of communication, whereas the non-Communist forces are divided and dispersed. The Chinese Communists also have a great superiority in manpower reserves. Without external assistance, and specifically without the support of American nuclear weapons, probably none of the non-Communist nations on China's periphery—with the possible exception of island countries, such as Japan, the Philippines, and Indonesia—would be able to defend themselves for more than a limited period if Communist China should decide to launch direct and full-scale aggression against them.

The only Asian power in the Far East which could, in theory, develop independent military strength which might counterbalance that of Communist China is Japan. But Japan, disarmed after World War II, is still militarily weak. Although it is now taking some steps to build up its defense forces, numerous factors—including a reluctance to pay the costs of arming, widespread pacifist and neutralist currents, and constitutional obstacles—have delayed the development of even a minimum of defensive strength. With close to 200,000 men now under arms, Japan under current plans is expected by mid-1961 to have 1,300 planes and a navy of 124,000 tons; it is doubtful that these minimum forces would provide it with an adequate basis for self-defense against a Communist attack in the event of major war. They certainly do not provide any counterbalance to Communist China's power elsewhere in the Far East. For the foreseeable future Japan, like all of the United States' Asian allies, will be dependent upon American support for its defense against attack.

With some half-million men under arms,[18] India is potentially capable of developing substantial, counterbalancing power, but its leaders are committed to devote as much as possible of India's limited resources to essential economic development programs, and, in any case, their philosophy of nonalignment in world affairs has led them consciously to avoid any appearance of military competition with Communist China. Furthermore, both India and Pakistan (the latter with close to 200,000 men in its regular armed forces plus about 60,000 state and security police) have appeared more concerned, at least until recently, with their dispute over

Kashmir than with a possible military threat from Communist China.

The two non-Communist nations in the Far East which currently have the strongest military forces are South Korea and the Chinese Nationalist regime on Taiwan. With over 600,000 well-armed ground troops and a small air force with about 100 fighter aircraft, including jet F-86s, South Korea possesses the strongest non-Communist military establishment on the periphery of Communist China. The Chinese Nationalists on Taiwan have a total of close to 600,000 troops in uniform, of whom about 465,000 are in active army, navy, air force, and marine units. Of roughly 300,000 in the ground forces, about one-third are stationed on the offshore islands. The Nationalists' air force has considerable strength; it includes over 500 aircraft, of which over 300 are F-84 and F-86 jet fighters and a few are bombers of World War II types.

The cost of maintaining these military establishments in South Korea and Taiwan, which are very large in proportion to their population and resources, is carried for the most part by the United States. Consequently, although the governments of both South Korea and Nationalist China have frequently talked of their desire to take offensive military action against the Communists, they are unable to do this without involving the United States and without the assurance of large-scale American assistance. Indeed, they cannot defend themselves against any major attack without the active participation of United States forces.

None of the non-Communist countries in Southeast Asia would be capable of more than a relatively brief defense on the ground if they should be attacked in force by Communist China, or by North Vietnam with Chinese Communist support. Compared with Peking's huge military machine, the regular armed forces in even the larger Southeast Asian nations are very small: Indonesia, 190,000; South Vietnam, 150,000; Thailand, 90,000; Burma, 65,000; the Philippines, about 35,000. (If semimilitary police forces are included, some of these figures should be higher; some estimates of Thailand's total forces run as high as 160,000.) With varying types of United States, British, and French support, local defense forces are being strengthened in a number of Southeast

Asian countries, from South Vietnam, Laos, and Cambodia to Thailand and Malaya. The purposes of the aid programs are limited; they are designed to build forces which can maintain internal security, strengthen defenses, and thereby deter a potential aggressor by making certain that he would face a determined local resistance. Even so, the economic burden of achieving these limited goals is an extremely heavy one. In the event of a large-scale Communist attack these countries probably could do no more than delay the invasion, unless effective support came from the United States or other outside powers.

U.S. Military Power in East Asia

After 1949 American strategic and political planning was forced to recognize the military imbalance which had been created in Asia by the rise to power of a strong Communist regime in China, the relative weakness of the nearby non-Communist countries, and the growing fear of Chinese Communist military ambitions stimulated by the Korean and Indo-Chinese wars. The United States gradually embarked upon a program of strengthening its own military position in Asia and attempted to build a counterbalance to Communist military power through a system of military bases, alliances, and aid programs.

The United States signed a military alliance with Australia and New Zealand (ANZUS) in 1951, and bilateral military pacts with Japan and the Philippines in 1951, with South Korea in 1953, and with Nationalist China in 1954. A multilateral Southeast Asia Collective Defense Treaty (SEATO, including Thailand, the Philippines, Pakistan, the United Kingdom, Australia, New Zealand, France, and the United States) was concluded in 1954. The "protective mantle" of SEATO was also extended to include South Vietnam, Cambodia, and Laos.

This series of treaties has committed the United States to help defend each of its new allies. In their wording the commitments are not as explicit or binding as the American commitment to NATO, but they are very strong nevertheless. In most of the agreements each of the signatories agrees, in the event of "armed attack" against the parties or areas specified by the agreement, to "act to meet the common danger in accordance with its constitutional processes." [19] The agreements with Japan, Korea, Nationalist China, and the Philippines give the United States the right to station American military forces in these countries, and the agreement with Japan authorizes the United States to use its forces based there for "the maintenance of international peace and security in the Far East" as well as for the defense of Japan.[20] The American commitment is strongest with respect to Nationalist China. The Joint Resolution on the defense of Taiwan, adopted by the United States Congress in 1955, gave the President prior authorization "to employ the Armed Forces of the United States as he deems necessary for the specific purpose of securing and protecting Formosa and the Pescadores" as well as "related positions and territories" which are "now in friendly hands" if "appropriate in assuring the defense of Formosa and the Pescadores." [21]

The United States has built up air and naval bases or facilities in Japan, Korea, Taiwan, and the Philippines and has also developed a major base on Okinawa under direct United States administration. From the American point of view, Japan and Okinawa are, without doubt, the most vital military positions in the Far East—Japan, as the principal supply base, and Okinawa, as its strongest complex of air bases in that part of the world. Major American naval bases are located in Japan and the Philippines, and there are important air bases in all four countries. These bases are backed up by more distant American bases located on Guam and elsewhere in the Pacific. The United States has also made the major contribution, in terms of financial support, equipment, and military advice, to the strengthening of local forces in South Korea, Japan, Nationalist China, the Philippines, South Vietnam, Laos, and Thailand.

The United States maintains only small ground forces of its own in Asia. Of American forces in the Pacific region totaling almost 550,000, about one-half are associated with the Pacific Fleet, and the bulk of United States combat ground forces is located in South Korea and Okinawa, in each of which there are about 50,000 American troops.[22]

Because of the weakness in manpower of the armed forces of the United States and its Asian allies, American military strategy in Asia has come to be based on the concept of a "mobile striking force," operating from bases in the island chain stretching from the Aleutians to the Philippines and ready to respond to a variety of emergencies when and where they arise.[23] This mobile strength is composed primarily of air and naval forces equipped with both conventional and atomic weapons. The core of United States naval strength in the area is the Seventh Fleet, which maintains a sizable force there at all times and can be built up rapidly in time of crisis. In 1958, at the height of the second Quemoy crisis, the Seventh Fleet's force in the Taiwan Strait area was enlarged to 70,000 men and about 50 combat ships, including 3 heavy cruisers, 6 aircraft carriers, and 40 destroyers. From a number of bases such as Guam, the United States Strategic Air Force is capable of striking at targets throughout the Far East. The 5th and 13th Air Forces operate with up-to-date jets out of Okinawa and the Philippines, and units of the Tactical Air Force can be moved rapidly to advanced bases throughout the area. In addition, on Taiwan and in South Korea the Air Force has installed Matador missiles, which have a range of over 500 miles and can carry conventional or atomic warheads.[24]

American strength in Asia is a powerful deterrent to large-scale aggression by Communist China. But because the ground forces of the United States and its Asian allies are relatively small in numbers, in the final analysis the single most important factor counterbalancing the huge Chinese Communist ground forces is the atomic weapons in the hands of American naval and air forces. Under present conditions it is essential for the United States to maintain a strong nuclear striking power in Asia. At the same time, the heavy reliance on atomic weapons creates serious dilemmas for American policy-makers. For one thing, political and psychological factors operating in Asia might limit the possibility of actually using atomic weapons even to resist a large-scale attack. For another, although nuclear power may deter Communist China from undertaking a direct military attack against certain areas, its value may be questionable in deterring Communist China from using other forms of military threat or pressure.

Peking's Military Power and Political Influence

Although a rough sort of balance has developed between American atomic weapons and Chinese Communist manpower, it is nevertheless clear that Communist China's growing military strength has substantially increased Peking's ability to pursue its foreign policy objectives. This is obvious in the cases of Tibet, Korea, and Vietnam. Chinese armies established Peking's control of Tibet and its influence over North Korea, and Chinese military support helped the Vietminh to secure control of North Vietnam. Although Communist China has not been able to take Taiwan by force, it has not hesitated to threaten it with attack.

Apart from these instances of the overt use of its military power, Peking's prestige and its ability to make its weight felt in world politics have steadily increased with the growth of its military strength. Despite the Chinese Communists' tactics of "competitive coexistence," no country on China's periphery, whether allied with the United States or militarily nonaligned, can overlook the fact that Peking, even when speaking softly, carries a big stick. To countries in Southeast Asia, the problems of dealing with local Communist movements, domestic insurrections, or border tensions are greatly magnified because of their fear of provoking military intervention by Communist China. The lengthening shadow of Peking's overwhelmingly superior military strength has certainly been a major factor influencing Burma and Cambodia, for example, to adopt a policy of nonalignment and partial accommodation in their relations with Communist China.

To understand the range of problems now posed by Communist China's military power, it is necessary to analyze its probable military intentions as well as its military strength and to consider many alternative situations which lie between the extremes of a calculated major war or a dependable, stable peace. It would be wrong to conclude that, since Communist China's ground forces are potentially capable of overrunning much of Asia, this is therefore the major danger, and yet it is clear that Peking is capable, even while pursuing tactics of "competitive coexistence," of using its military force in various ways to pursue its goals.

Large-Scale War

For numerous reasons, some of which were suggested in Chapters 4 and 5, the likelihood that Communist China will deliberately embark upon a major war to achieve its broad foreign policy goals appears remote at this time. It seems probable that Peking will try to avoid major war, while building up its power base at home and pursuing its principal aims abroad primarily by means other than overt military expansionism.

This does not mean, however, that there is no danger that a major war, involving Communist China, might occur. War between the United States and Communist China could break out, in one area in particular, as a result of miscalculation. That area is the Taiwan Strait.

Peking feels no political restraints which would limit its "right" to "liberate" Taiwan by force. It has repeatedly used military threats in this region and can be expected to continue using them. Because of its territorial claims, Peking regards the situation in the Taiwan Strait area as a domestic rather than an international issue, and consequently the Chinese Communists clearly feel that their general tactics of "peaceful coexistence" do not in any way inhibit the overt use of force in this area. They believe, with considerable justification, that many countries—in particular, many of the most important nonaligned nations—regard the threat of military action in this area in a different light from a threat of open aggression by Communist China against other Asian nations.

Peking is likely, therefore, to persist in using military threats to achieve its goals in the area of the Taiwan Strait. However, even here, while willing to run serious military risks, Peking appears anxious to avoid a full-scale conflict with the United States. But there is a real and continuing danger that in this area war may break out between Communist China and the United States through accident or miscalculation by either or both sides. The most direct danger of this happening centers on the offshore islands rather than Taiwan.

In terms of this danger, the situation of the offshore islands and that of Taiwan and the Pescadores need to be clearly differentiated. The hundred-mile stretch of water separating Taiwan from the mainland is a major obstacle to invasion. Because the United States is firmly committed to defend Taiwan and the Pescadores, any attack by the Chinese Communists on them could only follow a calculated decision to wage a large-scale war against the United States. It seems unlikely that the Chinese Communists will make such a decision, at least in the years immediately ahead, even though they can be expected to continue claiming and threatening Taiwan and the Pescadores.

The offshore islands present a quite different set of problems, not only because of the vague character of the American commitments, but more fundamentally because of their geographical position. The Chinese Communists can apply severe military pressure on the main offshore islands through prolonged artillery bombardment from the mainland, without actually invading them. Since 1949 the Chinese Communists have already done this twice, first in 1954-1955 and again in 1958, and each time the risks of war between the United States and Communist China have become more dangerous. During the 1958 crisis the United States found it necessary to use American naval vessels to help supply the offshore islands, by convoying Nationalist ships up to the three-mile limit of international waters, and there were serious risks that Communist artillery fire might hit American vessels. In both crises the threats and counterthreats, the pressures and counterpressures, built up to a high point. The national prestige of both sides was heavily involved, and unplanned and unforeseen incidents might have touched off a major conflict.[25] As long as the status of the offshore islands remains unchanged, future crises must be expected in this area, and this is the most important point at which the accidental outbreak of large-scale war is a constant danger.

If a major war involving Communist China were to break out, the consequences would be difficult to calculate. Conceivably, Peking might ignore the restraints which had limited its range of action prior to that event—including both the external restraints imposed by fear of American atomic power and self-imposed restraints arising out of its over-all political strategy. In this case it would presumably strike out in several directions, specifically against South Korea and Southeast Asia. It is by no means certain that even atomic weapons could stop an initial surge of Chinese military manpower into neighboring countries. The United States possesses weapons capable of devastating Communist China's domestic bases of power, and severe destruction within China, coupled with the attrition of Peking's troops abroad, might eventually force these forces to withdraw to Chinese territory. But even this outcome is not certain. There is no guarantee that, even if all the key centers of power in Communist China were destroyed, Chinese Communist military manpower might not still be spread out, living off the land and carrying out local military actions over large parts of Asia.

Limited War

Unless a major war were to break out elsewhere in the world, however, it now seems unlikely that Communist China will embark upon overt military aggression, even in Korea or Southeast Asia, in the foreseeable future. In Korea and Vietnam the clear demarcation lines between North and South, the commitments of the United States and other non-Communist nations to give active support to the defense of the existing non-Communist regimes, and the obvious possibility of American retaliation against the Chinese mainland, make it unlikely that Peking will now attempt to use its own forces, even in the guise of "volunteers," to extend its control in these two areas. There is a somewhat greater possibility that in these two countries Peking may attempt to build up the military strength of the local Communist regimes to such an extent that, in time, they could attempt independently to overrun the non-Communist parts of the countries. Theoretically, this might lead to a local or limited war, like the Korean War but with the Chinese Communists abstaining this time from direct intervention. This too seems relatively unlikely, however, as long as the United States remains pledged to support South Korea and South Vietnam.

Elsewhere in Southeast Asia, Peking may, from time to time, apply border pressure with its own troops, as it has already done against both Burma and India. Yet the possibility seems relatively slight that Communist China would deliberately choose to embark on overt, large-scale military aggression there over the next few years. For one thing, thinking ahead in long-range, revolutionary terms, the Chinese Communists unquestionably believe that there will be numerous opportunities for gradually expanding Communist and Chinese influence in Southeast Asia without incurring the risks and costs of overt aggression. And if Peking embarked on clear aggression, even against a nonaligned nation such as Burma, this might provoke the Western powers, and perhaps even India, into strong counteraction In its calculations Peking cannot ignore this risk.

Indirect Aggression or Military Subversion

Outside the Taiwan area the greatest immediate military danger arises from the possibility that Chinese Communists might decide, even while still subordinating military force to other instruments of policy in their general tactics, to give greater and more effective indirect, disguised military support to insurrectionary groups operating in the border regions on China's periphery or within its small and weak neighbors. This type of indirect aggression—it might be called military subversion—poses great dangers.

From 1954 until mid-1959 Communist China actually exercised considerable self-restraint in the sense that it refrained from exploiting fully the existing opportunities for aiding insurrections in neighboring countries. Clearly it considered it more profitable during this period to attempt to influence the existing non-Communist governments than to engage in any obvious attempts to promote military subversion; such attempts, it apparently felt, would antagonize these governments without offering any guarantee of success. In the latter half of 1959, however, Peking gave its blessing to the Pathet Lao when this Communist-led group resorted once again to insurrectionary tactics, with material support from North Vietnam, and this created a crisis which led the government of Laos to appeal for United Nations support.

As of the early autumn of 1959 it was not yet clear how far Peking was prepared to go either in aiding this particular revolt or in promoting similar types of indirect aggression elsewhere. If it should choose to do so, however, Peking could step up its efforts at military subversion in many ways and places. It could, for example, channel military aid to the Burmese Communist party, which, despite its current attempt to switch over from insurrection to political action, still maintains guerrilla units within Burma. It could train and arm members of minority groups within China who have racial kin in neighboring countries—the Kachins on the China-Burma border, and the Thais in China near the border of Thailand—to infiltrate neighboring countries and promote insurrections in them. The establishment of special Kachin and Thai "autonomous areas" as a part of Peking's program to give administrative identity to the national minorities within China has created fears in neighboring countries about Communist China's intentions, and there have been some reports of military training being given to Kachins and Thais in China.[26]

If potential guerrilla units do exist in China, they have not yet crossed into neighboring countries. Apparently, however, North Vietnam, with Peking's approval, gave both training and equipment to the Pathet Lao rebels who renewed their insurrection in Laos in mid-1959, and there is a real possibility that Peking might decide to do this itself rather than merely channeling support through North Vietnam.

If Peking were to embark upon a major program of promoting indirect aggression, it would certainly, in addition to providing covert military assistance and leadership, simultaneously adopt a threatening overt posture toward the governments concerned in order to create fears of direct Chinese intervention; in some respects Peking's public statements regarding Laos soon after the 1959 revolt broke out had this effect.

To date none of these possibilities has been exploited fully by Communist China. But in the foreseeable future indirect aggression through military subversion—on the general pattern indicated by the 1959 revolt in Laos—seems to be by far the most likely means by which Communist China might attempt to utilize its military strength directly to promote its ends in neighboring countries. Although overt armed aggression seems less likely, the prospect of limited wars certainly cannot be ruled out, however, and the less prepared the non-Communist nations are to cope with limited wars, the greater the risk of their occurring.

An estimate of the relative improbability of deliberate, large-scale military aggression by Peking must rest on the assumption that strong non-Communist states, particularly the United States, will continue to maintain clear and enforceable pledges of support for the defense of weak countries on China's periphery. In the absence of such pledges the Chinese Communists, or their allies in North Korea and North Vietnam, might well decide to increase their military pressure and even to launch sizable probing attacks. At the time of the attack on South Korea American intentions in respect to the defense of South Korea were by no means clear, and the Communist powers made a major miscalculation in assuming that the United States would not fight back. The chances of a new miscalculation of this sort, in Korea or Vietnam, appear to have been greatly reduced by clear demarcation lines and by firm pledges of outside aid against any attack across them. The chances of its happening elsewhere in the area have also been reduced by the military commitments which the United States and other powers have undertaken. Even in the case of Laos, with its many weaknesses, Peking cannot ignore the risk that overt Chinese aggression might lead the United States to retaliate directly against Communist China. In some respects, Burma, lacking any firm pledges of Western military support, appears to be the most exposed to Peking's military pressure. Yet Communist China's pressure has so far been limited to certain border areas in dispute between Burma and China, and here as elsewhere on China's borders the main military danger in the years immediately ahead is doubtless indirect aggression rather than any overt large-scale attack.

Political Problems Affecting the Defense of East Asia

As the United States attempts to maintain a satisfactory balance of power in Asia against Communist China by helping to defend Asian states which feel themselves threatened by Peking's military power, it faces problems which are of a quite different nature from comparable problems which it has faced in Europe. Political and economic instability are prevalent throughout much of Asia. Asian attitudes toward Communist China and the United States differ widely, and there is no political unity among non-Communist Asian states. Even among the United States' principal Asian allies, some countries have ambivalent feelings about their existing military ties with the United States. All these circumstances make the problems of security and defense particularly difficult in Asia. And these difficulties have been consciously exploited by Peking.

Since 1954, with their posture of "peaceful coexistence," the Chinese Communists have assiduously encouraged neutralism in an attempt to undermine the existing defense structure of the non-Communist countries of Asia. They have worked persistently toward the dissolution of Western-supported military alliances, the dismantling of American bases, and the prevention of even defensive rearmament in countries such as Japan. But Peking's machinations have not, by any means, been the only cause of opposition to Western-supported military programs. In many Asian countries deep currents of political emotion have led the nationalist leaders to oppose close association with Western strategy and to advocate nonalignment in world affairs. Through its "coexistence" policies Peking has merely attempted to nourish these emotions.

Within the broad region from Korea to Pakistan there have been wide differences in recent years between those countries which have criticized and those which have approved American efforts to build a collective security system. Many of the newly independent states have tended to minimize the possibility of any direct military threat arising from Communist China, have been critical of what they label "power politics," and have wished to avoid "military entanglements" with Western powers. When the United States' posture, in the eyes of the leaders of neutralist-inclined nations, has placed primary emphasis upon military policies designed to contain Chinese power, these leaders have often been antagonized. On the other hand, there are other countries which have felt directly threatened by Communist China and have strongly endorsed American strategic policies; some of them have urged the United States to assume an even stronger military posture against Communist China.

The Chinese Nationalist government on Taiwan and the anti-Communist governments in divided Korea and Vietnam obviously have special reasons for desiring maximum American military support and strong policies directed against Peking. The Communist threat to them is real and immediate, and their continued existence is wholly dependent on American military assistance. The leaders of Nationalist China and South Korea, furthermore, still think in offensive rather than purely defensive terms. The Philippines, because of its long history of American rule, likewise has a very special relationship with the United States. In international affairs, it often reflects American views more than prevalent Asian views, and it is strongly anti-Communist, partly because of its own domestic struggle with the Hukbalahap insurgents, and perhaps partly because it is predominantly a Catholic nation. The only country in Southeast Asia which escaped colonial rule, Thailand is unique in many respects; it has avoided the anticolonialism and exacerbated nationalism of those nations which have undergone colonial rule. In addition, it has long harbored a deep fear of China, partly because of uneasiness over the loyalties of its large Chinese minority. With a tradition of adjusting to the realities of power, Thailand has come to regard the United States as its protector in the period since World War II.

Occupied by American military forces after World War II, Japan has until recently been a ward of the United States, and only in the last few years has it begun to assert its full independence. At present its government supports American security policies, but this support is somewhat qualified, and there are significant neutralist and pacifist trends in Japanese political life. Laos, ostensibly neutral until recently, has received large-scale American military and economic assistance in the last few years, and, fearful of both its huge neighbor to the north and subversion at home, has moved steadily toward close alignment with the West. Malaya's present government is strongly anti-Communist; it is still fighting the remnants of Communist insurrection within its borders. However, even though it receives military support from Britain and other Commonwealth countries and is clearly aligned with the West, it has so far avoided direct military ties with the United States or with the American-supported alliance system. Pakistan has joined SEATO and the Baghdad Pact, but in deciding to do so it seemed to be motivated principally by its desire for American political and military support to strengthen its position in the conflict with India over Kashmir, rather than by fear of Peking or by any positive desire to help counterbalance Communist China's power.

India, Burma, Indonesia, Cambodia, Ceylon, Nepal, and Afghanistan are neutralist, and all have been critical of American military policies, in varying degrees, over the past decade. In Burma, Cambodia, and Nepal fear of Communist China and its potential menace have been extremely important in determining attitudes toward Peking, and their nonalignment has been motivated in large part by the desire to avoid provoking Peking. In India, Indonesia, Ceylon, and Afghanistan, however, there has been, at least until recently, little sense of any immediate military threat from Communist China, and consequently these countries have tended to regard American military policies in the Far East as a provocative and undesirable form of Western interference in Asian affairs. They have often argued that American policies have disturbed rather than preserved the peace. Some of these attitudes may now be changing very significantly, as a result of events in Tibet, on the Indian border, and in Laos, but changes in basic attitudes generally take place slowly. As of the early fall of 1959, while fear of Communist China and appreciation—or at least tolerance—of American security policies had obviously increased greatly in many Asian nations, the major neutralist leaders still seemed determined to follow a basic policy of nonalignment and to stay aloof from all military alliances.

Divisions among Non-Communist Asians

Serious internal divisions and frictions among the non-Communist nations of Asia, and even among those which have signed military pacts with the United States, have presented major obstacles to developing an effective collective security system in the region. They have made the formation of any NATO-like regional organization impossible, at least for the present. The South Korean government of Syngman Rhee is extremely hostile to Japan as a result of past Japanese colonialism; in 1959 this hostility was exacerbated by Japan's decision to repatriate many Koreans to North Korea. Japan is only slowly overcoming the antagonisms left behind by its occupation of Southeast Asia during World War II; anti-Japanese feelings have been particularly strong in the Philippines. Problems relating to the Overseas Chinese have created troublesome frictions in the relations of the Philippines, South Vietnam, and Thailand with Nationalist China. Because the nonaligned countries and Pakistan have recognized Communist China, Nationalist China has been bitter toward them. Burma and Indonesia are particularly hostile toward Nationalist China; both have charged Chiang K'ai-shek's government with intervening in their domestic affairs. Cambodia's relations with both South Vietnam and Thailand have been tense in recent years; border disputes have been both a symbol and a cause of deep distrust. There has long been a traditional hostility between Burma and Thailand, and it has been overcome only in part by recent friendly exchanges.

SEATO represents the only attempt at a regional pact among Asian states, and it suffers from serious weaknesses. Peking's propaganda attacks, denouncing it as a symbol of American "militarism" and "interventionism" in Asia, have had a considerable effect over the past five years, especially since the nonaligned countries have had their own reasons for opposing SEATO. The only two Southeast Asian members of SEATO—the Philippines and Thailand—are in many respects not typical of most Asian feelings, and their membership in SEATO may have separated them more sharply from other South and Southeast Asian states. Pakistan's membership has contributed little of value to the defense of Southeast Asia and has been one major reason for India's intense hostility to the pact.

Because of the French record in Indo-China, the inclusion of France has tended, in the eyes of some Asians, to identify SEATO with past European colonialism in Asia. SEATO's roster of five non-Asian members and only three Asian members has inevitably invited Asian criticism. It has been argued by some, in fact, that because of its divisive effects in South and Southeast Asia—in particular because of the fact that it has aroused highly critical reactions in India and Indonesia, the largest nations in that area—SEATO has brought more political losses than military gains.

The alliance has, however, produced some military advantages. It has, for example, made possible joint planning and training, exchange of intelligence, improvement of military base facilities, and standardization of weapons and military doctrine among its members. It has also made possible increased cooperation in strengthening antisubversion programs, although no general military pact was necessary for this. But in purely military terms SEATO has not resulted in a significant increase of strength in the area. The United States has not stationed new forces there, nor has any regional defense force been formed.

SEATO's main achievement has been the psychological reassurance which it has provided in mainland Southeast Asia—to Thailand, to the three non-Communist states of Indo-China, and perhaps even to certain nonmember states in the region—based on the United States' commitment to give support against either "armed attack" or "subversive activities directed from without." It can be argued, however, that this could have been accomplished through bilateral pacts or other arrangements which might well have had a less divisive political effect. It can also be argued that despite the SEATO pledges Southeast Asian nations may have doubts about exactly how the United States can and will honor its pledges as long as American strategy relies primarily upon mobile naval and air forces, designed to threaten nuclear retaliation against the centers of Communist power, rather than upon forces which can be brought to bear effectively within Southeast Asia in case Communist China increases its threats to that region.

Attitudes toward Atomic Weapons and U.S. Bases

The fact that the first two atomic bombs were dropped on an Asian country has made many Asians particularly hostile to any prospect of nuclear warfare. Sensitivity to atomic weapons is especially great in Japan, which together with India and other Asian countries has called for the banning of all nuclear weapons. The use of nuclear weapons by the United States even to repel overt aggression by Communist China in Southeast Asia might well create strong adverse reactions in many Asian countries, which could actually weaken the non-Communist position. There is no certainty, in fact, that the United States' allies in Southeast Asia, even if they were invaded by Chinese Communist forces, would approve the use of large-scale nuclear weapons on their own territory. Conceivably they might decide to submit to Chinese occupation if the only alternative appeared to be nuclear devastation. Also, these nations may well question how effective nuclear weapons, including small-scale tactical ones, would be against Communist guerrilla operations in the mountainous jungles which cover much of Southeast Asia.

Existing United States bases and military agreements in Asia have created many problems in American relations with the Philippines and Japan. The Filipinos seek to exercise a wider range of criminal jurisdiction over American servicemen stationed in their country; this and related issues have been a major symbol of resentment and a cause of growing friction in relations between the Philippines and the United States. The Japanese resent the seeming compromise of their sovereignty due to their lack of full control over the use of American bases on their territory. In demanding a revision of Japan's security treaty with the United States, many Japanese have used this issue to question the value of their government's basic pro-American policy, and in late 1959 the constitutionality of the agreements for establishing American bases in Japan was being tested in the Japanese courts. Japanese agitation for the return of Okinawa to Japanese administration, based in part upon local Okinawan grievances against the American administration there, has created additional complications in American-Japanese relations.

Economic Burden of Military Programs

At present, United States' military aid to Asian countries—including both "defense support" and direct military aid—far exceeds American assistance for economic development. The United States pays virtually all the costs of military equipment provided to its Asian allies, as well as a large part of the local costs required to maintain the existing military establishments in South Korea, Nationalist China, South Vietnam, Laos, and Thailand. Despite this large-scale aid, the burden of maintaining forces which are beyond the capacity of these nations to support has had a severe impact on the local economies in almost all of these countries.

The economies of South Korea, Nationalist China, South Vietnam, and Laos are so dependent upon United States support that it is difficult to see how these nations can become independently viable in the foreseeable future. This dependence is due, of course, to many factors, including the partitioning of these countries, the influx of refugees from Communist territory, and the disruptions of war. But it is also due fundamentally to the tremendous burden of military costs which these countries are now carrying. South Korea and Nationalist China probably cannot hope even to approach economic self-support as long as they maintain military forces so disproportionate to their populations and resources—even though these forces are small in comparison with Communist China's huge armies. Moreover, because military needs now receive first priority in these nations, urgently needed programs of economic development are considerably smaller and less effective than they might otherwise be. Some Asian critics of American military aid programs have charged that United States policies have tended to reinforce existing authoritarian tendencies and to encourage a primarily military orientation in these nations. Although such charges have often been exaggerated, the dangers which they suggest cannot be ignored.

While it is essential for the United States to help develop and maintain local defense forces in Asia, it is equally important—and for the long haul even more important—to help develop healthy economies and stable societies throughout the region. These objectives conflict in many respects, and this fact poses a basic dilemma. Sound economic and political development cannot proceed satisfactorily unless there is at least a minimum of security. Yet, if the demands of security absorb an excessive share of the energies and resources in Asian nations, the possibility of achieving sound economic and political development will be reduced, and this in itself could seriously threaten their future security.

Problems of American Policy

Underlying all of these specific problems is the subtle but immensely important problem of projecting a desirable image of the United States to an Asia deeply involved in a social, political, and economic revolution. Most Asians react viscerally and often bitterly against "Western military interventionism," "Big Power dominance," and "power politics." South Korea and Nationalist China, it is true, are notable exceptions; preoccupied with their own conflicts with the Communists, these two nations take a militant stand against communism and desire the United States to join them in an offensive to liberate their homelands. On the other hand, most Asian allies of the United States hope for an American policy which will be firm and at the same time defensive and nonprovocative. And almost all the nonaligned nations in Asia have urged the United States to be more conciliatory toward Communist China, to deemphasize military affairs, to make greater efforts to reduce military tensions, and to concentrate more of its effort on helping all the newly independent Asian nations to achieve their political, economic, and social aims. The Chinese Communists constantly portray United States policy as being primarily one of "military interventionism," involving a disguised form of Western colonialism, and over most of the past decade when they have attacked American moves in these terms, their propaganda has struck a considerable response among many Asians.

In view of all of these factors, the problem for the United States is to adopt a military posture which is neither weak nor excessively militant. A weak policy would tend to demoralize many countries in Asia; a posture which appears militant almost inevitably antagonizes many others.

The quest for security in Asia will be a long and difficult one. With the shadow of Communist China's great military power hanging over the region, there is little prospect of achieving absolute security, and the balance of power may remain precarious for a long time. Nevertheless, the attempt to achieve a more stable balance of forces must be sustained, and American policies should be constantly reviewed and adapted to cope with the complex political and economic as well as military factors which affect the security of Asia.

The American military posture should make it manifest to friends, opponents, and critics alike that the United States has both the capacity and the will to help the non-Communist nations resist any aggression from Communist China, but it should also avoid any provocation, "bomb-rattling," or excessive emphasis upon military affairs. It is certainly possible for the United States to follow this balanced policy. In quiet ways it can make its military capacities and intentions clear to both Peking and the non-Communist nations of Asia, without resorting to outright threats and military demonstrations which, in dramatizing the presence of Western power, also make the United States vulnerable to charges of "militarism."

While standing firm in its commitment to resist military aggression by Peking, the United States should also do all it can to avoid war with Communist China. For Asia a major war would be a disaster, whatever its military outcome. The risks of major war caused by accident or miscalculation are centered in the question of the offshore islands, and there are strong military as well as other arguments for modifying the present United States policy relating to them.

Under existing and foreseeable circumstances the United

States must continue to maintain a strong nuclear capacity in Asia as a deterrent to major war. Without this American capacity, the entire military balance would be upset, Communist China's massive manpower could dominate the area, and the chances of Peking's embarking on overt aggression might well be increased.

On the other hand, excessive or one-sided reliance on atomic weapons creates serious political and military liabilities for the United States. Peking may eventually gain access to these weapons, which would cancel at least some of the military advantages which the United States now enjoys. In addition, even now the actual use of nuclear weapons might have serious political effects, damaging the United States' position throughout the area, antagonizing key countries such as Japan and India, and frightening smaller countries into dissociating themselves from the United States. Atomic weapons by themselves are not well suited to provide "graduated deterrence" in Asia or to cope with the varied pressures or threats which Peking might use. These are strong reasons, therefore, for deemphasizing the role of nuclear weapons in American strategy in Asia and for reducing the United States' present reliance on them. To do this, however, it will be necessary to develop more adequate conventional forces capable of coping effectively both with limited war situations and with ambiguous acts of indirect aggression.

In part, this need can be met through continued help in developing local defense forces in the non-Communist countries of Asia. But, how far can this be carried? As has been emphasized, the capacities of these countries to support more effective military establishments are limited. If they are urged to concentrate their energies and resources on military problems to an extent which impairs their ability to cope with their fundamental problems of internal development, this course may eventually undermine their domestic stability. Such a policy would be self-defeating in the long run, even from the point of view of their future security.

Existing military forces in Taiwan and South Korea may already be excessive, and if possible they should be somewhat reduced. In many other countries, however, there is still a need to develop more effective local defense forces, and the

United States can and should assist the nonaligned countries as well as its Asian allies in developing their capacities for internal security and local defense. It has already begun to do this at the request of Burma and Indonesia, and this should be continued.

If the role of formal alliances is given less emphasis in American policy, it is probably feasible for the United States, in the military field, to broaden considerably its relationships with Asian nations by informal means and to encourage wider military cooperation even among Asian nations with very different political viewpoints. However, because of the limited membership of SEATO, excessive reliance on this alliance may prove to be a liability rather than an asset for the United States' relationships with the area as a whole. At present SEATO has a role to play, and a sudden dissolution of it might have seriously adverse repercussions among its Asian members. But, in the long run, if it is necessary to deemphasize SEATO in order to develop improved wider relationships throughout the region, this should be done.

In its efforts to build up the defenses of friendly nations in Asia, the United States must not forget that economic progress is at least as important as military strength, if not more so in the long run. It must strive therefore to achieve a sound balance between economic and military aid in its support of Asian nations. In some countries the emphasis is now heavily weighted toward military support, which creates risks not only of neglecting important problems of economic development but also of actually creating serious economic difficulties. Large-scale American military aid to Asian nations cannot be regarded as a substitute for economic aid but rather as a factor which calls for even greater efforts in the strictly economic field.

Whatever assistance the United States gives to these countries, there is no escaping the fact that their military potentialities are limited. Strong arguments can be made, therefore, in favor of developing and probably expanding the size of United States ground forces which can either be maintained in Asia or held in readiness to be moved there rapidly to cope with possible limited war situations. Although there may be some political disadvantages, as well as greater costs, involved in maintaining larger American forces in the area, a convincing argument can be made in favor of such a policy because it would relieve the United States of the necessity of relying on nuclear weapons as the primary deterrent to war in Asia. The recent development of the Strategic Army Corps, with its four divisions ready to be moved rapidly to deal with limited war situations anywhere in the world, is a step toward meeting this need.[27] But it seems clear, in view of the dimensions of the problems posed by Communist China's military manpower, that American conventional forces are not yet adequate to meet the possible challenge in Asia.

Since even limited wars seem relatively unlikely at present in Asia, the greatest immediate danger is that Peking will decide to give increased military support to indigenous insurrectionary groups in neighboring countries. Communist China's relationship to these insurrectionary forces is likely to be so ambiguous and disguised that threats of retaliation against China, by either atomic or conventional forces, may not be effective as a deterrent. The problem, therefore, will be to cope with such situations essentially as internal security problems. In long-range terms, the only effective answer to this kind of problem is for Asian nations to develop internal security forces adequate to maintain their own internal stability, even against insurrection supported from without.

It may be many years, however, before the countries which are vulnerable to this threat can protect themselves fully, and in the meantime situations—such as the one which developed in Laos in the latter half of 1959—could arise which might require direct United States support. If the threat is of moderate scope, support can be provided in the form of military advice and matériel. In situations of grave danger, however, the threatened governments might call upon the United States for direct assistance, including troops, and the United States should be prepared to provide such support if necessary. But it is difficult to improvise such an operation at the last minute, and it is by no means certain that American troops available in Asia would be able to operate with the necessary effectiveness. Little attention has been given to organizing and training units specifically to cope with guerrilla warfare in the jungle, to cooperate smoothly with local forces, or to be politically sensitive and discriminating in their relations with Asian populations. A number of small American combat groups should be specially trained and kept in readiness to perform such missions on request.

To meet the various situations which may arise in Asia, the United States clearly needs to maintain a number of bases there. But it is necessary to recognize the limitations which are imposed by political factors on the use of many of these bases, to weigh both the military advantages and the political disadvantages which they may involve, and to be ready to adapt and modify existing base agreements to serve the broad purposes of United States policy. Unless bases can be maintained on terms which underscore the mutual interest of the United States and the Asian host-nations, the actual utility of the bases is open to serious question. Under certain circumstances the United States might consider developing less exposed bases—for example, on Tinian or Saipan—as substitutes for existing forward bases. However, a minimum number of forward bases seems highly desirable, to meet the requirements both for limited wars and for nuclear retaliation, and every effort should be made to maintain them.

Although at present there is a great need for the United States to maintain and improve its own military capabilities in Asia, it can incur many political disadvantages by playing too large and too obvious a military role in the affairs of the region. It would be highly desirable, therefore, to encourage and support the development of international forces under United Nations auspices which could be brought to bear rapidly if and when conflicts occur in Asia. The prospects for organizing an effective United Nations police force seem slight at present, but other methods—including the wider use of United Nations observer groups—can help to deter conflicts by introducing a "United Nations presence" into the area. If conflicts should occur, United Nations observers can at least help to mobilize world opinion behind efforts to restore peace.

The long-run prospects for establishing and maintaining a more stable balance of power in Asia would be greatly improved if the two most important non-Communist nations in Asia, Japan and India, were to become increasingly willing and able to assume wider responsibilities for the defense of the small nations in the region. The responsibilities which the United States must now carry could then be substantially reduced, and its role in preserving peace in the region could be proportionately lessened. Currently, Japan and India possess neither the willingness nor the capacity to assume such responsibilities, and, at least for the present, many Asian nations would resist the idea of their attempting to assume them. It would be desirable, nevertheless, if these two nations were eventually to play more active roles in assuring the security of Northeast Asia and Southeast Asia, respectively.

Perhaps the ultimate military problem, in Asia as elsewhere, is that of disarmament. In the present atmosphere of Asia, however, there is little prospect of discovering useful approaches to it. Until existing conflicts of interest and tensions can be substantially reduced, any steps which might weaken the already unstable military position of the non-Communist nations in the region would be completely unrealistic.

In terms of the world-wide problem of disarmament, however, it is difficult to see how measures for arms control—including, for example, means of controlling nuclear weapons tests—can be made effective without including the territory and the military forces of Communist China within their scope.[28] Certainly Communist China would have to be included in any international inspection system if it were to be made effective. Any agreement which embraced the major Western powers but only one of the two major partners in the Sino-Soviet bloc would provide the Communists with such great opportunities for evasion that its enforceability would be dubious.

In the long run, if progress is to be made toward the regulation of armaments, the West will have to deal with Peking as well as Moscow on these questions. Furthermore, since the chief military problem in Asia today is the overwhelming predominance of Communist China's conventional ground forces, any arms control measures which concentrated on the control or limitation of nuclear weapons alone would not get to the root of the security problems in that part of the world.

Disarmament is, in any case, a problem for the future rather than for the immediate present in Asia. Before any real progress can be made toward arms control in that region, a more stable military balance must first be achieved. Only then, perhaps, can a basis be established for working gradually toward a reduction of military tensions, as a prerequisite for arms control measures which would include Communist China as well as the other major nations concerned with the power balance in Asia.

Chapter 7

COMMUNIST SUBVERSION AND THE POLITICAL STRUGGLE

Despite the grave problems posed by Communist China's growing military power, Peking's main impact upon most of Asia has so far been political rather than military. Peking's success has been a spur to revolutionary efforts throughout Asia, and the growth of indigenous Communist movements, and of forces which strengthen them, presents a fundamental challenge to the development of democratic societies.

Since 1949 Communist China has become, along with the Soviet Union, a major center for inspiration, support, and direction of Asian Communist movements. The impact of the Communist victory in China upon an Asia in ferment has been similar to, and perhaps stronger and more direct than, the earlier impact of the Bolshevik revolution of 1917. Asian Communists now look to Peking as well as Moscow for assistance and guidance. And the Chinese Communists themselves have given clear evidence of their determination to promote the spread of Communist regimes throughout Asia.

"People's Diplomacy" and Propaganda

A dictionary definition of the word "subvert" is "to undermine the morals, allegiance, or faith" of any group. Under this definition, even the proselytizers of Western democratic values might, in a sense, be considered subverters of many of the values of traditional societies in Asia. But there is an essential difference between "democratic subversion" and Communist subversion. Whereas the democratic faith advocates a peaceful evolution of society through action which receives the sanction of majority will and respects individual and minority rights, the Communist dogma calls for a conspiratorial and, if necessary, violent struggle by a minority to achieve power, establish its dictatorial rule, and impose its will upon society. The Communists relate virtually all their actions to their central revolutionary aim, and it is this that makes sinister and dangerous many activities which might otherwise represent normal and desirable aspirations.

Broadly speaking, the Chinese Communists' entire program of "people's diplomacy" has a strongly subversive purpose; it might, in fact, be called "overt subversion." Saying this does not imply that it is undesirable for non-Communist nations, Asian or Western, to develop cultural and other contacts with Communist China. Many types of contact can be extremely valuable, as a means of gaining an understanding of the Chinese Communists, possibly exerting a certain influence on them, and establishing some cooperative relationships, however limited, across existing barriers of hostility. It does mean, however, that from Peking's own viewpoint, its "people's diplomacy" is basically a political weapon, designed to promote its long-term national and revolutionary goals, and, because of the nature of these goals, even its cultural exchanges are frequently motivated by subversive aims.

In close coordination with the Soviet Union, Communist China has developed a massive program of international propaganda, with Asia as its particular target. Peking's activities throughout Asia are so extensive that only the principal efforts can be mentioned here.

A tremendous amount of Chinese Communist propaganda is distributed through conventional communications media. Peking's Foreign Languages Press produces large numbers of books for export in several Asian languages, including Japanese, Indonesian, Vietnamese, Thai, and Burmese. It regularly distributes abroad, at very low cost, many magazines and journals specially designed for foreign readers, among them prestige periodicals such as *People's China* and *China Pictorial*, which are printed in several Asian languages. Its radio programs beamed to the Far East alone totaled over 230 hours a week by 1957. Reports of the New China News Agency are widely distributed and used by Asian editors and commentators. And Chinese Communist films are given extensive showings throughout the region.

Peking has worked hard to establish a wide range of sympathetic or potentially sympathetic groups throughout Asia. These "front organizations" bring together thousands of non-Communists for the promotion of various Communist-sponsored causes, and they maintain numerous links with Peking and other Communist capitals. Some of these organizations, such as the Peace Committees and Asian-African Solidarity Committees (formerly Asian Solidarity Committees), are coordinated on a world-wide basis through Communist-dominated bureaus. Others, such as friendship societies and trade groups, stress the development of closer contacts with China rather than with the world-wide Communist movement.

The exchange of persons between Communist China and other Asian countries (and countries throughout the underdeveloped world) plays an important part in this program. In recent years thousands of hand-picked Chinese spokesmen have visited other Asian countries, as members of cultural and other delegations, and Peking has become a virtual Mecca for Asian visitors. Pilgrims to Communist China have included leading non-Communist politicians, labor leaders, writers, artists, scientists, leaders of women's and youth organizations, businessmen, and others. A large proportion seems to have been more impressed by Communist China's dynamism than by its totalitarian rule, and a great many have returned home enthusiastic in their praise of its accomplishments.

Peking's motives in promoting its "people's diplomacy" are clear. It aims to foster a favorable, or at least a benevolently tolerant, climate of opinion among key groups in other Asian countries toward Communist China, toward the Communist bloc as a whole, and toward local Communist movements. In effect, it attempts to cultivate fellow travelers and potential converts to serve as lobbyists in their own countries for the ideas and policies of the Communist bloc and as supporters of local Communist-led revolutions. Although it is not possible to measure the results of all these efforts, it is clear that Peking has achieved some notable propaganda successes.

Peking's Early Relations with the Communist Parties of Asia

The Chinese Communists' "agitation from above" takes its most visible form in "people's diplomacy," but this is not Peking's most important political activity. More important is its role, in collaboration with Moscow, in encouraging and supporting, through covert "agitation from below," the development of hard-core, disciplined Communist parties throughout Asia. Despite its assertions that "revolution is not for export," Peking has developed extensive and intimate relations with other Asian Communist parties, and it clearly regards these parties as the most important instruments for the eventual expansion of communism throughout Asia.

The Chinese Communists' missionary activity abroad has a long history, antedating 1949 by more than two decades, but it has acquired an entirely new impetus since they emerged in command of a strong state.

The founding of the Comintern at Moscow in March 1919 marked the beginning of a continuous Soviet effort to develop Communist parties and movements throughout the world. Unlike the pre-1917 Socialists, Lenin devoted special attention to the promotion of communism in Asia, and the establishment of the Chinese Communist party in 1921 was one of the Comintern's early accomplishments. Moscow became the primary center of guidance for the Communist movements abroad. Although there were periods—particularly in the 1930s and during World War II—when important Asian parties, including the Chinese party, operated almost entirely on their own, with only minimum contacts of any sort with Moscow, even then Moscow's general directives were rarely if ever questioned by Asian Communist leaders.

From the beginning, however, China was viewed by the Russian leaders as an important secondary base for Communist activities in Asia, and the Chinese party, acting in the name of the Comintern and under the over-all guidance of the Comintern's Far Eastern Bureau—set up in Shanghai in the early 1920s—soon expanded its own organizational links through many parts of Asia.[1] In addition to establishing close relations with Communists in Japan and Korea, the Chinese

SUBVERSION AND THE POLITICAL STRUGGLE   151

Communists also devoted particular attention to Southeast Asia. In 1926 they formed a South Seas (that is, Southeast Asia) Committee, and in the following year it was transformed into the "South Seas Communist party," for the specific function of maintaining liaison with revolutionary groups throughout Southeast Asia.

At about the same time the Pan-Pacific Trade Union Secretariat was established in China under Comintern leadership, as a regional directing organization. The South Seas Communist party, which had originally operated over a wide area including Indo-China, Burma, Thailand, Malaya, and Indonesia (then the Netherlands East Indies), was dissolved in 1930, when the Malayan and the Indo-Chinese Communist parties were formally established, but the Chinese party continued to maintain close links with Communists throughout the area. During this period the Communist movements in Malaya and Thailand, in particular, developed essentially as extensions of the Communist movement in China; from the start both were largely recruited from the Overseas Chinese.[2]

Prior to World War II Communist parties achieved only limited successes in the region from Korea to India. In many countries, severe police repression in the late 1920s and 1930s left the local Communist movements almost completely ineffective, and in some cases they all but disappeared. Then World War II offered these parties new opportunities. In many areas of Southeast Asia Communists assumed a leading role in organizing guerrilla resistance against the Japanese, and by their new appeal to growing nationalist feelings they built up a base of mass support in rural areas and acquired and trained a nucleus of armed force.

The Communists' "Hard" Policy after 1947

In 1947 the growing strength of Communist groups in postwar Asia and the highly fluid situation in many Asian countries led the Soviet Union to call for a militant policy of insurrection by Asian Communist parties, a shift which coincided with a new intransigence in Soviet actions elsewhere. This policy was publicly heralded by Andrei Zhdanov at the founding meeting of the Cominform in September and October 1947, which was called to revive the coordination of action among Communist parties everywhere. Although in its formal membership the Cominform was limited to the major Communist parties in Europe, Zhdanov gave strong emphasis to the revolutionary movements in Asia. He declared that as a result of the postwar "crisis of the colonial system" and "the rise of a powerful movement for national liberation in the colonies and dependencies," "armed resistance on the part of the colonial peoples" leading to "protracted colonial wars" was now developing.[3]

At that time Communist armed revolutions were well advanced in China and Indo-China, and Communist-led insurrections were taking place in the Philippines and India. Under the spur of the new policy Communist insurrections broke out shortly thereafter in Malaya, Burma, and Indonesia. In February 1948 two important Communist gatherings, attended by representatives of Communist parties throughout South and Southeast Asia, were held at Calcutta: the Southeast Asia Youth Conference, and the Second Congress of the Indian Communist party.[4] Apparently the new Cominform "line" was pressed home at these meetings, for almost immediately thereafter the Communist parties of South and Southeast Asia either adopted or intensified the strategy of militant insurrection.

In 1948, when the rash of Communist-led insurrections broke out in Southeast Asia, the Chinese Communists had not yet gained control of China, but they were pressing close to victory, and the influence of their example was already making itself felt in other Asian parties. Shortly after gaining power in 1949, the Chinese Communists vigorously asserted that their own revolutionary strategy should be the model which other Asian Communists should follow.

The holding at Peking, in November 1949, of a Conference of Asian and Australasian Trade Unions under the auspices of the Communist-led World Federation of Trade Unions symbolized both the new importance of Peking as a regional center for Asian communism and Moscow's willingness to delegate special responsibilities to the Chinese Communists.

The "Chinese Path" Propagated in 1949

At the November 1949 meeting in Peking Liu Shao-ch'i, second-ranking leader in the Chinese Communist party, proclaimed China's new mission. "The path taken by the Chinese people in defeating imperialism and its lackeys and in founding the People's Republic of China," he declared, "is the path that should be taken by the peoples of the various colonial and semicolonial countries in their fight for national independence and people's democracy." [5]

The full import of Liu's statement can be comprehended only if one keeps in mind the extraordinary emphasis which the Communist movement has always placed on the need to adopt a "correct" strategy for revolutionary struggle, one best suited to exploit existing conditions at any particular time. Ever since the Second Congress of the Comintern in 1920, Moscow had always defined the "correct" strategy, and Communist parties outside Russia had dutifully followed the strategic zigzags dictated by it. Major shifts had been decreed in 1921, 1928, 1935, and 1939 between so-called "left" and "right" strategies. In general terms, these shifts back and forth between "left" and "right" strategies were based upon Moscow's changing views on several basic issues. Should Communist parties press their struggle for power by tightening their organizations, following a militant policy, and concentrating their attacks upon domestic class enemies such as capitalism and feudalism, while restricting their efforts at mass organizations primarily to forming a "united front from below" of the most revolutionary classes, particularly the workers and peasants? Or should they attempt to form a broad "united front from above"? This meant cooperating with groups and parties representing major elements of the bourgeoisie, appealing to nationalism, focusing their attacks upon foreign imperialism, and emphasizing short-term piecemeal aims rather than ultimate Communist objectives. Each of these two broad alternatives could be and was defined in varying ways at different periods, but in general terms the shifts between "left" and "right" strategies hinged on these issues. In these terms Zhdanov's line of 1947 marked the shift to a new "left" strategy of militant struggle for power in as many countries as possible.

In his speech of November 1949 Liu Shao-ch'i spelled out in clear terms the current Chinese Communists' strategic prescription for Asian communism:

The path which led the Chinese people to victory is expressed in the following formula:

1. The working class must unite with all other classes, political parties, and organizations and individuals who are willing to oppose the oppression of imperialism and its lackeys, form a broad and nation-wide united front and wage a resolute fight against imperialism and its lackeys.

2. This nation-wide united front must be led by and built around the working class, which opposes imperialism most resolutely, most courageously, and most unselfishly, and its party, the Communist party, with the latter at its center. It must not be led by the wavering and compromising national bourgeoisie or the petty bourgeoisie and their parties.

3. In order to enable the working class and its party, the Communist party, to become the center for uniting all the forces throughout the country against imperialism and to competently lead the national united front to victory, it is necessary to build up through long struggles a Communist party which is armed with the theory of Marxism-Leninism, which understands strategy and tactics, practices self-criticism and strict discipline, and is closely linked with the masses.

4. It is necessary to set up wherever and whenever possible a national army which is led by the Communist party and is powerful and skillful in fighting the enemies. It is necessary to set up bases on which the liberation army relies for its activities and to make the mass struggles in the enemy-controlled areas and the armed struggles to coordinate with each other. Armed struggle is the main form of struggle for the national liberation struggles of many colonies and semicolonies.

This is the basic way followed and practiced in China by the Chinese people in winning victory. This way is the way of Mao Tse-tung which may also be the basic way for winning emancipation by the people of other colonial and semicolonial countries where similar conditions prevail.[6]

This Chinese revolutionary formula, proclaimed in 1949, placed primary emphasis upon two elements of strategy. The first was the clear focus upon imperialism as the central enemy and the call for a broad "united front" strategy combining features of both the "united front from above" and the "united front from below." Communist parties in Asia should strive to enlist support even among the "national bourgeoisie" in colonial and semicolonial areas because, Liu said, although "weak" and "vacillating," the national bourgeoisie "are opposed to imperialism within a certain period and to a certain extent." The "united front" in class terms should therefore include four classes: the workers, the peasants, the petty bourgeoisie and the national bourgeoisie. Instead of merely cooperating with major bourgeois parties and groups, as had generally been proposed under traditional "united front from above" tactics, the Chinese Communists urged the Communist parties to bring members of the national bourgeoisie directly into a national united front under Communist control, thus applying a "united front from below" approach even to capitalist groups as long as the latter are anti-imperialist. Their formula called, in short, for Asian Communists to capture effective control of local nationalist forces by concentrating their main attacks against external "imperialist" enemies to such an extent that even the "national bourgeoisie"—that is, native capitalist groups—could cooperate with or acquiesce in Communist leadership of the "liberation" movements.

A second important element in the Chinese formula—one which was particularly important in 1949 when Communist insurrections were spreading in many Asian countries—was the directive to organize Communist-led peasant armies operating from Communist-controlled rural bases. Implicitly, this strategy placed its central emphasis on the importance of the peasantry, and hence on agrarian policies, in the strategy of revolutionary struggle. Within China "armed revolution" based on rural "liberated areas" had been fundamental to Communist success, and Liu Shao-ch'i now stressed that "armed struggle can, and must, be the main force in the people's liberation struggles in many colonial and semicolonial countries." In passing, Liu qualified this statement by adding that revolutionary armies should be established "wherever and whenever possible," tacitly admitting that the

Chinese formula could probably be applied only "where similar conditions prevail."[7] This qualification received relatively little attention in 1949, however, when Communists throughout much of Asia were rushing to arms. It received more attention after 1951, when most of the insurrections had failed and many Communist parties in Asia had begun shifting to "peaceful" and noninsurrectionary tactics.

Until the latter half of 1949 it was not wholly clear whether Moscow approved of the Maoist formula. Although Zhdanov had endorsed the idea of armed insurrection in late 1947, the question of whether capitalists should be included in a national united front was subsequently debated in the Soviet Academy of Sciences as late as 1949.[8] Any doubts about Soviet attitudes toward the "Chinese path" were removed in 1949, however, when *Pravda* printed with approval Liu Shao-ch'i's formulation of strategy, and the Soviet Academy finally endorsed the idea of including major elements of the bourgeoisie in a broad united front strategy, in colonial and semicolonial areas.[9]

The Chinese Communists' emphasis upon "armed revolution" continued unchanged through 1951. In the autumn of 1951 on the occasion of the 30th anniversary of the founding of the party, Lu Ting-yi, head of the propaganda department of the Central Committee, reiterated Liu Shao-ch'i's statement of the Maoist strategy and added several new embellishments. "Mao Tse-tung's theory of the Chinese revolution," he said, "is a new development of Marxism-Leninism in the revolutions of the colonial and semicolonial countries and especially in the Chinese revolution. Mao Tse-tung's theory of the Chinese revolution has significance not only for China and Asia—it is of universal significance for the world Communist movement. It is indeed a new contribution to the treasury of Marxism-Leninism."[10]

Lu added, somewhat extravagantly, that "the classic type of revolution in imperialist countries is the October Revolution. The classic type of revolution in colonial and semicolonial countries is the Chinese revolution." "The study of Mao Tse-tung's theory of the Chinese revolution," he went on to say, "will help the Communists of various countries in their struggle against doctrinairism and empiricism to link together the universal truth of Marxism-Leninism and the concrete revolutionary practice of their respective countries, to overthrow imperialism and achieve the liberation of all mankind."

The Shift from Violence to Political Maneuver

By late 1951, however, the shift away from violence had already begun within several of the Asian Communist parties. From 1952 on the realities of world politics and the failure of insurrectionary tactics dictated a change of policy. Both Moscow and Peking endorsed this shift which was in line with the general change which was then taking place in their policies from "hard" to "soft" tactics. Thereafter Communist parties in Asia steadily deemphasized violence and insurrection and attempted to recover a greater flexibility of political maneuver. The idea of nonviolent revolutionary strategy now came increasingly to the fore. It was discussed by Stalin in his last writings, *Economic Problems of Socialism in the U.S.S.R.*, and was formally codified by Khrushchev at the Soviet 20th Party Congress in February 1956.[11]

According to Khrushchev, the working class, "by rallying round itself a toiling peasantry, the intelligentsia, and all patriotic forces, . . . has the possibility of inflicting a defeat on the reactionary antipopular forces and gaining a firm majority in Parliament, and converting it from an organ of bourgeois democracy into an instrument of genuine popular will." Violence was not renounced in principle; where police repression is severe, the Congress stated, the transition to socialism will be attended by "acute class revolutionary struggle." But Moscow's endorsement of the methods of parliamentary struggle implied approval of a very different strategy from that set forth by Liu Shao-ch'i in 1949.

After 1952 a parallel shift took place in Peking's party line. The Chinese Communists also played down the idea of violent revolution, and in 1954 they made the first of many official pronouncements that "revolution is not for export." However, the Chinese formula for a broad, four-class, united front was not rejected; it has, in fact, been accepted by most Asian Communist parties although they have adapted it to their own concrete situations, just as the Chinese adapted Soviet ideas to fit their needs.

Peking's Regional Influence in Asia

Since 1949 there has been a steady increase in the Chinese Communists' direct contacts with other Asian Communist parties and a significant growth in Peking's influence on their strategy. Moscow continues to be the primary headquarters of the world-wide Communist movement, but Peking's role appears, in effect, to have become that of a regional subheadquarters.

The Russians certainly have not abdicated their leadership in Asia. Doctrinal and strategic guidance for Communists everywhere still emanates from Moscow, and statements such as those of the 20th and 21st Congresses of the Soviet Communist party, or the Declaration of Communist and Workers' Parties in November 1957, serve as general directives for all Communist parties, with the notable exception of the Yugoslav party. In Asia both the Russians and the Chinese exert a significant influence on many of the local parties, and, as far as outsiders can know, in no case has there been a head-on clash between them. Conceivably, a serious rivalry could develop in the future, with disruptive effects on the entire Communist movement, but at present Peking and Moscow seem to be cooperating rather than competing in fostering the growth of Asian communism.

Yet Peking's influence is extensive and has definitely been on the upswing ever since 1949. Its direct ties with certain Asian parties have long been stronger than Moscow's, and there is considerable evidence that it has increasingly become a source of tactical guidance to certain others. Almost everywhere in Asia the example of the successful "Chinese path" to power has had a strong and continuing influence on the local Communist movements.

Brief histories of a number of Asian Communist parties, and details on the Chinese Communists' contacts with them, are contained in the Appendix, "Peking and the Communist Parties of Asia" (see pages 476-501). Here it is only possible to point out a few salient facts about the relationships between the Chinese Communist party and other Asian Communist movements.[12]

Peking's influence is strongest in those countries where the Chinese had a major role in the founding of the local parties and where ethnic Chinese make up the bulk of the Communist party membership. The Communist movements in Malaya (and Singapore) and Thailand are unquestionably within Peking's sphere of primary influence. The Malayan Communist party was founded in the early 1920s with the aid of Chinese Communist agents, and today over 95 per cent of its members are Overseas Chinese. Clearly, it looks upon the Chinese Communist party as its model. In Thailand, there are believed to be two party organizations. One is the relatively unimportant Communist Party of Thailand, with a small Thai membership. The other is the Chinese Communist Party in Thailand, which is many times larger and seemingly operates almost solely within the Overseas Chinese community.

Peking's influence is also very strong in the Communist parties which operate in the countries on two of its most sensitive flanks: Korea and Vietnam. Through the latter, its influence extends also into Laos, Cambodia, and northeast Thailand, areas where the Lao Dong or Labor party, as the Vietnamese Communist party is called, takes the lead—apparently under Peking's aegis and with its backing—in promoting the spread of communism.

Historically the Chinese Communists had much less influence than the Russians on the growth of communism in Korea. Even though a few Korean Communists worked during World War II with the Communist party in China, where they established a so-called "Yenan Independence Alliance," it was the Russians who occupied North Korea in 1945, set up a Communist regime there, and placed Kim Il-Sung and other Soviet protégés in power. Since the start of the Korean War, however, the Chinese—who bore the brunt of the fighting on the Communist side and kept a large occupation force in Korea until 1958—have strongly supported and influenced Kim Il-Sung's "Workers' party." Probably, Soviet influence is still greater than that of the Chinese in many respects, but Peking has given essential military support and large-scale economic aid to the Korean Communist regime, and its impact upon the Korean party has been extremely significant. Perhaps North Korea today can best be described as a Sino-Soviet condominium.

Peking obviously has developed a very special interest and influence in North Vietnam. Because of Vietnam's geographical, cultural, and historical ties with China, it has been greatly affected by modern Chinese political movements ever since 1911. Ho Chi-minh, although Moscow-trained, spent many years in China before World War II; he founded the Vietnam Revolutionary Youth Association in Canton in the 1920s and set up the Communist Party of Indo-China in Hong Kong in 1930. During World War II, he went from China to Indo-China to organize resistance against the Japanese, and, ironically, it was the Chinese Nationalists who backed him. The Chinese Communists apparently had few links with the Vietnamese Communists until 1949, but since then they have given them major military and economic support, and North Vietnam today is in many respects a satellite of Peking, more dependent on it than on Moscow. Peking seems to have exercised considerable restraint in its relationships with Hanoi, however; apparently it has encouraged the Vietnamese to play the primary role in directly supporting Communist-led groups such as the Pathet Lao guerrillas—and their above-ground political party, the Neo Lao Hak Xat—in Laos.

Both Peking and Moscow maintain close ties with, and exercise a strong influence over, the Japanese Communist party. While Moscow appears to be the main source of strategic guidance, however, Peking has clearly developed a very special relationship with the Japanese Communists since World War II. Nozaka, the present leader of the party and its principal strategist for the past decade, spent the last five years of World War II in China, where he organized a "Japanese Emancipation League" and set up a "Japanese Peasants' and Workers' School." Between 1952 and 1955 "Radio Free Japan," believed to have been located near Peking, served as a primary source of tactical guidance for the Japanese Communist party, and Tokuda, the Secretary General of the party in the immediate postwar period, fled to China when the party went underground, in the early 1950s, and died there in 1953.

Peking's influence elsewhere is less striking and probably less extensive. In Burma the Communist movement is relatively new and has been so fragmented during the past decade that undoubtedly Moscow and Peking have been almost as confused by it as the rest of the world. In 1946 the movement split into two parties—the "White Flag" Burma Communist party and the "Red Flag" Communist Party of Burma—and more recently it has also operated through various other organizations, both underground and aboveground, including the National United Front, which has become increasingly important as the Communists have attempted to switch over from insurrection to political maneuver. The ties between these various groups and the world Communist movement have been obscure. There is evidence, however, that the Burmese Communist party has sent several missions to China, and Burmese leaders have charged that the Chinese Communists have given covert support to the National United Front. In the Philippines, the Communist-led Hukbalahaps seem to have been isolated, for the most part, from both Moscow and Peking, but their rural strategy has resembled that of the Chinese Communists in certain important respects, and they are believed to have received some funds channeled through the Overseas Chinese.

Moscow's direct influence on the two largest and most important Communist parties in non-Communist countries of Asia—those in Indonesia and India—has long been far greater than Peking's. Yet even in these places the Chinese Communists' organizational contacts and ideological influence have steadily grown. In the faction-ridden Indian party there have been intense disputes over the relevance to India of the "thought of Mao Tse-tung." And in Indonesia the Chinese Communist Embassy in the period immediately after 1950 engaged in crude political meddling, before switching to more subtle means of exerting its influence.

In many places in Asia, however, because of widespread fears of China and dislike of the Overseas Chinese, Peking's support is not an unmixed blessing to the indigenous Communist movements. Some observers believe that the parties in

Korea, Vietnam, and Indonesia have all experienced internal conflicts during the past decade between groups with a greater or lesser identification with Peking and that in each case the groups which were allegedly most "pro-Peking" lost out. This kind of speculation is often based on rather slender evidence, yet it is doubtless true that in many Asian nations the Communist parties feel they must guard against becoming too closely identified with Peking.

Peking, on its part, certainly rates some of the Communist parties in Asia much higher than others as effective instruments to achieve its goals. Moreover, this rating has doubtless undergone a significant change during the past decade. Ten years ago when they were actively and overtly encouraging insurrections throughout Asia, the Chinese Communists probably regarded the prospects of the Communist parties in Malaya, Burma, and the Philippines as relatively favorable; in all of these areas the parties had developed strong guerrilla forces, operating from rural bases, and were able to threaten the survival of the existing non-Communist regimes. In recent years, however, the Asian parties which have generally been most successful are those which have concentrated on building up their aboveground apparatus and have pursued broad "united front" tactics.

In Indonesia the Communist party's membership is claimed to have jumped from 8,000 in 1952 to more than a million in 1957, and in the 1957 elections it emerged as the strongest single party on Java, the center of political power in Indonesia. In India the party, having doubled its membership between 1952 and 1957, emerged as the second strongest national party in the 1957 elections and won control of the state of Kerala; New Delhi removed this Communist regime in Kerala in mid-1959, but it remains to be seen what has happened to its grass-roots strength.

Much of the backing for the People's Action party, which won a landslide victory in Singapore's 1959 elections, was provided by Communist-manipulated and pro-Peking Chinese laborers and students. The Malayan Communist party can be expected to continue striving to gain complete control of the People's Action party and of the new State of Singapore, with the aim of converting it into a political satellite of Peking. In Laos the Communist-directed Pathet Lao, working through the aboveground Neo Lao Hak Xat, won most of the seats which it contested in the 1958 elections, adding a new political threat to the danger already posed by recalcitrant units of the former Pathet Lao army. Then, after the government of Laos had cracked down on the Pathet Lao, insurrection flared up again during the summer of 1959 in territory adjacent to North Vietnam and Communist China.

As long as they seem to be making gains through their "coexistence" tactics, both Peking and Moscow will doubtless encourage Asian Communist parties to build up their strength through overt political action. However, as shown by recent events in Laos, when peaceful tactics fail, those Communist parties which retain a nucleus of armed strength can always try to revert to violence, and in Malaya, Burma, and the Philippines as well as Laos, there are still small guerrilla units operating. Elsewhere, furthermore, there is always the danger that if the Communist parties in places such as Singapore, Indonesia, or India, should gain sufficient strength to attempt a coup, they might then be tempted to abandon "parliamentary" tactics and to attempt to seize power by violence.

By the latter half of 1959 leaders in Peking and Moscow, as well as the local leaders of Communist parties in many Asian areas, may have begun asking themselves whether or not a general shift to more militant tactics was desirable. Since 1958 the growth of local Communist parties appeared to have been checked, at least temporarily, in many places. In a wide range of Asian countries, including Pakistan, Burma, Indonesia, Thailand, and Laos, non-Communist military leaders, or political leaders with military backing, had assumed special powers, and in all of these places there had been a clampdown on Communist activities. Where this clampdown hurt the Communists most, the local Communist parties did, in fact, become more militant. When the government of Laos moved to bring the last Pathet Lao military units under effective control, the Communists in Laos reverted once again to open insurrection, and in India the Communists instigated violent riots in Calcutta after the

Kerala administration had been dismissed. It was still not clear in the early autumn of 1959, however, whether these actions were merely local reactions to stronger anti-Communist measures, or whether they foreshadowed more militant Communist tactics on a broad scale. Nor was it clear whether the new anti-Communist measures in many Asian countries were substantially reducing the basic Communist threat. The new political importance of anti-Communist military leaders was clearly due in large part to the total or partial breakdown of democratic institutions and processes, and it remains to be seen whether the new regimes will be able to strike successfully at the root causes of Communist growth.

The Limits of External Aid

Although both the Russians and Chinese can encourage, advise, and in various under-the-board ways support the numerous Communist parties in Asia, they cannot fight their political battles for them. Among political analysts in the West are some who appear to believe that tremendous revolutionary movements, anywhere in the world, can be manufactured virtually out of thin air by a few remarkable agents sent by Moscow and Peking and that revolution in Asia can be explained almost wholly in terms of decisions made in the Kremlin or the Forbidden City. Without underestimating the importance of either Soviet or Chinese guidance and assistance, it is clear that external support is in most cases only a marginal factor in the development of communism in Asian countries. In the final analysis, the success or failure of most Asian Communist parties in building up their strength will depend on fundamental social, economic, and political forces in the countries where they operate and on the success or failure of non-Communist political groups in meeting the basic problems of their countries.

Communist regimes can be placed in power by foreign armies, of course, as they were by the Russians not only in Eastern Europe but also in North Korea after World War II. And in countries immediately adjacent to the Communist bloc, such as Laos, material as well as other forms of aid can be channeled across the border, particularly when Communist insurrectionary groups are able to establish bases in border regions. But the Communists in Peking are not in the position of puppeteers capable of manipulating major forces within all the nations throughout Asia merely by tugging on a few strings. However, while keeping in mind the limitations on Peking's influence, it is still essential to recognize that Communist China has contributed, and will continue to contribute, substantially to the growth of communism throughout Asia.

The Types of Chinese Assistance to Asian Communists

Although no open organization has been established in Asia, equivalent to the Europe-centered Cominform, which was dissolved in 1956, since 1949 Peking has become the headquarters for an increasing number of Communist and Communist-front organizations which appear to have a regional responsibility. Immediately after 1949 the Trade Union Liaison Bureau for Asia and Australasia, newly established in Peking, seemed destined to serve as the key organizational center for Communist activities in Asia, but there is little evidence that it has done so. Several other headquarters organizations for coordinating activities throughout the region have been set up in China, and there is no firm evidence that any single organization serves as the directing center. Actually, some of the most important direct contacts between Chinese and other Asian Communist leaders may take place rather informally. Each May and October important Communists from all over the region make pilgrimages to Peking to participate in the Chinese May Day and National Day celebrations. Furthermore, the stream of Communist visitors to Peking, as to Moscow, is not restricted to any particular time, but is almost continuous. Peking's embassies, particularly in Rangoon and Djakarta, undoubtedly also play an important role in maintaining liaison between the Chinese Communists and other Asian parties.

With the notable exceptions of North Korea and North Vietnam, the actual assistance which Peking has given to most other Asian Communist parties has not been primarily material. Peking's financial aid has apparently been of some importance to the Communist parties or their front organizations in Indonesia, Burma, the Philippines, Japan, and perhaps elsewhere. And in the latter half of 1959, military supplies from North Vietnam, which itself relies on supplies from Communist China, clearly bolstered the Pathet Lao rebels in Laos. But in over-all terms, intangible assistance, in the form of political and moral support, inspiration, encouragement, and guidance, is probably more significant than material aid, in Asia as a whole. The most revolutionary influence emanating from Peking may simply be the force of the ideas which the Chinese regime represents—the doctrine, the faith, the ideology, and the example which inspire fanatic dedication on the part of Communist converts all over Asia.

The growth of indigenous Communist strength throughout Asia is undoubtedly regarded by Peking as the primary means of achieving its long-term revolutionary aims. And because of the tremendous domestic problems and internal instability in most Asian countries, the leaders in Peking must have found considerable cause for encouragement during 1957 and 1958, when political instability and the prospects for Communist success appeared to increase considerably in many Asian countries. In Indonesia, Laos, and Singapore a real danger emerged that Communist parties or Communist-dominated coalitions might even achieve power through legal electoral processes. In Burma, the breakup of the AFPFL seemed to open up new opportunities for the Communists. In Pakistan, Nepal, Ceylon, and other countries acute instability posed serious new problems which the Communists could be expected to try to exploit. Since the start of 1959, it is true, a somewhat greater measure of stability appears to have been achieved in some of these places, but the danger posed by Communist parties throughout Asia will certainly be a continuing one.

Other Forms of Chinese Subversive Activity

Although the Asian Communist parties are undoubtedly regarded by Peking as the principal instruments of revolution, the Chinese Communists also have at their disposal other subversive and revolutionary tools which they have not yet used to the full. Several prominent Asian political figures, after defeat at home, have sought asylum in Communist China. Among them are Pridi Phanomyong, a prominent political leader in Thailand in the 1930s, and Premier at the time of Phibul's coup in 1947; Nai Prasert Sapsunthorn, the one member of the Proletarian party elected to parliament in Thailand after World War II; K. I. Singh, onetime leader of an unsuccessful revolt in Nepal; and Naw Seng, a Kachin who was a senior officer in the Burmese army prior to rebelling against the government. Of these, only K. I. Singh has so far returned to his homeland. An enigmatic figure, Singh was Prime Minister briefly and then strongly opposed the government; he has alternately appeared both pro- and anti-Communist. He was defeated in the elections of early 1959, but it is difficult to predict what role he may play in the future.

The Chinese Communists also have sizable Kachin and Thai minorities within their borders; a few of them have been infiltrated into Burma and Thailand and, according to some reports, "Chinese" Kachins have urged the Burmese Kachins to secede. There has also been some infiltration from Chinese-controlled Tibet into Nepal. And, of course, there are about 10 million Overseas Chinese with great economic power scattered throughout Southeast Asian countries; their situation and potential role will be discussed in Chapter 8. In terms of the ultimate objective of establishing indigenous Communist regimes in other Asian countries, none of these possible instruments of subversion, including even the Overseas Chinese (except in Singapore, Malaya, and possibly Thailand), can be regarded by Peking as of primary importance, at least by comparison with the importance of local Communist parties, but they can be utilized to create situations of instability and to provide support to the indigenous Communist movements. To some extent they have already been used for these purposes.

Subversion in Peking's Foreign Policy

Even if, in the years immediately ahead, the Communist movements and other subversive elements do not acquire political control in other Asian countries, they can still be expected to contribute significant support to Peking's foreign policy. Both the Communist parties and the large number of Communist-influenced front groups in Asia give consistent backing to Peking's and Moscow's foreign policy. They help to mold local public opinion and endeavor to influence their governments' policies in ways favorable to the world Communist movement.

Between 1954, when Peking switched wholeheartedly to a "peaceful coexistence" line, and 1959, when revolt broke out in Laos, the Chinese Communists did not, it is true, support revolutionary groups outside China's borders. This "restraint" can be explained by the high priority which they attached to establishing friendly relations with non-Communist governments in Asia. To achieve their short-term diplomatic aims, the Chinese Communists officially disavowed all subversive activity and made many diplomatic pledges that "revolution is not for export," and in practice they were extremely cautious in providing material support to revolutionary groups.

In some instances Chinese Communist policies between 1954 and 1959 may, in fact, have actually hurt rather than helped other Asian Communist parties. Peking's wooing of Nehru's government after 1954, its prompt recognition of an anti-Communist government in newly independent Malaya in 1957, and its attentive interest in the Japanese Socialist party may have embarrassed, and harmed to some extent, the position of the Communist parties in India, Malaya, and Japan. In this period Peking probably hoped, however, that by establishing friendly relations with non-Communist governments and parties it could aid indigenous Communist parties in the long run. Its friendly gestures toward the Indonesian government, for example, seemed to have aided the Indonesian Communists to win greater tolerance on the goverment's part and greater respectability among the general public, and the Chinese Communists may still be convinced that in many instances a friendly posture toward anti-Communist governments can provide backing to the Communist parties' current united front, parliamentary tactics.

As of the autumn of 1959 it is not clear, however, whether Peking's political backing of the Pathet Lao rebels in Laos represents merely an exception to the general policy Communist China has pursued during the past five years or whether it marks a basic change of policy foreshadowing a period of more open support by Peking to Communist subversion throughout Asia.

The Problem of Countering Subversion

Dealing effectively with Communist subversion is clearly one of the basic and most difficult problems in countering Communist China's growing influence in Asia. It must be recognized, however, that Peking's influence on other Asian Communist parties may be exerted with considerable effect through intangible as well as through material means and that there is no practical way of eliminating at its source the ideological inspiration and support which emanate from Communist China. Before 1949 countering Soviet influence in China required, above all, effective means to help China solve its domestic problems; similarly, today the problem of combating Chinese Communist influence in Asia requires coming to grips with the problems which concern the peasants of Java and Luzon, the intellectuals of Tokyo and Rangoon, the workers of Calcutta and Kuala Lumpur, and the students of Singapore and New Delhi. When the social and political system in any Asian nation fails to cope with existing problems, this provides the Communists with great opportunities to exploit the resentments of disappointed nationalism and frustrated social aspirations. The programs and promises which draw the dissatisfied, the discontented, and the frustrated to communism can be met only by programs and ideals which inspire faith and support for alternative programs.

There is in addition, of course, a more limited but nonetheless serious police problem posed by Communist subversion. It focuses on the need to combat illegal activities conducted by Communist party organizations and to find more effective means to prevent indigenous Communists from obtaining material assistance from Communist China, North Vietnam, or elsewhere. Most of the nations in the region need to improve their internal security apparatus substantially. A great deal of useful experience in antisubversion techniques has already been accumulated within Asian countries—in the Philippines, Malaya, and elsewhere—and Asian governments should share their experience and cooperate more closely in meeting this problem. In this field SEATO has made a valuable contribution, and some countries, such as Malaya and Thailand, have developed their cooperation outside the SEATO framework. Much more needs to be done in the field of domestic security, however, preferably on a still wider basis than at present. At best, of course, police measures deal with symptoms rather than with the basic causes of subversion. The causes can best be attacked in positive ways, by helping build viable and vigorous societies, able to develop political, social, and economic strength.

Through both governmental and private action the United States is already aiding these countries in many ways, but it must face the challenge to do far more than it has. Many other countries—those of the British Commonwealth, the socialist democracies of Scandinavia, the larger Asian countries such as Japan and India, and others—can also make very great contributions to the development of Asian nations. In many cases these nations may be better situated than the United States to provide the kind of assistance needed, and much more should be done to encourage a cooperative approach, both within and without the United Nations, to many of the problems of economic and cultural development. But the United States itself must assume a major responsibility for assisting the development of Asian nations.

Present American aid programs, while substantial, fall far short of the urgent needs. With the exception of India, almost none of the underdeveloped nations in Asia has even approached a "breakthrough" in its economic development—the stage at which its development "takes off" and begins to generate a substantial development momentum of its own. In comparison with Communist China, many of these nations are still stagnating. Although a great deal of knowledge has been acquired in recent years about the problems of economic development, the need remains for both the non-Communist Asian nations themselves, and for other nations which can help them, to prove that they possess the will and the dedication essential to develop the necessary trained manpower, and allocate the required resources, to meet the problems adequately.

The question of how the United States and other nations can best assist the nations of Asia in their political development is, if anything, even more difficult. Yet, the democracies start with many advantages. In the newly independent nations of Asia most of the non-Communist leaders look to the West for political inspiration. They share with the democracies many basic political values, and they have deliberately borrowed numerous parliamentary and other democratic institutions. However, Western political values and institutions cannot be simply transplanted without major adaptation; recent developments in Burma, Indonesia, Thailand, Pakistan, and elsewhere have made this quite apparent. In time, democratic values can certainly be translated into new institutional forms and processes, but this requires both the building of new types of national institutions and the development of political organizations and methods which can function effectively at the grass-roots level, where the Communists labor most assiduously to build up their mass organizations.

The political problems, perhaps even more than the economic ones, must in the final analysis be solved by the people themselves in these Asian nations. But Americans and others who have had many years of pragmatic experience in developing and applying a democratic approach to political problems can provide valuable assistance to help these nations generate a self-sustaining political dynamism of their own. If the non-Communist national leaders fail to solve their countries' most pressing problems, disillusion will surely grow. Then Communist China's achievements in creating economic and military strength by ruthless totalitarian methods will loom ever larger, and Peking will certainly be eager to train other nations in Asia in its own school of totalitarianism.

Chapter 8

THE OVERSEAS CHINESE

There are about 11 or 12 million Chinese living outside the borders of Communist China, not including those on Taiwan, Hong Kong, or Macao, and roughly 10 million of them live in Southeast Asia. A large majority of these Overseas Chinese is unassimilated; they regard themselves as Chinese, and their primary loyalties are toward China as their homeland. Throughout Southeast Asia they have great economic power.

Southeast Asian governments, newly independent and nationalistic, fear possible political subversion by their Chinese minorities, and they also resent the concentration of economic power in the hands of unassimilated, alien groups. Consequently, they have subjected the Overseas Chinese to increasingly severe restrictions and controls. In most places anti-Chinese discrimination has been designed to limit the Chinese in their economic activity, but the control measures adopted also aim to hasten the assimilation, or at least the integration, of Chinese minorities into the local societies. These discriminatory measures have injured the Overseas Chinese, but have not undermined their economic power, because the Chinese in Southeast Asia are highly skilled in evading restrictions. In some areas current policies are probably facilitating assimilation, but in others the discrimination is so extreme that it is more likely to impede integration, at least in the short run. The most significant evidences of current assimilation are to be found in Thailand. Elsewhere the problems are still great, and progress toward integration is slow.

The primary aim of the typical Overseas Chinese businessman or merchant is economic self-preservation; ideology and politics are generally secondary. However, in Singapore and Malaya, where the Overseas Chinese form a large proportion of the total population, they have now emerged for the first time as a major political force, and they will doubtless play a large part in deciding the political future of the area. In other areas, particularly where they constitute small minorities, which are politically weak despite their great wealth and economic power, they have felt very vulnerable to persecution and have generally abstained from direct participation in local politics. But they have increasingly been tempted to look abroad for external support, and this has made them susceptible to being manipulated and used by political groups in China, not only as a factor in China's own political struggles, but also as an instrument through which China can influence political developments in Southeast Asian countries.

Although both the Chinese Nationalists and the Communists have competed actively for control of the Overseas Chinese, neither side has won a total victory. The Overseas Chinese are highly opportunistic and have shifted their political loyalties several times in response to changing situations and pressures. Nevertheless, it is clear that since 1949 there has been a very great increase in pro-Peking sentiment among the Chinese in many Southeast Asian nations. "Pro-Peking" is a more accurate term than "pro-Communist," since ideology is frequently not basic in determining their political orientation.

Origins of the Overseas Chinese

Although the "Overseas Chinese problem" has become acute only in recent years, since the establishment of newly independent nations throughout Southeast Asia and the rise to power of a strong Communist government in China, it has a very long history.

The migration of Chinese to Southeast Asia started many centuries ago, in response to local population pressures, rather than to Chinese official policy. It can be viewed as one of many examples of the steady expansion of the Chinese from their original heartland in the "Middle Kingdom." What is now South China was populated by Chinese migrants pushing southward overland. Ancestors of the present inhabitants of North Vietnam, Laos, Thailand, and Burma once lived in lands which are now Chinese, before they were forced to retreat southward to their present homelands by the tide of Chinese migration. Manchuria was also populated largely by overland migrants from North China, most of whom moved north in the nineteenth and twentieth centuries. The migration by sea routes to Southeast Asia was a part of this broader picture.

There were important enclaves of Chinese living in Southeast Asia from the sixteenth century onward. During the nineteenth century, as European colonial rulers turned to developing the economic potentialities of the region, the flow of Chinese steadily increased. It kept rising through the late 1920s and then was brought virtually to a halt by World War II and by subsequent immigration restrictions imposed by the newly independent nations of Southeast Asia. Except for a brief period in 1946-1947, when there was a temporary spurt of large-scale migration, no significant flow of Chinese to Southeast Asia has taken place in recent years; only a trickle of legal and illegal migration has continued.

Over 90 per cent of the Overseas Chinese came from the two Chinese coastal provinces of Fukien and Kwangtung. Economic pressures at home led the residents of these overpopulated, mountainous provinces to seek economic opportunities abroad, and they turned seaward, attracted by the lure of underpopulated Southeast Asia with its rich resources. Until the mid-nineteenth century the imperial government in China usually restricted or even prohibited emigration, and the migrants, who went abroad as individuals or in small groups, had to fend for themselves. In the late nineteenth century, however, the Chinese government began for the first time to take an active interest in its nationals abroad.

The region in China from which the Overseas Chinese emigrated is divided into numerous small areas, each of which has its own dialect and its own clannish loyalties. The emigrants took their dialects and clannishness abroad with them, and consequently Chinese communities in Southeast Asia are far from homogeneous, even though their members share a common Chinese culture which sets them apart from the local populace. These communities are usually divided into many subgroups which tend to retain their dialects and their distinctive customs. In their relations with local authorities, however, the Overseas Chinese have generally acted with some degree of unity.

Among the Overseas Chinese in Southeast Asia, the five most important dialect groups are the Hokkiens, Teochius, Cantonese, Hakkas, and Hailams. The 2.5 million Hokkiens, from the Amoy region of southern Fukien, are the largest group, and they are numerically predominant among the Chinese in Malaya, Singapore, Indonesia, Burma, and the Philippines. The Teochius, from the Swatow region of northern Kwangtung, number roughly 2.3 million and form the largest Chinese group in Thailand, Cambodia, and Laos. The Cantonese, from central Kwangtung, totaling about 1.7 million, are the biggest group in Vietnam and rank second in Malaya and Singapore as well as in Cambodia and Laos. The Hakkas, regarded as a minority group even in their home provinces of Fukien and Kwangtung, total close to 1.5 million in Southeast Asia; they constitute the biggest group in North Borneo, Sarawak, and Brunei, and the second largest in Indonesia and Thailand. The Hailams, from Hainan Island, are scattered throughout many areas of Southeast Asia and number about 600 thousand in the region as a whole. Much of the daily life and internal politics of Overseas Chinese centers in the numerous institutions and associations which these dialect groups have established wherever they live.

Distribution of the Overseas Chinese

The far-from-even distribution of Overseas Chinese throughout Southeast Asia is not surprising; the migration was not planned, but developed in response to opportunities for employment and to the haphazard traditions of migration which gradually developed.

Today the main areas of concentration are Malaya, Singapore, Thailand, and Indonesia.

OVERSEAS CHINESE IN SOUTHERN ASIA [1]

	Ethnic Chinese	Percentage of total population
Malaya	2,365,000	37.8
Singapore	965,000	76.6
Thailand	2,360,000	11.3
British Borneo	270,000	27.0
Cambodia	230,000	5.5
South Vietnam	780,000	6.2
North Vietnam	50,000	0.4
Indonesia	2,250,000	2.7
Burma	320,000	1.6
Philippines	270,000	1.2
Laos	10,000	0.6

In terms of their potential political significance, the number of Overseas Chinese in various countries is less important than their ratio to the total population in each area. In all of Southeast Asia the Overseas Chinese constitute only about 5 per cent of the total population, but in Singapore, Malaya, Thailand, and British Borneo they are a very significant portion of the population.

Singapore is a Chinese city. In the colony as a whole the million or so Chinese make up over three-quarters of its total population. Here the other groups—Malays, Indians, and Europeans—are the minorities. In Malaya between 2 to 2.5 million Chinese constitute close to 40 per cent of the population, being only slightly outnumbered by the Malays. If Singapore and Malaya are considered as a joint economic and political unit, as was the practice until recent political developments separated them, the Overseas Chinese outnumber the Malays. In Thailand the 2 to 2.5 million Chinese comprise over 10 per cent of the population.[2] And on the island of Borneo the Chinese in North Borneo, Sarawak, and Brunei, totaling between 200,000 and 300,000, form 20 to 30 per cent of the population.

Elsewhere the Overseas Chinese are a relatively small part of the total population. In Cambodia the 200,000 to 250,000 Overseas Chinese make up about 6 per cent of the population. In Vietnam the 800,000-plus Chinese constituted until recently only a little over 3 per cent of the population of Vietnam as a whole. Most of them, however, lived in what is now South Vietnam, and after the partition of the country some of those in the north moved south. The 780,000 Chinese in South Vietnam now account for over 6 per cent of the total population, and there are currently only 35,000 to 50,000 in the North.[3] In no other Southeast Asian country do the Overseas Chinese exceed 3 per cent of the population. Even in Indonesia, with over 2 million, they total only 2 to 3 per cent of the population, although on Sumatra they make up 5 per cent and on Indonesian Borneo 9 per cent. The 300,000 or more Overseas Chinese in Burma, and the slightly smaller number who live in the Philippines, comprise less than 2 per cent of the population in each instance. In Laos the 10,000 Overseas Chinese are a numerically unimportant group. It is fortunate for the countries immediately adjacent to China's southern borders, including North Vietnam, Laos, and Burma, that they have the smallest percentages of Overseas Chinese in their populations.

Economic and Social Position of the Overseas Chinese

In almost every Southeast Asian country the economic importance of the Overseas Chinese is far greater than their numerical strength. Many of the Chinese have achieved great economic success. Although most were poor and illiterate at home, they came from a culture which put a high value on hard work and thrift, as well as on economic skills. From the start, they had phenomenal success in competition with the local peoples whose cultures, developed in a rich tropical environment, placed a much lower rating on the value of diligence and material gain. Among the Overseas Chinese "rags-to-riches" success stories have been common. Some, of course, failed to advance themselves, but most of those who went to Southeast Asia have been able to improve their own economic status and to make substantial contributions to their families in China.

Despite a certain ambivalence in their attitudes toward the Chinese, the European colonial regimes generally encouraged them to migrate to Southeast Asia, and the Chinese made an enormous contribution to the economic development of the region. In addition, their remittances to their families back home helped to raise living standards in their native villages above those in other parts of South China. Emigrant remittances came to constitute a vital item in China's international balance of payments, in some years prior to World War II totaling over $100 million annually.[4]

Almost everywhere in Southeast Asia the Overseas Chinese have gradually become the dominant commercial class, even where they make up only a small percentage of the population. They own a very large percentage of the small retail stores and workshops, as well as a sizable proportion of the large commercial firms, in the area. They have traditionally controlled the milling and sale of rice, the staple food. They were formerly important in money-lending, but they play a smaller role in this today, partly because of restrictions which have been imposed on them. They have also had a major part in developing large-scale enterprises. Under the prewar colonial regimes European capital was foremost in the development of basic raw materials, but the role of the Overseas Chinese in the production of rubber, tin, teak, and many other commodities was second in importance only to that of the Europeans and far overshadowed that of local people. In foreign trade the Overseas Chinese also assumed control of most of the trade that was not transacted by large European firms. They have, in fact, entered most of the lucrative occupations in Southeast Asia—relatively few have gone into agriculture—and where they are especially numerous, as in Singapore, Malaya, and Thailand, they constitute the bulk of the urban industrial and working class as well.

The economic success of the Overseas Chinese in Southeast Asia has had far-reaching social results.[5] Under colonial rule European administrators and businessmen dominated the social structure and monopolized political and economic power at the top. To the extent that they shared political power, it was with the native aristocracy. More recently, since independence, political power has passed to new groups of native nationalists, many of whom derive from the old aristocracy. During all of this time the native inhabitants have made up the bulk of the farming class and other lower-class, noncommercial segments of society, at the bottom of the social scale. Both under colonial rule and since independence, the Overseas Chinese—and to a lesser extent other alien groups including the Indians—have constituted the bulk of the commercial "middle class." To be sure, they have not played the traditional role performed by the middle class in Western societies, but they have served as the principal economic middlemen or intermediaries between the political rulers and the mass of the local population. In recent years, as an indigenous middle class has begun to emerge in some countries, the continuing domination of economic life by the Overseas Chinese has become increasingly galling to many political groups and leaders.

Assimilation and Integration

The resentments of Southeast Asians against the Overseas Chinese would be less strong today if the Chinese had been assimilated to a greater extent into the local cultures and societies. Although probably most of those who went to Southeast Asia before 1900 were assimilated, a great majority of Overseas Chinese in the area today are relatively recent migrants who have remained clearly alien, preserving their language and traditions, maintaining their separate identities, and retaining close links with their homeland.

In the early years of Chinese migration most migrants were men, and many married local women, even when they continued to support other wives in their home villages. This intermarriage led to a great deal of assimilation, and today there is a Chinese strain in a sizable proportion of the indigenous populations of Thailand, the Philippines, Burma, Cambodia, and Vietnam. In most places except Thailand, however, the assimilation process declined steadily after 1900.

A process of acculturation—which is often a first step toward assimilation—has taken place somewhat more widely than full assimilation. In scattered areas in Southeast Asia there are groups of Chinese who have adopted many of the customs of either the local people or past colonial rulers and have severed most if not all ties with China. Many have given up the Chinese language in favor of Southeast Asian or European languages. In some places these acculturated groups form a majority of the Overseas Chinese; elsewhere, they have dissociated themselves in many ways from the majority. However, even though groups like the "peranakan" in Indonesia, the "baba" in Malaya, and the "Straits Chinese" in both Singapore and Malaya have closely identified themselves with the countries of their residence, they have nevertheless remained separate and distinct from the population as a whole and are still almost universally regarded as Chinese, albeit a special kind of Chinese.

There have always been impediments to either assimilation or acculturation of the Chinese in Southeast Asia. These barriers increased substantially in the period between 1900 and World War II. Although during the past decade they may have decreased somewhat, they are still very great.

Foremost among the traditional barriers, perhaps, has been the distinctiveness of Chinese culture and the deep-rooted Chinese sense of cultural superiority. Islam, which predominates in much of Southeast Asia, has also been a serious obstacle to the assimilation of the pork-eating Chinese. And the colonial policy of treating the Chinese as a group apart also discouraged assimilation.

After the turn of the century, new factors further impeded the integration of the Chinese into the local societies. As migration increased, the percentage of China-born persons in Overseas Chinese communities rose rapidly, and the increase in the number of women immigrants led to a steady decline in the proportion of mixed marriages. The Chinese government's growing interest in the Overseas Chinese, and the development of modern Chinese nationalism, which had a strong impact on the Chinese abroad, strengthened political ties between China and the Overseas Chinese. Nationalism stimulated the expansion of Chinese schools abroad, as well as the use of *kuo yü*—the officially approved lingua franca of modern China—all of which tended to increase the "Chineseness" of the Overseas Chinese.

In the past decade the situation has changed once again in many respects. As a result of the cutting off of migration during World War II, and the subsequent decline of two-way travel, the number of China-born Overseas Chinese is steadily decreasing. At present, close to three-quarters of all Chinese in the major Overseas Chinese communities in Southeast Asia are local-born persons, rather than China-born; in time practically all will have been born abroad.

Most Overseas Chinese now think of their future in terms of permanent settlement abroad. In many areas this change clearly favors integration, but in others, such as Singapore and Malaya, the Chinese have not as yet become any less Chinese in outlook as a result of settling down.

In many parts of Southeast Asia new pressures toward integration and assimilation are now exerted by the educational and other policies which have been adopted by the newly independent nations in the region. The Overseas Chinese resent many of these policies, however, and they are still pushed and pulled by influences from their homeland. Despite the many factors encouraging integration, therefore, a large majority of Overseas Chinese continues to live, act, and feel as Chinese; they are regarded by the local people as Chinese, even when they hold local citizenship, as many do.

Political Life of Overseas Chinese

The Overseas Chinese in Southeast Asia have traditionally avoided becoming involved in local politics. Under colonial regimes they frequently achieved a measure of autonomy as separate communities, but they generally tried to keep to a minimum their dealings with the colonial authorities. This does not mean, however, that the Overseas Chinese were "apolitical"; a complex political life was carried on within their own communities.

Since the turn of the century these communities have been increasingly organized into dialect associations, clan groups, occupational guilds, secret societies, welfare societies, chambers of commerce, and other institutions. Now, the Overseas Chinese are undoubtedly among the most highly organized people in the world, and their intramural politics have been and are intense. But in their relationships with the local societies they have generally—in the past—restricted their external political activities to dealings with the existing authorities through designated representatives, usually, in recent years, the heads of Chinese chambers of commerce or other associations representing the entire Overseas Chinese community in any area. These relationships have often resembled the conduct of foreign relations, rather than participation in domestic politics.

Since the turn of the century, however, successive governments in China have shown an increasing interest in the Chinese abroad, and the Overseas Chinese have become more and more involved in the political affairs of their homeland. Strongly influenced by the growth of modern Chinese nationalism, and increasingly hopeful of obtaining support from their home government, Chinese abroad have been closely linked with almost all important political movements in modern China, and they have played an important role in many of them, particularly by helping to finance revolutionary activities. They gave major financial support to Sun Yat-sen's revolutionary efforts and later to the Nationalist government, especially during the Sino-Japanese War.

Chinese Nationalism and Homeland Politics

The first important signs of Chinese governmental interest in the Overseas Chinese became evident in the last days of the Ch'ing Dynasty. In 1905 a special commissioner was sent to Southeast Asia, and he tried actively to encourage the development of Chinese education. This aim was pursued with increasing energy and enthusiasm by subsequent Chinese governments, particularly by the Chinese Nationalists after 1928. The Nationalist government registered and subsidized many Chinese schools in Southeast Asia and promoted the use of *kuo yü* through them. After the 1911 revolution, the practice of bringing representatives of the Overseas Chinese into the new legislative bodies organized in China became firmly established. Overseas Chinese were included in China's Senate in 1913,[6] and from 1928 onward the Nationalists followed this same practice. After World War II the Nationalist government organized election districts among the Overseas Chinese and allotted them 65 seats in China's National Assembly, 19 in the Legislative Yuan, and

8 in the Control Yuan.[7] It also established an Overseas Chinese Affairs Commission to deal with all matters affecting Chinese abroad, and the Kuomintang organized party branches throughout Southeast Asia. The Nationalists attempted both to support the Overseas Chinese in their dealings with local governments and to win their political and financial support.

Chinese governments have always regarded all persons of Chinese race and culture as Chinese. The first Chinese law on citizenship, adopted in 1909, based nationality on the principle of *jus sanguinis,* and this principle was retained in the revised laws of 1912, 1914, and 1929.[8] Successive Chinese governments have consistently maintained, therefore, that all persons of Chinese blood are Chinese citizens, regardless of their place of birth or other citizenship they may hold. Before World War II the dual citizenship held by Overseas Chinese did not greatly concern the colonial authorities in Southeast Asia—although the Dutch in 1911 forced the Chinese government to agree, at least in form, that East Indies law would be conclusive in determining Dutch or Chinese nationality for Chinese residing in the Indies.[9] As one Southeast Asian nation after another has achieved independence, however, many of their political leaders have come to regard the dual nationality of their Chinese minorities as a major problem.

Southeast Asian Nationalism and Restrictions on the Overseas Chinese

The steady increase of nationalist feelings among the Overseas Chinese, and the forging of closer political ties between them and China, have coincided with the growth of local nationalism among the indigenous peoples of Southeast Asia. It has been inevitable that these trends should come into conflict. Even before the growth of modern nationalism in Southeast Asia there were undercurrents of resentment against the economic power and social exclusiveness of the Overseas Chinese. Although normally the Chinese lived peaceably side by side with the indigenous peoples, there were periodic campaigns of anti-Chinese persecution, and even a few instances of massacres. With the growth of nationalism, resentments have increased. Many of the new political leaders in Southeast Asia now regard the position of the Chinese—economically strong but alien in culture and status—as intolerable for modern nations, and they therefore feel that the Chinese must be restricted and controlled.

Restrictions on the Overseas Chinese in Southeast Asia started many years ago. Even under colonial regimes the Chinese had to contend with numerous limitations on their places of residence and their activities, but these generally did not prevent them from succeeding in their economic endeavors. Prior to World War II stringent controls were imposed first in Thailand, the only independent country in the region. Then after the war the newly independent nations of Southeast Asia began imposing all sorts of controls on their Chinese minorities—measures which the individual countries consider essential to their national welfare but which the Chinese regard as unreasonable persecution.

Throughout Southeast Asia—with considerable variation from country to country—steps have been taken to restrict Chinese immigration, education, and economic power, to deal with the problems of citizenship, and to promote political integration. The new restrictions on immigration have virtually put an end to any significant inflow of Chinese. Most countries have barred certain occupations and economic activities to the Chinese; in some cases this has been applied only to Chinese aliens, in others, to all persons of Chinese race, regardless of citizenship. Restrictions on Chinese education have been widely adopted. And many frankly discriminatory levies have pressed the Chinese financially. In a few countries drastic steps have been taken to force the Chinese entirely out of important economic activities, in order to transfer local enterprises into the hands of indigenous people and thus to promote the development of a class of native businessmen and entrepreneurs. In several countries attempts have been made to eliminate the problem of dual citizenship either by requiring the Overseas Chinese to make a choice of citizenship or by forcing the local-born Chinese to accept local citizenship.

Most of the Southeast Asian governments have pursued

the contradictory aims of reducing the economic power of the Overseas Chinese, regardless of their citizenship or the degree of their identification with their adopted countries, and assimilating or integrating them into the national life as rapidly as possible. The conflict between these objectives generally remains unresolved. Economic restrictions have tended to alienate the Overseas Chinese, to make them feel more vulnerable and persecuted, and to stimulate them to look for external backing; consequently, they have often made the task of integration more difficult than ever. Moreover, it has not been possible to legislate into existence local groups capable of suddenly taking over many of the economic functions traditionally performed by the Chinese. And the Overseas Chinese themselves have fought for economic survival in every possible way, evading or circumventing restrictions by methods such as bribing corrupt officials or employing local "fronts" to cover their activities. As a result, the restrictions have often left the Overseas Chinese feeling persecuted and the local leaders frustrated.

Communist China's Aims

On coming to power, the Chinese Communists inherited from previous Chinese regimes the idea that all people of Chinese blood and culture, wherever they reside, are a part of the national entity of China, for whom the government of China is responsible. In the years immediately following 1949 this was one of the major themes of public statements on the Overseas Chinese emanating from Peking. The Common Program, which outlined Chinese Communist policies in the autumn of 1949, stated: "The Central People's Government of the People's Republic of China shall do its utmost to protect the legitimate rights and interests of Chinese residing abroad." [10] Shortly thereafter a Chinese Communist spokesman on foreign affairs asserted: "We will not tolerate any insult or injustice done to our fellow countrymen on foreign soils." [11] Up to 1954 Chinese Communist statements were often marked by a threatening tone. In late 1951, for example, Premier Chou En-lai declared: "Lawful rights and interests of these people [the Overseas Chinese], as a result of unreasonable discrimination and even persecution on the part of certain countries, have been seriously infringed. This cannot but arouse serious attention and deep concern of the Chinese people." [12]

The Chinese Communists have also inherited the belief, held by virtually all political groups in modern China, that the backing of the Overseas Chinese is important to China's domestic politics. In a sense, the struggle since 1949 between the Communists and the Nationalists for political influence among the Overseas Chinese is simply an extension of the civil war in China. Each side considers it psychologically and politically important to obtain positive support from the Chinese abroad. Undoubtedly this is due in part to the fact that the Overseas Chinese played such an important role in backing the Sun Yat-sen revolution. With conditions changed both in China and abroad, there is little prospect that they could play a similar role again, even if they wished to, but in Chinese eyes they continue to have a symbolic importance disproportionate to their real political importance in homeland affairs. The Nationalists regard anti-Communist Overseas Chinese as a symbol of continuing resistance to the Peking regime, while the Communists appear to feel that Overseas Chinese support is symbolically necessary for the ratification of their succession to power in China.

The Overseas Chinese are very important in relation to the two Chinese provinces from which most of them come. According to Peking, within China there are over 10 million dependents of Overseas Chinese, mostly in Kwangtung and Fukien.[13] The flow of influence between Southeast Asia and these two Chinese provinces is a two-way proposition. Peking has acknowledged that the relatives of Overseas Chinese are a special group in China, and it has modified some of its nation-wide policies in various ways to give them special treatment. The financial support of this group depends upon remittances from abroad, and any decrease in these remittances automatically affects not only the welfare of the families directly concerned, but also the entire economy of the two provinces. Perhaps even more important, funds sent home by Overseas Chinese provide Peking with a major source of foreign exchange, one which is especially important because Communist China faces a difficult balance of payments problem.

Overseas Chinese and Peking's Foreign Policy

Peking clearly regards the Overseas Chinese as a useful instrument in its foreign policy toward their countries of residence, particularly in Southeast Asia. It has attempted to use them in varying ways. In the first years after 1949 it frequently accused foreign countries of persecuting their Chinese minorities. Apparently, it hoped by threats and pressures to influence the policies of Southeast Asian governments toward both the Overseas Chinese and Communist China itself. Since 1954 and the shift to a "soft" line, however, this threatening approach has been played down.

On occasion the Overseas Chinese have been used as a bargaining counter in Communist China's relations with countries which consider them to be a major problem. Since 1954 Peking has stressed its willingness to make concessions on issues affecting the Overseas Chinese, particularly if it can obtain a *quid pro quo,* or gain political capital and thereby promote closer relations with Southeast Asian nations. The most notable example of this has been the Chinese Communists' approach to the dual citizenship question. The signing in April 1955 of an agreement on dual citizenship with Indonesia was one of the most important moves made by Peking when it began its drive to establish friendly relations with the nonaligned Asian nations. By making concessions at an opportune time during the Bandung Conference, it achieved significant propaganda gains.

It is obvious that Peking now views the dual nationality problem as an important lever in its foreign policy toward Southeast Asia. Significantly, instead of making a declaration of general policy applicable to all Overseas Chinese, the Chinese Communists have insisted on conducting bilateral negotiations with any country which is concerned with the citizenship problem. Chou En-lai has intimated that Peking may regard this issue as a means of securing recognition from countries such as Thailand and the Philippines. In 1955 he stated that the treaty with Indonesia "serves as an example for settling questions of dual nationality by our country and other Southeast Asian countries," [14] and he emphasized that Peking is ready to "settle" the citizenship issue "first with Southeast Asian countries which have established diplomatic relations with us." [15]

The Shift in Peking's Policy in 1954-1955

The shift which took place during 1954-1955 in Peking's approach to the Overseas Chinese was an important aspect of the broader change then occurring in its foreign policy tactics. Undoubtedly it was also due to Peking's increasing realization that while the Overseas Chinese are useful, they create some real problems for the Chinese Communists in their relations with Southeast Asia. During 1954-1955 the leaders of India, Burma, and Indonesia all discussed the Overseas Chinese problem with the Chinese Communists, and their representations—those made by Nehru were doubtless considered to be most important by Peking, even though India itself does not have a significant Chinese minority—probably helped to convince Peking that a change of policy was desirable.[16]

This shift was marked by an important change of tone in official Chinese statements on the Overseas Chinese. "There are some 12 million Chinese residing outside of the country," Chou En-lai said in September 1954. "For the past few years, they have been under very difficult conditions in the countries which are unfriendly to China. We hope that these countries will not discriminate against the Overseas Chinese and will respect their legitimate rights and interests." He went on to say:

For our part, we are willing to urge the Overseas Chinese to respect the laws of the governments and the social customs of all the countries in which they live. It is worth pointing out that the question of the nationality of the Overseas Chinese is one which the reactionary governments of China in the past never tried to solve. This placed the Overseas Chinese in a difficult situation and often led to discord between China and the countries concerned. To improve this situation, we are prepared to settle this question.[17]

This markedly conciliatory tone has continued in most official statements. On numerous occasions since 1954 Peking has officially stated that Overseas Chinese should refrain from interfering in the local politics of Southeast Asian countries, and it has disclaimed any intention of using the Overseas Chinese as an instrument of subversion. In 1955, for example, Chou En-lai declared: "Some people say that there are over ten million Overseas Chinese whose dual nationality might be taken advantage of for carrying out subversive activities. . . . China has no intention whatsoever to subvert the governments of its neighboring countries." [18] During 1954-1955 Chou also gave specific assurances to this effect to the leaders of India, Burma, Indonesia, Cambodia, Thailand, and the Philippines.

Since 1955 Peking has exhorted Overseas Chinese to make positive efforts to promote friendship between their countries of residence and Communist China. In 1957 Chou En-lai stated that on his recent trip through Southeast Asia he had urged Overseas Chinese to "work for closer friendship with the people among whom they have come to live and strive for still more cordial relations between China and the country in which they reside." [19] This approach, although reassuring to the governments in Southeast Asia, did not suggest that Communist China had completely renounced the hope of using the Overseas Chinese as an instrument of its policy; it indicated, rather, a change of attitude on how the instrument could best be used.

Peking has continued to appeal to the Overseas Chinese to keep up their contacts with China. In the same month, September 1954, when Chou En-lai was assuring Southeast Asians of Communist China's willingness to "solve" the dual nationality question, Ho Hsiang-ning, Chairman of the Overseas Chinese Affairs Commission in Peking, speaking directly to Overseas Chinese, urged them to develop closer ties with their homeland. "Nobody can sever the bond which ties the Chinese residents abroad to the fatherland," she declared. "Mainland China is the homeland of all Chinese residents abroad." [20]

Chinese Communist Policies and Programs

Chinese Communist policy toward the Overseas Chinese cannot, in any case, be judged solely or primarily from official statements. The Chinese Communists' actions show that since 1949 they have worked energetically to capture the loyalty of the Overseas Chinese. They also show that Peking's efforts were actually being stepped up markedly during 1954-1955, at the very time it was adopting a conciliatory public posture on this issue.

Both the Common Program of 1949 and the constitution of 1954 enjoin the government of Communist China to "protect" the "legitimate rights and interests of Chinese residents abroad." [21] Overseas Chinese have been included in China's official population figures beginning with the census of 1953. Peking's electoral law allocates 30 seats to representatives of Overseas Chinese in Communist China's National People's Congress, and their representatives from all over the world have sat in the Congress ever since 1954, even though Peking appoints these representatives rather than arranging elections abroad, in order to minimize adverse reactions in Southeast Asia.[22]

The two most important bodies in Communist China dealing with Overseas Chinese affairs are the United Front Department of the Communist Party Central Committee, which has conducted political activities among Overseas Chinese for many years, starting long before 1949, and the Overseas Chinese Affairs Commission under the State Council, which was established in 1949. These two agencies direct and coordinate Peking's programs among both the Overseas Chinese abroad and their relatives at home.

Within China, almost all returned Overseas Chinese and dependents of those residing abroad have been organized into Returned Overseas Chinese Associations, under a national headquarters which has held periodic conferences and in 1956 convened its first formal Congress. "Associations in various places," said an official of the All-China Returned Overseas Chinese Association at its 1956 Congress, "should tighten the links between returned Overseas Chinese and dependents of Overseas Chinese and our countrymen abroad," as well as mobilize those in China to "participate in the socialist construction of the mainland." [23] Abroad, the organizational links between the Overseas Chinese and Peking are numerous, and the Chinese Communist party itself maintains an underground apparatus among Overseas Chinese. The prime targets in the Communists' efforts to infiltrate, influence, and control Chinese communities abroad are the numerous and long-standing associations which exist in every Overseas Chinese community. Frequently these efforts are made directly by Peking's embassies or its economic missions.

Communist China has conducted a large-scale propaganda effort directed at the Overseas Chinese through every possible channel, including personal contacts, the written word, and radio. In this it obtains invaluable help from a few leading Overseas Chinese businessmen who have become fellow travelers. It has developed numerous publications and radio programs for the Overseas Chinese and has even established a special news agency—the China News Service—aimed primarily at Chinese abroad. All propaganda directed toward the Overseas Chinese attempts to appeal to their nationalism and patriotism. This, in fact, is its main theme, and Marxist theories are played down except in propaganda directed toward Overseas Chinese youth, who are more susceptible than their elders to ideological appeals.

Peking has also made a deliberate effort to buy Overseas Chinese political support. In some Southeast Asian countries, for example, Chinese Communist banks follow liberal loan policies but establish political preconditions for loans, requiring the recipients to send their children to pro-Communist schools, hire only pro-Communist employees, and fly the Chinese Communist flag on Peking's National Day.

The Chinese Communists have also made some modifications of their domestic policies in applying them in the home villages of Overseas Chinese, as a mark of special consideration for the relatives of Chinese abroad. After the land reform, for example, they began to restore "civil rights" to former landlords among the relatives of Overseas Chinese earlier than to other ex-landlords. And even since the 1958 campaign to build the new communes, Ho Hsiang-ning has attempted to reassure Overseas Chinese that their "right of private ownership" over clothing, tools, furniture, bank deposits, and monetary remittances "will be protected now and in the future." [24] These concessions have not been very significant in practice, however. The relatives of the Overseas Chinese have been collectivized, socialized, and communized like everyone else, and this has had a highly adverse effect on the attitudes of large numbers of Chinese abroad.

Overseas Chinese Students

The Chinese Communists have made great efforts to encourage pro-Peking teaching in the Chinese schools in Southeast Asia. In addition, they have paid special attention to attracting Overseas Chinese students for study in China, and they have had considerable success, by appealing to patriotism and by subsidizing those who wish to return to the mainland. The lack of Chinese institutions of higher education in Southeast Asia and the low quality of many Chinese-language high schools in the region have helped Peking in this program. Moreover, students from abroad are welcomed to China with great fanfare and receive preference in college placement. Between 1949 and mid-1957, according to Peking's claims, roughly 40,000 Chinese students of high school or college level returned to China; of these about 8,000 entered institutions of higher learning.[25]

Apparently Peking's main motive in attracting Overseas Chinese students has been to make use of their skills in its development programs within China. The shortage of middle schools has been a serious bottleneck in the expansion of China's educational system, and Peking has wanted to attract students from abroad to help fill its growing universities. Very few of these students have so far returned to Southeast Asia; most of them have been unable to do so, in any case, because their return has generally been barred by the countries they left. They now provide a reservoir, however, of indoctrinated, trained persons whom Peking may some day attempt to use in promoting its purposes in Southeast Asia.

In the past few years the number of students returning

to Communist China has dropped off. This has been due in part to unfavorable reports from some of the students who have gone there. In 1958 a fairly large group came out to Hong Kong and denounced the Peking regime publicly. The development of alternative opportunities for higher education has been another important reason for the decline. The Nationalists have attracted an increasing number of Overseas Chinese students to Taiwan, and in Hong Kong several Chinese colleges have been developed in recent years. And even in Southeast Asia one small Chinese institution of higher education has recently been established, in Singapore. In addition, Peking has started urging some Overseas Chinese students to stay abroad to attend available educational institutions in their countries of residence.

Overseas Chinese Remittances and Investments

Peking has given a high priority to the aim of maximizing Overseas Chinese remittances to China. At the start, it used crude blackmail, but this proved to be self-defeating, and since 1954-1955 it has emphasized policies of attraction. The blackmail campaign reached its peak during the Korean War.[26] By jailing or threatening relatives of Overseas Chinese and, in effect, demanding ransom, the Communists extracted millions of dollars from Chinese abroad, but, in doing this, they alienated many of them. Since late 1954 Peking's banks have been making every effort to encourage and facilitate remittances by more normal techniques. Pressures are still applied on the Overseas Chinese, both by their organized relatives at home and by Peking's representatives abroad. In general, however, the methods now used are very different from the ones used earlier. Despite all these efforts remittances are considerably below prewar levels, but they still provide a substantial source of foreign exchange.[27]

In the field of investments Peking's policies have been particularly interesting. It has established a number of special state-controlled investment companies, designed particularly to attract Overseas Chinese capital and channel it into certain types of industrial and other developmental projects. In 1955, in a move highly unusual for a Communist country,

Peking merged these companies into several large Overseas Chinese Investment Corporations and issued a public guarantee that all Overseas Chinese investors in them would be guaranteed an annual 8 per cent return on their investments and could retain ownership of their shares even after the Chinese economy as a whole had been socialized. It is difficult to know how much capital has been attracted from abroad through this device. Peking has reported numerous factories built by Overseas Chinese investments in China, but no overall figures have been released.[28]

Probably investments in China by the Overseas Chinese have increased, as Peking claims, since these new policies were adopted. However, the current level of investments is certainly well below the peak levels of prewar years, and it is unlikely to return to prewar levels in the foreseeable future. China is now almost wholly socialized, and the communization program will probably further discourage the Overseas Chinese from making investments in their home districts. In addition, Peking has recently advised Overseas Chinese to invest in local industries abroad.

Significance of Peking's Concessions

The Chinese Communists' various policies designed to strengthen the ties between Overseas Chinese and their homeland give cause for skepticism about the significance of the concessions which Peking has made to Southeast Asian countries on issues relating to the Overseas Chinese. Some of the concessions are certainly important, but they do not provide the sole key to Peking's aims.

To date, the most significant of these concessions has been the Sino-Indonesian treaty of 1955 [29] on the question of dual nationality. This treaty is especially important because it constitutes the first official recognition by any modern Chinese government of the principle that Overseas Chinese can renounce their Chinese citizenship and that this renunciation will be accepted by China under certain conditions.

It is doubtful, however, that the formula on which the treaty is based will really "solve" the citizenship problem from Indonesia's point of view, even though it gave the Indonesian government most of what it asked for. Many Indonesians outside the government have recognized this, and soon after the text of the treaty was published it was subjected to severe criticism by many political groups in Indonesia. Although it is actually too early to judge what the effects of its implementation will be—it was not ratified until late 1957 and the period of implementation will not be completed until two years after the first steps to put it into effect—certain of its features appear to be undesirable from Indonesia's point of view.

The treaty specifies that within the two-year period of implementation each person holding dual Chinese-Indonesian citizenship shall choose the citizenship of either Communist China or Indonesia; in choosing one he will renounce the other.[30] Under this principle of "active choice," if a person takes no steps, he will be considered to have chosen the citizenship of his father. A larger number of Overseas Chinese in Indonesia may well become or remain Chinese citizens under this formula than would be the case under the principle of "passive choice," which Indonesia had attempted to apply to its Chinese residents during 1949-1951. According to the principle of "passive choice," those who do not specifically reject Indonesian citizenship acquire it automatically. Whether the principle of "active choice" actually works to Indonesia's disadvantage, however, will depend largely on the way in which it is implemented.

Another basic shortcoming of the treaty is the stipulation that any Chinese who chooses Indonesian citizenship may later regain Chinese citizenship merely by returning to Communist China and establishing permanent residence there. This makes it possible for Chinese to adopt Indonesian citizenship purely as a matter of expediency, without a genuine transfer of loyalty, secure in the knowledge that they are not cutting their ties with China irrevocably.

An even more fundamental objection is the fact that the treaty does not actually establish *jus soli* as the underlying principle of Indonesian citizenship and therefore perpetuates the existence of a large, permanent, and alien Chinese community. The children of Overseas Chinese who choose Indonesian citizenship under the treaty will, it is true, become

Indonesian citizens, but the descendants of those who choose Chinese citizenship will be Chinese, even if they are born in Indonesia.

All things considered, the formula of the treaty appears to be far from ideal, from Indonesia's point of view, even though it contains some important concessions by Peking. There has been no indication since 1955 that other Southeast Asian countries regard it as a desirable model to follow, and it seems unlikely to provide a basis for dealing with the dual nationality problem elsewhere.[31]

The Overseas Chinese as an Instrument of Political Influence

Peking's recent policy of publicly urging the Overseas Chinese to stay out of local politics, observe local customs, and come to terms with Southeast Asian nationalism represents another important concession. It indicates an increasing awareness on the part of the Chinese Communists that in most of Southeast Asia visible interference by the Overseas Chinese in local politics may, instead of promoting Peking's long-term objectives, merely antagonize existing governments in the area, compromise the local Communist movements, and lead to increased persecution of the Overseas Chinese. In 1958 Peking went further than ever before in its new line of conciliation. In February 1958, for example, Ho Hsiang-ning, in a speech to China's National People's Congress, stated:

In order to carry out the spirit of the Five Principles of peaceful coexistence more satisfactorily, we should, in regard to our work for Chinese residents living abroad, first settle the question of their dual nationality in an appropriate manner so as to promote friendly relations between China and the countries in which they reside and to facilitate them to live there permanently. We hold that Overseas Chinese should choose the nationality of the country in which they reside on the basis of the voluntary principle and be loyal to that country and its people. As for those who wish to remain Chinese subjects, we ask them to continue to observe the policy, law, and regulations of the country in which they reside and to respect the customs and habits of the local people. Overseas Chinese should be encouraged to invest commercial capital in local industries and to cooperate with native capitalists to help develop the independent national economy of the countries in which they live. Children of Overseas Chinese should study local languages, geography, and history and acquire certain skills so that they may enter high schools or earn a living there.[32]

Since late 1954, moreover, Peking has generally exercised restraint in accepting the increasingly restrictive policies toward the Overseas Chinese in the neutralist countries of Southeast Asia. It has occasionally protested the treatment of Overseas Chinese, as when it denounced the arrests made by the government of Thailand in late 1958, but it has refrained from using the full weight of its influence to press Southeast Asian nations to moderate their discriminatory policies.

Peking's new line cannot simply be taken at face value, however. It has little relevance to Singapore and Malaya, where the Chinese Communists regard the Overseas Chinese as their main hope for the ultimate establishment of Communist-controlled regimes. And throughout Southeast Asia Peking continues to foster ever closer ties with Chinese who retain their Chinese citizenship and still maintains links even with those who acquire local citizenship.

Many of the Overseas Chinese who are oriented toward Peking provide the Chinese Communists with valuable intelligence about the countries where they live. Some serve as agents for Peking's trade drive in Southeast Asia; they have been used to promote the sale of Chinese Communist goods and, in some instances, to boycott the goods of competitors such as Japan. Others provide a source of funds to the Chinese Communists, and they have been used as a channel for the transmission of financial aid to local Communist movements.

If Peking decides to reverse its present "soft" approach, furthermore, it will have available large numbers of Peking-oriented Overseas Chinese to manipulate for disruptive purposes to a far greater extent than it has had in recent years. Even where the Overseas Chinese, as vulnerable minorities, wish to avoid being pushed into risky political actions, Peking might still be able to manipulate many of them to corrupt, confuse, and divide local non-Communist political groups. Under normal peacetime conditions a large proportion of the Overseas Chinese undoubtedly would refuse to jeopardize their own economic interests in order to serve Peking as an organized fifth column; in the event of war, however, many of them might be induced to play this role. During World War II nationalistic Overseas Chinese were very active in anti-Japanese guerrilla resistance movements, and if Communist China became involved in war in Southeast Asia, it could—and undoubtedly would—attempt to organize pro-Peking Overseas Chinese into militant local action groups.

Competition between the Chinese Communists and Nationalists

The Chinese Nationalists have continued to compete actively for the loyalty of Chinese abroad, and they still have a considerable political influence among some Overseas Chinese groups. The relative success of Communist and Nationalist efforts in this competition has been significantly affected over the past decade by a number of factors: the attitudes of individual governments in Southeast Asia toward communism, the reaction of the Overseas Chinese to Peking's policies, the influence of personal ties with Taiwan and the China mainland, and the impact of major world events on Southeast Asia.

In a sense, this Communist-Nationalist competition impinges directly upon only a minority of the Overseas Chinese, and it is somewhat misleading to think of all the Chinese in Southeast Asia aligning themselves politically in any clearcut fashion. Probably a majority still manages to stay fairly aloof from direct political involvement. The majority is swayed, however, by the minority which is directly involved, since the latter includes most community and opinion leaders. And it is among the minority that the contest for influence is waged. In almost every Southeast Asian country there are still hard-core groups of pro-Nationalist as well as pro-Peking adherents. The principal barometer of their relative success is the shifting alignment of leaders in opinion-forming organizations—the regional associations, schools, newspapers, and other social institutions.

In Southeast Asia as a whole, although the barometer of Communist success has been somewhat erratic during the past decade, the rise of Communist influence has been very great since 1949, and pro-Peking groups are now predominant. The Communist victory in 1949 touched off a strong pro-Peking trend, as the Overseas Chinese almost instinctively shifted their support to the new regime in their homeland. During the Korean War, this trend was partially reversed, largely as a result of Peking's extortion of money from Overseas Chinese, its violent treatment of many of their relatives in its revolutionary mass campaigns, and its confiscation of their land and property at home. Since then, however, each of Peking's international successes has impelled many Overseas Chinese to shift their loyalty toward Communist China, and this drift has been only partially counteracted by the disaffection caused by Peking's domestic policies.

In each country of Southeast Asia, however, the political attitudes and policies of the local governments have also exerted a strong influence on the attitudes of the Overseas Chinese. Where local governments have established relations with Peking, where Chinese Communist embassies or trade missions operate, where local Communist movements have made headway, or where, for whatever reasons, the governments have been strongly hostile to the Chinese Nationalists —Indonesia, Burma, and Cambodia, for example—the pro-Peking elements have achieved a clear ascendancy among the Overseas Chinese. Where the local governments have been strongly and consistently anti-Communist, and where the Chinese Nationalists continue to maintain embassies, pro-Peking elements have been kept in check to a greater extent. Only in the Philippines and South Vietnam, however, have pro-Nationalist groups managed to retain a position of clear ascendancy. Almost everywhere else, including anti-Communist Thailand, pro-Peking groups now appear to have the stronger influence.

Peking has certain fundamental advantages which are almost certain to be increasingly felt in the long run. The basic impulse among the Overseas Chinese is to accommodate to the fact of political power. It is clear to most of them that Communist China has become a major power and that in the foreseeable future the Nationalists have little prospect of returning to power on the mainland. Moreover, Peking, rather than Taipei, controls their home villages on the China mainland, and this impels large numbers of them to come to terms with the Communists, despite the damage which Peking's domestic policies inflict on their own interests and those of their families.

Taiwan and Hong Kong

Even though Peking enjoys great advantages in this competition, as long as there are significant groups of Chinese in Southeast Asia who resist Communist blandishments and pressures and yet insist upon retaining ties with their traditional culture, Taiwan will continue to play a role of considerable importance. Its potential as a political rallying point will probably decline, but as long as it remains free of Communist control, it will undoubtedly be regarded by many Chinese abroad as a repository of traditional Chinese culture and an important center of non-Communist education. In the past eight years the number of Overseas Chinese students studying in Taiwan's high schools and colleges has grown from under 100 to over 8,000 [33] despite the decline of hopes that the Nationalists might soon return to the mainland and the steady increase in Peking's influence over the Overseas Chinese.

The position of the British colony of Hong Kong in relation to the Overseas Chinese is also an important one. As the last remnant (together with nearby Portuguese Macao) of Western colonialism on the China coast, Hong Kong is a political anachronism, but it has nevertheless played a remarkable role over the past decade. It has been a major point of contact between the West and Communist China, an important entrepôt for world trade, a growing industrial center, a refuge for politically minded Chinese who are both antiCommunist and non-Kuomintang, and a haven for several hundreds of thousands of refugees from Communist China. Peking has infiltrated the labor movement, schools, and press of Hong Kong, and on a few occasions, as during the Quemoy crisis of 1958, it has brought considerable political pressure to bear on the colony. But it has so far refrained from making a major issue of Hong Kong's status, partly because the continued existence of the colony has been useful to it in many respects and partly because it has not wished to provoke a head-on clash with the British, who have made firm pledges to defend Hong Kong against attack.

There are close to three million Chinese, who constitute 99 per cent of the population, living under British protection in Hong Kong. Well over a million of them have moved there during or since the period of Communist take-over on the mainland, and, as in past periods of upheaval in China, Hong Kong is again a kind of safety valve for refugees from China.[34]

Among the refugees, there are many non-Communist intellectuals who have attempted to make Hong Kong a new center of Chinese education and learning. The colleges they have founded are attracting an increasing number of Overseas Chinese students. There are also in Hong Kong a significant number of politically minded youth, as well as some former non-Communist Chinese leaders; despite British efforts to discourage political activities which might provoke Peking, these political refugees have attempted to keep alive democratic political ideas and ideals both among the refugees in Hong Kong and among the Overseas Chinese. The attempts of such people to organize a so-called "Third Force" have been ill-fated, but nevertheless they have represented one effort by Chinese who are neither Communists nor Nationalists to think constructively about the problems of their country.

Hong Kong is the primary channel for contacts of all sorts between Overseas Chinese and their home districts on the mainland. It is a major center for the production of non-Communist books, magazines, and motion pictures for the Overseas Chinese market. And it is a focal point for business organizations which link Overseas Chinese merchants all over the world.

Although Hong Kong's future is difficult to predict, its economy has shown a remarkable resilience, and today it is an important center of Chinese free enterprise and free trade. As its commerce with mainland China—its original *raison d'être*—has declined, Hong Kong has expanded its entrepôt trade with countries in Southeast Asia and elsewhere, and in the past decade it has seen a notable development of new industries based largely on the skills, capital, and labor of refugee Chinese. Yet Hong Kong stands out as a political symbol of the colonial past, and undoubtedly Peking will some day turn its attention to it. Although the most important parts of the colony, including the island of Hong Kong and the Kowloon Peninsula, were ceded outright to Britain in 1842 and 1860, its largest area, the New Territories, was leased only for the period 1898-1997, and without the New Territories, Hong Kong's viability and tenability would be questionable if Peking applied strong pressure.

It is difficult, therefore, to foresee what Hong Kong's future will be four decades from now, when the New Territories lease expires, and the colony may well come under strong Chinese Communist pressure long before that. For the present, however, the British remain committed to hold Hong Kong, and their determination to hold it is backed not only by a majority of the Chinese in the colony but also by large numbers of Overseas Chinese as well. Even though the United States has apparently not assumed any direct commitment to help defend Hong Kong, a strong argument can be made that the future of this area—with a population larger and far more productive than that of many countries such as Laos where the United States has assumed major defensive responsibilities—should be a matter of concern to American as well as British policy. Conceivably, the interests of the people in Hong Kong might best be served if steps were taken in the years ahead to transform the colony gradually into a self-governing area, backed by some sort of United Nations or other international support.

The Future of the Overseas Chinese

In long-range terms, the crucial political question concerning the Overseas Chinese is not whether they will maintain ties with Peking, Taipei, or Hong Kong, or whether they will be pro-Peking or pro-Nationalist. Rather it is whether they will be integrated into the Southeast Asian countries in which they live or will continue to be alien groups with a primary attachment to their Chinese homeland. The outlook for integration varies markedly from country to country.

In Singapore the prospects appear to be very poor. There the overwhelmingly Chinese population has become increasingly militant in asserting its "Chineseness." The Malayan Communist party and the Communist-influenced People's Action party have made every effort to arouse Chinese nationalistic feelings among the youth and working class, and the "preservation of Chinese culture" has become a major rallying cry even among conservative Chinese businessmen. Most of the Chinese in Singapore now hold local citizenship and have voting rights, and political power has been shifting steadily into the hands of groups which have a strong sense of identification with China and are oriented primarily toward Peking.[35]

In Malaya the decline of the Communist guerrillas, mainly Chinese, and the establishment of a governing coalition of Malays and Chinese, reaffirmed in the elections of 1959, have greatly improved the short-run prospects for building a viable Malayan state. But the present arrangements may prove artificial and unstable in the long run. Though the Chinese dominate the economy, the Malays still hold a privileged political position inherited from British rule, and many government policies reflect Malay attitudes more than Chinese desires. Even in the conservative Malayan Chinese Association, a strong partner in the ruling Alliance group, there are significant undercurrents of opposition to pro-Malay policies. Many of its members resent the present policies in education; although these policies are designed to lay the basis for a genuine nonracial or multiracial Malayan nationhood, many Chinese feel that their immediate effect is adverse to Chinese interests. Further, the Chinese have been unsuccessful in their efforts to have Chinese accepted as an official language, along with Malay.[36]

The Chinese population in Malaya has so far not been able to make its weight fully felt on political issues; as a result of past citizenship laws, its voting power is not commensurate with its numerical strength. However, with the changes in citizenship laws enacted at the time of independence, noncitizen Chinese living in Malaya in September 1957 received the right to register as citizens after eight years of continuous residence, and all persons born in Malaya since independence have automatically acquired its citizenship on the basis of the *jus soli* principle. During the first year after independence over 800,000 Chinese acquired Malayan citizenship.[37] In the future the voting power of the Chinese will increase steadily, and undoubtedly Chinese numerical strength and economic power will be gradually translated more effectively into political influence. The consequences of this are not entirely predictable. If genuine cooperation between Chinese and Malays, based upon mutual accommodation, can be consolidated over the next few years, the Chinese in Malaya may increasingly identify themselves with the new multiracial state. If, however, the Chinese come to feel that the Malays have used their political advantage unfairly, they may become increasingly defensive and look for ways to retaliate politically. If this should tempt them to strengthen their ties with their Chinese homeland, the consequences could be dangerous for Malaya.

In the Philippines and South Vietnam the Overseas Chinese now feel pushed to the wall by the severe economic measures taken against them in recent years by the two governments.[38] A Philippine law of 1954 requires that all retail businesses owned by aliens (other than United States citizens) be liquidated prior to the death or retirement of the present owners or, in the case of corporations and partnerships, prior to 1964. Although the Chinese have resorted to innumerable means of evasion, many face the inevitable prospect of liquidation. If Philippine laws on naturalization made it reasonably easy to take out local citizenship, a large number of Overseas Chinese might do so, but under existing laws this is impractical for the majority.

The steps which were taken against the Chinese by the government of South Vietnam in 1956 were only slightly less severe than those in the Philippines. A new ordinance of that year automatically declared all local-born Chinese to be

Vietnamese citizens; no choice was offered, as in Indonesia. The government then banned aliens from eleven important fields of business, giving them from six months to a year to liquidate their enterprises. The Chinese reaction to these sudden, arbitrary steps combined strong opposition to registration as citizens and passive but fairly effective resistance to the economic restrictions. The resulting dislocation of the economy forced the Vietnamese government to backtrack somewhat, and subsequently, in practice, it has allowed many Chinese to continue operating in some of the banned economic activities, often through fairly obvious subterfuges. But the Chinese have been seriously hurt economically, and many are extremely embittered. An increasing number, however, have decided that there is no alternative but to register as Vietnamese citizens.

In neither the Philippines nor South Vietnam have the Overseas Chinese been able to secure effective backing or protection from outside. Because of the two governments' strong anti-Communist attitudes, open appeals to Peking have been impossible. The Chinese Nationalists have made representations on their behalf, but they have not had a very significant influence on either Philippine or Vietnamese policies, even though they have created frictions between Nationalist China and these two countries. In both countries the Overseas Chinese feel persecuted and isolated. But both the Philippine and Vietnamese governments appear determined to follow through with these tough policies, in order to "solve" the "Overseas Chinese problem." If they exert excessive pressures on the resident Chinese groups, however, they may actually make it more difficult to integrate them into national life; the Chinese, if pushed too hard, may look increasingly to outside support to bolster their position.

In Indonesia, Burma, and Cambodia the Chinese Communists maintain diplomatic or other government missions. There Peking's influence has increased steadily in recent years, and many Chinese have been induced to strengthen their ties with their homeland. In Burma Chinese Communist banks have been particularly active in buying the allegiance of the Chinese with loans offered on political conditions. In Cambodia the Chinese Communist economic aid mission, soon after it was established in 1956, set about placing pro-Peking teachers and textbooks in Chinese schools, as part of an energetic propaganda campaign among the entire Chinese community. The strong reaction from Prince Sihanouk Norodom and his government led the Chinese Communists to reduce this obvious manipulation, however, and during his visit to Peking in 1958 Sihanouk elicited renewed pledges from Chou En-lai against using the Overseas Chinese to interfere in Cambodia's politics.[39] In Indonesia the Chinese Communist Embassy has been extremely active among the Overseas Chinese and has steadily increased Peking's influence among them.

In both Burma and Indonesia the governments have condemned the Chinese Nationalists much more severely than the Communists for using the Overseas Chinese to interfere in local affairs, and they have taken strong action against pro-Nationalist activities. In 1958 the government of Burma banned all Nationalist organizations.[40] The Indonesian government went even further and decided to shut down newspapers, schools, and other organizations run by pro-Nationalist Overseas Chinese.[41]

Indonesia and Cambodia have combined economic and other pressures on the Overseas Chinese with expanded opportunities to take out local citizenship, but in both countries the Chinese have discovered that acquiring local citizenship is by no means a complete solution to their problems. In 1956 Cambodia closed 16 economic occupations to Chinese citizens and simultaneously opened the way for many Chinese to qualify for citizenship. However, when a large number of Chinese applied for citizenship, the naturalization requirements were raised. In Indonesia many forms of economic discrimination against the Chinese—in the issuance of import licenses, loans, and authorizations for many kinds of economic activity—are in practice based on race rather than citizenship. Until recently the Chinese have been successful in circumventing most of these discriminatory measures, principally by the use of native Indonesians as "fronts," but they are nonetheless bitter about the pressure on them.

In late 1957 and throughout 1958 Indonesia greatly increased its pressure against resident Chinese. It adopted new measures which expanded restrictions on employing aliens and required special work permits of alien employees. At the same time the government took drastic steps to restrict and regulate Chinese education, cutting back the number of alien schools and forbidding alien-run schools to admit students of Indonesian nationality. They also banned all Chinese newspapers, although later a few were allowed to resume publication. A number of pro-Kuomintang Chinese were arrested, and numerous Chinese enterprises of various sorts were seized.[42] Whether these measures—which were probably motivated in part by the desire to force resident Chinese to take out Indonesian citizenship and identify themselves with Indonesia—will be effective remains to be seen. As long as the Overseas Chinese are discriminated against on the basis of race rather than citizenship, it is questionable whether they will choose genuinely to identify themselves politically with Indonesia, even if a majority should adopt Indonesian citizenship.

It is in Thailand that the most significant process of assimilation anywhere in Southeast Asia is currently going forward, despite a long history of severe local restrictions on Chinese residents. Several factors help to explain this. Chinese and Thai cultures appear to be relatively compatible, with no major cultural barriers as in Muslim areas. The Thais have deliberately promoted assimilation. Under Thai citizenship laws based on the principle of *jus soli,* Chinese born in Thailand have automatically become Thai citizens (except for a brief period, 1953-1956, when one parent was required to hold Thai citizenship). Thailand has long devoted serious attention to the problem of the Chinese schools; its policies, although resented by the Chinese, have worked strongly toward assimilation. In recent years, for example, the Thais have banned all Chinese-run schools above the primary school level, although in 1958 they decided to allow one Chinese-supported middle school to be opened. Even the primary schools run by Chinese must teach according to a government-approved curriculum and use Thai as their primary language of instruction, with Chinese taught merely as a secondary language.

In Thailand, as elsewhere, many economic restrictions, including the banning of a number of occupations, have been directed against the Chinese. But even though Overseas Chinese interests have been affected adversely, the Chinese have not been pushed to the wall, and in practice many of the restrictions amount to little more than disguised taxation against enterprises which continue to be run by Chinese. In Thailand's loose, informal society the Chinese have found a great deal of room for maneuver in their dealings with the Thais. One remarkable development during recent years has been the formation of many large Sino-Thai companies—actually alliances between leading Thai politicians and Chinese businessmen—in which the Chinese furnish the business skills while the Thais provide political protection.

Even in Thailand, however, there is still a large group of Overseas Chinese who are alien, both legally and culturally. These unassimilated Chinese are bitter about the restrictions and levies imposed on them and would undoubtedly welcome outside support if it could help them to improve their position. They have been strongly affected by competing influences from both the Chinese Communists and Nationalists, and their political orientation has been highly volatile. Recently both Peking and Taipei have intensified their activities among the Chinese in Thailand. The Nationalists have the advantage of maintaining an embassy in Bangkok, but Peking, with the advantage of growing prestige and power, has for several years been increasing its influence through propaganda and trade. In 1958 the Thai police estimated that well over half the Overseas Chinese there were pro-Peking.[43] Repressive measures against pro-Communist Chinese—including a number of arrests and the closing of several newspapers—were stepped up after Sarit's coup in 1958, and in 1959 new restrictions were imposed on trade with Communist China, but Peking's influence remains strong, nevertheless.

It is by no means easy to predict what the future holds for the Overseas Chinese. Peking will surely continue to regard them as a useful instrument of its foreign policy, although of secondary importance except in Singapore and Malaya, but as long as the Chinese Communists pursue tactics of "peaceful coexistence," Peking seems likely to pursue a generally conciliatory line in matters concerning the Overseas Chinese. In the long run, the key question—whether the Overseas Chinese in Southeast Asia can be genuinely integrated into their countries of residence—will probably be decided more by what Southeast Asian governments do than by what the Chinese Communists attempt to do. As long as large numbers of Overseas Chinese remain primarily attached to their homeland, however, Peking may decide some day to utilize them much more actively than at present for its subversive purposes, and this could pose a very serious threat to the nations of Southeast Asia.

Implications for United States Policy

Some observers have exaggerated the dimensions of the Overseas Chinese problem by implying that the future of all Southeast Asia may well be determined by whether the Chinese there are oriented toward Communist China or Nationalist China. Others have suggested that the American decision on recognition or nonrecognition of Communist China will be the key factor in determining the future political role of the Overseas Chinese. In fact, the Chinese are likely to be a major factor in determining the future only in two or possibly three countries—in Singapore and Malaya and perhaps in Thailand. Even in these three areas there are many complex influences at work on the Overseas Chinese, and United States nonrecognition policy is likely, at most, to have a marginal effect.

The major problem is one of integrating and, if possible, ultimately assimilating the Overseas Chinese into the nations in which they are now living. In its policies the United States should give full support to the nations of Southeast Asia in their efforts to achieve this. American policy may be severely limited in what it can actually do, since most of the countries in Southeast Asia regard the Overseas Chinese as a purely domestic concern and resent anything that looks like outside interference. But the United States can and should make it clear that it fully endorses the idea of integration.

It might be desirable, theoretically, if Peking could be

pressed to make a generalized declaration renouncing any claims of dual citizenship affecting Overseas Chinese who become citizens of Southeast Asian nations. For the newly independent nations this would be preferable to Peking's present insistence on negotiating the issue country by country. But any initiative in this direction can come only from the Southeast Asian nations themselves.

It would certainly be desirable for the nations in Southeast Asia to work out more reasonable, enlightened, and effective assimilation policies, concentrating on educating their Chinese minorities genuinely to accept local citizenship and minimizing those forms of economic and other discrimination which are most likely to create bitter antagonisms. To this end, American organizations can and should help these nations strengthen their efforts in the field of education in ways which increase their ability to satisfy the needs of the oncoming generations, both indigenous and Overseas Chinese, and contribute to the development of a common national allegiance.

At best, however, the full integration of the Overseas Chinese into the nations of Southeast Asia will take many years, and their full assimilation, even under favorable circumstances, may require several generations. In the near future large numbers of Overseas Chinese will maintain many and varied links with their homeland, and their political outlook should be a matter of continuing concern. The United States should continue, therefore, to encourage and support those institutions and groups, both in Taiwan and Hong Kong, which, by developing school facilities, books, magazines, and motion pictures to meet Chinese needs, can provide the Overseas Chinese with sources of education and culture other than those offered by Peking. Such efforts should not, however, be allowed to hinder or obstruct the steady integration of the Chinese minorities into the local societies, for this process offers the only lasting solution to a problem which is of great importance to the welfare of Southeast Asia as well as the Overseas Chinese themselves.

CHAPTER 9

TRADE, AID, AND ECONOMIC COMPETITION

OVER THE PAST SEVERAL years the Sino-Soviet bloc has carried out a concerted campaign to promote its broad international objectives by economic means, and in this campaign Communist China has steadily assumed a role of increasing importance.

Both Moscow and Peking proclaim that the Communist bloc can and will outproduce the West. The result, they declare, will be to alter the whole balance of world forces decisively in the Communists' favor and to convince the underdeveloped countries everywhere of the superiority of communism. "Some economically underdeveloped countries are not confident in their ability to develop their own national economy," Peking asserted during 1958, but "China's experience provides convincing proof that once the people of a country have become masters of their own destiny and follow the socialist path, they are able to develop their national economy at a rate never before known in their history." [1]

The Communist nations have also been expanding their trade and aid programs as important instruments of their foreign policy, particularly toward the underdeveloped areas. Economic and political motives are inextricably mixed in the Sino-Soviet bloc's economic foreign policies, but it is clear that both Moscow and Peking attach a high priority to their political objectives. "We value trade least for economic reasons and most for political purposes," Khrushchev has said bluntly.[2]

The Communists hope that their current policies will help them to build up their prestige in the underdeveloped nations and will encourage these nations to reduce their existing ties with the West and to pursue policies of nonalignment. "Greater economic cooperation among Asian and African countries" should be developed, Peking stated in 1958, so that these countries can "free themselves quickly from the economic enslavement by imperialism and drive off the waves of the U.S. economic crisis." [3]

The Communists have generally adopted a cooperative, reasonable, and even generous posture in their offers of trade and aid, but in several instances Peking has also applied strong economic pressures to achieve political ends. There is little doubt that if the underdeveloped nations should become economically dependent on the Communist bloc to a significant degree, they would be exposed to serious risks.

The Soviet Union, possessing the greatest economic strength within the Communist bloc, has naturally taken the lead in promoting the new policy of economic "competitive coexistence." But despite its own domestic economic problems and the extremely low living standards of its own people, Communist China has also made great efforts to develop its own trade and aid programs in the underdeveloped areas of the world.

Peking's Foreign Economic Policies

Communist China's foreign economic policies have reflected closely the tremendous changes of the past decade in its domestic economy, and they have paralleled the development of its general foreign policy. Peking's decision to "lean to one side" in international politics led to a radical realignment of China's economic ties away from the West and toward the Soviet bloc. With the progress of its economic development, Peking's need to obtain equipment and supplies from abroad and its capacity to participate in international trade have steadily grown. As a result, its economic role both within the Sino-Soviet bloc and in the bloc's relations with the non-Communist world has become increasingly important.

Economic factors have served in many ways to cement the Sino-Soviet alliance. Communist China's trade has been closely integrated with that of the bloc, and Soviet technical and other assistance has helped forge special ties between the bloc's two major partners. In recent years trade and other economic links have also increased between Communist China and Russia's East European satellites. There is little doubt, however, that economic issues also create important problems between Moscow and Peking. Decisions on the types and amounts of Soviet aid to Communist China have required protracted negotiations, and Russia's financial assistance to Peking has been surprisingly small when measured against China's needs. By keeping its economic dependence on Moscow to a minimum, Peking has strengthened its capacity for independent action in foreign policy, but this has increased the strains on the Chinese domestic economy and may well have created significant tensions between Peking and Moscow. So far, however, any such strains have been subordinated to the broader interests of Sino-Soviet solidarity, and in many respects China's economy is becoming more and more integrated with that of the bloc.

In the years immediately after 1949 Communist China's economic contacts with the non-Communist world declined rapidly, partly as a result of Peking's deliberate decision to "lean to one side" and partly because of the economic restrictions on China trade that were imposed by the major non-Communist trading nations in retaliation for Peking's role in the Korean War. Since 1952, however, and particularly since 1955, the Chinese Communists, in line with their over-all foreign policy shift to tactics of "peaceful coexistence," have made strenuous efforts to restore and expand their trade with nations outside the Communist bloc. These efforts can be explained in part by China's economic needs, but the high priority which the Chinese Communists have attached to expanding their economic relations with the underdeveloped nations is clearly designed also to serve and support a political purpose—that of neutralizing and attracting the nonaligned countries of Asia and Africa.[4] Peking has openly used trade as a weapon of political pressure against Japan. Its recent trade drive in Southeast Asia bears the earmarks of cutthroat competition through dumping; although the objectives of this drive are not wholly clear, its political potentialities are disturbing. And, at least until 1957, when the major trading nations (except the United States) reduced their restrictions against trade with China to the level applied to other Communist states, Peking constantly attempted to use the trade issue as a means of creating political frictions among the non-Communist countries.

Growth of Peking's Foreign Trade

In the decade since 1949 Communist China's foreign trade has more than doubled, and it is now greater than under any previous Chinese regime. Industrialization has required large amounts of imported capital goods, equipment, and raw materials, and to pay for needed imports the Communists have had to export an increasing volume of agricultural and other products. It is estimated that Communist China's foreign trade rose from 1.8 billion dollars in 1950 to 2.7 billion dollars in 1952, on the eve of its first Five Year Plan, and then to almost 4.3 billion dollars in 1957, the final year of the Plan.[5] During the five years of the first Plan it grew by almost 60 per cent.

This impressive increase does not mean that Communist China's trade will necessarily continue to grow with equal rapidity in the future. The highest rate of increase occurred in the early years of Peking's trade expansion program, and since 1955 the total volume has leveled off. As a matter of fact, from 4.7 billion dollars in 1955, it dropped to 4.6 billion dollars in 1956, and then to 4.3 billion dollars in 1957. In 1958 it rose to a level of perhaps 4.9 billion dollars, but its growth is likely to be slower in the future than it was up to 1955. Nonetheless, the development of Communist China's foreign trade has been impressive; it is now considerably above the prewar peak and amounts to over 10 per cent of China's national income.

The most important single factor motivating Communist China's trade drive undoubtedly has been Peking's pressing need to support its program of industrialization. From 1.59 billion dollars in 1952, on the eve of the first Five Year Plan, imports rose to a peak of 2.56 billion dollars in 1955. In 1957, they amounted to 2.02 billion dollars, and during the

Plan period as a whole they averaged close to two billion dollars a year.

The commodity composition of China's imports has changed radically over the past decade. The Communists have cut the importation of consumer goods to a minimum, reserving most of their scarce foreign exchange for imports of machinery and industrial raw materials. Recently they have been forced by economic necessity to increase imports in some categories of essential consumer goods, and since 1957 they have attempted to conserve foreign exchange by relying on Chinese-manufactured capital goods as much as possible, but these trends have merely qualified rather than altered the basic emphasis in their import policy.

Imports

In recent years Peking has not published any detailed breakdown of foreign trade by commodities, but it has stated that during the first Plan about 60 per cent of its total imports consisted of "machines and equipment" (broadly defined), 30 per cent of basic raw materials for industry and agriculture (of which metals made up roughly one-third), and the remaining 10 per cent of consumer goods.[6]

Large-scale imports of capital goods have been absolutely essential to Peking's industrialization program. During 1953-1957, for example, China produced only 60 per cent of its needs for all types of machinery and equipment; the remaining 40 per cent had to be imported, almost wholly from the Soviet bloc.[7] During the first four years of the Five Year Plan, according to official claims, Communist China produced 72,000 machine tools and imported 22,000; the latter figure included a large proportion of its needs for highly complicated and specialized machine tools. During the same period it imported roughly 1,600 railway cars, 16,000 tractors, 40,000 trucks, and 1,400 mining drills. Without these and similar imports Communist China could not have carried through its first Five Year Plan.

Imports of key raw materials have also been vital to Peking's economic development program. During the past few years the Chinese Communists have imported roughly

5 million tons of iron and steel, averaging approximately 700,000 tons a year; between 6 and 7 million tons of petroleum, amounting to well over half of China's total petroleum needs; and almost 300,000 tons of nonferrous metals, providing a major portion of China's needs for essential items such as copper and aluminum.[8] All of these imports have come principally from the Communist bloc. From non-Communist countries Peking has purchased large amounts of other essential raw materials, particularly chemical fertilizers, cotton, and rubber. Total fertilizer imports have amounted to between 3 and 4 million tons over the past few years; in 1956 Peking imported more than 700,000 tons, or two-thirds, of all chemical fertilizers used in that year. Cotton imports have fluctuated in inverse ratio to the success or failure of domestic crops; during 1953-1956 they totaled almost 180,000 tons, and in 1955 alone over 80,000 tons were imported. During the first Plan Peking imported about 50,000 tons of rubber annually from Ceylon, but recently purchases from Ceylon have dropped off somewhat, partly because rubber is becoming increasingly important in China's trade with both Malaya and Indonesia. As stated earlier, consumer goods have been relatively unimportant among Peking's imports, but some commodities, such as sugar, kerosene, and pharmaceuticals, have been imported in significant quantities.

As Communist China's own industry develops, its need for some imports will decline, but its total import requirements are likely to increase as new needs develop. Imports of petroleum and chemical fertilizers, for example, have risen steadily in recent years. In late 1957 Peking declared that by 1962 it hopes to reduce the percentage of imports of machinery and equipment from 40 to 30 per cent of its over-all requirements in this vital field, but its total needs, and therefore its total imports, will almost certainly continue to grow even in this category.[9]

Exports

Communist China's ability to import depends primarily upon its ability to export, and Peking has made extraordinary efforts to promote exports, at great cost to consumers within

China. According to Yeh Chi-chuang, Minister of Foreign Trade, the Chinese Communist Party Central Committee and State Council defined a policy in 1954 which assigns a clear-cut priority to exports over domestic consumption in many fields.[10] Under this policy "commodities that are not essential to the livelihood of the people" should be exported in "as large a quantity as possible" "with the surplus [that is, after exports] for domestic sales." Other commodities which are more important to consumers in China "but short of an urgent demand on the domestic market" should be "reduced in domestic sales to make a bigger export possible." Only in the case of certain vital commodities "essential to the livelihood of the people and of which short supply exists in the domestic market" should exports be limited by quotas. Even in this third category the quotas set have been large enough to allow sizable exports of commodities which, because they are in very short supply, are strictly rationed within China, such as food grains, pork, vegetable oils, and cotton cloth.

By strenuous efforts Peking was able to raise its total exports from 1.15 billion dollars in 1952 to a peak of 2.35 billion dollars in 1956. But then they dropped to 2.28 billion dollars in 1957 and the Chinese Communists now face serious problems in further expanding their exports to support a rising level of total trade.

As in the past, the bulk of China's exports consists of agricultural produce, and consequently Peking's export policies have placed a heavy burden on the rural sector of the Chinese economy. In recent years about 75 per cent of all Chinese exports have consisted of agricultural commodities in raw or processed form, the remaining 25 per cent being made up of mineral products and manufactured goods.[11] The Communists have attempted to maximize sales abroad of all of China's many traditional export products—including soybeans, miscellaneous food products, tung oil, various types of vegetable oils, eggs and other dairy products, hog bristles, animals and animal products, silk and tea, tin and tungsten, antimony and manganese, handicrafts, and numerous miscellaneous products, such as fiber goods, straw, braid, human hair, hairnets, and so on.[12] In addition, Peking has forced consumers at home to tighten their belts so that it could step up exports of grain, pork, and vegetable oils—basic items in the Chinese diet. The Chinese Communists exported over 4 million tons of grain during 1953-1956, averaging roughly a million tons a year (exclusive of soybean exports, which also averaged about a million tons a year), and its pork exports during the same period ran well over 100,000 tons annually.[13] Export of these commodities, which are rationed in China, imposed a serious strain on the domestic economy during the last years of the first Plan period, and in 1957 Peking was forced to cut its export quotas, as compared with 1956, from 1,320,000 tons to 780,000 tons for grain and from 162,000 tons to 77,000 tons for pork.[14] In 1957 Peking also announced a policy of maximizing its exports of manufactured goods and raw materials in relation to exports of agricultural products.[15] This does not necessarily foreshadow any absolute decline in agricultural exports, but it does mean that manufactured goods exports will probably continue to rise.

A slow but steady increase in the export of Chinese manufactured products has actually been taking place for several years. Exports in this category still constitute only a relatively small percentage of China's over-all trade, but the trend is one of great potential significance. In addition to many types of manufactured consumer goods, the Chinese Communists are now selling some capital goods abroad, in both the Soviet bloc and in non-Communist countries.

One Communist source stated in 1957 that China's exports of cotton cloth amounted to about 600 million yards annually.[16] If this figure was correct, Peking was then exporting roughly 10 per cent of its total cotton cloth output, during a period of severe domestic shortages and rationing. Probably its actual exports were somewhat below this figure: the United States Department of Agriculture estimates that in 1958 Peking exported about 450 million yards of cotton fabrics.[17] In any case, however, Communist China's exports of cotton textiles to Southeast Asia have been rising steadily. It has also exported some steel (in 1956 steel exports were reported at 200,000 tons, but they have probably declined somewhat since then). In addition, it has begun exporting various types of machinery and equipment, including entire textile mills and other plants. The range of other manufactured goods exported has grown tremendously and now includes (in addition to several types of textiles): cement and building materials, flat glass, enamelware and pottery, fountain pens, sewing machines and bicycles, flashlights, typewriters, thermos flasks, radios and phonographs, tape recorders, wrist watches and clocks, adding machines, small electric motors, cigarettes, canned foods, and a wide variety of other products.[18]

Peking's future ability to expand its exports will depend directly on the growth of China's domestic economy. It will also depend on how far the Communists feel they can go in curtailing domestic consumption in order to foster exports. The Chinese Communists have already demonstrated their willingness and ability to export sizable quantities of items which are in short supply within China, but future decisions on how far it can do so are likely to be determined by complex political calculations as much as by economic conditions.

Economic Relations with the Communist Bloc

Even more striking than the over-all growth of China's foreign trade has been the revolutionary change in its direction. Since 1949 Peking has radically reoriented the country's foreign economic relations away from the West and toward the Communist bloc, and China's development of large-scale industry has been directly geared to Soviet promises to help build many of its key projects by providing technical assistance and selling essential equipment to China. Soviet credits for economic development purposes have been limited, however, and for the most part Communist China has had to pay its own way, exporting agricultural and other commodities to the Soviet bloc in exchange for equipment and technical assistance.

The basis for Sino-Soviet economic cooperation was first defined in early 1950. At that time the Russians extended a five-year, 300-million-dollar loan to Peking, promised to help build or rehabilitate 50 specific projects in China,[19] and signed their first barter agreement with the Chinese. Shortly thereafter, when Communist China entered the Korean War,

Moscow began supplying Peking with large quantities of military equipment. Then, in 1952, when the Chinese Communists started preparing for their first Five Year Plan, and it became clear that the Plan's whole scope and character would depend on Soviet assistance, Peking sent a high-powered delegation to negotiate with the Russians in Moscow. The negotiations dragged on from late 1952 until mid-1953, and they undoubtedly involved hard bargaining. Finally, in late 1953, after the death of Stalin and after China's first Plan had officially been under way for many months, the Russians agreed to help build an additional 91 industrial and other projects in China. These 141 (50 plus 91) Soviet "aid projects" (the term "aid project" implies technical assistance and supply commitments, not necessarily any financial aid) formed the cornerstone of China's first Five Year Plan.[20]

The number of Soviet "aid projects" has been boosted several times since 1953. In 1954 Khrushchev and Bulganin, making the first visit of any top Soviet leaders to China, raised the total to 156. They also announced a second Soviet loan, equivalent to 130 million dollars, and promised to provide China with 100 million dollars in supplies and equipment, above and beyond previous commitments.[21] In 1956 Mikoyan visited China and promised Soviet assistance for 55 more projects, requiring an additional 625 million dollars of Russian equipment and supplies. The total number of Soviet "aid projects" during the first Plan was thus raised to 211.[22]

In 1958 the Russians made new commitments to help China in its second Five Year Plan period. In August a Sino-Soviet agreement signed in Moscow committed the Russians to give technical assistance for 47 more projects.[23] And in early 1959 a new list of 78 projects was added.[24] For these latest projects only part of the equipment is to be provided by the Russians; much of it will be manufactured in China.

Trade with the Communist Bloc

To pay for Communist bloc "aid," Communist China has redirected a very high proportion of its trade toward the bloc. This shift had begun before the Korean War, and although it was hastened by the restrictions which the United States and its allies imposed on trade with China in 1950-1951, it was not caused by them. It was the result of a deliberate decision by Peking's leaders to integrate China's economy to a maximum degree with the Communist bloc. The consequences of this decision have been remarkable.

Before World War II China traded almost entirely with the West and Japan. Its trade with the Soviet Union generally amounted to one per cent or less of its total trade, and its trade with East European countries was even smaller. After 1949 the share of the Communist bloc in China's foreign trade rose to 33.48 per cent in 1950 and then to 78.08 per cent in 1952; it reached a peak of 82 per cent in 1955, before declining to 75.3 per cent in 1956.[25] In monetary terms, according to Chinese Communist data, Peking's trade with the entire Communist bloc increased from 590 million dollars in 1950, to 2.14 billion dollars in 1952, to a peak of 3.8 billion dollars in 1955, before dropping to 3.5 billion dollars in 1956.[26]

Peking has published figures on its trade with the Soviet Union during 1956 which reveal both the character of this trade and its great importance to China.[27] Of Soviet exports to China in that year, 70.9 per cent consisted of machinery and equipment (including complete sets of equipment for plants in China), 11.7 per cent of petroleum products, and 8.5 per cent of ferrous metals. Of Communist China's exports to the Soviet Union, 40.4 per cent consisted of foodstuffs (including raw materials for foodstuffs), 16.5 per cent of nonferrous and rare metals, 12.3 per cent of textiles, 7.7 per cent of raw materials for textiles, and 3.4 per cent of animal by-products. This pattern has continued. Basically, China is exchanging its agricultural products and raw materials for Soviet capital goods and industrial raw materials.

There are some curious discrepancies between Chinese and Soviet figures, however. In publishing ruble figures for Sino-Soviet trade in 1956, Peking reported a total of 6.99 billion rubles, or 1.75 billion dollars at official exchange rates.[28] These figures, together with published percentages on the relative value of Soviet and satellite trade, indicate a total

Communist China-bloc trade of 2.68 billion dollars in 1956. Soviet sources have published a figure of 5.99 billion rubles, or 1.50 billion dollars, for Sino-Soviet trade in 1956, indicating a total Soviet-plus-satellite trade of 2.25 billion dollars.[29] On the other hand, official Chinese Communist statistics on total foreign trade, stated in yüan, and the published figures on the percentage of China's trade which was carried on with the Communist bloc, indicate, as stated above, that Peking's total trade with the bloc in 1956 was 3.46 billion dollars. It is difficult to explain these discrepancies. Possibly some important elements in Sino-Soviet trade, such as Soviet exports of military equipment to China, may be excluded from certain of these figures. Or possibly the discrepancies arise because of the difficulty of converting rubles and yüan into dollars at official exchange rates when, in fact, the figures represent barter transactions, and very little is known about pricing practices in Sino-Soviet barter arrangements.

Soviet figures indicate, in any case, that in 1956 Communist China accounted for over one-fifth of total Soviet trade and ranked first among Moscow's trading partners in that year, ahead even of East Germany, Czechoslovakia, and Poland.[30] After 1956, however, several new trends appeared. China's trade with Russia declined noticeably in 1957, and the Chinese found it necessary to maintain a large export surplus in Sino-Soviet trade, but Peking's trade with Eastern Europe continued to rise steadily.

According to Soviet statistics, trade between Communist China and the U.S.S.R. dropped from 1.50 billion dollars in 1956 to 1.28 billion dollars in 1957. Of this total, Peking's exports accounted for 738 million dollars, while its imports from the Soviet Union ran to only 544 million dollars.[31] The Chinese Communists, in short, had to maintain an export surplus in trade with the U.S.S.R. of almost 200 million dollars. By contrast, because of increasing economic demands by the satellites on Soviet resources, Moscow in 1956 had a large export surplus, exceeding 600 million dollars, in its trade with Eastern Europe.

In late 1958 Chinese Communist statements indicated that Peking's export surplus in its trade with the U.S.S.R. was still growing. Its exports to the Soviet Union in 1958 were expected to be 23 per cent higher than 1957, while its imports from the Soviet Union were expected to rise by only 12 per cent.[32] These percentages, if applied to the Soviet figures cited earlier, suggest that Sino-Soviet trade in 1958 totaled about 1.5 billion dollars, with China's exports amounting to 900 million dollars and its imports 600 million dollars, putting Peking's export surplus at about 300 million dollars. As a further indication of the new trend, Peking stated in early 1959 that during 1958 trade with the U.S.S.R. had constituted only 40-plus per cent of China's total trade, in contrast with 50 per cent in the immediately preceding years.[33]

The necessity of helping China industrialize is undoubtedly a major factor in Moscow's economic planning, particularly in view of the competitive demands on Soviet resources imposed by the East European satellites, by domestic consumers in Russia, and by Moscow's growing markets in underdeveloped areas. But there is little evidence that this burden has been excessive for the Soviet economy. There is evidence, however, that Chinese demands for industrial equipment and supplies have imposed a definite strain on some of the East European satellites.[34]

Peking has been steadily increasing its barter trade with East European countries. When China's first Five Year Plan got under way in 1953, of the 75.49 per cent of its total trade which was with the bloc, 56.39 per cent was with the U.S.S.R., 16.58 per cent with the East European Communist states, and 2.52 per cent with Asian Communist states. By 1957, however, Communist China's trade with the Soviet Union had dropped to about 50 per cent of its total foreign trade, while trade with other Communist states had risen to about 25 per cent; in 1958 the Soviet share apparently dropped still further to a little over 40 per cent. By 1958 East Germany and Poland ranked second and third, after the Soviet Union, in Communist China's foreign trade. The growing importance of this trade may be one reason for Peking's increasing political interest in Eastern Europe since 1956; it has undoubtedly increased Peking's concern about maintaining bloc solidarity.

Integration with Soviet Bloc

Political factors clearly motivated Peking's drastic reorientation of its trade toward the Soviet bloc immediately after 1949, and trade with the bloc has doubtless involved economic disadvantages as well as advantages. There is some evidence—not conclusive but at least suggestive—that because of high transport costs, and possibly also because of the Russians' superior bargaining position, Communist China may have had to accept relatively poor terms of trade in exchanges with the Soviet Union. According to Peking's Minister of Foreign Trade, except for "some necessary readjustments" the prices of the major commodities in Sino-Soviet trade were the same in 1957 as those established in the first agreement in 1950.[35] While it is difficult to compute and balance the numerous price changes which have occurred on the international market since 1950, the Chinese Communists have been defensive in arguing the advantages of maintaining fixed prices. Soviet goods are often sold within China at prices far higher than those which obtain in nearby international markets. And the discrepancy between Soviet and Chinese figures on the value of Sino-Soviet trade may conceivably be the result, in part at least, of pricing policies or exchange rates which favor the Soviet Union.

On the other hand, Communist China has certainly benefited from the stability provided by its annual barter agreements with the Soviet Union and other Communist states. Through these agreements it has had assured sources of supply for equipment and materials essential to its economic development program, and this has facilitated its long-range planning. In Peking's view this advantage probably outweighs any possible disadvantages.

In 1958 Communist China and the other Asian Communist states, although not members of the Communists' Mutual Economic Assistance Council in Europe, attended its meetings and "expressed readiness to take an active part in the economic cooperation of the socialist countries."[36] After making pledges to "strengthen this cooperation" the Chinese Communists in late 1957 began signing long-term trade treaties, extending for more than one year, with other Communist governments. By early 1959 it had signed long-term agreements with Bulgaria, Poland, Rumania, Hungary, North Korea, and North Vietnam,[37] and Peking has stated that it intends to sign similar long-term treaties with the U.S.S.R. and other Communist states in the future. In 1958 Communist China and Russia signed a general Treaty of Commerce and Navigation,[38] and a long-term trade agreement between the two countries will probably be forthcoming.

These steps toward closer trade integration between China and the Communist bloc do not mean, however, that trade with the bloc will necessarily continue to rise in proportion to China's total foreign trade. Since 1955 Peking's trade with other Communist countries has actually declined somewhat in relation to its total trade, and even though the bulk of China's trade will doubtless continue to be with the bloc, trade with non-Communist countries will probably rise slowly in proportion to China's total trade, for both political and economic reasons.

Peking may well shift some of its trade to non-Communist countries in order to support the bloc's current economic drive in underdeveloped areas. In addition, strictly economic motives may impel Peking to procure larger amounts of equipment and industrial raw materials from either the West or Japan. And as Communist China increases its exports of manufactured goods, it may be compelled to search for new markets in non-Communist countries. In recent years, it is true, Chinese Communist exports of such commodities to bloc countries have increased. Between 1952 and 1956, for example, exports of textiles rose from 3.5 per cent to 12.3 per cent of China's total exports to the Soviet Union;[39] in the same period, processed foods rose from 13.8 per cent to 23.8 per cent of its total exports to the U.S.S.R., while unprocessed food materials dropped from 30.2 per cent to 3.4 per cent. However, the ability of bloc countries to absorb China's manufactured goods may not be unlimited, and the main demand for Chinese manufactured goods may well be in the underdeveloped areas of Asia and Africa in the years immediately ahead. All these factors may lead Peking to exert greater efforts to increase its trade outside the Communist bloc, and they provide strong economic reasons, reinforcing the existing political ones, for Peking to pursue its "competitive coexistence" policy toward non-Communist areas.

Soviet "Aid" to China

Communist China will doubtless remain dependent on the Soviet bloc, however, as the principal source of supply for the most essential equipment and supplies which it needs in order to develop its new large-scale industries. This is clearly indicated by the programming of Soviet "aid" to China. Of the 211 major "aid projects" that Moscow had promised by the end of Communist China's first Five Year Plan, only some 140 were scheduled to be started, and only about 60 were to be finished, during the first Plan period. Taking into account the new projects added to the list in 1958 and early 1959, between 200 and 300 projects must be either started or completed during the second Five Year Plan, and Peking will doubtless buy most of the necessary equipment from the U.S.S.R. Most of these projects are for the development of heavy industries which require a large amount of imported machines and equipment. Among them are steel and other metallurgical plants; machine tool and engineering plants; iron, coal, and other mines; automotive, tractor, and aeronautical factories; chemical, synthetic, and plastics plants; factories for electrical and radio equipment; petroleum installations and refineries; railway and other transportation projects; and scientific research institutes.

All these Soviet "aid projects" are planned on the basis of specific Soviet commitments to sell certain equipment and provide the necessary technical assistance. In early 1956 Khrushchev stated that the U.S.S.R. had promised to supply 1.4 billion dollars' worth of equipment and supplies for 156 projects in China.[40] Later in 1956 Mikoyan made a further commitment in the amount of 625 million dollars.[41] Through 1957, therefore, the Soviet Union had guaranteed to supply China with well over 2 billion dollars' worth of equipment and supplies for the construction of key development projects. Then, in the Sino-Soviet agreement of early 1959, Moscow committed itself to supply an additional 1.5 billion dollars more in equipment and supplies during the coming nine years, an amount which averages out to roughly 140 million dollars a year.[42]

Technical assistance has been extremely important in the aid Communist China has received from the Communist bloc —from the East European nations as well as from the Soviet Union. Some sources estimate that perhaps 10,000 to 20,000 advisers and technicians from the bloc have been sent to work in China. According to the Chinese Communists themselves, by 1957 the Soviet Union alone had sent 7,000.[43] (Military advisers and technicians, if included, might swell the figure substantially.) There seems to have been a falling off in the number of Soviet experts in China since 1957, but they continue to be extremely important to Peking's economic plans. Perhaps the most succinct statement on the vital role that Soviet technical assistance has played in China was made in 1955 by Li Fu-ch'un, Chairman of Peking's State Planning Commission:

On the 156 [the total at that time] industrial projects which the Soviet Union is helping us to build she assists us through the whole process from start to finish, from geological surveying, selecting construction sites, collecting basic data for designing, designing, directing the work of construction, installation, and getting into production, and supplying technical information on new types of products, right down to directing the work of the manufacturing of new products.[44]

Soviet advisers have also played an important part in helping the Chinese Communists establish or reorganize their industrial management systems, planning organizations, budgetary methods, tax systems, labor organizations, and wage systems. They have helped the Chinese develop their educational system, stressing technical and scientific training, and Peking claims that with Soviet help it was able to increase the number of Chinese "technicians," broadly defined, from 170,000 in 1952 to 800,000 in 1957.[45] In the seven years up to June 1957 over 7,000 Chinese university and graduate students went to other Communist countries to obtain various types of training, principally in scientific and technical fields, and most of them went to the Soviet Union.[46] The Sino-Soviet Scientific and Technical Cooperation Commission, established in 1954, had by 1956 supplied the Chinese Communists with 600 kinds of blueprints for factories, shops, and enterprises, 1,700 working drawings for the production and installation of machines, and other important technical data.[47] And in early 1958 a Sino-Soviet protocol on technical and scientific research called for an extensive program of cooperative research during China's second Five Year Plan.

Numerous other examples of Sino-Soviet economic cooperation can be cited. Over the past decade the Chinese and Russians have signed agreements covering many fields: telecommunications; mails; joint management of the Changchun Railway in Manchuria; joint operation of Sino-Soviet companies in the fields of petroleum and nonferrous metals in Sinkiang, shipbuilding in Manchuria, and international aviation; through railway traffic linking China and Russia; construction of power plants in China; construction of two new railways linking the two countries via Sinkiang and Outer Mongolia; development of atomic energy for peaceful purposes in China; joint control of plant diseases and insect pests; joint investigation and development of the Amur River valley; and mutual use of waterways bordering the two countries.[48] The joint operation of the Changchun Railway and the establishment of joint stock companies in China were clearly objectionable to Peking, and in 1954 the Soviet Union agreed to return these enterprises to sole Chinese ownership and control, with China compensating the Soviet government for its shares in the enterprises. But most of the other forms of economic cooperation that Peking and Moscow have agreed upon seems to have been of a type genuinely desired by the Chinese Communists.

Soviet Financial Aid and Peking's Balance of Payments

One field in which Soviet "aid" has been surprisingly small, however, is that of financing. The Soviet Union has not given Communist China a single free grant for economic development, as far as is known on the basis of the public record, and even the volume of Soviet loans and credits for economic purposes has been relatively small in relation to China's needs.

In mid-1957 the Chinese Communists stated that they had received loans and credits of all kinds from the Soviet Union totaling about 2.24 billion dollars, of which about 1.31 billion dollars had been received during the first Five Year Plan, 1953-1957.[49] Of this total, however, only the 430 million dollars included in the loans of 1950 and 1954 can definitely be identified as long-term economic loans, and these have now been expended. The 300 million dollar loan in 1950 was for a five-year period, averaging only 60 million dollars a year; since 1954 the Chinese Communists have been repaying it, together with interest charges of one per cent, in annual installments that will continue through 1963. The second publicly announced loan, made in 1954, amounted to 130 million dollars,[50] and it, too, has now been used up. The fact that these two loans are the only ones which have been made public suggests that most if not all the balance of the 2.24 billion dollars in Soviet credits has consisted of transactions other than loans for China's economic development. It seems likely, in fact, that the large and unexplained balance represents charges against the Chinese for Russian military equipment and services, as well as for the Soviet shares in the joint stock companies which were turned over to exclusive Chinese ownership during 1954-1955.

By the end of its first Five Year Plan Communist China had, in fact, definitely used up all past Soviet loans and credits. Figures for the amounts of Soviet credit actually utilized by Communist China in each year can only be estimated up to 1956, but since 1956 Peking has published specific figures in its budget on receipts from foreign loans. According to these figures, Communist China received only 50 million dollars in foreign aid in 1956, 10 million dollars in 1957, and nothing in 1958.[51] By contrast, it is estimated that Chinese repayments (including servicing charges) for past Soviet loans and credits totaled 260 million dollars in 1956 and 271 million dollars in 1957.[52] This is only part of the total aid picture, furthermore; during this same period Communist China's own foreign aid programs have grown to sizable proportions. Peking's budgets indicate that China gave out 165 million dollars in aid to foreign countries in 1955, 171 million dollars in 1956, 192 million dollars in

1957, and 116 million dollars in 1958. Then, in 1959, it announced plans for expending 253 million dollars for foreign aid in a single year.[53]

It is not surprising, therefore, that throughout this period Peking has encountered increasingly serious balance-of-payments problems. From 1950 through 1955 it was able consistently to maintain annual import surpluses, but since 1955, as receipts from foreign loans have declined and repayments for past loans have fallen due, Peking's export surpluses have steadily grown. In 1956 its export surplus amounted to 115 million dollars, and in 1957 it rose to 261 million dollars.

On the basis of rough estimates, it now appears that during 1953-1957 Communist China's own foreign aid programs plus the servicing and repayment of Soviet loans and credits actually exceeded its receipts from all types of Soviet financial assistance during 1953-1957. In general terms, China's major receipts in its balance of payments during the first Five Year Plan probably consisted of: 9.92 billion dollars from exports; 1.32 billion dollars from Soviet loans and credits of all sorts; and over 800 million dollars from miscellaneous receipts (including Overseas Chinese remittances and expenditures of foreigners in China).[54] During the same period Peking's major payments abroad were, roughly: 10.64 billion dollars for imports; 760 million dollars for servicing and repayment of Soviet loans and credits; and 647 million dollars for foreign aid from China to other countries.

In the light of China's strained balance-of-payments situation, it is surprising that Moscow has not made larger economic loans to Peking to ease its financial problems. Recently, it is true, the Russians have apparently helped the Chinese somewhat by granting them limited short-term trading credits. In 1957, for example, they agreed to let the Chinese postpone for a year some of their scheduled 1957 exports to Russia, and in 1958 Mikoyan revealed that the Russians normally permit a sizable lag in Chinese deliveries. Mikoyan claimed that discussions of payment problems are not initiated until Communist China is more than 75 million dollars behind in its deliveries,[55] asserting that Moscow not only tries to take all the exports that Peking can deliver, but that it also reduces its own output of certain commodities by 2 or 3 per cent so that it can absorb additional exports from China. But this kind of assistance is very different from the granting of long-term economic loans.

After Mao Tse-tung's visit to the U.S.S.R. in November 1957, and again after Khrushchev's talks in Moscow with China's top economic planners in May 1958, many outside observers expected that further Soviet loans to China would be announced. None had been forthcoming by the autumn of 1959.

As China embarked on its second Five Year Plan, it appeared, therefore, to be proceeding almost completely on a pay-as-you-go basis, and this may have been an important factor behind the radical changes in domestic policies which Peking introduced during 1957-1958. The dramatic decisions to set up decentralized, small-scale, labor-intensive industries, to mobilize labor on a mass scale for irrigation and other projects requiring little capital investment, and to regiment China's population and resources further by establishing the communes may all be related, in some respects at least, to the fact that by 1958 Communist China was carrying out its development programs without long-term foreign loans.

Peking's Trade with Non-Communist Countries

Peking's first serious steps toward developing trade with non-Communist nations were taken in 1952, at about the time of the Moscow economic conference. This was when the Russians began developing the idea of economic competition with the West, and Peking followed the Soviet lead. The Chinese Communists also had special reasons of their own for wanting to promote trade outside the bloc. The Western restrictions imposed on China trade during 1950-1951 multiplied Peking's difficulties in obtaining certain needed industrial equipment, raw materials, and other commodities; they were clearly hurting, and the Chinese Communists were determined to have them removed.[56] Apparently Peking also felt that by attacking the trade restrictions it could create friction between the United States and other major non-

Communist nations that disagreed over the extent to which trade with China should be restricted.

At the 1952 Moscow conference, Chinese Communist representatives signed "trade agreements" with private businessmen from 11 non-Communist countries, including Great Britain, France, West Germany, Belgium, Netherlands, Switzerland, and Italy. In many respects, these "agreements" were merely propaganda documents, since existing Western restrictions prevented their implementation, but they were important in that they marked the beginning of Peking's efforts to restore trade relations with Europe. At about the same time Peking also began to promote its trade with Asian countries.[57] As early as 1951 it had concluded limited barter agreements with India and had begun purchasing rubber from Ceylon. The sale of rubber to Communist China was barred by the Western nations at that time, but Ceylon, not being a member of the United Nations, did not feel obligated to follow its recommendations regarding the restriction of trade with Communist China. After the Moscow conference Communist China signed a "trade agreement" in June 1952 with a group of Japanese businessmen who passed through Peking on their way home from Moscow, calling for trade between Communist China and Japan of 30 million pounds sterling each way. Then in late 1952 it signed an important, five-year trade agreement to exchange Chinese rice for Ceylon rubber, and in the same year it also signed a new agreement with India. From then on, efforts to promote trade with Asian countries steadily increased. In 1953 Peking concluded its first trade agreement with Indonesia and agreed with Pakistan to exchange Chinese coal for Pakistan's cotton. In 1954 it sent special trade missions to Burma, Indonesia, and India, and it signed a three-year trade pact with Burma, as well as renewing its agreements with Ceylon, India, and Indonesia. In 1955, the year of the Bandung Conference, it began to show interest in trade with the Middle East and sent trade missions to Egypt and Syria.

Since 1955 the Chinese Communists have energetically promoted trade with an increasing number of non-Communist countries, and the obstacles to trade with Communist China have steadily diminished. In many important non-

Communist countries, including Great Britain and Japan, pressure to relax the special controls on China trade grew rapidly after the Korean truce of 1953, and soon these countries proceeded to ease their restrictions by removing many items from their lists of restricted strategic goods. Finally, in mid-1957 there was a general relaxation of controls, and the major trading nations, other than the United States, placed their trade with China on the same footing as trade with all Communist bloc countries, eliminating the special restrictions which had previously been applied to China. The United States—the only major trading country which at any time completely forbade all trade with Communist China—has continued its total embargo, but since 1957 the American position has been of greater symbolic than practical significance.

At present Communist China is trading with over 80 non-Communist countries and areas.[58] By early 1959 it had concluded intergovernmental trade agreements not only with all of the Communist bloc countries, but also with India, Afghanistan, Ceylon, Burma, Indonesia, Cambodia, the United Arab Republic (both Egypt and Syria), Lebanon, Finland, Sweden, Denmark, Nepal, Yemen, Tunis, Morocco, Iraq, and Sudan. It had also concluded barter arrangements with the government of Pakistan as well as semiofficial trade agreements with business groups in many other countries.

As a result of all its promotion efforts, Communist China's trade with the non-Communist world has grown steadily. Even though it still represents only about one-quarter of Peking's total trade, it is once again at about the same level, measured in dollars, as it was in 1948, the year before the Communists came to power.

Chinese Communist figures indicate that trade with non-Communist areas was about 1.17 billion dollars in 1950, dropped to 601 million dollars in 1952, and then rose to 1.13 billion dollars in 1956. The United States Department of Commerce has published figures, compiled from the official trade statistics of non-Communist countries, which indicate that it totaled 987 million dollars in 1950, dropped to 638 million dollars in 1952, and then rose to 1.05 billion dollars in 1956 and 1.14 billion dollars in 1957.[59] These figures cannot be reconciled completely, but whichever figures are accepted, it is clear that Peking's trade with the non-Communist world has risen to about one billion dollars yearly.

During the past few years Communist China has consistently maintained a sizable export surplus, ranging from about 100 million to 200 million dollars per year, in its trade with non-Communist countries. A part of the foreign exchange which it has earned from this trade has consisted of sterling, Swiss francs, Hong Kong dollars, and Malayan dollars, all fairly easily converted in international markets; apparently Peking has used at least a portion of these earnings to help make up its deficit in commodity trade with the Communist bloc and, when Western trade restrictions were at their peak, to buy some goods indirectly from the West through Soviet bloc countries. The need to earn foreign exchange for these and similar purposes has been one important reason for Peking's strenuous efforts to promote trade outside the bloc.

Another of Peking's motives has been the desire to purchase certain key commodities. In recent years Communist China's major imports from the non-Communist world have included chemical fertilizers, crude rubber, cotton and wool, scientific instruments of various sorts, and miscellaneous dyestuffs and chemicals, all of which are of great importance to the Chinese economy. Its largest exports to non-Communist countries have been agricultural commodities: soybeans, grain, vegetable oils, fruits and vegetables, pork and live pigs, dairy products and eggs, tea, pig bristles, feathers, tung oil, plant seeds, and silk. Iron ore and coal, which China once sold abroad in substantial quantities, and which the Communists hope again to export in larger quantities in the future, have been small. However, its export of manufactured goods, especially to underdeveloped countries, have risen rapidly since 1955.

Peking's Trade with Asian Countries

Peking's trade with Europe seems to have relatively few political undertones. Particularly since the removal of the differential restrictions on China trade, it has been essentially a matter-of-fact exchange of goods on a businesslike basis. But Communist China's trade policies toward both Japan and the underdeveloped countries carry strong political implications; in some instances, political motives seem to be at least as important, or even more important, than economic aims.

Peking has made a deliberate effort to develop its trade with countries in Asia and Africa, and it often publishes figures or percentages on its trade with the "Asian-African" area as a whole. It has stated, for example, that during the first Five Year Plan trade with this area constituted 16 per cent of its total foreign trade; by comparison, its trade with the West, mainly with Europe, totaled only about 9 per cent.[60]

According to the United States Department of Commerce figures, Peking's trade with all non-Communist countries in Asia, the Middle East, and Africa totaled 716 million dollars in 1956, while its trade with all OEEC countries (the Organization of European Economic Cooperation—Western Europe minus Spain plus Turkey) was only 362 million dollars. This has, generally speaking, been a persistent ratio, so that roughly two-thirds of Peking's total trade with non-Communist areas (including about one-half of its imports from such areas and close to three-quarters of its exports to them) is now being carried on with countries in Asia and Africa.

The Chinese Communists' motives for fostering trade with particular countries vary, but Peking seems to assume, in general terms, that a growing trade will enhance Communist China's prestige and influence and pave the way for closer political relations with countries throughout Asia and Africa. In addition, Peking has attempted to gain political capital in some countries by helping them dispose of burdensome export surpluses. In other cases it has set out to capture important markets for manufactured goods from Western countries and also from Japan and India. And in its dealings with Japan it has attempted to use trade not only to obtain diplomatic recognition and other political concessions, but also as a weapon to influence domestic politics in Japan.

Trade with Japan

Peking's political purposes have been most obvious in the case of Japan. After the first private "trade agreement" of 1952 Communist China concluded two similar agreements with Japanese businessmen in 1953 and 1955, and thereafter trade between China and Japan grew slowly but steadily, from a low of roughly 15 million dollars in 1952 to about 150 million dollars in 1956. In this period economic motivations appeared to be fairly strong on both sides. The Chinese Communists obtained valuable manufactured goods from Japan, including chemical fertilizers, insecticides, textile machinery, cement, synthetic and other textile yarns and fabrics, and miscellaneous chemicals, machines, and instruments. The Japanese imported from China needed agricultural products and raw materials, including large quantities of soybeans, rice, and salt, and lesser quantities of magnesia clinker, silk, tung oil, coal, and rosin.[61]

Although in 1956 trade with Communist China constituted only about 2 per cent of Japan's total foreign trade, many Japanese indulged in wishful thinking, harking back nostalgically to prewar days, when roughly one-fifth of Japan's total trade was with China. They ignored the fact that the Chinese Communists no longer import large quantities of consumer goods, such as textiles, and disregarded many other factors which make it highly unlikely that Sino-Japanese trade can be restored to the prewar level. Even those Japanese who were more realistic looked forward to a steadily increasing trade with Communist China; some predicted that by 1962 trade with Peking could rise to 280 million dollars each way.

While encouraging this optimism in Japan, the Chinese Communists proceeded to use trade as a weapon to exact political concessions from the Japanese government. In opening negotiations with Japanese business representatives for a fourth nonofficial "trade agreement," in the fall of 1957, Peking began to press hard for its political demands. After the Chinese Communists had exerted strong pressure, to the point of breaking off negotiations temporarily, the Japanese government, although not a direct participant, indicated a willingness to concede a number of Peking's demands. It agreed, for example, to an exchange of permanent nonofficial trade missions, and it also indicated that it would exempt members of the Chinese Communist trade mission from the fingerprinting requirement which Peking found objectionable. After months of negotiation, Japanese business representatives finally signed an agreement calling for trade each way of about 100 million dollars in 1958.[62] In February 1958 representatives of the Japanese iron and steel industry also signed an important agreement with the Chinese Communists providing for the exchange of Japanese steel products for Chinese iron ore and coal (plus, as was later indicated, rice), to a total of close to 300 million dollars each way over the five-year period 1958-1962.[63]

These two agreements appeared to lay the basis for a mutually profitable expansion of Sino-Japanese trade. Then Peking balked at a purely political issue—the refusal of the Japanese government to guarantee protection for the flag of Communist China. In May it denounced the Kishi government in violent terms and broke off all trade relations. This drastic step was followed by numerous other pressures, including a refusal to sign a new fisheries agreement when the previous nonofficial agreement expired in June.

Apparently Peking was convinced that strong economic pressures would force the Japanese government to make additional political concessions; perhaps it even hoped that Japan would withdraw its recognition from the Chinese Nationalist government and would establish diplomatic relations with Peking. Nationalist China also reacted strongly to the flag issue, however, and brought strong pressure to bear on Japan, threatening to cut off trade. Since Japan's trade with Taiwan was still slightly larger than that with Communist China in 1957, the Nationalists' pressure had a real effect.

Clearly Peking also hoped that its tough policy would help the Japanese Socialists in the forthcoming elections, but in this it made a bad miscalculation. If anything, its threats may actually have hurt the Socialists; in any case Premier Kishi's party won the election handily. Despite this setback, since the spring of 1958 the Chinese Communists have remained adamant, demanding an apology for an alleged act of desecration against the Chinese Communist flag in Japan and calling on the Japanese people to oppose the Kishi government. Even after Tokyo had decided in late 1958 and early 1959 to offer certain further concessions, the Chinese Communists showed no signs of softening their stand. In new and strong statements they now indicated that the establishment of diplomatic relations between Peking and Tokyo —and the withdrawal of recognition from the Nationalist government—would be a prerequisite for reopening trade.

The economic results of these crude political maneuvers were felt promptly. In 1957 Sino-Japanese trade dropped to 141 million dollars, and after the rupture in May 1958 it ceased completely. What the final outcome of the present deadlock will be is still far from clear. Peking's demonstrated ability and willingness to manipulate trade for political purposes have given many Japanese second thoughts about the risks of becoming overdependent upon trade with China. On the other hand, a prolonged stoppage of trade may eventually build up new pressures within Japan on the Kishi government, impelling it to grant additional political concessions to Communist China, since the desire to develop trade with the China mainland is still strong within Japan.

Trade with Other Asian Countries

Communist China's trade with other Asian countries has risen steadily, particularly since 1955, but only in a few instances has Peking attempted to exert overt economic pressure such as that directed against Japan. Between 1954 and 1957 trade with the broad area from Pakistan to Japan—Burma, Cambodia, Ceylon, Hong Kong, India, Indonesia, Japan, Malaya, Pakistan, Sarawak, Taiwan, Thailand, and the Philippines—rose from about 425 million dollars to over 610 millions. The major part of this increase was due to rising Chinese Communist exports; from under 250 million dollars in 1954 they rose to over 410 millions in 1957, while imports from the same area only increased from a little over 175 million dollars to about 200 millions. Between 1954 and 1957 Peking's trade with the underdeveloped non-Communist countries in the Far East and Southeast Asia increased by over 75 per cent, at a rate more than three times as fast as the increase in Japan's trade with the same region in the same period.[64]

Hong Kong is Communist China's largest trading partner in the non-Communist world. It obtains much of its food and other requirements from mainland China, and it also serves as a major entrepôt for Peking's trade with many other areas. During the Korean War Hong Kong was a major channel for Chinese Communist imports from the non-Communist world. In its peak year, 1951, Hong Kong's trade with mainland China totaled 432 million dollars; of this total Hong Kong's exports to Communist China were 281 million dollars, while its imports were only 151 millions. Then, after the war, Hong Kong's trade with mainland China dropped sharply, reaching a low of 189 million dollars in 1955, and its character was greatly changed. From Peking's viewpoint Hong Kong became primarily a place to earn exchange and an entrepôt for exports to widely scattered non-Communist markets. By 1957, although Hong Kong's trade with Peking had risen to 220 million dollars, its exports to Communist China reached a new low of 22 million dollars, while Peking's exports to Hong Kong—roughly one-third of which are reexported—reached a new high of 198 million dollars. Since 1956 Chinese Communist textiles and other manufactured goods have become increasingly important in Peking's trade with Hong Kong; they have seriously affected local Hong Kong industries, reduced Japanese markets in Hong Kong, and cut into Hong Kong's exports to Southeast Asia.

The Chinese Communists have ranged far and wide in developing their foreign trade. In the Middle East, for example, Sino-Egyptian trade is particularly important. Between 1956 and 1957 this trade, based primarily upon an exchange of Chinese manufactured goods for Egyptian cotton, jumped from 35 million dollars to 63 millions and served as an important symbol of growing friendliness at that time between Asian communism and Middle Eastern neutralism. Peking has also fostered and developed considerable trade with all the major South Asian nations. In this region China-Pakistan trade, based largely upon an exchange of Chinese coal for Pakistan cotton, has been especially significant. In the seven years up to 1957 Communist China bought some

200,000 tons of cotton from Pakistan,[65] and in 1958 the two countries concluded a large new coal-for-cotton barter deal. Probably the most significant development of trade between China and any underdeveloped area, however, has been in the Southeast Asian region.

Prior to 1955 Burma's trade with Communist China was negligible, amounting in 1954 to less than one million dollars. After the signing of a three-year trade agreement in 1954, it rose to almost 20 million dollars in 1955 and over 30 millions in 1956, before settling to a level of 20 to 30 millions in 1957. At first Communist China, like the Soviet Union and some East European satellites, purchased sizable quantities of Burmese rice, at a time when Burma was having difficulties in selling its chief export product. More recently rice has declined in importance to Sino-Burmese trade, and Peking has been obtaining cotton, rubber, and other commodities from Burma and in return exporting sizable amounts of manufactured goods to it. In 1956 the Chinese Communists agreed to help build a textile mill in Burma with over 20,000 spindles and almost 200 looms; in late 1957 it agreed to build a second mill with 40,000 spindles.[66]

Communist China's trade with Indonesia has risen rapidly, mainly as a consequence of trade agreements signed in 1953 and 1956, from two million dollars in 1953 to 53 millions in 1957. It has consisted largely of an exchange of Chinese manufactured goods for Indonesian agricultural products and raw materials. Peking's exports of cotton textiles to Indonesia —by far the most important Chinese export commodity in this trade—rose from 8.4 million yards in 1954 to 100 million yards in 1957.[67] The Chinese have also sold a wide variety of other manufactured products to the Indonesians, including consumer goods, machines, and appliances. Copra, sugar, and (since 1957) rubber have constituted the main Indonesian exports to Communist China, but Indonesia has also sold smaller quantities of pepper, rattan, hemp, and citronella oil. In 1956 Indonesia had difficulty meeting its export commitments, and Peking came to its assistance by extending the time limit for settling past trade deficits.[68] Apparently this difficulty has diminished since 1957 with the growth of Indonesian rubber exports to Communist China.

Since 1952 Peking's trade with Ceylon has been based primarily on an exchange of Chinese rice for Ceylon rubber. In 1952 when Ceylon had difficulty in marketing its rubber at the prices which it hoped for, Peking stepped in with an offer to buy a large amount at prices well above those prevailing on the world market. A five-year agreement, covering the years 1953-1957, called for an annual exchange of 50,000 tons of rubber for 270,000 tons of rice.[69] Under this agreement trade between the two countries rose from less than one million dollars in 1950 to 95 millions in 1953; it dropped to 70 million dollars in 1954 and then leveled off between 40 million and 70 million dollars during 1955 and 1957. When the first agreement expired, a new one-year pact was signed in 1957, calling for a minimum trade of 20 million dollars each way, with Ceylon providing rubber plus some other commodities and Communist China sending 200,000 tons of rice annually plus various manufactured goods, including iron and steel.[70] Although the price Peking agreed to pay for rubber this time was lower than previously, the Chinese Communists offset this in part by announcing an economic aid program to Ceylon. This trade will doubtless continue to be important to both countries, although Peking's purchases of Ceylon rubber seemed likely to decline somewhat because of its increased imports from Indonesia and Malaya.

China has long had a sizable trade with Singapore-Malaya, based in part on the Overseas Chinese demand for its consumer goods. In 1949, when the Chinese Communists came to power, their total trade with Malaya was 37 million dollars, of which 34 millions represented Chinese exports to Malaya. During 1950-1951, after the Korean War had started but before restrictions on China trade were made effective, trade between Communist China and Singapore-Malaya jumped to over 70 million dollars annually, 30 to 40 million dollars of which consisted of Malayan exports to Peking, largely of rubber. Then, when Great Britain cut off rubber exports to Communist China, the trade declined, returning to the previous pattern; between 1953 and 1955 it averaged 30 to 40 million dollars a year, most of which consisted of imports from Communist China. During this period Peking looked on Singapore-Malaya, like Hong Kong, primarily as a place to earn foreign exchange. Since 1955, however, the Chinese Communists have vigorously pushed the export of their textiles and other manufactured goods to Singapore-Malaya. As a result of this, and of the reopening of the rubber trade in 1956, the total two-way trade jumped to 76 million dollars in 1957, of which exports from Communist China were 52 million dollars and exports from Singapore-Malaya 24 millions. This trade continued its rapid rise in 1958, and the Malayan and Singapore governments, alarmed by the possible impact of Peking's exports on their local economies, decided in late 1958 to restrict cement and textile imports from Communist China, as well as to limit Chinese Communist banking operations in Malaya.[71]

Communist China's recorded trade with other Southeast Asian nations has been relatively small. In the case of the Philippines and South Vietnam, this is due in large part to their restrictions on trade with Peking. Thailand's imports from China have been greater than is indicated by official trade statistics, however, since the statistics do not register the increase in purchases of Chinese Communist goods through Hong Kong. During 1958 the Thais became increasingly disturbed by Chinese Communist goods flooding their markets, and in early 1959 Thailand, like Malaya, imposed new restrictions on imports from Communist China.[72] Although small so far, Communist China's trade with Cambodia can probably be expected to increase substantially in the future, as a result of the establishment of formal diplomatic relations in 1958.

Peking's trade with Southeast Asia is striking for many reasons. It differs greatly from the general pattern of China's foreign trade. In Southeast Asia Communist China is rapidly becoming a large-scale exporter of manufactured goods and a buyer of agricultural products and raw materials. It apparently is making a major effort to capture control of the markets for many manufactured goods in that region. This became particularly obvious in 1958 when, after the cutting off of its trade with Japan, Peking resorted to drastic price cutting in order to capture markets in Southeast Asia. It started selling textiles and numerous other manufactured goods at prices 5 to 10 per cent below the prices for comparable Japanese and Indian goods, and this aggressive export policy caused immediate damage to both Japanese and Indian sales in Burma, Malaya, Singapore, and Ceylon, and even in Cambodia and Thailand. Peking pressed Overseas Chinese businessmen to push the sale of its goods, and in some places it urged them specifically to boycott Japanese goods. As a result, Communist China's trade with the region rose substantially during 1958, to the detriment of both Japan and India.

In early 1959, however, Peking was confronted with new obstacles in its trade drive in Singapore-Malaya and Thailand, and apparently it also encountered significant problems within China in collecting and handling export products, probably because of serious domestic dislocations caused by the "great leap forward" and the communization campaign. There was little reason to assume, however, that the apparent slowdown in its export drive was likely to be more than temporary.

There are several possible explanations for Communist China's recent cutthroat competition for export markets in Southeast Asia. Peking's need for foreign exchange has become increasingly urgent as its balance of payments situation has become more difficult, and the rupture of trade with Japan probably stimulated the Chinese Communists to increase their efforts in Southeast Asia. There is also ample evidence that Peking believes its exports—especially of manufactured goods and, most of all, of capital goods—will buy prestige and political influence in underdeveloped areas, and that it regards its export drive as an essential weapon in pursuing its tactics of "competitive coexistence."

There is also the ominous possibility that Peking has deliberately embarked on a campaign of dumping to drive Western, Japanese, and Indian competition out of Southeast Asian markets, in order to tie the region as closely as possible to Communist China, making it increasingly susceptible to pressures from Peking. However, Peking's capacity to export is still limited, and although it is likely to grow, Chinese Communist leaders will probably not be able, at least for some years, to think seriously about attempting to dominate Southeast Asia's trade. Trade with Communist China still constitutes only a very small percentage of the total trade of the major Southeast Asian nations. In 1957, for example, it accounted for 7 per cent of Ceylon's total trade, 4 per cent of Burma's, 3 per cent of Indonesia's and Malaya's, and even less in all other countries in the area.[73] The Chinese Communists have a long way to go before they can hope to establish a really dominant trade position in Southeast Asia.

Peking's Foreign Aid Programs

Peking's foreign aid policies illustrate even more dramatically than its trade drive both the growing role of economic factors in Communist China's foreign policy and the willingness of China's leaders to make economic sacrifices to promote their political aims. It is remarkable that Peking, despite the strained economic situation within China, is now giving much more foreign aid than it is receiving. From 1953, when it started its foreign aid programs, until 1956 all of Peking's foreign aid was granted to neighboring Communist states. Since 1956, however, it has extended economic aid to a number of free-world countries and has assumed an increasingly significant role in this aspect of economic competition in the underdeveloped areas of the world as well as in the trade competition between the Communist and non-Communist nations.

The amount of foreign aid which Communist China extended during its first Five Year Plan was substantial. It probably totaled about 647 million dollars; this was a very large sum, even though a part of it may have represented merely a writing off of Chinese costs incurred in assisting the North Korean regime during the Korean War. Specific figures are lacking for Chinese foreign aid during 1953-1955, but it can be estimated at about 118 million dollars during 1953-1954 and 166 millions in 1955.[74] Peking's budgets for later years include concrete statistics on its foreign aid, which amounted to 171 million dollars in 1956, 192 million dollars in 1957, and 116 million dollars in 1958. The 1959 budget called for expenditures of 253 million dollars on foreign aid.[75] The total amount of publicly announced Chinese grants of economic aid during 1953-1957 was 779 million dollars, although under some of the grants included in this figure deliveries have continued since 1957.[76] Of this total, the sum of 724 million dollars was granted by Peking to other Communist countries—North Korea, North Vietnam, Outer Mongolia, and Hungary—but 55 million dollars went to non-Communist countries in the Asian-African area—Cambodia, Nepal, Ceylon, and Egypt.

All of these grants, extended during Peking's first Five Year Plan, were made as free gifts, rather than as credits or loans. This is doubly striking because all Soviet financial assistance to Peking has been on a loan rather than a grant basis. Only recently has Communist China started emphasizing loans as well as grants in its foreign aid program.

Aid to Communist States

Peking's ventures into the foreign aid field began in November 1953 with a grant of roughly 338 million dollars to North Korea, for use over a four-year period, 1954-1957, for economic rehabilitation after the Korean War.[77] A similar grant, also of approximately 338 million dollars, was made in July 1955 to North Vietnam; this too was for postwar rehabilitation and was to be used during the period 1955-1959.[78] In August 1956 Communist China gave a grant to Outer Mongolia of 40 million dollars to help in building industrial and other projects during 1956-1959.[79] After the Soviet suppression of the Hungarian revolt Peking, in November 1956, extended a grant of 7.5 million dollars to the Kadar government.[80] During 1953-1957 other Chinese Communist assistance to governments within the Soviet bloc included a long-term credit to Albania in December 1954,[81] about which no details are known, and a long-term credit of 25 million dollars to Hungary in May 1957; the latter bears an interest rate of 2 per cent and is to be repaid in ten years starting in 1960.[82]

Since launching its second Five Year Plan, Peking has announced large new aid programs to its Communist neighbors in Asia. In the autumn of 1958 it extended two long-term loans to North Korea;[83] the amounts were not revealed, but it was announced that they would be used to purchase textile and industrial paper-bag mills in China and to help pay the North Korean share of the costs of a large Sino-Soviet hydroelectric project on the Yalu River. Later in 1958 Peking extended a long-term loan of 25 million dollars to Outer Mongolia, to be used during 1956-1961 for the construction of power plants, bridges, several factories, and other projects, and to be repaid over 15 years starting in 1962.[84] In early 1959 Communist China announced a new program of aid to North Vietnam, for the construction of 49 industrial and communications enterprises, including iron and steel, power, fertilizer, and textile plants, coal mines, and railroads. To help construct these enterprises, Peking extended North Vietnam a loan amounting to roughly 127 million dollars—to be repaid in ten years, starting in 1967, at one per cent interest—as well as a new grant of approximately 42 million dollars.[85]

Through this aid to Communist countries Peking has demonstrated its ability to carry out fairly large-scale programs of foreign aid. It has been supplying to all of these recipients of its aid sizable quantities of manufactured consumer and capital goods as well as industrial raw materials, including many specific items which the Chinese themselves must import. Peking has sent North Korea locomotives, freight and passenger cars, communications equipment, machinery, agricultural implements, metal products, electric motors, textile machinery, chemical raw materials, building materials, cement, coal, steel, cotton fabrics, paper, miscellaneous consumer goods, and grain. Similar types of equipment and commodities have been sent to North Vietnam, including the materials needed to restore or construct textile mills, leather tanneries, electrical equipment factories, agricultural implement plants, paper mills, factories to produce medical equipment, petroleum installations, railway lines, conservation works, and meteorological stations. In Outer Mongolia the Chinese Communists are helping build a textile plant, a brick kiln, a plywood factory, a glass works, and numerous other installations, including a stadium, a gymnasium, and housing.

Technical assistance has also been an important part of Peking's aid programs to North Korea, North Vietnam, and

Outer Mongolia. The Chinese army railway corps has helped to restore transportation in North Korea and North Vietnam, and many Chinese civilian technicians have been sent to all three countries. A significant number of workers and technicians from these areas have been sent to Communist China for training, and a fairly large flow of Chinese workers has gone to Outer Mongolia—over 10,000, reportedly, in the one-year period preceding August 1956.[86]

These economic aid programs have doubtless reinforced Peking's influence in important areas adjacent to China; it is significant that Communist China has given more aid than the Soviet Union to North Korea and North Vietnam. Beyond this, Peking's aid programs are suggestive of its potential ability to extend economic aid to countries outside of the Communist bloc on a larger scale than heretofore if its leaders should decide to do so.

Aid to Non-Communist Nations

Peking's programs of economic assistance to non-Communist countries have so far been relatively small, but they are of considerable importance, nonetheless. Communist China has made significant grants to Cambodia, Nepal, and Ceylon, designed to reinforce its general policy of encouraging nonalignment in South and Southeast Asia, to foster closer Chinese relations with the recipient nations, and to expand China's influence throughout the area. It has made loans to Burma and Indonesia as well as Ceylon, with similar aims in view. It has also made a grant to Egypt and a loan to Yemen, which reflect its increasing interest and influence in the Middle East. None of these grants or loans has been very large if one compares them with the economic aid extended either by the major Western countries or by the Soviet Union, but they are large enough to be of real importance to some of the smaller recipient countries, and they have certainly enhanced China's role in the economic competition between the Communist bloc and the West.

Peking's first aid program to a non-Communist country was started in 1956. In June of that year it made a grant of 22.4 million dollars to Cambodia, to be delivered during the next two to three years.[87] The Chinese promised to send the necessary equipment and technicians to build four factories —a textile mill, a cement plant, a paper mill, and a plywood factory. Chinese aid to Cambodia also has included various types of commodities and supplies. The first inventory of goods requested included textiles, round iron bars, cement, paper, pottery, and porcelain; the government of Cambodia stated it would sell these supplies through local businessmen. A part of the Chinese 1956 grant to Cambodia has apparently taken the form, therefore, of commodities which the Cambodian government can sell to finance various of its own programs, while another part has been allocated to build four factories with the help of Chinese technicians. In 1958, when Cambodia and Communist China established formal diplomatic relations, Peking intimated its willingness to undertake new projects in Cambodia, including a small iron and steel mill.

In October 1956 Communist China agreed to provide Nepal, over a three-year period, with about 12.6 million dollars, one-third in foreign exchange and two-thirds in commodities, equipment, and supplies, to be determined by negotiation.[88] As in the case of its other aid agreements, Peking laid great stress on the assertion that "no conditions whatsoever" were attached to the assistance. A unique feature of the Nepal agreement is its specific stipulation that no Chinese technical personnel are to be sent to Nepal—an indication of Nepalese sensitivity about maintaining its nonaligned position and suspicion about the possible political implications of accepting Chinese technicians.

The November 1956 crisis in Egypt brought forth a new grant of Chinese economic aid. Shortly after the Anglo-French invasion at Suez, Peking announced a grant to Egypt of roughly 4.7 million dollars in cash.[89] At the same time it speeded up its freight shipments under a recently concluded Sino-Egyptian trade agreement. Essentially this was an emergency assistance program, provided as evidence of Communist China's support for the Nasser regime.

In September 1957 Communist China gave Ceylon a grant of approximately 15.75 million dollars, with "no strings attached," to be drawn on during 1958-1962, primarily for the improvement of rubber plantations.[90] Once again, as in the case of Cambodia and Nepal, the recipient was a small, nonaligned country. In addition, there was a special reason for Peking to make a grant to Ceylon at this particular time. Upon signing a new rubber-for-rice barter pact, the Chinese had insisted on setting a lower price for Ceylonese rubber, and the grant served to offset any sense of grievance.

Although no Chinese offers of grants to Laos have been officially announced, the Communist-oriented Pathet Lao have repeatedly urged the Laotian government to request aid from Peking. Their actions suggest that, at least until recently, Communist China would have been willing to extend aid to Laos if the Laotian government had been willing to accept it.

In its trade with Southeast Asia Communist China has also given some short-term trading credit in special circumstances, as in the case of Indonesia. When the Indonesians fell behind in their deliveries to China under the 1954 trade protocol, the Chinese, in November 1956, allowed them to stretch out the fulfillment of these obligations over the next three years, 1957-1959.[91]

Starting in late 1957 and early 1958, the Chinese Communists added a new element in their foreign aid programs when they began offering long-term loans to several non-Communist countries. Their largest offers have been made to Indonesia. A long-term credit of 11.2 million dollars was made to the Indonesians in the spring of 1958, to cover imports of rice and textiles from Communist China.[92] In early 1959 Indonesia was reportedly considering the offer of another 40 million dollars in Chinese loans, possibly to include the costs of a textile factory and a steel mill.[93] Early in 1958, also, a Burmese Deputy Premier returning home from China announced that the Chinese Communists had granted Burma a loan equivalent to about 4 million dollars, at 2.5 per cent interest, to help expand the Burmese textile industry.[94] At about the same time Peking signed an agreement with Yemen for a long-term loan of about 16.38 million dollars for the construction by the Chinese of a motor road, a textile mill, a cigarette factory, and other plants, with the participation of Chinese technicians and workers.[95] In March 1958 Ceylon received a Chinese Communist offer of a loan of roughly 10 million dollars for rehabilitation of flood damaged areas, and the Ceylonese accepted it in September. This loan is to be delivered in four annual installments and repaid over ten years starting in 1961, with interest at 2.5 per cent.[96]

All these grants and loans to non-Communist countries do not add up to an amount in any way comparable to the volume of foreign aid currently provided to non-Communist nations in Asian and African areas either by Western nations or by the Soviet Union. But this fact may not be particularly relevant or important. There is no doubt that even the present volume of Communist China's foreign aid does much to bolster its prestige and reinforce its general foreign policy, and Peking may be able to continue expanding its foreign aid in the future.

In relation to Communist China's small national income, furthermore, Peking's total foreign aid is already very substantial. If, in fact, foreign economic aid is measured as a percentage of national income, Peking's current annual rate of total economic aid takes a slice out of Communist China's economic output which is comparable to that which the United States is allocating to its foreign economic aid programs.[97] The Chinese Communists' willingness, despite the tremendous demands on their limited resources, to extend any aid at all to small non-Communist countries is eloquent testimony to their determination to pursue the goals of the Communist bloc's current tactics of "competitive coexistence."

Implications for United States Policy

In the long-term economic competition which is now under way between the Communist bloc and the West, clearly it is the Soviet Union's economic policies which pose the greatest problems for the United States and other Western countries. But the role of Communist China in the competition is already a significant one, and it is Peking rather than Moscow which poses the new challenges in much of Asia, particularly in regard to Japan and Southeast Asia.

In working out effective means to meet the specific problems raised by Peking's policies, there are several fundamental facts that should be borne in mind. Despite the dangers of political influence, pressure, and manipulation which the Communist bloc's current economic policies create, it should be recognized frankly that in many respects a shift of emphasis on the Communists' part from threats of military action to economic competition is highly desirable from the point of view of the non-Communist countries. Even though it is impossible to accept Moscow's and Peking's bland assurances that their trade and aid have no subversive intent, it is clearly better for the West to meet the Communist powers in a primarily economic competition rather than in a military conflict. To the extent that this is feasible, therefore, it should be welcomed. The United States and other democratic nations possess economic resources, skills, and capacities far exceeding those of the Communist bloc. They should therefore approach this competition with self-confidence, even though there is still an urgent need for a greater understanding of the nature of the competition and for a greater willingness and resolution to devote the necessary skills and resources to it.

It must also be recognized that, as a developing country, Communist China will inevitably expand its foreign economic relations over the coming years, and it would be unrealistic to ignore this fact. For economic as well as political reasons, Peking will undoubtedly be impelled to develop its foreign trade steadily, and for economic as well as political reasons, many non-Communist countries can be expected to favor increased trade with Communist China. Furthermore, the development of certain types of trade between non-Communist nations and Communist China can be of economic benefit to both sides, and some types of economic aid projects even from Communist countries may make a significant enough economic contribution to the recipient nations that they will regard them as desirable even when balanced against the potential political risks. It is only realistic to expect, therefore, that many of the nonaligned countries in Asia will be receptive to offers of trade and aid from Peking and other members of the Communist bloc as well as from the West. It would be a mistake for the United States to pressure them to change their views; any pressure would, in all probability, merely tend to estrange them from the West and would thereby directly help the Communist bloc to achieve its political ends. An increased recognition of the political dangers involved in relations with the bloc can only grow out of the direct experience of the nations in Asia.

The United States will not find it useful in the long run, therefore, to concentrate on a negative effort to induce these countries to cut off their economic relations with Peking. Instead it should focus its attention on the further development of its own economic relations, through both trade and aid, with all the Asian countries. In this effort, it should not be preoccupied solely with countering specific Communist moves. Instead, the United States should plan its own trade and aid policies effectively to meet the genuine economic needs of the countries involved. If this is done successfully, the influence of the Communist bloc's economic policies will in most instances be automatically countered.

Because Communist China's foreign economic policies are strongly based upon political ambitions as well as economic motives, however, and because Peking has already demonstrated its capacity to use economic pressure and manipulation for political purposes, its policies create special problems which may require special counteraction. For example, the United States and other major trading nations may find it necessary to work out with Asian nations agreements or understandings about how to meet, by cooperative action, unfair Communist trading practices such as price cutting and dumping. The Communists' willingness to exploit certain marketing difficulties of the raw-material-producing countries underlines the desirability of developing more effective international action to deal with this special problem. The United States government should also have in reserve more effective measures by which it can prevent preemptive buying by the Communists on a scale which might make some of these countries excessively dependent upon the Communist bloc. In the case of Japan, with its great dependence on world trade, it is clearly desirable for the American government to make serious efforts to help it develop greater trade with all non-Communist countries, including the United States, and to liberalize American trade policies for this purpose. And the United States should be prepared, in case the Communists suddenly apply damaging economic pressure on Japan or countries in a similar situation, to step in and assist them by special emergency aid if necessary.

The desirability of continuing the present total ban on all United States trade with Communist China is questionable, however. Although there was a strong economic justification for enforcing stringent restrictions on trade with Communist China while the Korean War was still in progress, and while the major non-Communist trading countries were willing to cooperate in implementing them, the continuation of the American embargo has little real economic meaning now. All other major trading countries have removed the special restrictions on trade with China and now merely apply the same restrictions on strictly strategic items which they apply in their trade with all Communist nations. Peking can buy the kind of nonstrategic goods it might wish to purchase in the United States from many other industrial trading nations in the non-Communist world. Today, therefore, the significance of the American embargo is principally political and psychological, and for much of the world it appears to be mainly a symbol of American intransigence. Whereas several years ago the United States might have been able to use the trade issue for direct bargaining in relations with Communist China, it no longer has any leverage with this issue.

Communist China's economy is now, and in the foreseeable future will probably continue to be, oriented basically toward the U.S.S.R., and this is a significant factor cementing the Sino-Soviet alliance. However, Sino-Soviet economic relations pose certain problems for Peking and may actually give rise to subsurface tensions. This raises numerous questions about what Western policies would be most desirable, even assuming that these policies can at best have only a marginal influence on the Sino-Soviet alliance. On this, there are basically two quite different viewpoints. The one, which has shaped United States policy, maintains that it is desirable to isolate Communist China as much as possible from the non-Communist world because this may tend to exacerbate any Sino-Soviet frictions. The other, predominant in Britain and in most Western countries, maintains that increased economic contacts between Peking and the West would not only bring economic benefits to both sides but might, in the long run, produce some slight psychological or political benefits for the West, by influencing both the Chinese Communists' interpretation of their national interests and their general attitudes toward the West. Although any immediate hope of splitting Peking from Moscow seems completely unrealistic, the possibility of achieving some slight benefits through trade with Communist China is one which deserves more serious American consideration.

Economic relations are not likely, in any case, to be of decisive importance in direct United States-China relations. But in the long run they may well be of very great importance in the relations of both the United States and Communist China with those areas on China's periphery which constitute the principal arenas of long-term competition between Washington and Peking.

Chapter 10

COMMUNIST CHINA'S FOREIGN POLICY: JAPAN AND KOREA

EVER SINCE THE Chinese Communists came to power in 1949, they have regarded Japan as a major target in their efforts to expand Communist influence in Asia. Despite its defeat in World War II and its present military weakness, Japan still possesses impressive assets: a crucial strategic position, a dynamic population of over 90 millions, a valuable accumulation of technological skills, a developed and growing industrial economy, and the highest standard of living in Asia. Japan in the Far East, like Germany in Central Europe, occupies a key position and represents a major obstacle to the spread of communism.

Many factors influence Chinese Communist attitudes toward Japan. Wholly apart from the bitterness created in China by the Japanese invasions of the 1930s and 1940s, Japan's record since the Sino-Japanese War of 1894-1895 predisposes any Chinese regime to view it as a potential, if not an actual, threat to its security. Japan is the only nation in the Far East which is theoretically capable of developing sufficient military power to serve as a counterbalance to Communist China. In addition, a strong, modern, industrial, and non-Communist Japan represents, by its very existence, a major competitor to Communist China. It constitutes a challenge in economic and political terms, and potentially in ideological and military terms as well, to the Communist path which Peking proclaims as the future salvation of all Asia.

From Peking's viewpoint, the challenge and potential threat posed by Japan have been increased by its rapid postwar recovery, the predominance of American influence there, and the role of Japan as an important base of United States military power in the Far East. Japan's alignment with the United States and the presence of American influence and power in Japan and South Korea constitute, in Peking's view, basic obstacles to the achievement of both its national aims and its ideological goals.

Chinese Communist Aims

One of Peking's ultimate goals is a Communist-ruled Japan. In the long run, the Chinese Communists hope to bring about Japan's detachment from the West and its incorporation into the Sino-Soviet bloc. A complete realignment of this sort would alter fundamentally the political, economic, and strategic situation in the Far East.

Immediately after 1949 the Chinese Communists may have believed that this objective could be achieved in a relatively short period of time. They soon concluded otherwise, however, and since the Korean War they have been less sanguine about an early fulfillment of their maximum aims. In recent years they have set their sights lower, but they have nevertheless labored persistently to influence and change Japan's policies and political orientation. They have tried in every way possible to weaken its ties with the United States and to reinforce neutralist and pacifist sentiment among the Japanese. They have worked to open up many channels of influence to both government and public opinion, and they have encouraged almost all those political forces in Japan which, even though non-Communist, agree with at least some of Peking's immediate goals.

In a fundamental sense, however, the Chinese Communists' ability to influence Japan during the past decade has been limited. Under the Allied Occupation the United States held a controlling position in Japan. Since 1952, when the Japanese regained control of their own affairs through the signing of a peace treaty, every Cabinet has regarded close alignment with the United States as a basic requirement of Japan's foreign policy, and successive governments have followed the United States' lead in refusing to recognize the Peking regime. In the absence of formal intergovernmental relations the Chinese Communists have been circumscribed in their approaches to the Japanese. As a consequence, they have devoted a major effort to reestablishing diplomatic relations with Japan, and this has been one of their most important immediate aims.

The lack of formal relations has by no means prevented Peking from cultivating extensive unofficial and quasi-official relations with Japan, however. In addition to maintaining close contacts with the Japanese Communist party, it has developed many types of relations with numerous other Japanese organizations and political groups. Japan has, in fact, been the most fertile field for the cultivation of Peking's "people's diplomacy." Many unofficial delegations ("unofficial" on the Japanese side) have been exchanged, and numerous front groups have been encouraged in Japan. Chinese leaders have done a great deal of quasi-diplomatic negotiating with Japanese individuals and groups representing powerful political forces and economic interests. By 1957 over 40 unofficial "agreements" had reportedly been signed between the Chinese Communists and various Japanese organizations or groups on trade, fisheries, and many other matters.

Since 1952 the Japanese, on their part, have been groping toward a new role in international affairs, in a world fundamentally altered by World War II and the growth of Chinese and American power in the Far East. Within Japan a new experiment in democratic government and party politics has been taking place, and foreign policy issues have become enmeshed in domestic politics to an unprecedented degree.

Among Japanese political groups there are wide differences of opinion about foreign policy in general and specifically about the nature of the relationship Japan should develop with both the United States and Communist China. Peking has done its utmost to manipulate and exploit the existing political cleavages on this basic issue.

The Chinese Communists have found many ways to apply indirect pressure on the Japanese government as well as to influence Japanese public opinion. Issues relating to trade, fishing rights, prisoners of war, and war criminals have been deliberately manipulated by Peking for political purposes, and questions relating to disarmament and rearmament, atomic weapons, American bases in Japan, and the status of Okinawa have been exploited for propaganda aims. Japanese and Chinese interests inevitably impinge closely on each other, as a result of geography, history, and economics, and Peking has worked persistently to take advantage of this fact.

Peking's Tactics

The numerous shifts in Chinese Communist tactics toward Japan over the past decade have paralleled broader and more basic changes in Peking's foreign policy. They have also been based on Peking's assessments of how changes in the total balance of international forces have affected Japan, as well as on the Chinese Communists' concrete experience in dealing with many Japanese groups and individuals.

Immediately after 1949 both the Chinese and Russian Communist leaders appeared to be preoccupied with the potential security problem posed by a Japan allied with the United States, and apparently they concluded that a military attack by the North Korean regime, supported by militant action on the part of the Japanese Communist party, could effect a drastic change in the entire balance of power in Northeast Asia. Not long after the signing of the Sino-Soviet treaty of February 1950, which was aimed specifically at Japan and implicitly at the United States,[1] Moscow, backed by Peking, directed the Japanese Communist party to attempt to seize power by violence in early 1950; and in June 1950 the North Koreans invaded South Korea.

The Communist propaganda line toward the conservative Yoshida government was an extremely hostile one in this period. Peking applauded the Soviet demands for the arraignment of a number of leading Japanese as war criminals. It supported the Russians' adamant opposition to any peace treaty with Japan except on Moscow's own terms, and it consistently maintained that no treaty would be valid unless it included Communist China as a signatory. The Chinese Communists also appealed repeatedly to the Japanese people to oppose the Yoshida government, and they demanded the withdrawal of all American occupation forces from Japan.

Both at home and in Southeast Asia, Chinese Communist propaganda portrayed the Yoshida government as a rising military threat.

During this early period Peking clearly regarded the Japanese Communist party as its principal instrument for influencing developments within Japan.[2] The Communists' success in Japan's 1949 elections in winning almost 10 per cent of the vote, and electing 35 members to the lower house of the Diet, apparently led both Peking and Moscow to overestimate their strength. In any case, Peking paid little attention until later to the possibilities of allying itself with other political groups in Japan.

Sino-Soviet policy toward Japan during 1949 and 1950 was a gamble which failed. The Korean War resulted in a stalemate and alerted much of the world to the military threat of communism in the Far East and elsewhere. The Japanese Communists' policy of violence met with harsh countermeasures, and popular support for the Communists dropped off rapidly. And at the San Francisco conference of 1951 the Western allies proceeded, despite Peking's protests and Soviet obstructionism, to sign a peace treaty with Japan.[3] Forced to conclude that they could not achieve their aims through violence and subversion, at least not without incurring much greater risks and costs than they were then willing to accept, Moscow and Peking were compelled to revise their strategy toward Japan drastically, and they shifted to a policy of political maneuver.

Japanese Attitudes and Policies

Even prior to the shift in Sino-Soviet policy there was already a widespread feeling among the Japanese that Tokyo must sooner or later establish relations with the new power that had arisen on the China mainland. In 1950 Premier Yoshida had told the Diet that he was prepared to send trade representatives to Communist China as soon as Allied Headquarters would permit it, and in early 1951 he expressed the view that, in Japan's relations with China, geography and economics would eventually prevail over "ideological differences and artificial trade barriers."[4] However, as a result of the Korean War, American policy toward Communist China steadily hardened after June 1950, and the United States strongly disapproved of the Japanese recognizing or having other dealings with Peking.

The existence of two Chinese governments greatly complicated the drafting of the Japanese peace treaty in 1951.[5] Unable to agree on which Chinese government should take part in the peace conference, the major Allies decided to exclude both. When they finally drafted the treaty they inserted an article obligating Japan to sign, during the next three years, a bilateral treaty with any state which had been qualified to sign the original treaty but had not done so. They also hit upon the formula of having Japan renounce all title and claim to Taiwan and the Pescadores without specifying to what government or authority these territories should pass.

In theory, Japan was left free to sign a treaty with either Peking or Taipei. Actually, however, this freedom of choice was illusory, and Yoshida frankly told the Diet that the decision was up to the Allies;[6] the Japanese government felt, in short, that it had no alternative but to follow the American lead. Secretary Dulles visited Japan to clarify the American position in late 1951, while ratification of the Japanese peace treaty was still pending in Washington, and on December 24 Yoshida wrote Dulles promising that his government would sign a treaty with the Nationalist government on Taiwan as soon as possible and would refrain from establishing relations with the Chinese Communist regime.[7] When the letters exchanged between Yoshida and Dulles were published in early 1952, they evoked strong criticism from all the opposition parties in Japan, much of which was based upon the fear that Yoshida's commitments would affect the development of Sino-Japanese trade adversely. In April 1952, however, the Japanese government proceeded to sign a treaty with the Nationalists, which was made applicable to all territory controlled by the Nationalists, at that time or in the future.

Ever since then the Japanese government, in trying to shape its policy toward China, has been caught in a vortex of strong competing pressures. The United States has stood firm against recognition of Peking. Within Japan widespread sentiment, in the ruling party as well as in the opposition, has favored the development of increased contacts with Communist China. Nationalist China has used its influence to forestall the establishment of political relations between Tokyo and Peking. And the Chinese Communists have tried persistently to exploit these conflicts and have pressed for recognition on their own terms.

Peking's "People's Diplomacy"

After the failure of its early militant policy toward Japan, Peking initiated an energetic campaign of "people's diplomacy," concentrating to begin with on the trade issue. In June 1952 it signed its first private "trade agreement" with a group of Japanese businessmen. This was hailed by Peking as an important step toward normalizing relations, but, in fact, it was designed primarily to apply pressure on the Japanese government to remove the existing trade restrictions. The agreement divided the goods to be exchanged into three categories, and the Chinese commodities most desired by the Japanese were to be provided only in exchange for exports which Tokyo, following the American example, had restricted or banned.[8]

In the autumn of 1952 various Japanese groups were represented at the "Asian and Pacific Peace Conference" held in Peking, where in addition to propagating their new "coexistence" line, the Communists devoted primary attention to the alleged dangers of Japan's remilitarization.[9] At the same time the Chinese Communists stepped up their attacks on Yoshida as a "tool of the United States," denouncing him for betraying Japan's "true interests" and calling on the Japanese people to oppose his government and its policies.

In this period Peking still seemed to regard the Japanese Communist party as the main instrument of its policy toward Japan, and "Radio Free Japan" was set up in that year, presumably in or near Peking. However, after the Diet elections held in the autumn of 1952, in which the Communists won only 2.5 per cent of the vote and failed to win a single seat, Peking began to turn its attention increasingly to other Japanese groups. In late 1952 it took up the unresolved issue of the Japanese prisoners of war still held in China as a means of opening up new and wider channels of influence in Japan.

The initiative on the prisoner of war issue came from Peking. The official *People's Daily* announced in December 1952 that there were still 30,000 Japanese residents in China and that if the Japanese would provide shipping, Communist China would facilitate their repatriation.[10] Peking then proceeded to define detailed and specific procedures which would have to be followed. Despite the fact that the Japanese National Council for the Repatriation of Japanese Nationals Overseas had offered to send a delegation to discuss the issue, the Chinese Red Cross Society insisted that a group be sent by three other organizations: the Japan-China Friendship Association, the Japan Peace Liaison Committee, and the Japanese Red Cross Society.[11] The Chinese Communists specified, furthermore, that the delegation include a particular person known for leftist, pro-Peking views, whom the Japanese government had refused a passport. In short, they attempted, successfully, to embarrass the Japanese government and to achieve a maximum propaganda impact from their move. After some delay Tokyo acquiesced, and representatives from the designated organizations finally proceeded to China. In February 1953 they reached an agreement with the Chinese, and during March and April the first repatriated groups reached Japan. They had been carefully selected to include the most well-indoctrinated and pro-Communist Japanese detainees, and their praise of Communist China had a substantial impact on Japanese opinion.

Other important contacts also developed during 1952 and 1953. A Japan-China Fisheries Association, formed in Tokyo, proposed to send a delegation to Peking. The Sino-Japanese Trade Promotion Council offered to hold trade fairs in China. The General Council of Japanese Labor Unions proposed an exchange of information with the All-China Federation of Trade Unions. And the Japan Council of Science established contact with the Academy of Science in Peking. As these and other contacts developed, the Japanese government found itself in an embarrassingly defensive position.

On the Japanese political scene steady gains were made during this period by left-wing groups which strongly favored developing relations with Peking and chose to make China policy a major domestic political issue. In the elections of early 1953 Yoshida was reelected and the Japanese Communist party took only one Diet seat, but the Socialists made substantial gains and in their campaigning attacked Yoshida for being subservient to the United States in his policy toward China, as well as in other matters. The left-wing Socialists called for the abrogation of Japan's treaty with Nationalist China, the recognition of Peking, and concrete steps to implement the 1952 "trade agreement" by reducing existing restrictions on trade with mainland China. The right-wing Socialists were more moderate, but they too called for increased Sino-Japanese trade. Almost every political group in Japan favored this, in fact. Even conservative politicians like Hatoyama accused Yoshida of being afraid to promote China trade because of excessive deference to American opinion.

Interest in China trade grew steadily during 1953, partly as a result of Japanese fears that the ending of the Korean War and the resulting decline in American military procurement in Japan would aggravate Japan's balance of payments problem. Within the Diet a Dietmen's League for the Promotion of Sino-Japanese Trade was organized, and many business groups stepped up their efforts to promote trade with China.[12] In mid-1953 the Sino-Japanese Trade Promotion Association and the Japan-China Trade Promotion Council asked Peking to extend the first "trade agreement" for six months, and in July the lower house of the Diet unanimously passed a joint resolution in favor of reducing Japan's restrictions on China trade at least to the level maintained by the major Western European nations, which was considerably lower than that maintained by Japan in deference to American policy.[13]

Sino-Soviet Moves toward Formal Relations

Late in 1953 the Sino-Soviet bloc began making its first tentative moves toward the reestablishment of diplomatic relations with Japan. The initiative for this came primarily from Moscow, however, and for many reasons the Chinese Communists were less eager than the Russians to deal with

Yoshida. Most important, Japan's treaty with Nationalist China created obstacles to relations which were far more difficult to resolve than any existing barriers to Russo-Japanese relations. Nevertheless, Chinese Communist leaders told Japanese politicians visiting China in the autumn of 1953 that Peking was willing to establish relations with Japan if the existing obstacles could be removed. But at the same time Premier Chou En-lai emphasized that Japan's alleged subservience to the United States and its relations with the Nationalists prevented the immediate restoration of relations.[14] Also in this period Kuo Mo-jo, head of the Chinese Academy of Sciences, told representatives of the Dietmen's League for the Promotion of Sino-Japanese Trade that a nonaggression pact between Communist China and Japan would be desirable, but he too implied, as Chou had, that Japan must first cut its ties with the Nationalists.[15] Communist China was asking a high price, therefore, for reestablishment of Sino-Japanese relations. Since the Yoshida government was clearly unwilling to pay this price, Peking was obviously directing its appeals to the extreme left in Japanese politics. It was also trying to broaden its contacts in Japan, and in this it had considerable success. The delegation sent by the Dietmen's League was the first important group representing all the major parties in Japan to visit Peking, and it signed the second private "trade agreement" between Communist China and the Japanese.

In October 1953 Peking announced that the repatriation program had been completed, at least on an organized group basis, and this announcement evoked a very mixed reaction in Japan. Several thousand Japanese still remained in China, and in the minds of many people the issue was by no means completely solved. On the other hand, there was widespread gratitude for the return of 26,000 detainees, and as an expression of appreciation the Japanese Red Cross proposed inviting a delegation from the Chinese Red Cross to visit Japan. In May 1954 the Diet passed a resolution backing this idea; in August the Japanese Foreign Office gave its approval, and the Chinese Red Cross delegation arrived in October.

This delegation was the first major group from Communist China to visit Japan, and its visit was another important milestone in the development of Peking's informal "people's diplomacy." [16] It met numerous Japanese groups, established wide contacts, and even held unofficial conversations with the Japanese Minister of Welfare. Soon after its return to China articles appeared in the Chinese press stating that Communist China could establish relations with any legitimate Japanese government—with the proviso that Japan's relations with the Nationalists be terminated—even though Peking continued to defame Yoshida.[17]

Then in October 1954 the Sino-Soviet bloc made a major move toward the reestablishment of relations with Japan. During a visit by Khrushchev and Bulganin to Peking, the Chinese and Russian leaders issued an important joint declaration calling for the normalization of relations with Japan; it implied a readiness to deal with Yoshida without, however, defining the conditions in any detail.[18] At the same time, through an influential delegation of Japanese Diet members which was visiting Peking, the Chinese Communists made additional overtures. Premier Chou En-lai told the members of this delegation that China wished to sign a peace treaty and establish relations with their country as soon as it became truly independent, democratic, and free, once again implying that Japan's close ties with the United States still made this impossible, and stated that then it would be possible to conclude a Sino-Japanese nonaggression treaty. In further conciliatory gestures, Chou declared that Communist China was prepared to settle the unresolved war criminal issue, and he also suggested that a Japanese mission come to Peking to discuss the fisheries problem. In late 1954, responding to the hopes which these statements aroused, private groups in Japan established a National Council for the Restoration of Diplomatic Relations with the Soviet Union and China, a Japan-China Fishery Problems Council, and an International Trade Promotion Association.

At this point a change of government in Japan raised still higher the hopes of those Japanese who favored increased contacts with Communist China. In the caretaker government formed in December 1954, both Hatoyama, as Premier, and Shigemitsu, as Foreign Minister, made public statements favoring increased trade and other contacts with Communist

China. They differed, however, in their views on the possibility of establishing political relations with Peking. Hatoyama said he saw no reason why relations could not be established with both Peking and Taipei, proposing, in effect, a kind of "two Chinas" policy, while Shigemitsu expressed the opinion that formal diplomatic relations with Peking would probably not be possible as long as Japan maintained relations with Nationalist China. No major changes in Japan's policy toward China occurred, but in the brief period preceding the new elections Hatoyama eased the restrictions on travel to mainland China, agreed to permit a Chinese Communist trade delegation to visit Japan, and approved the idea of a Japanese private fishery delegation going to China.[19]

During this period Peking also moderated its position somewhat. In January 1955 Chou En-lai reportedly told Shozo Murata, President of the International Trade Promotion Association, then visiting Peking, that the Chinese Communists wished to continue promoting increased trade and cultural exchange with Japan, despite Japan's recognition of Nationalist China. Toward Hatoyama himself, however, Peking at first adopted a definitely unfriendly line, calling upon all "democratic" forces in Japan to oppose him. Then, after he had won the elections held in February 1955, this line was toned down. The elections had made it clear that, despite Socialist gains, the conservatives would continue to dominate politics in Japan for some time. Although Hatoyama's "two Chinas" formula was denounced by Peking, his views at least suggested that there might be increased room for maneuver in Peking's approaches to Tokyo.

Attempts to Achieve De Facto *Relations*

During the following months, as Peking moderated its hostility toward Hatoyama, the Chinese Communists began, in effect, working steadily toward the establishment of some kind of *de facto* relations with the Japanese government, as a preliminary step toward formal diplomatic relations in the future. At the Bandung conference in early 1955, for example, the Chinese Communists established direct contact with the Japanese delegation, and Chou En-lai reportedly assured Japan's chief delegate that Peking recognized that the Hatoyama government was representative of the Japanese people.[20] Soon thereafter, in May 1955, the first Chinese Communist trade delegation to visit Japan signed a third private "trade agreement," which followed the pattern of the first two but emphasized the desirability of an exchange of permanent trade missions between Japan and Communist China and called for intergovernmental agreements on trade and payments.[21] In April Japanese fishing interests sent a delegation to Communist China, where it signed an agreement with the Chinese and supported Peking's statements that an intergovernmental agreement would be more satisfactory.[22]

From early 1955 until mid-1956 the Chinese Communists pressed in every way they could for the establishment of *de facto* relations with the Japanese government, while Hatoyama appeared to be groping for some formula to facilitate increased contacts and relations with the Communist bloc without compromising Japan's basic commitment to maintain close relations with the United States, which remained the keystone of Japanese foreign policy.

In June 1955 the Japanese government took the initiative, through its consulate in Geneva, in proposing talks on repatriation, specifying, however, that such talks should not be construed to imply recognition. In a letter to the Peking government it claimed that Communist China was still detaining 47,000 Japanese, including 1,000 war criminals, 6,000 other known Japanese citizens, and 40,000 unaccounted-for prisoners of war.[23] On August 15 Peking's Ministry of Foreign Affairs replied with a statement which asserted that only 6,000 Japanese remained in China.[24] It declared bluntly that Japanese war criminals would be dealt with according to Chinese law, and it raised the countercharge that the rights of tens of thousands of Chinese in Japan were being infringed. At the same time, however, it said that Communist China would be willing to negotiate with the Japanese government on trade, cultural contacts, and the rights of citizens in both countries, as well as on other matters. And two days later Chou En-lai qualified the somewhat harsh tone of the August 15 statement by telling a group of Japanese newsmen that although his government rejected the idea of "two Chinas" and objected to Japan's maintaining relations with the Nationalists, it was nevertheless possible to take certain steps toward normalizing relations.[25] He also said explicitly, for the first time, that the San Francisco peace treaty would be no obstacle to the signing of a peace treaty between Japan and Communist China.

During the summer of 1955 Peking made several other moves which indicated its desire to establish *de facto* relations. In July, for example, Chou En-lai, in an interview with a group of Japanese returning home from a "peace conference" in Helsinki, indicated that he would like to meet with a representative of Hatoyama to discuss the normalization of relations. However, at about the same time, the Chinese Communists also raised new issues as bargaining counters, including the question of reparations for war damages in China and the alleged problem of protecting the rights of Chinese living in Japan.

New Attempts to Achieve Diplomatic Relations

Then in late 1955 Peking seemingly altered its objective and raised its price for the solution of outstanding problems between China and Japan. The fundamental issue, it began saying, in effect, was the establishment of full *de jure* relations. Unless and until diplomatic relations were restored, it implied, the solution of concrete problems relating to trade, fisheries, and repatriation would have to be deferred.

While this complicated political maneuvering was taking place, Peking also stepped up greatly its campaign of "people's diplomacy." During 1955 over 800 Japanese visited mainland China,[26] and many were given full red carpet treatment, including interviews with Mao Tse-tung, Liu Shao-ch'i, or Chou En-lai. In October, in his first interview with a Japanese visitor, Mao met Fusanosuke Kuhara, head of a group representing the National Council for the Restoration of Diplomatic Relations with China and the Soviet Union, and reportedly suggested that Japan send an envoy of ambassadorial rank to discuss the restoration of relations. During the same month Mao told a delegation of Diet members that such questions as the repatriation issue could be settled only after the state of war between Japan and China was ended.[27] Later in the autumn he gave an interview to a delegation from the Japanese League for Protection of the Constitution. In all of these quasi-official discussions Mao and other Chinese Communist leaders, while emphasizing the need to establish diplomatic relations before solving concrete problems, worked persistently to get Japanese to associate themselves with Peking's policies. Many of the Japanese delegations visiting China signed joint communiqués with various Chinese groups, and Peking exploited this new propaganda device to the utmost. The traffic between Japan and China was not all one-way, furthermore. In December 1955, for example, Kuo Mo-jo headed a Chinese science delegation to Japan, reportedly with great propaganda success; according to Peking, the Japanese Minister of Education expressed regret that he could not entertain Kuo as a state guest.[28] This "people's diplomacy" had a significant influence upon Japanese public opinion, reinforcing pressures in Japan in favor of establishing relations with Peking. At the same time, sympathy in Japan for the Chinese Nationalists was declining, especially after the Nationalists' veto of Outer Mongolia's application for membership in the United Nations had led to a Soviet veto of Japan's request for admission. Following this incident, the Socialist party called a special conference to discuss the recognition of Communist China.

Meanwhile, Russo-Japanese talks on reestablishing relations were proceeding in London. Started in mid-1955, these talks proved to be long and tortuous, and many basic issues, including the territorial ones, remained unsolved. Finally, however, after Moscow had applied strong pressure by imposing new restrictions on Japanese fishing rights, the two governments agreed in late 1956 to end the state of war and establish diplomatic relations, deferring solution of many problems. This raised the hopes of some Japanese that relations with Peking could also be restored, but the obstacles to this—in particular, the strong opposition of the United States government, and Japan's relations with the Nationalist government on Taiwan—made these hopes unrealistic.

New Tactical Changes by Peking

In the spring of 1956 Peking apparently abandoned all early expectations of achieving *de jure* relations with Japan and reverted to its earlier policy of seeking some basis for *de facto* dealings with the Japanese government on specific problems. Once again it began making conciliatory gestures. In May 1956 Chou En-lai told a group of visiting Japanese that Peking now planned to repatriate a majority of the Japanese war criminals still held in China, utilizing the good offices of the Red Cross and other "people's" organizations in both China and Japan. In June Peking announced that at its April meeting the National People's Congress had decided upon a new policy of leniency.[29] Procedures for repatriation were then worked out, and by late August 1,017 of the 1,062 Japanese war criminals known to have been held in Communist China had been returned to Japan.

In May 1956 the Chinese Communists also agreed, after discussions with a private Japanese delegation, to extend the period covered by the Sino-Japanese Fisheries agreement. The Japanese delegation, on its part, agreed to sign a joint communiqué with the Chinese Communists calling for an intergovernmental agreement on fishing problems in the future.[30] During the same month the Chinese extended the third private "trade agreement" for another year,[31] and the Japanese negotiators agreed, with the approval of their government, that permanent trade missions of a private, nondiplomatic type should be exchanged in the future between Communist China and Japan. The flow of Japanese visitors to Communist China also grew. During 1956 over 1,200 Japanese visited the China mainland.[32] The majority were non-Communists, and they included many important public figures. Among them were a delegation of Japanese military men led by Saburo Endo and a second delegation of Japanese industrialists and businessmen. Peking also kept applying direct psychological pressures on the Japanese government. In October 1956 Mao Tse-tung, Chou En-lai, and Liu Shao-ch'i reportedly suggested not only that Hatoyama pay a visit to Peking on his way to Moscow, but also that former

Premier Yoshida, who had been the target of some of their bitterest attacks, visit Communist China.

Peking and the Japanese Socialists

One of the Chinese Communists' aims in all these statements, interviews, and informal negotiations was to mobilize support within Japan for steps toward the establishment of formal relations, and by 1956 Peking clearly regarded the Socialist party in Japan as its most useful channel for this campaign. In their quasi-diplomatic talks with various Socialist leaders, such as those in October 1956 with Seichi Katsumata, head of the Socialist party's Diet policy committee, the Chinese Communists spelled out their conditions for establishing formal relations with Tokyo. Reportedly, Katsumata carried a letter to Chou from Suzuki, head of the Socialist party, expressing hope for early normalization of relations, and then he took back a letter in reply from Chou. In effect, these talks and exchanges constituted a form of negotiation between Communist China and the leaders of Japan's major opposition party, and, as such, they created numerous embarrassments and complications for the Japanese government.

The complications were particularly serious when the Socialists proceeded to take action, as they did after the Katsumata visit to Peking. In late 1956 the Socialists stated explicitly that Japan should sever its relations with the Nationalists. They also organized a nation-wide campaign for the early establishment of diplomatic relations with Communist China and announced their intention to send a special mission of Socialist Dietmen to Peking for further discussions on this question.[33]

In the autumn of 1956 preliminary negotiations were begun in Peking, at the same time that a Japanese trade exhibit was opened there, for a fourth private Sino-Japanese "trade agreement." The negotiations soon bogged down, however, because of Peking's objections to the Japanese regulations requiring the fingerprinting of members of any Chinese trade mission, as of all long-term visitors. The Chinese Communists nevertheless agreed to extend the third agreement temporarily, until May 1957,[34] and at a Japanese reception in Peking Chou En-lai stimulated new hopes by intimating that China was interested in technical cooperation with Japan.[35] Many Japanese were quick to respond to hints of this sort, and in the following months several Japanese groups started investigating the possibilities for technical cooperation in a number of different fields.

Pressure on the Kishi Government

After each change of government in Japan the Chinese Communists have apparently reviewed their Japan policy and have modified their tactics to fit the new situation. After Kishi had formed a new Cabinet in February 1957, Peking, to judge by its actions, decided that it should attempt to strengthen its alignment with the Socialists in order to use their advocacy of relations with Communist China to exert increasing pressure upon the Japanese government.[36] The Japanese Socialists were quite willing, for their own purposes, to cooperate.

In April 1957 a Japanese Socialist good-will mission to China, headed by Inejiro Asanuma, Secretary General of the party, agreed to issue an important joint statement with the Chinese People's Institute of Foreign Affairs condemning the policy of the Japanese government. "The two sides . . . agree," this statement said, "that the time has come for the governments of Japan and the People's Republic of China to restore diplomatic relations as soon as possible, formally and completely. . . . The Good-Will Mission of the Japanese Socialist party explained the basic policy of the Japanese Socialist party to be nonrecognition of the existence of two Chinas. Taiwan is China's internal question. . . . Certain existing agreements between the people's organizations of the two countries, together with matters on which agreement might be reached, should be developed into agreements between the two governments at the earliest possible date." [37] The statement also called for the dissolution of all military blocs, the signing of a Sino-Japanese peace treaty, the conclusion of a collective peace pact for the Pacific area including Japan, Communist China, the Soviet Union, and the

United States, and the banning of all atomic weapons. According to some reports, Mao also indicated at this time a willingness to revise the 1950 Sino-Soviet alliance, if and when a Pacific security pact could be signed.

When Kishi first came to power, Peking's attitude toward him appeared to be uncertain. Although he had shown no inclination to consider changing Japan's nonrecognition policy, he had advocated increased trade with mainland China, which was a hopeful sign from Peking's point of view. But before a half year had passed, Peking had begun to show strong hostility toward him. As Premier, Kishi set about defining a new basis for closer and more nearly equal relations between Japan and the United States, and during a visit to Washington he secured several concessions, including a promise of an early withdrawal of United States troops from Japan. This trend, as well as a good-will tour which Kishi made throughout Southeast Asia, was disturbing to Peking. Most upsetting of all was the fact that Kishi visited Taiwan, where he held friendly talks with Chiang K'ai-shek. The Chinese Communists reacted strongly to what they regarded as an unfriendly act, and they accused Kishi of backing Chiang in his hopes to return to the mainland.[38] From then on, Chinese Communist hostility mounted steadily. Asserting that "Japan today is under the control of the United States," Chou En-lai, in an interview with Japanese correspondents in late July 1957, accused Kishi of visiting the United States merely "to curry favor with his American masters by slinging mud at New China." [39]

Like virtually all Japanese leaders, Kishi favored increased trade with Communist China, and in July 1957 his government followed the lead of Britain and the other major Western European nations and greatly reduced its restrictions on trade with Communist China, in effect removing the so-called "China differential" and placing trade with Communist China on the same basis as trade with the rest of the Communist bloc. This step, which Peking had long demanded, left the Chinese Communists far from satisfied, however, and despite the signing of several important private contracts and other agreements with the Japanese in the next few months, Peking soon began injecting all sorts of political problems into the trade issue as a means of pressuring Japan to change its entire policy toward China.

In August 1957 the Chinese Communists canceled their plans for holding trade fairs in Japan in protest against Japanese laws requiring the fingerprinting of long-term visitors.[40] Then, the negotiations for a fourth private "trade agreement," started in September, were adjourned in the following month, without having resolved several key questions, including the number of persons to be permitted in the proposed trade missions and the issue concerning fingerprinting requirements.

In February 1958 the Japanese government made a significant concession, offering to modify its fingerprinting regulations. In the same month Peking once again raised Japanese hopes for increased trade. It signed a five-year contract with representatives of Japan's steel industry calling for the exchange of Chinese coal and iron ore for Japanese steel,[41] and it agreed to resume negotiations for a fourth over-all "trade agreement." Finally, in March, the fourth "trade agreement" was signed.[42] However, the text of the agreement (and an official memorandum attached to it) included, in addition to the previous Japanese concessions such as the exchange of nonofficial trade missions, several other provisions—among them the right of the trade missions to fly their national flags—which Tokyo firmly opposed. Again the Chinese Communists were deliberately applying pressure upon the Japanese Foreign Office.

The pressures which Peking exerted on the Kishi government through these trade negotiations were supplemented by a steady increase in its contacts with important Japanese groups and individuals. The total number of Japanese visitors to Communist China in 1957 was more than 1,600, even higher than in 1956. Peking also continued its quasi-diplomatic negotiations with the Japanese Socialist party. Chinese leaders held long talks with Hachiro Arita, an adviser to the Socialist party, in September and entertained Yoshio Suzuki, head of the party, in December.[43] And a spate of joint communiqués signed by influential Japanese groups came out of Peking.

Peking's Embargo and Other Pressures in 1958 and 1959

In early 1958 Peking's pressures on Kishi mounted, reaching a peak between March and May, just on the eve of Japan's national elections. At the same time the Chinese Nationalists brought strong pressures to bear to discourage Tokyo from making concessions to Peking. Soon after the signing of the fourth "trade agreement," the Chinese Nationalists expressed vehement objections and began taking retaliatory steps against Japanese trade. Kishi responded by giving assurances to the Nationalists that his government was not changing its China policy, and Aichi, Secretary General of Kishi's Cabinet, made a public statement in April which emphasized that "the Japanese government at the present time does not recognize the Communist Chinese government" and "has no intention of according diplomatic immunity" to its trade mission. "Care will be taken," he said, "to prevent the misunderstanding that the setting up of a trade mission means *de facto* recognition of Communist China, but at the same time assistance and cooperation will be extended within the limits defined under national laws. ... Since the government does not now recognize Communist China, the right of the trade mission to raise its flag will not be recognized." [44]

Peking's reaction to this statement was violent. It denounced Kishi in extreme terms and refused to discuss any new trade agreement until existing "obstacles" were removed. Then after an incident at Nagasaki in which a Chinese Communist flag was desecrated, Communist China completely halted all trade with Japan and canceled all existing trade contracts. This drastic step was followed by other sanctions against Japan. The Chinese Communists seized a number of Japanese fishing vessels and refused to renew the fisheries agreement which expired in June. Peking's Foreign Minister Ch'en Yi lashed out at Kishi as a man who had shown "his true colors as an imperialist"; anyone, he asserted, who thought Communist China must trade with Japan was experiencing "the hallucination of an idiot." [45]

Peking apparently hoped that these pressures would either help the Socialists to achieve victory in the forthcoming elections or, at least, would force the Japanese government to make further concessions. However, this new get-tough policy, like the violence of 1949-1950, appeared to boomerang. It probably hurt rather than helped the Socialists in the elections; in any case, the Socialists failed to make the gains which many observers had predicted. Kishi refused to be bludgeoned into any major change of policy, and Peking's crude use of its trade weapon evoked widespread criticism in Japan.

Despite these setbacks, Peking decided to keep up the pressure against Japan rather than retreat. Perhaps it felt that, having gone so far, it could not back down. In June the Peking *People's Daily* stated: "The wishful thinking of the Nobusuke Kishi government is like this: if cultural contacts between the people of the two countries go on as usual while its policy of hostility toward the Chinese people remains unchanged, it may claim that this is an expression of weakness of the Chinese people. On the other hand, if cultural contacts between the Chinese and Japanese people are actually affected by it, it may pass on the responsibility to the Chinese people, thereby provoking the Japanese people's dissatisfaction with China. We must warn the Nobusuke Kishi government that this trick will get it nowhere." [46] At the same time, Peking kept making hopeful predictions. In July the Peking *People's Daily* declared: "We believe that the struggle of the Japanese people for friendship with China and normal relations between the two countries, like their struggle for peace, independence, and democracy, will overcome all obstacles and difficulties and gain final victory." [47]

Simultaneously, the Chinese Communists were stepping up their competition against Japanese trade with Southeast Asia. Peking probably had several reasons for its new export drive, but Japanese anxieties mounted in direct proportion to the increase in Chinese exports to Southeast Asia. Peking's trade policies in that region were certainly viewed by at least some Japanese businessmen as a punitive measure aimed specifically at Japan. Cultural and other exchanges declined immediately following the trade ban, but then in the latter half of 1958 the Chinese Communists again stepped up their wooing of the Japanese Socialists and other groups which advocated restoring Sino-Japanese relations and abrogating Japan's security pact with the United States.

In September 1958, when the Socialists issued a policy statement calling for new steps to break the deadlock between Japan and Communist China, Peking applauded loudly.[48] Soon thereafter it applied new propaganda pressure on the Kishi government, and once again it obtained support from various Japanese groups, including the Japanese National Council for the Restoration of Diplomatic Relations with China and the Japan-China Friendship Association. In November Ch'en Yi called on the Japanese people to force Kishi to abrogate Japan's security treaty with the United States,[49] and this theme became increasingly strident in early 1959. Peking's propaganda campaign supporting this idea was closely coordinated with Soviet diplomatic notes advising Japan to adopt a neutralist policy.[50] Within Japan the Japan-China Friendship Association launched a major movement for abrogating the treaty with the United States and restoring relations with Peking.

On the eve of local elections in Japan in early 1959 this pressure reached a new peak. Peking signed joint communiqués of major importance, reiterating the Communists' stock themes, with both the Japanese Communist party and the Socialist party. The Socialists pledged themselves to press for recognition of Communist China, abrogation of Japan's security pact with the United States and its treaty with the Nationalists, and the conclusion of a collective peace pact including Communist China, the Soviet Union, the United States, and Japan.[51]

Despite this external pressure, and the growing agitation within Japan for revision of the security treaty with the United States, the Kishi government more than held its own in the local elections of 1959. But Peking showed no signs of retreating from its hard policy. It maintained its ban on all trade, implying that this would continue until diplomatic relations were restored, and it appeared determined to continue its tough line indefinitely. In the late summer of 1959 there were some signs that Peking was once again considering new approaches to the Japanese. In August Premier Chou En-lai and Foreign Minister Ch'en Yi invited two senior politicians of Japan's ruling Liberal-Democratic party —former Premier Tanzan Ishibashi and former Education Minister Kenzo Matsumura—to visit Communist China. This was interpreted by some as a step toward talks concerning a resumption of trade, but it produced no immediate results.

It is difficult to predict what effects the existing deadlock, if prolonged, will have on Japanese public opinion. While Peking's embargo has evoked strong criticism of Chinese Communist policy among some Japanese, other Japanese place the chief blame for the rupture of trade on the Kishi government.

Opinions and Attitudes in Japan

There are so many Japanese organizations and groups which are pro-Peking in their orientation that the Chinese Communists can rely on strong continuing support within Japan for many of their policies. Organizations such as the Japan-China Friendship Association, the Japan Peace Liaison Committee, the Japanese National Council for the Restoration of Diplomatic Relations with China, the Japanese Red Cross, the Japan International Trade Promotion Association, the Dietmen's League for the Promotion of Sino-Japanese Trade, the Japan-China Cultural Exchange Association, the Japan-China Music and Dancing Society, the Japan-China Cinema Society, the Japan-China Translations Society, the League for the Protection of the Constitution, the National Council for Banning Atomic and Hydrogen Bombs, the Asian Solidarity Committee, the China Research Institute, the Society for Research on Contemporary China, and numerous other groups consistently present a favorable image of the Peking regime or advocate closer contacts with mainland China. The "China lobby" is a powerful force within Japan.

Peking's propaganda attempts with considerable success to appeal to a wide variety of groups, and it obtains some response from Japanese of all political colorations. The Chinese Communists' opposition to atomic weapons, criticism of American bases and forces in Japan, support for the return of Okinawa to Japanese jurisdiction, appeals to "Asianism," warnings against the remilitarization of Japan, and endorsement of neutralism—all evoke favorable responses from large numbers of Japanese.

According to public opinion surveys, a great majority of Japanese favor increased trade with Communist China, and a sizable proportion of the public opposes Kishi's nonrecognition policy. In one newspaper poll of 1958, 53 per cent of those interviewed favored the immediate establishment of diplomatic relations with Peking, and 70 per cent favored such relations in the future.[52] Quite a few Japanese appear to incline in a general way toward some sort of "two Chinas" policy, which would involve the establishment of relations with both the Communist and Nationalist regimes.

Despite the risks of generalizing about national attitudes, it seems apparent that most Japanese feel that important cultural bonds link their country with China and believe that isolation from contact with Communist China is "unnatural." There appears to be relatively little fear of Communist China in Japan, and few Japanese view Peking as a military threat. Many Japanese feel that as a result of long experience they "know how to handle" the Chinese. At the same time, a large number of Japanese are greatly impressed by developments in Communist China since 1949, especially by the Communists' success as political organizers, their discipline, and their economic progress. There is a tendency among many Japanese to underrate the importance of ideology in international affairs and to feel that Communist China is very different from the Soviet Union, despite the fact that both are Communist-ruled. Some Japanese have a sense of guilt about Japan's past record of aggression against China, and this predisposes them to support conciliatory policies toward Peking.[53] Special factors impel particular groups to promote closer relations with Communist China with an almost missionary zeal. Many businessmen, even though they are conservatives in their own party affiliations, fervently believe that trade should be developed wherever possible, without regard to politics. Marxism has a very wide influence among students in Japan, and most intellectuals strongly support closer ties with Peking. In addition, the Communist party and, more important, the Socialist party have consistently attacked the China policy of Japan's conservative governments. On this issue, the Socialist party is not completely unified; the currently dominant left-wing leaders are much more pro-Peking than the right-wing Socialists. But the ruling Liberal-Democratic party also has many internal differences over China policy, and some conservatives go almost as far as the Socialists in urging closer relations with Communist China.

The China Issue in Japan's Domestic Politics and Foreign Policy

Successive governments in Japan have been, and are likely to continue to be, vulnerable on the issue of China policy. The leaders of the Liberal-Democratic party have felt compelled to make campaign pledges both to promote trade with Communist China and to "try to normalize or adjust diplomatic relations with the countries with which such relations have not been resumed," [54] but they have moved with extreme caution and deliberation. Peking's recent pressures on Japan have doubtless reinforced this caution, but over most of the past decade it has been due in large part to the United States' firm opposition to relations with Peking. This fact has made the Liberal-Democratic leaders vulnerable to the charge that their China policy is really more American than Japanese in its origin. There is no doubt that Japan would have moved more rapidly toward establishing formal relations with Peking if Washington had been less insistent in pressing its views. As C. Martin Wilbur has written, actually "all Japanese political parties favor trade and diplomatic relations with Communist China"; they "disagree only on the manner and timing" and on the importance they attach to coordinating their policies with Washington.[55]

Over recent years, in a predictable resurgence of nationalist feeling, the Japanese have moved steadily toward greater "independence" in their foreign policy. To Japan's present conservative leaders, this implies the "adjustment" of Japanese-American relations in many respects but within the framework of continued close cooperation with the United States. At present their primary concern is to modify those policies or arrangements which most clearly symbolize Japan's postwar subservience, including the security treaty between Japan and the United States and the status of Okinawa. It would not be surprising, however, if over the years ahead issues relating to China policy come to be included in this list with increasing frequency, since Japan's perspective on China is inevitably different from that of the United States. In his New Year's message of 1958 Premier Kishi declared: "There are situations when one cannot simply assume that Japan's position as a nation of Asia and her stand as one of the free nations will be identical. In such circumstances, if a choice must be made, I think Japan must approach the problem from the viewpoint of Asia." [56] Peking's crude pressures on Japan since early 1958 may well have pushed the present Japanese government temporarily closer to the views of the United States government on policy toward China, but there seems little doubt that the long-run pressures on Japan "as a nation of Asia" will push it toward establishing relations with Peking.

If the Socialists should achieve power in Japan, major changes in Japan's foreign policy would immediately follow. The Socialists are committed to make far-reaching changes in Japan's relations with America, to establish diplomatic relations with Peking, and to assume a neutralist posture in world affairs. Once in power, their views on foreign policy might well undergo significant modifications, but there is little reason to doubt that they would follow the general policy which they now advocate, thereby fundamentally altering the balance between the United States, Communist China, and Japan in Northeast Asia. A shift of this drastic nature is not imminent. At present the Socialists hold only about one-third of the seats in the Diet, and they failed to improve their position in the 1958 and 1959 elections. Yet any estimate of future possibilities would be unrealistic if it overlooked the possibility that the Socialists may eventually be able to gain in strength and influence in Japan's political life.

Possible Consequences of Changes in Japan's Policies

If Japan, whether under a conservative or Socialist government, should decide to move toward closer relations with the Chinese Communist regime, what consequences would this probably have?

If recognition of Peking by Tokyo took place in the face of strong American disapproval, or if in Japanese eyes it symbolized a split with the United States, it might have very far-reaching effects upon Japan's whole political position. If, however, changes in China policy were coordinated between the Japanese and Americans, or if the United States acknowledged the existence of special factors inducing Japan to deal with Communist China and minimized the over-all political significance of such a move, there is no reason why the recognition of Communist China by the Japanese would inevitably alter Japan's fundamental position or undermine its present cooperation with the United States.

The establishment of formal diplomatic relations between Japan and Communist China, in and of itself, would probably not greatly increase the dangers of Communist subversion within Japan. The informal and nonofficial channels of contact between Communist China and Japan are already extensive, and the opening of a Chinese Communist Embassy in Tokyo would add little to their effectiveness. Whether or not the Japanese can effectively counter Peking's efforts at subversion will depend primarily on other factors, on the basic political, economic, and social strength of their national life, as well as on the vigilance of Japanese government authorities.

The Danger of Economic Dependence

One question which is frequently, and legitimately, asked is what the effects would be of closer economic relations between Japan and China. In many respects the Chinese Communist and Japanese economies are now complementary, and a large-scale exchange of Japanese manufactured goods for Chinese raw materials would certainly be profitable to both countries. If diplomatic relations should be established, would trade grow rapidly? If so, what would be the economic and political effects on Japan?

The establishment of "normal" political relations between Japan and Communist China would doubtless lead to some increase in trade between the two countries, at least by comparison with the level reached just before the rupture of trade relations. Even under ideal conditions, however, this trade seems unlikely to grow as fast as many optimistic Japanese businessmen have hoped. Peking's basic economic orientation toward the Communist bloc, its difficulties in increasing exports of the kind of commodities which the Japanese want, its foreign exchange problems, and its severe restrictions against importing manufactured consumer goods would limit the growth of Sino-Japanese trade, even if existing political obstacles were removed. The China market is not likely, therefore, to be "the answer," as many Japanese have hoped, to Japan's basic export problem. In many respects the existence of political barriers, on which the low level of trade can be blamed, has encouraged many Japanese to harbor illusions about the China market. It can be argued that the removal of political barriers might, in the long run, foster a greater realism in Japan about trade with Communist China. It would certainly reduce the importance of what is now a very troublesome issue in domestic Japanese politics.

Nevertheless, under favorable conditions, trade between Communist China and Japan would certainly rise, despite the many limiting factors, and both Japan and Communist China would regard this as beneficial, in strictly economic terms. To the extent that Peking could buy Japanese manufactured products, and Japan could obtain coal, iron, or other basic materials more cheaply in China than elsewhere, Japan would profit. From the Japanese viewpoint, increased Sino-Japanese trade might, it is true, by accelerating Peking's program of industrialization, help to build up Communist China as a competitor to Japan, but it would at the same time help the Japanese in coping with their own economic problems.

The basic danger which would arise from increased Sino-Japanese trade would be the possibility that if Japan became progressively more dependent upon the mainland of China, either for raw materials or for markets, the Chinese Communists' ability to use trade as a political weapon against Japan would steadily increase. Most Japanese tended to discount this danger before 1958, but having seen Peking's crude manipulation of trade for political purposes in the past two years, many Japanese are now at least aware of the risks. But these risks should not be exaggerated; few Japanese even today take them as seriously as do many Americans, and this is understandable. In 1957, before the rupture of relations, Sino-Japanese trade amounted to only some 2 per cent of Japan's total foreign trade, and there is little possibility of Japan becoming dangerously dependent on China unless this trade should be expanded many times over. Furthermore, since Japan's total trade is growing steadily, Sino-Japanese trade could increase substantially without becoming a very large part of Japan's trade. The risks of dependence are also diminished by the availability of alternative sources of supply, in the United States and elsewhere, for the commodities which the Japanese wish to import in larger quantities from the mainland of China. Even, therefore, if Japan's trade with China grew considerably, and then were again cut off suddenly by Peking, the Japanese would probably not find it excessively difficult to meet their import needs from these alternative sources. Actually, if the Chinese Communists should decide to import substantially larger quantities of capital goods from Japan, conceivably they themselves might in some degree become dependent on Japan, in strictly economic terms; conceivably this might impose certain limits upon their ability to manipulate trade for political purposes.

The fact remains, however, that the Chinese Communists, with their total state control over foreign trade, may be able, in the future as in the past, to exert economic pressure against Japan for political purposes. And since it is only realistic to predict that they will continue striving to achieve their basic objectives—to weaken the ties between Japan and the United States, to bring Japan steadily closer to the Communist bloc, and to encourage the growth of Communist-oriented forces within Japan—they can be expected to use economic as well as other weapons to achieve these goals.

The United States and Future Japanese Relations with China

The attitudes and policies of the United States will have an important influence both on the extent to which Japan may turn toward Communist China for trade and on the degree to which this trade may make Japan vulnerable to pressures from Peking. If the United States encourages a steady expansion of Japanese-American trade, unquestionably the appeal of the China market to the Japanese will be lessened, and the possibility of Japan becoming increasingly dependent on China will be held to a minimum. Even if Sino-Japanese trade is resumed and grows to substantial proportions, a continuing close political and economic association between the United States and Japan, and firm American assurances to the Japanese that they can look to the United States for economic assistance if the Chinese should again apply economic pressure, would greatly reduce Peking's capacity to influence Japan by manipulating or threatening to manipulate trade in the future.

American interests will be served best in the long run if Japan emerges as a stable, strong, independent, and democratically oriented state, serving as a general counterweight to Communist China in Northeast Asia, competing against the Chinese Communists' expanding influence in Southeast Asia, and acting as a responsible ally of the West. Japan's current willingness to follow the United States' lead on most international issues, and to provide important military bases for American forces, does not mean that it is effectively playing these roles at present. The Japanese are only beginning to regain their national self-confidence and have only recently begun to develop an independent foreign policy. They have been reluctant to assume responsibility even for their own defense, to say nothing of the general security of Northeast Asia. Although they have begun to repair the damage which they inflicted on their relations with other Asian nations in World War II, they have not yet demonstrated a capacity to be a dynamic and constructive influence, capable of competing against Peking throughout the Far East. If Japan is to play an important role in that region, it must be more than a ward of the United States, and the United States, on its part, must be willing to encourage and support greater Japanese initiative and independence in international affairs. This will require adjustments in both American and Japanese foreign policy.

United States policy should aim, whenever possible, to work out joint Japanese-American policies, representing a genuinely cooperative effort to meet the major current problems in the Far East, including those created by the emergence of a strong Communist regime in China. In respect to China, the aim of the United States should be to develop joint policies which will reflect the views and interests of both Japan and the United States. Mere acquiescence by Japan in American decisions will not be an adequate or effective response to the enormous problems facing the non-Communist nations in Asia.

It would clearly be desirable for the United States, instead of unilaterally defining its own policies toward China and then urging the Japanese to shape their policies accordingly, to make greater efforts to formulate joint policies which can obtain more positive and enthusiastic Japanese support. Despite Peking's embargo against Japan and the growing realism that it has stimulated among some Japanese, in the long run the pressures and factors impelling the Japanese to establish relations with their most powerful Asian neighbor may well be irresistible. The wise course for the United States would be to adopt a more flexible posture and then, in consultation with the Japanese, to explore possible ways by which Tokyo, with American backing, could take more initiative in its dealings with Peking, with the aim of breaking the present trade deadlock and moving slowly toward the ultimate establishment of relations on a basis which would not compromise the fundamental interests of either Japan or the United States. If the United States does not attempt this, there will probably come a day, sooner or later, when the Japanese will be persuaded or compelled to modify their policy toward China, despite American objections. Such a parting of the ways on China policy would inevitably highlight the conflicts between Japan's "position as a nation of Asia and her stand as one of the free nations" and would strain instead of strengthen the alignment of Japan with the United States, an alignment which is vital both to the United States and the future of Asia.

Korea—Focus of Great Power Rivalry

Situated at a crucial crossroads in Northeast Asia, Korea has long been a focus of international rivalries. The Chinese, the Japanese, and the Russians have competed in projecting their influence into this small but strategic peninsula, and much of Korea's history is the story of its struggle, not always successful, to maintain its independence against external pressures.

China's interest in the peninsula dates back at least two thousand years, and over the centuries the Chinese have left a strong cultural mark on the language, customs, and institutions of Korea. Even though Korea has evolved a distinctive national culture, in a fundamental sense it also belongs to the Sinic, or Chinese, cultural sphere.

As early as the Han Dynasty, in the second century B.C., the Chinese annexed a part of what is now Korea, and for four centuries thereafter they exercised direct control over this territory. From then until the late nineteenth century, whenever they had a strong government, the Chinese periodically exerted political pressure on the Koreans. Even in the nineteenth century Peking still claimed suzerainty over the peninsula, although by this time the claim had relatively little meaning, since China's power and influence were clearly waning.

The decline of Chinese influence in Northeast Asia brought little gain to the Koreans, however, for both Russia and Japan competed to replace China as the dominant power. At the end of the Sino-Japanese War of 1894-1895 Japan compelled China to recognize Korea's complete independence. Ten years later, after the Russo-Japanese War, it forced the Russians to acknowledge Japan's "paramount political, military, and economic interests" [57] in Korea, and, with their hands freed by this double victory, the Japanese first established a protectorate over the peninsula and then finally annexed it in 1910.

This historical background helps to explain much that has happened in and to Korea since World War II. For the Koreans, V-J Day meant liberation from the Japanese and the opportunity to reassert their independence. But for the great powers it meant the appearance of a new power vacuum in Northeast Asia, and the contest for Korea began once again. First, Russian forces pressed southward, while the United States undertook the occupation of South Korea. This resulted in a divided nation and led to a tense "cold war" confrontation of Soviet and American power along the 38th Parallel, with the Russians backing a Soviet-installed Communist regime in the North, and the United States supporting Syngman Rhee's government in the South.

China was little involved in these developments until after the Communists came to power. Then, however, it was virtually inevitable that a resurgent China, allied with the Soviet Union, would renew its interest in Korea. Less than a year after setting up their regime in Peking, and within a few months of signing an alliance with the Soviet Union, the Chinese Communists were called upon by the Russians to intervene militarily in Korea. They sent a huge force to bail out the Soviet-supported North Korean regime when it appeared to be on the verge of defeat by the United Nations forces after its abortive aggression against the South.

The Chinese Communist intervention in Korea in the autumn of 1950 may have been motivated in part by a real fear that the security of their new regime would be endangered by a total defeat of the North Koreans. Whatever their motives then, it has become clear since 1950 that Peking is committed to supporting the North Korean regime indefinitely as a buffer state along China's northeastern frontier. In effect, it appears to share with the Soviet Union a condominium over North Korea.

Although the fighting was brought to a halt in Korea in 1953, in the years since then there has been no progress toward reunifying the peninsula. While giving large-scale aid for the rehabilitation and economic development of North Korea, Peking and Moscow have blocked all efforts by the United Nations to unify the country through free elections. Refusing to make any concessions on their part, the Chinese Communists have repeatedly tried to exert pressure on the United States, and on the other countries which fought under the United Nations' mandate in defense of South Korea, to withdraw their military forces and their political and economic support from Rhee's regime. In 1958 Peking increased its pressure on the United States by withdrawing its troops and calling on the Americans to do likewise. The Chinese withdrawal does not represent any diminution, however, of Peking's interest in, and commitment to, North Korea.

Today the Chinese Communists certainly regard North Korea as an ally of considerable importance, and they are giving major assistance to building its strength. Having failed to achieve their aims by direct aggression, both the Chinese and Korean Communists, as well as the Russians, now seem to accept the military stalemate, at least for the time being. But they continue to exert unremitting political pressure on both the United States and the South Korean regime. Apparently resigned to a long-term competition between the two Korean regimes, they are concentrating their efforts on building up the North, while doing all they can to subvert the South.

To the non-Communist nations Korea has been, and remains, an extremely important symbol of their common determination to resist Communist military aggression. It is also a symbol of the continuing power struggle between the Communist and non-Communist nations and of the fact that this struggle is not likely to be resolved in the foreseeable future.

Barring the possibility of a major war, the prospect in Korea is for a long-term economic and political struggle between the two Korean regimes and a continuing confrontation of Sino-Soviet and American power. The situation, in short, is a stalemate.

Even if this stalemate continues, it is not likely to be static, however, since the political and economic competition will continue relentlessly. The United States bears a heavy responsibility in this long-term competitive struggle, and it must take the lead in helping the South Koreans build up their political and economic strength and in probing for the Communists' psychological weaknesses. It must continue to shield Korea with the mantle of its strategic protection. Through the United Nations, it should continue pressing for any steps, however small, which might lead toward the ultimate reunification of Korea. In Korea itself it should increase its efforts to support sound economic growth and democratic political progress. And, to strengthen Korea's international position, it should do everything possible to help heal the serious breach between the Koreans and Japanese and to encourage the development of new contacts and ties between South Korea and the other non-Communist nations of Asia.

Chapter 11

COMMUNIST CHINA AND SOUTH AND SOUTHEAST ASIA

COMMUNIST CHINA'S DETERMINATION to expand its influence in South and Southeast Asia has been apparent ever since 1949, and over the past decade Peking has had a tremendous impact on these two areas. The Chinese Communists' growing power, political dynamism, and economic growth have created both fear and attraction in the nations to its south. Peking has consciously attempted both to woo and attract, and to threaten and intimidate, nations in these areas, and it has made its influence felt through very diverse tactics.

As has already been emphasized in earlier chapters, Peking has numerous instruments of policy at its command, and its use of them has varied according to the over-all tactics it has adopted, and the scale of priorities it has set in different situations and at different times. Several major shifts in its policies over the past decade have greatly affected its relations with the nations of South and Southeast Asia.

In 1949 the Chinese Communists openly proclaimed their aim of promoting armed revolts throughout these areas, and after extending their rule to China's southern border, they proceeded to give large-scale assistance to the Vietminh. They showed relatively little concern about their relations with the existing non-Communist governments in these areas and seemed preoccupied with encouraging immediate Communist insurrections. These revolutionary policies did not succeed in any wide area, but Peking was able to help consolidate Communist rule in the northern half of Indo-China, and the integration of North Vietnam into the Communist bloc has been the only significant territorial addition to the bloc during the past decade.

The most striking shift in Communist China's policies toward South and Southeast Asia occurred during 1952-1954. When Peking, along with Moscow, evolved new tactics of "competitive coexistence," the nations of South and Southeast Asia became a special target of their efforts at attraction. Under these new policies the Communist bloc played down its revolutionary aims and laid primary stress upon achieving certain short-run goals through influencing the existing governments in these areas. As these new tactics evolved, Peking, as the main Asian member of the bloc, worked hard to develop an effective policy of attraction, directed particularly toward the nonaligned nations of South and Southeast Asia, and while the "Bandung spirit" was at its height, between 1955 and 1957, the Chinese Communists achieved some significant gains.

Then from late 1957 on the general hardening of Sino-Soviet policies began to have a noticeable effect on Peking's relations with the nations of South and Southeast Asia—even though the more militant posture adopted by both Moscow and Peking seemed directed primarily at the West, rather than at the Asian and African countries. But until 1959, despite a cooling of Peking's relations even with those Asian countries it had been cultivating most assiduously, the Chinese Communists in general adhered to the idea of positively wooing these countries, and these tactics imposed certain definite restraints on their use of militant threats and pressures to achieve their aims.

In 1959, however, a significant change took place. After the Tibetan revolt Peking showed a new militancy in its policies toward South and Southeast Asia and, seemingly indifferent to the loss of the good will it had built up over the previous five years, it began to exert new pressures on India and Laos. As of the early autumn of 1959 it was difficult to predict, however, whether these moves were signs of a major shift in tactics or merely temporary deviations from the "peaceful coexistence" line.

There were a number of possible explanations for Peking's actions which suggested that perhaps the Chinese Communists' pressures on India and Laos were primarily aberrations from the "competitive coexistence" line rather than an indication that these tactics had been deliberately abandoned. Peking's pressure on the Indian border, for example, may well have been essentially a side-effect of the Tibetan revolt. In the latter half of 1959 the Chinese Communists were encountering continued resistance in Tibet, and they may have decided that sealing off Tibet from the outside world required a show of strength on the border, regardless of its effect on Sino-Indian relations. It seemed apparent, also, that world sympathy for the Tibetans and India's decision to give sanctuary to the Dalai Lama and over 13,000 of his followers angered the Chinese Communist leaders, and this may have been a factor impelling them to react strongly and emotionally, regardless of the immediate consequences. In the case of Laos, the renewed outbreak of insurrection on the part of the Pathet Lao rebels, aided by North Vietnam and with strong moral support from Communist China, may have been a rather desperate response by the Communists to the increasingly effective action taken by the government of Laos in early 1959 to bring the Pathet Lao under control. It is conceivable, also, that Peking in the summer of 1959 was less than wholly enthusiastic about Khrushchev's scheduled trip to the United States and wished to demonstrate to the world that Communist China's power, and claims, would have to be taken into consideration before any major Soviet-American moves could be made toward reducing tensions and stabilizing the world situation on the basis of the existing *status quo*.

Whatever the Chinese motives for creating new tensions in the latter part of 1959, Peking's actions clearly had a profound impact on attitudes toward China throughout most of South and Southeast Asia, and as a result the "Bandung spirit" is not likely soon to regain its former luster. Among many Indians and others apprehension and suspicion of Peking have replaced the trust, good will, and wishful thinking which the Chinese Communists previously worked hard to cultivate.

Despite this change in attitudes, however, it is nonetheless possible that after attempting to make certain limited gains, Peking may well try to repair the damage it has caused to the slogans of "coexistence" and to reemphasize once more its positive approaches to the nations of South and Southeast Asia. Or, it may follow a new kind of "coexistence policy"— one which involves less attraction and more pressures—while still trying to achieve some of its most important short-term goals by encouraging neutralism or nonalignment in these areas. Conceivably, Peking may believe that since nonalignment is often based on fear or a feeling that accommodation is a necessity, as well as on positive attraction, threats as well as blandishments may contribute to its growth.

It seems likely, in fact, that even if it does step up its pressures on neighboring countries, Peking, in working toward its short-term aims, will continue placing great emphasis on further developing its relations with the existing governments in South and Southeast Asia. It is essential, therefore, to understand the tactics it has pursued in dealing with these governments in the recent past—especially in the period between 1954 and the Tibetan revolt.

Coexistence and Attraction

In 1954 Peking initiated an energetic political and economic offensive in South and Southeast Asia in the name of the "five principles of peaceful coexistence" and "Asian solidarity" (or "Asian-African solidarity"). It worked hard for several years to establish close relations with as many as possible of the existing non-Communist governments. And it tried in every way possible to neutralize South and Southeast Asia, to reduce Western influence there, and to build up Communist China's political prestige and economic position. Throughout this period the Chinese Communists did more than adopt a tolerant attitude toward neutralism or nonalignment;[1] they became active sponsors of it. They also tried to exploit in every way possible the residue of anti-Western feeling remaining after long years of colonial rule. And they assiduously propagated the idea that all Asians, whether nationalist or Communist in their politics, are linked by special bonds and share common interests and should therefore band together against "Western imperialism."

Internal developments within Communist China have been a vital factor in Peking's policy toward South and Southeast

Asia; they may, in fact, have had as great or even a greater impact than Peking's foreign policies. One basic premise underlying the entire Sino-Soviet strategy of "competitive coexistence" has been the belief that, if the Communist nations can develop their economies at a rate substantially higher than that of the non-Communist countries, this fact in itself will have decisive psychological and political consequences. Peking and Moscow apparently believe their economic successes can persuade other nations, particularly in the underdeveloped areas, not only to accommodate their policies to the Communist bloc's growing power but also to emulate their revolutionary example. There is no doubt that the dynamism, discipline, and economic growth which Peking has already demonstrated have, in fact, had a very great impact upon many nations in South and Southeast Asia.

In its policy toward South and Southeast Asia Peking between 1954 and 1959 generally assumed a nonmilitant and conciliatory posture, while still building up its own military power rapidly. It made numerous gestures toward removing causes of friction, while still protecting Chinese interests forcefully. And it emphasized issues on which Communist China and other Asian nations could take a common stand, while still pursuing its own brand of power politics. Starting in 1954, Chou En-lai conducted a free-wheeling and extremely skillful diplomatic campaign to promote Peking's new policy in South and Southeast Asia. In early 1954 a Sino-Indian agreement on Tibet was signed. Then, after Communist China had played a large role in the Geneva Conference on Indo-China, Chou made important visits to both India and Burma, where he signed joint communiqués with Nehru and U Nu embodying the "five principles of peaceful coexistence" as the prime symbol of the new relationships developing between the nonaligned nations and the Communist powers. Chou's prominent role at the Bandung Conference in Indonesia, in early 1955, was one highlight of his subsequent diplomatic campaign. Another was his grand tour of South and Southeast Asia, in 1956-1957, when he visited North Vietnam, Cambodia, India, Burma, Pakistan, Afghanistan, Nepal, and Ceylon.[2] In this period the stream of important Asian leaders visiting Peking included the Prime

Ministers of India, Burma, and Indonesia, as well as leaders from many other countries, including Cambodia and Laos, which had not officially recognized Peking. Supplementing these intergovernmental contacts, Peking also energetically pushed its "people's diplomacy" in much of South and Southeast Asia.

By 1957 the Chinese Communists had established diplomatic relations with all the countries of South Asia—India, Pakistan, Nepal, and Ceylon.[3] They had also formed diplomatic ties with Afghanistan, which is sometimes considered to be a part of South Asia. In Southeast Asia Peking was able to develop diplomatic relations with the three nonaligned countries in the region—Burma, Indonesia, and Cambodia. It had little success, however, in developing contacts with the four countries which are most clearly aligned with the West—South Vietnam, the Philippines, Thailand, and Malaya. These four states, all of which maintain close military links with the West, have pursued a consistent policy of nonrecognition toward Peking and have restricted contacts of all sorts with the Chinese Communists. With Laos, which until recently vacillated between neutrality and alignment with the West, Peking at one time developed significant official contacts, but since 1958 Laos has steadily strengthened its ties with the West.

Official diplomatic or political relations have been only one channel of Peking's influence. In ways already described, the Chinese Communists have used many other instruments of policy—military power, Communist subversion, the Overseas Chinese, trade, and economic aid—to further their interests and expand their influence in South and Southeast Asia. Even while propagating the slogan of "competitive coexistence," they have continued exerting limited military pressure along China's borders, promoting subversion by covert and disguised means, and expanding their economic influence through trade and aid.

Despite Peking's nonmilitant posture in the years following its shift to "coexistence" tactics, apprehension about Communist China's growing military power has without doubt exerted a strong and continuing influence throughout much of the region. Fear of Peking has substantially increased since early 1959, especially in those countries closest to China's borders, but even before 1959 uneasiness about Peking's strength, and uncertainty about its intentions, were factors which helped to shape basic attitudes, not only in those nations which aligned themselves with the West, but also in some of the neutralist nations which have tried in every way to "get along" with their powerful neighbor. Instead of relying on fear alone, however, Peking, at least until 1959, endeavored by promoting the "Bandung spirit" to allay the fears of its power and to attract the peoples of South and Southeast Asia by more positive appeals. To understand the basis for these appeals, it is necessary to consider the fundamental forces now at work in these areas.

Basic Attitudes in South and Southeast Asia

From Pakistan to the Philippines most of South and Southeast Asia is undergoing a fundamental political, social, and economic revolution, an upheaval caused largely by the impact of the West and directed in many respects against the West. With the notable exception of Thailand, the entire area was dominated by Western colonialism until World War II. Then Southeast Asia was conquered by Japan, and the Japanese occupation helped to shatter the structure of Western colonial power, giving added impetus to the growing strength of anticolonialism and nationalism. By the end of the war nationalism had become the dominant political force in South and Southeast Asia, and within a very few years after the war most of the nations in the region had achieved their independence, leaving only a few pockets of colonial rule.

The recent colonial past has left a heritage of attitudes and emotions which have continued to shape the outlook of the small elite groups which control most of these newly independent nations. Anticolonial feeling has been strong throughout the region. It has affected even those nations which are militarily aligned with the West; although over the past decade they have generally defended the United States against the frequently made charges of excessive interference in Asia, they nevertheless have joined the Asian and

African nations in opposing the remnants of old-style colonialism anywhere in the world. Militant anticolonialism has been an important factor impelling some leaders in the nonaligned nations to feel that certain basic American policies in Asia—including nonrecognition of Peking and the building up of military alliances against Communist China—have represented Western interference of an undesirable sort.

In almost every nation in South and Southeast Asia there is sensitivity to race prejudice. In subtle ways feelings about race and racial discrimination have influenced the assessments which their leaders have made of the motives and aims of both Communist China and the United States. In recent years appeals for "Asian solidarity" against the West and propaganda stressing racial discrimination in the United States have evoked a fairly wide and sympathetic response.

Indigenous cultural traditions have strongly affected the views of some leaders in the region toward "power politics" and the "cold war." The Gandhian tradition of nonviolence in India and Hinayana (Theravada) Buddhism in Burma, to cite two concrete examples, have helped to mold the opinions of leaders in these two countries toward the basic East-West struggle—even though the results have not always been entirely consistent or logical.

Marxism has had a deep and widespread influence among intellectuals in many countries in the area. Although the Communist movements vary greatly in strength from one country to another, in the region as a whole communism presents the greatest ideological challenge to nationalism. Moreover, the influence of Marxism extends far beyond the organized Communist movements; it has also helped to shape the outlook of many nationalist leaders.

Most of the leaders in South and Southeast Asia subscribe to "socialism" of one kind or another. Many hope to create societies which can best be described as "socialist democracies," combining free and representative government with varying degrees of state economic planning. For the most part, they still look primarily to the West for their models, and they are attempting to adapt Western experience to their own needs, but few accept any specific Western model without qualification, and they have encountered great difficulties in attempting to transplant Western institutions in their countries. Many, while rejecting communism as a system of power, have felt that the Communists' experience in the Soviet Union and China has considerable relevance to their own problems. Moreover, in some respects, events and developments during the past two to three years have shaken their own self-confidence and their faith in democratic processes. In one country after another parliamentary government has faltered or failed, and almost everywhere economic achievements have lagged far behind the "revolution of rising expectations" which has swept through the area. Because of these and other factors, the ideological and political issues which are at stake in the world-wide conflict between the Communist bloc and the West have seemed much less clear-cut to many leaders in South and Southeast Asia than they have appeared in either Washington or Peking.

One of the most pervasive influences in the region has been the idea of nonalignment, or "neutralism." Over the past decade the leaders of India, Burma, Indonesia, Ceylon, Nepal, and Cambodia have been "neutralist," even though many of them have rejected this particular term. Laos has also belonged to the neutralist group; in a sense it still does even though it has steadily strengthened its ties with the United States. In South Vietnam, the Philippines, Thailand, Pakistan, and Malaya the dominant groups have opposed neutralism, but in several of these countries there have been neutralist currents of some significance.

Neutralism is a complex phenomenon in South and Southeast Asia, and in recent years it has meant different things in different countries.[4] Its basic common denominator, however, has been the idea of nonalignment—the avoidance of military alliances—in the struggle between the Communist bloc and the non-Communist world. The outstanding leaders in the nonaligned nations in South and Southeast Asia are all fundamentally nationalists, and most of them strongly oppose communism within their own countries, but many have refused to be anti-Communist in their foreign policies, even when fighting communism at home.

The causes of neutralism in these areas have been varied. The widespread emotions and attitudes already described—

anticolonialism in particular—have contributed to it in much of the region, but it cannot be explained by them alone. Many intensely nationalist leaders have believed that aligning their countries with either major bloc would involve subordinating their policies to those of one or the other of the great powers, thereby compromising the independence which they have so recently attained. Others have genuinely felt that they cannot subscribe fully to the ideological or political positions of either of the major blocs. Most of the leaders who have fitted this category actually have had stronger ideological affinities with the West than with communism, but they have not wished to identify themselves wholly with either side. Many have felt that their countries are so weak, and so overwhelmed with internal problems, that they must avoid any sort of international involvement which might divert resources and energies from their main tasks at home. Others have believed that Communist China's great power leaves them no alternative but to accommodate their policies to placate Peking—at least to the point of avoiding any provocation. Some have been convinced that "positive neutralism" can help to maintain peace, ease international tensions, and prevent conflicts between the major powers. For them, nonalignment has not been a passive attitude, but rather it has expressed a desire to play an active, mediating role in world affairs.

Many of Communist China's greatest political gains in South and Southeast Asia between 1954 and 1959 can be traced directly to its tactical decision to endorse neutralism— as a desirable policy for others, not for itself—and dealing with the various forms of neutralism has been a major problem for the United States. Over the past decade the American government has, it is true, maintained friendly relations with all the nonaligned nations in South and Southeast Asia and has provided some of them with large-scale economic assistance. However, the priority which American policy-makers have generally given to the need for building a system of mutual military security directed against potential aggression by Communist China has at times resulted in ambiguity and vacillation in Washington's attitudes toward the nonaligned nations; this has made many of the leaders of these nations critical of American policies and has inevitably complicated American relations with them.

If only because of its dominant position in South Asia, India has held a special place in Peking's policy. Undoubtedly, the Chinese Communists regard India, like Japan, as a major competitor for influence throughout Asia, but between 1954 and 1959 they attempted to work toward many of their aims by cooperating with the Indians. In this period both Peking and New Delhi played up the elements of cooperation in their relations and rarely acknowledged they were in any way engaged in a competition. Yet, in a fundamental sense Communist China and India are competitors throughout the entire region. In South Asia the conflict of their interests has become most obvious in the Himalayan region where the two countries touch, but Peking has also tried persistently to increase its influence on all of India's neighbors. In Southeast Asia competition between them will unquestionably be a major factor influencing the shape of things to come. Historically, both China and India have exerted significant cultural, economic, and political influences in Southeast Asia. Today, Peking is clearly attempting to establish its own predominance in that region, and in many respects its influence appears to have grown more rapidly than India's.

The Importance of Southeast Asia

Southeast Asia is a crossroads area, and repeatedly it has been controlled or decisively affected by external power and influences. Culturally fragmented and politically divided, it has frequently constituted a power vacuum, inviting the intervention of foreign powers.

The lure of Southeast Asia is tremendous, today as in the past. Its total population, slightly larger than that of the United States, is spread over a vast and rich tropical area, extending more than 3,000 miles from east to west and over 2,000 miles from north to south. It lies astride some of the world's most strategic lines of sea and air communication. Except for a few crowded areas, such as Indo-China's Red River Valley, Central Luzon, and Java, it is generally underpopulated—in striking contrast to the largest Asian nations,

China, India, and Japan, all three of which have been attracted in varying degrees and ways by its economic potential.

For many years Southeast Asia has been Asia's rice bowl, and its surplus, currently amounting to between three and four million tons annually, has helped meet the needs of nearby deficit areas.[5] It possesses great wealth in natural resources. Although these resources have been only partially exploited, Southeast Asia nevertheless supplies approximately 90 per cent of the world's crude rubber, 60 per cent of its tin, and 80 per cent of its copra and coconut oil. It is the world's largest exporter of rice, quinine, kapok, teak, pepper, and tapioca flour, and it also exports sizable quantities of sugar, tea, coffee, tobacco, sisal, fruits, spices, natural resins and gums, petroleum, iron ore, and bauxite. Yet, in terms of its economic potential, Southeast Asia is still very underdeveloped. Agriculture, which currently provides 70 per cent of its total production, could yield much more, and industrialization has barely started. All these economic and strategic factors have attracted European and Japanese colonialism in the past, and they invite Communist China's attention today.

Culturally, both South and Southeast Asia are more heterogeneous than Europe. They are fragmented by many racial, linguistic, religious, and other differences. And politically, both areas are disunited; despite efforts to promote regional cooperation, little progress has been made toward effective political regionalism. There are numerous antagonisms within the region, the result both of past conflicts and present rivalries. And in their approaches to the broad problems of international relations, the local leaders represent widely differing outlooks; the contrasts between Indian and Filipino foreign policies over the past decade, for example, have probably been as great as those which have divided any two non-Communist countries anywhere. Because of this diversity, it is essential to examine Peking's relations with South and Southeast Asia on a country-by-country basis, at least to the extent of pointing out some of the special factors which have shaped its relations with individual countries.

Vietnam

Historically, China's influence has been greater in Vietnam than in any other country in Southeast Asia. Vietnam is the only Southeast Asian nation which might, like Korea in Northeast Asia, be classified as belonging basically to the area of Sinic culture; its culture represents a blending of indigenous and Chinese elements. Like the Thais, Laotians, and Burmans, the Vietnamese migrated southward from China many centuries ago, and the term "Viet" probably derives from Yüeh, the name of an ancient state in China. Over the past 2,000 years Chinese conquerors have repeatedly incorporated part or all of what is now Vietnam into the Chinese empire, and the Vietnamese have repeatedly attempted to assert their independence or autonomy.[6] From the first Chinese conquest in the third century B.C. until the establishment of French control in the nineteenth century, Vietnam's political relationship to China generally alternated between direct subjugation and vassalage. The Chinese exercised direct control over at least part of what is now Vietnam during 221-214 B.C., 111 B.C.-40 A.D., 43-543 A.D., 603-938 A.D., and 1407-1427 A.D.; thereafter, the Vietnamese acknowledged China's suzerainty until 1885, when the French gained control. Over long periods important areas of Vietnam, including Tongking and Annam, were administered as parts of China, and since the first migration of Chinese to the area took place in the third century B.C. there have been numerous periods of substantial Chinese colonization.

Although the Ch'ing or Manchu Dynasty, which came to power in China in the seventeenth century, was more interested in expanding its rule in Central Asia than in Southeast Asia, like every strong Chinese dynasty it also showed great interest in areas to the south. It imposed a tributary status on Vietnam, as well as on Laos, Siam, and Burma, and it treated all these countries as buffer areas. The Ch'ing rulers carried out several invasions of Vietnam, and on numerous occasions they intervened directly in its internal struggles. Until 1885 the rulers of Vietnam received investiture from Peking, and they were expected to visit the Chinese capital every four years and to send tribute missions to China every two years.

During the period of French rule in Indo-China the Chinese were forced to renounce all their claims to Indo-China, and the French, taking advantage of China's weakness, actually marked out a sphere of influence in the South China provinces of Kwangsi and Yunnan. But even under French rule Vietnamese politics remained closely linked with China, and the development of modern revolutionary and nationalist movements followed parallel lines in the two countries.

When World War II weakened the French position in Indo-China, the Chinese again sought to expand their influence there. In accordance with decisions made at the Potsdam Conference in 1945, Chinese Nationalist forces occupied northern Vietnam immediately after the defeat of Japan and attempted, unsuccessfully, to install the Vietnamese Nationalist party in power. Then the Kuomintang government exacted numerous concessions from the French, including special privileges for the Chinese living in Vietnam, before agreeing to withdraw in 1946. This postwar occupation left a residue of bitter feelings against the Chinese among both the Vietnamese and the French.

Communist China's ambitions in Vietnam have been nourished, therefore, by China's historic traditions as well as by revolutionary zeal. Almost all strong Chinese governments have regarded Vietnam both as a strategic buffer and as a natural sphere of China's influence; the present Peking regime is no exception. But, in addition, the Chinese Communists have had special ideological and political bonds with the Communist-led Vietminh and have regarded them as comrades in a world-wide revolutionary movement.

The Chinese Communists recognized the Vietminh-created "Democratic Republic of Vietnam" in early 1950, even before the Soviet Union did, and they began almost immediately to provide it with military support.[7] Then at the Geneva Conference of 1954 the Chinese Communists played a major role in working out the truce formula which led to a division of Vietnam and the incorporation of its northern half into the Communist bloc.

Since 1954 Peking has devoted major resources to the

building up of North Vietnam as a close ally. It has provided substantial economic aid to the Vietnamese, has assisted them in building up their communications and industries, and has helped them expand and equip their armed forces. Apparently, however, Peking has been cautious about intervening directly in their domestic political affairs. Traditional Vietnamese hostility toward the Chinese has not been completely eliminated merely because the leaders of the two countries now have a close ideological and political affinity. This may, in fact, have been one factor which deterred Peking from intervening directly in 1953-1954, although there were other factors which were probably more important, including Peking's desire to avoid an open military conflict with the United States, and its decision to shift to tactics of "coexistence."

Today Peking clearly regards North Vietnam as a firm ally and a valuable base for expanding Communist influence elsewhere in Southeast Asia. It apparently finds it expedient to leave the initiative for Communist activities in South Vietnam and Laos largely in North Vietnamese hands, even though Communist strategy toward both these areas is doubtless formulated jointly in Peking and Hanoi. The Chinese Communists give full backing to North Vietnam's moves, however, and Hanoi's policies are coordinated closely with Peking's general strategy.

At the time of the partition in 1954 Chinese and Vietnamese Communist leaders may have believed that the regime in North Vietnam would be able to achieve political control over the South fairly soon, either through nation-wide elections, which the Geneva agreements called for, or through subversion. The success with which Diem's regime in South Vietnam, with strong American backing, has consolidated its rule has frustrated any such hope, however. And South Vietnam, which was not a signatory to this part of the Geneva agreement, has refused to agree to nation-wide elections which the Communists, through their totalitarian control over a majority of Vietnam's total population, might well expect to win in the absence of effective guarantees for free elections.

North Vietnam, with Chinese Communist backing, has

continued to press for elections on its own terms. And since 1958 it has made an increasing number of overtures to Diem's regime for more trade and other contacts between North and South.[8] At the same time, however, it has stepped up its subversive activities in South Vietnam and has supported the Pathet Lao's insurrection in Laos. All of these moves have been backed by Peking and coordinated with similar moves made by the Communist regime in North Korea. In effect, the Communists now appear to regard the struggle between the North Vietnamese and South Vietnamese regimes as one of long-term economic and political competition, but, as recent Vietnamese pressures on Laos indicate, they can be expected to probe any weak spots on North Vietnam's periphery.

India

Communist China's relations with India have gone through several distinct phases since 1949. When they first came to power, the Chinese Communists showed open hostility and contempt for India's non-Communist leaders. Then in 1954 they began a major campaign to promote friendly relations with India, hoping thereby to expand their influence throughout the underdeveloped and uncommitted areas of the world. More recently, ever since the hardening of Peking's policies in 1957, the Chinese Communists' deference to Indian attitudes has steadily decreased and in the 1959 border crisis Peking adopted a threatening attitude which had profoundly adverse effects on Indian feelings toward China.

In the period after the "five principles of peaceful coexistence" were first unveiled in the Sino-Indian agreement of 1954, both the Indians and the Chinese Communists went to great lengths to stress their common Asian heritage, highlighting the contacts which have taken place between their two countries in the past. Actually, however, Indian and Chinese cultures are very different, as an increasing number of Indians have recognized. And, despite the transmission of Buddhism from India to China almost two millennia ago, relations between the two countries were minimal until recently.

In the early years of the present century contacts increased slowly. After 1911 Indian intellectuals became interested in the nationalist movement in China, and Tagore's visit to China in the 1920s aroused a new interest in the past relations between the two nations. When Nehru visited China in 1939, he showed strong sympathy for the Chinese struggle against Japan. However, when Chiang K'ai-shek visited India in 1942, although he evoked some expressions of Indian sympathy, he was unable to persuade the Indian nationalists, then immersed in their own struggle for independence, to support the war against Japan. After the war diplomatic relations were established for the first time in 1947, but the Indians soon lost all enthusiasm for the Chinese Nationalist regime. When the Communists came to power in 1949, the Indian government immediately adopted a friendly attitude toward the Peking regime, and India was the second non-Communist country to recognize it.

From the start Indian leaders viewed the Communist revolution in China primarily as a part of a general Asian revolt against colonialism and backwardness rather than as a part of an expansionist world-wide revolutionary movement. As they saw it, the Communists had won the civil war in China, and other nations should refrain from interfering in China's affairs. They minimized the possibility of any threat from Communist China to India or, for that matter, to any Asian nation. And they reasoned that unfriendly policies would merely antagonize the Chinese Communists, make them more belligerent, and force them into increasing dependence on the Soviet Union. In the Indian view the policy of nonalignment, which had been adopted even before the events of 1949, called for active efforts to develop friendly relations with both Communist and non-Communist countries. New Delhi's attitude toward Peking was a logical expression of this basic approach to world affairs, and the Indians began immediately to enlarge their contacts with Communist China through cultural exchanges and trade as well as through diplomacy.

From 1949 until 1954 the initiative for promoting friendly

relations came primarily from the Indians, and India became Communist China's most important supporter in the non-Communist world. It acted repeatedly as a voluntary advocate for Peking's interests and attempted to mediate between Peking and the West. At first, Communist China by no means fully reciprocated this enthusiasm for developing closer relations, however, and it ignored Indian attitudes and interests whenever it chose to do so. In 1949 Peking was still labeling Nehru, along with all non-Communist Asian leaders, as a "running dog" of "imperialism," to be overthown by the Indian Communists as soon as possible.[9] In 1950 the Chinese Communists invaded Tibet without even informing the Indians, although India had urged peaceful negotiations between the Chinese and Tibetans. To a mildly reproachful note deploring this resort to force, Communist China replied by accusing the Indian leaders of being "affected by foreign influences hostile to China in Tibet," and it proceeded with its military occupation.[10]

Communist China's attitudes began to change somewhat in 1951, when it signed its first trade contracts with India and approved of several important exchange visits. Then from 1952 on Peking began seriously to cultivate its "people's diplomacy" and trade with India. In late 1952, however, it spurned the Indian attempts to work out a compromise on the prisoner-of-war issue in Korea, and it denounced Krishna Menon's formula as "this illegal resolution which has as its basic content the United States 'principle of voluntary repatriation' under an Indian cloak." [11]

None of Peking's actions, not even its invasion of Tibet, altered New Delhi's resolve to be friendly toward Communist China. In fact, Indian leaders in one situation after another actively opposed Western policies toward China, and they were indefatigable in attempting to mediate between Peking and the West. Although India had endorsed the original United Nations intervention in Korea, it warned the West that any advance beyond the 38th Parallel would bring Communist China into the war, and when Peking did intervene, the Indians opposed the United Nations resolution branding Communist China as an aggressor. From 1950 on India pressed repeatedly for the seating of Communist

China in the United Nations. It opposed the United States "neutralization" of Taiwan in 1950 and endorsed Peking's claims to the island. It also criticized strongly the peace treaty with Japan, partly because it had been negotiated without the participation of Communist China. In 1952 India played the role of a mediator in the complicated efforts to achieve a truce in Korea. And in 1954 it opposed what it considered to be United States intervention in Indo-China and showed considerable sympathy for the Vietminh and their Chinese Communist supporters. Indian diplomats also played an important behind-the-scenes role in the Geneva negotiations on Indo-China in 1954. Throughout this period, fundamental disagreements on policy toward China were a major obstacle to close Indian-American relations, probably second in importance only to differences over Kashmir and American aid to Pakistan. As one major study of Indian-American relations put it, "at the heart of Indian-American differences over East Asia" has been "the so-called 'China Question,' which the two countries approach from profoundly divergent perspectives." [12]

The signing of the Sino-Indian agreement on Tibet in 1954 initiated a "honeymoon period" for Peking and New Delhi, and the initiative for closer relations now came from Peking as well as New Delhi.[13] The leaders of the two largest Asian nations became cosponsors of the "five principles of peaceful coexistence," publicly affirming their joint opposition to colonialism, military pacts, atomic weapons, and many other aspects of Western policies in Asia. Chou En-lai's visit to New Delhi in mid-1954, Nehru's visit to Peking later in the same year, and the cooperation of these two leaders at the Bandung Conference of 1955 had a strong impact upon the entire situation in Asia. New Delhi supported the Chinese Communists' claims to Taiwan, and Peking backed up Indian claims to Goa. Both attacked SEATO, the Baghdad Pact, and other United States-sponsored military alliances. They glossed over their basic differences in ideology and foreign policy, stressing areas of common agreement. Peking made some concessions to India. It seemingly ignored Nehru's uncompromising opposition to the Communists within India, and gave repeated assurances that it would not interfere in the domestic affairs of other nations. When Nehru raised specific issues, such as the activities of Overseas Chinese, which were causing apprehension in Southeast Asia, Chou's responses were conciliatory and reasonable. It was the Indians, however, who made the most significant real concessions, particularly in regard to Tibet.

Tensions in the Himalayan Region

The Chinese invasion of Tibet in 1950 caused sharp differences between China and India, and it shocked many Indians deeply. Though India at no time disputed China's suzerainty there, it had inherited from the British a special interest and special position in Tibet, and at first the Indians tended to regard Tibet as an important buffer area. In 1950 the Indians, following the British example, still maintained a special political representative, trade agencies, postal and telegraph installations, and even a small military contingent in Tibet. Yet when the Chinese Communists decided to "liberate" Tibet by force, although the Indian government protested, it felt that it must sacrifice its interests there for the broader aim of good relations with Peking. When, after considerable delay, an agreement on Tibet was signed by the Indians and the Chinese Communists in 1954, New Delhi agreed in effect to abandon completely its special position and special interests in Tibet.

Ever since 1950 the Himalayan frontier region has been the main area where Peking's policies have created concern on the part of India. Many Indians, military leaders in particular, were sensitive from the start about China's growing power just north of their borders, realizing that pressures from Tibet could increase and that Chinese economic and political penetration of the Himalayan area would affect Indian security adversely.[14] Until 1959, however, although a few minor incidents involving Chinese troops occurred on India's borders, the principal irritant and cause of apprehension was Peking's game of "mapsmanship"—which some Indians labeled "cartographic aggression." Numerous maps published in Communist China showed fairly large portions of India's Northeast Frontier Agency, Bhutan, and Ladakh (in Kashmir) within China's boundaries.[15] In response to Indian diplomatic inquiries about these maps, Peking blandly claimed that they were merely old ones drawn up by the Nationalists. But the Chinese Communists persisted in issuing such maps and refused to make it clear that they accepted India's existing boundaries, such as the McMahon line.

Apprehension about the border regions led India gradually to build up its frontier defenses all along its northern boundaries—in Ladakh, Uttar Pradesh, and the northeast frontier area. It also stimulated the Indians to cement their ties with the small independent or autonomous areas in the Himalayan region. In 1949 and 1950 India signed treaties with Bhutan and Sikkim, strengthening its control over their foreign relations. Nehru also made it clear that he regarded Bhutan as being within India's own frontier for defense purposes, and in Sikkim India acquired the right to station Indian troops and to "take such measures as it considers necessary for the defense" of that small state.[16] As a result of these moves, Bhutan and Sikkim became protectorates of India, as they were previously of Britain.

India also took steps to strengthen its relations with Nepal, and in 1950 it signed a treaty with the Nepalese calling for consultation in the event of any external threat to either signatory. Thereafter, India provided Nepal substantial economic aid, helped to improve its army and defenses, and exercised varying degrees of control over its foreign trade. It also exerted a strong and continuing influence upon political developments within Nepal.

Meanwhile, however, Peking also pursued an energetic program to build up its own influence in Nepal, and, as a result, this small landlocked neutralist nation became an important arena of competition between China and India.

In the past Nepal, like almost all the small countries on China's periphery, has periodically been subjected to strong Chinese pressure or influence.[17] In the late eighteenth century a quarrel over Tibet led China to invade Nepal. After their defeat in this war the Nepalese were forced to acknowledge Chinese suzerainty, and from then until 1910 they were required to pay tribute to China every five years. On the other hand, in the 1850s Nepal defeated Tibet in a war and forced the Tibetans to pay annual tribute to Nepal, to grant it certain extraterritorial rights, and to permit the stationing of Nepalese troops in Tibet at several trading stations. These relationships with Tibet and China were extremely important. They were actually less important to Nepal, however, than Nepal's ties with British India. The British authorities in India converted Nepal into a protectorate and exercised a paramount influence there until 1947. Then the Indians extended their influence into the vacuum created by the British withdrawal.

The Chinese Communist occupation of Tibet in 1950 almost immediately had repercussions on Nepal. It confronted the Nepalese with the problem of infiltration, and they began strengthening their border security system to counter pressures from the north. In 1953 Tibet stopped its annual tribute payments to Nepal.[18] Then, after the Sino-Indian agreement on Tibet, the Chinese Communists initiated conversations with the Nepalese in 1954, aimed at the establishment of formal relations. At Bandung, the meeting of the Chinese and Nepalese delegates laid the groundwork for serious negotiations, and finally in mid-1955 a Chinese Communist delegation visited Katmandu where it signed an agreement in which the two governments recognized each other and agreed to exchange Ambassadors [19]—although, for the time being, in deference to India, they agreed that their representatives in New Delhi were to serve concurrently as Ambassadors to each other. In 1956 a new Sino-Nepalese treaty, with an accompanying exchange of notes, put an end to all special Nepalese rights in Tibet, including the right to station Nepalese military contingents there; [20] it provided, however, for the establishment of Nepalese trading posts in Tibet and similar Chinese posts in Nepal, and for the opening of consulates in both Lhasa and Katmandu. In late 1956, when Nepal's Prime Minister visited Peking, the Chinese Communists announced a sizable grant of economic aid to the Nepalese—without "strings" and without Chinese technicians. Chou En-lai made a return trip to Katmandu in early 1957, and thereafter numerous cultural and other contacts developed. Despite India's desire that other countries restrict their direct dealings with the Nepalese to a minimum, Communist China worked steadily to develop its own contacts and channels of influence in Nepal.

The growth of Chinese influence in Nepal disturbed many Indians. Until 1959, however, its principal effect on Nepal was probably the reinforcing of its policy of nonalignment. As a small and weak nation, which has only recently begun to develop its own foreign relations, Nepal has been extremely wary of influences from both north and south.

While a few Indians viewed all of China's efforts to expand its influence in the Himalayan region with suspicion and apprehension from the start, tensions in this area were consciously played down by both Peking and New Delhi until 1959. The Indian government, pursuing its policy of nonalignment, tended to regard border frictions in the Himalayan area as no more than minor irritants, and most Indians seemed to feel that any open clash of Chinese and Indian interests would be unthinkable. Then in 1959 India received a rude shock. The Tibetan rebellion and Peking's subsequent actions on the India border created acute tensions in Sino-Indian relations, which significantly altered the character of relations between the two countries and affected attitudes in ways which will doubtless have consequences for some time to come.

New Antagonisms in Sino-Indian Relations

The cordiality in relations between India and Communist China, which reached its peak soon after the Bandung Conference, started undergoing a significant cooling off in 1957. Many developments within Communist China—such as the repression of intellectuals after the "hundred flowers" episode of 1957 and the communization of the villages in 1958— shocked the Indians. Indian opinion was adversely affected by Peking's attitudes toward the Hungarian uprising in 1956, by its campaign of vituperation against Tito in 1958, and by other evidences of the hardening of its policies. In this period, many Indian leaders, including Nehru, also showed increasing concern about the growth of communism in India, and became increasingly aware of the Indian Communist party's links with the international Communist movement. Slowly, they also became more aware of the competition between India and Communist China for influence throughout South and Southeast Asia, a contest between different political and economic philosophies the outcome of which will greatly affect all of the underdeveloped countries of the world.

Then, the Tibetan revolt in early 1959 had a tremendous impact on India—and on most of South and Southeast Asia—and evoked widespread and bitter criticism of the Chinese Communists' policies. Peking's brutal suppression of the revolt, and its scrapping of the 1951 Sino-Tibetan agreement which had promised local autonomy, were openly denounced. Even Nehru, while emphasizing the necessity for maintaining friendly relations between India and Communist China, was extremely critical of Peking; he bluntly rejected the Chinese Communists' charges that Indians had instigated the revolt in Tibet and decided to grant refuge to the Dalai Lama and over 13,000 Tibetan refugees. Peking fanned the deep resentments in India by claiming that the revolt had been plotted from the Indian hill-city of Kalimpong and by assailing so-called Indian "expansionists."

In the months that followed, frictions and tensions in the frontier region grew, reaching a high point in August and September. In late August Nehru brought the border issue into the open and told the Indian people for the first time about a series of border clashes which had occurred. He accused the Chinese of penetrating the Indian border at two points in the Northeast Frontier Agency and of having actually built a road through Indian territory in Ladakh. Shortly thereafter, the Indian government published a White Paper recounting a long history of diplomatic exchanges concerning the border. Charges and countercharges then became increasingly acrimonious on both sides. The Chinese Communists accused India of numerous incursions into territory claimed by China, asserted that Indian policy was "two-faced," and called, in effect, for a renegotiation of the entire frontier. Nehru accused Peking of "aggression," declaring that the Chinese were motivated by the "pride and arrogance of might"; he also reaffirmed India's determination to defend not only its own territory but also Bhutan and Sikkim. While stressing the need to negotiate a settlement of border disputes, he asserted that India would only consider minor adjustments in the frontier, and he rejected Peking's claims to thousands of miles of Indian territory, as indicated by Chinese Communist maps.

The effects of all these developments on Indian attitudes toward China were very great, and in some respects this began to influence Indian policies. With a new awareness of the security problem posed by Peking, the Indians stepped up their efforts to strengthen their defenses in the north and to form even closer ties with the small Himalayan states between India and Tibet. Yet, there was little sign of any immediate change in the basic principles underlying India's foreign policy. Indian leaders and diplomats reaffirmed their policy of nonalignment and restated their belief that Communist China should be brought into the United Nations. They refused to back the Dalai Lama's plea for United Nations support for Tibet's freedom and reiterated their view that Tibet is legally Chinese territory. In short, despite their new suspicion and hostility toward Peking, they persisted in their firm adherence to the essential concepts of their own particular form of neutralism.

Pakistan and Ceylon

Pakistan recognized the Peking regime in early 1950, soon after it came to power, and exchanged Ambassadors with it in 1951. In the following years, the Chinese Communists' desire to buy cotton, and the Pakistanis' eagerness to sell it, led to a significant growth of trade between the two countries. Exploiting the fact that China possesses a sizable Muslim population, Peking also attempted to foster closer relations by encouraging contacts between various Muslim organizations in the two countries.

In 1954 Pakistan's decision to join SEATO was denounced by Peking, but this did not seem to affect relations between the two countries very much. Actually, in joining the alliance, the Pakistanis had their eyes focused primarily on New Delhi and Moscow, rather than on Peking, and they showed little fear of Communist China or hostility toward it. On the Kashmir question which has preoccupied the Pakistanis above all else, Peking has stressed the need to reach a settlement through negotiation, a stand which has contrasted with Moscow's unequivocal support of the Indians. In the years between 1954 and 1959, while relations between Communist China and Pakistan were considerably less cordial than those between Peking and the nonaligned countries, they were nevertheless correct and relatively friendly, and in some respects they were particularly important as a symbol of Peking's declared readiness to deal even with those Asian countries belonging to the U.S.-supported, anti-Communist alliances.

In its dealings with Ceylon Communist China from the start assiduously fostered neutralism, and by doing so it undoubtedly reinforced the existing neutralist forces there. The government of Ceylon recognized Peking in early 1950 and although formal diplomatic relations were not established until 1956, important economic exchanges developed much earlier. Rubber has clearly been the most important factor in relations between Communist China and Ceylon ever since 1952 when the two countries signed a five-year agreement for the exchange of rice for rubber. Ceylon's decision to supply China with rubber at that time had significant political as well as economic implications, since the United States was working tirelessly to develop effective economic sanctions against Peking. Ever since 1952 trade between Communist China and Ceylon has been important to both countries; trade with Communist China represents a larger share of Ceylon's total foreign trade, in fact, than it does in the case of any other South or Southeast Asian country. Until fairly recently religion has also been a factor in Sino-Ceylonese relations, and over the past decade there have been a number of contacts and exchanges between Peking's government-controlled religious organizations and Buddhist groups in Ceylon. Since the Dalai Lama's bitter denunciations of Peking, however, the Chinese Communists' ability to exploit Buddhism for political purposes has doubtless declined sharply.

As long as Sir John Kotelawala was Prime Minister, the government of Ceylon, although inclined toward nonalignment, was openly critical of some aspects of Communist China's foreign policy. At the Bandung Conference, Kotelawala assailed Communist colonialism and even attempted to promote his own formula for a "two Chinas" solution of the Taiwan issue. After 1956, however, Ceylon, under the premiership of S. W. R. D. Bandaranaike, moved steadily toward a nonaligned position, and Peking did all it could to encourage this trend. Following the agreement to exchange diplomatic representatives, Chou En-lai visited Ceylon in early 1957; later in the year Communist China signed a new trade agreement with Ceylon and made a sizable economic grant to it. In 1958 it gave further economic assistance in the form of a loan. Since then, however, Ceylon has been affected, as have almost all South and Southeast Asian nations, by the events in Tibet and on India's northern border.

Burma

As a prime mover, together with India and Indonesia, in the Colombo group of South and Southeast Asian nations (the other members being Ceylon and Pakistan), Burma over most of the past decade has been one of the main sponsors of neutralism in the area, and as such it has been a primary target of Peking's "coexistence" policy. Burma was the first non-Communist nation to recognize Communist China, and it had special reasons for doing so. In addition to any ideological or emotional predisposition, such as India's, to view the Chinese Communists primarily as Asians rather than as Communists, fear of China has from the start been a basic element in Burmese attitudes toward Peking. Ever since 1949 Burmese leaders have had a deep apprehension, rooted in history, about the influence which their powerful neighbor to the north might try to bring to bear upon them.[21]

The Burmese policy of nonalignment—which at different times has been labeled "neutrality," "nonpartisanship," and an "independent course"—took clear shape only in late 1949, when the Communists were consolidating their power in China. Just one week before Burma recognized Peking, Prime Minister U Nu declared that Burma certainly did not have to adopt communism "merely because Chinese Communists are overrunning China," but, he warned, "our tiny nation cannot have the effrontery to quarrel with any power." [22] In some respects Burma's policy toward China might better be called one of nonprovocation rather than neutralism.

For many centuries the Chinese impact upon Burma has been very great. Not only the Burmans, but also minority groups such as the Chins, Kachins, and Shans, and possibly the Karens, came originally from what is now China and were forced southward under steady Chinese pressure, starting as early as the second century B.C. Some of the small states first formed in Burma are believed to have been tributary to the T'ang Dynasty, between the seventh and tenth centuries A.D. When Burma was unified under the Pagan Dynasty, in the eleventh century, it probably paid tribute to the Nanchao Kingdom in China, which was itself tributary to the Sung Dynasty. Later the Mongols, after absorbing Nanchao, twice attacked Burma and helped to undermine the Pagan state. The Ming rulers of China attempted to exercise suzerainty over the states of Upper and Eastern Burma during most of their reign, at least until the late fifteenth century. And in the late eighteenth century the Manchus tried to reimpose vassalage on Burma. After the Burmese had defeated the Manchus in the period of the "four invasions," the two countries finally agreed to an exchange of missions every ten years. China's rulers regarded these missions as a symbol of Burma's vassalage, but the Burmese consistently denied that they were really tributary to China.[23]

In the nineteenth century the British moved into Burma, motivated in considerable part by an interest in trade with southwest China. After deciding to annex Upper Burma, however, they immediately encountered problems in their relations with the Chinese, and in order to come to terms with Peking they signed a treaty with China in 1886, calling for the establishment of one commission to demarcate the boundary and another to promote trade. Surprisingly, the British in this treaty acknowledged the Chinese claim that Burma had been a vassal by agreeing that, "as it has been the practice of Burma to send decennial missions to China," this practice would be continued.[24]

The boundary problem proved to be a difficult one to resolve, however. In 1894, after a partial survey had been carried out, a convention was signed demarcating one part of the boundary, but the area north of 25°35′N (the latitude of Myitkyina) was left undefined.[25] In 1895, in retaliation for China's having ceded to France territory which it had agreed in the previous year not to cede to any third power, the British ended the "tributary" missions to China, forced the Chinese to lease them the border district of Namwan, and insisted on setting up another boundary commission. During 1897-1900 this new commission surveyed the border area north of the Shan states. However, some 200 miles of the frontier, in the area of the Wa states, were again left undefined; many conflicting boundary claims remained unresolved; and disputes continued. In 1934 still another commission, under a Swiss officer named Colonel Iselin, who was appointed by the League of Nations, undertook to define the border, but it was forced to abandon its efforts when the Sino-Japanese war broke out, and its findings were never put into effect. Then in mid-1941 the frontier in the Wa states area was clarified by a Sino-British exchange of notes, but the Chinese proceeded almost immediately to ignore this agreement and tried to reopen negotiations. Only when World War II broke out, and Britain and China became allies, did the border issue fall into the background temporarily.

During the war, Burma was extremely important to China—the Burma Road, once it was opened up, became the main overland supply route to China—and immediately after the war the Chinese Nationalist government again reasserted its territorial claims. In 1946 a Chinese force which had occupied a region south of Myitkyina finally withdrew only after the British had threatened to attack it by air.[26] In 1949 the new Burmese state, which had achieved independence less than two years previously and was tottering under the blows of Communist, Karen, and other revolts, had every reason to view with deep apprehension the new Communist regime in China.

Since 1949 the border issue has inevitably reemerged, and numerous other issues have also complicated Sino-Burmese relations. But Peking to date has refrained from taking extreme measures. There are a number of possible explanations for this fact. Immediately after 1949 the Chinese Communists were heavily preoccupied elsewhere, and there was no direct challenge from Western military power in Burma, as there was in both Korea and Vietnam. Moreover, the Communist movement within Burma was so fragmented that Peking would probably have had difficulty in giving it effective support even if it had wished to do so. Then after 1954, because of their shift to "competitive coexistence," the Chinese Communists clearly observed self-imposed restraints and in general emphasized the carrot over the stick in their approaches to Burma.

After 1949 both official relations and "people's diplomacy" developed slowly between Communist China and Burma. Then a big change occurred in 1954. In that year a trade agreement was concluded, Chou En-lai visited Rangoon, where he and U Nu signed a joint communiqué endorsing the "five principles," and U Nu made a return visit to Peking. Agreement was reached during 1954 on the establishment of consulates, the opening up of air and highway communications, and China's purchase of Burmese rice.[27] It was also agreed that each government should urge its nationals living in the other country to abide by all local laws, that they should negotiate on the citizenship of these nationals, and that they should settle all border problems amicably. During his stay in Peking U Nu also assured China that the Burmese would never allow their country to be used as a base for subversion or military action against China.

Both trade and religion were important factors in the development of closer relations in this period. China's purchases of rice were very helpful to Burma during a period when Rangoon was having marketing difficulties, and although trade in rice subsequently declined, general trade continued to develop. Peking attempted to exploit Buddhism in various ways. During the 2,500th anniversary of Buddhism in 1956-1957, for example, the Chinese Communists sent to Burma a tooth reputed to have come from the mouth of

Buddha, thus, as one writer has remarked, putting "teeth into their diplomacy."[28]

One of the most important factors influencing the development of Sino-Burmese relations in earlier years was the question of the 10,000 or more Chinese Nationalist soldiers who fled to Burma after 1949. These troops, which refused to be disarmed, added greatly to the already grave difficulties which beset the Burmese government in its efforts to pacify the country. Rangoon feared that Communist China might use the presence of the Nationalist troops in the Shan states as a pretext for direct intervention. The support that these troops were receiving from Taiwan made the government of Burma extremely hostile to the Chinese Nationalists, and its suspicions that the United States was also assisting them created serious tensions in Burmese-American relations, which led the government of Burma to ask the United States economic aid mission to leave the country. Peking did not intervene, however, and finally in 1953 Burma raised the issue in the United Nations, where a resolution was adopted condemning the presence of foreign troops on Burmese soil.[29] The United States, Nationalist China, and Thailand then cooperated in evacuating some of these troops from Burma. This reduced the problem, but it did not eliminate it, and for several years Burmese attitudes toward Communist China and Taiwan, and toward the United States as well, were greatly influenced by this protracted dispute.

Although Peking refrained from direct intervention over this issue, it has used other channels, some subtle and some not so subtle, to exert pressure on Burma, and under the surface of cordial relations a deep sense of uneasiness has continued to plague the Burmese, reinforcing their determination to avoid provoking Peking in any way.

Clandestine contacts between Burmese Communists and China, large-scale illegal immigration into Burma from China, the establishment by Peking of autonomous minority areas bordering Burma, the presence in China of the Kachin rebel Naw Seng, reports of Chinese encouragement for Kachin separatism, the manipulation by the Chinese Communist Embassy and banks of the Overseas Chinese, and Chinese support for Communist-infiltrated Burmese parties such as the National United Front—all these have worried Burma's leaders and continue to worry them today.[30] And despite Peking's seemingly conciliatory attitude whenever the Burmese have raised basic political issues, the most important of these issues remain unresolved. For example, no steps have yet been taken to settle the problem of Overseas Chinese citizenship in Burma, and the border issue—the most troublesome problem in Sino-Burmese relations—also awaits a final solution.

As early as 1951 the Burmese were disturbed by maps coming out of Peking, which, like former Nationalist maps, showed as Chinese territory four disputed areas: the northern frontier above Myitkyina; the Irrawaddy-Salween watershed farther south (including an area containing the villages of Hpimaw, Gawlun, and Kangkang); the so-called Namwan Assigned Tract; and the contested Wa state region.[31] Then, after Chinese Communist troops made several incursions across the border into Burma, the boundary dispute became a public issue, and U Nu discussed it in detail during his second trip to Peking in late 1956. According to U Nu, Peking indicated at that time, that, if it received the Namwan Assigned Tract and the three villages mentioned, it would renounce all other claims. However, no definite agreement has yet been reached. One cause of delay has been opposition within Burma to the idea of giving away any territory, but apparently Peking has also been inclined to delay any final solution of the border issue, perhaps as a means of continuing to apply pressure in order to keep the Burmese uneasy and off balance. As it has recently demonstrated on Tibet's border with India, Peking can step up its pressures at any time, if it so chooses.

Partly because they fear Peking, many Burmese, at least until recently, have been outspokenly critical of United States policy toward China. They have been less critical of SEATO, it is true, than have the Indians or Indonesians. In fact, even though they have wanted no part in SEATO for themselves, some Burmese leaders have clearly felt that American efforts to strengthen military security in the area have had definite advantages for Burma, to the extent that they have restrained Peking without provoking it. Nevertheless, most Burmese leaders have disagreed fundamentally with the United States nonrecognition policy and opposition to the seating of Communist China in the United Nations. U Nu publicly asserted in 1954: "I feel that most of the tensions in East Asia will be relaxed if an understanding can be brought about between the People's Republic of China and the United States of America," [32] and he consistently tried to facilitate such an understanding, on several occasions endeavoring to play a mediating role between Peking and Washington. Since late 1958, however, a subtle change has been taking place in Burma's neutralism. While continuing to adhere to a policy of nonalignment, Burma's new military leaders, headed by Ne Win, have steadily strengthened their ties with the West.

Indonesia

The driving force of anticolonialism has been particularly strong in Indonesia's foreign policy. The claim to West Irian, or Dutch New Guinea, has been virtually a national obsession, and many Indonesian leaders have tended to judge foreign nations by their stand on this issue. Peking, recognizing this, has given Djakarta enthusiastic propaganda support on the West Irian issue,[33] demanding that the Dutch simply get out and turn over the territory to Indonesia. While the United States has endeavored to take into account the interests of the Dutch, the Australians, and the local inhabitants, as well as the Indonesian claims, Peking has not been plagued by such complications and has found it easy to endorse the Indonesian view that this question is a clear-cut issue of righteous Asian nationalism versus nefarious European colonialism. Many Indonesians, on their part, have tended, like the Indians—at least until recently—to view the revolution in China fundamentally in terms of the Asian revolution against imperialism, and they have strongly supported Peking's claims to Taiwan, while criticizing almost every aspect of United States policy toward China.

During 1958, after a serious revolt under anti-Communist leaders had broken out against the Sukarno government, Peking made further political gains by strongly condemning the rebellion and offering to help the government against the rebels.[34] When evidence was uncovered of aid being delivered to the rebels by Taiwan-based planes, the Indonesians' bitterness and hostility toward the Chinese Nationalists, and the resulting suspicion of United States policy, clearly redounded to Peking's advantage. During this same period the Chinese Communists also wooed Indonesia by extending its sizable credits.

Although it is difficult to know how much the domestic strength of the Communist Party of Indonesia has influenced the government's attitude toward Communist China, or, conversely, how much the development of cordial relations between Peking and Djakarta has facilitated the growth of communism within the country, there seems little doubt that these factors have been interrelated. For some years, the Indonesian Communist party has been among the most vocal supporters of many of Sukarno's domestic and foreign policies—including the claim to West Irian, anti-Dutch measures in general, the policy of nonalignment, the development of friendly relations with the Communist bloc, and the idea of "guided democracy." As it emerged as the strongest single party on the island of Java, its growing strength undoubtedly had a significant impact on the foreign policies of Indonesia's successive non-Communist governments. Since 1958, however, military leaders such as Nasution have played an increasingly important role in making Indonesian policy, and they seem to have reduced, or at least contained, the Communists' influence.

Another factor which has influenced Indonesian policies has been the fact that both the personality of Communist China's top leaders and Peking's domestic development programs have had a strong impact upon many Indonesian leaders, including Sukarno. When Chou En-lai stayed on in Indonesia after the Bandung Conference in 1955 to pay an official "state visit," he made a very favorable impression, and the visit produced a joint statement in which the Indonesians associated themselves with the "five principles." Later in the same year Prime Minister Ali Sastroamidjojo visited Communist China, and in 1956 Sukarno made an official tour of both the Soviet Union and Communist China. Sukarno was profoundly impressed by the disciplined activity which he observed in China. Then in early 1957, shortly after returning from this trip, he announced his "conception" of "guided democracy." "Guided democracy" was not, in any sense, borrowed directly from the Chinese Communist political model; on the contrary, it appeared to be an attempt, however uncertain, to combine deep-rooted and traditional Indonesian practices with Western ideas of representative government. However, it did express an urgent desire to find some new political formula to mobilize the country for more effective action, and in his search for a new formula Sukarno may well have been spurred by the contrast between the organized dynamism he saw in China and Indonesia's discouraging disunity and stagnation.

Unlike the small countries bordering Communist China, Indonesia appears, until recently, to have had little or no feeling of a potential military threat from the Chinese Communists. Peking is a long way off, and Indonesia is separated from the mainland by bodies of water. Undoubtedly, this fact has significantly influenced Djakarta's attitude toward SEATO and other military pacts. Like India, Indonesia has tended to view all military alliances in Asia as provocative Western intervention into Asian affairs. However, this attitude may now be changing somewhat, as a result of the Tibetan revolt and the Sino-Indian border clashes. In 1959 Indonesia purchased some arms from the United States, and its new military leaders now seem to be increasingly wary of both local communism and Peking. They have continued, however, to endorse Peking's claims to Taiwan and to support the seating of Communist China in the United Nations.

The issue which has caused the most serious apprehension to Indonesia in its relations with China is the problem of the Overseas Chinese. However, Peking's willingness to compromise on this issue, as evidenced by the signing of a treaty on dual nationality in 1955, had a significant impact upon Indonesian leaders. This was probably, in fact, Peking's most effective single move in its campaign to court Indonesia, but whether or not Peking will continue its conciliatory policy on this issue over the long run remains to be seen.

Cambodia and Laos

Cambodia is a relatively recent recruit into the camp of nonaligned nations maintaining relations with Peking. Although Peking's post-Bandung policies clearly helped to draw Cambodia toward neutralism, essentially it is the contrast between Cambodia's weakness and Communist China's power which has convinced Cambodia's dominant political leader, Prince Norodom Sihanouk, that his country's survival demands a policy of cautious nonprovocation toward Peking.

Prince Sihanouk has expressed perhaps more candidly and succinctly than any other Southeast Asian leader the rationale which has motivated a small and weak country on Communist China's periphery to adopt a policy of nonalignment and partial accommodation to Peking. Writing in mid-1958, he said:

If I have no particular liking for communism, neither have I any cause or means to join a crusade—even a moral one—against the nations that have adopted that ideology and which since 1954 have not given my country sufficient grounds for complaint. It would be absurd to suppose that a tiny country like mine, geographically situated as it is, would risk provoking the Chinese and Soviet colossi now that planes fly so fast and rockets so far. . . . Our neutrality has been imposed on us by necessity. A glance at a map of our part of the world will show that we are wedged in between two medium-sized nations of the Western bloc and only thinly screened by Laos from the scrutiny of two countries of the Eastern bloc, North Vietnam and the vast People's Republic of China. What choice have we but to try to maintain an equal balance between the "blocs"? Are we "pro-Red"? Our neutrality is neither complaisance nor surrender to anyone. . . . We are not a "breach" in the Western bloc merely because we cannot be a "rampart." In the event of a world conflict, we might very well become one of the first victims of a harsh occupation. In that case, the "free world" would have other things to do besides undertaking our liberation—or rather the liberation of what little remained of us. Are we selfish or "wrong-minded" in thinking as we do? I maintain that we are merely being realistic. By practicing genuine neutrality which eliminates any pretext for aggression we have a chance of not bringing down a storm on our heads; and a storm can be dangerous where there is no lightning-conductor.[35]

Peking began cultivating Norodom Sihanouk at the Bandung Conference, where Chou En-lai took part in an informal meeting with representatives of Cambodia, India, and North Vietnam, in which all present pledged their respect for Cambodia's sovereignty.[36] Thereafter, both Chou and Nehru gently led Cambodia along the road to "neutrality." Soon after Bandung Sihanouk publicly stated that he favored recognizing Peking in due time.[37] While visiting Peking the following year, he stressed his country's nonalignment and his disapproval of SEATO. Then in mid-1956 Peking announced a grant of economic assistance to Cambodia—its first grant to any non-Communist country. A trade agreement was also signed between them in 1956, and economic missions were exchanged between the two countries. Chou En-lai visited Cambodia later that year, and while there he publicly urged the Overseas Chinese to keep out of politics. Finally, in mid-1958 Sihanouk decided to establish formal diplomatic relations with Communist China. Following this decision he made a second trip to Peking, where once again the Chinese Communists reiterated their pledges not to interfere in Cambodia's domestic affairs and offered additional economic assistance.[38] These moves came at a time when Cambodia was embroiled in border disputes with both Thailand and South Vietnam, and Sihanouk was doubtless influenced by the strong moral support which Peking gave to his country in these affairs.

Both Communist China and North Vietnam at one time also endeavored to woo Laos, but competing efforts by the United States were more successful, and as Laos moved toward closer association with the West, the Communists stepped up their efforts to subvert it.

At Bandung both Chou En-lai and the Premier of North Vietnam, in a meeting with the Laotian Prime Minister, made pledges to respect the sovereignty of Laos—pledges which soon proved to have little meaning. Subsequently, the Communist-led Pathet Lao movement, presumably with Peking's approval, urged the Laotian government to accept economic assistance from Peking and to establish diplomatic relations with it. In this period, Peking also backed the idea of settling the civil conflict between the Pathet Lao forces and the Laotian government by forming a coalition government to include several Pathet Lao leaders.[39]

Threatened internally, and subjected to pressure by both Hanoi and Peking, the Laotian government finally did agree to a settlement on this basis, and immediately afterward, Prime Minister Souvanna Phouma flew to Peking where, in a joint communiqué with Chou En-lai, he pledged Laos to a "policy of peace and neutrality." [40] In 1956 Souvanna Phouma described Laos as having "a neutral, but not a neutralist position." "Ours is a position," he declared, "of complete neutrality like Switzerland's. . . . There is no question of neutrality between two philosophies, but neutrality between two military blocs. Neutrality is for us a vital necessity." [41]

At that time Laos appeared to be following a path similar to Cambodia's. Then, starting in late 1958, the Laotian government, under Prime Minister Phoui Sananikone, embarked on a very different course; it decided to align itself far more closely with the West. Unlike Cambodia, Laos in this period faced a growing threat from Communists both at home and abroad. In early 1959 the political maneuvering of the Pathet Lao movement stimulated the non-Communist groups in Laos to vote special powers to the government for a one-year period in order to stabilize the internal situation. Then Peking and Hanoi stepped up their pressures from abroad, and in the summer of 1959 insurrection led by the Pathet Lao, with moral support from both Hanoi and Peking, broke out once again.

As these pressures mounted, the leaders of Laos, realizing that continued independence was impossible without external aid, turned to the United States for help. In response, the United States has poured large amounts of both military and economic aid into that small country. Then in September 1959, as the threat posed by the Pathet Lao rebels and their Vietnamese supporters grew to dangerous proportions, the government of Laos accused North Vietnam of aggression. It appealed to the United Nations for help, and in response the Security Council dispatched a special subcommittee to make an on-the-spot inquiry into Laos' charges. As of the autumn of 1959 it was difficult to predict the future course of events in Laos, but it seemed clear that in its struggle for survival the government of Laos had been forced to place increased reliance upon support by the West.

South Vietnam, the Philippines, Thailand, and Malaya

South Vietnam, the Philippines, Thailand, and Malaya have consistently held attitudes and pursued policies very different from those of the nonaligned nations. All four nations have long regarded Peking's military power and subversive activities as a direct and serious threat which demands positive counteraction rather than accommodation. They have made clear their belief that close alignment with the West and military support from the non-Communist powers are essential to their independence and integrity. They have opposed recognition of the Peking regime, and although their attitudes toward United States policy in Asia have varied in some respects, all four have endorsed general policies of active resistance against the dangers of Communist expansionism.

Directly threatened by the Peking-backed regime in North Vietnam, South Vietnam would have had little hope of surviving, to say nothing of achieving its ultimate aim of unifying the country under a democratic non-Communist government, without strong American backing. Unlike Syngman Rhee in Korea, however, Ngo Dinh Diem's posture toward Communist China has not been a bellicose one. He apparently has felt that new military conflict would more likely lead to disaster than to national unification; like the Communists, he seems in practice to have accepted the idea of a long-term political and economic competition between North and South. Clearly, however, he has believed that strong United States economic and military support to the anti-Communist states in the area is essential to prevent any new Communist military aggression.

In some respects the most militantly anti-Communist nation in the area has been the Philippines. Its government has fully endorsed United States policy toward Communist China, and its leaders have been adamant in their stand against recognition of Communist China. Some Philippine leaders have implied that their country might well continue a policy of nonrecognition even if the United States abandoned its opposition to relations with Peking. Despite the physical separation of the Philippines from the Asian mainland by the South China Sea, its leaders have shared with American policy-makers the acute sense of military threat which led to the formation of SEATO, and public opinion in the Philippines has consistently favored strengthening of the alliance. In short, its leaders have strongly backed the development of effective security measures to counter the threat of Chinese Communist aggression and have opposed the trend toward nonalignment in South and Southeast Asia.

Among some Filipinos, however, attitudes toward contacts with Communist China have altered to a degree over the past two years or so, in a period when Philippine-American relations have been strained. In 1958 a trip to Peking by Manila's Vice-Mayor Jesus Marcos Roces aroused considerable public interest about Communist China.[42] Roces' trip probably heightened the Filipinos' awareness of the tremendous changes in China, but, in a sense, it may also have reinforced their underlying fears of the Chinese and antagonism to communism.

Thailand has also been very conscious of the dangers posed by a strong Communist China. Thai leaders have been apprehensive ever since 1949 both about subversion and about a potential military threat from Peking.[43] Their fears have been aroused by many facts and developments. Communist activity is extensive among Thailand's powerful Chinese minority—which forms a larger percentage of the population than in any major Southeast Asian area except Singapore-Malaya. The Vietminh have successfully infiltrated the large Vietnamese minority in northeast Thailand; and the Malayan Communist guerrillas have used one area of south Thailand as a base. Peking has established a Thai Autonomous Area in the Sipsongpanna district of China just north of Thailand's border, and there have been many rumors of a Communist-sponsored "Free Thai movement" in China. Also Communist China has given political asylum to Pridi Phanomyong, who was one of Thailand's two foremost political leaders during the 1930s and 1940s until he was ousted in a coup engineered by Phibul.

Like its neighbors, Thailand has experienced pressure from China repeatedly in the past. Many centuries ago this pressure forced the Thais to move from China to their present homeland, and thereafter it compelled Thailand periodically to acknowledge a tributary relationship to Peking. Until 1946 the Thais avoided establishing formal diplomatic relations with China, and when the Chinese Nationalists then opened an Embassy at Bangkok, the initial impact upon the Overseas Chinese there was disruptive and disturbing.

Thailand's response to the rise of Communist China has been very different from that of Burma and Cambodia. In 1950 it decided to align itself closely with the United States, and in 1954 it joined SEATO. Unlike the nations which have only recently achieved independence after long years of colonial rule, Thailand has not been motivated by intense anticolonialism, and it encounters no serious emotional or psychological barriers to close cooperation with a strong Western power.

The Thais have a long history of independent diplomacy, and over the years they have acquired a realistic—some would say "opportunistic"—view of military and political power. Throughout the colonial period Thailand upheld its position as a buffer state in the heart of Southeast Asia by playing off its British and French neighbors against each other. Its decision in 1950 to align itself closely with the United States represented a realistic adjustment, similar to many it had made in the past, to a new power situation. Recently, Marshal Sarit's government has taken many steps to strengthen Thailand's relations with the United States, to clamp down on communism at home, and to halt the drift toward neutralism which became noticeable during 1957-1958 among some Thai politicians. Yet, in many respects, a close alignment with one great power represents a break with Thailand's tradition as a buffer state, and it is conceivable that Thai leaders might at some future time decide to move toward a more neutralist position, or at least to try to deal directly with both Communist China and the United States. In 1956 Thailand's Foreign Minister, Prince Wan, asserted: "The

Thai Government is not blind. It realizes that the Peiping regime has *de facto* control over the majority of the Chinese people. But being a small nation, Thailand has to wait for the United Nations to admit Communist China before extending recognition." [44]

The Malayan government's attitude toward the Chinese Communists has been shaped primarily by the continuing rebellion of the China-oriented Malayan Communist party against the government and by the fact that close to one-half of Malaya's population is Chinese in origin. Because of their problems at home, the present Malay leaders of the country have good reason to be extremely wary of opening up any new channels for Chinese Communist influence. Before Malaya achieved independence in 1957, the British, despite their recognition of the Peking regime, were adamant in refusing to admit any Chinese Communist representatives into Malaya. Soon after independence Prime Minister Tengku Abdul Rahman declared that the Communist insurrection in Mayala must be ended before his government would even consider establishing diplomatic relations with Peking.[45] Malaya still needs substantial military support from Britain and the Commonwealth in its fight against the Communists within its borders, and consequently it has shown no desire to become nonaligned or to disassociate itself from Western military aid. To date, however, it has avoided participating in SEATO, and despite the policies of the present government there are some groups within Malaya which have favored increased contacts with Communist China.

Peking and the "Committed" Countries

In its policies toward the "committed" countries Peking has tried persistently to foster "creeping neutralism." In 1955 at Bandung the Chinese Communists indicated that they hoped to find some basis for establishing diplomatic relations with Thailand and the Philippines, and in 1957 Peking promptly recognized the new Malayan government. Communist China has energetically promoted trade with several of the "committed" countries—in 1956 an unofficial Singapore-Malaya trade mission was invited to Peking—and during

1957-1958 its exports to Malaya and Thailand grew so rapidly that both countries felt compelled to restrict them. It has also fostered other contacts. A number of Thai individuals and groups have visited Peking, and although to date the Chinese Communists have had relatively few contacts with the Philippines, the trip to Peking by the Vice-Mayor of Manila was significant. As of the autumn of 1959, however, none of these contacts had significantly corroded the anti-Communist position of the "committed" countries or weakened their ties with the United States and the West.

Implications for United States Policy

Throughout the past decade a dilemma for the United States has been posed by the conflict between the real need for effective collective security measures in South and Southeast Asia to counterbalance the growing power of Communist China and the equally important need to cultivate closer relations with the nonaligned nations which, for varying reasons, have opposed military pacts, have criticized anti-Communist policies, have maintained that the chances of conflict can be minimized by granting Peking an international status commensurate with its size and strength, and have urged reducing tensions through promoting a rapprochement between the major Communist and non-Communist powers.

The United States' firm opposition to Chinese Communist expansionism, and the military, political, moral, and economic support which it has furnished to South Vietnam, Thailand, the Philippines, Laos, and Pakistan, have been vital factors in the effort to deter Peking from military adventures in South and Southeast Asia. American security policies have helped to preserve the sovereignty and integrity of these states, and they have been a major factor in deterring the Chinese Communists from adopting more aggressive policies. Even the small nonaligned nations, such as Burma and Cambodia, have profited indirectly from American security policies, and despite their criticisms of United States policies many of their leaders have not been unaware of this fact.

On the other hand, differences in attitudes and policies

toward China have, on many occasions, been a serious irritant in American relations with the major nonaligned countries of South and Southeast Asia, and at times they have tended to reinforce an undesirable image of the United States in that part of the world. Frequently, they have nourished deep-rooted suspicions about American motives in Asia and have served as an unfortunate symbol, particularly in the United Nations and other international bodies, of the divergencies of world outlook which have tended to divide the United States from the nonaligned nations.

Because of the impact of recent events on prevailing attitudes in South and Southeast Asia, differences over China policy may well be less of an irritant in American relations with the nonaligned nations in the period immediately ahead than they have been over the past decade. Yet on issues such as recognition of Peking, and its seating in the United Nations, there is every indication that the neutralist countries will continue to be critical of American policies, and the existence of basic differences on how the non-Communist nations should deal with Peking cannot but detract from the effectiveness of joint measures to deal with the many problems posed by Communist China.

How would United States relations with South and Southeast Asia be affected, first, by rigidly maintaining present policy toward China, or second, by modifying it substantially? Could the United States adjust its China policy in such a way as to promote a broader consensus between itself and the nonaligned nations without seriously weakening or undercutting its relationships with the "committed" nations?

It is difficult, of course, to attempt to answer questions of this sort without examining both the precise nature of various alternative policies and the specific circumstances in which changes of policy might occur. Yet it seems clear that if the United States should adopt new policies toward China which the nonaligned nations regarded as more "flexible" and "reasonable" than its current ones, this would help further to close the gap between our policies and theirs and would probably enhance the possibilities of obtaining greater approval and support from these nations for the United States' general purposes in Asia. Even if new moves in American policy produced no real "solutions" to the basic problems in Sino-American relations, if they at least helped to shift to Peking the onus for the present stalemate in these relations, this might in itself be an important gain. On the other hand, if changes in the United States policy toward China went so far, or were made in such a way, that either the "committed" countries or the small neutralist nations interpreted them as a sign of any fundamental weakening of the United States' determination to oppose Chinese Communist aggression, or as an indication of a slackening of American efforts to counterbalance Peking's growing power and influence, such changes might well undermine the morale and the stability of these countries.

In considering possible changes in United States policy toward China, it is necessary, therefore, to estimate whether, on balance, a more "flexible" policy, if carried out under favorable circumstances, would produce a net gain or a net loss. Some argue that at present the possible gains in relations with South and Southeast Asia from making any significant modifications of existing policies—affecting, for example, the future of the offshore islands, the Chinese seat in the United Nations, or the question of recognition—would be intangible and insubstantial while the possible psychological and political damages might be real and significant. This view is open to serious question, however. Actually, the gains to the United States from a broadening of the consensus between itself and the Asian nations on how to deal effectively with Communist China might be very substantial, and the danger that greater tactical flexibility on the part of the United States in its direct dealings with China would weaken the position of the "committed" nations of South and Southeast Asia should not be exaggerated.

So long as the United States remains firm in its commitments to protect the fundamental interests of the "committed" nations, there is no essential reason why a tactical modification of American policy toward China on specific issues such as the offshore islands, United Nations representation, or recognition should have any significant adverse effect on these nations, or on American relations with them. If the United States should decide to modify its present policies on these issues, it could certainly make it entirely clear to the "committed" nations that a greater "flexibility" in American policy did not imply any weakening of the basic United States determination to protect them against Chinese Communist expansionism.

In any case, whether the United States decides to modify its present policy toward China or maintains it unchanged, it would be a great error, and self-defeating in the long run, for Americans to judge the nations of South and Southeast Asia, or to determine over-all United States policies toward them, according to the degree to which their particular policies toward China conform to current American policy. In South and Southeast Asia as a whole, the essential commitment of the United States must be to encourage and support all non-Communist governments, whether "committed" or nonaligned, in their own national programs of political and economic development.

Communist China casts a lengthening shadow over the future of the whole region. Its persistent efforts to expand its influence make it essential for the United States to devote major efforts to the tasks of counterbalancing Peking's power and coping with the problems posed by the Overseas Chinese, Communist subversion, and Peking's economic penetration. This can best be done by steadily developing closer cooperation between the United States and all the non-Communist nations of the region, whatever their individual tactical approaches to the problems of dealing with Peking.

One important criterion for judging specific American policies toward China problems should be the degree to which they make it more or less difficult for South and Southeast Asian nations to identify their own aims and interests with the broad purposes of American policy. If by adopting a more flexible attitude toward some of the issues involved in its China policy the United States can demonstrate to these nations its positive desire to explore all possible means of generally reducing the existing tensions in Asia, without sacrificing any of the essential interests of the non-Communist nations in order to appease Peking, it is very possible that the American posture and the free world position in Asia as a whole could thereby be significantly improved.

CHAPTER 12

THE SINO-SOVIET ALLIANCE

DURING THE PAST DECADE the Sino-Soviet alliance has become a crucial factor in world politics, and it is no longer realistic to examine the power and aims of either the Soviet Union or Communist China in isolation. These two powers, ruling some 850 million people and comprising the strategic "heartland" of Eurasia, have forged an intimate association—ideological, military, political, and economic—and now pursue joint or coordinated policies toward the non-Communist world. The support which they give each other adds greatly to the capacities of both nations to pursue their common aims.

Numerous common interests have welded the two partners into a strong alliance. However, beneath the façade of monolithic unity, the relationship between Peking and Moscow has by no means been a static one. It has, in fact, been undergoing constant adjustment and change. It is necessary, therefore, in evaluating the strength and purposes of Communist China to take a careful look at the nature of the bonds which link the two countries, the ways in which each partner is influenced by its own outlook and interests, and the sources of actual or potential friction and divergence between them.

The questions most frequently asked about the future of the Sino-Soviet alliance are generally formulated in terms of extremes. Will Peking and Moscow maintain a monolithic unity? Or will the Chinese Communists eventually break with the Russians as the Yugoslavs did in 1948? These questions are certainly relevant, but they may not reveal the practical issues which are likely to be most important during the period immediately ahead. The limited evidence which we have suggests that, like all alliances, even strong ones, the

Sino-Soviet partnership has not been completely monolithic. The evidence available also indicates that in recent years the alliance has grown stronger rather than weaker, and there appears to be little immediate prospect of an open split between the two allies. Probably the most meaningful question now is whether, within the framework of a continuing alliance, there are likely to be significant shifts in relationships, or important strains and tensions, which may affect the alliance and the policies of the two partners. To approach this question realistically, it is necessary to examine how the partnership has evolved in recent years, to define the nature of possible problems, tensions, or divergent interests which may arise within the alliance in the years ahead, and to assess the significance that possible future changes in relations between the two allies may have for the non-Communist world.

Early Relations between the Chinese Communists and Moscow

Although the Sino-Soviet alliance came into formal existence only in 1950 with the signing of a Treaty of Friendship, Alliance, and Mutual Assistance, its origins must be traced to links which were formed thirty years earlier, when the first Comintern representatives reached China. These agents helped a handful of Chinese intellectuals to organize the Chinese Communist party in 1921, and throughout the 1920s Moscow played a decisive role both in selecting the local leadership and in determining the domestic strategy of the Chinese party. During this early period Soviet policies toward China were extremely complex. While maintaining diplomatic relations until 1927 with the weak Chinese national government in Peking, the Russians also supported, with advisers and material aid, the revolutionary efforts of both the Nationalist party and the Communist party, which cooperated in a revolutionary alliance from 1923 until 1927. The relationship of the Chinese Communists to Moscow was further complicated by the bitter struggles then going on within the Soviet party, particularly by the Stalin-Trotsky contest for power. These struggles were intimately related to debates over the correct revolutionary strategy to follow in

China, and they had a profound impact upon the Chinese party.

Following the Nationalist-Communist split of 1927 within China, Soviet advisers were forced to leave the country, and the Chinese Communists themselves were repressed by the Nationalists and driven underground. Then, after a confused period of shifting policies and leadership, the Chinese party, thrown largely onto its own resources, developed an indigenous strategy of armed revolution organized from rural bases. It established revolutionary bases first in the East China province of Kiangsi and later, after the "Long March," in Shensi Province in the Northwest. Mao Tse-tung, who favored a peasant-based revolutionary strategy, emerged from this period of confusion as the party's chief strategist. Mao, who had never been in Moscow, had gained his leadership without Soviet assistance, and his power was based, therefore, on internal rather than Soviet support.

The relationships which developed between the Chinese Communists and Moscow during the 1930s and 1940s, up to the end of World War II, are still obscure in many respects. However, there is no definite evidence that Moscow seriously attempted to intervene in the internal politics of the Chinese Communists, who were then isolated in remote rural areas. In their struggle to expand the area under their control, first in the Northwest, and then, after the start of the Japanese war, throughout the North China countryside—where a vacuum had been created by the Nationalist military withdrawal and the Japanese failure to consolidate control in rural areas—the Chinese Communists fought their own battles, with no significant outside material support. Guidance from Moscow no longer played a decisive role, as it had in earlier years, in determining the leadership and in shaping the domestic strategy of the Communist party in China. The Chinese Communists developed their own unique strategy of guerrilla warfare and built up their own revolutionary strength.

Even in this period, however, the ideological, personal, and other intangible bonds which had linked the Chinese Communist party to Moscow from the start remained strong. According to a top Chinese Communist leader writing in

1949, Mao himself had not made any systematic study of Stalin's many works on China before World War II but had "been able to reach the same conclusions as Stalin on many fundamental problems through his own independent thinking." [1] Still, a large proportion of the top Chinese Communist leaders had received some training in the Soviet Union, and there was never any serious doubt about the fidelity of the party to Moscow. On all major international issues the Chinese Communists adhered faithfully to the line emanating from Moscow, and they supported every major shift in Soviet foreign policy. In their own major policy shifts—for example, in their decision in 1936-1937 to form a second temporary alliance with the Nationalists to fight the Japanese—the Chinese Communists closely followed shifts which had previously taken place in the Russian and Comintern line. Soviet material aid to China during the Sino-Japanese War was channeled to the Nationalist government rather than to the Communists, but there is no significant evidence that the Chinese Communists did not give consistent allegiance to Moscow or that Moscow lost faith in their loyalty.

During the last two years of the war, it is true, Stalin and Molotov made certain deprecatory remarks about the Chinese Communists to American diplomatic representatives. According to Ambassador Patrick J. Hurley, they said that "the Chinese Communists are not in fact Communists at all" and that the "Soviet Union is not supporting the Chinese Communist party." [2] But these statements may well have been deliberately calculated to mislead the United States. At the same time, however, they may also have reflected a certain lack of confidence on the part of the Soviet leaders in the ability of the Chinese Communists to play a primary role in the conflict with Japan, as well as a feeling that Chinese Communist interests had to be subordinated in Soviet policy because of the immediate need for a unified anti-Japanese war effort in China under Nationalist leadership.

Postwar Developments

There is substantial evidence that during and immediately after the war Soviet leaders were uncertain about the Chinese

Communists' prospects. Certainly, at that time the Russians did not rely on the Chinese Communist party as the principal instrument of their policy in China. With almost no reference to the Chinese Communist movement, the Soviet leaders pressed for the reestablishment of Russia's special rights in China, such as had existed under past Tsarist regimes. At the Yalta Conference in February 1945 Stalin extracted from Great Britain and the United States the promise that, in return for Soviet entry into the war with Japan, the Soviet Union would recover "the former rights of Russia violated by the treacherous attack of Japan in 1904" (including the reestablishment of joint Sino-Soviet control over the major railways in Manchuria, a lease on Port Arthur as a naval base, and the internationalization of Dairen, as well as recovery of the Kurile Islands and the southern part of Sakhalin from Japan).[3] He also insisted that China agree to recognize the *status quo* of Outer Mongolia—that is, its separation from China and its status as a nominally independent satellite of the Soviet Union. The Chinese Nationalist government acquiesced in these terms, and in August 1945 it signed a treaty and exchanged several notes with the Soviet Union in which China agreed that the major Manchurian railways should be placed under joint Sino-Soviet ownership for thirty years, Port Arthur should be jointly used as a naval base, and Dairen should be turned into a free port, with half of its port facilities leased free of charge to the Russians.[4] The Nationalists also agreed to recognize the independence of the "Mongolian People's Republic" if a plebiscite confirmed the Mongolians' desire for this status. In return, the Russians reaffirmed their recognition of China's full sovereignty in Manchuria, pledged noninterference in Chinese internal affairs, and promised to give moral and military support only to the Nationalist government.

Despite Moscow's political pledges, the Soviet troops which occupied Manchuria began immediately after the war to remove a large portion of the Japanese-built industries and equipment in that region, claiming it as "war booty." Although the Russians' own pressing need for industrial equipment was undoubtedly one motive for this policy, the dismantling of industries in Manchuria also seemed to suggest either a lack of confidence that the Chinese Communists could soon achieve control of Manchuria or a belief that an industrially strong Manchuria under the control of any Chinese regime, whether Nationalist or Communist, was not desirable from the Soviet viewpoint.

Top-ranking Yugoslav Communists have claimed that there was a basic disagreement between Moscow and the Chinese Communists on strategy in China in the immediate postwar period. In his authorized biography of Tito, Vladimir Dedijer asserts that in 1948 Stalin told a Yugoslav delegation that, after the war, "we told them [the Chinese Communists] bluntly that we considered the development of the uprising in China had no prospect and that the Chinese comrades should seek a *modus vivendi* with Chiang K'ai-shek, that they should join the Chiang K'ai-shek government and dissolve their army."[5] Reportedly, Stalin added: "The Chinese comrades agreed here with the views of the Soviet comrades but went back to China and acted quite otherwise." There are several aspects of Stalin's statement as quoted by Dedijer, including his alleged advice to the Chinese Communists to disband their army, as well as his reported admission that "we were wrong," which are not wholly credible. Nevertheless, the Yugoslav Communists' belief that in this period there was a basic difference between Soviet advice and Chinese Communist actions may have a basis in fact.

Whatever doubts or lack of confidence the Soviet leaders may have felt about the Communists in China immediately after the end of the war did not deter them from giving substantial material assistance to the Chinese Communists during 1945-1946. Immediately after Soviet troops occupied Manchuria and a part of Inner Mongolia, the Chinese Communists shifted an important segment of their party leadership and military forces to that region, where they received extremely valuable assistance from the Russians in their revolutionary struggle. The Soviet troops delayed their evacuation from several key points and then timed their departure so that Chinese Communist forces were able to move in before the Nationalists and take possession of large stocks of surrendered Japanese arms and equipment.[6] Even with these arms, it is true, the Communists were still inferior in military strength to the Nationalist forces which eventually moved into Manchuria, and the reasons for ultimate Communist success must be sought in the complex development of political, economic, and social, as well as military, forces in China. Nevertheless, the indirect military aid which the Russians gave the Chinese Communists in Manchuria after the war had an important and direct effect on the situation in China and helped the Communists substantially in building up their strength.

There is no indication that the Chinese Communists questioned the basic importance of close alignment with Moscow at any time during this period, and more than a year before they came to power in 1949 they defined their commitment to accept Soviet leadership in very clear terms. One of the most important statements of this commitment was made in November 1948 by Liu Shao-ch'i. In his article "On Internationalism and Nationalism," Liu expressed the Chinese Communists' unequivocal support for the Soviet leaders' world view and international policies and endorsed the crackdown on Tito which had taken place earlier in the year. "Communists will be betraying the proletariat and Communism and playing the game of the imperialists all over the world and will make themselves pawns of the imperialists," Liu said, "if, after their own nation has been freed from imperialist oppression, the Communists . . . reject the international unity of the proletariat and working people and . . . oppose the Socialist Soviet Union." [7] Then, in an essay "On People's Democratic Dictatorship," published in July 1949, Mao Tse-tung proclaimed his celebrated "lean to one side" doctrine. "The gunfire of the October Revolution sent us Marxism-Leninism," [8] he said. "Travel the road of the Russians—this was the conclusion." Mao rejected the idea of accepting aid from the non-Communist countries even if it should be offered. "Internationally, we belong to the anti-imperialist front, headed by the U.S.S.R.," he said, and "we can only look for genuine and friendly aid from that front and not from the imperialist front." [9]

By early 1949, some months before Mao had set up a national government, the Chinese Communist authorities in Manchuria had begun dealing with the Russians on a formal intergovernmental level. Kao Kang, top Communist leader in the region, headed a Chinese industrial and commercial mission to Moscow and signed an agreement to regulate Manchurian trade with the Soviet Union. The Russians continued to maintain diplomatic relations with the Nationalists during this period, however, and even though the Communist victory in the Chinese civil war was clearly imminent, they negotiated with the Nationalists throughout 1949 to secure special Soviet economic rights in Sinkiang.[10] Stalin was apparently still determined to guarantee Russian, as distinct from Communist, interests in China, and this ambition, which he continued to press even after 1949, had a significant influence on Sino-Soviet relations throughout the period of Stalin's rule.

The Alliance and Stalin's Policies

When the Chinese Communist government was formally established on October 1, 1949, the Soviet Union immediately recognized it, with the satellites following suit, and in the next few months the initial framework of Sino-Soviet relations was worked out in detail. In December Mao Tse-tung paid his first visit to the U.S.S.R., and during his nine-week stay a number of important Sino-Soviet agreements were concluded. Most important was the 30-year Treaty of Friendship, Alliance, and Mutual Assistance, signed in February 1950. In this political and military alliance the Chinese and Russians agreed that if either ally were "attacked by Japan or any state allied with it" (the latter phrase clearly referred to the United States), the other partner would "immediately render military and other assistance by all means at its disposal."[11] This treaty gave Communist China strong, though not unqualified, military backing. By a separate agreement the Russians gave Communist China economic backing through a five-year 300 million dollar loan. During the same period important trade and other economic arrangements were also worked out.

In return for Soviet support, Communist China had to make major concessions. Stalin was still concerned about establishing Russia's "special rights" in China, even though

China was now under Communist rule. An agreement signed in February 1950 provided for joint Sino-Soviet administration of the principal railways in Manchuria, as well as for joint use of the naval base at Port Arthur, either until a peace treaty with Japan could be concluded or, at the latest, until the end of 1952. Later agreements called for the establishment of several long-term joint stock companies, to operate mostly in China's borderlands, where the Russians had traditionally pressed for special rights. These included: two companies to exploit petroleum and nonferrous metals in Sinkiang, a company to build and repair ships in Dairen, and a civil aviation company to provide services between Communist China and the U.S.S.R. The Chinese Communists also agreed, in an exchange of notes in February, to accept the *status quo*—that is, Soviet-dominated "independence"—in Outer Mongolia. At Moscow Stalin and Mao probably also discussed plans for bringing South Korea under Communist control—although there was no indication of this at the time.

The first real test of the Sino-Soviet alliance came less than a half-year later with the outbreak of the Korean War, and, whatever pullings and haulings may have taken place behind the scenes, the partnership weathered the test successfully. Entering the war to make good Soviet miscalculations and rescue the North Korean regime, the Chinese Communists did the bulk of the fighting to preserve the Communist bloc's interests. Peking's willingness to bear the brunt of the conflict enabled the Russians to avoid direct involvement, and in return Moscow poured in large amounts of military supplies and equipment, which helped the Chinese Communists not only to fight the war but also to modernize and build up their army and air force. Furthermore, Peking's alliance with the Soviet Union and the Russians' possession of atomic weapons were undoubtedly major factors which deterred the West from direct attacks against Communist bases in Manchuria, and the war remained a limited one. (The United States' desire to avoid an all-out war, and the unwillingness of its allies to support attacks beyond the Yalu, were other important factors, of course, which contributed to the decision to limit the war.) It is clear, however, that the major risks and costs of the war had to be borne primarily by the Chinese Communists, and this may have been less than wholly satisfactory to Peking.

In the autumn of 1952 Chinese Communist and Russian leaders again sat down together to discuss a wide range of problems, in their most important meeting since Mao's 1949-1950 visit. In September, while Premier Chou En-lai was in Moscow, the two governments announced that the Manchurian railways would be returned to sole Chinese management by the end of 1952, as agreed in 1950.[12] They also revealed, however, that the Russians would stay on beyond 1952 in joint control of the naval base at Port Arthur, allegedly at Peking's "request." Because the Korean War was still going on and Communist China had no strong navy of its own, Peking may genuinely have wished the Russians to continue using and maintaining the base, but Chinese Communist leaders probably had mixed feelings about prolonging the special Russian rights on Chinese soil.

A large delegation of Chinese experts, whom Chou left behind in Moscow, continued negotiating with the Russians until mid-1953. Liu Shao-ch'i attended the 19th Congress of the Soviet Communist party in October 1952 and stayed on in Russia until January 1953, and he may also have taken part in the negotiations. Apparently, there was hard bargaining, particularly over economic matters, and the aid offered by the Russians may have fallen considerably short of what the Chinese Communists hoped for. Peking had formally launched its first Five Year Plan at the start of 1953, while the negotiations were still in progress, and it could not determine the scope of the Plan until it knew how much economic assistance would be forthcoming from the Russians. Finally, after the negotiations had dragged on for many months, the results were announced in the autumn of 1953. The Russians committed themselves to help the Chinese by providing equipment and technical assistance for a large number of key development projects, which made it possible for Peking to proceed with its Five Year Plan. But there was no announcement of any new financial aid to supplement the Soviet loan of 1950. (An agreement on the construction of a new railway linking China and the Soviet Union was also signed in this period, in late 1952, but it was not publicly announced until 1954.) [13]

The Moscow discussions must also have dealt with the problem of terminating the Korean War. Later developments suggest that the Chinese Communists were probably more eager than Stalin to end the war and extricate themselves from it. Until Stalin's death in March 1953 the truce talks in Korea had remained deadlocked, but only four days after Stalin's death Chou En-lai put forth new proposals, very similar to the proposals previously advanced by India and rejected by the Communist powers, which made possible a solution of the main issues still outstanding.

Throughout Stalin's last years, although the alliance remained solid and a public posture of monolithic unity and enthusiastic cooperation was carefully maintained, there clearly must have been strains and frictions beneath the surface. Soviet primacy and superiority were highlighted at all times by both partners in the alliance. The Chinese Communists, on their part, engaged in enthusiastic adulation of Stalin and of almost everything about the Soviet Union, going to extraordinary lengths to indoctrinate their people in Stalinism and pro-Soviet feelings. At the same time, however, Peking was paying a sizable price for Soviet support, and apparently Stalin withheld both the level of assistance and the political status which the Chinese Communists wished for. According to Polish sources, Khrushchev, in a speech in Warsaw made after his decision to promote "de-Stalinization," specifically accused Stalin of having been responsible for serious strains in Sino-Soviet relations.[14]

After Stalin

Mao Tse-tung's prestige within the Communist bloc started to rise even before Stalin's death, but, perhaps because of domestic and international uncertainties, Stalin's successors began almost immediately to show increasing deference to the Chinese Communists. Over a period of time they made a number of important concessions to China and granted it some additional economic aid. Undoubtedly, the Russians' steps to improve relations since the spring of 1953 have helped to strengthen the Sino-Soviet alliance by removing some of the previous sources of friction. They have also contributed to a steady rise in Peking's influence and prestige within the Communist bloc.

An increased Soviet sensitivity to Chinese Communist pride was apparent at Stalin's funeral, at which Chou En-lai marched in a place of honor, along with top Soviet leaders. Almost immediately a perceptible change in tone began to creep into Soviet statements about the "great Chinese people." Even more important to the Chinese, the Russians found it desirable to make definite concessions.

The first visit of any top-level Soviet leaders to Communist China took place in the autumn of 1954. Khrushchev and Bulganin, soon to emerge in the top positions in Moscow, paid unprecedented deference to Communist China when they went to Peking in September-October of that year. Khrushchev called Communist China a "great power" and declared that "after the Great October Socialist Revolution, the victory of the Chinese people's revolution is the most outstanding event in world history," one which has "immense" significance for the "peoples of Asia." [15] He praised the Chinese Communists for having "creatively applied" Marxism-Leninism and proclaimed that "the Soviet Union and the People's Republic of China are the invulnerable bastion of the camp of peace, democracy, and socialism."

During Khrushchev's 1954 visit the Russians agreed to sell China all their shares in the Sino-Soviet joint-stock companies and to return Port Arthur to sole Chinese control by the end of 1955. They announced a second Soviet loan of 130 million dollars as well as an increase in the number of "Soviet aid" projects in China. They also agreed to cooperate in constructing another major railway, to link China and the Soviet Union through Sinkiang. And in two major joint declarations they gave strong endorsement to many of Peking's objectives, including the recovery of Taiwan.[16] Somewhat over a year later, in the spring of 1956, Mikoyan visited Communist China and promised a substantial increase in the number of Chinese industrial projects to be built with Russian help.[17]

These developments were tangible signs of a significant

adjustment which appeared to be taking place in Sino-Soviet relations after 1953. The Russians began to pay more attention to Chinese Communist feelings and interests, and Peking started to assume greater independence and initiative in Communist bloc affairs. This process gained a startling momentum following Khrushchev's dramatic attack on Stalin at the 20th Party Congress of the Soviet party in February 1956.

Peking and "De-Stalinization"

Khrushchev's decision to "de-Stalinize" the Soviet party set in motion a process which soon led to a loosening of controls throughout the Communist bloc, and it marked the beginning of a critical period of instability in bloc affairs. Stalin's heavy-handed dominance and his insistence upon tight Soviet control, particularly in the East European satellites, had created numerous fundamental tensions within the bloc, which had been clearly revealed by Tito's struggle against Moscow after 1948, the Berlin uprising in 1953, and many less obvious signs. By 1955 Khrushchev had apparently decided to meet these problems by relaxing Moscow's controls, denouncing the symbol of past Soviet dominance, and seeking a reconciliation with Yugoslavia. But the unprecedented violence of Khrushchev's denunciation of Stalin and Stalinism sent a shock throughout the entire world Communist movement and gave a sudden impetus to the development of what Italian Communist leader Togliatti called "polycentric Communism." [18] It touched off the Poznan riots, the crisis in Soviet-Polish relations, and the Hungarian uprising. Finally, it raised the whole issue of the future unity of the Communist bloc.

At almost every stage in these turbulent events the Chinese Communist leaders gave evidence that, instead of being content merely to parrot Moscow's line, they were determined to make their own independent evaluations and to define their own position.[19] Despite the obscurity which surrounds most Communist bloc affairs, it is clear that during 1956-1957 Peking assumed a new and very significant political role as a mediator or conciliator between Moscow and the East European satellites. Apparently, Communist China took considerable initiative in defining political and ideological positions for the bloc as a whole. And as a result it emerged into a position much closer to parity with the Soviet Union in the leadership of the bloc, at least in political and ideological terms.

From the start Peking's reaction to Khrushchev's February 1956 denunciation of Stalin was somewhat cool. Its leaders and press were slow in reacting at all, but finally the Chinese Politburo's views were made known in an article entitled "On the Historical Experience of the Dictatorship of the Proletariat," published in early April.[20] These views differed considerably from those which Khrushchev had revealed at the 20th Congress. Although, the article stated, Stalin had "exaggerated his own role" and had made "unrealistic and erroneous decisions on certain important matters" (including "in particular a wrong decision on the question of Yugoslavia"), he had nonetheless "creatively applied and developed Marxism-Leninism." "Some people," it said, "consider that Stalin was wrong in everything; this is a grave misconception. Stalin was a great Marxist-Leninist, yet at the same time a Marxist-Leninist who committed several gross errors without realizing they were errors." The article went on to criticize Stalin for maintaining that the principal target of Communist revolutionaries should be "middle-of-the-road" social and political forces; this formula, it said, had been "crudely applied" in China until the Chinese Communists worked out their own program calling for "winning over" and "neutralizing" the "middle-of-the-road" forces. But, the article continued, "Stalin's works should, as before, still be seriously studied and . . . we should accept as an important historical legacy all that is of value in them, especially those many works in which he defended Leninism and correctly summarized the experience of building up the Soviet Union."

There were undoubtedly many reasons why the Chinese Communists decided to take this middle position, instead of accepting Khrushchev's initial, general condemnation. In 1956 the Chinese Communists were, in a sense, passing through a Stalinist stage of their own. They had explicitly modeled many of their policies on Stalin's, and an outright repudiation of Stalin could have led to the questioning of many of their own current policies. Peking may also have feared that the attack on Stalin could have repercussions affecting Mao Tse-tung's position within China, since for many years Mao had played a comparable, although by no means identical, role as the foremost party leader. In addition, the Chinese Communist leaders, then and subsequently, seem to have shown a greater concern than Stalin's successors in the Soviet Union about the prime importance of doctrine and ideology in the Communist system. This may have deterred them from approving any blanket condemnation of the man who for years had been idolized as the principal oracle of world communism. And, unlike Khrushchev, the Chinese Communists had no compelling domestic reasons to discredit Stalin's past leadership. By the end of 1956 Khrushchev, too, had apparently come to the conclusion that his initial condemnation of Stalin was too sweeping; in any case, he began moderating his extreme stand and moved closer to the Chinese position.

Communist China and the Crisis in Eastern Europe

During 1956, as rumblings of discontent and revolt grew stronger in Eastern Europe, Communist China became directly involved for the first time in Soviet-satellite relations. By the autumn of 1956 Peking was playing a major role in the dramatic events which centered on Poland and Hungary. Its views appeared to be extremely influential in the formulation of Soviet policies and of policies for the entire Communist bloc.

As the crisis within the bloc approached a climax, the Poles, and probably other East Europeans as well, looked increasingly to Peking, hoping to obtain support of their attempts to achieve a greater degree of internal independence and increased acceptance of their own particular "roads to socialism." The 20th Congress had endorsed the concept of "differing roads," but apparently Khrushchev expected it to apply to new recruits to the bloc, not to countries already in it. In many respects, however, Communist China had become a symbol to East Europeans of the possibility of exercising a greater degree of national independence within the bloc.

On their part, the Chinese Communist leaders were clearly becoming more and more disturbed by the danger of disintegration, or at least disruption, of the bloc in Eastern Europe. Their own security and prestige were intimately linked to the unity of the bloc as a whole, and apparently Peking even feared that the situation in Eastern Europe could lead to the outbreak of a war, ultimately involving China.[21] Eastern Europe was also becoming increasingly important in Communist China's trade; any serious disruption of trade with that area would have hampered China's own economic program. The Chinese Communists also may have been wary of possible repercussions in China. In any case, effective intervention in Eastern Europe would increase Peking's international stature and influence.

For the Soviet leaders, concerned above all to bring a dangerous situation under control, Chinese Communist assistance was extremely valuable. Perhaps they purposely delegated a special role to the Chinese, who, being remote and not directly involved, could speak in support of bloc unity with a semblance of disinterestedness impossible for Moscow.

The Chinese Communists, despite their consistent support of many basic aspects of Stalinism, had from the start favored allowing significant national variations in the application of Marxism-Leninism in each country. They had always asserted that their own revolution had special characteristics, and during 1949-1951 they had publicly stressed the originality of Mao's revolutionary strategy and its contribution to the "treasury of Marxism-Leninism." Stalinism remained the fundamental model for their post-1949 development, but one criticism they made of Stalin was, as they stated in December 1956, that "sometimes he . . . intervened mistakenly with many grave consequences in the internal affairs of certain brother countries and parties."[22] In practice, the Chinese Communists had experimented a good deal, making numerous important innovations in applying Soviet experience to China. Since Stalin's death, furthermore, the Chinese Communists had tended increasingly to highlight their own innovations, while the Russians paid public tribute more and more frequently to their originality. In late 1955, for example, a Chinese Communist publication stated:

One of Mao Tse-tung's brilliant contributions to the storehouse of Marxism is the principle that under certain socio-historic conditions, in a state in which the proletariat has gained power, it can carry out a basic transformation of the capitalist elements in accordance with Socialist principles. None of the previous classics of Marxism-Leninism contain this type of theory, and no other state in the world has ever had this experience. In the Soviet Union and the people's democracies of Southern and Eastern Europe, capitalism is being eradicated by violent and forceful means. However, because of the concrete conditions of our country, we are able to arrive at the same goal—the eradication of capitalism—by peaceful methods of Socialist transformation.[23]

One of the resolutions of the Soviet 20th Party Congress had endorsed and given credit to Communist China for having "introduced many special features into its form of Socialist construction." [24] In a speech to the 8th Congress of the Chinese Communist party, in the autumn of 1956, Mikoyan went much further. The Chinese Communists have not only "creatively applied" basic Marxism-Leninism, he said, but have also developed "distinctive new forms and methods of building socialism" which "have not been tried in other countries." He paid tribute to Peking for having avoided "some of our mistakes," for using "unique methods" to "transform private capitalist enterprises into state-capitalist enterprises," and for working out "a general policy of gradual transition to socialism." [25] The Chinese Communists, Mikoyan said, "have made a major contribution to Marxist-Leninist theory" and have "refuted the insinuations made by enemies of our cause—the opportunists—that Marxism-Leninism is suitable for Russia but not for other countries, for Europe, but not for Asia." "Each country," he added, "has its own distinctive features and brings its own elements to bear in making the transition to socialism."

The right of a Communist state to follow its own distinctive transition to socialism and to enjoy a significant degree of internal independence was at the root of the crises in Poland and Hungary in the autumn of 1956. In both Poland and Hungary the Communists pressed for greater freedom from Soviet control over their internal affairs, while the Soviet leaders attempted to retain as much control as possible. By its intervention in these crises, Communist China apparently attempted to define a workable compromise formula which would place limits both upon the Russians in exercising their power over the satellites and upon the satellites in pressing for independence from Moscow.

According to Polish sources, as tension mounted between Warsaw and Moscow from April 1956 on, Communist China gave considerable encouragement to the Poles' aspirations for autonomy. Edward Ochab, the Polish leader who attended the 8th Congress of the Chinese Communist party in September 1956, is reported to have conferred at length with Mao Tse-tung. Allegedly Mao urged the Poles "to obtain internal independence and to develop their own socialism as the Yugoslavs had done." [26] Earlier, the Chinese Communists, following Moscow's example, had established relations with Belgrade, and by 1956 they were going further than the Russians in giving the Yugoslavs credit for their experiments with workers' councils, which Moscow still condemned as "anti-Marxist."

In October 1956, when the crisis reached its peak, Mao, according to Polish sources, advised Moscow against military intervention "if the Polish revolution got out of hand," and reportedly he later telegraphed the Polish leaders, in January 1957, to inform them of this fact.[27] The crisis in Poland reached its climax, in any case, during the second half of October, with Gomulka's coming to power. Finally, a delegation of top Soviet leaders headed by Khrushchev made an unannounced trip to Warsaw, and a compromise was hammered out across the conference table; it provided for somewhat greater "equality" for the Poles yet it held Poland within the Communist bloc.

The crisis in Hungary, which came to a head a few days later, took a different course, and from the Communist bloc point of view it got completely out of hand. It soon became apparent that the Hungarians would not be satisfied with a compromise on the Polish model. Disorder turned into revolution, and Imre Nagy was swept along toward the popular goals of complete independence, free elections, rejection of communism, and secession from the bloc.

During the crisis, on October 30, the Soviet leaders issued an important declaration which appeared to grant many concessions to the Hungarians. In this statement they spoke of a "commonwealth of Socialist nations," a concept which, though not entirely new in Communist parlance, had certainly never received great stress previously. "United by the Communist ideals of building a Socialist society and by the principles of proletarian internationalism," the declaration said, "the countries of the great commonwealth of Socialist nations can build their mutual relations only on the principle of complete equality, of respect for territorial integrity, state independence and sovereignty, and of noninterferrence in one another's internal affairs." [28] The "five principles," which had been one of Peking's major theme songs since 1954, echoed strongly in this statement.

Moscow's declaration failed to slow the momentum of the Hungarian revolution, however, and on November 1 Nagy promised to withdraw from the Warsaw Pact and take Hungary out of the Communist bloc. In the eyes of both Peking and Moscow, this was going much too far. The Russians proceeded to launch a full-scale military assault on Budapest, while the West was preoccupied, diverted, and split by the Suez invasion, which had started on October 29. Peking gave its prompt and full endorsement both to the Soviet military suppression of the Hungarian revolution and to the principles outlined in Moscow's declaration of October 30.

Peking's Mediation and Ideological Initiative

In the months that followed these climactic events, the Chinese Communists made it clear that in their view it was necessary to work out a formula for bloc relations which would restrain both the "tendency toward great-nation chauvinism" (that is, the Soviet Union) and excessive small-nation "nationalism" (that is, the East Europeans); in many respects they still appeared, at this time, to be as much concerned with the former as with the latter. In November, for example, the official Peking news agency, commenting on Polish-Russian relations, stated: "In future relations between Socialist countries, if only the bigger nations pay more attention to avoiding the mistake of big-nation chauvinism (this is the main thing), and the smaller nations avoid the mistake of nationalism (this is also important), friendship and solidarity based upon equality will undoubtedly become consolidated." [29]

On December 29, 1956, the Chinese Politburo publicly set forth its views once again in an editorial, "More on the Historical Experience of the Dictatorship of the Proletariat." This document, which in some respects was a response to Tito's statements on the Hungarian crisis, was perhaps the most important attempt to define a new basis for relations between Communist states to appear anywhere in the Communist bloc during this period. The Soviet revolution, it stated, ushered in a "new era" in history, but not all "Soviet experience" is universally applicable.[30] "One part is fundamental and of universal significance," but the "other part is not of universal significance," and the Soviet Union has "also had its mistakes and failures." Although "Stalin's mistakes take second place to his achievements," his "tendency toward great-nation chauvinism" and the fact that he "even intervened mistakenly" in "the internal affairs of certain brother countries and parties" were errors which had "grave consequences." For 39 years, it declared, the U.S.S.R. has rightly been "the center of the international Communist movement," but in the Socialist system there should be "relations of equality" and a "genuine, not nominal, exchange of views." Stalin's mistakes, it asserted, should not be blamed on the Socialist system.

However, the editorial continued, although it is "understandable that the Yugoslav comrades bear a particular resentment against Stalin's mistakes" and admirable that they have "stuck to socialism under difficult conditions," and although China has "no wish to interfere in the internal affairs of Yugoslavia," nevertheless Tito's views on Hungary are not "well balanced or objective." "Each Communist party must educate its members and the people in a spirit of internationalism, because the true national interests of all peoples call for friendly cooperation among nations. On the other hand, each Communist party must represent the legitimate national interests and sentiments of its own people." The "nationalist tendencies in smaller countries" are undesirable, but, "to strengthen the international solidarity of the Socialist countries, each Communist party must respect the national interests and sentiments of other countries. This is of special importance for the Communist party of a larger country in its relations with that of a smaller country."

In this same statement the Chinese Communists also undertook to define what they considered to be of "universal significance" in "Soviet experience." "The path of the October Revolution," they said, "reflects the general laws of revolution and construction at a particular stage in the long course of the development of human society. It is not only the road for the proletariat of the Soviet Union, but also the road which the proletariat of all countries must travel to gain victory." The "path of the October Revolution" consists essentially, they declared, of the following "universal truths of Marxism-Leninism which are generally applicable" in all countries:

1. The advanced members of the proletariat organize themselves into a Communist party which takes Marxism-Leninism as its guide to action, builds itself up along the lines of democratic centralism, establishes close links with the masses, strives to become the core of the laboring masses, and educates its party members and the masses of people in Marxism-Leninism.

2. The proletariat, under the leadership of the Communist party, rallying all the laboring people, takes political power from the bourgeoisie by means of revolutionary struggle.

3. After the victory of the revolution, the proletariat, under the leadership of the Communist party, rallying the broad mass of people on the basis of a worker-peasant alliance, establishes a dictatorship of the proletariat over the landlord and capitalist classes, crushes the resistance of the counterrevolutionaries, carries out the nationalization of industry and the step-by-step collectivization of agriculture, thereby eliminating the system of exploitation, private ownership of the means of production, and classes.

4. The state, led by the proletariat and the Communist party,

leads the people in the planned development of Socialist economy and culture, and on this basis gradually raises the people's living standard and actively prepares and works for the transition to Communist society.

5. The state, led by the proletariat and the Communist party, resolutely opposes imperialist aggression, recognizes the equality of all nations and defends world peace, firmly adheres to the principles of proletarian internationalism, strives to win the help of the laboring people of all countries, and at the same time strives to help them and all oppressed nations.

Almost immediately after this Politburo statement was published, Chou En-lai suddenly interrupted an important tour he was then making through South and Southeast Asia and flew via Peking first to Moscow and then to Poland and Hungary, presumably to see what he could do to facilitate a compromise solution. According to Polish sources, he spelled out the Chinese position to Gomulka and promised him Peking's moral support on the condition that Poland avoid any split like Yugoslavia's in 1948.[31] In Budapest he gave full backing to Kadar's regime, and after returning to Moscow he and the Russians issued an important joint communiqué on January 19, 1957. While emphasizing the "supreme interests" of the bloc and the importance of its efforts to achieve "victory in the common struggle for the triumph of communism," this declaration also endorsed Peking's "five principles" as the proper basis for international relations and asserted that "the Socialist countries are independent and sovereign states and relations between them are based upon the Leninist principle of national equality." [32]

In late February 1957 the Chinese Communists made a new independent effort to define the correct ideological basis for solving the internal problems of nations within the Communist bloc. Mao Tse-tung's speech "On the Correct Handling of Contradictions among the People" (published only in mid-1957, and then in revised form) was at least as important as the Politburo's 1956 statements.[33] It remains the most authoritative effort by any Communist leader to define the concept of "contradictions" within Communist-ruled states.

Earlier, the Chinese Politburo's statement of April 1956

had dealt to some extent with the problem of "contradictions," a subject on which Mao had written extensively as early as the 1930s. "Some naïve ideas," it stated, "seem to suggest that contradictions no longer exist in a Socialist society." [34] This is wrong, it said. "Socialist society also develops through contradictions between the productive forces and the relations of production"; "when old contradictions are solved new ones will arise"; "not everybody will be perfect, even when a Communist society is established."

The Chinese views on this problem were spelled out further by the Politburo in December 1956. The new declaration distinguished between "contradictions among the people and contradictions between the enemy and ourselves." Contradictions "between Socialist countries," it declared, are only a "partial contradiction of interests . . . whose solution must, first and foremost, be subordinated to the over-all interests of the struggle against the enemy." [35]

Then, in his February 1957 speech, Mao admitted that "certain people in our country were delighted when the Hungarian events took place," and he undertook a thorough and detailed discussion of the problem of "contradictions." [36] This speech, which dealt primarily with internal tensions and conflicts within China, revealed that Mao had apparently decided that China's own "contradictions" could best be handled by a loosening of controls, in line with a formula which he described as one of "unity-criticism-unity." Later, Peking attempted to apply this policy in China by encouraging free expression, in May and June 1957, but it soon was alarmed by the upsurge of criticism and reversed its more liberal course after only one month of "relaxation." Mao's speech also had far-reaching implications for the bloc as a whole, for his admission that "certain contradictions do exist between the government and the masses" even in a Communist country could not be ignored in other Communist nations.

Moscow's first reaction apparently was to reject Peking's concept of "contradictions" within Communist states. In its initial version of the Chinese April 1956 statement *Pravda* omitted all references to contradictions within Socialist society, although it did include them in a later version. Then in the spring of 1957 in an interview for an American television network, Khrushchev rejected Mao's assertion that there are "contradictions in socialism," and his statement to this effect was, in turn, omitted by the Chinese in their version of his interview.[37]

Finally, in a major speech in March 1957 Chou En-lai summarized the Chinese Communists' views on intrabloc relations. "The Soviet Union is not only the first triumphant Socialist country," he said, "but also the most powerful and experienced Socialist country; it has been giving the most significant help to other Socialist countries. Therefore, the Soviet Union has naturally become the center around which the Socialist countries are united."[38] "China, the Soviet Union, and all Socialist countries," he declared, "are bound by a fraternal friendship and have the obligation of assisting each other"; "no force on earth can separate us." But, he said:

Of course, the superiority of the Socialist system by no means implies that there will be no difficulty in our work, nor does it ensure that we will commit no mistakes in our work. . . . The Socialist countries are united by the common ideal and aim of communism, therefore their relations are based on the principles of proletarian internationalism. The Socialist countries are at the same time independent sovereign states, therefore their relations are based also on the Marxist-Leninist principle of national equality. . . . There are no essential contradictions or clash of interests between the Socialist states. . . . Great-nation chauvinism and narrow nationalist tendencies have given rise to a certain amount of estrangement and misunderstanding . . . but now these shortcomings and mistakes are being corrected. . . . Moreover, these differences can be resolved and, on the common basis of Marxism-Leninism, a unanimity can be reached gradually through comradely discussions and consultation. Even if no unanimity can be reached for the time being, it would be normal to reserve the differences while upholding our solidarity.

During early 1957 the Chinese Communists' role in bloc affairs unquestionably continued to be a mediating and moderating one. Peking credited Poland with "rectifying mistakes of doctrinairism in its past and at the same time combating mistakes of revisionism."[39] Premier Cyrankiewicz paid a state visit to China in April, and Mao Tse-tung stated that he would make a reciprocal visit to Warsaw during the summer of 1957. The Chinese Communists asserted that Hungary also was "resolutely rectifying all the mistakes made by the former leadership." And Peking voiced only "comradely" criticism of Tito.

Hardening of the Sino-Soviet Line

Then in late 1957 the Chinese Communists began to change their tune. They started to give more unequivocal backing to the primacy of the Soviet party, to place a stronger emphasis on "bloc unity," and to take a much harsher line against "disrupting" influences.

There is little to indicate just how and when the new "hard" Sino-Soviet line was worked out. The cancellation of Mao's scheduled trip to Poland suggests that the hardening had begun by mid-1957. The new line first became clear, however, at the conference of Communist states and parties which was held in Moscow in November 1957 during the celebration of the fortieth anniversary of the October Revolution.

The tone of Mao Tse-tung's speeches at Moscow was quite different from that of Chinese Communist statements made earlier in 1957. Mao now put much less stress on the need for "equality" and "independence." While reiterating that the "Chinese revolution has its own national characteristics," [40] he emphasized that China had "made full use of the rich experience of the Communist party and the people of the Soviet Union." He no longer underlined the importance of national peculiarities in developing socialism; instead, he asserted that "the urgent task is to oppose revisionist deviations." "We share the same destiny and the same life-spring with the Soviet Union and the entire Socialist camp," he declared, and "we regard it as the sacred international obligation of all Socialist countries to strengthen the solidarity of the Socialist countries headed by the Soviet Union." Furthermore, he asserted, [41] "the Socialist force has surpassed the imperialist force. . . . Our Socialist camp should have a leader, and this is the Soviet Union. The enemy also has a leader, and this is America. If there is no leader, the strength will be weakened."

The same emphasis was reflected in the Declaration of Twelve Communist and Workers' Parties, signed by representatives from all Communist-ruled states except Yugoslavia, which was one of two major statements issued at the close of the November conference. Reiterating some of the Chinese and Soviet statements of previous months, this declaration did assert that "the forms of the transition of different countries from capitalism to socialism may vary," [42] and that "all issues pertaining to relations among Socialist countries can be fully settled through comradely discussion, with strict observance of the principles of Socialist internationalism." But its main emphasis was on unity. "Strengthening the unity and fraternal cooperation of the Socialist countries and of the Communist and Workers' parties of all countries and closing of the ranks of the international working class, national liberation and democratic movements take on a special importance in the present situation," it declared. Communists must make a "determined struggle to overcome the survivals of bourgeois nationalism and chauvinism"; "it is necessary above all to strengthen the unity of Communist and Workers' parties of all countries." The declaration also listed nine "general laws," "applicable in all countries" for the "processes of the Socialist revolution"; these "laws" were little more than a rewording of the five "universal truths" set forth in the Chinese Communist statement of December 1956.[43]

Mao Tse-tung doubtless played an important role in the drafting of the Declaration of the Twelve Parties. According to Friedrich Ebert, of the East German SED, it was prepared jointly by the Communist Party of the Soviet Union and the Chinese Communist party.[44] Polish sources asserted that Gomulka, after a long conference with Mao in Moscow, came away "disappointed" because of Mao's backing of a "hard line in favor of Communist conformity." In mid-1958 the Yugoslavs claimed that Mao had forced through certain revisions of the declaration, which stressed the importance of the Soviet role in the bloc, and that these changes and China's general support for the new hard line were important factors in producing a policy declaration unacceptable to Yugoslavia.[45] The Chinese Communists themselves, at a Party Congress held in May 1958, hailed the declaration as one which

> sums up the experience of the international Communist movement in the past century, especially in the past 40 years; expounds the common principles which the Communist parties of all countries must abide by in the Socialist revolution and in Socialist construction; puts forward the basic policy of the Communist parties in rallying the broad masses of the people to the struggle for peace, democracy, and socialism; it lays the ideological and political foundation for solidarity among the Communist parties and strengthens the unity of the Socialist camp headed by the Soviet Union.[46]

It is not clear, however, whether the primary initiative for the new line came from the Soviet or the Chinese leadership. Either or both may have decided by late 1957 that a harder line was desirable in order to maintain bloc unity. In May and June 1957 the Chinese Communists had been dismayed by unexpected criticism of their regime within China, during their "let all flowers bloom" campaign, and in late 1957 they were engaged in a tough crackdown in their "anti-rightist" campaign. There have been some suggestions that Khrushchev had been challenged in his own party by Stalinists who charged that his policies of relaxation were responsible for events in Eastern Europe. In mid-1957 Khrushchev had demoted Molotov and other members of an alleged "anti-Party group," and Marshal Zhukov was dismissed just before the November meeting.

Both Moscow and Peking may have decided by late 1957 that the time was ripe for the adoption of a more aggressive posture in their approaches to the non-Communist world and that a tightening of discipline within the bloc was a prerequisite for this. The Russians had tested an ICBM in August and then launched their first Sputniks in October and November, and the harder line had been foreshadowed in statements of the Soviet Communist party prior to the November conference. Mao, in his Moscow speeches, emphasized the international importance of the Sputnik launchings and declared, in effect, that the Communist bloc should now seize the strategic initiative:

> I consider that the present world situation has reached a new turning point. There are now two winds in the world: the east wind and the west wind. There is a saying in China: "If the east wind does not prevail over the west wind, then the west wind will prevail over the east wind." I think the characteristic of the current situation is that the east wind prevails over the west wind; that is, the strength of socialism exceeds the strength of imperialism.[47]

Within the bloc, the spotlight turned in early 1958 to the Yugoslavs, who had refused to sign the November declaration —although they did sign the accompanying broader statement issued in the name of the world-wide Communist movement. In a new draft party program, published in March 1958, the Yugoslavs expressed strong criticism of many Sino-Soviet policies and practices, opposed all blocs including the Communist bloc, and favored peaceful evolution toward socialism. Moscow and Peking responded by launching a concentrated propaganda attack against the Yugoslav party and against "revisionism" in general. Although Moscow opened the attack, its criticism was relatively mild in comparison with the vituperation which issued from Peking, starting with an editorial in the *People's Daily* on May 5. Whether on their own initiative or in agreement with the Russians, the Chinese Communists went much further than Moscow in accusing Tito of trying to subvert the Communist bloc. They labeled the Yugoslav party's program as "anti-Marxist-Leninist" and "out-and-out revisionist." It "substitutes sophistry for revolutionary materialistic dialectics" and "substitutes the reactionary theory of the state and reactionary bourgeois nationalism for revolutionary proletarian internationalism," they said.[48] It "takes up the cudgels for monopoly capital and tries to obliterate the fundamental differences between the capitalist and socialist systems." Peking accused the Yugoslavs of "speaking like the reactionaries of all countries and the Chinese bourgeois rightists." It also went further than Moscow when it asserted that the Cominform resolutions of 1948 on Yugoslavia had been "basically correct."

This new preoccupation with revisionism represented a great change from Peking's earlier emphasis. In December 1956 the Chinese Communists had put almost all their emphasis upon combating doctrinairism rather than revisionism, asserting that "while resolutely opposing doctrinairism we must at the same time resolutely oppose revisionism." [49] In February 1957, it is true, Mao Tse-tung had placed greater stress on the dangers of revisionism, stating that "while criticizing doctrinairism, we should at the same time direct our attention to criticizing revisionism," [50] and adding that "revisionism, or rightist opportunism, is a bourgeois trend of thought which is even more dangerous than doctrinairism." In actual fact, however, at that time he had devoted almost all his attention to doctrinairism. The big change had come in November 1957, when Mao asserted with clear conviction that, "at present, the urgent task is to oppose revisionist tendencies." [51] After May 1958, Peking's attacks on revisionism became increasingly violent, and there was a significant difference in degree, acknowledged by both Peking and Moscow, between the Chinese Communist and Soviet attacks.

Whether or not the Russians and the Chinese actually agreed in November 1957 that they should attempt to seize the initiative in 1958 by adopting tougher policies toward the non-Communist world, the Sino-Soviet posture in successive crises since early 1958—in Iraq, Lebanon, the Taiwan Strait, and Berlin—suggests that this was in fact their intention.

Increased Chinese Communist Stature in Bloc Affairs

Since this period of rapid change started, there has been widespread speculation that Communist China has capitalized on its increased prestige within the bloc by extracting promises of additional Soviet backing for its aims. There has been no indication, however, that Peking has been able to obtain any increase in Soviet financial aid. The Chinese Communists, it is true, sent observers to the Communist bloc economic conference held at Moscow in May 1958 and agreed to participate in steps to coordinate and integrate the bloc economies. And in late 1958 and early 1959 the Russians agreed to help the Chinese construct a sizable number of important new development projects. Still, it is surprising that no new Soviet financial aid has been forthcoming. Since 1957 the assistance which the Russians have promised for the new projects is actually more limited than that offered in its previous promises.

There have been some indications since 1957, however, that the Chinese Communists may have been able to use their increased leverage to extract promises for additional military and political support from Moscow. A high-ranking delegation of Chinese military experts followed Mao Tse-tung to Moscow in November 1957. There was no indication at the time of what they had discussed with the Russians, but then in May 1958 Communist China's Foreign Minister announced that Peking intended to obtain nuclear weapons "in the future," and in the same month the head of the Chinese Academy of Sciences declared that Communist China planned to launch an earth satellite.[52] It is still not entirely clear whether these statements indicated that the Chinese Communists had obtained new Soviet promises of military aid, and if so in exactly what form; in the summer of 1959, however, Khrushchev reportedly claimed that Russia had already sent rockets to China.[53]

The circumstances surrounding Khrushchev's secret trip to Peking at the end of July 1958 raised numerous questions about Communist China's influence in the formulation of bloc policies. The trip was widely interpreted at the time as dramatic evidence of Peking's increased leverage on Moscow, but its real significance seems rather less clear now than the initial reactions to it seemed to suggest. In late July Khrushchev, maneuvering for a summit conference on the Lebanon crisis, agreed to a Western proposal that the arrangements for this conference be worked out within the framework of the Security Council of the United Nations, which would have given Nationalist China a voice in planning it. Then at the end of July he made his sudden trip to Peking, where on August 3 he and Mao issued a rather uninformative joint communiqué which underlined Sino-Soviet "unanimous agreement" on world issues, condemned "revisionism" once again as the "chief danger in the Communist movement," and proposed a heads-of-government meeting of the great powers—pointedly omitting any reference to the United Nations in this connection.[54] Upon returning to Moscow, Khrushchev frankly abandoned the idea of arranging a summit meeting within the framework of the Security Council and proposed, instead, a special session of the General Assembly. He also strongly reemphasized the international importance of Communist China. "The policy of ignoring the People's Republic of China is a folly," he declared. "This great power exists, is gaining strength, and is developing irrespective of whether it is ignored or not by certain governments." [55]

Moscow's shift on the question of a summit conference was widely interpreted as being the result of pressure from Mao. A close examination of the record shows, however, that Khrushchev's acceptance of a summit meeting within a Security Council framework had always been qualified, that he had begun to change his position even before his trip to Peking, and that the Chinese Communists had consistently supported the changing Soviet line. From the start, Mao may not have liked the idea of Nationalist China taking part in arranging a summit meeting, but there is no concrete evidence of divergent Chinese and Soviet views on this issue.[56] Nevertheless, it is significant that Khrushchev felt it desirable, at that particular time, to fly to Peking to reemphasize Sino-Soviet solidarity and to obtain renewed pledges of Chinese support, and this in itself was an important sign of Communist China's increasingly influential role in bloc affairs.

Khrushchev's visit to Peking also gave rise to speculation that the Chinese Communists—who had just completed a large and major conference of their top military leaders—wished to obtain Soviet backing for a policy of increased military pressure in the Taiwan Strait. Whether or not a specific agreement on this subject was concluded between Mao and Khrushchev, within three weeks after their meeting, the Chinese Communists did, in fact, open up an intense bombardment of Quemoy, and by their ominous threats to "liberate" the offshore islands and Taiwan they kept the world poised on the brink of war for over a month. In this crisis the Russians gave Peking stronger political and diplomatic backing than ever before. They fully endorsed all of the Chinese Communists' claims, and at the height of the crisis Khrushchev stated that "an attack on the People's Republic of China . . . is an attack on the Soviet Union." [57]

In the autumn of 1959 the importance placed upon relations with Peking by the Russians was once again highlighted when Khrushchev announced that immediately after visiting the United States he would fly to Peking to take part in the Chinese Communists' celebration of the tenth anniversary of the founding of their regime.

However one interprets all these developments, it is clear that Communist China's prestige and influence within the Communist bloc have increased greatly over the past three or four years, and this has doubtless improved Peking's ability to influence Soviet policy. At the same time, new links and commitments have developed between Moscow and Peking, making their policies more interdependent and interreacting than ever before. Yet, under the surface important strains and frictions certainly remain, and some of them may become increasingly significant in the future. Any attempt to view the future of the alliance must, therefore, take account of both the cohesive and divisive elements in it.

Ideology

Ideology is a basic foundation of the Sino-Soviet alliance. Although a common ideology may not alone provide a cement strong enough to hold together a political alliance between Communist partners, as Tito's case proves, it would be a mistake to underestimate the importance of ideology in relations between Peking and Moscow. The sharing by Chinese Communist and Soviet leaders of common values, premises, prejudices, hopes, and fears has certainly been a fundamental unifying factor in their alliance.

Over recent years, however, subtle changes have been taking place in the ideological relationships within the alliance, and they may be of considerable importance for the future. Despite their firm and consistent support of orthodox Marxism-Leninism and their tendency to give Stalin even more credit than the Russian leaders have since 1953, the Chinese Communists have increasingly become innovators and independent interpreters of the common creed. In some respects, Mao has emerged since Stalin's death as the leading apostle of Communist ideology. Many of the bloc's most important ideological statements in recent years have emanated from Peking, and Communist China's policies and programs have created a new model which differs in significant respects from that of the Soviet Union. The Chinese Communists' distinctive revolutionary strategy evolved during their struggle for power, their "new forms and methods of building socialism," and their formula for intrabloc relations—all have contributed to raising Peking's ideological stature within the bloc.

Peking's communization campaign, in particular, has raised many ideological questions for the future, questions which are by no means wholly resolved. When the Chinese Communists first announced this campaign, the extravagance of their statements raised a very real question as to whether they were consciously attempting to put China in the forefront of the Communist bloc in terms of Socialist "advancement." Subsequently, the Russians appear to have put a damper on any Chinese pretensions of this sort by reemphasizing the role of Soviet leadership in the building of communism, but it remains to be seen what the long-run ideological effects of Peking's communization program will be on the bloc.

Peking's first major statements on the communization program implied that Communist China was making a very rapid spurt ahead toward ultimate communism. "It seems that the attainment of communism in China is no longer a remote future event," stated the Central Committee in August 1958; "we should actively use the form of people's communes to explore the practical road of transition to communism." [58] In reaction to this announcement and the entire communization program, many East Europeans privately expressed amazement and shock, and the Yugoslavs openly denounced the communes as having "nothing in common with Marxism." Publicly, Moscow was remarkably silent, but top Soviet leaders made some remarks to Westerners which suggested a notable lack of enthusiasm. According to Senator Hubert

Humphrey, Khrushchev, in an interview in Moscow, called the communes "old fashioned" and "reactionary." Reportedly he also declared: "We tried that right after the revolution. It just doesn't work. That system is not nearly so good as the state farms and the collective farms." [59]

What went on behind the scenes between Moscow and Peking in the following months is not known. But in December 1958 the Chinese Communist Central Committee issued a second major statement which, while endorsing the communization program in general, called for a halt to some of the initial excesses, proposed a slowdown in the implementation of some features of the program, and outlined a process of consolidating the rural communes already established. The tone of this resolution was quite different in important respects from the Central Committee's August statement. Even though it asserted that "it is of course not proper to ignore or even impede this course of development and relegate communism to the distant future," it also declared that the completion of the building of socialism in China "will not be very soon," and that the "transition from socialism to communism is quite a long and complicated process of development." [60] Then, at the 21st Congress of the Soviet Communist party in February 1959, Khrushchev outlined dramatic new economic goals in the Soviet Seven Year Plan and declared, somewhat pointedly, that it is necessary for all Communist states to pass through a gradual process of socialization before moving on to the building of communism. He also specifically emphasized that the U.S.S.R. itself is moving steadily ahead toward communism. All that Khrushchev said was then dutifully endorsed by Peking's official *People's Daily,* which hailed Khrushchev's "majestic program for the all-out building of communism" and denounced those who "exert all their efforts to seek and create imaginary 'differences' between the Chinese Communist party and the Soviet Communist party." [61]

The fact remains, however, that the communization program is taking the Chinese Communists along a path quite different from that of the Soviet Union, and Peking is creating a distinct model for the "transition to communism" which differs substantially from the Soviet formula. To date there is little or no indication that other Communist leaders are inclined to follow the Chinese model, however. Most, in fact, seem to have been more repelled than attracted by the communes. But it is probably still too early to judge what the reactions within the bloc will be in the long run. Conceivably the commune program might be labeled as a serious deviation. On the other hand, if the program succeeds it might substantially enhance the Chinese Communists' stature as successful innovators and ideological leaders. Or perhaps it may merely promote acceptance within the bloc of very different "roads of transition to communism." In any event, however, it has introduced a significant new ideological element into intrabloc affairs.

Political Coordination

In addition to being linked by ideology, Peking and Moscow share many common goals, and they derive strong political support from each other. Their ability to coordinate both strategy and tactics on a world-wide basis is invaluable to both partners. Since 1949 the Soviet and Chinese Communist leaders have closely integrated successive changes in their general strategy—for example, the shift to "competitive coexistence" after the Korean War, the implementation of their trade and aid policies toward the nonaligned and underdeveloped countries, and the stepping up of pressure against the West since 1957. They have given full backing to each other not only on broad questions such as disarmament or control of nuclear weapons, but also on specific tactics toward Korea, Japan, Southeast Asia, the Middle East, Germany, and most other areas, and have closely coordinated the timing of their separate moves. During 1958 the skill with which they shifted the focus of world tension rapidly from Iraq and Lebanon to Taiwan and then to Berlin, keeping the West off balance, illustrated the advantages which accrue to an alliance of partners facing outward from opposite ends of the Eurasian continent.

One of the strongest incentives for Peking and Moscow to keep their partnership intact is undoubtedly the realization that both the Soviet Union and Communist China would pay a heavy price if they split apart. If the alliance broke up, Peking would almost certainly have to give up many of its major long-term aims in Asia. With an unfriendly Soviet Union on its border, Communist China would be surrounded and vulnerable. Conversely, the Soviet Union would pay a tremendous political price if its most important ally became openly estranged. Most particularly, Moscow's entire strategy toward the non-Western world might be gravely compromised, if not undermined, if its principal Asian ally repudiated the alliance.

These compelling reasons for holding the alliance together do not automatically eliminate all differences between the two partners on strategy and tactics, however, and it is unlikely that Peking and Moscow always agree on all their aims or on the priorities, timing, or methods of achieving their various aims. Some Yugoslavs have maintained that the Russians, despite their consistent verbal support of Peking's claims to a seat in the United Nations and other international bodies, have actually not been eager to see Communist China emerge as a full-fledged member of the international community, preferring to have Peking remain dependent upon Moscow as its advocate in international affairs. Although for a number of reasons this seems improbable, the Russians have appeared at times to be rather perfunctory in their advocacy of Communist China's "rights" in the international community. When they vetoed Japan's admission to the United Nations, many observers were surprised that they used this issue only to strengthen their own position in bargaining for the restoration of Soviet-Japanese relations and failed to demand the seating of Communist China in the United Nations as the price for Japan's entry. At other times, the Soviet Union has apparently found it expedient to evade issues relating to Communist China's area of special interest. In early 1958, for example, the Soviet proposals on space control called for eliminating all Western military bases in Europe, Africa, and the Middle East but omitted all mention of the Far East. Peking's opinions and interests may have raised significant complications for Moscow on other occasions, imposing certain limitations on the Russians' flexibility in formulating their policies.

There is little doubt that the Soviet Union and Communist China have rated the Taiwan issue differently in their scale of priorities. From Peking's point of view, control over Taiwan is a basic national aim, which it considers to be of prime importance, and it has been willing to take serious military risks to achieve it. The Russians, on the other hand, probably feel that Taiwan is not worth the risk of a major war, which might well involve them. Many observers believe that Moscow has restrained Peking in its efforts to take Taiwan, and this is certainly possible. Certain events in early 1955 suggested the possibility of differences, or at least a lack of coordination, in their approaches to the Taiwan issue. Whereas the Soviet Union proposed an international conference on Taiwan, almost immediately thereafter the Chinese Communists, who insist that Taiwan is a domestic issue, proceeded to initiate bilateral talks with the United States about "relaxing tension" in the Taiwan area. Since then, however, and particularly since 1958, Peking seems to have obtained increasingly strong Soviet backing for its aims in regard to Taiwan, and this has been one important yardstick of Communist China's increasing weight within the Communist bloc.

Soviet and Chinese Communist policies toward South Asia, Southeast Asia, and the Middle East—in fact, toward the "colonial" and "semicolonial" areas as a whole—have generally been closely coordinated and mutually supporting in recent years. Even though both Peking and Moscow probably have considered this coordination to be essential, the Chinese Communists may have had mixed feelings about many Soviet activities in areas which Peking probably considers to be within its sphere of primary influence. Chou En-lai's energetic diplomatic campaign in Southeast Asia, launched in 1954, was immediately followed in 1955 by Khrushchev's spectacular tour of the area. In 1955 the Chinese Communists began building up an Asian solidarity movement, under their own primary influence, and then in 1958, when the Russians joined it, it was converted into an Afro-Asian solidarity movement, and its center of gravity was shifted to the Middle East, where Soviet rather than Chinese influence has been predominant in it. Perhaps both the Russian and Chinese leaders have viewed this coordination with satisfaction; yet one cannot rule out the possibility that their interests may also be competitive, to some degree at least, in these areas.

In the autumn of 1959 Moscow's reaction to the Chinese-Indian border dispute suggested that Peking's pressures on India—coming on the eve of Khrushchev's visit to the United States, when the Russians were attempting to "ease tensions" internationally—did not have Soviet backing. On September 9 the official Soviet news agency, in its first mention of the dispute, called on both sides to reach a settlement "in the spirit of friendship." What was remarkable about the statement was the fact that the Russians deliberately avoided taking sides in the dispute.

The relations of Communist China and the Soviet Union with Communist parties throughout Asia may also raise delicate problems within the alliance. Although there appears now to be more cooperation than competition in their backing of these parties, the existence of two major headquarters and two models for world revolution may some day raise important questions about where and how broad policies for the Communist movement are to be formulated, where the tactical direction of individual Asian parties is to be centered, and which "path" or model is to be followed in varying situations. Although the Chinese Communists themselves have underlined the importance of having "a leader" and have supported the Soviet party in this role, Peking's own influence has also steadily grown, and diffusion of authority may create conflicts even if both Moscow and Peking consciously attempt to avoid them. The Russians and Chinese may eventually find it necessary to define separate spheres of primary influence more clearly than they apparently have done so far.

Military and Economic Relations

Neither ideological stresses nor problems of policy coordination are likely to determine the future of the Sino-Soviet alliance, however; military and economic factors will probably be far more crucial. Over the past ten years the military bond between the U.S.S.R. and Communist China has without doubt been one of the strongest factors of cohesion in the alliance, and the relative military power of the two partners will certainly be a decisive factor in their future relations.

The Soviet Union has provided, and continues to provide, Communist China with large-scale military assistance, which has enabled Peking to build up its forces to their present level of effectiveness. From Moscow's point of view, there are great advantages in having a strong ally in Asia. A military alliance controlling the heartland of Eurasia, with interior lines of communication, has long been the dream—or the nightmare—of military strategists. And the Chinese Communists' contribution to the alliance, in terms of manpower as well as territory, is a tremendous one. From Peking's viewpoint, Soviet assistance has been essential. Communist China lacks the ability to manufacture on a large scale many vital elements of military equipment such as aircraft parts, and it is not self-sufficient in such basic raw materials as petroleum. Even more important, it cannot yet produce nuclear weapons. Peking is clearly the junior partner in a military sense, therefore, and theoretically the Russians could almost cripple Communist China's capacity to fight a modern war merely by cutting off certain crucial supplies.

The Chinese Communists are steadily building up their capacity to produce essential military equipment, but they have little prospect in the near future of catching up with the U.S.S.R. or the West in the crucial field of nuclear weapons. They are clearly eager to increase their military power by gaining possession of atomic weapons, and they probably aim eventually to develop an independent capacity to produce such weapons. But as of mid-1959 there was no evidence that they had yet obtained them, and despite Khrushchev's claim that rockets had been sent to China and the reports that Peking was reorganizing its forces into pentomic units, Moscow still seemed reluctant to share its atomic arsenal.

The complicated question of sharing advanced military technology may well prove to be among the most delicate issues in Sino-Soviet relations. If Moscow should hold back and refuse to share its atomic weapons with Communist China under any circumstances, this might well undermine the Chinese Communists' confidence in their ally. On the other hand, if the Russians should feel compelled to give Peking atomic weapons without adequate controls attached, the Chinese Communists might then pursue their own objectives in Asia more boldly, with fewer restraints exercised from Moscow. Differences over this issue might conceivably lead the Soviet Union and Communist China to adopt divergent positions on a number of issues, such as the limitation and inspection of armaments.

The changing character of Sino-Soviet economic relations also raises questions about possible strains between the two partners in the future. Without large-scale Soviet technical assistance, or without access to Russian supplies and equipment, the Chinese Communists could not, it is true, have carried out their development programs of the past decade. China's pattern of trade, furthermore, makes it highly dependent in some respects on the U.S.S.R. and the East European satellites. Yet the Chinese Communists' "dependence" should not be exaggerated. They have paid their own way financially, and the total amount of loans and credits they have received from the Russians has been small. By 1958 all past Soviet loans had been used up, and the Chinese Communists' export surpluses in trade with the Soviet Union were steadily rising.

Even if the Russians in their dealings with Peking justify the low level of their financial assistance by pointing to the burdens they have assumed elsewhere, in Eastern Europe and in the underdeveloped countries, the Chinese Communists may still be dissatisfied at having to carry their tremendous load without Soviet financial help. It is true that by relying primarily on their resources the Chinese Communists have safeguarded their economic independence, and perhaps they have not wanted to be too much in Moscow's debt. But the necessity of relying on China's own resources has added greatly to Peking's economic problems, and in all likelihood it would welcome more generous assistance from the U.S.S.R. Moscow's relative parsimony may well imply that it has had certain reservations about helping the Chinese Communists develop their economy too rapidly. And if Peking must continue paying its own way, at great cost to its people, its leaders may wonder whether it would be desirable to expand their trade and other economic contacts with countries outside the Communist bloc.

Relations with Other Communist States

Developments within the bloc during 1956-1957 suggest that under certain circumstances Peking might find it advantageous to act as a counterweight to the Soviet Union in Eastern Europe. The tendency of the East European Communists to look to China for support, and Peking's initiative in attempting to stabilize Soviet-satellite relations, introduced a new dimension into bloc affairs during that period. And despite the Russians' military and economic predominance, the Chinese Communists made their ideological and political influence felt to a significant degree. Since late 1957, it is true, Peking's strong support of bloc unity under Moscow's leadership and its increasingly doctrinaire policies at home and abroad have apparently made East European Communists much less sanguine about the possibility of Peking's protecting them against Moscow's demands for subservience. But if Communist China ever consciously attempted to challenge Soviet leadership, it might try to manipulate the East European nations for its own purposes.

In Outer Mongolia Soviet influence is predominant now, as it has been ever since the early 1920s. But this is an area of traditionally strong Chinese interest, and since 1949 Peking has increased markedly its contacts with Ulan Bator. In 1952 the Soviet Union, Communist China, and Outer Mongolia agreed to construct a railway connecting Russia and China via Mongolia. In the same year, Premier Tsedenbal made his first visit to China, and Outer Mongolia and China signed a ten-year agreement on economic and cultural cooperation. Since then political, cultural, and economic relations between Peking and Ulan Bator have increased steadily. The opening of the railway in early 1956, a rapid growth of trade, the initiation of a Chinese economic aid program to Ulan Bator, and the migration of several thousand Chinese workers to Outer Mongolia have substantially increased Chinese contacts and influence.

Although Peking has not attempted to challenge the predominant Soviet position, the Chinese Communists may not have abandoned China's traditional interest in Outer Mongolia. According to one Western interviewer, Mao asserted in 1936, for example, that, "when the people's revolution has been victorious in China the Outer Mongolian Republic will automatically become a part of the Chinese federation, at their own will." [62] And in 1944 he reportedly declared: "Our national government must first recognize Outer Mongolia as an autonomous national state in accordance with the promise Dr. Sun Yat-sen gave all national minorities. . . . I hope and have no doubt that they will rejoin China the moment the national government lives up to the promise of the founder of the Republic and the Kuomintang." [63]

There are actually more Mongols in China than in Outer Mongolia. Those in China have been organized by the Chinese into an "Inner Mongolian Autonomous Region," where, despite their growing political role, the Mongols are outnumbered by, and dominated by, the "Han" Chinese. While there has been no evidence yet of Mongol Irredentism, either in China or Outer Mongolia, there has been some increase of contacts across the border, and these may well continue to grow. The border itself, it may be noted, has never been officially demarcated.

Although for many decades before 1949 Korea was an area of conflict between Chinese and Russian strategic interests, today both Peking and Moscow exercise a strong influence in North Korea, and apparently they agree, either tacitly or explicitly, to share control of this satellite. The Soviet military occupation after World War II and the Chinese Communist occupation during and after the Korean War gave both Moscow and Peking a very direct role in Korean affairs, and, although pro-Soviet leaders now occupy the top positions in the North Korean regime, Communist China's economic support to the Korean Communists appears to be greater than Russia's. Perhaps the two powers will continue sharing influence and responsibility in this area, but this situation could conceivably lead to numerous problems and frictions, particularly if the general relationship between Moscow and Peking should become strained.

It seems almost inevitable that in the long run Peking's influence will predominate in North Vietnam, through trade, military support, and political and economic aid. But in certain conceivable situations Hanoi might consciously attempt to call upon the Soviet Union for support to counterbalance Chinese influence, much as the East European satellites looked hopefully to Peking for backing during their quarrels with Moscow in 1956 and 1957. In this, as in many other situations, the mere existence of two strong power centers within the Communist bloc introduces into bloc affairs a new element which was absent before 1949.

Other Contacts: The Borderlands and Communist Party Politics

China's borderlands, stretching from Manchuria to Sinkiang, have traditionally been a focus of conflicting Russian and Chinese ambitions. The mutual antagonism characteristic of pre-1949 Sino-Russian relations was nourished by rivalries in this area. However, since Stalin's death and Moscow's abandonment of its special interests in Manchuria and Sinkiang, Peking has steadily consolidated its control in the entire area along its frontier with Russia. Manchuria has been fully integrated into China proper, and "autonomous" regions under Peking's firm political control have been established in Inner Mongolia and Sinkiang. New communications, trade, and administrative links now bind all of these areas more closely to China. In Sinkiang the Soviet-oriented group of Uighurs and Kazakhs, who obtained Russian aid in their rebellion of 1944 against China and established an autonomous regime in the Ili region, have been brought under control by Peking, and the Ili region has been reintegrated with the rest of Sinkiang. The entire border region has become increasingly important in Peking's economic development program in recent years, and it has seen a steady flow of Chinese capital and labor, as well as Chinese troops, administrators, and settlers.

Some observers believe that, if anything, the traditional pressure from the Soviet Union toward China's borderlands may have been reversed, giving way to a potential outward pressure from China. It is at least possible that the Chinese drive to open up and develop the borderlands may cause some concern to Soviet leaders. Several West European politicians who have talked with Khrushchev have implied that the Soviet leaders are disturbed even now about China's explosive population growth and its possible implications for the Amur and Maritime Provinces (which Russia annexed from China in 1858 and 1860), as well as Siberia, which are still relatively underpopulated.[64]

Since 1949 there has been a steady increase of party contacts between the Chinese Communists and the Russians, and today political influence undoubtedly flows both ways. Soviet advisers as well as technicians have played a very important role within Communist China in a wide range of activities. There is little substantial evidence, however, that Moscow has been able to manipulate the political situation in China or that it has attempted to capitalize on whatever struggles for influence may have taken place within the Chinese Communist hierarchy. Perhaps the Russians, chastened by their experience with the Yugoslavs, have been wary about trying to infiltrate the party structure in China in the way that they did in the East European satellites. Almost certainly the cohesiveness of Peking's top leadership has limited Moscow's ability to influence developments in China by supporting particular individuals or groups within the Chinese party leadership.

Since 1956 there has been some speculation that Chinese Communist influence may have played a role in the struggles for power within the Soviet party; Polish sources have claimed, for example, that Peking has been involved in factional struggles between Khrushchev and "Stalinist" elements.[65] Some observers have argued that competing leaders within the Soviet party have looked for support to Peking, and it is claimed that Peking has backed up Khrushchev against both Malenkov and Molotov. Again there is little or no concrete evidence to support speculation of this sort. Yet, in theory, domestic party rivalries could conceivably become important in the relations between Moscow and Peking.

These and many other imponderable factors will affect the

future of the Sino-Soviet alliance. At present, however, strong ties—ideological, political, military, and economic—unite Peking and Moscow. Soviet and Chinese leaders share a common ideology and common aims. Both partners derive very great advantages from their alliance, and both would pay a tremendous price if the alliance were dissolved. For these reasons, it seems highly unrealistic to formulate policy on the expectation of a split between them. Yet their relationship is not a simple or uncomplicated one. Under the surface there are significant tensions, problems, and differences of outlook. And as the alliance continues to evolve, there will certainly be continuing changes in its internal relationships, and these could affect not only the policies of each of the partners but also the policies of the entire Communist bloc toward the outside world.

Implications for U.S. Policy

The nature of the Sino-Soviet alliance today clearly makes it unrealistic to believe that any foreseeable changes in United States policy toward China—for example, recognition of the Peking regime or the development of trade and other contacts with Communist China—could promote a split between Peking and Moscow in the near future. At best, United States policy toward China can probably have only a marginal influence on Peking's alliance with Moscow. If serious frictions should develop between the two partners they would doubtless arise out of tensions and problems within the Communist bloc rather than from outside wooing or prodding. Moreover, unless or until such frictions grow substantially from within, Peking is likely to be highly suspicious of any wooing, and extremely sensitive to any prodding, by a major Western power.

The dimensions of the challenge which Communist China presents in Asia can only be understood if the basic solidarity and strength of the Sino-Soviet alliance are appreciated fully. In dealing with Communist China over the years ahead, the United States will have to deal, not with Communist China alone, but with China backed by the power of the U.S.S.R.

Even if this estimate of bloc solidarity is accepted as a

fundamental premise of policy-making, however, it is also clear that relations between Peking and Moscow have steadily become more complex as Communist China's stature within the bloc has increased, and it is desirable, therefore, to ask whether United States policy toward China might be able to influence these relations at least in marginal ways. Might there be advantages to the United States, in its relations with the Communist bloc as a whole, from entering into direct dealings with Peking?

Many supporters of present American policy toward Communist China maintain that the best way to promote increased tensions or frictions within the Peking-Moscow axis is to isolate the Chinese Communist regime as much as possible from the outside world, forcing it into a position of maximum dependence on Moscow. It is difficult to say, however, that this kind of pressure has brought significant results over the past decade. In fact, even though the Sino-Soviet relationship has become increasingly complex, in a fundamental sense it may well be stronger now than it was in Stalin's lifetime.

It is equally difficult to provide convincing support for the alternative proposition—that increased acceptance of the Peking regime into the international community of nations, or expanded contacts between the United States and Communist China, would necessarily produce desirable results. Nevertheless, taking a long-range view, it is at least possible that the attitudes of leaders in Peking might be affected gradually, in ways desirable from the American viewpoint, by greater contacts with and improved knowledge of the United States and other major Western powers. Conceivably, increased contact with the West might eventually influence in some degree their assessment of the liabilities as well as the assets inherent in their present relationship with Moscow. Perhaps more important, from a short-run tactical point of view, the chances of exploiting differences and strains between the Soviet Union and Communist China might well be increased if the United States could deal directly with both members of the alliance. Differences in priorities, and difficulties of coordination, might come more into the open, and the United States might then be able actively, directly, and simultaneously to probe the positions of both Peking and Moscow. The Russians, in their dealings with the Western alliance, certainly find numerous opportunities to exploit differences among its members. The problems of policy coordination between Moscow and Peking are doubtless less complex than those within the Western alliance, but nevertheless the United States could do more than at present to probe them.

In many respects Peking is now the more doctrinaire and militant partner in the Sino-Soviet alliance. Communist China is still in a relatively early stage of its development and is strongly affected by its recent revolutionary past. It is still very much a "have-not" nation, whereas by contrast the U.S.S.R. may be increasingly inclined to avoid risks in order to preserve the economic gains it has already made. Peking is also, relatively speaking, a more unsatisfied power than the U.S.S.R., in terms of its national territorial claims and its desires for international status. These differences should not be ignored in the formulation of United States policy. In the years ahead, situations could arise in which the Soviet Union might have definite reservations about supporting the Chinese Communists' aspirations; under such circumstances it would be desirable for the United States, while maintaining direct channels of communication with both Moscow and Peking, to encourage the Russians to exert a restraining influence on the Chinese.

Chapter 13

TAIWAN AND THE CHINESE NATIONALIST REGIME

The Taiwan Strait has been a focal point of political and military tension ever since 1949. On one side of the strait is the island of Taiwan, present seat of the Chinese Nationalist government. Protected by strong American commitments to assist in its defense and bolstered by large-scale American aid, the Republic of China maintains its claim to be the legitimate government of all China and still looks forward to its "return to the mainland." On the other side is the Communist-run People's Republic of China. Peking regards the destruction of the Nationalist regime and the bringing of Taiwan under its control as one of its basic aims, a necessary final step in the unification of China, and it therefore demands the "liberation" of Taiwan. The United States is deeply involved in the continuing civil war between these two protagonists. Twice during the past decade, in 1954-1955 and again in 1958, the struggle has erupted in fighting over the small Nationalist-held offshore islands. Although American commitments to help defend Taiwan do not specifically extend to the offshore islands, the Communists' repeated threats to invade them, the Nationalists' resolve to hold them, and Washington's deliberately ambiguous policy toward them have twice brought the United States and Communist China to the brink of war.

The problems arising out of this situation are among the most complex and difficult which face United States policymakers anywhere in the world. The clashes of interests seem irreconcilable, the risks of open conflict are real, and the stakes involved are very great.

Land and People

Taiwan, or Formosa, is a rich semitropical island, lying some 100 miles from the mainland of China, about 400 miles from Okinawa, and less than 250 miles from the northern tip of the Philippines. Its 13,836 square miles now support a population of over 10 million people, concentrated on the coastal plain on the west side of the island, in the lee of high mountains which rise to the east. Approximately halfway between Taiwan and the China mainland are the Pescadores (Penghus), which have long been attached administratively to Taiwan. The offshore islands lie close to the China mainland. The Quemoy (Kinmen) and Matsu groups are located strategically along the Fukien coast adjacent to two major Chinese Communist ports, Amoy and Foochow. Most of the offshore islands have traditionally been attached to Fukien Province, but since its move to Taiwan the Nationalist government has held them and developed them into heavily fortified military positions.

The present population of Taiwan is Chinese, except for some 100,000 descendants of the aboriginal pre-Chinese tribes. There are important differences, however, between the 8 million local "Taiwanese," descended from early Chinese migrants, and the 2 million "mainlanders," most of whom came only in 1949. The Taiwanese have strong local roots. Even before the Japanese conquest in 1895 mainland China's political control over Taiwan was often fairly loose. Then, during their half-century of colonial rule, the Japanese had a significant cultural impact upon the Taiwanese, and the links between Taiwan and the mainland were substantially weakened. The 8 million local inhabitants now regard themselves, therefore, as "Taiwanese" as well as Chinese—or one might say they think of themselves as a special kind of Chinese. By contrast, the 2 million recent migrants from the mainland consider themselves basically to be temporary refugees. Most of them speak dialects different from the Hokkien or Hakka native to the majority of the Taiwanese. And, while clinging to the hope of returning to their homes on the mainland, most have been reluctant to sink deep roots in Taiwan.

Early Chinese Rule

Both the Nationalists and the Communists regard Taiwan as unquestionably Chinese territory, and they base their claims on the history of the island. The first Chinese contacts with Taiwan took place in the seventh century, according to Chinese sources.[1] In the thirteenth century the Yüan Dynasty gained control of the Pescadores, and during the fourteenth and fifteenth centuries Chinese migration to Taiwan began. Finally, during the seventeenth century, the Manchu (Ch'ing) Dynasty established its political control over Taiwan.

Throughout the seventeenth century Taiwan's history was extremely complex. Various outside powers and dissident Chinese forces vied for control, and the situation at that time paralleled the present state of affairs in many respects. In the early part of that century the Portuguese, Spanish, and Dutch all attempted to establish trading posts on the island; eventually the Spanish and Dutch occupied parts of it, and ultimately the Dutch achieved a supremacy which lasted for over 30 years. Their control was brought to an end only after the struggle for power on the mainland extended to Taiwan. After the Manchus had defeated the Ming Dynasty, a loyalist partisan of the Mings, Cheng Ch'eng-kung (Koxinga), fled across the Taiwan Strait with his army, conquering Taiwan in 1661-1662. For over 20 years Cheng and his descendants held the island against the Manchus, and pro-Ming refugees from the mainland swelled Taiwan's Chinese population to 200,000, roughly eight times the number who had migrated to the island previously. Finally, in 1682-1683 the Manchus captured Taiwan.[2] The local dynasty which Cheng had founded capitulated, and Taiwan was incorporated into Fukien Province.

During the next two centuries Manchu control of Taiwan was continuous, but at times it was fairly loose, and there were frequent rebellions against Peking's rule. Between the late seventeenth and late nineteenth centuries over a dozen important uprisings and numerous lesser disorders directed against the Manchu authorities were fomented either by the Chinese or by the aborigines. But over the years Manchu rule grew stronger, and Chinese immigration, which was especially large in the nineteenth century, bound Taiwan more closely to the mainland. By the end of the nineteenth century there were between 2 and 3 million Chinese on the island, and in 1885 Taiwan's status was raised when it was constituted as a separate province.[3]

Japanese Rule

Only ten years later China lost this new province. In the Treaty of Shimonoseki, at the end of the Sino-Japanese War of 1894-1895, China was forced to cede both Taiwan and the Pescadores to Japan. The Chinese on Taiwan opposed this and attempted to set up an "independent Island Republic" acknowledging Manchu suzerainty,[4] but the republic was short-lived. It took the Japanese several years to "pacify" the island, however, and they were plagued by serious disorders until 1902. Even after that, there were sporadic outbursts, as well as several armed revolts, instigated both by the Taiwanese Chinese and by the local aborigines. But eventually the Japanese successfully integrated Taiwan into their empire. They stopped almost all immigration from mainland China, and the large rise in Taiwan's population between 1895 and 1945—from between 2 and 3 million to roughly 6 million—resulted primarily from a natural increase.[5] Thousands of Japanese migrated to Taiwan as colonial administrators and businessmen. Ultimately there were 300,000 of them occupying all the key governmental and managerial posts on the island, and they consciously attempted to "Japanize" the Chinese.

Economically, Taiwan proved to be a highly successful colonial venture for Japan. The Japanese developed the resources of the island, constructing excellent transportation, communications, and hydroelectric power systems. They did a great deal to develop agriculture, concentrating especially on rice and sugar, and Taiwan's large agricultural surpluses were exported to Japan. Eventually, the island became an appendage of the Japanese economy, and nine-tenths of its trade was with Japan. From the mid-1930s onward the Japanese also put increasing emphasis upon industrial development on Taiwan. Attempting to build up the island as a self-supporting base for Japan's imperial ventures in Southeast Asia, they developed cement, aluminum, oil refining, and other important industries.[6]

Under Japanese rule the Taiwanese enjoyed a higher standard of living, greater law and order, a higher literacy rate, and better public health protection than did the Chinese on the mainland. They enjoyed few opportunities for cultural development, however, and had virtually no opportunities for political self-expression. They deeply resented their treatment as inferior colonial subjects and remained unruly throughout the period of Japanese rule.

Restoration of Chinese Rule

To Chinese leaders on the mainland Japan's encroachments on China were an ever-present symbol of national humiliation, and the recovery of all the territories taken by Japan was a primary national aim. During World War II the major allies pledged themselves to support this aim. At Cairo in December 1943 Roosevelt, Churchill, and Chiang K'ai-shek jointly declared as their "purpose" that "all the territories Japan has stolen from the Chinese, such as Manchuria, Formosa and the Pescadores, shall be restored to the Republic of China."[7] The U.S.S.R. also approved this objective in the Potsdam Proclamation of July 1945. In August 1945, after the Japanese government accepted the Potsdam terms as a basis for surrender, MacArthur's General Order No. 1 directed that Chiang K'ai-shek should receive the surrender of Japanese forces on Taiwan.[8] In September 1945 Chinese Nationalist forces took control of the island.

The record of Chinese Nationalist administration of Taiwan in the years immediately after 1945 was a disillusioning one.[9] Although some competent Chinese technicians from the mainland tried to begin repairing the damage caused by Allied bombing during the war, incompetent military and civilian officials proceeded to mismanage the island and antagonize the local population. At first the Taiwanese had welcomed the Nationalist officials as liberators, but within two years they became openly rebellious against the mainland officials who acted like conquerors and exploited the island as carpetbaggers. The Nationalist government took over monopolistic control of the economy from the 300,000 Japanese, who were repatriated. The economy was seriously disrupted, and the political administration deteriorated rapidly.

In February 1947 Taiwanese resentment exploded in revolt. Rioters attacked the occupation authorities, and a Taiwanese "Committee for the Settlement of the February 28th Incident" was set up. The Nationalist commander, Ch'en Yi, at first gave the appearance of accepting some of their demands, but then, after military reinforcements had arrived from the mainland, he launched a brutal suppression campaign in which an estimated 10,000 Taiwanese were killed.[10] After 50 years of colonial rule Taiwan had very few men of political experience and sophistication, and of these few a large proportion were killed in 1947.

Almost immediately after this disaster Chiang K'ai-shek removed Ch'en Yi, and under a more competent governor Taiwan was reconstituted as a regular province of China.[11] Some Taiwanese were brought into the administration, and efforts at reform were undertaken. But the Nationalist government, engaged in bitter civil war with the Communists on the mainland, was becoming more and more demoralized and could pay little attention to Taiwan's needs.

Refuge for the Nationalists

When the Nationalists transferred the seat of their government to Taiwan in late 1949, most observers felt that it was only a matter of time before the Communists would take over. The Nationalists were disorganized and discredited, and Taiwan was still suffering from the deterioration of recent years. And in early 1950 the United States disassociated itself militarily from Chiang K'ai-shek's regime and its Taiwan refuge. In January 1950 President Truman declared that the United States had "no predatory designs on Formosa or any other Chinese territory," did not have "any intention of utilizing its armed forces to interfere in the present situation," and would "not provide military aid or advice to the Chinese forces on Formosa." [12] When he made this statement,

Chinese Communist troops were already preparing for an amphibious assault against Taiwan.

Then the Korean War, and the United States reaction to it, basically altered the entire situation affecting Taiwan. On June 27, 1950, President Truman announced an about-face in American policy. Asserting that "the attack upon Korea makes it plain beyond all doubt that communism has passed beyond the use of subversion to conquer independent nations and will now use armed invasion and war," Truman declared that "in these circumstances the occupation of Formosa by Communist forces would be a direct threat to the security of the Pacific area."[13] He announced a policy designed to "neutralize" Taiwan. "I have ordered the Seventh Fleet to prevent any attack on Formosa," Truman said, and "I am calling upon the Chinese Government on Formosa to cease all air and sea operations against the mainland." He also reopened the question of Taiwan's legal status. "The determination of the future status of Formosa," he said, "must await the restoration of security in the Pacific, a peace settlement with Japan, or consideration by the United Nations." Following this policy shift, and particularly after the Chinese Communist intervention in the Korean War, Washington initiated a new program of large-scale military and economic assistance to the Nationalist government on Taiwan.

This radical change in United States policy gave the Nationalists a new lease on life. Even prior to this the disastrous defeats suffered on the mainland had led many of the Nationalist leaders to examine the causes of their past failures and had stimulated them to embark on many needed measures of reorganization and reform. Then, with American assistance, the Nationalist regime began to remake itself into a going concern. In the past decade it has come a long way from the low point of 1949. It has created an effective administrative apparatus. It has reorganized and retrained its military forces, converting them into a military establishment of considerable strength. And it has initiated a fairly impressive economic development program which has increased production to levels well above those attained under Japanese rule. Despite its progress in many fields, however, the Nationalist regime still suffers from the heritage of the past, and it faces many difficult problems in the future.

Chiang and the Present Nationalist Regime

The Nationalist government of today defies any simple classification. It has been called "the best government in Asia," and it has also been denounced, for example, by ex-Governor K. C. Wu, as a "police state." [14] Actually, it is neither, in any complete sense. It is a government which blends and compromises numerous conflicting strands: traditional Chinese ideas of paternalistic authoritarianism, Western ideas of parliamentary representative government, and Soviet ideas of mass organization and political control.

The structure of its government is parliamentary in form and combines features borrowed from both the British cabinet system and the American presidential system with certain traditional Chinese institutions. However, the Kuomintang or Nationalist party remains a Leninist-type mass organization, based on the concept of "democratic centralism" borrowed from the Communists. But these facts do not explain the realities of political power on Taiwan today. The basic character of the regime can only be understood in terms of the dominating position and personality of Chiang K'ai-shek, president of the Republic, leader of the party, and the real source of all political power.

Chiang K'ai-shek is a man with an unshakable belief in his own destiny and a stubborn confidence that the future of China rests in his own hands. Reconquest of the mainland is his fundamental aim, and despite past defeats he remains dedicated to this primary objective. He thinks of himself in old Confucian terms as a leader who, because he carries the primary burden of responsibility, also has the right to demand absolute personal loyalty in return. Virtually every policy decision of any importance is made either by him personally or by his immediate entourage.

The dominating force of Chiang's personality and the loyalty which he demands have in many respects been a source of strength to the Nationalist regime since 1949. On the small island of Taiwan, his influence has been more pervasive than it ever was on the mainland, and personal loyalty to "the leader" has served as a mortar to keep the varied elements of the regime together, minimizing internal cleavages and disunity.[15] Clearly, however, Chiang's domination of the regime is also a source of weakness, if one looks into the future. He has retarded the growth of other leadership and prevented the development of political institutions with real vitality by inhibiting initiative and creativeness among his subordinates. Eventually his passing from the scene—he is now 72—is likely to be followed by considerable confusion and uncertainty.

In late 1958, not long after Mao Tse-tung had announced his intention—subsequently carried out—of giving up the chairmanship of the Communist regime, Chiang K'ai-shek declared that he would relinquish the presidency of the Nationalist government in May 1960 when his present term of office expires.[16] In the past, Chiang has given up top posts in the government without actually letting go of any of his political authority, however, and there is every reason to believe that he will continue to keep the reins of power in his own hands as long as he is physically able to do so, whatever his formal position.

There is really no leader on the horizon who seems able to assume Chiang's unique role. The most likely successor to his formal position as top leader is Ch'en Ch'eng, a close associate for many years, who since 1949 has been, first, Governor of Taiwan, then Vice-President, and, since 1958, Premier as well as Vice-President. Ch'en has proved an able, competent administrator, but there is little likelihood that he can assume Chiang's mantle in any real sense. Another possible contender for the succession is one of Chiang's sons, Chiang Ching-kuo, who controls numerous elements of power —including the secret police, the political officers in the army, and the major mass youth organization. Chiang Ching-kuo may have ambitions to succeed his father, but many Nationalist leaders would resist the idea of transferring their loyalty from father to son.

In all likelihood, therefore, the symbol which Chiang K'ai-shek represents—a symbol of hope for return to the mainland

and of unity within the Kuomintang's ranks—will either disappear or be greatly weakened upon his death. Temporarily, this may weaken the Nationalist regime considerably. But it may also permit new ideas and leadership to emerge and encourage a reassessment by Nationalist leaders of the realities of their situation on Taiwan. In the long run this could further the interests of the regime even though it might alter its character in many ways.

The Kuomintang

The Kuomintang party organization under Chiang is a mass political organization which ever since 1924 has been based upon Soviet political concepts. It monopolizes a majority of the key political and military positions on Taiwan. Despite some concessions to the forms of multiparty democracy, the Nationalists have not tolerated the development of any significant opposition; the two other small parties on Taiwan, the Young China party and Social Democratic party, lack any substance of real power or influence. Actually, the Kuomintang has tightened rather than loosened its internal party controls in recent years. Many Nationalist leaders blame past defeats on the mainland primarily on their inability to infuse effective discipline into the Kuomintang rather than upon any failure to develop multiparty democracy, and consequently efforts at party reform since 1950 have concentrated on strengthening the party as a "democratic centralist" mass organization. In its ideological appeals, the Kuomintang clings to slogans first formulated by Sun Yat-sen, which have lost much of their force of attraction for Chinese on Taiwan or elsewhere. Although Sun's "Three People's Principles" have undergone some reinterpretation in recent years, there is little sign at present of ideological vigor. One very significant change has taken place within the Kuomintang since 1949, however. There has been a steady recruitment of local Taiwanese into the party's membership, and with a large percentage of Taiwanese members the party will probably develop closer links with local problems and local people than in the past.

Government Administration

The government on Taiwan today presents great contrasts with the Nationalists' past administrative record on the mainland. Major corruption has been eliminated, and efficiency has been substantially improved. The government has demonstrated a capacity to rule which was clearly lacking during its last days on the mainland.

Progress has been made in introducing some of the forms of local representative government on Taiwan. Genuine elections are now held for representative councils and executives at the county and municipal levels, as well as for a provincial representative body. A majority of these local elective positions is held by Taiwanese, and in the elections of early 1958 almost four-fifths of the eligible electorate went to the polls.[17] This has not yet altered the monopoly of real political power which is held by mainlanders and Kuomintang members, however. Almost all top positions in the central government are still held by Kuomintang leaders who came with Chiang from the mainland, and at the local level, although a few non-Kuomintang politicians have defeated Kuomintang members in election contests, the large majority of those elected are Taiwanese members of the party.

At the highest level the government administration is a complicated, top-heavy bureaucracy. The superstructure of a national government is maintained above the Taiwan provincial government as a symbol of the Nationalists' claim to be the government of all China and of their hope to return to the mainland. This results in a cumbersome structure and deprives the Taiwanese of any significant participation in the decision-making process, since the central government remains the preserve of mainlanders for the most part.

The Nationalists also maintain an elaborate system of police supervision and political control. They justify this apparatus as a necessary means of coping with the danger of subversion, which is real, but it also prevents the growth of any legitimate political opposition or of genuinely democratic processes.[18] The degree of control exercised over the population cannot be compared with the totalitarianism of Chinese Communist control across the Taiwan Strait, however. On

Taiwan there is some criticism of the administration in the press and in political bodies such as the legislative Yüan and Provincial Council, and nonpolitical citizens are relatively little affected by the control apparatus. One might say that, while retaining the instruments of totalitarian rule, the Nationalists utilize them with relative restraint. The average citizen on Taiwan enjoys a fairly high degree of personal freedom and has acquired an increasing number of formal political rights, even though his real political freedom is still limited and his actual political power or influence is severely restricted.

The presence of men of widely differing political views within the Nationalist government, and even within the Kuomintang party organization, testifies to the far from monolithic character of the regime. Liberal democratic elements and elements with strong totalitarian proclivities exist side by side, and a certain balance between these disparate elements prevents the regime from being either genuinely democratic or genuinely totalitarian. However, in recent years its ability to attract the support of intellectuals and youth both at home and abroad has been affected adversely by the disgrace which has befallen several leading figures popularly regarded as political liberals, among them, former Governor K. C. Wu and General Sun Li-jen.[19]

The Nationalist regime has not, in fact, provided an effective rallying point for intellectuals and youth among the large number of anti-Communist but non-Kuomintang Chinese who are scattered all over the world, in Hong Kong and elsewhere. Recently, it is true, a few prominent intellectuals, such as the scholar and former diplomat Hu Shih, have been attracted back to Taiwan, but the Nationalists have retained a deep apprehension about subversion, and a fundamental prejudice against all who in the past have not given unqualified support to the Kuomintang, and they still pursue policies which in practice tend to discourage contacts between Taiwan and Chinese exiles elsewhere.

Despite its shortcomings, however, the Nationalist regime appears to have achieved a fairly high degree of political stability on Taiwan, at least by comparison with a decade ago. To the two million mainlanders it remains the focus of hope for return to the mainland. Although the resentments of the Taiwanese are difficult to assess, since they cannot be freely expressed, they appear to have steadily decreased. The Nationalists have made a deliberate effort to improve relations between mainlanders and Taiwanese and have made some concessions to them. At the lower levels in the government, party, and army, the role of Taiwanese has become steadily more important, and the regime has come increasingly to rely on them in many respects.

The Taiwanese

It is difficult to know what the real political attitudes and aspirations of the Taiwanese are today. It seems probable that a majority continues to regard the Nationalists fundamentally as a group of outsiders. Clearly they still have many resentments and grievances and would like to achieve a greater degree of self-rule, political power, and governmental responsibility. However, there are few visible signs of the bitter hostility of earlier years, and although the existing resentments may be greater than appears on the surface, there is almost no indication that they have given rise to any significant pro-Communist feeling. The Peking regime has supported a so-called "Taiwan Democratic Self-Government League" on the mainland, but it has never been much more than a name. It has had no visible impact on Taiwan, and in late 1957 its leader was denounced by the Communists as a "rightist."[20] Actually, Peking's political appeals are directed more to the mainland refugees than to the local Taiwanese. It has little basis for appealing to the Taiwanese; they already enjoy a far higher standard of living and considerably more political freedom than they could expect under Communist rule, and, in any case, they would like less, not more, control by mainlanders.

A small Taiwanese independence movement, first formed in late 1948, has been based in Tokyo for the past decade.[21] It was set up in 1948 by Dr. Thomas Liao and several other Taiwanese intellectuals who had fled from their home island after the 1947 revolt. In 1950, a Formosan Democratic Independence party was formed, and in late 1955 these Taiwanese dissidents organized a "Provisional Government of the Republic of Formosa" in Tokyo. In early 1956 they "declared Formosa's independence" and "elected" Liao as President. Although there is no firm basis for judging whether or not this group of exiles speaks for any substantial body of feeling on Taiwan, it is possible that they evoke considerable secret sympathy from some Taiwanese intellectuals.[22] But since they lack any important organizational base and have almost no prospect at present of gaining access to the sources of military and political power, there appears to be little immediate possibility of a successful Taiwanese independence movement developing on the island.

Many foreign observers believe that if the Taiwanese were in a position freely to determine their own political future, they would choose either independence or autonomy or some sort of United Nations-sponsored trusteeship status (possibly under either United States or Japanese supervision). As long as no such alternatives are available to them, however, there seems little doubt that they prefer a continuation of Nationalist rule to control by Peking, and at present these appear to be the only alternatives in sight.[23]

Economic Development

The Nationalists' accomplishments in the social and economic fields during the past decade are more impressive, in many respects, than their political achievements.[24] There has been a marked improvement in economic stability, and numerous development projects have been undertaken by the Nationalists with American assistance. Production has increased to new highs. The standard of living—already one of the highest in Asia (exceeded only by Japan and Malaya) —has risen, and the island's economy has grown at an impressive rate.

Agriculture, the foundation of Taiwan's economy, has undergone substantial development. Food output has been increasing by an average of about 5 per cent annually during the past few years.[25] In addition, the government has implemented a notable program of social reform in the countryside. As early as 1949 Governor Ch'en Ch'eng took the initiative in implementing an excellent land reform program. In its first stage land rents were limited to a maximum of 37.5 per cent of the main crop, and tenants were ensured reasonable security of land tenure. Subsequently, large amounts of government land and landlord holdings above a fixed acreage have been sold to tenant farmers on reasonable terms. This program, carried out in an orderly and peaceful manner, with compensation for dispossessed landlords, has benefited about 75 per cent of Taiwan's farm families and has reduced the incidence of tenant farming from 41 per cent to 16 per cent of the farm acreage on the island.[26]

In the program of agricultural improvement and development on Taiwan, an important role has been played by a unique and highly successful Sino-American organization, the Joint Commission on Rural Reconstruction. Supported by American funds and technicians, but largely manned by Chinese, this organization carried out 2,258 projects between 1949 and 1957. It has achieved marked progress in almost every field of rural improvement—irrigation and water control, forestry and soil conservation, rural health, crop improvement, mechanization, and many others.

Total agricultural output on Taiwan increased by 32 per cent between 1950 and 1956. Between 1949 and 1957 the output of rice rose from 1.2 million tons to 1.8 million tons, and sugar production increased from 626 thousand tons to 866 thousand tons.[27] Sugar production is still considerably below the peak figure under Japanese rule, but this is largely because sugar-cane planting has been restricted in favor of other more urgently needed crops, and because the export of sugar has been hampered by international quotas. However, rice output in 1957 exceeded the peak figure during the Japanese period by over 400,000 tons.

Taiwan's industrial development has also been impressive. During 1953-1956, the period of Taiwan's first Four Year Plan, many new factories were constructed, and by 1956 total industrial output had risen by 132 per cent compared with 1950.[28] The increase in output between 1949 and 1957 was very large in a wide range of industries: from 45,800 tons to 215,000 tons in fertilizers, 291,000 tons to 604,000 tons in cement, from 29 million to 155 million square meters in cloth, from under 2,000 tons to almost 28,000 tons in cotton yarn, from 1.6 million tons to 2.9 million tons in coal, from 854 million kwh to 2.5 billion kwh in electricity, and from under 3,000 tons to almost 60,000 tons in paper.

Hard work not only by members of the Nationalist administration, but also by a large number of well-qualified non-political technicians, both mainlanders and Taiwanese, together with large-scale American economic assistance, has resulted in an over-all rate of economic growth on Taiwan which has been one of the highest in Asia during the past few years. Between 1950 and 1956 Taiwan's gross national product increased by 66 per cent.[29] And in 1957 its national income rose by over 7 per cent (in constant 1956 prices).[30] As these figures indicate, Taiwan's rate of economic growth in recent years has been approximately the same as the rates achieved by Japan and Communist China and is far higher than those of most other Asian countries.

Despite this evidence of progress, however, Taiwan faces many economic problems and uncertainties. Stating the basic problem simply, Taiwan has become an economic dependency of the United States, and even though present economic planning aims to make the island self-supporting, there is little prospect that it can achieve this goal in the forseeable future. The heavy economic burden of the Nationalists' large military establishment, the very high rate of population growth, and other fundamental problems create difficulties which have no easy solutions.

Population Problem

Taiwan's population problem raises some of the most difficult questions about the future. The sudden influx of two million mainlanders imposed a tremendous strain on the resources of a small island, but a more fundamental and continuing problem is created by the high rate of population growth. Taiwan's net annual increase of population is now estimated to be about 3.5 per cent a year![31] Due in large part to improved medical facilities and a rising standard of living, this phenomenal rate will probably continue for some years, since the Nationalist regime is not attempting to promote birth control or other policies to restrict population growth. And if present growth rates continue, Taiwan's population will double over the next generation.

Taiwan's ability to increase agricultural output to support such a rapid growth in population is definitely limited. Most of the cultivable land on the island is already in use, and per-acre yields are already extremely high. Some land now under dry farming can be made more productive through irrigation—the Nationalists' ambitious Shihmen Dam project is an illustration of possibilities along this line—and yields can be increased somewhat through further technical improvements, but as optimum conditions are approached the rate of increase in agricultural output will almost inevitably slow down.

Increased industrialization can help to solve the island's problems, but the possibilities of attracting private investment for this purpose are also limited at present. One major deterrent to large-scale foreign private investment is the uncertainty about Taiwan's future. Another is the fact that despite some liberalization of the Nationalist regime's laws and regulations affecting private enterprise, the climate for private investment is still not one which attracts large-scale investment from abroad; the government's role in the economy is an extremely pervasive one. Significantly, Overseas Chinese have invested far less capital in Taiwan than in Hong Kong and elsewhere in the past few years. Taiwan's recent industrial development has been made possible primarily by the large inflow of American government aid, and unless this assistance is continued on a large scale, the rate of industrialization is likely to decline rather than rise.

Furthermore, industrialization in itself cannot provide a complete answer to Taiwan's basic economic problems. The island has a large gap in its international balance of payments, which has been filled during recent years by United States aid. In 1957, for example, Taiwan's imports totaled 252 million dollars, while its exports were only 169 millions. Of the 252 million dollars in imports, 99 millions were so-called "U.S. aid imports," as compared with 154 millions of normal "commercial imports." [32] Taiwan's traditional exports, furthermore, have consisted largely of agricultural products, and the prospects for increasing such exports are limited. Exports of industrial goods have increased substantially in recent years, but in finding and holding markets for its manufactured products Taiwan faces stiff and growing competition from Japan, Communist China, and Hong Kong, to say nothing of the major non-Asian competitors for Asian markets.

The Economic Burden of the Military

Another of Taiwan's fundamental economic problems is created by the heavy burden imposed by the Nationalists' military establishment. For an island with a total population of 10 million—1/65 the population base of the Chinese Communist regime—to support roughly 600,000 men in uniform is a highly abnormal situation, to say the least, and the economic load could not be borne at all without large-scale American assistance. The United States provides the Nationalists, on a free grant basis, with most of its military "hardware"—that is, major equipment and supplies. In addition, the bulk of American "economic aid" to Taiwan is classified as "defense support," required to bolster the economy so that it can support the military establishment. In the fiscal year 1958, for example, of the 60 million dollars of economic aid to Taiwan which the International Cooperation Administration "obligated" during the year, 57 million dollars was classified as "defense support" and only 3 million as "technical cooperation." [33] This is somewhat misleading, since the "defense support" included large amounts of commodities required by the civilian economy, as well as equipment for industrial development projects, in addition to commodities needed by the military—which was formerly called "direct forces support." Nevertheless, a very large share of the "economic aid" has been required simply to support the military establishment, and the Nationalist government's budget depends heavily upon the "counterpart funds" derived from the local sale of United States aid imports. A huge percentage of all government expenditures on Taiwan—about four-fifths of central government expenditures and over one-half of the expenditures of government at every level, central, provincial, and local—goes to support the military establishment.

Taiwan's Dependence on United States Aid

Because of the extraordinary burdens which Taiwan's economy has supported, the island has been, and remains today, fundamentally dependent on large-scale American assistance. Since no official figures are published on direct military aid, it is not possible to give an exact figure for the total assistance over the past decade, but it has certainly exceeded two billion dollars. "Economic" aid alone totaled 817 million dollars in actual "expenditures" (and 909 millions in "obligated" funds) between April 1949 and June 1958.[34] During the six years through the fiscal year 1957 it averaged between 90 million and 100 million dollars annually. And military aid was more than double economic aid during much of this period. In at least some years, therefore, total American aid to Taiwan exceeded 300 million dollars, or over 30 dollars per capita. In the fiscal year 1958 economic aid "expenditures" were reduced to 68 million dollars (obligations during the year were 60 million dollars),[35] but the offshore islands crisis of late 1958 required a stepping up of deliveries of military assistance.

If United States aid to Taiwan were suddenly ended, the results would be disastrous for both the Nationalist regime and the people of Taiwan. Even if the island's economic development can be stepped up, and its dependence upon the United States thereby reduced gradually, there is little possibility that it will be able to stand on its own feet economically in the years immediately ahead. Separated from both the China mainland and Japan, burdened with a large and expanding population, supporting a very large military establishment, and caught in the vortex of international rivalries in Asia, the Nationalist regime will require continuing external economic support for the foreseeable future in order to survive.

Military Position

The military position of the Nationalist regime is comparable in many respects to its economic position. During the past decade the Nationalists have made impressive progress in building up their military strength, but, in view of the great military power of the Communist regime on the mainland, there is little doubt that, if external support and protection—now provided by the United States—were removed, Taiwan would soon fall under Chinese Communist control.

A decade ago the bulk of the Nationalist troops who fled the mainland were not much more than a disorganized and demoralized rabble. Since then—and particularly since the establishment of a United States Military Assistance Advisory Group on Taiwan in May 1951—they have been reorganized into a respectable fighting force. Of the 600,000 men in uniform, approximately 465,000 can be classified as combat forces: 300,000 effective ground troops; 80,000 in the air force; 60,00 in the navy; 25,000 in the marines. Roughly one-third of the combat ground forces are stationed on the offshore islands, and the balance are on Taiwan itself.

The Nationalists have energetically attacked many of the problems which formerly plagued their military forces and have greatly improved their effectiveness. They have instituted an honest and effective supply system. They have retired large numbers of useless, supernumerary military officers. They have improved the treatment of rank and file troops. Through intensive training they have maintained their forces at a fairly high level of combat readiness. They have worked out improved coordination between the various components of their forces.

What the morale of the Nationalist troops would be under conditions of large-scale combat is not wholly predictable, however. The political officer system within the forces, modeled on the Communist system of commissars, has helped to ensure discipline and has exposed the troops to intensive political indoctrination. But it has also caused resentments among the rank and file which are difficult to assess. Political factors still play a major role in the assignment of top command posts, and the disgrace inflicted upon Sun Li-jen—one of the most "nonpolitical" of the Nationalist generals—was a blow to those officers who favored the steady development of less personalized command relationships. To the extent that it has been tested in recent years, however, the morale of the Nationalist forces has stood up well. In the offshore islands crises of 1954-1955 and 1958 the troops performed creditably under fire. And in 1958 particularly Nationalist pilots outperformed, man-for-man, their Chinese Communist adversaries.

Until recently it was widely assumed that in time the Nationalist forces would steadily decline in effectiveness as the troops who had come from the mainland became superannuated. Since 1953, however, a local conscription system appears to have "solved"—at least temporarily—the replacement problem. At present, over one-third of the Nationalist forces consist of Taiwanese youth, and the average age of the forces has been brought down to 26.[36]

The steady replacement of refugee mainland troops with local Taiwanese recruits may eventually have far-reaching effects on the character of the forces of Taiwan. During the past decade the morale of the troops who came from the mainland in 1949 has been bolstered by the hope of an early return to the mainland. But an army composed of local Taiwanese is likely to have quite different attitudes. In spite of indoctrination in the idea of active struggle against the Communists on the mainland, Taiwanese troops almost certainly will see their main purpose as that of defending their homes on Taiwan and avoiding conflict with the Peking regime. Furthermore, it is highly questionable whether local recruitment from a population of ten million can support indefinitely a military establishment of the present size.

In realistic terms, even though the Nationalists now have one of the strongest non-Communist military establishments in Asia, surpassed in the Far East only by that of South Korea, Taiwan cannot defend itself against the huge armies of Communist China without outside assistance. It is quite clear, in fact, that since 1950 the most important deterrents to a Communist attack on the island have been the American commitment to defend Taiwan—a commitment backed by the Seventh Fleet—and the water barrier which separates Taiwan from the mainland.

"Return to the Mainland"

If the primary mission of the Nationalists' armed forces were defined purely in terms of defending Taiwan, there seems little doubt that the size of these forces—and the economic burden they impose upon the island's economy— could be considerably reduced, provided the United States maintained its pledge to defend the island with American naval and air forces. However, Chiang and other top Nationalist leaders have strongly resisted any major reorientation of their basic outlook which would imply abandonment, or even any extended postponement, of their fundamental aim of returning to the mainland. Chiang maintains that large forces would be crucial in the event of major conflict, for use against the China mainland or elsewhere in Asia, and this consideration, especially urgent during the Korean War, apparently influenced American planners in their own estimates of the desirability of building up a large Nationalist military establishment.

Chiang believes that the world-wide conflict between the Communist and non-Communist blocs will inevitably lead to new military conflicts and that the only real choice lies between local wars and a world war. He asserts that because of popular disaffection the Peking regime is actually weak despite its outward appearance of strength, and he maintains that if the mainland were attacked from without effective internal opposition to the regime would develop rapidly. He professes to believe that Nationalist forces could attack the Peking regime with no more than political and logistical support from the United States, although he may actually believe that a large-scale conflict between his forces and the Communists would almost inevitably lead to full-scale American participation. "If the democracies wish to prevent the outbreak of an all-out world war and to save mankind from a major calamity," Chiang stated in *Soviet Russia in China —A Summing Up at Seventy,* published in 1957, "the only way is to substitute a local war in East Asia for an all-out world war and to fight a war with conventional weapons instead of a war of annihilation with thermonuclear weapons." [37] "All we need" from the Western nations, he said, "is moral and material assistance and the supply of arms and technical aid."

Communist China's Aims and Tactics

If Chiang shows an unwavering determination to return to the mainland, the Chinese Communists are equally firm in their determination to gain control of Taiwan. Peking has varied its tactics over the past decade, but it has shown no sign of abandoning this central aim.

In 1949 and early 1950 the Chinese Communists actively prepared for what they predicted would be the "biggest campaign in the history of modern Chinese warfare," [38] and they appeared confident of their ability to capture Taiwan. Then in June 1950 the American "neutralization" of the Taiwan Strait blocked the achievement of this aim and evoked violent propaganda attacks against the United States. From 1950 until 1955 Peking made repeated threats against both the Nationalist regime and the United States and talked almost constantly of "liberating" Taiwan by force. Accusing the United States of having "turned Taiwan into a United States colony as well as a military base for attacking our country," Chou En-lai in 1954 warned, for example, that "if any foreign aggressors dare to prevent the Chinese people from liberating Taiwan, if they dare to infringe upon our sovereignty and violate our territorial integrity, if they dare to interfere in our internal affairs, they must take upon themselves all the grave consequences of such acts of aggression." [39] He labeled the "Chiang K'ai-shek clique of national betrayal" as "public enemies of the Chinese people."

Peking's Shift in Tactics

The intensity of this propaganda campaign was moderated for a time, while the Chinese Communists were preoccupied elsewhere. Then, after the fighting had been halted in Korea and Vietnam, and Peking could again devote primary attention to Taiwan, Communist China applied strong military pressure to the offshore islands in late 1954 and early 1955. This pressure brought about the evacuation of the Tachen Islands by the Nationalists, but it also led the United States to extend its commitments to support the Nationalist regime. By early 1955, apparently having realized that it could not achieve its aims by threats alone, Peking decided to shift to a new kind of policy.

The first move in this shift was Chou En-lai's public offer, made at the time of the Bandung Conference in April 1955, to "sit down and enter into negotiations with the United States Government to discuss the question of relaxing tension in the Far East, and especially the question of relaxing tension in the Taiwan area." [40] In July Chou declared that Peking was willing to negotiate directly with "the responsible local authorities" on Taiwan for a "peaceful liberation" of the island.[41] A year later, in June 1956, he reiterated the Communists' willingness to negotiate "with the Taiwan authorities on specific steps and terms for peaceful liberation of Taiwan," and added that "we hope the Taiwan authorities will send their representatives to Peking or other appropriate places, at a time which they consider appropriate, to begin these talks with us." [42] "Patriots belong to one family," Chou declared. He announced a "policy of no punishment for past deeds," offered rewards for "meritorious services" by defectors from the Nationalists, and warned the mainlanders on Taiwan that "only thus can they escape the fate of leading the life of exiles in foreign lands, being looked down on by others." Later in 1956 Chou was quoted as offering even Chiang K'ai-shek a high post under the Peking regime.[43] None of these blandishments appeared to have any substantial effect on the Nationalists, however, and there were almost no defections from either the leaders of the regime or the rank and file of its forces.

During 1957 Peking began to shift its line once again. It started to show increased apprehension about the possibility of the United States adopting some sort of "two Chinas" policy, and it sought now to drive a wedge between the Nationalists and the United States with repeated warnings that the Americans were entirely undependable allies. The

United States, Chou said in early 1957, "has instigated a group of people claiming to represent so-called Free China or so-called independent Taiwan to overthrow the Taiwan authorities, in an attempt to turn Taiwan into a United States dependency like Honolulu." [44] "If the United States can launch a movement to overthrow the authorities in Taiwan," Chou warned, "why could it not abandon tomorrow the self-termed Free China or independent Taiwan elements? . . . All decent Chinese should unite," he declared, "as patriotic members of one big family and together fight against and crush the schemes of United States imperialism."

Then in the late summer of 1958, in another switch of tactics, Peking again applied military pressure, threatening, as in 1954-1955, to invade the offshore islands. This time it combined military pressure with continued efforts to attract Nationalist leaders and with warnings against an imminent abandonment of the Nationalist regime by the United States. "Chinese problems must be settled by us Chinese alone," said the top Chinese military commander, P'eng Teh-huai, in a statement directed to Taiwan.

There is only one China, not two, in the world. On this we agree. All Chinese people, including you and compatriots abroad, absolutely will not allow the American plot to forcibly create two Chinas to come true. . . . All patriots have a future and should not be afraid of the imperialists. Of course we are not advising you to break with the Americans right away. That would be an unrealistic idea. We only hope that you will not yield to American pressure, submit to their every whim and will, lose your sovereign rights, and so finally be deprived of a shelter in the world and thrown into the sea. These words of ours are well intentioned and bear no ill will. You will come to understand them by and by.[45]

In addition to making general propaganda declarations of this sort, the Chinese Communists, through agents in Hong Kong and elsewhere, made a great number of appeals to Nationalist leaders through private correspondence during this period.[46] Once again, however, neither threats nor blandishments were successful, and after pushing the crisis to the brink of large-scale war, the Chinese Communists decided to slacken their pressure and agreed to initiate further negotiations with the United States.

In the light of Peking's past actions and statements, there is every reason to believe that it will continue its efforts to achieve control over Taiwan by every available means. Even though it may continue negotiating with the United States about "relaxing tension in the Taiwan area," it is not likely to make any major concessions in these negotiations. It may well be willing in the future, as in the past, to risk war over Taiwan. It can certainly be expected to create new situations of tension and to work persistently to drive a wedge between the Nationalists and the rest of the non-Communist world. It is likely to resist any moves which might tend to stabilize the existing situation in the Taiwan Strait. Most probably, however, it will seek to gain its ends without a direct military conflict with the United States.

United States Policy and Taiwan

The development of United States policy toward Taiwan has gone through several stages during the past decade. In many respects, it has evolved in direct response to military crises caused by Chinese Communist threats, and each crisis has evoked new, or newly defined, commitments from the United States government.

The American government has made firm commitments to defend Taiwan and the Pescadores against Communist attack, but at the same time it has dissociated itself from the Nationalists' fundamental aim of returning to the mainland by force, and it has maintained an ambiguous position in relation to the offshore islands. There are also other basic ambiguities in American policy toward Taiwan. For example, although the United States continues to recognize the Nationalist regime as the *de jure* government of all China, it maintains that the legal status of Taiwan and the Pescadores—the only territory, other than the offshore islands, now under Nationalist control—has not been finally settled, implying that the islands may not be Chinese territory at all. This position would seem to suggest that the future of Taiwan is very much an open question. Yet other aspects of American policy imply that United States attitudes toward Taiwan are unchangeable and that there is little room for any major modification of policy, even for negotiating purposes.

In the Cairo Declaration and Potsdam Proclamation the major Allied Powers in World War II declared it to be their "purpose" that Taiwan and the Pescadores "shall be restored to the Republic of China," and the Japanese instrument of surrender accepted the Potsdam Proclamation as a basis for peace. MacArthur's General Order No. 1 instructed the Japanese to surrender Taiwan to Chiang K'ai-shek's government, and the Nationalists took over the administration of the island immediately after the war. Pending the formalization of their status by a treaty with Japan, therefore, Taiwan and the Pescadores became a *de facto* part of the Republic of China in 1945, and thereafter they were treated as such by the United States, as well as by the other major powers, until 1950.[47]

Then in June 1950, after the start of the Korean War, President Truman reversed United States policy and declared that "the determination of the future status of Formosa must await the restoration of security in the Pacific, a peace settlement with Japan, or consideration by the United Nations." [48] Communist China reacted violently against this move and accused the United States of committing aggression against China. The United States responded by proposing that the General Assembly consider the Taiwan situation, but Communist China declared that the United Nations had no right to concern itself with a purely "domestic" Chinese problem.

The view that Taiwan's legal status is still undefined has been maintained by the United States ever since 1950.[49] It was incorporated into the Japanese peace treaty, signed in 1951 and ratified in 1952. This treaty declared that Japan had renounced all "right, title, and claim" to Formosa, but it did not state that sovereignty over Taiwan and the Pescadores had actually been transferred to China.

Despite this view of Taiwan's uncertain legal status, the United States steadily increased its support to the Nationalist regime from 1950 onward, and in 1954, during the first offshore islands crisis, Washington decided to sign a Mutual Defense Treaty with the Nationalist regime. This treaty, signed in December 1954, and ratified in the following spring, strengthened American ties with the Nationalists, but at the same time it limited the flexibility of United States policy in respect to the future of Taiwan. It did not, however, alter Washington's view of the legal status of the island. The treaty merely stated that "for the purposes of Article II and V [defining mutual defense commitments] the term 'territorial' and 'territories' shall mean in respect of the Republic of China, Taiwan and the Pescadores." [50] The offshore islands were not covered by the treaty.

In January 1955 the United States Congress, at Eisenhower's request, passed a joint resolution authorizing the President to use American forces to defend Taiwan and the Pescadores. This constituted a stronger American commitment to Taiwan than to any other area in Asia. Again, no specific mention was made of the offshore islands, but the resolution stated that the authority of the President was "to include the securing and protection of such related positions and territories of that area now in friendly hands and the taking of such other measures as he judges to be required or appropriate in assuring the defense of Formosa and the Pescadores." [51] This, in effect, left it to the discretion of the President to decide whether or not American forces would be used to defend the offshore islands.

At the same time that the United States government assumed these new commitments, however, it also attempted to impose restraints upon the Nationalist government which would deter it from embarking upon military adventures against the mainland. In December 1954, in an important exchange of notes between Washington and Taipei, the United States recognized that the Nationalists possess "the inherent right of self-defense" with respect not only to Taiwan and the Pescadores, but also to "other territory" (that is, the offshore islands) under their control.[52] On their part, however, the Nationalists agreed to accept significant limitations on their ability to take independent military action. "In view of the obligations of the two Parties under the said treaty," the notes declared, "and of the fact that the use of force from either of these areas by either of the Parties affects the other, it is agreed that such use of force will be a matter of joint agreement, subject to action of an emergency character which is clearly an exercise of the inherent right of self-defense."

The second offshore islands crisis, in September and October 1958, once more raised certain basic questions about United States policy, particularly in regard to the offshore islands where the immediate threat of conflict was again centered. On September 11, at the height of the crisis, President Eisenhower implied that, despite the absence of any specific commitment, the United States was fully prepared to help defend the offshore islands as well as Taiwan and the Pescadores. "Today," he said, "the Chinese Communists announce, repeatedly and officially, that their military operations against Quemoy are preliminary to attack on Formosa. So it is clear that the Formosa Straits resolution of 1955 applies to the present situation." [53] Failure to help defend the offshore islands, he implied, would constitute dangerous "appeasement" in the face of "aggression." On September 30, however, Secretary Dulles stated that it was "rather foolish" for the Nationalists to maintain such large forces on the offshore islands, asserting that it would "not be wise" to keep them there if a reasonably dependable cease fire could be arranged.[54] The United States attitude toward the Nationalist build-up of strength on the offshore islands, he said, was one of "acquiescence . . . not of approval." On October 1 Chiang K'ai-shek said he was "incredulous" at Dulles' statement. "I doubt that his remarks could be construed to mean that he would expect us to reduce our garrison forces on the offshore islands," and even if that were the case, he added, "it would only be a unilateral declaration and my government would be under no obligation to accept it." [55] On October 10 Chiang reiterated his pledge to fight back to the mainland. "I am sure," he said, "since we have already won this first round, we can follow up by winning the second round in the battle of the Taiwan Strait. And then we can further launch our counterattack to deliver our compatriots on the mainland from Communist tyranny and to complete our common task of national reconstruction." [56]

On October 14, when asked if he intended "to urge Chiang K'ai-shek to reduce the military strength of forces on Quemoy," Dulles replied that "we have no plans whatsoever for urging him to do that"; "I would not want to give the impression," he said, "that we are pressing or plan to press the Republic of China to do something against its better judgment."[57] Shortly thereafter, he flew to Taiwan, where on October 23 he issued a joint statement with Chiang K'ai-shek. This communiqué declared that the offshore islands are "closely related" to the defense of Taiwan—a statement which appeared to give added American backing to the Nationalists' determination to defend them but avoided any explicit commitment by the United States to participate in their defense.[58] It also declared, however, that the "use of force" would not be the "principal means" for restoring freedom to the people on the China mainland—a statement which seemed to place further restraints upon the Nationalists, yet avoided any explicit renunciation by them of the use of force to achieve their aim of returning to the mainland.

This sequence of events and statements during 1958 highlighted the dilemmas, ambiguities, and uncertainties inherent in the United States' policy toward the Taiwan area. It did not, however, resolve them. The United States' ultimate purposes and objectives in the Taiwan area are still open to varying interpretations.

The Danger of Conflict—Offshore Islands

The situation in the Taiwan Strait remains an explosive one which involves a continuing danger of a major conflict between the United States and Communist China. The focal point of this danger is the offshore islands, and it is essential to make a clear distinction between these islands and Taiwan (including the Pescadores) in stating the policy issues, as well as in defining the United States' commitments and interests.

The major offshore islands lie within sight of the China coast. In administrative practice they have traditionally been a part of the mainland. They do not have a large indigenous population. Quemoy, for example, has less than 50,000 inhabitants—only slightly more than half the number of troops defending the island—and they could certainly be evacuated if the larger issues of war or peace made this necessary. An overwhelming majority of world opinion accepts Peking's claims to these islands. A majority even of the United States' closest allies feels that a war over the offshore islands would be a disaster; if such a war were to occur, the United States would find itself in a dangerously isolated position. War over the offshore islands might well expand into an all-out war involving the United States and the Soviet Union, since defense of the islands against full-scale attack would probably require retaliatory action against the mainland, and the Russians are pledged to support Peking in that event.

The offshore islands constitute, in Eisenhower's words, a "thorn" in the side of Communist China. Until recently they have been used by the Nationalists to harass shipping entering or leaving two of the Communists' major ports, as well as for infiltration and guerrilla activity against the mainland. Any strong Chinese government on the mainland, whatever its political character, would consider these islands important to its security and would feel under strong compulsion to assert its control over them.

The importance of the offshore islands to the Nationalists is primarily psychological. In military terms, although useful to the Nationalists as forward posts, they are not essential to the defense of Taiwan. In fact, the stationing of roughly one-third of the Nationalists' best troops on the islands is probably both unwise and dangerous to the defense of Taiwan itself. The real importance of the islands to the Nationalists is the fact that they symbolize the hope of returning to the mainland.

The United States has become involved in the offshore islands question through no choice of its own. American policy-makers have felt that any definite commitment to the defense of the islands would be unjustifiable, politically and strategically. Yet because the Nationalists have insisted upon holding the islands and building them up militarily—with, as Secretary Dulles put it, American acquiescence but not approval—it has been felt that, if the United States renounced any intention to defend the islands, this would merely invite Communist China to attack. The events of recent years indicate, however, that the American policy of ambiguity makes it difficult to avoid helping the Nationalists to defend the islands if they should be subjected to major attack. Failure to defend them would, in effect, reveal the United States position as a bluff, and having a bluff called could have adverse effects on the American position throughout Asia.

Another unfavorable aspect of the situation is the fact that the United States has little control over it. Communist China can create a situation of crisis and tension whenever it chooses, merely by intensifying the bombardment of Quemoy. As was shown during the crisis of 1958, it can threaten the survival of the Nationalist garrison without committing any troops to an actual attack. Each offshore islands crisis has had a seriously divisive effect upon the non-Communist world; for this reason, if for no other, Peking can be expected periodically to create new crises. It was predictable after the crisis of 1954-1955 that military pressure would be renewed, at a time of Peking's choosing. And now, even though the 1958 crisis has receded into the background, it is predictable that a repeat performance will take place at some future time, unless the offshore islands situation is somehow changed in the meantime. Probably Peking will do all it can to complicate any efforts to change the existing situation, by sporadically shelling the islands or exerting other pressures on them. If and when it decides to create another major crisis over the islands, it may well choose a time when the United States and the Soviet Union are heavily engaged elsewhere.

The danger of a crisis over the offshore islands touching off a major war involving the United States is very real, even though Peking probably would not attack the islands with that explicit intention. What is possible is that through threats and counterthreats, pressure and counterpressure, tension might build up to such a degree that some accident could trigger off a war; in this situation each side might feel that its prestige was so deeply involved as to render any retreat or compromise impossible. During the second offshore islands crisis the risks of war were clearly greater than in the first, because both sides did in fact increase their threats and military pressure. In 1958, for example, the Chinese Communist air force took a limited part in attacking the offshore islands, and the United States Seventh Fleet convoyed supplies up to the three-mile limit, well within range of Communist artillery.[59] And in any future crisis, the risks are likely to be even greater.

The situation of Taiwan is quite different because of the 100 miles of water separating it from the mainland, the Chinese Communists' lack of modern naval strength, and the firm United States commitment to defend the island. These factors mean that for Peking to apply direct military pressures—as contrasted with military threats alone—against Taiwan, it would have to make a conscious decision to challenge the full weight of American power. It seems unlikely that the Chinese Communists will choose to do this in the foreseeable future. Consequently, whereas the offshore islands situation and the American involvement in it create serious risks of war between Communist China and the United States, the American commitment to Taiwan is a formidable deterrent which probably helps greatly to reduce the danger of war over Taiwan itself.

A Divergence of American and Chinese Nationalist Interests

Although the basic conflict in the Taiwan area is between the United States and Nationalist China on one side and Communist China on the other, there is also a divergence in outlook, interests, and aims between the United States and the present leaders of Nationalist China which cannot be overlooked. Whereas the United States has repeatedly made it clear that its immediate objective is to achieve an end to military hostilities in the region in order to stabilize the existing situation and reduce the chances of armed conflict, the Chinese Nationalists, like the Communists, view the present situation as merely a lull in the Chinese civil war and look forward to continuing the struggle, by military means if necessary. Because of this basic divergence, specific problems, such as that of the offshore islands, are inevitably viewed in very different perspectives by Washington and Taipei. And, when the United States' policy of seeking a stabilization of the area conflicts with the Nationalists' aim of returning to the mainland, relations between Washington and Taipei are unavoidably affected in an adverse way. This has been an extremely important consideration in the formulation of American policy. Although the United States has induced the Nationalists to accept some restraints on their freedom of action, American policy-makers have been very reluctant to consider any major policy changes which might evoke a strongly unfavorable Nationalist response.

World Opinion

The international implications of policy toward the Taiwan area must also be given great weight. Some Americans maintain that any sign of compromise by the United States in this area would dangerously weaken the non-Communist position in Asia as a whole. In fact, however, it seems clear that the present situation, particularly in regard to the offshore islands, involves more liabilities than assets for the United States in its effect on world opinion. Most of the world is critical in varying degrees of American policy toward the Taiwan area, and it constitutes, in fact, a glaring example of an almost completely unilateral policy. If modifications of American policy toward Taiwan were actually interpreted as a sign of weakening support for resistance against communism throughout the region, this would, of course, create uncertainty about United States aims and intentions, but certainly modifications could be made in such a way that this could be avoided. On the other hand, if a major conflict between the United States and Communist China should break out in the Taiwan area, and particularly if it should be triggered by a crisis over the offshore islands, the effects on even the closest Asian allies of the United States might be extremely adverse.

No other country has assumed any obligations to come to the defense of Taiwan, and the economic and military aid upon which the Nationalist regime's survival depends comes entirely from the United States. Although 45 countries still maintain diplomatic relations with the Nationalist regime [60] —more than have recognized the Peking regime to date—in many cases this is an indication of deference to the United

States rather than a sign of positive support for the Nationalists. Many nonaligned nations are highly critical of American policy toward Taiwan, and most of the United States' major allies are critical of at least some aspects of it. Here again, however, a distinction between Taiwan itself and the offshore islands is of great importance. Probably a majority of non-Communist nations now understand and in some degree approve, either publicly or tacitly, the United States' determination to prevent a Communist military conquest of Taiwan, although many of these same countries reject the Nationalists' claim to be the government of all China. However, a very large majority of world opinion feels that the offshore islands are not worth the risk of war and that if their transfer to Peking's control would reduce the likelihood of a military conflict in the area then the transfer should be made.

Basic United States Interests

It is essential that the basic interests and aims of the United States in the Taiwan area be clearly defined. The primary American interest is to prevent the conquest of Taiwan and the Pescadores by the Chinese Communists. The United States has made a firm commitment to this end, and there are compelling reasons to uphold it.

One basic factor involved is the United States' strategic interest in Taiwan, an interest which has increased greatly since the United States decided to base its defense in the Western Pacific on a chain of island bases stretching from the Aleutians to the Philippines. On January 24, 1955, President Eisenhower defined this interest as follows:

In unfriendly hands, Formosa and the Pescadores would seriously dislocate the existing, even if unstable, balance of moral, economic, and military forces upon which the peace of the Pacific depends. It would create a breach in the island chain of the Western Pacific that constitutes, for the United States and other free nations, the geographical backbone of their security structure in that ocean. In addition, this breach would interrupt north-south communications between other important elements of that barrier, and damage the economic life of countries friendly to us.[61]

When the Communists first came to power on the China mainland, American policy-makers felt that, however desirable it might be for strategic purposes to deny Taiwan to the Communists, the United States did not then have the military forces available to undertake this commitment. Until the outbreak of the Korean War, therefore, the United States avoided any commitments to defend Taiwan. Former Secretary of State Dean Acheson has asserted, in fact, in a statement on China policy made in September 1958, that on four occasions between 1948 and 1950 the highest American military authorities concluded that it was not essential to the United States' vital interests that Taiwan be retained in friendly hands.[62] Then the Communist attack on South Korea altered the situation abruptly. As a result of this Soviet-planned aggression, the balance of forces in the entire Pacific area was greatly changed, and the United States felt compelled to broaden its strategic commitments and to increase its military strength in the Far East. Now, there can be little doubt that, if the Chinese Communists gained control of Taiwan and built it into a major military base, the existing United States security system in Asia would be seriously impaired. The Japanese used Taiwan as a base for extensive operations during World War II, and if the Chinese Communists took control of it, a real threat could be posed to nearby areas such as the Philippines and Okinawa.

The basic security interest of the United States in Taiwan does not extend to the offshore islands, however, and even in regard to Taiwan itself that interest may well be primarily one of denial rather than of positive need. The United States has never claimed that its own security interests demand the retention of the offshore islands in friendly hands. Nor has it ever claimed that its own strategic interests require the use of Taiwan as a military base for its own forces. In actual fact, the United States has not built up important bases of its own on Taiwan. What has been defined as essential to American strategy is to deny to the Chinese Communists the use of Taiwan as a military base. In purely military terms, therefore, if general policy considerations make it desirable for the United States to dissociate itself from the defense of the offshore islands or even to consider the possibility of an internationally backed military neutralization of Taiwan itself, neither of these ideas would be incompatible with American security interests.

The United States also has important political and moral interests in Taiwan, however. The 10 million people on Taiwan—more than the population of many nations which are represented in the United Nations—clearly oppose any idea of submitting to Chinese Communist rule and would unquestionably suffer if they were brought forcibly under Communist control against their wishes. To abandon them to conquest by Peking would violate basic principles and aims which underlie American policy. Despite Communist China's claims to Taiwan, it is wholly consistent with the United States' attachment to the principle of self-determination to support the right of the people on Taiwan to decide their own political future. If this is intervention in the affairs of a foreign nation—and many of those who recognize Peking's claims to Taiwan label it such—it is an intervention which can be fully justified if the complex historical, political, and moral factors now involved in the Taiwan situation are taken into account.

Furthermore, if the United States, after making firm pledges to come to the defense of Taiwan, were now to abandon the island and renege on this basic commitment, a step of this grave nature might well undermine the faith of much of the world in the future reliability of American promises. The effects of this could be very serious on the United States' relations, not only with its allies, but even with those countries which are most critical of Washington's current policy toward China.

To say that the United States has a basic interest in preventing a Chinese Communist military conquest of Taiwan is not to say, however, that the United States should support either the idea of a continuing military struggle to recover control of the mainland or the Nationalists' claim to be the sole legal government of China. The United States has already dissociated itself from the Nationalists' aim to reconquer the mainland, and American policy regarding the legal status of Taiwan and of the Nationalist government should be determined in the future in the light of the broader requirements of American policy toward China and Asia as a whole.

The Future Development of Taiwan

The United States interest in Taiwan is not merely a negative one, however. Denying a territory to the Communists is not a sufficient basis in and of itself for shaping American policy toward any area, and American policy should be concerned positively with the future of the people on Taiwan. The United States should do all it can in positive ways to help build Taiwan into an example both of effective and democratic rule and of successful economic development.

Since there is no realistic prospect, in the foreseeable future, of the Nationalist regime either returning to the mainland or achieving complete economic self-support on Taiwan, the United States must continue giving it large-scale assistance. This support should be directed primarily to strengthening Taiwan's political system, its social structure, and its economy through improved utilization of its human and material potential.

The relationship between a large nation and any political regime which is dependent in many respects on it can be extremely complex, and relations between the United States and Taiwan will require a conscious exercise of restraint on the American side. The United States cannot escape the fact, however, that because of the Nationalist regime's basic dependence on American military, political, and economic support, anything the United States decides to do or not to do in relation to Taiwan will have a significant influence on the future of the island and its population. With this heavy responsibility for the very survival of a non-Communist Taiwan, the United States can and should use its support in such a way as to give positive backing to trends and developments which are most desirable for the future welfare of the people on the island and which can strengthen the political and economic base for a viable democratic regime.

Despite the recent improvement in mainlander-Taiwanese relations on Taiwan, there is still a great need for the Nationalists to broaden the base of their rule and to provide greater opportunities for political self-expression and participation in the processes of self-government on the part of the Taiwanese. Even though the role of the Taiwanese has already grown substantially, at the lower levels of the Kuomintang, the army, and local government, the Taiwanese are not likely to identify themselves in any full sense with the Nationalist regime until they feel that the centers of real authority at the top are more widely representative of their interests and sentiments than at present. In the long run it is both possible and desirable for the Taiwanese to participate increasingly in their government and to identify their loyalties with it and for the mainlanders to become increasingly "Taiwanized" by identifying their interests and sentiments more and more with Taiwan rather than their former mainland homes. An evolution of this sort would doubtless make it desirable to discard the present two-layered governmental structure, which maintains an expensive, cumbersome, and unrepresentative national government on top of a local provincial government.

The problem of broadening the political base on Taiwan concerns much more than just the question of improving mainlander-Taiwanese relations, however. There is also a need to develop new and younger political leadership drawn from among both mainlanders and Taiwanese, to encourage a freer expression of new political ideas, and to foster genuinely democratic groups and processes in order to infuse greater vitality into political life on Taiwan. Although the continuing danger of Communist subversion cannot be overlooked, there is also a need for increased respect for the rule of law and a gradual elimination by the Nationalists of those totalitarian features of their regime which they have borrowed from the Communists in order to fight communism. To attack successfully the problems of Taiwan's future development, the Nationalists also need to attract the talents of many of the non-Communist Chinese exiles who are now scattered elsewhere throughout the non-Communist world. And there is a pressing need to revitalize the intellectual life on the island.

If Taiwan is to make real progress toward economic viability, the present facts of its economic life will have to be faced frankly, and effective efforts to develop both industry and agriculture will have to be continued, and in fact stepped up. This requires the adoption of an effective birth control program, for example, as well as steps to improve the investment climate in order to attract both Overseas Chinese and foreign development capital. In addition, if the military establishment should be viewed primarily in defensive rather than offensive terms, it undoubtedly could be cut back in some measure so that greater efforts and resources can be devoted to building up Taiwan's economic base and improving the welfare of its people. However, because of the continuing military threat posed by Peking's ambitions, even if Taiwan's military establishment can be cut back, it will still be much larger than the island's economy can reasonably be expected to support, and the United States will have to continue giving substantial military as well as economic aid. Nevertheless, more can and should be done to help Taiwan progress toward increased economic independence, and this is essential to future strength and self-respect.

For the Nationalist regime to work effectively toward these goals, undoubtedly its leaders will eventually have to rethink their position and their goals, recognizing frankly that reconquest of the mainland is not a realistic objective in the predictable future and that they should therefore concentrate on strengthening and developing their position on Taiwan. Even though Chiang K'ai-shek and other Nationalist leaders have so far strongly resisted such a reorientation, the United States should work persistently to encourage it. This is not only desirable for the future welfare of the people on Taiwan; in the long run it could have a significant impact on the China mainland. The continued existence and development of a strong democratic regime on Taiwan—whatever its international status—might in time affect the China mainland far more than futile and hollow threats of a military invasion.

Disengagement from the Offshore Islands

The conflict of Chinese Communist and American interests in the Taiwan Strait area is the most immediate and specific cause of the current state of exacerbated tension between the United States and Communist China. It has twice brought Communist China and the United States to the brink of war. The basic conflict arises over Taiwan itself, and since the interests of the United States demand a continuing commitment to the defense of Taiwan, this cause of tension is likely to persist for a long time to come. As emphasized previously, however, the greatest risk of war centers on the offshore islands. And if the United States genuinely hopes to reduce the danger of conflict and work toward a stabilization of the situation in the Taiwan Strait, more positive steps must be taken to disengage American interests from the offshore islands.

There is little hope at present for stabilizing the situation in the Taiwan Strait through direct negotiations with the Chinese Communists. Ever since 1955 the United States has negotiated with Peking's representatives, in both Geneva and Warsaw, in an attempt to persuade Peking to accept a "cease fire" in the Taiwan Strait, but the Chinese Communists have adamantly refused to agree, on the grounds that this might cast doubt on their claim to Taiwan.[63] Peking is not likely to change its views on this issue. If any "cease fire" is to be achieved in the foreseeable future, therefore, it will undoubtedly have to be a *de facto* rather than a *de jure* one.

The United States government has publicly stated that in its view it is "foolish" for the Nationalists to keep large forces on the offshore islands, implying that it would favor a military disengagement if the Nationalists would agree. It has, in fact, made efforts to persuade Chiang K'ai-shek to accept this view.[64] But so far the Nationalists have refused even to consider giving up the islands.

In this situation there appears to be no alternative to using more positive measures of persuasion to induce the Nationalists to modify their position. Only after the offshore islands are evacuated can a clear and unambiguous line of defense be established between Taiwan and the mainland. It is important that this be done before another military crisis over the offshore islands explodes, since a withdrawal while the pressure is off could have a favorable psychological and political impact on most of Asia, whereas a retreat under military pressure might have seriously damaging effects.

In view of the Nationalists' emotional attachment to the offshore islands—described in September 1958 by the then Under Secretary of State Christian Herter as "pathological" [65] —this is, of course, easier said than done. But it certainly can be done. The Nationalists could not continue defending the offshore islands without American acquiescence and material support. Because the United States has failed to make clear its own determination to disassociate American interests completely from the offshore islands, the Nationalists have been able to assume that by remaining adamant they could deter the United States from adopting a clear position of the sort which American interests demand and that, as long as the American position remains ambiguous, the United States is likely in time of crisis to be compelled by the pressures of the moment to help prevent a successful Communist invasion of the offshore islands.

Clearly, if the United States does take more affirmative action to achieve a disengagement from the offshore islands, there may be strains between Washington and Taipei. Some observers have even predicted that such action might risk undermining the Nationalist regime. Arguing that the morale of the present Nationalist leaders is founded on the myth that they will soon return to the mainland, these observers have asserted that if they were forced to withdraw from the offshore islands, the myth would be destroyed and morale would disintegrate. They have warned that some Nationalist leaders might try to make political deals with the Communists on the mainland.

Clearly, many Nationalist leaders will resist acknowledging that reinvasion of the mainland is not a practical aim for the immediate future—although others have obviously reconciled themselves privately to the realities of the situation—and it is inevitable that such an adjustment would involve some disillusionment. It is neither inevitable nor probable, however, that this would undermine the Nationalist regime, or cause major defections from Taiwan to the Communists. The will to survive will remain, and in view of the increasing evidence of the harsh realities of Communist rule on the mainland, particularly since 1957, there is probably less danger now than formerly that any significant number of Nationalist leaders will try to come to terms with Peking, even if circumstances force them to conclude that reinvasion of the mainland is not an attainable goal for the foreseeable future.

Broader International Support for Taiwan's Defense

One basic reason for the weakness of the United States' present position in the Taiwan Strait area is the fact that it obtains almost no enthusiastic or positive backing from any other major nation, Asian or Western. If the offshore islands situation could be resolved, however, this might greatly improve the possibility of obtaining stronger international support for American policy toward the area. Even the United States' most important allies have been unwilling to associate themselves with the present American and Chinese Nationalist position, since this might involve them in the existing offshore situation. If, however, a line of defense for Taiwan could be clearly established in the Taiwan Strait, the United States might then be able to convince at least some of its allies to commit themselves to the defense of Taiwan and the Pescadores. Certainly, the United States should try to do this, in the hope of broadening the base of international support—at least political, if not military—for the defense of Taiwan, and it ought to do this at the same time that it tries to persuade the Nationalists to disengage their forces from the offshore islands.

Disengagement from the offshore islands might also improve the possibility of obtaining wider and more positive support within the United Nations for the idea of a military neutralization of the Taiwan Strait. If there were such support, world opinion could be mobilized more effectively to oppose any possible violation of the peace in that area by the Communists in the future.

All of these developments could help to stabilize the situation in the Taiwan Strait and reduce the risks of war, even if Peking persists in rejecting a formal cease fire and continues to make verbal threats against Taiwan. A tactical withdrawal could, in short, actually strengthen the non-Communist position in the area, rather than weaken it.

The Future Status of Taiwan and the Nationalist Regime

For the past decade the United States has continued its recognition of the Nationalist regime as the legitimate government of all China. At the same time the American government has maintained that the legal status of Taiwan and the Pescadores remains unsettled and that in theory it could be determined either by the United Nations or by the countries which signed the San Francisco Peace Treaty with Japan. Many other nations have, of course, recognized the Peking regime as the legitimate government of all China. Some have acknowledged Peking's claims to Taiwan, but others, including Britain, have supported the American contention that Taiwan's legal status remains undecided. The Nationalist regime has continued to occupy China's seat in the United Nations, but support has slowly but steadily risen for transferring this seat to Peking.

Over the past decade this confusing and ambiguous situation has been the cause of many complications and frictions within the entire international community and has given rise to a number of unofficial proposals that adjustments be made in a *de jure* or legal sense to fit the *de facto* changes in the political situation since 1949. Many proposals have been put forward for a "two Chinas" solution.

In actual fact, of course, there have been two Chinas for a full decade. But since both Chinese regimes have continued claiming jurisdiction over all of China, the rest of the world has had to choose between them, and formal relations with one have precluded relations with the other. The supporters of the idea of recognizing two Chinas have argued that, since both regimes are likely to survive for the foreseeable future, it would be desirable for the international community to accept the authority of each over the territory it now controls and to establish relations with both on this basis. Essentially, the "two Chinas" idea implies that while the Chinese Communist regime should be accepted as the governing authority on the mainland, Taiwan under Nationalist rule should now, after a decade of existence apart from the mainland, be regarded as a separate state.

A number of unofficial proposals have been made, calling for positive United Nations action to determine or redefine Taiwan's status. It has been proposed, for example, that the United Nations should establish a trusteeship over Taiwan or conduct an internationally sponsored plebiscite to determine the future of the island. The supporters of these proposals have generally been vague as to how they might be implemented, however, and have seemingly ignored some basic facts. Both the Chinese Communists and the Nationalists assert that Taiwan is an integral part of China, reject the idea that Taiwan can be legally alienated from the mainland, and deny that the United Nations has any right to consider Taiwan's status. If the United Nations were to attempt either to carry out a plebiscite or to establish a trusteeship over Taiwan, perhaps Peking could do no more than protest, but the Nationalists undoubtedly could and would resist actively. As long as the United Nations lacks the capability of imposing such measures on any area in the face of local resistance, it is difficult to see how these proposals can be considered seriously.

Even if both Peking and Taipei continue opposing the "two Chinas" idea, however, the United States and other major non-Communist nations can decide for themselves how they will view and treat the jurisdiction and status of both the "People's Republic of China" on the mainland and the "Republic of China" on Taiwan. If, for example, the United States concluded that it was no longer justifiable or desirable to accept the fiction that the Nationalists still have jurisdiction over the mainland, it could redefine its own view of the Nationalist regime's status in any of several alternative ways. It could, for example, decide to treat it as either the *de facto* or *de jure* government of a new autonomous or independent state. Or, alternatively, it could continue recognizing it as the government of the "Republic of China," accepting its jurisdiction over Taiwan, but without recognizing its claim still to have authority on the mainland of China.

This latter formula was, in effect, incorporated into the

peace treaty signed between Japan and Nationalist China in 1952, when the Japanese recognized the Nationalists' sovereignty only over "all the territories which are now, or hereafter may be" under its control.

Despite, therefore, the seeming impossibility of discovering any formula for redefining the status of Taiwan which would be acceptable to Taipei, Peking, or the international community in general, this does not preclude the United States from adjusting its own policies to take account of the realities of Taiwan's situation today. If the requirements of the United States' over-all policy toward China and Asia demand changes in American policy toward Taiwan, there are choices, in short, other than continuing to acknowledge the Nationalists' jurisdiction over the mainland or deciding to concede Peking its claim to Taiwan. Whether these choices should be seriously considered depends on what broad policies the United States decides to pursue toward China—both Chinas. Policy toward Taiwan and the Nationalist regime must be fitted into this broader context.

Chapter 14

THE POLICY OF NONRECOGNITION

IN RECENT YEARS controversy in the United States over policy toward China has focused primarily on whether diplomatic, commercial, or other contacts should be established with Peking. Above all, it has centered on one question: "Should the United States recognize Communist China or should it continue its policy of nonrecognition?" [1]

The importance of the recognition question has been grossly exaggerated by many Americans. Some proponents of continued nonrecognition argue, in effect, that this is such an essential keystone for United States policy that changing it might undermine the entire American effort to check the expansion of Chinese Communist influence in East Asia. On the other hand, some supporters of recognition seem to imply that, if only formal diplomatic relations could be established with Peking, then somehow, suddenly, the entire situation in Asia might radically change so that a genuine *modus vivendi* could be worked out between the United States and Communist China. Both these extreme views overstate the importance of recognition policy and tend to obscure the long-term problem of dealing with Communist China. Since the recognition issue has figured so largely in American debate over policy toward China, however, it is essential to analyze carefully the arguments both for and against continuing a policy of nonrecognition.

The case for nonrecognition has been presented most eloquently in the Department of State's official pronouncements on policy toward China. Perhaps the clearest and most complete statements in recent years have been Secretary of State John Foster Dulles' speech on China policy delivered at San Francisco on June 28, 1957,[2] and a Department of State

430

memorandum entitled "United States Policy regarding Nonrecognition of Communist China," which was sent to all American diplomatic missions abroad in 1958.[3]

The rationale for nonrecognition is carefully formulated in these statements. Numerous arguments are presented to bolster the view that American recognition of Peking—or the establishment of trade and cultural contacts with Communist China—would have widely adverse effects, perhaps even disastrous effects, on the entire non-Communist position in Asia. The judgments which underlie this view are phrased in such categorical and forceful terms that one might conclude there is no reasonable basis for any alternative judgments pointing toward different conclusions. This is certainly not the case, however. Essentially, the question of recognition is a matter of tactics, and there is wide ground for differing views on the possible consequences of either continuing an adamant opposition to recognition or moving toward recognition. Many complex issues are involved in this broad question, and each deserves careful examination.

The Nature of Recognition

One important area of controversy concerns the nature of recognition itself. During recent years the State Department has strongly supported the view that recognition should be looked on as "an instrument of national policy" and that, therefore, in Mr. Dulles' words, "there is nothing automatic about it."[4] Elaborating this view, the State Department has argued that recognition must be clearly defined as "a privilege and not a right."

There is a good deal of disagreement among specialists on international law about the criteria which can or should be applied in the recognition of governments. Since international practice in this field has never been standardized or generally agreed upon, however, the basic contention that recognition is, in the final analysis, a matter of national policy, not governed by clear international law, cannot be disputed. There is a sizable body of opinion, nonetheless, which believes that it would be highly desirable for the United States, and other nations as well, to base their recognition policy on so-called "objective tests"—such as the degree to which a new government exercises effective *de facto* control over its territory, represents "the will of the nation," and is willing and able to fulfill its international obligations.[5] Those who support this view argue that when recognition is based on "subjective" factors—such as moral approval or disapproval of a new government, or the political advantage in recognizing or not recognizing it—this introduces uncertainty and confusion into international transactions without any commensurate gains. They also assert that nonrecognition has never been an effective instrument for bargaining, conducting political warfare, or exerting pressure against a new government and that attempts to use it for these purposes are likely to be unsuccessful and may produce unwanted and undesirable political results.

It can be argued, therefore, that the United States should be prepared to recognize any government if and when that government fulfills certain basic "objective tests," making clear that this does not in any sense imply moral approval or disapproval.

In relation specifically to Communist China, however, although this might have been possible a decade ago, there is little doubt now, after ten years in which nonrecognition has been used as a weapon of political pressure against the Peking regime, that if and when the United States recognizes Communist China this act will have significant political implications and repercussions. The attempt to use nonrecognition as an instrument of pressure against Communist China has created a situation in which the act of recognizing the Peking regime, if and when it takes place, will undoubtedly have a greater political impact than it otherwise would have had. This fact can be used as an argument, of course, for never recognizing Communist China. It is also possible to argue, however, that the decision on whether to recognize Peking must be based on many other considerations and factors and that the American government's adamant opposition to recognition over the past decade, by giving the act a kind of moral significance which should have been avoided, has greatly and unnecessarily complicated the problem of evolving a rational policy toward China.

"Tests" for Recognition

Although the State Department, in justifying its current China policy, has placed a great emphasis on the political nature of recognition policy, it nonetheless takes cognizance of the "tests often cited in international law." It argues strongly that the Chinese Communist regime fails to qualify for recognition even under the most widely accepted tests. It asserts, for example, that the Chinese Communists "have not completed their conquest of the country" because the Nationalist regime remains in control of Taiwan. While conceding that there is "no reason to believe that the Chinese Communist regime is on the verge of collapse," it argues that there is "equally no reason to accept its present rule in mainland China as permanent." The Peking regime represents only a "tiny minority" of the Chinese people, it declares, and it certainly does not represent "the will of the populace, substantially declared." Moreover, it points out, the Chinese Communists have violated numerous agreements—including the Korean armistice, the Geneva agreements of 1954, and the 1955 Sino-American agreement (in which Peking pledged itself to permit all Americans in China to return home "expeditiously")—and has shown "no intention to honor its international obligations."

The implication that in reality the Chinese Communists have yet to establish *de facto* control over China is an example of the kind of justification for current American policy which has made an unfavorable impression on much of the world and has evoked widespread charges that United States policy toward China is "unrealistic." Actually, the Chinese Communists' present control over the mainland of China cannot be seriously questioned, and the argument that the Nationalist regime's continued existence proves that the Communists "have not completed their conquest of the country" appears specious to most of world opinion, since clearly it is United States support of the Nationalists which has prevented Peking from achieving control of Taiwan. Furthermore, although no government anywhere is necessarily "permanent," the Peking regime undoubtedly must be viewed as being at least as permanent—in terms of the limited time span which is relevant to planning policy and conducting diplomatic relations—as many other governments, including other Communist regimes, which the United States feels it desirable or necessary to recognize.

Many of the arguments used to oppose recognizing Communist China seem to imply that recognition of a government or the establishment of diplomatic relations with it are irrevocable acts. This obviously is not the case. Even if the United States recognizes Peking and exchanges representatives with it, if at some future time the Chinese Communists appear to be on the verge of overthrow or collapse, American policy would then, of course, have to be reexamined. In short, if, contrary to present expectations, the Peking regime proves to be short-lived, the United States would certainly be free to reshape its policies accordingly.

The argument that the Chinese Communist regime does not represent the "will of the nation, substantially declared," is a valid one if this Jeffersonian criterion for recognizing a government is interpreted literally to mean that a regime must be democratic to deserve American recognition. Clearly it has not been generally applied in this sense by the United States government, however. Normally, it has been interpreted to mean that any new government, whether democratic or dictatorial, should control its people sufficiently to obtain acquiescence and obedience, before the United States will recognize it. If it had been generally applied in any wider sense, the United States would not maintain relations, as it does today, with a wide range of dictatorial governments, both Communist and non-Communist. And if it is now applied in its more limited sense, the Peking regime doubtless passes this test in much the same way as the other Communist governments recognized by the United States.

Similarly, Communist China's record of honoring international obligations is little different from that of other Communist governments which the United States has recognized. The problem of dealing with all of these states is extraordinarily difficult because none of them can be counted on to honor their international agreements except insofar as they consider it expedient or are induced by international pressures of various sorts to do so. Peking has clearly violated many of the provisions of the two important agreements which the United States, despite its policy of nonrecognition, has made with it during the past decade—the Korean armistice and the Sino-American agreement of 1955 on the reciprocal return of citizens.[6] Yet, even though these agreements have been only partially observed, they have at least served a limited purpose, in halting the fighting in Korea and in helping to pry loose most of the Americans imprisoned in China.

The United States' approach to the Communist bloc as a whole—with the notable exception of Communist China—implies a belief that although agreements with Communist nations are far from dependable and must be backed by the sanction of power, nevertheless there are advantages in maintaining relations with these nations and in regulating relations through formal agreements when possible. It is difficult to see why this should not apply to Communist China as well as to the other nations in the Communist orbit. Yet instead of dealing with Peking as it does with the rest of the bloc, the United States has publicly applied the label of "outlaw" or "gangster" nation to Communist China.[7] It is highly doubtful that deliberate treatment of Communist China as an "outlaw" nation is likely to make it more amenable to the idea of honoring its agreements. On the contrary, it can be argued that, if the Chinese Communists were brought increasingly into the community of nations, and into relationships regulated by international law, possibly this might subject them increasingly to pressures which might help induce them to honor their international agreements to a greater extent than at present.

The Value of Continuous Contact

The State Department's official declarations on policy toward China point out, quite rightly, that recognition is not an absolute prerequisite to dealing with Communist China. During the past decade the American government has, in fact, negotiated at length with Peking's representatives at Panmunjom, Geneva, and Warsaw. The State Department goes further, however, and argues that there would be "no tangible benefits" from recognition. This can be seriously questioned.

Many non-Communist nations, and at least some American critics of present United States policy toward China, believe that there can be definite advantages in maintaining continuous diplomatic contacts even with governments which are clearly hostile. It can be argued, in fact, that it is especially important to maintain contacts with those nations which, like Communist China, pose the greatest problems for American policy. It is essential that the United States make its own intentions clear at all times to the Chinese Communists and that it probe Peking's intentions in every possible way; it is doubtful if this can be done effectively without continuous diplomatic contacts. Limited and sporadic negotiations, such as those which the United States has conducted with the Chinese Communists in the past, can hardly serve the same purposes as uninterrupted diplomatic relations.[8] Actually, because the United States has lacked channels of its own for continuing contact with Peking, on numerous occasions in the past ten years it has had to rely on others—particularly the British—to serve as its spokesmen. On other occasions, some of the uncommitted nations have attempted to act as self-appointed intermediaries between the United States and Communist China. Even though these efforts have generally been well intentioned, serious questions can be raised about the desirability of relying on others to express and interpret the American position in dealings with Peking.

Few people question the necessity of maintaining channels of continuous contact in American-Soviet relations, and it is difficult to accept the thesis that there would be no advantages in having similar channels in relations with Communist China. Dealing with Peking over the years ahead will present many of the same problems as dealing with Moscow, and lack of contact may simply magnify these problems.

Still another point deserves consideration. Possibly the United States' policy of nonrecognition is itself a factor reinforcing the Chinese Communists' inclination to be unyielding and recalcitrant, even over minor issues, thereby adding to the difficulties of negotiating successfully on any problems. Whenever a negotiable issue arises between the United States and Communist China, Peking can adopt an uncompromising position, in order to bargain for American recognition, and can attempt to justify its own unreasonableness by pointing to the United States' unyielding position on the recognition question.

Possible Steps Short of Full De Jure *Recognition*

Perhaps the strongest argument against any immediate or precipitate step toward full *de jure* recognition of the Peking regime by the United States is one which is not generally used by official spokesmen for present American policy. It is simply this: If the United States were to recognize Communist China tomorrow, it is almost certain that Peking would not reciprocate by "recognizing" the United States, unless the American government were willing to concede Taiwan to the Communists. The Chinese Communists have made it quite clear that, from their viewpoint, the United States' commitment to defend Taiwan is a fundamental obstacle to the establishment of diplomatic relations between Communist China and the United States, for the present, at least. Since the defense of Taiwan is essential to United States interests, there is little immediate prospect of finding a basis for establishing formal relations with Peking even if the United States government decides that this is desirable. Under these conditions, if the United States were to extend full *de jure* recognition to the Peking regime only to have Peking refuse to reciprocate, there would be little or nothing gained, while the losses might be substantial, from the American point of view.

This does not mean, however, that the United States cannot or should not modify its present adamant opposition to recognition of Communist China or that it is impossible to take steps which point in the direction of ultimate recognition and the establishment of relations with Peking at some time in the future. If the United States should decide to move in this direction, there are a number of steps it could take, even assuming that Peking is unwilling to change its position.

At any time of its own choosing, the United States could, for example, make clear that it recognizes Peking's *de facto* control of the mainland of China while specifically rejecting Communist China's claim to Taiwan. This would require, of course, a redefinition of the United States' view of the Nationalist regime's status and jurisdiction, such as was suggested in Chapter 13.

The United States could go further, at an appropriate time, by letting both Communist China and other nations know that it would be willing to extend formal *de jure* recognition to the Peking regime, accepting its rule on the mainland of China and establishing diplomatic relations with it—it being understood that the United States would continue to maintain relations with the Nationalist regime on Taiwan—if and when there were assurances that Communist China would reciprocate and establish relations with the United States on this basis. If Peking responded favorably to such a move, this would imply a far greater willingness on its part to accept a *de facto* truce in the Taiwan Strait and to acquiesce in the separation of Taiwan from the mainland than it has shown to date. Probably the Chinese Communists' initial reaction would be to reject such a proposal, but even so the United States would have improved and strengthened its position. By demonstrating its willingness to recognize and deal with Peking on the basis of the existing *de facto* situation, the United States could effectively counter the widespread charges that American policy toward China is "unrealistic," and this would undoubtedly help to shift to Peking the onus for the continuing lack of relations. It would create a situation, in short, in which it was up to Peking to decide whether it wished to establish diplomatic relations with the United States on terms set by the United States, and in this situation the Chinese Communists might be impelled over a period of time to move gradually toward the idea of establishing relations on terms acceptable to the United States.

The Political Effects of Recognition Policy

The supporters of continuing nonrecognition argue that those who propose a course of action such as that suggested above overlook the value of nonrecognition as an instrument of pressure against Peking and ignore the possible adverse consequence of a shift toward a policy of recognition. The State Department asserts categorically that nonrecognition is an essential political weapon which the United States must continue using against the Peking regime and that American recognition of Communist China would have dangerously adverse effects on the political situation throughout Asia. It argues that recognition would weaken anti-Communist elements on the mainland of China, undermine the Nationalist regime on Taiwan, discourage pro-Nationalist groups among the Overseas Chinese, and seriously harm the entire free-world position in the area. These arguments must be given careful consideration.

"In the effort to block Peiping's attempts to extend Communist rule in Asia," the State Department says, "the withholding of diplomatic recognition is an important factor." One "basic purpose" of nonrecognition is to "deny" Communist China the "advantages" of "access to international councils" and "international standing and prestige," thereby helping to "limit its ability to threaten the security of the area." It argues that nonrecognition of Peking, combined with American support of the Nationalists, "keeps alive the hopes of those Chinese who are determined eventually to free their country from Communist rule." Recognition would, in Dulles' view, "immensely discourage" people on the mainland of China who are anti-Communist. Furthermore, according to the State Department, nonrecognition can help to "hasten the passing" of the Chinese Communist regime. Recognition of Peking, it is also argued, "would seriously cripple, if not destroy altogether," the Nationalist regime on Taiwan. Dulles emphasized that the United States is "honor bound" to give the Nationalists "a full measure of loyalty" and that American recognition of Peking would leave them feeling "betrayed."

As to the effect on other Asian nations of American recognition of Peking, the State Department declares bluntly that it would have such an "adverse effect on the other free governments of Asia" that it "could be disastrous to the free world." South Korea and South Vietnam, it says, "would be confused and demoralized" and "might reason that their only hope for survival lay in desperate measures, not caring whether these threatened the peace of the area and the world." It also argues that other governments "further removed from China" "would see in American recognition of Communist China the first step in the withdrawal of the United States from the Far East," and warns that "probably" some of them would "seek the best terms obtainable from Peking." All of this, it predicts, would place the free-world position in Asia in "the gravest peril."

In the State Department's view recognition of Peking would also "have such a profound effect on the Overseas Chinese that it would make inevitable the transfer of loyalties of large numbers to the Communist side," which "would undermine the ability" of Southeast Asian nations "to resist the pressures" of Communist influence and would "seriously retard" their efforts to build healthy, free societies. Finally, it warns, American recognition of the Chinese Communist regime would have an adverse effect upon the entire free world; it would be interpreted "as damaging evidence of a serious difference of opinion within the free world on how to deal with the expansionist forces of international Communism."

Many critics of current American policy toward China, both in the United States and abroad, hold that the possible political consequences of both nonrecognition and recognition have been so greatly exaggerated in statements of this sort that the issue has acquired a symbolic importance all out of proportion to its real significance. Estimating these consequences is, of course, a matter of judgment, and there is good reason to avoid being categorical. In examining the many issues relevant to recognition policy, however, it is certainly possible to form judgments which differ greatly from many of those quoted above.

First of all, it seems highly doubtful that American nonrecognition, although it may handicap Peking to a limited extent, can really play a significant, positive role in blocking Communist China's attempts to extend its influence throughout Asia. As has been emphasized throughout this book, preventing the spread of Chinese Communist influence depends on much more basic factors; moreover, despite American nonrecognition, Peking has steadily expanded its political and economic relations in Asia, particularly with the nonaligned nations which are likely to be most vulnerable or susceptible to Chinese Communist pressures and influence. Overestimating what the policy of nonrecognition can be expected to accomplish may well divert effort and attention from the real problems which must be faced.

Undoubtedly, Peking's exclusion from international councils does pose certain problems for it—although apparently the Chinese Communists do not consider them serious enough to force them to make major compromises to gain access to these councils. At the same time, Peking's exclusion also poses problems for the non-Communist nations as well. There are, for example, many international issues which cannot be seriously considered without the participation of Communist China. In Chapter 6 it was pointed out, for example, that if progress is to be made on the problem of the control of armaments—and specifically on the problem of inspection and control of atomic weapons—there is little doubt that eventually Communist China will have to be included in the negotiating process at some point. On many of the most important unresolved international problems in Asia—such as the problem of political unification in both Korea and Vietnam—there is now a stalemate, but if these issues become negotiable in the future, Communist China clearly must be included in any serious international consideration of them.

Effects on the China Mainland

There is little to sustain the belief that nonrecognition can contribute significantly to "hastening the passing" of the Peking regime, as the State Department maintains. Undoubtedly, American recognition of Communist China would discourage those on the mainland who still cling to the unrealistic hope that a sudden change of government may be brought about by external intervention. But it is doubtful that American nonrecognition contributes positively to the growth of an anti-Communist movement on the mainland of China or increases the chances that an effective internal opposition to the Peking regime will emerge. It is possible, in fact, that the United States' present posture toward China actually makes it easier, in some degree, for Peking to arouse nationalist and antiforeign feelings and to mobilize active support for its anti-American policies.

As has been emphasized already, there is clear evidence of considerable dissidence in Communist China, caused by resentments against Peking's revolutionary policies at home, not by any American influence, but unless and until the Communists' structure of power weakens from within, the prospects for effective organized opposition are slim. Conditions on the mainland, rather than anything the United States does, will be decisive in determining whether effective opposition to the Communists develops in the future. Furthermore, there is little evidence to support the idea that a significant number of anti-Communists on the mainland of China, faced with the realities of Peking's power, still pin their hopes on the idea that the Nationalists might come back. For those who may still look to Taiwan with hope, the island can serve as the symbol of an alternative to Communist rule as long as it stays out of Communist hands, regardless of whether the United States recognizes Peking or not.

Effects on the Nationalist Regime

The fear that United States recognition of Peking, or any other major change in current American policy toward China for that matter, would have a severe impact upon the Chinese Nationalist regime, has undoubtedly been a major factor shaping American policy in recent years. As was stated in Chapter 13, the United States cannot shape its entire policy toward China on the basis of a vain hope of avoiding the problems which changes of policy will inevitably involve. Without any doubt, the Nationalists must undergo a difficult psychological and emotional adjustment to bring their aspirations more into line with the military, political, and economic realities of the situation which they face. What the United States must do is attempt to facilitate this adjustment. It must remain firm in its basic commitment to protect Taiwan from Communist attack—this is what it is "honor bound" to do—and take positive measures to counteract or soften the adverse impact on the Nationalists' morale which adjustments in over-all United States policy will doubtless have. If this is done, there is certainly no reason to believe that even major changes in American policy would actually "cripple" or "destroy" the Nationalist regime. It simply means that both the United States and the Nationalists must face up to, and in every possible way prepare for, the difficulties which a period of transition in their relations may involve.

Effects on Other Asian Nations

The flat assertion that American recognition of Peking would have an effect on the rest of the non-Communist nations of Asia that would be "disastrous to the free world" seems wholly unjustified. The reaction of different nations in the region would vary considerably, but many would approve of changes in American policy toward China, and there is no reason why such changes should have a "disastrous" effect on any of them.

In view of the symbolic importance which the recognition question has acquired in recent years, however, the United States must certainly give careful consideration to how, if moves are made in the direction of recognizing Peking, it can demonstrate convincingly to all the non-Communist nations in the region that such moves are not "the first step in the withdrawal of the United States from the Far East." Surely, however, it would be possible for the United States to do this, by reemphasizing its firm support for its Asian allies, most particularly South Korea and South Vietnam as well as Taiwan, in ways which would prevent these nations from being demoralized. It should be made clear to these countries which lie directly in the shadow of Chinese Communist power that while the United States will continue supporting their development and will defend them from attack, American policy will avoid extremes.

As for the other nations in the region, many, including India and virtually all of the other nonaligned nations, and probably Japan as well, would doubtless approve of American moves in the direction of recognizing the Peking regime. It seems probable, in fact, despite the recent change of attitude toward China in these countries, that if the United States were to abandon its adamant opposition to recognizing Communist China, the general American posture in Asia would be improved in their eyes. Conceivably, by narrowing the gap between American policies and theirs, this could help lay a basis for increased cooperation between the United States and these nations in facing many of the concrete problems posed by Peking. Far from being "disastrous," a change of American policy toward China might actually open up new opportunities for strengthening the non-Communist position in Asia.

Effects on the Overseas Chinese

The problem of the Overseas Chinese, and its implications for American policy toward China, have been discussed in detail in Chapter 8. As stated there, in the long run American recognition policy is not likely to have a decisive influence on the political orientation of most Overseas Chinese. Their attitudes and political roles will be determined by much more immediate factors, including the policies of the governments of Southeast Asia toward them, their own assessment of their economic self-interest, their estimate of the realities of world power, and their reaction to Communist China's policies at home and abroad. American nonrecognition of Peking has not been notably effective in preventing a pro-Peking swing among the Overseas Chinese in several key areas, including Singapore, Indonesia, Burma, and Thailand. Although American recognition of Communist China might add, to a degree, to the pressures impelling the Overseas Chinese in some areas to shift their allegiance to Peking, it would doubtless be no more than a marginal factor.

The crucial question for the future relating to the Overseas Chinese is whether the governments of Southeast Asian nations can evolve effective policies for integrating their Chinese minorities into the local societies. The focus of American policy toward the Overseas Chinese, therefore, should be on supporting the efforts of Southeast Asian governments to achieve this end. Since effective integration may take generations, many Overseas Chinese will undoubtedly continue maintaining ties with their homeland for years to come, and it is certainly desirable that as many as possible be attracted toward Taiwan rather than Communist China. As Peking's power and influence grow, however, Taiwan will have little basis for serving as a symbol of political and military power. Its main attraction will be as a center of traditional Chinese culture and a place where the children of Overseas Chinese can obtain a non-Communist education. This attraction would not be destroyed by a change in the United States' policy of recognition.

Moreover, if the political significance of the Overseas Chinese is viewed in a wider perspective, it seems clear that in most of Southeast Asia, although they create serious problems for the local governments, they do not present a major political threat. The exceptions are Singapore, Malaya, and Thailand; in these three areas, there is a serious danger of political subversion by the Overseas Chinese. The American policy of nonrecognition toward Peking has little bearing on the causes of this danger, however, and it does little to solve the problem. What is needed in these areas are effective local policies and measures, which can and should be evolved irrespective of American recognition policy toward China.

The possible implications, for these areas, of United States policy toward China cannot be ignored, however. It can certainly be argued, in fact, that until the governments of Singapore, Malaya, and Thailand achieve a higher degree of political stability, and develop more effective measures and techniques for coping with possible Overseas Chinese subversion, they would be well advised to continue limiting their contacts with Peking and refraining from establishing formal diplomatic relations with Communist China. If the United States contemplates recognizing Peking, therefore, it would be desirable to urge these governments not to feel that they should automatically follow the American lead; they should be encouraged to determine their recognition policies on the basis of their own particular situations and unique problems and assured that they can rely on firm American support of whatever policies they decide to pursue toward Peking.

The Problem of China's Seat in the United Nations

Perhaps the most unconvincing of all the official arguments used to justify the current American policy of nonrecognition is the allegation that American recognition would have an adverse effect upon the entire free world, because it would be interpreted "as damaging evidence of a serious difference of opinion within the free world on how to deal with the expansionist forces of international Communism." Actually, a strong case can be made that the opposite is true; throughout the past decade there have been many "serious differences" on policy toward China. Differences not only on recognition policy but, even more important, on the question of whether Peking should be seated in the United Nations have clearly highlighted the disagreements among the free world nations on how best to deal with communism, and unquestionably these issues have been divisive and damaging in their effect on the United States' relations with many non-Communist nations.

Differences on China policy have been an important area of disagreement between the United States and some of its closest allies, including Britain and Canada. The major nonaligned nations of Asia, such as India, have consistently, and often vigorously, criticized American policy toward China. To the American critics of current China policy, this fact is one of the most convincing arguments for changes in present policy—changes which could lay the basis for wider international agreement and broader multilateral approaches to the problems of dealing with Peking.

The perennial issue of whether the Nationalists or the Communists should occupy China's seat in the United Nations has been perhaps the most important focus of controversy about China policy between the United States and many other non-Communist countries. The Soviet Union first raised this issue in early 1950, proposing that the Peking regime be seated at once in place of the Nationalists. Then in the fall of 1950 India took the initiative in urging this step. Since then the question of seating China has been raised, either by one of the nations of the Communist bloc or by India, in virtually every session of every United Nations body to which China belongs.[9] The United States has consistently taken the lead in mobilizing opposition to the seating of Peking, and by strenuously urging all of its allies and friends within the United Nations to support the American view, it has been able so far to defeat every attempt made to oust the Nationalists.

Differing Views on the Effects of Seating Communist China

The United States government has given extraordinary attention to this issue, maintaining that it is of utmost importance. Currently, in fact, the official American view is that the seating of Communist China in the United Nations "would vitiate, if not destroy, the United Nations as an instrument for the maintenance of international peace." In recent years this extreme position has been reiterated on every possible occasion. In June 1957, for example, Secretary of State Dulles, asserting that the United Nations is "not a reformatory for bad governments," declared that if the Peking regime was seated, this would "implant in the United Nations the seeds of its own destruction." Communist China cannot qualify for membership, he argued, because it "has a record of successive armed aggressions," "today stands condemned by the United Nations as an aggressor," and still "defies the United Nations decision to reunify Korea."

Even though the United States has managed so far to persuade a majority of United Nations members to vote against considering the seating of Peking, however, few nations agree fully with the extreme American position as defined in recent years. The position has, in fact, been challenged on many grounds, by critics in the United States as well as elsewhere.

The argument that the seating of Communist China would "vitiate" the United Nations can certainly be challenged. Since the Soviet Union already possesses the veto power in the Security Council, there is actually little reason to believe that one additional Communist veto would fundamentally upset the existing balance of power in the organization or basically alter the nature of the problem which the non-

Communist nations already face in dealing with the Communist bloc within the United Nations.

The seating of Peking would doubtless add somewhat to the influence of the Communist bloc in the United Nations. Conceivably, it might bolster the Communists' attempts to influence or manipulate the Asian-African bloc. On the other hand, some would argue, there might be gains as well as losses if Communist China were brought into the United Nations. At the Bandung Conference of 1955 the Chinese Communists felt it necessary to make some concessions in their efforts to woo the Asian and African nations, and if Communist China were seated in the United Nations, there is no reason to believe that the flow of influence would be a one-way street. Conceivably, the non-Communist nations in the Asian-African group might be able to exert a certain influence upon Chinese Communist policies, as well as the reverse.

It would be a mistake to overestimate the influence which membership in the United Nations, in and of itself, can have upon the policies of any nation (witness the Soviet Union). Nonetheless, it is possible to argue that Communist China, if seated in the United Nations, might be somewhat more influenced than at present by the restraints of world opinion and might feel compelled to give more deference to the United Nations Charter and resolutions. As long as it is excluded, it will certainly continue to deny—as it has throughout the past decade—that the United Nations has any jurisdiction over any problems involving China.

One basis for disagreement on this whole issue is a difference of viewpoint or philosophy on the nature of the United Nations and the role it can play in international affairs. If the United Nations were to be viewed as an organization restricted to righteous, moral, and democratic states—if, in short, the specifications for membership laid down in the Charter were applied in a literal sense—then clearly the seating of Communist China, or, for that matter, of other Communist nations, would be difficult to justify. Most of the Communist countries have already been seated, however, and for some years the trend in international opinion about the United Nations has been toward the idea of universal membership. Those who have supported this trend feel that, although the United Nations certainly is not a "reformatory for bad governments," neither can it be considered an alliance or club restricted to good governments. They argue that, even though there is little prospect of immediately resolving the basic conflicts between the Communist and non-Communist worlds, nonetheless there is real value in bringing the democratic and Communist nations together in an organization where many problems can at least be discussed at the conference table.

A Possible American Position

Even if one accepts the generalized arguments in favor of seating Communist China in the United Nations, however, there is one specific and important fact which should not be overlooked. Peking was branded as an aggressor by the United Nations for its intervention in Korea. And it still adamantly opposes and obstructs implementation of the United Nations' decisions on the reunification of Korea through free elections. It continues, in short, openly to defy the United Nations.

The fact that Communist China has yet to "purge" itself of aggression in Korea is one of the strongest arguments used by those who oppose seating it in the United Nations. Not enough attention has been given, however, to how Peking might be expected to "purge" itself. There is little merit in the idea that a nation, once branded an aggressor, should be permanently excluded from the community of nations. On the other hand, before seating a nation found guilty of aggression, the United Nations can certainly require that it halt its aggression and comply with the United Nations' decisions on how a settlement should be made.

In adamantly opposing the seating of Peking in the United Nations, however, the United States has often made it appear that nothing the Chinese Communists might reasonably be expected to do could "purge" them of their aggression in Korea. Consequently, American opposition to the seating of Peking has appeared to be absolute rather than conditional.

A good case can be made that if the United States and the

United Nations genuinely hope to induce Peking to make concessions regarding Korea, the Chinese Communists must be convinced that they can qualify for United Nations membership by fulfilling certain conditions. The United States would be on sound ground if it made clear that, while opposing the seating of the Chinese Communists until Peking adopts a more compliant attitude, it would accept a majority decision on seating Peking if the Chinese Communists were to fulfill whatever the United Nations defines as "substantial compliance" with its requirements. Whether these requirements should include full acceptance by Peking of the United Nations' current formula for unification of Korea by free elections, or something less ideal but more attainable, should be determined by the will of the majority of members in the United Nations.

Acceptance of the Majority Will

Whatever position the United States itself chooses to adopt on the seating of Peking in the United Nations, it must be recognized that this issue is not, in the final analysis, subject to United States control, since it concerns the whole international community within the United Nations. For the American government to expend a great deal of political capital in attempting to guarantee that its own views shall prevail, or for it to imply that its entire attitude toward the United Nations might depend upon this one issue, is extremely unwise. This, in effect, is what the United States has done in recent years. Although when the question first arose, the United States indicated that it would accept the majority's decision within the United Nations, whatever that decision might be, subsequently the American position has hardened, and United States representatives have threatened to use the veto if necessary to bar Communist China from a seat in the United Nations.[10]

The legal aspects of the issue are by no means clear, and there are differing opinions on whether the veto is applicable in the Security Council to a question of seating representatives or passing on their credentials. In the view of some, a vote on the seating of Communist China would be procedural rather than substantive, and therefore the veto would not be applicable. Within the General Assembly there is, of course, no power of veto, and consequently if the Assembly were to vote in favor of seating Communist China, the United States could not block it. The Assembly could decide this question by a majority vote, unless it specifically determined that it should be treated as an "important" question requiring a two-thirds vote. In the event Peking were seated in the Assembly, if the United States tried to bar Communist China from the Security Council by attempting to use the veto, this would risk seriously straining or splitting the organization and would almost certainly have divisive effects tending to weaken rather than strengthen the entire non-Communist position.

All of these facts make it desirable for the United States to make it entirely clear that, even if American representatives in the United Nations continue to vote against the seating of Peking, they will not attempt to use the veto, and will, therefore, in the final analysis, accept the majority decision.

Opposition to the American Position

Looking into the future, it is difficult to avoid the conclusion that, whatever the American government does, a majority of the United Nations membership is likely some day to vote for the seating of Peking. So far, by exerting strong pressure on its friends and allies, the United States has been able to hold together majority support for its own position. Nevertheless, opposition to the American view has gradually increased, as indicated by the annual votes in the General Assembly on deferring debate on the seating of Communist China. In 1956 the vote was 47 for, 24 against, and 8 abstained; in 1957 it was 48 for, 27 against, and 6 abstained; in 1958 it was 44 for, 28 against, and 9 abstained; and in 1959 it was 44 for, 29 against, and 9 abstained. Even today the United States would clearly be in a minority without the solid support of the Latin American bloc, which has 20 votes. In the 1958 vote only 5 of 12 Asian members in the United Nations, 4 of 14 Middle Eastern members,

7 of 16 non-Communist European members, and 8 of the United States' 13 NATO allies voted to support the American position.[11] And in 1959 the solid support of the Latin American bloc was eroded for the first time when Cuba abstained.

Despite all the arguments against "inevitability," therefore, it is a fair prediction that, if the United States is not able to evolve a position which can obtain wider international support, the vote will eventually go against it. Conceivably, it may be possible to defer this for several years. On the other hand, it might happen suddenly. If, for example, the British Labor party, which has strongly supported the idea of seating Communist China in the United Nations, came to power, the British might soon shift their policy and vote against the United States. Even one such major defection from the American side might well lead to a rapid disintegration of the entire position.

A "Two Chinas" Formula in the United Nations

In realistic terms, the alternatives which the United States faces on this issue—if one looks more than a year or two ahead—are probably either the eventual seating of Communist China in the place of the Nationalists, or the active exploration of some alternative approach behind which international support can be rallied. One alternative would be a "two Chinas" formula in the United Nations. Under such a formula, it might be possible to link the seating of the "People's Republic of China" (the Communists) in the Security Council and General Assembly with the admission of the "Republic of China" (the Nationalists) as a new state in the General Assembly. It is by no means clear that this idea could be carried out, but in view of the probable alternative it certainly seems worth attempting. Its feasibility would depend entirely on whether broad support could be organized for it. In the short run it would certainly be blocked. Both the Chinese Communists and Nationalists would oppose it, and even if support could be developed for the idea, the Soviet Union could be expected to block its implementation by vetoing the admission of Nationalist

China as a new state (the admission of new states is subject to the veto). Conceivably, therefore, the immediate result of attempting to implement a "two Chinas" formula within the United Nations might simply be a temporary deadlock, perhaps one in which neither Chinese regime was represented for a period of time. Such a result would not necessarily be undesirable, however. It might create a situation, in fact, which would tend over the long run to exert pressure on the international community in general, and on both Communist and Nationalist China in particular, to accept the idea of having both mainland China and Taiwan represented in the United Nations. A deadlock on this issue might also open up the basic question of the composition of the Security Council, and conceivably it might be possible eventually to gain acceptance for the idea of making India as well as China a permanent member of the Security Council, thus giving Asia a more equitable representation in that body.

Trade and Other Contacts

For almost a decade the United States has attempted not only to ostracize the Peking regime politically but also to restrict the development of economic and all other types of contacts between the Chinese Communists and the non-Communist world. On the United States' part, this has involved continuing measures of economic warfare against Peking and an almost total ban on all other types of even unofficial contact. In his June 1957 speech on China policy, Secretary of States Dulles outlined the official rationale for these measures. Arguing that "trade with Communist China is not a normal trade," because it is government-controlled, and that in any case there is little likelihood of it developing in "any appreciable" quantity, he declared: "Whatever others may do, the United States, which has heavy security commitments in the China area, ought not build up the military power of its potential enemy." "We also doubt," he said, "the value of cultural exchanges." Peking favors cultural exchanges with the United States, he argued, because it believes that if the Americans permitted such exchanges, then "it would be difficult for China's close neighbors not to follow," and if they did follow suit, this would "add greatly to their danger."

Several years ago the argument that the United States' ban on trade with Communist China was an important measure to help slow down Peking's build-up of its military power had real meaning. But, if the present situation is viewed realistically, it has little validity today. While the Korean War was in progress, there were good reasons to mobilize the most important trading nations in the non-Communist world to apply economic sanctions against Communist China. Although no other major nation followed the American lead in banning all trade, a large number of non-Communist countries, following a United Nations recommendation, did adopt special restrictions on trade with Communist China, as a wartime measure. After the end of the fighting in Korea, however, virtually all the important trading nations, other than the United States, steadily reduced their restrictions and finally, in 1957, most of them decided to eliminate all special restrictions on trade with Communist China, retaining only those restrictions applying to trade with the Communist bloc as a whole. They decided, in short, to eliminate the so-called "China differential" and to restrict in their trade with Communist China only the basic strategic items which are barred in trade with the Soviet Union and its satellites.

Today, therefore, the United States' total embargo on trade with Communist China has little more than a symbolic significance. Peking can buy from countries such as Britain, Germany, or Japan the kind of nonstrategic goods which it might wish to buy from the United States.[12] It is doubtful, therefore, that the American embargo now serves any significant economic purpose. In this situation it is difficult to see why the United States should not alter its present policy and, like the other major non-Communist nations, apply to Communist China the same restrictions on strategic items which it applies to trade with the rest of the Communist bloc, permitting trade in nonstrategic items to develop. What is the justification now, it can be asked, for treating Communist China differently from the Soviet Union and other Communist states?

Until fairly recently it might have been possible for the United States to try to use the trade issue for bargaining purposes in negotiations with the Chinese Communists, by offering a relaxation in American trade restrictions in return for Chinese concessions. Now, however, the United States no longer has any real bargaining power on this issue. This is a good example of how an inflexible approach has prevented the United States from bargaining—and perhaps achieving some gains through compromise before its position was undercut by the predictable actions of others. Today perhaps the main significance of the United States' continuation of its total embargo on trade with Communist China is the fact that it probably symbolizes, in the eyes of much of the world, the basic inflexibility of United States policy toward China.

If the United States were to modify its present ban on trade with Peking, probably, as Secretary Dulles argued, the actual volume of Sino-American trade would not be very large in the foreseeable future, since Peking has good reasons for channeling most of its trade elsewhere. Yet, as suggested in Chapter 9, there might conceivably be some psychological and political, as well as economic, benefits from whatever trade could be developed.

The United States government's policy of almost totally forbidding cultural and other contacts with Communist China can also be seriously questioned, and it has, in fact, been widely challenged by the American press during recent years. Quite clearly there is a sizable body of private opinion in the United States which firmly believes that it would be desirable for the United States government not to block all contacts but instead to do all it can to make it possible for American correspondents, scholars, and the like to visit, observe, and report on Communist China—as on all other major nations, whether friendly or hostile. Whatever United States policy toward China may be, it is argued, there is a need for greater knowledge and public understanding in the United States about the rapid and momentous changes which are now taking place in Communist China, and this need demands positive steps on the part of the American government to open up greater channels of contact. Possibly, there might be minor advantages, also, in broadening Communist China's knowledge of the outside world, just as there seem to have been in our development of cultural exchanges with the Soviet Union, Poland, and Yugoslavia.

In the view of critics of current American policy, furthermore, the kind of minor incidents which inevitably result from existing policy—for example, the banning of a panda, sought by an American zoo, because it originated in Communist China, and the indictment of an American stamp dealer because he imported Chinese Communist stamps— make the United States look slightly ridiculous in the eyes of world opinion.

The question of whether the United States government should allow and facilitate visits by American newsmen to Communist China has aroused more controversy in the United States than perhaps any other single issue arising from the current policy of restricting contacts, and the State Department's handling of this issue has been widely criticized.

For reasons of their own, the Chinese Communists took the initiative in 1956 in pressing the United States government to modify its existing travel restrictions by extending specific invitations to a number of American newsmen to visit and report on mainland China. The State Department's initial reaction was to reaffirm its long-standing opposition to any travel to Communist China, and at first it denied passports to these newsmen. In the months that followed, criticism of this stand steadily mounted, and finally, in the fall of 1957, the State Department issued passports valid for travel to Communist China to a limited number of American newsmen. In announcing this decision, however, the United States government took special pains to point out that it would not make any agreement with the Chinese Communists which would assure them of reciprocity for their newsmen,[13] on the grounds that under American immigration laws each visa application made by a person from a Communist country must be considered individually on its own merit. Reacting bitterly, Peking retaliated by reneging on its earlier invitations to American newsmen. By the early autumn of 1959 only one American newsman with a properly validated passport had actually been admitted to mainland China by the Peking authorities, and no Chinese Communist newsmen had yet applied for American visas.

The State Department's handling of this issue can be looked at from two quite different perspectives. If the aim of the United States government was merely to counter Peking's pressure for an exchange of correspondents, and to shift the onus for blocking such an exchange from the United States to Communist China, the State Department's course of action was quite understandable and defensible. If, however, it is really felt desirable to facilitate American newsmen going to Communist China, the United States government could and should have pursued a different line of action, avoiding moves which might unnecessarily provoke Peking and pressing the issue in every way possible.

Despite existing immigration regulations, the United States government can devise ways of assuring Peking of reciprocal treatment for a limited group of Chinese Communist newsmen, if this is a prerequisite for inducing Peking to admit American newsmen into Communist China. In practice the United States Attorney General, who is responsible for making decisions on the admission of Communists, normally follows the State Department's recommendations, and in fact the State Department has already worked out ways and means, in other cases, to allow the admission of certain Chinese Communists to the United States. Approval has been given, for example, to the convocation of the 1961 General Assembly of the International Astronomical Union in the United States, with the understanding that Chinese Communist representatives will be allowed to attend.[14]

If, in short, the United States government should decide to seize the initiative in promoting certain types of unofficial contacts with Communist China, it could press much harder than it has to date to overcome the many obstacles which now exist. Peking would undoubtedly try to obtain political concessions from the United States, and the American government need not and should not pay any significant political price merely to establish limited channels of unofficial contact. Undoubtedly, however, a willingness to make limited concessions—such as reciprocity in the case of an exchange of newsmen—will be a prerequisite for any serious effort to open up increased channels of contact, and if greater contacts are desirable, such concessions are justifiable.

Even though all of these issues, and particularly those relating to recognition policy and China's seat in the United Nations, are unquestionably important, none of them gets to the heart of the problem of deciding what policy the United States should pursue toward China. They are essentially tactical issues, and unless questions of broad strategy are answered first, debate over tactical issues is likely to be fruitless, since tactics which appear logical and desirable in the context of one general approach may be illogical and unwise in terms of another.

Chapter 15

THE CHOICES BEFORE THE UNITED STATES

In the face of Peking's challenge in Asia, what broad policy should the United States adopt in dealing with China? What goals can the United States legitimately pursue? What strategy should it follow?

These are essential questions which must be answered, however difficult they may be. But before they can be examined rationally, it is indispensable to state clearly the fundamental premises which should underlie any American policy toward China. The entire discussion so far has dealt with issues relevant to defining these premises, and no attempt will be made here to recapitulate in detail the many conclusions already put forward. However, the essential propositions which should be kept in mind in formulating broad policy toward China deserve to be reiterated.

The Chinese Communist regime now exercises effective, albeit ruthless, totalitarian control over the mainland of China. In the years immediately ahead there is little prospect, therefore, either for an overthrow of the Peking regime from within or for a return to the mainland by the Chinese Nationalists.

More than this, the Chinese Communists are rapidly building up their economic and military strength. Communist China's rate of economic growth now appears to be almost double that of India, and in a few years Peking will probably have built a base of heavy industries overshadowing that of Japan. While Communist China, despite many internal difficulties, appears to be surging ahead, most Southeast Asian nations are still struggling to get their programs of economic development under way. The Chinese Communists' military strength is growing more rapidly than that of all other countries in the Far East and South and Southeast Asia combined, and their command of military technology is far outstripping that of their neighbors. If present trends continue, Peking's power and influence relative to its neighbors will be far greater a decade from now than it is today.

Unquestionably, the Chinese Communists will continue striving to achieve Great Power status and will work persistently to promote the spread of communism in Asia. In the struggle to achieve these ends, Peking has already used, and will continue using, all the instruments of foreign policy at its command, including diplomacy, political maneuver, subversion, trade, and economic aid, as well as military power.

Communist China's military power is clearly an important component in its over-all foreign policy strategy. As its power grows, Peking may be tempted to exert increasing pressure on its weak neighbors, and if it believes it can use force to make local gains without fearing a large-scale war, it may do so. Peking's growing power may also increase the opportunities for Communist subversion in neighboring countries, particularly if the Chinese Communists attempt to support insurrectionary groups in these countries by throwing a mantle of strategic protection over them. On the other hand, military power is not the only weapon in Peking's arsenal, and the Communists undoubtedly wish to avoid a major war. If, therefore, United States policies can successfully counterbalance the growth of Peking's power and prestige, and if the general balance of world power does not shift disastrously in favor of the Communist bloc, Chinese Communist expansionism is more likely to take political and economic rather than military forms in the years immediately ahead. Instead of attempting overt military expansionism, Peking seems more likely, in short, to promote revolutionary subversion and to expand its influence through conventional diplomacy, "people's diplomacy," trade, and aid.

In its efforts to promote communism in Asia, Peking can count on continued backing from Moscow. Although there are differences and tensions between Communist China and the Soviet Union, there is little chance of an open split between them within the next few years, and the Sino-Soviet alliance undoubtedly will hold together for the predictable future.

From Peking's viewpoint, the United States is the main obstacle blocking the achievement of its broad foreign policy objectives in Asia, and it will try in every possible way, therefore, to weaken the American position throughout the region. The Chinese Communists frankly state that their hope is ultimately to eliminate American influence entirely from the Western Pacific.

It is eminently clear that Communist China represents the most dangerous threat to American political and economic, as well as security, interests throughout Asia. If the United States is to achieve its aims in the region—to prevent the domination of Asia by any single state, to support the principles of independence and self-determination in that area, and to encourage the political and economic growth of democratic, non-Communist states—it must not only evolve adequate security measures to deter Chinese Communist military expansionism; it must also devote primary attention to the need for more positive and effective measures to assist in developing viable, independent, non-Communist states.

Because of the basic conflict between American and Chinese Communist purposes, the United States must, in short, dedicate itself to a long-term competition to counter the expansion of Peking's influence. This competition may involve a delicate and dangerous balance of military force, but if war can be avoided, the future of Asia will be determined largely by the outcome of an intense and prolonged competition of opposing ideological, psychological, political, and economic forces in the entire region on China's periphery.

For some years, the situation in Asia is likely to involve serious risks of war between the United States and Communist China. These risks may even increase in the decade ahead. Since it is clear that American purposes in the region might be defeated by the outbreak of major war with Communist China, as well as by appeasement, United States policy should strive to avoid both these calamitous extremes.

In summary, the United States should accept and act on the basis of several fundamental propositions. Effective, long-term competition against Peking's influence throughout Asia will be a precondition for avoiding war. If a military balance can be maintained, the outcome of this competition will depend fundamentally on whether the major non-Communist nations on China's periphery succeed or fail in their programs to build viable states. Consequently, the United States must put forth a major effort to support these nations, not only in their efforts to preserve their independence, but also in their attempts to realize their potential for political and economic growth. Such support, to be effective, will have to be given on terms and for purposes which these nations desire. In the case of the nonaligned countries, the United States must accept the fact that even if the principles which underlie their policies toward China differ from those on which American policy is based, it is nonetheless important to back them up and help them achieve their own aims as they see them. This—rather than an attempt to urge these countries to line up in support of existing American policies toward China—should be the primary emphasis in the United States' efforts to offset Peking's influence.

Numerous countries besides the United States have a vital stake in the outcome of the competition with Communist China. Many of them have views on how to deal with Peking which are different from those which underlie current United States policy. Even though these differences cannot be fully resolved, clearly the United States should try to evolve policies which have as wide a base of international agreement and support as possible. Obviously, it is too much at present to expect a general consensus to emerge among the major non-Communist nations concerned with Asia on how to deal with Communist China. For the long haul, however, it is important to work toward such a consensus and to evolve new multilateral approaches to the major problems which Peking poses.

It is important, too, for the United States to adopt positions in its policy toward China which are tenable for more than a brief period of time. The competition with Peking requires the building of positions of real strength—political and economic as well as military—and if American policy is based on positions lacking international support, which are obviously vulnerable to steady erosion or sudden collapse, there is little chance that it will be effective in the long run. Without a sound basis of international support, the appearance of strength may prove temporary and illusory.

Broad Policy Alternatives

These premises and propositions do not automatically provide a clear answer to the question: What broad strategy should the United States follow in its policy toward China? They do, however, provide a realistic starting point for examining the alternatives.

There are substantial risks of oversimplification and distortion in attempting to define and label broad policy alternatives, but it is possible nonetheless to distinguish at least four general approaches to China policy which have been seriously proposed at one time or another, either in the United States or elsewhere. For convenience, these four alternatives can be given the following labels: full accommodation to Communist China; a "liberation" policy involving all-out pressure against Peking; a policy aimed at isolating Peking and applying limited pressure against it; and a "two Chinas" policy aimed at stabilizing and gaining international acceptance for a new *status quo* based on a divided China. Each of these alternatives must be considered, at least briefly.

A Policy of Accommodation

In theory, the idea of attempting to work rapidly toward some sort of full accommodation to Communist China might sound attractive to some, and many leaders of Asian and African countries have argued, in effect, that this is what the United States should do. For a number of important reasons, however, there is no basis for the United States to view such a policy as a practicable or desirable alternative in the foreseeable future.

The Taiwan issue constitutes a fundamental obstacle to full accommodation to Communist China, and it is likely to remain so for a considerable period of time. By definition, full accommodation would require the elimination of the most serious causes of present dispute between the United

States and Communist China. Clearly, it could not be achieved unless the United States were willing to accept Peking's claims to Taiwan, liquidate American commitments to the Nationalist regime, and allow the Communists to deal with Taiwan as a purely "domestic problem." The many arguments against such a course of action have already been set forth in Chapter 13.

After the events of the past decade, if the United States were now to abandon Taiwan and the Nationalist regime completely, this, in addition to violating and discrediting fundamental principles which underlie the United States' entire policy toward Asia, would risk undermining the American strategic position in the area and demoralizing those Asian nations allied to and dependent upon the United States. Undoubtedly it would alarm and weaken even the nonaligned nations in the area. It might, in fact, set in motion forces threatening the whole American and non-Communist position throughout Asia.

Furthermore, if one analyzes Peking's foreign policy aims, strategy, and tactics realistically, it seems clear that, even if the Taiwan issue did not exist, there would be little basis at present for expecting the Chinese Communists to make the basic compromises and adjustments which would be necessary for a genuine, stable, and lasting *modus vivendi* to be achieved in Asia. Under existing conditions, therefore, if the United States attempted to appease Peking by abandoning its commitments to Taiwan, the Chinese Communists, instead of being propitiated, would probably respond by challenging the entire American and non-Communist position in Asia even more openly and militantly than they do at present.

During the past decade, the main support for a policy of full accommodation has come, not from within the United States, but rather from certain leaders in the nonaligned countries, leaders who have shaped their own national policies to this end and have urged the United States to follow their example. In recent years, however, these leaders appear to have become increasingly realistic in their assessment of Communist China's motives and aims. Consequently, even if they continue urging the United States to be more conciliatory in its policy toward Peking, as they may well do, they probably will understand more fully than before the obstacles to a full accommodation to Communist China on the United States' part.

A "Liberation" Policy

At the other extreme, a "liberation" policy would require all-out pressure against the Peking regime, involving the use of every practicable means to subvert and disrupt Communist rule on the China mainland, with the aim of bringing about either an overthrow of the Peking regime from within or a return to the mainland by the Chinese Nationalists. There is no basis for believing that a "liberation" policy of this sort would be any more practicable or desirable than a policy of full accommodation. While retaining faith that the totalitarian rule of Chinese Communism can and will be changed ultimately, it is essential to recognize that the Peking regime is both viable and strong today. There is no realistic basis for hoping that, short of a major war, even all-out pressure against the Chinese Communist regime would result in a successful internal revolution against Peking or a reinstatement of the Chinese Nationalist regime on the mainland. On the contrary, all-out pressure against Peking would doubtless stimulate the Chinese Communists to adopt increasingly severe repressive measures at home and pursue more aggressive policies abroad. It would involve great risks of provoking major war between the United States and Communist China, a war which would probably expand into a world-wide struggle involving the Soviet Union. In a global conflict, the United States would have to concentrate first on eliminating the Soviet Union, the more dangerous opponent, and conceivably Communist China could achieve its immediate aims in Asia while the United States was fighting the Soviet Union, primarily in Europe and the Middle East. The political as well as military consequences of such a war could be disastrous, whoever might ultimately "win" it in a limited military sense.

Actually, almost the only serious proponents of an all-out "liberation" policy have been the leaders of Nationalist

China and South Korea. Chiang K'ai-shek and Syngman Rhee in particular have been the personal embodiment of the idea of a militant struggle to "liberate" all the territories which the Communists now control in Asia, by renewed military struggle if necessary, and they have urged the United States to support such a policy.

Instead of adopting such a policy, the United States government has in practice felt compelled to impose direct and specific restraints upon both Chiang and Rhee to prevent them from taking action which might lead to all-out war against Communist China. At times during the past decade, however, some very prominent Americans have urged action which could easily have led to a warlike policy of "liberation," and on several occasions pronouncements by the American government have seriously disturbed its closest allies, raising questions as to whether American official thinking was moving toward acceptance of a militant policy of "liberation," with all of its risks of war. In particular, during the "Great Debate" on the Korean War in 1951, the proposals made publicly by some Americans that the war be expanded—by a blockade of China and attacks against the mainland—seemed to imply a belief that the Peking regime could be easily destroyed if the United States were only willing to attack it directly. Then, after a new administration under President Eisenhower had assumed office, the American government ostensibly "unleashed" Chiang K'ai-shek in early 1953 and attempted to emphasize a "new positive foreign policy" of "liberation" rather than mere "containment."

In fact, this "liberation" idea was from the start more of a psychological warfare tactic than a sign of real changes in United States policy. Soon after "unleashing" Chiang, the American government proceeded to restrain both him and Rhee, and in recent years the whole "liberation" theme has fallen into the background. Especially since the Hungarian revolution, when the United States was deterred from supporting a major anti-Communist revolt by the clear risk of war with the Soviet Union, the "liberation" slogan has had little concrete meaning. Yet, hints of the idea periodically recur in official American statements on policy toward China.

In June 1957, for example, Secretary of State Dulles declared, "We can confidently assume that international communism's rule of strict conformity is, in China as elsewhere, a passing and not a perpetual state. We owe it to ourselves, our allies, and the Chinese people to do all that we can to contribute to that passing."[1] In this and similar statements, however, the idea of "liberation" appears to represent merely a hope for eventual revolt from below in Communist China, or a mellowing from within, rather than a policy for the United States actively to pursue.

A Policy of "Limited Pressure"

Despite statements of this sort, in practice the United States government has consistently and consciously avoided moving toward any "liberation" policy of all-out pressure, recognizing that such a policy would be both dangerous and impracticable. Ever since 1950, however, the United States has actually followed a policy which has involved steady and persistent, even if limited, pressure against Peking. Officially, this policy was described by the head of the China Desk in the State Department in 1954 as one of "pressure and diplomatic isolation."[2] It might best be labeled, in fact, as a policy of "limited pressure."

The supporters of this policy, emphasizing that American and Chinese Communist aims clash throughout Asia and that a state of "semiwar"[3] continues between the United States and Peking, maintain that it is desirable for the United States to do everything it can, while still avoiding military conflict, to isolate the Peking regime diplomatically and prevent, or at least delay, its acceptance into the international community of nations. They strongly support continued psychological, political, and economic pressures against Peking, with the aim of weakening Communist China in any way possible and detracting from its international prestige and influence. And they argue that all the basic components of current American policy toward China are essential: adamant opposition to recognition of Peking and continued support for the claim of the Nationalist regime to be the *de jure* government of all China; unrelenting opposition to the seating of Communist China in the United Nations or any other international bodies; and the prohibition of commercial, cultural, and virtually every other type of contact between the United States and Communist China. The United States' policy toward Taiwan, including military and economic support for the Nationalist regime, the pledge to defend Taiwan, and neutralization of the Taiwan Strait, is, in this general approach, a corollary to the policy of pressure against Peking.

Many, if not most, supporters of this policy recognize that involvement in an armed conflict over the offshore islands is undesirable from the American viewpoint, but they argue that, because of the Nationalists' strong opposition to evacuating the islands, it is difficult to see how American interests can be disengaged. In this situation, they say, the United States cannot allow Peking to take the offshore islands by force, and thus they accept, in effect, the existence of an implicit American commitment to defend the islands, despite the fact that the American government has deliberately avoided any explicit commitment on this issue.

American policy-makers have reacted strongly against the oft-made charges that they have been "inflexible" in their approach to China policy. In practice, however, they have consistently maintained in recent years that any substantial change of any important aspect of American policy toward China would result in undermining the whole policy, thus weakening the entire non-Communist position in Asia. They have also argued that not only should the United States itself "abstain from any act to encourage the Chinese Communist regime, morally, politically, or materially," thus quarantining Peking as completely as possible, but that it should also do everything possible to persuade other non-Communist countries to apply the same policy of "pressure and diplomatic isolation."

American Attitudes

During recent years, a large majority of the most articulate spokesmen on China policy in the United States has strongly supported the existing policy, vigorously opposing all proposals for change. The late Secretary of State John Foster Dulles and former Assistant Secretary of State Walter S. Robertson, the principal architects of current China policy, defended the policy repeatedly and eloquently. Congress has shown a remarkable and almost unique unanimity in recording its approval of continued nonrecognition of Peking and opposition to the seating of Communist China in the United Nations. A number of organizations, such as the Committee of One Million against the Admission of Communist China to the United Nations, have worked assiduously to mobilize public support for current policy and to discourage serious consideration of any alternatives.

Some of the most widely repeated arguments used in support of existing policy have been based upon an emotional and moralistic condemnation of the Chinese Communist regime. It is not surprising that these arguments have evoked a strong response. The American people, with a profound and well-founded aversion to communism anywhere, appear to have developed a particularly intense resentment against the Chinese Communists. This can be partially explained by the fact that the Communists' advent to power in China marked the end of a long period in which innumerable friendly ties, unique in their character, had developed between the American and Chinese peoples. American feelings have been legitimately aroused by the Peking regime's deliberate mistreatment of captured or detained citizens and soldiers over the past decade. Perhaps most important, the war in Korea, involving heavy American casualties, greatly increased the aversion of many Americans to the Chinese Communists—even though American resentments have been directed primarily against the Peking regime, not the Chinese people. This residue of bitterness has undoubtedly been a major factor influencing American attitudes toward Communist China ever since the war.

Emotional feelings and moral aversion are not, in and of themselves, a sufficient or valid basis for determining the United States' aims, strategy, and tactics in any major area of foreign policy, however. On this, both policy-makers responsible for China policy and nearly all critics of that policy agree, at least in theory. Where they differ is in their judgments on how best to meet the challenge and counter the threat which the Peking regime poses. Their differences, in short, concern strategy and tactics.

Major Criticisms of the Policy of "Limited Pressure"

The basic criticisms of current American policy toward China can be stated fairly simply. First, and in the view of many critics most important, it does little to lessen military tensions in Asia and in some respects it tends to heighten them, diverting attention from the all-important task of building political and economic strength in the non-Communist nations of the area. Beyond this, it clearly involves certain undesirable and unnecessary risks of war. Second, it lacks the broad base of international support which is essential to build a strong position for successful long-term competition throughout Asia. Instead of providing a desirable framework for growing cooperation in meeting the Chinese Communist challenge, it has in fact created significant divisive strains between the United States and many other non-Communist nations, including some of its close allies. Third, it is based on positions which will probably be subject to steady erosion and on fictions which will be difficult to sustain in the years ahead. In all likelihood, therefore, it will prove untenable over the long run. Finally, it is inflexible, despite arguments to the contrary, and provides little room for adjustment, adaptation, and maneuver, all of which are essential if American policy is to cope successfully with opponents as agile as the Chinese Communists and with the demands of a rapidly changing situation throughout Asia.

As has been repeatedly emphasized, American involvement in the offshore islands clearly involves risks and creates tensions which are both unnecessary and undesirable. The ambiguity and vulnerability of the situation create the greatest dangers of accidental war anywhere on China's periphery. It is a situation over which the United States has almost no control. And each new crisis which arises over these islands strains the relations between the United States and most of the non-Communist world. By disassociating itself from the defense of the offshore islands, and working toward a disengagement of the Nationalist forces from them, the United States would not, of course, escape other risks or eliminate other tensions, either in the Taiwan area or elsewhere on China's periphery. On the contrary, in meeting its heavy responsibilities for the defense of Taiwan, South Korea, South Vietnam, and other Asian countries, the United States must face many serious and unavoidable risks. The wise course, in this situation, would be to concentrate on defending those positions which are essential, strengthening them by building international support, and avoiding entanglements in situations which are both divisive and unessential.

Involvement in the offshore islands question has been only one of the several aspects of American policy toward China which have caused strains between the United States and other major non-Communist nations. Some of the United States' most important allies, including Britain, and many of the key nonaligned nations, including India, disagree in fundamental respects with the entire American approach to China. Because of this, both in its relations with these countries and within the United Nations the American government has paid a sizable political price. By rigidly holding to its own views, and attempting to force them on others, the United States has failed to obtain wide support even for those aspects of American policy toward China which are indispensable. Not a single one of the United States' major allies, for example, has publicly pledged itself to the defense of Taiwan, and where, as in the United Nations, it has been possible so far to obtain the minimum support required to sustain the American position, this "support" in reality has often represented grudging acquiescence rather than strong positive backing.

Despite the vigorous efforts of the United States government to hold the line, its policy toward Communist China has been steadily eroded by the actions of other countries. The policy of economic pressure against Peking has already been undermined. In 1957 the other major trading nations decided to part company with the United States and abandoned the special restrictions which they previously had imposed on trade with Communist China. Despite the United States' continuing nonrecognition of Peking, a growing number of other countries have established diplomatic or other contacts with the Chinese Communists. Within the United Nations, support for seating Peking has grown slowly but steadily, and it seems almost certain that ultimately the present American position will be undercut. If this happens, and if Peking is seated in the face of unyielding United States opposition, this will be a major blow not only to American policy toward China but to American leadership in a broader sense. Very likely, in fact, if the United States persists in an all-or-nothing approach of no compromise, attempting to defend positions without broad international support, rather than adapting its policies so as to gain maximum backing, this may merely result in one small defeat after another for American policy.

A "Two Chinas" Policy

Is there a practical alternative to the general policy which the United States has followed for almost a decade? Supporters of current policy, warning that any changes in current policy may have dire consequences, say "no." Their critics, while acknowledging that new approaches may involve many uncertainties, say "yes." A majority of these critics, or at least the most responsible ones, are drawn to the idea of some sort of "two Chinas" policy.

There are many variations on the "two Chinas" idea, but in essence it is simply this. The dangers and liabilities of current policy demand a change of approach, it is argued. Yet, although it is not desirable to shore up the hollow fiction that the Nationalist regime still exercises jurisdiction over all China, neither is it desirable to recognize Peking on its own terms, abandoning Taiwan to the Communists. Instead, the United States should attempt to stabilize a new *status quo*, based on the indisputable fact that there are now two Chinese regimes. It should work toward the international recognition and acceptance of both these regimes, in the United Nations as well as in the world at large. On this basis, it is argued, the United States should strive to reduce the existing tensions and risks of war in the Taiwan Strait, by seeking to achieve a genuine truce there, even if it is only a *de facto* one, and bolster its neutralization of the Strait with wider international backing. Then, it should do everything possible to deemphasize the direct military confrontation of American and Chinese Communist power in the Taiwan area, so that the United States can focus its primary attention on the manifold problems of effectively countering Peking's influence throughout Asia.

Few proponents of this approach would maintain that there is any neat formula for achieving these aims quickly or easily. Nevertheless, it is possible, they believe, to take certain definite steps toward achieving them. And even if the aims cannot be fully achieved in the foreseeable future, there may be positive gains merely from moving in this direction.

In speculating about how this approach, untested and untried, might be developed in the future, there are tremendous obstacles to outlining in any detail the exact sequence of specific moves which might be made. Nonetheless, one can outline in general terms a number of possible steps. They could include any or all of the following:

Increased efforts to open up certain channels of nonofficial contact with Communist China and the gradual relaxation of existing restrictions on trade, except on strategic goods.

Effective action to persuade the Nationalists to evacuate the offshore islands and decisive moves to disassociate the United States from their defense.

Efforts to induce some of the United States' major allies to commit themselves to the defense of Taiwan, as well as to persuade a larger number of nations that neutralization of the Taiwan Strait should be an international responsibility.

Moves to redefine the United States' view of the status of the "Republic of China" on Taiwan, which would make it clear that, while recognizing the Nationalist regime's authority over Taiwan and the Pescadores and reemphasizing its pledge to defend these islands, the United States no longer recognizes the Nationalists' claim to be the government of the mainland of China.

Action to indicate that the United States acknowledges the *de facto* control of the "People's Republic of China" on the mainland, but that it specifically rejects Peking's claim to Taiwan. Either simultaneously with this action, or at an appropriate later time, the United States might indicate a willingness to consider formally recognizing the Peking regime, and establishing relations with it, if the Chinese Communists, accepting the fact that the United States intends to continue defending and supporting the Nationalists, were willing to reciprocate.

An effort within the United Nations to link the seating of Peking with the simultaneous admission of Nationalist China as a new member, conditional upon Communist China purging itself of aggression in Korea by fulfilling certain clearly defined requirements, which should be determined by the United Nations. The United States should continue opposing the seating of Peking except on these terms, but at the same time it should be willing to accept the majority view, whatever it might be, on the question of China's seat in the United Nations.

None of these moves would "solve" the basic problems of dealing with China. Each would, in fact, create new problems. Nevertheless, by moving in this direction, thus altering its basic posture toward China, the United States could reduce many of the dangers and liabilities inherent in its current policy and could enlist wider international support for creating and preserving a more stable situation in the Far East.

An "Asia Policy"

Even if the United States decides to move toward a "two Chinas" policy, it should not proceed unilaterally in this new course. What is needed, above all, is a basic decision that, instead of adopting rigid positions without consultation with others, the United States should actively explore, with all the major non-Communist countries on whom the future of Asia depends, the possibilities for finding broader ground for common action and cooperation. If the United States is wise and flexible enough to pay greater deference to the attitudes and opinions of these nations, they will almost certainly respond by showing a greater understanding of American purposes in Asia and an increased willingness to cooperate for common ends.

What is needed to meet the challenge of Communist China

is, fundamentally, not so much an effective China policy as an effective Asia policy in the broader sense. In such a policy, the United States must make clear that, while continuing to maintain and strengthen the existing security structure in Asia, it is determined to do all it can to help all of the non-Communist states in the area, whether allied with the West or nonaligned, to build strong, viable states. If this becomes the primary focus of policy, the situation in the Taiwan Strait and tactical issues such as recognition and China's seat in the United Nations will be seen in proper perspective.

Communist China is one of the most dynamic and dangerous forces at work in the world today. Not content with attempting to change almost overnight the ancient patterns of life within China, its leaders have dedicated themselves to pushing forward what Mao Tse-tung calls the "wheel of history" throughout the world, and particularly in Asia. The crucial long-range question is whether the ideas, values, and institutions which Peking represents will triumph, or whether the non-Communist countries in Asia, with assistance from the United States and other nations, can achieve their aspirations to grow as free societies based on democratic values. The question, in short, is whether "the east wind prevails over the west wind," as Mao confidently proclaims, or whether "the west wind will prevail over the east wind." This question presents a challenge which will demand of the United States a far larger commitment of its national resources—intellectual and moral as well as material—than it has so far made.

Appendix

PEKING AND THE COMMUNIST PARTIES OF ASIA

Korea

THE HISTORY OF the relationships between the Chinese and Korean Communist parties is unusually obscure, but some basic facts are known. The Communist party in Korea, like those in China and Japan, was formally established under the Comintern's aegis and came under the direction of its Far Eastern Bureau at Shanghai. From its founding in 1925 it had only a brief three years of existence before Moscow ordered it disbanded in 1928, apparently because the Russian leaders felt that it was concerned more with the struggle for independence than with the fight for communism. Within Korea the party was severely repressed by the Japanese police.

During the following 17 years the Korean movement consisted principally of a small number of intellectuals in exile who operated both in and from the Soviet Union and China; in China particularly, they cooperated with several of the more important groups of Korean nationalists. Some Korean Communists in China joined the Kuomintang; later others fought with Chinese Communist guerrillas against the Japanese, particularly in Manchuria. During World War II one group of Korean Communists, trained by the Chinese Communists, established a so-called Yenan Independence Alliance in Chinese Communist territory.[1]

The Korean Communist exiles in the Soviet Union, such as Kim Il-Sung, were the ones, however, who eventually emerged as the key figures in the postwar period. When the Russians occupied North Korea in 1945, they placed Soviet-trained Korean Communists in the most important positions in the new regime. But the Korean Communists in China also returned home in 1945, and when a formal government was first established under Kim Il-Sung, the Korean Communist party and the Yenan Independence Alliance merged to form the Workers' party (called the North Korean Workers' party in 1946, it was renamed the Korean Workers' party in 1949).

During the Soviet occupation of North Korea, which lasted until 1948, the predominance of Soviet influence over Korean Communist affairs was complete. However, after the Communist victory in China and especially after Peking's participation in the Korean War, Chinese influence grew substantially. From late 1950 until mid-1953 Chinese Communist troops bore the main brunt of the fighting in Korea, and large numbers of Chinese soldiers remained on garrison duty there until 1958. In the years following the 1953 truce, Chinese economic, cultural, military, and other relations with the Korean Communists expanded steadily, and now Peking and Moscow appear to exercise a kind of condominium over the North Korean regime. This situation of divided influence has given rise to much speculation about rivalry between allegedly pro-Soviet and pro-Chinese groups within the Korean party.

One of the principal causes of this speculation was a drastic purge which was carried out in North Korea immediately after the 1953 truce, when 12 senior government officials, including Foreign Minister Pak Heung-Yeung, were arrested, and seven members of the Central Committee were expelled from the party. In the view of some observers, this purge weakened pro-Chinese elements in the Korean party and strengthened the position of those who are oriented primarily toward the Soviet Union, but the evidence for these and similar views is by no means conclusive. Although it is certainly possible, in the light of historic Chinese-Russian rivalry over Korea, that serious Sino-Soviet frictions could develop concerning relations with the Korean Communist leadership, it seems likely that at present the Korean Communists are dependent upon and receive guidance from both Moscow and Peking.

In South Korea, where the Communist party is banned, there has been very little effective political action by the Communists since the 1953 truce. A Communist underground continues to exist, particularly in urban areas, and many agents are sent from North Korea, but the Communists' activities are mainly in the field of espionage, and their opportunities for political agitation are limited. Espionage and disruptive activity have apparently been stepped up, however, since 1957.

Japan

Since World War II a special relationship appears to have developed between the Chinese and Japanese Communist parties. There were some contacts between the Chinese and Japanese Communists in the years immediately following the founding of the Japanese Communist party under Comintern sponsorship in 1922, but they did not become particularly important only until the 1940s. In its early years the Japanese Communist party looked constantly to the Comintern for funds and instructions.

In the late 1920s and early 1930s the Communist party in Japan was almost destroyed by mass arrests and severe police repression, but one important Japanese Communist leader, Nozaka, managed to obtain his release from prison and went into exile in the Soviet Union. In 1940, after nine years in Russia, Nozaka went to China and joined the Communists at Yenan. There he helped in many ways to lay the groundwork for the Japanese Communists' initial struggle in postwar Japan. In addition to taking charge of the Chinese Communists' psychological warfare against Japanese troops in China, as well as the indoctrination of Japanese prisoners of war, Nozaka established in Yenan a "Japanese Peasants' and Workers' School" to train Japanese Communists, issued appeals to the Japanese people, and organized a "Japanese Emancipation League." [2] Immediately after the war he returned to Japan, where MacArthur had legalized all parties, and at a party Congress in late 1945 he emerged as the party's principal strategist, although Tokuda, released from jail by the Occupation, was elected Secretary General of the party.[3]

In the years 1946-1950 the strategy of the Japanese Communist party called for nonviolent political action and gradualism. Based on the idea of "peaceful revolution" rather than "armed struggle," its program called for a two-stage revolution (the first stage being a "bourgeois democratic" revolution) and, perhaps under Maoist influence, for a broad united front, including important elements of the bourgeoisie. Even after many other Asian parties had shifted to insurrectionary tactics in 1948, the Japanese Communists persisted in their gradualist policy for almost two years. They were making considerable headway at that time through their peaceful tactics; in the 1949 elections they won 9.6 per cent of the votes, more than in any subsequent election.

Then Moscow intervened. Possibly because of plans for war in Korea, the Cominform in January 1950 denounced the Japanese party's gradualist line and directed it to make a sudden and radical shift to violence.[4] The Japanese Communists complied, after Moscow's call for violence had been endorsed by Peking, and then began to organize riots and prepare for civil war. The Japanese government and the Occupation took immediate counteraction, however, and the members of the Central Committee were banned from public life and forced underground. Although the Japanese Communists tried to form revolutionary groups trained in Chinese Communist guerrilla tactics. their new violent tactics failed; they alienated most of the Japanese people, and intense factionalism arose within the party's own ranks.

From 1950 until 1955 the top Japanese Communist leaders remained underground, and the party continued its unsuccessful attempts to carry out the prescribed strategy of violence. "Radio Free Japan," believed to have been located in China near Peking, was established in 1952, and it served as a primary source of guidance for the Japanese Communists until 1955, when it was shut down. Peking's new stature was reflected in a message which the Japanese Communists sent to the Chinese Communists on China's National Day celebration in 1951: "We will learn unswervingly from the Chinese people the course you have traversed," it said, "and in answer to your expectations of us, we will lead to victory our struggle for national independence, democracy, and peace." [5] At some time during this period Tokuda slipped away to Peking, where he died in 1953.

It was not until 1955, when the top leaders reemerged from the underground and Nozaka took over party leadership as first secretary, that the Japanese Communists reverted fully to peaceful tactics. The party then denounced its recent "ultraleftist adventurism" and began again to concentrate on open political maneuver, on appeals to trade unions and intellectuals, and on efforts to form a United People's Liberation Front. Nozaka proclaimed the Japanese Communist party's continuing allegiance to both Moscow and Peking, emphasizing "the importance and need . . . of listening to the words of the people and parties of the two countries." [6] By this time, however, while ultimate strategic direction still appeared to be centered in Moscow, Peking seemed to have become increasingly important as the source of much day-to-day tactical guidance for the Japanese Communists.

Since 1955 the Japanese Communist party has tried to attract popular support by "legitimate" political action rather than by violence and subversion. It has propagated slogans such as "peace, independence, and democracy" and has attempted—without success so far—to form a united front with the far larger and more powerful Socialist party. However, even though it has rebuilt an effective propaganda machine and has had considerable success in manipulating front organizations, its real political power is still limited. In 1958 at its Seventh Party Congress—the first since 1947—the party's leaders were unable to agree on a party platform, an indication of the continuing problem of factionalism. There has been little growth in the party's membership in recent years; it now totals 60,000 to 80,000 and is composed mainly of urban intellectuals, white-collar workers, and industrial workers.[7] Since the national elections of 1958, when the Communists lost one seat in the lower house, the party has held only three Diet seats—one in the lower house and two in the upper house—out of a total Diet membership of 717 in both houses.

Because of the relative weakness and ineffectiveness of the Japanese Communist party, Moscow and Peking have devoted increasing attention, since about 1953, to the Japanese Socialist party, and especially to its most radical left-wing members, in their attempts to influence political developments in Japan. The Communists in Japan have also worked hard to win the cooperation of the Socialists on many specific issues, such as the elimination of United States' bases and the renewal of trade with mainland China.

Vietnam

The close interrelationship of revolutionary activity in Vietnam and China, and the extension of Vietnamese revolutionary influence into other areas of Southeast Asia, have both been constant themes in the history of the Vietnamese Communist movement.

The establishment of the first revolutionary parties in Vietnam (then Indo-China) can be traced directly to the impact of the Chinese revolution of 1911. Although Ho Chi-minh, long the outstanding Vietnamese Communist leader, was French-inspired and Moscow-trained, he became involved in Chinese revolutionary activities early in his career. During the pre-1927 period of Communist-Kuomintang alliance in China, Ho worked under Comintern advisers who had been assigned by Moscow to the Kuomintang. It was in Canton that he helped found the Vietnam Revolutionary Youth Association, the first step toward creating a Communist party for Indo-China.[8] In 1927 Ho fled to Moscow, after Chiang K'ai-shek's suppression of the Communists in China, but soon he was sent out again as a revolutionary organizer, and he operated from Hong Kong, Thailand, and other bases in Southeast Asia. Finally, in 1930 he formed the Communist Party of Indo-China in Hong Kong, and it was recognized by the Comintern.[9]

Harassed by the French police, the Vietnamese party made only limited progress in Indo-China during the 1930s, and when World War II broke out, its top leaders again took refuge in China. By an irony of history, it was the Kuomintang which aided Ho and his followers during the war. In its attempts to organize resistance to the Japanese in Indo-China, the Kuomintang supported Vietnamese of every political coloration, and the Vietminh (Vietnam Independence League) was organized in 1941 at a conference of Vietnamese revolutionaries convoked by the Kuomintang in South China. Although subsequently Ho was held under arrest for a short time in China, he finally volunteered in 1943 to go into Indo-China to carry out anti-Japanese revolutionary activities. It was then that he assumed the pseudonym Ho Chi-minh by which he has been known ever since.[10]

By the end of the war Ho had achieved control of a well-organized nationalist movement in Indo-China, and immediately after the surrender of the Japanese, he successfully established a Vietminh-dominated regime, despite the attempts of the Chinese Nationalists—during their postwar occupation of North Indo-China—to install members of the Vietnamese Nationalist party in control. Then, in 1946, after negotiations with the French for independence broke down, he embarked on a full-scale revolutionary war for independence.

During the years just before 1949 there apparently were few significant contacts between the Vietminh and the Chinese Communists, but close relations were established as soon as the Chinese Communists' armies reached the borders of Vietnam. Almost immediately the Chinese began to give various forms of assistance to the Vietminh, including equipment, supplies, and the training of personnel in China.[11] This assistance, stepped up greatly after the Korean armistice in 1953, enabled the Vietminh to shift from guerrilla fighting to large-scale mobile warfare, and by 1954 Ho and his followers had achieved complete control of North Vietnam. Meanwhile, the Communist party reappeared in Vietnam in 1951 as the Lao Dong, or Labor party; whatever doubt there had been about the Communists' complete control over both the Vietminh and its united front organization, the Lien Viet, completely disappeared.

Relations between the Lao Dong party and the Chinese Communist party appear to be extremely close. In many respects, in fact, the North Vietnam regime seems more a satellite of Communist China than of the Soviet Union, despite the fact that it, like the Chinese Communist party, acknowledges Moscow's primacy. Vietminh policies and programs have borne a striking resemblance to Chinese Communist precedents, and a number of top leaders in North Vietnam, such as Vo Nguyen Giap, were trained in China.[12]

It is difficult to assess the speculation that in North Vietnam, as in North Korea, there have been factional divisions between pro-Soviet and pro-Chinese groups. There certainly is a long history of Vietnamese resentment and wariness toward the Chinese, and in the past Ho himself has expressed such feelings.[13] When Ho replaced Truong Chinh—reputedly the leader of a "pro-Chinese" faction—as party General Secretary in 1956, this was interpreted by some observers to be a curtailment of Chinese influence. Yet, although Lao Dong party leaders may have certain reservations about allowing Chinese influence to become too strong in North Vietnam, at present cooperation between Communist leaders in Peking and Hanoi is unquestionably close.

In South Vietnam, as in South Korea, the non-Communist regime has taken strong action to suppress Communist organizations. The Communist party has been banned since early 1955, when Ngo Dinh Diem's government felt strong enough to enforce this step, and the 1956 constitution declared communism to be in violation of the principles of the regime.[14] When the Vietminh moved north, however, they left behind some trained guerrillas and agitators, and these underground units are continuing their intimidation and propaganda, particularly at the village level, and they still agitate among certain intellectual groups critical of the Diem regime.

Laos and Cambodia

Laos and Cambodia are certainly regarded by the Communist leaders of North Vietnam as within their special sphere of revolutionary activity, and possibly the Vietnamese have some responsibility for Communist activities in nearby northeast Thailand, which has a large Vietnamese minority that is predominantly pro-Vietminh in political sympathies.[15] The Chinese Communists also have a large stake in Laos and Cambodia, however, and they have played an important role in evolving strategy toward them, but it is the Vietnamese Communists who have taken the lead in aiding pro-Communist movements in these two areas.

The Free Lao (Lao Issarak) movement in Laos and Free Kmer (Kmer Issarak) movement in Cambodia came into existence as left-wing independence movements soon after the end of World War II. Both were subsequently excluded from the local groups to which the French turned over political power, and they therefore attempted to operate, with Vietminh assistance, from headquarters in Thailand. Later they were able to shift their activities directly to Laos and Cambodia. In 1950 the Free Lao set up the Pathet Lao United Front, and the Free Kmer established a Kmer Issarak Front, and in 1951 joint organizations were established, linking both of them clearly with the Vietminh. Since then, the Vietminh's control and direction of their revolutionary struggles has been nearly complete, and both organizations have operated as Communist-led front groups.

In Cambodia, the Kmer Issarak group has made almost no real progress in challenging the popular leadership of Prince Norodom Sihanouk. Geographically separated from North Vietnam, it has not been able to organize effective guerrilla activity. Neither the so-called "People's Group" of ex-Kmer Issarak elements, who ran candidates in the 1955 Cambodian elections, nor the Communist-led Pracheachon (Nationalist) party, which contested the 1958 elections, was able to win a single seat in the Cambodian parliament.[16]

In Laos, however, the Pathet Lao movement has presented a major threat to the government and to the non-Communist parties. Aided by the Vietminh military invasion of Laos in 1953 while the Indo-China War was still in progress, the Pathet Lao developed strong guerrilla resistance forces and in 1954 established control of the two northern provinces of Phong Saly and Sam Neua, adjacent to both North Vietnam and Communist China. Material support and advisers from the Vietminh, plus training of personnel in North Vietnam, enabled the Pathet Lao to prevent the integration of these two provinces into the new state, as had been specified in the Geneva agreements of 1954. From 1954 until 1957 neither the Pathet Lao nor the government of Laos was able to gain a military victory. In 1955, in a major shift of strategy, the Pathet Lao leaders opened negotiations for a settlement which would give their movement legal status throughout the country and would allot seats to it in a coalition government. Under an agreement of late 1957 Phong Saly and Sam Neua were to be reintegrated under the central government, while 1,500 of the Pathet Lao's 9,000 or so armed men were to be incorporated into the national army and the rest demobilized. In return, the Pathet Lao movement gained legal status, was permitted to organize as a political party called the Neo Lao Hak Xat (Lao Patriotic Front), and obtained two cabinet posts, including one for the top Pathet Lao leader, Prince Souphanouvong. The Neo Lao Hak Xat almost immediately proved its organizational strength and political appeal by winning 9 out of 13 seats which it contested in supplementary elections held in early 1958 for 20 new seats in parliament.[17]

After the 1958 elections the Neo Lao Hak Xat held 9 seats in the Assembly and dominated a nominally neutralist opposition bloc of 19 deputies, out of a total Assembly membership of 59; in the 1958 elections this Communist-dominated, antigovernment coalition gained 40 per cent of the popular vote. Taking advantage of its legal status, the Neo Lao Hak Xat worked hard to build popular support for the next general elections, scheduled for late 1959 or early 1960. It energetically pursued, in short, the new Communist line of revolution via the ballot box. At the same time, however, the Pathet Lao movement retained an underground organization capable of renewed insurrection and delayed the integration of its troops into the national army. Then, when the government of Laos attempted to restrict its activities and bring it under better control in 1959, it reverted once again to insurrection. In May 1959 the government had to use force to make one 750-man battalion of the old Pathet Lao army surrender, and it was unable to disarm other recalcitrant units. In midsummer serious fighting broke out in the areas adjacent to North Vietnam and Communist China.[18]

Throughout this period Neo Lao Hak Xat leaders have repeatedly indicated that they continue to maintain primary ties with both Communist China and North Vietnam. They have made regular pilgrimages to Hanoi whenever important decisions have had to be made, and they have consistently pressed the Laotian government to accept economic aid from Peking, as a first step toward establishing diplomatic relations.

The growing strength of the Communists in Laos since 1958 has stimulated greater cooperation among non-Communist political groups and increased efforts to counter Communist activities. In mid-1958 the ruling Nationalist party merged with the Independent party to form a new Lao Union party under Prince Souvanna Phouma, who was then Premier. In the autumn of 1958 Phoui Sananikone took over as Premier, excluded the Neo

Lao Hak Xat from his Cabinet, and stepped up the efforts of non-Communist groups to organize popular support.[19] And in mid-1959 the government clamped down on the Neo Lao Hak Xat leaders, arresting many after the Pathet Lao reverted to insurrection. The threat posed by the Communists in Laos continues to be very serious, however, and it is a double-barreled one. If allowed to operate aboveground, they pose a threat at the polls. When forced underground, they can pursue their goals by violence, as they are now once again doing.

Malaya

Since its inception the Communist movement in Malaya and Singapore has been Chinese-inspired and Chinese in composition. The Chinese Communist party first sent agitators to Malaya in the early 1920s, following the 1923 Kuomintang-Communist alliance within China; at the start they went under the auspices of the Kuomintang, which also sent its own agents. In 1926 the Communists established in Singapore the Nanyang (South Seas) General Labor Union under direct Chinese Communist control, and in 1927 Communist agents sent from China organized the Nanyang Communist party in Malaya, under the direct supervision of the Chinese Communist party.[20] Three years later, in 1930, this organization was dissolved when the Malayan Communist party was formed by the Far Eastern Bureau of the Comintern, acting through its southern branch at Hong Kong. The ties between the Chinese Communists and the Malayan Communists—who were also racially Chinese—were temporarily disrupted in the early 1930s by police repression of both the Shanghai Bureau of the Comintern and its Hong Kong organization, but in 1936 new agents were sent from China to organize an anti-Japanese popular front in Malaya. When the Sino-Japanese War broke out in 1937, a functioning united front group took shape, including both Communists and other major Chinese political groups in Malaya and Singapore.

The most spectacular spurt in the growth of the Communist movement in Malaya took place from 1941 on, following the Japanese invasion of Southeast Asia.[21] The Chinese leaders of the Malayan Communist party withdrew to the jungle, where they rapidly built up an effective guerrilla force—the Malayan People's Anti-Japanese Army—and led the resistance movement against the Japanese. Under a 1943 agreement with the British they promised to accept military orders from the British commanders in Southeast Asia, and in return they were provided with British arms.

Despite this agreement the Malayan Communist party in 1943 made clear its long-range goals by adopting a nine-point program, anti-British as well as anti-Japanese, which called for the eventual establishment of a Malayan republic allied with Russia and China. And during the latter years of the war the Malayan Communists increasingly stressed their aim of carrying out "national liberation" and establishing a "People's Democratic Republic," even though their public platform appeared to be only mildly "progressive." By late 1945 the Malayan Communist party and its army controlled wide areas of Malaya, and in the interim period between the Japanese surrender and British reoccupation it came into the open and set up village "People's Committees" all over the country. Then, when the British returned, only a part of the Malayan People's Anti-Japanese Army—the "open" section—turned in its arms and demobilized. An estimated 4,000 men in its "secret" section cached their weapons, and those who were demobilized were organized into "Ex-Comrades Associations." The party leadership secretly adopted a program for the eventual overthrow of the government, by violence if necessary, and through the Communist-controlled General Labor Union, which they organized in both Singapore and Malaya, they began to attract increasing support from among urban workers. During the next three years, operating both as a legal party and underground, they made rapid progress, despite a shake-up in top leadership during 1947 in which Loi Tek, wartime party chief, was accused of secret collaboration with the Japanese and was replaced as Secretary General by Chin Peng.

In March 1948, immediately after the regional Communist meetings at Calcutta, the Malayan party embarked on a new campaign of insurrection and terrorism. In April and May it called major strikes, first in Singapore and then in Malaya, and mobilized its "secret" military units. In June government authorities in both Singapore and Malaya issued drastic Emergency Regulations, the Communist party was banned, and the Malayan Communist leaders disappeared once again into the jungle, where they launched a full-scale civil war.

At the start of this struggle the Communists had perhaps 3,000 to 4,000 guerrillas in their army—renamed first the Malayan People's Anti-British Army and then the Malayan Races Liberation Army. Essentially, what they attempted to do was to apply in Malaya the Chinese Communists' successful experience in establishing a rural base for revolutionary military operations.

They projected a three-phase struggle, moving from guerrilla warfare to the capture of outposts and finally to the establishment of consolidated "liberated areas." But because of the drastic measures taken against them by the British, with Malayan and some Chinese support, they were never able to progress beyond the first of these phases. They did, however, terrorize much of Malaya, and they organized thousands of Chinese squatters on the edge of the jungle into "Min Yuen" units (variously estimated between 10,000 and 100,000) to support their guerrilla forces.[22] The British responded to the Communists' terrorism by carrying out a massive resettlement of the squatters into barbed-wire-enclosed "New Villages," and they adopted vigorous new tactics which proved steadily more effective as the conflict dragged on.

After several years of indiscriminate violence and terrorism the Malayan Communist party began to realize the difficulties of achieving success by violence alone. In October 1951 the party's leaders made a decision (which, like other party directives, did not reach isolated jungle outposts until almost a year later) to put greater emphasis upon political warfare, to attempt to deemphasize somewhat the Chinese character of their movement, and to work toward an anti-British united front of all races, including the Malays and the Indians, and of all classes, including a large segment of the bourgeoisie.[23] In late 1952 they decided further to limit their violence by concentrating their terrorist attacks against government forces rather than attacking the civilian population at random. And from 1954 on they made intensive new efforts to penetrate labor and student groups in urban centers, particularly in Singapore.

Then in mid-1955 the Communists offered to end the war by negotiation. Since that time the Malayan party has repeatedly attempted to obtain a settlement which would allow it to emerge from the jungle and function as a legal political group, while the government authorities in Malaya and Singapore have offered amnesty only on the basis of complete surrender. Talks between the chief ministers of Malaya and Singapore and Chin Peng in December 1955 broke down over this basic difference. In subsequent offers to negotiate, in 1956 and 1957, the Communists have continued refusing simply to surrender, while the government has continued to offer pardon only to individuals and has refused to grant an amnesty to the party as an organization.

A Communist courier link between China and Malaya is believed to exist, but concrete ties between the Malayan Communist party and the Chinese Communist party are believed to have been tenuous during this entire period, because of the extreme isolation of the Malayan guerrillas in the jungle. However, 95 per cent of the estimated 5,000 members of the Malayan Communist party are racially Chinese, the party's leaders have been clearly Peking-oriented, and its program has borrowed heavily from Chinese Communist experience. The Chinese character of communism in Malaya is underlined by the fact that the government's amnesty terms have offered the alternative of reindoctrination and resettlement in Malaya or repatriation to China. Reportedly, the Communists themselves have offered to send back to China those who could not stand the hardships of prolonged jungle warfare.

Ever since the adoption in 1955 of a new program designed to appeal to Malays and Indians as well as Chinese, the Malayan Communists have attempted to broaden their political support. They have worked persistently to infiltrate labor unions, youth and student groups, and political parties. In late 1958, when they celebrated the tenth anniversary of their "national liberation war," they called, without success, for a "national consultative conference" of all political parties in Malaya, including the Communist party.[24]

The achievement of independence by Malaya in August 1957 appeared to cut the ground from under many of the Communists' appeals. Since then, Communist surrenders have increased, and the party's guerrilla strength has declined steadily in the face of pressures exerted by the new government, under Tungku Abdul Rahman, with strong British Commonwealth support.[25] In 1958 it was estimated that the number of guerrillas in the jungle had been reduced to less than 1,300, about 500 of whom were believed to be across the border in Thailand, where the headquarters of the Malayan Communist party has been located for some years. Then in mid-1959 the Malayan government announced that there were less than 300 guerrillas still operating in Malaya.[26]

Armed guerrilla insurrection no longer poses a major threat in Malaya, but the government was unable to end the "Emergency" in 1958, as it had hoped, and the danger of political subversion is still great.

Singapore

While the Communists' guerrilla efforts in Malaya have steadily declined, in Singapore the party has had increasing success since 1955 in its new efforts at political penetration. In a relatively brief period after 1955, it was able to achieve predominance in the field of labor organization by building up new unions among unorganized Chinese workers, and it established tight control over the militantly nationalistic and pro-Peking students of the Chinese high schools. Using these workers and students to foment riots and disorders, the Communists have seriously threatened the internal security of Singapore.[27]

The Communists have also joined with other left-wing politicians to support the People's Action party, formed in 1954, which emerged as the strongest political group in the municipal elections in Singapore in 1957, electing the mayor and achieving control of the city council.[28] In 1957 the government arrested several key leaders within the People's Action party, and the police tried to clamp down on Communist activity in Singapore unions and schools, yet the People's Action party's strength has steadily grown. In the mid-1959 elections for a new Assembly to take over local rule from the British, it won by a landslide, winning 43 out of 51 seats.[29] Having demonstrated its political power, it insisted that the British authorities release the party members who had previously been arrested, and then it proceeded to establish the first government of Singapore as a semi-independent, self-governing state.

Within the People's Action party there has been an intense political struggle. The leftist but non-Communist faction under Lee Kuan-yew—the chairman of the party who became Prime Minister of Singapore in June 1959—has increased its efforts, with some success, to cut down Communist influence in the party's organization. But the base of the party rests fundamentally on pro-Peking Chinese labor and student groups, and it is in these groups that the Communists' influence is strongest.

If, as is clearly possible, the Communists should succeed in achieving dominance within the People's Action party, and through it over the new State of Singapore, political control of the strategic crossroads of Southeast Asia would pass into the hands of a regime which would be, to say the least, very friendly to Peking and which would doubtless attempt by easy stages to turn Singapore into a Communist and Chinese state likely to accept a large degree of direction from Peking. Until Singapore actually receives its complete independence, the British will, it is true, have the option of revoking its constitution in order to forestall such a course of events, but this would create many serious difficulties and might create as many problems as it solved. The Communist threat in Singapore cannot really be

Thailand

The Communist movement in Thailand, like that in Malaya, has been and remains basically Chinese in its inspiration, orientation, and membership. In contrast to the problem in Malaya, however, the threat of communism has not grown to alarming proportions in Thailand. The Communist party has, in fact, been a rather small and shadowy force in Thai life.

The first attempts to form a Communist party in Thailand were made by agitators sent out from China in the late 1920s and early 1930s, and it is believed that a formal party organization was finally established there in the 1930s. The party did little more than circulate a few leaflets in the 1930s, however, and even during World War II it remained unimportant.[30] In 1946, when the official ban on the party was lifted after 13 years, the Communists came into the open briefly, and one alleged Communist was elected to parliament as representative of a Communist-front group called the Proletarian party, but after the coup which brought Phibul Songgram to power in 1947 the party was suppressed once again. Since then it has continued some publishing activity and has surreptitiously distributed a few propaganda pamphlets. It has not, however, developed important strength, partly because the government has been dominated by small military cliques while the mass of the population has been politically apathetic and partly because the suppression of subversive activities has become increasingly severe and effective in recent years.

In Thailand, Communist activities have been confined almost wholly to the Overseas Chinese community. It is believed that there are really two Communist party organizations in Thailand (doubt on this point illustrates how little is known about the Communist movement there). One of them, the Chinese Communist party in Thailand, may have as many as 5,000 Chinese members, whereas the local Communist Party of Thailand probably does not have more than 200 Thai members.[31]

After a new legalization of political parties by Phibul in 1955, there was a brief period during which political activities in Thailand increased, and a number of small leftist parties gained some adherents.[32] Among the latter the Economist party (which with three other parties made up the so-called Socialist Front) was clearly Marxist and pro-Peking; its leader, Thep Chotinuchit, visited Peking in defiance of governmental restrictions, and the Chinese Communists undoubtedly hoped to penetrate and utilize it. Then, however, in the fall of 1958 Field Marshal Sarit Thanarat, in a new military coup, ousted Phibul, dissolved the National Assembly, and instituted a tight dictatorship, banning all political parties and stepping up efforts to suppress Communist activities.[33] As a result, there appears to be less immediate danger of Communist political success in Thailand, at least among the Thais, than almost anywhere else in Southeast Asia.

The Philippines

The Communist Party of the Philippines, first organized in the early 1930s and accepted into the Comintern in 1932, remained a small and relatively unimportant group until World War II. During the war, however, it was able to appeal to Filipino nationalism and by attracting the support of many peasants who hated both the Japanese and unscrupulous Filipino landlords it organized extensive guerrilla resistance. As a consequence, it emerged after V-J Day with considerable armed strength, which it then tried to exploit to gain political power. It continued building up this strength, particularly in central Luzon, by pursuing guerrilla tactics and making promises of agrarian reform until by 1949 it controlled a guerrilla army of almost 11,000 men. Apparently the party had real hopes of seizing power by 1952.[34] In 1948 President Quirino had proclaimed a general amnesty for all Hukbalahaps (the Communist-led guerrilla organization, the former Anti-Japanese People's Army, which in 1950 was renamed the People's Liberation Army), but subsequent negotiations with Communist leader Luis Taruc broke down, and thereafter both the Huks' revolutionary efforts and the government's program of military and police suppression were intensified. After 1950, with Ramón Magsaysay as Secretary of National Defense, the anti-Huk campaign gained ground steadily. Improved military measures were accompanied by political, social, and economic reforms and by a program for resettling land-poor farmers, all of which greatly reduced the Communists' political appeal. In 1953 the Communists asked for a truce to consider the government's surrender terms, but their request was rejected. The election of Magsaysay as President in 1953, which was followed by sincere efforts at government reform, and the surrender of Luis Taruc in 1954, which had a demoralizing effect on the Communist party organization, led to a further decline in Huk strength.[35]

By 1958, although the Huk rebellion was not entirely ended, it was estimated that the party's membership had dropped to 700, and the party's armed strength had dwindled to about 500 men.[36] As elsewhere, in recent years the Communists in the Philippines have turned increasingly to political penetration and "legal struggle." Although outlawed, the party still has some influence in labor unions and youth organizations as well as among tenant farmer groups. It is not now a major threat to the Philippines, but there is a danger that the political deterioration which has set in since the death of Magsaysay might provide it with new opportunities.

The relationship between the Chinese Communists and the Communist-led insurrection of the Hukbalahaps has apparently not been direct or close. Some financial assistance from the Chinese Communists appears to have been channeled to the Huks via pro-Communist elements among the Overseas Chinese, however, and, perhaps more important, the Chinese Communists' experience with revolution based upon agrarian revolt has provided a model for a Hukbalahap strategy.

Indonesia

Chinese Communist assistance to the Communist movement in Indonesia has likewise consisted primarily of ideological inspiration, together with some financial support, and, as in the case of the Philippines, it is a new, postwar phenomenon. The Indonesian Communist party has a long history of its own—it was formally established by a few Dutch organizers in 1920, even before the Communist party was founded in China—and throughout its history it has been linked with Moscow. Since 1949, however, Chinese Communist influence has made itself increasingly felt in Indonesia, as elsewhere in Asia.

In the early 1920s the Indonesian Communist party emerged as one of the chief spokesmen for growing Indonesian nationalism. Its attempted revolt in 1926-1927 failed, however, and this defeat was followed by a split which divided the Communist movement into an orthodox, Comintern-linked party and a "nationalist" Communist group under Tan Malaka. Tan Malaka exerted considerable influence immediately after World War II, but the mainstream of Indonesian communism remained under the control of others who were loyal to Moscow. The Indonesian

Communist party had already begun to recover somewhat from its 1927 defeat when Musso, one of its exiled leaders, returned to Indonesia from Russia in 1935.[37] During a brief stay in Indonesia Musso started organizing a new illegal underground party organization, many members of which also joined nationalist organizations, and this period is now regarded by Indonesian Communists as the beginning of their popular front strategy. The growth of the party was slow, however, and even at the end of World War II it was still relatively weak.

In October 1945 the Communist Party of Indonesia was reestablished in Djakarta, and in the following year many exiled leaders returned, most of them from the Soviet Union. In 1946 Sardjono became head of the party, with Alimin—who had returned from exile after spending ten years with the Chinese Communists—acting, in effect, as coleader. During the following two years the party pursued a policy of "united front from above," cooperating with non-Communist leftist parties in forming the Sajap Kiri (left wing) in Parliament and supporting a series of left-wing Cabinets. The Premier of one of these Cabinets, Sjarifuddin, later revealed that he had for years been a secret Communist. However, when a Cabinet excluding the Sajap Kiri was formed in early 1945, the left-wing coalition began to fall apart, and the Communists' position, which had rested principally upon parliamentary struggle rather than mass support, was greatly weakened.

In February 1948 Indonesian Communist representatives attended the Calcutta meetings. Later in the year Musso, newly returned to Indonesia, attacked Alimin and called for a program which showed considerable Maoist influence. Revolution in Indonesia, Musso asserted, should go through a preliminary bourgeois democratic stage during which capitalism would still be needed; it should confiscate the land of rich peasants and implement a program of land to the tillers; and it should be based upon an alliance of workers, poor and middle peasants, and petty bourgeoisie.[38] Shortly after Musso's return the government, alarmed by the Communists' activities, undertook to disarm some pro-Communist army units, and this precipitated a Communist-led insurrection in 1948. But again revolt failed, as it had twenty years earlier. Musso was killed, and the party fell into a state of disrepute and dissension.

Resuming leadership of the party, Alimin once again attempted to rebuild a united front, but he had little success. Then in 1950 important changes started, and the party began to strengthen its organization among the masses—in a turn to the "united front from below." In 1951 it adopted a new party program which had a strong Maoist flavor; it called for a transitional people's democratic revolution and a four-class coalition, including the national bourgeoisie. Within the party a younger group of energetic leaders, among them Aidit, began to grow in influence. In 1952 Aidit spelled out in detail the idea of a four-class national united front, and in 1953 he took over as the party's Secretary General.[39]

Since then the Indonesian Communists have made rapid progress. Party membership jumped from 8,000 in 1952 to a claimed one million plus in late 1957.[40] Through mass organizations of labor, peasants, women, and students, the Communists have built very wide electoral support. In the 1955 national elections they polled 6 million votes, thereby becoming the fourth strongest national party, and in the 1957 local elections they received 8 million votes, emerging as the strongest party on Java, the center of political power in Indonesia.[41] Throughout this period they have supported a series of non-Communist Cabinets, even though they themselves have not secured posts in them.

By 1958 it appeared possible that the Communists might be able to win the national elections scheduled for 1959. And when rebellions by various non-Communist groups—motivated both by regional feelings and by anticommunism—broke out in early 1958, the Communists, by giving strong support to Sukarno, seemed to reinforce still further their already strong position.

Then in late 1958 Nasution and other military leaders rose to positions of increased influence in Indonesia and began gradually to limit Communist activities. Before the end of the year it was announced that the 1959 elections would be postponed.[42] And in June 1959 the army severely limited the activities of political parties and dissolved the parliament. Shortly thereafter, Sukarno, with the army's backing, restored Indonesia's 1945 constitution, under which he has enormous powers, and set about trying to implement his "concept" of "guided democracy."

These recent developments seem to have checked somewhat the growth of the Communists' strength in Indonesia. Yet even though Nasution and other army leaders appear determined to reduce the Communists' influence, the mass base of the Communist party remains intact, and there is no reason to suppose that it has suddenly lost all of its appeal to large segments of the population. Until non-Communist political groups develop far greater strength, there will be a continuing danger that the Communists might gain control of the country.

Undoubtedly the most important Chinese Communist influence on the development of communism in Indonesia during this period has been ideological. In formulating their program for mass organization and a broad united front, the Indonesian Communists have borrowed much from the Chinese Communists, despite the fact that they have restricted themselves, for the present, to peaceful rather than insurrectionary methods and even though they specify that, because of differing conditions, revolution in Indonesia must be different in many respects from revolution in China.

Beyond this, the Chinese Communists are believed by competent authorities to have provided substantial financial support to the Indonesian Communists, through their Embassy in Djakarta and through local Overseas Chinese.[43] The first Chinese Communist Ambassador sent to Indonesia in 1950, Wang Yen-shu, had formerly been a resident of Indonesia and a member of the Communist party, and as Ambassador he engaged in flagrant pro-Communist activities.[44] Since 1952, although the Chinese Embassy has adopted more subtle methods, there is little doubt that Chinese support to the Indonesian Communists has continued.

On the other hand, there is some basis for believing that the Indonesian Communists, for tactical reasons, have wished to avoid becoming identified too closely, in the eyes of their nationalistic compatriots, with either Communist China or the unpopular Overseas Chinese community in Indonesia. Some of the most prominent Indonesian-Chinese members of the party, such as Tan Ling Djie, were dropped from posts of party responsibility in 1953, at the same time that Aidit replaced Alimin as party chief. And Aidit himself now places great stress on the equal importance of both Moscow and Peking to his party; in doing so he is probably stating the truth rather than merely hedging on the delicate question of political orientation.

Burma

In view of Burma's proximity to Communist China, it is surprising in a sense that the Chinese Communists have not exploited more fully than they have the ready-made opportunities to give large-scale material support to the Communist movement there. Chinese Communist support to Burmese communism has been much more limited than that given to the Vietminh. One explanation may be found in the chaotic and divided character of the Communist movement in Burma. Despite the great impact of Marxism on the entire Burmese nationalist movement, the Communist party in Burma was one of the last to be organized in Asia, and it has had a history of extreme factionalism.

Established during World War II under the leadership of Than Tun and Thakin Soe, the Communist party joined with the Socialists in forming the Anti-Fascist Peoples Freedom League (AFPFL) which was aided by the British during the war and then led the postwar movement for independence against the British. In 1946, however, Thakin Soe denounced Than Tun as an opportunist and organized the Communist Party of Burma, separate from Than Tun's Burma Communist party. The AFPFL subsequently expelled the Communists from its membership in 1947, and in March 1948, after the regional Communist meetings in Calcutta, both Than Tun's "White Flag" Communists and Thakin Soe's "Red Flag" Communists went into rebellion against the government. To further complicate the situation, one group from the wartime paramilitary organization called the People's Volunteer Organization—the "White Band PVO"—joined the Communists in their rebellion of July 1948. In late 1948 a group of Karens rebelled, and subsequently their National Defense Organization cooperated at times with the Communists. And shortly afterward a large group of Chinese Kuomintang troops, who had fled from China in 1949 and refused to surrender, embarked on a war of their own against the government of Burma.

The new government of Burma tottered and almost fell under these successive blows. If the Communist rebels had been able to achieve unity, they could perhaps have taken control of the country. If the Chinese Communists had intervened as they did in Indo-China—and the presence of Kuomintang troops in Burma could have served as a pretext for intervention—this almost certainly would have turned the tide in the rebels' favor. Neither of these developments took place, however, and from 1951 on the government of Burma gradually but steadily regained control of the situation, while the rebels' strength declined. The "Red Flag" Communists before long became relatively unimportant. The "White Flag" Communists continued to harass the government, but by 1957 almost 29,000 rebels had surrendered, and the Communists' armed strength had been reduced to under 1,000 men.

After 1953 Thakin Tun's Burma Communist party sought repeatedly to negotiate with the government, in order to regain its former legal status, but Premier U Nu and the other top AFPFL leaders insisted that the Communists must simply surrender. Frustrated in these efforts, the Communists then began to expand their aboveground political activities through Communist-front parties. The most important of these has been the Burma Workers' and Peasants' party, founded in 1950 [45] and renamed as the Burma Workers' party in 1958; it has constituted the most influential aboveground segment of the Communist movement and is the strongest element in a parliamentary group called the National United Front. Since 1958 another segment of the Communist movement has also operated aboveground; about one-half of the People's Comrades party (that is, the "White Band PVO") came into the open in August 1958. This aboveground apparatus has steadily built up its strength, both in parliament and among labor and peasant groups, while Communist guerrilla strength in Burma has been declining. In early 1959 the Burma Communist party was estimated to have about 5,000 members, the Communist Party of Burma around 1,000, and the underground half of the People's Comrades party about 1,000, while the Communist membership of the National United Front was believed to be somewhat under 5,000 and that of the aboveground People's Comrades party about 1,000.[46]

The Communists' chances for political success in Burma were limited as long as the AFPFL, which had far greater popular support, held together, but in mid-1958 their opportunities for political maneuver were increased when a factional dispute between U Nu and two of his deputy prime ministers—U Kyaw Nyein and U Ba Swe—resulted in a breakup of the AFPFL. Suddenly, the National United Front, holding over 40 of the 250 seats in the Chamber of Deputies, acquired a key position in the balance of power in parliament, and U Nu was forced to rely on its support to maintain his premiership when his position was openly challenged by the Kyaw Nyein-Ba Swe group.[47] During this same period, when Than Tun again initiated negotiations with the government through intermediaries, U Nu reportedly gave assurances for the first time that the rebels belonging to the Burma Communist party would be allowed to operate aboveground if they gave up their arms and ceased their rebellion. Than Tun held out for the highest possible price, however, demanding the legalization of his party.[48] The remaining "Red Flag" Communists, under Thakin Soe, also still held out adamantly against surrender. However, about half of the Communists in the People's Comrades party decided to give up their arms and surrender, in order to switch to aboveground political activities.

The net result of these confused developments was to undermine seriously that degree of political stability which the AFPFL had been able to maintain prior to 1958, and a real threat developed that the political situation would deteriorate rapidly. Then, in the autumn of 1958, General Ne Win, commander of the army, took over the premiership from U Nu, and the military came to the fore in the government in Burma as it had previously in Indonesia. In late 1958 and early 1959 Ne Win proceeded to clamp down vigorously on the Communists, stepping up antiguerrilla measures and arresting some members of the National United Front. At the same time he took energetic steps to clean up the government.[49] Since then, the political situation in Burma has clearly improved, and the immediate danger that the Communists might be able to exploit the break-up of the AFPFL appears to have declined. But the political future is clouded by the bitter competition now going on among the non-Communist politicians in Burma, and it is still uncertain whether the transition from military to civilian rule can be made easily or successfully in the near future.

The complex development of the Communist movement in Burma since World War II has undoubtedly confused Moscow and Peking as well as the rest of the world, and the relationship between the Burmese Communists and both the Russians and Chinese has been fairly obscure. Nevertheless, even though the Chinese Communists have not intervened openly or directly in these developments or, as far as is known, given significant material aid to the Burmese guerrillas, there have been some important contacts between the Burma Communist party and the Chinese Communists,[50] the Burmese Communists' program has borrowed heavily in ideological terms from the Chinese, and the Chinese have given some assistance to the legal Communist groups operating within the National United Front. The Burmese press has reported in detail numerous missions sent by the Burma Communist party to China; one mission is said to have stayed there for two years. And it has been charged that Burmese Communists have been receiving military training in Yunnan Province, adjacent to Burma, since 1951. In addition, the AFPFL and U Nu himself have accused certain foreign embassies (meaning the Chinese and Russian embassies) of giving financial support to the National United Front.

India

Contacts between the Communist parties of China and India have never been close. From the time of its founding as an all-India party in 1933 until after World War II, the Indian Communist party looked solely to Moscow (sometimes via London) for inspiration and guidance, and it faithfully followed, with fairly disastrous effects upon its own position in India, the numerous policy zigzags decreed by the Russians. Even since World War II the Indian Communist movement appears to have remained outside the Chinese Communists' sphere of special interest and organizational influence, but its postwar history is an excellent illustration of the ideological impact which the Chinese Communists have had beyond the immediate periphery of China.

During 1946-1947 the Indian party vacillated between "right" and "left" tactics, but when B. T. Ranadive replaced P. C. Joshi as General Secretary, after the Calcutta meetings of 1948, it embarked upon an extreme "left" program of terrorism and violent strikes in urban areas. This policy resulted in serious setbacks and a substantial decline in party strength, however, and it was challenged almost at once by the Andhra faction of the party, led by Rajeshwar Rao, which favored a Maoist type of strategy based on rural peasant rebellions. As early as 1946 the Andhra provincial committee of the party had assumed leadership of a peasant uprising in the Telengana district of Hyderabad, and by 1948 this rebellion, which was to continue into 1951, was having considerable success. In June 1948 the Andhra leaders submitted an anti-Ranadive document to the Politburo of the party proposing a program closely modeled on the Chinese Communist experience. It called for reliance upon the peasantry, rural guerrilla warfare, inclusion of the rich peasants and "national" bourgeoisie in a broad united front, and focus on imperialism and feudalism as the central enemies.

From the outset Ranadive strongly opposed many aspects of this new line, especially the idea of cooperating with important elements of the bourgeoisie, and in mid-1949, before the Russians had made clear their attitude toward Mao's ideas, he openly attacked and ridiculed Mao Tse-tung to the extent of labeling his ideas "reactionary," "horrifying," and even "counterrevolutionary." [51] Shortly thereafter, however, Moscow endorsed Peking's line and specifically warned the Indian Communists that they would make a grave mistake if they did not ally themselves with anti-imperialistic segments of the bourgeoisie. In January 1950 the

Cominform, in a public rebuke to the Indian Communist party, instructed it to form the broadest type of united front, following the Chinese path—without, however, specifying that it should also follow a policy of violence.[52] A few months later, in June 1950, Rao replaced Ranadive as General Secretary.

The predominance of the Andhra group was shortlived. By 1951 the Telengana rebellion was dying out, and the party adopted a new program which rejected both the Ranadive idea of urban insurrection and the Andhra idea of peasant guerrilla warfare, while still retaining a Maoist emphasis on united front tactics. The new program called for a nonviolent struggle to achieve a "government of people's democracy" and a coalition of "all antifeudal and anti-imperialist forces." This, the party declared, constituted "a path which we do not and cannot name as either Russian or Chinese." [53] Almost immediately, Ajoy Ghosh, who was identified with neither "right" nor "left," became General Secretary in place of Rao.

Since 1951 the Indian Communist party has continued to be plagued by factionalism, the existing leadership has been challenged from both "right" and "left," and the party program has undergone numerous modifications in its details. But Ghosh has remained as General Secretary, and the basic line calling for nonviolent political struggle and a broad antiimperialist united front has remained unchanged.

Although not yet able to challenge seriously the dominant role of Nehru's Congress party, the Indian Communist party has made substantial gains.[54] Party membership had grown to about 125,000 by the end of 1957, and an estimated 250,000 by the end of 1958, and in the 1957 national elections it doubled its vote of 1952, receiving more votes than any other opposition party. In the State of Kerala it won a plurality and then set up a Communist-led government under E. M. S. Namboodiripad, which gave it the distinction of being the only Communist government freely voted into power anywhere in the world except in San Marino. It also emerged as the largest of the opposition parties in the national parliament as well as in the state parliaments of Andhra and West Bengal.

In 1958 the Indian Communists placed even greater emphasis on peaceful and parliamentary struggle. The party adopted a new constitution which asserted that it "strives to achieve full democracy and socialism by peaceful means," and it dispensed with such typically Communist titles as "politburo" and "cell." It also stepped up its campaign to organize support both among educated unemployed and laboring groups, where it was already strongest, and among the peasants. It also gave increased attention to parliamentary activity and worked persistently toward forming a united front with other opposition parties. Between the 1957 general elections and the Amritsar Party Congress in the spring of 1958, the party nearly doubled its membership, raising it to a total of about 250,000—two-thirds of which were concentrated in Kerala, Andhra, and West Bengal. In short, it made steady gains by following the current world-wide Communist strategy stressing revolution by ballots rather than bullets.

During this same period opposition to communism also tended to grow stronger and more vocal in India, however. The Indian parliament kept a close watch on developments in Kerala, and finally, after the violent disorders there in mid-1959, the central government dismissed the Communist administration in that state. The Indian Communists' parroting of Peking's claims that the 1959 revolt in Tibet had been engineered from Indian territory aroused strong Indian feelings against the Communists. Nehru and many other Indians bitterly denounced the Communist party for its foreign allegiance, and in the latter half of 1959 anti-Communist feelings were on the upswing in India.

NOTES

SCMP: *Survey of the China Mainland Press.*
NCNA: New China News Agency.
ECMM: *Extracts from China Mainland Magazines.*
AUFS: American Universities Field Staff.

Chapter 2. Communist China, A Totalitarian Political Power

1. New China News Agency (NCNA), Moscow, November 6, 1957.

2. See Chao Kuo-chün, "Leadership in the Chinese Communist Party," *The Annals of the American Academy of Political and Social Science* (hereafter, *The Annals*), vol. 321, January 1959, pp. 41 ff.

3. See H. F. Schurmann, "Organization and Response in Communist China," *The Annals*, same, pp. 51 ff.

4. See Robert J. Lifton, " 'Thought Reform' of Western Civilians in Chinese Communist Prisons," *Psychiatry*, vol. 19, May 1956, pp. 173 ff., and "Thought Reform of Chinese Intellectuals: A Psychiatric Evaluation," *Journal of Asian Studies*, vol. 16, November 1956, pp. 75 ff., for a psychiatrist's analysis of techniques used.

5. See A. Doak Barnett, "Hsüeh Hsi—Weapon of Ideological Revolution in China," American Universities Field Staff (AUFS) Report ADB-3-54, Hong Kong, March 5, 1954.

6. A good summary of early steps toward communization is in *China News Analysis*, No. 246, September 26, 1958. For one of the few American eyewitness descriptions of the communes, see articles by John Strohm, *New York World-Telegram and Sun*, October 13-18, 1958.

7. For text of Central Committee's August 29, 1958, "Resolution on the Establishment of People's Communes in Rural Areas," see *Peking Review*, September 16, 1958.

8. For text of Central Committee's December 10, 1958, "Resolution on Questions Concerning People's Communes," see "Sixth Plenary Session of 8th Central Committee of Chinese Communist

Party," *Current Background,* No. 542, December 29, 1958 (NCNA, December 17, 1958).

9. See, for example, "Public Mess Halls in Communist China," *Current Background,* No. 538, December 12, 1958; "Cultural Activities in People's Communes," *Current Background,* No. 539, December 15, 1958; and "Collective Life for School Children in Communist China," *Current Background,* No. 540, December 18, 1958.

10. To cite a few examples: a top leader in Sinkiang talked in December 1957 of "clamors for independence" and "for the establishment of independent republics" (Saifudin speech, Peking *People's Daily,* December 26, 1957, SCMP 1689, January 13, 1958); another Chinese leader in January 1958 attacked minority groups with "separatist ideas" who desire "the right of self-determination" or "independence" (Liu Ko-p'ing speech, Peking *People's Daily,* January 11, 1958, *Survey of the Mainland China Press* [SCMP] 1698, January 24, 1958). See also "Recent Reports on Tibet," *Current Background,* No. 490, February 7, 1958; "Some Statements on Minority Peoples," *Current Background,* No. 500, March 31, 1958; "Local Nationalism in Tibet," *Current Background,* No. 512, July 10, 1958; and " 'Reactionary' Minority Religious Leaders in Tsinghai and Kansu," *Current Background,* No. 549, February 3, 1959.

11. The Chinese Communists' official line on the Tibetan revolt of 1959 is briefly summarized in the State Council's order dissolving the local government of Tibet; for text, see *New York Times,* March 29, 1959. For the text of the Dalai Lama's first public indictment of Peking, see *New York Times,* June 21, 1959.

12. This policy was apparently first outlined by Mao at a Supreme State Conference on May 2, 1956; it was made public in a speech entitled "Let All Flowers Bloom Together, Let Diverse Schools of Thought Contend," made on May 26, 1956, by Lu Ting-yi, chief of the Propaganda Department of the Chinese Communist Central Committee. For text of Lu's speech, see *Current Background,* No. 406, August 15, 1956.

13. In Mao's February 27, 1957, speech, "On the Correct Handling of Contradictions among the People," text in *Current Background,* No. 458, June 20, 1957.

14. See Peking *People's Daily,* editorial, July 1, 1957, SCMP 1567, July 11, 1957.

15. See, for example, "The Rightists Surrender," *Current Background,* No. 470, July 26, 1957; "Confessions of Leading Rightists Meet Unfavorable Response," *Current Background,* No. 475,

August 28, 1957; and "Report on the Rectification Campaign" by Teng Hsiao-p'ing, Secretary General of the Central Committee, *Current Background*, No. 477, October 25, 1957.

16. See Roderick MacFarquhar, "Communist China's Intra-Party Dispute," *Pacific Affairs*, vol. 31, December 1958, pp. 323 ff.

17. Communiqué of the November 28-December 10, 1958, Wuchang meeting of the Chinese Communist Central Committee, text in NCNA, December 17, 1958, *Current Background*, No. 542, December 29, 1958.

Chapter 3. Economic Development

1. See speech by A. I. Mikoyan in Peking, September 17, 1956, in "Greetings from the Soviet Union," *Current Background*, No. 415, October 8, 1956.

2. For a summary of Peking's official claims in this period, see *New China's Economic Achievements, 1949-1952* (Peking: Foreign Languages Press, 1952).

3. See "The General Line," *Current Background*, No. 285, May 5, 1954; and "Address before the National Congress of All-China Federation of Industrial and Commercial Circles," by Li Wei-han, *Current Background*, No. 267, November 15, 1953.

4. See Li Fu-ch'un speech to the National People's Congress, July 5-6, 1955, "Report on the First Five Year Plan for the Development of the National Economy," *Current Background*, No. 355, July 12, 1955. This and other important articles are also in *New China Advances to Socialism* (Peking: Foreign Languages Press, 1956).

5. This and following data are from Li Fu-ch'un speech, same as above. Henceforth, "dollars," unless otherwise indicated, refers to "U.S. dollars."

Throughout this book Chinese monetary figures have been converted to United States dollars at the Chinese Communist official exchange rate, which currently is US $1.00 = Yüan 2.367. This is an artificial rate, since there is no free exchange of these currencies; undoubtedly it exaggerates the value of the Chinese figures somewhat, although probably not to the extent of distorting the over-all economic picture excessively. A few ruble figures from Soviet sources have been converted at the official rate of US $1.00 = 4.00 rubles; this probably involves a considerably greater distortion.

The term "capital construction" is a budgetary term referring to the government's fixed capital expenditures, whether for economic, social, military, or administrative purposes; it also includes expenditures for repair and replacement of capital assets.

"Above-norm" projects are ones involving new investments above certain "investment norms" which range from 1.25 million dollars for projects in some light industries to 4.22 million dollars in heavy industries, such as iron and steel.

6. Good general sources giving claims on the first Plan period, include: "Report on the Second Five Year Plan," by Premier Chou En-lai, to the 8th National Congress on September 16, 1956, in *Current Background,* No. 413, October 5, 1956; "Proposals on the Second Five Year Plan for the Development of the National Economy," adopted by the Party Congress on September 27, 1956, in *Current Background,* No. 413, October 5, 1956; "Draft Plan for the Development of the National Economy in 1958," a report by Po Yi-po to the National People's Congress on February 3, 1958, in *Current Background,* No. 494, February 19, 1958; and "The Implementation of the State Budget for 1957 and the Draft State Budget for 1958," a report by Li Hsien-nien to the National People's Congress on February 1, 1958, in *Current Background,* No. 493, February 17, 1958.

7. The Chinese Communist figures for national income used in this study are from the following sources. Series in constant prices: figures for 1952-1956 from *Peking Review,* April 8, 1958; figure for 1957 is derived from a reported over-all increase of 53 per cent over 1952, given in *Extracts from China Mainland Magazines* (ECMM), No. 132, June 16, 1958. Series in current prices: figures for 1953-1956 are derived from percentage data given in *Peking Review* cited above; figure for 1957 is derived on the basis of a statement giving total national income for 1953-1957, given in ECMM No. 136, July 21, 1958.

8. See William W. Hollister, *China's Gross National Product and Social Accounts, 1950-1957* (Glencoe: The Free Press, 1958), especially pp. 2, 13, 132, 133.

9. T. C. Liu, "Structural Changes in the Economy on the Chinese Mainland, 1933 to 1952-57," Papers and Proceedings, *American Economic Review,* vol. 49, May 1959, pp. 84-93. For additional work on China's gross national product, see Alexander Eckstein, "Communist China's National Product in 1952," *The Review of Economics and Statistics,* vol. 40, May 1958, pp. 127-139.

10. See Wilfred Malenbaum, "India and China, Contrasts in Development Performance," *American Economic Review,* vol. 49, June 1959, pp. 284-309.

11. Based on Table IV-1, p. 45 in Jerome B. Cohen, *Japan's Postwar Economy* (Bloomington: Indiana University Press, 1958).

12. See "Proposals on the Second Five Year Plan for the Development of the National Economy," adopted by the 8th Party Congress on September 27, 1956, in *Current Background*, No. 413, October 5, 1956.

13. See A. D. Barnett, "The Metamorphosis of Private Enterprise in Communist China," AUFS Report ADB-1-54, Hong Kong, January 10, 1954.

14. See A. D. Barnett, "China's Road to Collectivization," *Journal of Farm Economics*, vol. 35, May 1953, pp. 188-202.

15. See Liu Shao-ch'i's Political Report to the 8th Party Congress in "Speeches by Mao Tse-tung and Liu Shao-ch'i," in *Current Background*, No. 412, September 28, 1956.

16. The 1952 figures are from "Communiqué on the Fulfillment of the Economic Plan for 1955," issued by the State Statistical Bureau on June 14, 1956, in *Current Background*, No. 429, November 26, 1956. The 1957 figures are from "Communiqué on China's Economic Growth in 1958," issued by the State Statistical Bureau on April 14, 1959, in *Current Background*, No. 558, April 20, 1959.

17. The First Plan target for petroleum output was 2.01 million tons of crude oil; claimed 1957 output was only 1.46 million tons. For an interesting over-all report on China's oil situation, see *Petroleum Press Service*, February 1959, pp. 62-64.

18. Cotton yarn 1952 figure is from "Communiqué," on 1955, cited in Note 16 above; cotton piece goods 1952 figure is from Li Fu-ch'un "Report" cited in Note 4 above. Cotton yarn figure for 1957 is from *People's Daily*, January 1, 1958. Cotton piece goods 1957 figure is from "Final Accounts for 1956 and the 1957 State Budget," a report by Li Hsien-nien to the National People's Congress on July 29, 1957, in *Current Background*, No. 464, July 5, 1957.

19. For detailed data on wages and standard of living, see *Income and Standard of Living in Mainland China*, 2 vols., by Cheng Chu-yuan (Hong Kong: Communist China Problem Research Series, Union Research Institute, 1957).

20. Chou En-lai's "Report on Work of the Government," delivered June 26, 1957, to National People's Congress, in *Current Background*, No. 463, July 2, 1957.

21. Po Yi-po report, in *Current Background*, No. 494, February 19, 1958, cited in Note 6 above.

22. *China News Analysis*, No. 61, November 26, 1954.

23. For example, Liu Shao-ch'i, NCNA, September 29, 1958.

24. See Lawrence Krader and John S. Aird, *What Do We Know about the Population on Mainland China?*, mimeographed (Washington, D.C.: Bureau of the Census, 1958).

25. See Ma Yin-ch'u, "A New Theory of Population," *Current Background,* No. 469, March 27, 1958.

26. Peking *Daily Worker,* December 30, 1957, SCMP 1693.

27. E. Stuart Kirby, "China's Population Problem," *Problems of Communism,* vol. 7, March-April 1958, pp. 36-41.

28. Alexander Eckstein, *Conditions and Prospects for Economic Growth in Communist China* (Cambridge: Center for International Studies, Massachusetts Institute of Technology, 1954), p. 91.

29. This and subsequent budget data are from official Chinese Communist budget reports, including those by Po Yi-po on February 13, 1953, Teng Hsiao-p'ing on June 16, 1954, Li Hsien-nien on July 6, 1955, June 15, 1956, June 29, 1957, and February 1, 1958. These are contained in the *Current Background* series.

30. See F. C. Iklé, *The Growth of China's Scientific and Technical Manpower,* ASTIA Document Number AD 123545 (Santa Monica, Calif.: The RAND Corporation, April 24, 1957).

31. Chou En-lai, "Report" of June 26, 1957; see Note 20 above.

32. For an analysis of some of the problems of planning early in the first Plan period, see Ronald Hsia, *Economic Planning in Communist China* (New York: Institute of Pacific Relations, 1955).

33. "Proposals on the Second Five Year Plan," in *Current Background,* No. 413, see Note 6 above.

34. See Chou En-lai "Report" of June 26, 1957, in *Current Background,* No. 463, cited in Note 20 above.

35. See Liu Shao-ch'i report on "The Present Situation, the Party's General Line for Socialist Construction and Its Future Tasks," made on May 5, 1958, to the 2nd session of the 8th Party Congress, in *Current Background,* No. 507, June 2, 1958.

36. See "Communiqué on China's Economic Growth in 1958," cited in Note 16 above, and *New York Times,* August 27, 1959.

37. State Statistical Bureau mid-1958 report in *Peking Review,* August 12, 1958.

38. NCNA, February 23, 1958, SCMP 1719, February 26, 1958.

39. See Note 36 above.

40. See, for example, *Peking Review,* May 27, 1958; *China News Analysis,* July 11, 1958; and Richard Moorsteen, "Economic Prospects for Communist China," *World Politics,* vol. 9, January 1959, pp. 192-220.

41. See, for example, *U.S. News and World Report,* January 30, 1959, pp. 68 ff.

Chapter 4. The Roots of Mao's Strategy

1. Chou En-lai, "The Present International Situation, China's Foreign Policy, and the Question of the Liberation of Taiwan," report to the National People's Congress, June 28, 1956, *Current Background,* No. 395, July 5, 1956.

2. NCNA, March 17, 1954.

3. Liu Shao-ch'i November 16, 1949, speech, NCNA, November 23, 1949; and Lu Ting-yi, "The World Significance of the Chinese Democratic United Front," July 1, 1951, *Current Background,* No. 89, July 5, 1951.

4. See Chou En-lai speech of April 28, 1954, at the Geneva Conference, NCNA, April 28, 1954, SCMP 797. Chou in effect is saying that all powers other than China should keep hands off Asia. Peking's revolutionary motives for adopting this attitude are, of course, very different from the motives underlying the Monroe Doctrine.

5. See John K. Fairbank and S. Y. Teng, "On the Ch'ing Tributary System," *Harvard Journal of Asiatic Studies,* vol. 6, June 1941, pp. 135-246.

6. Mao Tse-tung speech, September 21, 1949, to the People's Political Consultative Conference, *China Digest,* October 5, 1949.

7. Mao Tse-tung speech, November 6, 1957, in Moscow to the Supreme Soviet of the U.S.S.R., *Current Background,* No. 480, November 13, 1957.

8. See Benjamin Schwartz, "On the Originality of Mao Tsetung," *Foreign Affairs,* vol. 34, October 1955, pp. 67-76. The degree to which Mao has been a genuine ideological innovator is a highly controversial subject among specialists on China, but it is clear, at least, that Chinese Communist spokesmen have claimed that he has made important ideological innovations, and Soviet leaders have accepted at least some of these claims.

9. Lu Ting-yi, article cited, see Note 3 above.

10. Liu Shao-ch'i, *Internationalism and Nationalism* (Peking: Foreign Languages Press, 1949), p. 32.

11. Same, p. 33.

12. Mao Tse-tung, *On People's Democratic Dictatorship,* English Language Series (Peking: New China News Agency, 1949), p. 7.

13. Liu Shao-ch'i speech, "The Significance of the October

Revolution," November 6, 1957, in *Current Background,* No. 480, November 13, 1957.

14. See Chapter 5, p. 100.

15. Mao Tse-tung, *Selected Works* (New York: International Publishers, 1954), vol. 1, p. 75.

16. Mao Tse-tung, *Strategic Problems of China's Revolutionary War* (Yenan, 1941), pp. 1 and 5-6. (This work by Mao is also serialized in *China Digest,* May 17-September 21, 1949.)

17. P'eng Teh-huai, NCNA May 13, 1955, SCMP 1048, May 14-16, 1955.

18. Mao, *Strategic Problems of China's Revolutionary War,* cited in Note 16 above, p. 51.

19. Same, p. 35.

20. Same, p. 46.

21. In early 1959, however, Peking on two occasions strongly protested to South Vietnam, which also claims the islands, charging that a South Vietnamese vessel had mistreated and kidnaped Chinese fishermen on the islands and had desecrated the Chinese flag. NCNA, February 27 and April 5, 1959; and *Peking Review,* March 3, 1959.

22. Mao Tse-tung, "The Chinese Revolution and the Chinese Communist Party" (December 15, 1939, version), *Current Background,* No. 135, November 10, 1951.

23. Edgar Snow, *Red Star over China* (New York: Random House, 1944), p. 96.

24. Chou En-lai, speech cited in Note 4 above.

25. Liu Shao-ch'i speech on February 13, 1953, "3rd Anniversary of the Sino-Soviet Treaty of Friendship, Alliance, and Mutual Assistance," *Current Background,* No. 229, February 20, 1953.

Chapter 5. Evolving Tactics in Foreign Policy

1. Mao Tse-tung, July 1949, *On People's Democratic Dictatorship,* cited in Note 12 of Chapter 4, p. 13.

2. Liu Shao-ch'i speech on November 16, 1949, NCNA, November 23, 1949.

3. "The Observer," in *China Digest,* November 30, 1949, commenting on the conference.

4. See Ko Pai-nien, "New China's Foreign Policy," *China Digest,* November 2, 1949.

5. Art. 2 and Art. 3, "The Common Program," *China Digest,* October 5, 1949, supplement.

6. Same, Art. 54.

510   COMMUNIST CHINA AND ASIA

7. Same, Art. 56.

8. See "Diplomatic Relations of Communist China," *Current Background*, No. 440, March 12, 1957.

9. Chou En-lai statement on June 28, 1950, commenting on President Truman's June 27 statement. Text in *People's China*, July 16, 1950.

10. Chou En-lai, "Fight for the Consolidation and Development of the Chinese People's Victory," speech on September 30, 1950, to a cadres meeting of the National Committee of the People's Political Consultative Conference, *Current Background*, No. 12, October 5, 1950.

11. K. M. Panikkar, *In Two Chinas* (London: G. Allen and Unwin, 1955), pp. 110 ff.

12. Wu Hsiu-ch'uan speech at the United Nations Security Council, November 28, 1950, *Current Background*, No. 36, December 5, 1950.

13. See "How to Understand the United States," in *Current Affairs Handbook* of November 5, 1950, text in *Current Background*, No. 32, November 29, 1950. This article exhorts the Chinese people to: "Hate the United States, for she is the deadly enemy of the Chinese people. . . . Despise the United States, for she is a rotten imperialist nation, the headquarters of reactionary degeneracy in the whole world. . . . Look with contempt upon the United States, for she is a paper tiger and can be fully defeated."

14. Richard P. Stebbins, *The United States in World Affairs, 1952* (New York: Harper, for the Council on Foreign Relations, 1953), p. 43.

15. Text of message of the conference to the United Nations, NCNA, October 12, 1952, SCMP 433, October 14-15, 1952. For the texts of major reports and speeches at the conference, see *People's China*, October 16, 1952, supplement.

16. See Dai Shen-yu, "Peking and Indo-China's Destiny," *The Western Political Quarterly*, vol. 7, September 1954, pp. 346-368.

17. Text in NCNA April 29, 1954, SCMP 786, April 29, 1954.

18. Quoted in Peking *People's Daily* editorial of July 2, 1954; in SCMP 841, July 3-4, 1954.

19. Chou En-lai: "Now that the flames of war in Korea and Indo-China have been put out one after another, the United States aggressive group has intensified its use of the traitorous Chiang K'ai-shek group in Taiwan to enlarge the war of harassment and destruction against China's homeland and sea coast. . . . Taiwan is China's sacred and inviolable territory. . . . The Chinese people must liberate Taiwan." Speech on September 23, 1954, to National

People's Congress, *Current Background,* No. 296, September 28, 1954.

20. For a detailed report and evaluation of the Bandung Conference by the author, who attended the conference as a reporter, see A. D. Barnett, "Chou En-lai at Bandung," AUFS Report ADB-4-55, Djakarta, May 4, 1955; and "Asia and Africa in Session," AUFS Report ADB-5-55, Surabaja, May 18, 1955. Unless otherwise indicated, the following data and quotes are from these reports. See also George McT. Kahin, *The Asian-African Conference* (Ithaca, N.Y.: Cornell University Press, 1956).

21. See especially Chapter 12.

22. Mao Tse-tung speech on November 18, 1957, in Moscow, in "Mao Tse-tung on Imperialists and Reactionaries," *Current Background,* No. 534, November 12, 1958.

23. The Chinese campaign against the Yugoslavs was launched by an editorial entitled "Modern Revisionism Must Be Condemned," in the Peking *People's Daily,* May 5, 1958; in SCMP 1767, May 8, 1958 (where the title is translated "Modern Revisionism Must Be Criticized").

Chapter 6. Military Strength and the Balance of Power

1. Text in *Sino-Soviet Treaty and Agreements* (Peking: Foreign Languages Press, 1951), pp. 5-8. The wording of Art. 1 is as follows: "In the event of one of the Contracting Parties being attacked by Japan or any state allied with her and thus being involved in a state of war, the other Contracting Party shall immediately render military and other assistance by all means at its disposal."

2. Khrushchev message of September 7, 1958, to President Eisenhower, text in *New York Times,* September 9, 1958. In elaborating and explaining this pledge, Khrushchev later stated: "The Soviet Union will come to the aid of the Chinese People's Republic if the Chinese People's Republic is attacked from without or, more concretely, if the U.S.A. attacks the Chinese People's Republic.... However, we have not interfered and do not intend to interfere in the civil war which the Chinese people are waging against the Chiang K'ai-shekite clique." *Pravda,* October 6, 1958, in *Current Digest of the Soviet Press,* vol. 10, November 12, 1958.

3. See "Military Service Law," *Current Background,* No. 344, August 8, 1955; and "Report on the Draft Military Service Law," by P'eng Teh-huai, *Current Background,* No. 337, July 20, 1955.

4. See "Development of People's Militia in Communist China—

The 'Everyone a Soldier' Movement," *Current Background*, No. 530, October 31, 1958.

5. The official figure, 1950 to May 1958, is 6.8 million; NCNA, May 22, 1958.

6. See NCNA, July 10, 1958, SCMP 1811, July 15, 1958.

7. John R. Gibson, "Formosa Furor," in *Wall Street Journal*, August 13, 1958.

8. Admiral Herbert G. Hopwood on April 24, 1958, stated that the Chinese Communists had been building their own submarines at Shanghai for about two years. *Washington Post and Times-Herald*, April 25, 1958.

9. See S. M. Chiu, "The Chinese Communist Army in Transition," *Far Eastern Survey*, vol. 27, November 1958, pp. 168-175.

10. *Current Affairs Handbook*, November 5, 1950, in *Current Background*, No. 32, November 29, 1950.

11. K. M. Panikkar, *In Two Chinas* (London: G. Allen and Unwin, 1955), p. 108.

12. Ch'en Yi made this statement on May 10, 1958, in an interview with German correspondents. In *Die Welt* of May 12, 1958, one correspondent quotes Ch'en as saying: "At the moment China does not own atomic weapons, but we shall have them in the future." The *Stuttgarter Zeitung* correspondent, in a story also published on May 12, reported—without directly quoting—that Ch'en said: "No Asian country possesses long range atomic weapons, not even China. If the U. S. should station such weapons in Asia, Peking would examine if China, too, must have nuclear weapons, because such American weapons would be chiefly directed against China." This latter version is somewhat more qualified than that in *Die Welt*.

13. A. M. Rosenthal, *New York Times*, August 18, 1958.

14. John L. Steele, *Life*, July 13, 1959, p. 36, and *New York Times*, September 18, 1959.

15. P'eng Teh-huai speech in Warsaw on May 12, 1955, NCNA, May 13, 1955, SCMP 1048, May 14-16, 1955. In early 1959 the Chinese Communists also made a specific commitment to support East Germany. In a Sino-German Joint Communiqué signed in Peking on January 27, they stated: "The Government of the Republic of China emphatically declared that it would regard any assault on the German Democratic Republic by the imperialist countries as an attack on the socialist camp and would give all-out support to the German Democratic Republic in repulsing such an assault." NCNA January 27, 1959, SCMP January 30, 1959.

16. Yeh Chien-ying speech on October 6, 1950, "The Interna-

tional Situation Today," *Current Background,* No. 41, December 18, 1950.

17. For a summary of the Sino-Korean statements announcing the decision that Chinese troops would be withdrawn, see NCNA, February 20, 1958.

18. For figures on the forces of South Asian nations, see John M. Lindbeck, "The China Problem Today," in "Contemporary China and the Chinese," *The Annals,* vol. 321, January 1959, pp. 9-19.

19. Art. III (1) of Southeast Asia Collective Defense Treaty, text in *Collective Defense in Southeast Asia* (London: Oxford University Press, 1956).

20. Art. I of 1951 Security Treaty between the United States and Japan, text in *The Department of State Bulletin,* vol. 25, no. 638, September 17, 1951, p. 454.

21. Public Law 4, 84th Congress, 1st Session, *Documents on American Foreign Relations, 1955* (New York: Harper, for the Council on Foreign Relations, 1956).

22. For a breakdown of all United States forces in the Pacific, see chart in *New York Times,* September 21, 1958.

23. See Secretary of State Dulles' radio "Report from Asia," on March 8, 1955, *The Department of State Bulletin,* vol. 32, no. 821, March 21, 1955, pp. 459-464; and his March 15, 1955, news conference, *The Department of State Bulletin,* vol. 32, no. 822, March 28, 1955, pp. 526-527.

24. New York *Herald Tribune,* January 22, 1958.

25. Paul H. Nitze, in an article on "Brinkmanship and the Averting of War," points out that by the second offshore islands crisis in 1958 the situation had changed considerably, as compared with 1954-1955, and that then it was "not we but the Russians" who were "pursuing a policy of brinkmanship." *Military Policy Papers, December 1958* (Washington, D.C.: The Washington Center of Foreign Policy Research, 1958), p. 52.

26. See, for example, Richard Butwell, "Communist Liaison in Southeast Asia," *United Asia* (Bombay), vol. 6, June 1954, pp. 146-151.

27. See "Peace or Piecemeal?," United States *Army Information Digest,* June 1958.

28. On February 22, 1959, Assistant Secretary of State Walter S. Robertson stated that "if it were possible to establish a sound workable system for controlling armaments or nuclear tests or surprise attacks—a system that truly protected our national security—then, of course, I believe Red China should be included."

He stressed the fact that such a system would have to be "sound" and "workable" and underlined the fact that Peking has "repeatedly broken promises" over the past decade. *Disarmament and Foreign Policy,* Hearings before a Subcommittee of the Committee on Foreign Relations, United States Senate, 86th Congress (Washington, D.C.: U.S. Government Printing Office, 1959).

Chapter 7. Communist Subversion and the Political Struggle

1. See Richard Butwell, "Communist Liaison in Southeast Asia," *United Asia* (Bombay), vol. 6, June 1954, pp. 146-151.

2. Virginia Thompson and Richard Adloff, *The Left Wing in Southeast Asia* (New York: Institute of Pacific Relations, Sloane, 1950), pp. 51 and 123.

3. Cominform journal, *For a Lasting Peace; For a People's Democracy,* November 10, 1947.

4. Captain Malcolm Kennedy, *A History of Communism in East Asia* (New York: Praeger, 1957), p. 359.

5. Liu Shao-ch'i November 16, 1949, speech, NCNA, November 23, 1949.

6. Same.

7. Same.

8. John H. Kautsky, "Indian Communist Party Strategy since 1947," *Pacific Affairs,* vol. 28, June 1955, pp. 145-160.

9. *Pravda* in June 1949 reprinted Liu Shao-ch'i's *Internationalism and Nationalism.* In the subsequent months both *Pravda* and the Cominform journal printed a number of theoretical statements by Mao Tse-tung and Chu Teh, and on January 27, 1950, the Cominform journal published Liu Shao-ch'i's November 16, 1949, speech.

10. Lu Ting-yi, "The World Significance of the Chinese Democratic United Front," July 1, 1951, *Current Background,* No. 89, July 5, 1951.

11. The following quotations are from Khrushchev's February 14, 1956, speech, as released by Tass, text in *New York Times,* February 15, 1956.

12. For sources on the Asian Communist parties and the Chinese party's relationships with them, see Appendix and Bibliographic Note.

Chapter 8. The Overseas Chinese

1. Based on table in G. William Skinner, "Overseas Chinese in Southeast Asia," *The Annals,* vol. 321, January 1959, p. 137. Esti-

mates of the number of Overseas Chinese vary considerably. This is due in part to the lack of dependable demographic data and in part to differing criteria for determining who is Chinese. The most commonly used figure for the total number of Overseas Chinese in all areas is 13 million; Skinner's research indicates that 11 or 12 million would be closer to the real figure.

2. Skinner's recent estimate for Thailand's Overseas Chinese (2,360,000, 11.3 per cent of population) is considerably lower than estimates generally accepted in the past. This is partly a result of greater discrimination in determining who should be considered a Chinese. The most commonly accepted estimate in recent years has been about 3 million.

3. Bernard F. Fall, in "Vietnam's Chinese Problem," *Far Eastern Survey*, vol. 27, May 1958, pp. 65-72, states that South Vietnam has 800,000 Overseas Chinese, making up almost 8 per cent of the population.

4. Hsiao Chi-jung, *Revenue and Disbursement of Communist China* (Hong Kong: Union Research Institute, 1954), p. 82. Estimates for periods before 1921 are contained in C. F. Remer, *The Foreign Trade of China* (Shanghai, 1926), pp. 215-221.

5. See Cora Du Bois, *Social Forces in Southeast Asia* (Minneapolis: University of Minnesota Press, 1949), pp. 25-42.

6. *Collective Defense in Southeast Asia*, A Report of a Study Group of the Royal Institute of International Affairs (London: Oxford University Press, 1956), chapter on "China and the Overseas Chinese," p. 82.

7. *China Handbook 1950* (New York: Rockport Press, 1950), p. 24.

8. *Collective Defense in Southeast Asia*, cited in Note 6 above, p. 81.

9. Donald E. Willmott, *The National Status of the Chinese in Indonesia*, Interim Report Series (Ithaca, N.Y.: Southeast Asia Program, Cornell University, 1956), pp. 12-13.

10. Art. 58, text in *China Digest*, October 5, 1949, supplement.

11. Ko Pai-nien, "New China's Foreign Policy," *China Digest*, November 2, 1949.

12. Chou En-lai, "Political Report" made on October 23, 1951, to National People's Congress, in *Current Background*, No. 134, November 5, 1951.

13. Ho Hsiang-ning, "Rising Patriotism of Overseas Chinese," *Current Background*, No. 467, July 15, 1957.

14. "Premier Chou En-lai's Report on Asian-African Conference," May 13, 1955, to the Standing Committee of the National

People's Congress, *Current Background,* No. 328, May 17, 1955.

15. Chou En-lai's "Report on Government Work," made on September 24, 1954, to the National People's Congress, *Current Background,* No. 296, September 28, 1954.

16. See, for example, *New York Times,* October 25 and 31, November 1 and 14, 1954.

17. See Note 15 above.

18. See Note 14 above.

19. Chou En-lai, "Report on Visit to 11 Countries in Asia and Europe," made on March 5, 1957, to the National Committee of the People's Political Consultative Conference, *Current Background,* No. 439, March 8, 1957.

20. NCNA, September 26, 1954, SCMP 898, September 29, 1954.

21. Constitution of the People's Republic of China, Art. 98, text in *Current Background,* No. 297, October 5, 1954.

22. For apportionment and distribution of Overseas Chinese representation, see "Composition of the 1st National People's Congress," *Current Background,* No. 290, September 5, 1954.

23. "Chuang Hsi-chuan Reports on the Basic Tasks of the National Returned Overseas Chinese Association," *Current Background,* No. 427, November 13, 1956.

24. Ho Hsiang-ning message to Overseas Chinese, NCNA, December 31, 1958.

25. Ho Hsiang-ning, "Rising Patriotism of Overseas Chinese," speech made on July 11, 1957, to the National People's Congress, *Current Background,* No. 467, July 15, 1957.

26. See, for example, *New York Times,* January 7, 1951.

27. Solomon Adler, *The Chinese Economy* (New York: Monthly Review Press, 1957), pp. 228-229, estimates that remittances are now about US $110-US $140 million a year; cited in Leng Shao Chuan, "Communist China's Economic Relations with Southeast Asia," *Far Eastern Survey,* vol. 28, January 1959, pp. 1-11. Even though this figure undoubtedly includes both family remittances and investments, it may be too high.

28. Peking has made numerous statements which, although giving only fragmentary information, indicate that the Chinese Communists regard these investments as quite important to their programs in some areas of South China. It has stated, for example, that Overseas Chinese investments made up 10 per cent of all funds invested in local industry in Kwangtung and Kwangsi in 1955, that by 1956 44 factories had been established by the Overseas Chinese in these two provinces, and that during 1958 close to US $30 million was invested by Overseas Chinese in agricultural,

industrial, and welfare projects in 38 counties in China. See *Current Background,* No. 467, July 15, 1957; and NCNA, February 3, 1959.

29. The following discussion is based principally on the author's own research and observations in Indonesia during 1955. See A. D. Barnett, AUFS Report ADB-7-55, Djakarta, May 28, 1955. For a somewhat different interpretation, see Willmott, cited in Note 9 above.

30. For text of treaty, see *Current Background,* No. 326, April 27, 1955, or Willmott, cited above.

31. Willmott, cited above, p. 44, states that "the treaty was a success," since the Indonesian government "was able to achieve virtually all of its aims," that "many of the objections raised" have been "either exaggerated or groundless," and that other Southeast Asian countries "might also seek treaties with China, following the precedent of this treaty." This view of the treaty seems overoptimistic, however, and there has been no indication to date that other Southeast Asian nations are attracted by its formula.

32. Ho Hsiang-ning speech to the National People's Congress made on February 6, 1958, *Current Background,* No. 503, April 10, 1958.

33. Ralph N. Clough, "United States China Policy," *The Annals,* vol. 321, January 1959, pp. 20-28.

34. See Dr. S. G. Davis, *Hong Kong in Its Geographical Setting* (London: Collins, 1949), pp. 90 ff.; and A. D. Barnett, "Social Osmosis—Refugees in Hong Kong," AUFS Report ADB-3-53, Hong Kong, December 15, 1953.

35. See A. D. Barnett, AUFS Reports ADB-7-8-55, Singapore, July 7, 1955; and ADB-9-55, Singapore, July 11, 1955.

36. See Gerald P. Dartford, "Malaya: Problems of a Polyglot Society," *Current History,* vol. 34, June 1958, pp. 346-351.

37. *Free China Review,* November 1958.

38. See Albert Ravenholt, "Chinese in the Philippines—An Alien Business and Middle Class," AUFS Report AR-12-55, Manila, December 9, 1955; and Bernard F. Fall, "Vietnam's Chinese Problem," *Far Eastern Survey,* vol. 27, May 1958, pp. 65-72.

39. See text of speeches on August 16, 1958, by Prince Sihanouk Norodom and Chou En-lai, NCNA, August 16, 1958.

40. NCNA, March 15, 1958.

41. *New York Times,* October 11, 1958.

42. *Free China Review,* February 1958, and November 1958.
43. *New York Times,* September 22, 1958.

Chapter 9. Trade, Aid, and Economic Competition

1. Editorial in *Peking Review,* September 30, 1958.
2. *The Communist Economic Threat,* Department of State Publication 6777 (Washington, D.C.; March 1959), p. 2.
3. *Ta Kung Pao,* April 28, 1958, NCNA, April 28, 1958.
4. For a good statement of Peking's conciliatory official posture regarding trade and aid, see Chou En-lai's speech of June 28, 1956, to the National People's Congress, "The Present International Situation, China's Foreign Policy, and the Question of the Liberation of Taiwan," *Current Background,* No. 395, July 5, 1956. See also article by Chu Jung-fu in *World Culture,* October 5, 1954, *Current Background,* No. 307, December 6, 1954, which indicates one of Peking's political motives in fostering trade. Chu says: "We have also exerted efforts in the development of business relations with the Asian nations which have not yet recognized our Government, promoting intercourse and understanding, and developing trade with them, and creating favorable conditions for the establishment of normal relations."
5. The fragmentary character of official Chinese Communist data on trade makes it necessary to derive estimates by rather involved calculations, applying Peking's official percentage figures on trade increases, etc., to the available figures. The figures used in this chapter on Communist China's trade are derived on the basis of the following data. Figures on total trade and total imports and exports for 1956 are from Yeh Chi-chuang, "The Foreign Trade of China," report to the National People's Congress on July 11, 1957, *Current Background,* No. 468, July 22, 1957; similar figures for 1957 are from *Peking Review,* June 17, 1958. (See also: Shigeyoshi Takami, "Prospects for Trade with Continental China," *Contemporary Japan,* vol. 15, April 1958, pp. 208-223.) The figure on total trade for 1954 is from *Foreign Trade of the People's Republic of China* (Peking: China Committee for the Promotion of International Trade, 1956). All other figures on total trade and imports in years prior to 1956 are derived by using indices covering several years which are included in the following sources: *Trade with China, A Practical Guide,* by Ta Kung Pao (Hong Kong, 1957), 1950-1955 over-all index; *Asia Keizai Jumpo* (Tokyo, March 1, 1957), 1950-1955 indices of total trade, imports and exports, obtained by Japanese at a Canton

trade fair; and *China Reconstructs* (September 1956), 1950-1955 index. Over-all Chinese figures on trade with the Soviet bloc and free world are then derived by taking these figures on total trade and applying to them official percentage figures for Communist China's trade with the Soviet bloc and free world each year. The most detailed set of percentages of this sort is in *Vneshiaia Torgovlia*, No. 5 (Moscow, 1956); and *Razvitie Ekonomiki Stran Narodnoi Demokratii Azii* (Moscow, 1956). All figures have been converted to dollars at the official exchange rate of $1.00 equals 2.367 Yüan. For a detailed table of estimates of Communist China's trade, see the Appendix of A. D. Barnett, *Communist Economic Strategy: The Rise of Mainland China* (Washington, D.C.: National Planning Association, 1959).

6. NCNA, July 11, 1957, SCMP 1577, July 25, 1957; and Po Yi-po report to the National People's Congress on July 1, 1957, "Working of the National Economic Plan . . . ," *Current Background*, No. 465, July 9, 1957.

7. This figure and import figures which follow are also from NCNA, July 11, 1957, SCMP 1577, July 25, 1957. See also NCNA, June 5, 1957, SCMP 1544; and Li Hsien-nien report to National People's Congress, "Final Accounts for 1956 and the 1957 State Budget," June 29, 1957, NCNA, June 29, 1957, *Current Background*, No. 464, July 5, 1957.

8. Same. Chinese Communist statements are not entirely clear, however, on whether the period covered by these figures is 1953-1956 or a somewhat longer period. See also *New York Times*, July 5, 1956.

9. See, for example, Po Yi-po speech of August 9, 1958, NCNA, August 10, 1958, SCMP 1590, August 14, 1957.

10. Yeh Chi-chuang report of July 11, 1957, *Current Background*, No. 468, July 22, 1957.

11. Po Yi-po, July 1, 1957, report, *Current Background*, No. 465, July 9, 1957.

12. For data on exports compiled from fragmentary sources, see Robert F. Dernberger, "The International Trade of Communist China," in C. F. Remer, ed., *Three Essays on the International Economics of Communist China* (Ann Arbor: University of Michigan Press, 1958); on p. 138 there is reproduced a useful table from Cheng Chu-yuan, "The Export Potentiality of Communist China," *China Weekly*, February 20, 1956.

13. Yeh, cited in Note 10 above, *Current Background*, No. 468, July 22, 1957.

14. Po Yi-po, July 1, 1957, report, *Current Background*, No. 465, July 9, 1957.

15. Po Yi-po, August 9, 1957, speech, NCNA, August 10, 1958, SCMP 1590, August 14, 1957.

16. Tsai Chin, "Prospect of Export of China's Cotton Piece-Goods," *Ching Chi Tao Pao*, June 24, 1957, ECMM No. 92, July 27, 1957. See also Yeh, cited above, *Current Background*, No. 468, July 22, 1957.

17. The United States Department of Agriculture also estimates that during 1953-1957 Communist China's total exports of cotton yarn and fabrics expanded about eightfold. Bernice M. Hornbeck, *Communist China's Cotton Textile Exports*, Foreign Agricultural Service, FAS-M-52 (Washington, D.C.: U.S. Department of Agriculture, April 1959). See also Takashi Murayano (Director of Research, All Japan Spinners' Association), "Communist China's Cotton Textile Industry—Present and Future," mimeographed, August 1, 1958.

18. J. Graham Parsons (Deputy Assistant Secretary of State for Far Eastern Affairs), "Foreign Trade: Welfare or Warfare," speech given on September 25, 1958, to the Far East-America Council of Commerce and Industry, New York, mimeographed.

19. For text of loan agreement, see *Current Background*, No. 62, March 5, 1951. The statement that 50 projects were decided upon in 1950 is in Li Fu-ch'un, "Report on the First Five Year Plan for the Development of the National Economy," made July 5-6, 1955, to the National People's Congress, *Current Background*, No. 335, July 12, 1955.

20. See "Great Aid Given by Soviet Union to Our Economic Construction," *Chinese Youth Journal*, November 6, 1953, SCMP 701, September 4, 1953.

21. Text of communiqué on the negotiations between China and the Soviet Union, October 12, 1954, SCMP 906, October 12, 1954.

22. Text of Sino-Soviet communiqué of April 7, 1956, SCMP 1265, April 11, 1956.

23. Agreement of August 8, 1958, NCNA, August 11, 1958, SCMP 1833, August 15, 1958; see also *Peking Review*, November 11, 1958.

24. Agreement of February 7, 1959, NCNA, February 7, 1959, SCMP 1953, February 13, 1959.

25. See *Vneshiaia Torgovlia*, No. 5, 1956 (Moscow, 1956) and *Razvitie Ekonomiki Stran Narodnoi Demokratii Azii* (Moscow, 1956).

26. These figures are based on the author's calculations; see Note 5 above.

27. "Achievements in Sino-Soviet Trade over the Past Eight Years," Peking *Ta Kung Pao,* January 1, 1958, SCMP 1704, February 3, 1958.

28. Same.

29. *Vneshiaia Torgovlia SSSR 1956* (annual supplement), *Vneshtorg* (Moscow, 1958), p. 9.

30. "Soviet Trade with Socialist Countries," article from *Vneshiaia Torgovlia,* No. 11, 1957 (Moscow, 1957), *Current Digest of the Soviet Press,* vol. 10, March 19, 1958, p. 16.

31. *New York Times,* November 2, 1958.

32. *Peking Review,* November 18, 1958.

33. Article by Li Chiang on Sino-Soviet cooperation in Peking *People's Daily,* February 14, 1959, SCMP, February 19, 1959. However, in the *Peking Review* as late as November 11, 1958, the figure being used was still 50 per cent.

34. See Jan Wszelaki, *Communist Economic Strategy: The Role of East-Central Europe* (Washington, D.C.: National Planning Association, 1959), especially Chapter 10, "Economic Relations with the Chinese Orbit."

35. Yeh, cited in Note 10 above, *Current Background,* No. 468, July 22, 1957.

36. May 24, 1958, communiqué issued by the Communists' Council for Economic Mutual Assistance, text in *New York Times,* May 25, 1958.

37. See *China Reconstructs,* December 1958.

38. Treaty signed April 23, 1958, text in *Peking Review,* April 29, 1958.

39. Same as Note 27 above.

40. Excerpts from Khrushchev speech released by Tass, February 14, 1956, text in *New York Times,* February 15, 1956.

41. Same as Note 22 above.

42. Same as Note 24 above.

43. "Sino-Soviet Cooperation," *Peking Review,* April 29, 1958.

44. Li Fu-ch'un July 5-6, 1955, speech, *Current Background,* No. 335, July 12, 1955.

45. *New York Times,* October 3, 1957.

46. Chou En-lai June 26, 1957, speech to National People's Congress, *Current Background,* No. 463, July 2, 1957.

47. Peking *People's Daily,* November 5, 1956, SCMP 1416, November 23, 1956.

48. A list of Sino-Soviet agreements between 1949 and 1957 is

contained in "Agreements between Communist China and Foreign Countries," *Current Background,* No. 545, January 20, 1959. For data on atomic energy agreement, see Peking *People's Daily,* November 5, 1956, SCMP 1416, November 23, 1956; for data on Amur agreement, see NCNA, March 4, 1958, SCMP 1726, March 7, 1958.

49. Li Hsien-nien, "Final Accounts for 1956 and the 1957 State Budget," report to National People's Congress, June 29, 1957, *Current Background,* No. 464, July 5, 1957.

50. See Note 21 above.

51. Same as Note 49 above, and Li Hsien-nien April 27, 1959 report, cited in Note 53 below. (It can be estimated that Soviet credits and loans to China during 1953-1955 were as follows: 1953—US $185 million; 1954—US $373 million; and 1955—US $700 million. Budget data for these years give figures for total receipts and a breakdown of receipts other than foreign aid; presumably the difference between these figures represented foreign aid. The large 1954-1955 figures thereby derived probably represent in large part the charges for Soviet military aid to China and the sale to China of the Russian shares in Sino-Soviet joint enterprises in China.

52. These estimates of Chinese servicing and repayments of Soviet loans are derived as follows. Budget data for these years include figures on total debt servicing, including both domestic and foreign, which amounted to US $305 million in 1956 and US $354 million in 1957. It is estimated that servicing charges on domestic debt, including all known bond issues, amounted to US $45 million in 1956 and US $80 million in 1957. The estimates of servicing and repayment of Soviet loans are derived by subtracting the latter figures from the former ones.

53. Figures from official budget statements: Li Hsien-nien report on June 15, 1956, "The 1955 Final State Accounts and the 1956 State Budget of Communist China," *Current Background,* No. 392, June 26, 1956; Li Hsien-nien, report to the National People's Congress on June 29, 1957, "Final Accounts for 1956 and the 1957 State Budget," *Current Background,* No. 464, July 5, 1957; Li Hsien-nien, report to the National People's Congress on February 1, 1958, *Current Background,* No. 493, February 17, 1958; and Li Hsien-nien, "Report on Final State Accounts, 1958, and the Draft State Budget, 1959," report to the National People's Congress on April 21, 1959, *Current Background,* No. 562, April 27, 1959.

54. See Appendix Table on Estimated Balance of Payments,

1953-1957, in A. D. Barnett, *Communist Economic Strategy: The Rise of Mainland China*.

55. Anastas I. Mikoyan in interview with Adlai E. Stevenson, *New York Times*, October 2, 1958.

56. For background on these restrictions, see *The Strategic Trade Control System 1948-1956*, Mutual Defense Assistance Control Act of 1951, Ninth Report to Congress (Washington, D.C.: International Cooperation Administration, June 28, 1957).

57. Useful data on Communist China's trade agreements are contained in Hsin Ying, *The Foreign Trade of Communist China*, Communist China Problem Research Series (Hong Kong: Union Research Institute, March 1954); Robert F. Dernberger, "The International Trade of Communist China," in C. F. Remer, ed., *Three Essays on the International Economics of Communist China* (Ann Arbor: University of Michigan Press, 1958); and Leng Shao Chuan, "Communist China's Economic Relations with Southeast Asia," *Far Eastern Survey*, vol. 28, January 1959, pp. 1-11.

58. Article by Yeh Chi-chuang, *Peking Review*, October 7, 1958.

59. United States Department of Commerce trade sheets, *Value Series* and *Country-by-Commodity Series*. The figures on China's free world trade used in the discussion which follows are from these sheets, unless otherwise noted. The Commerce Department figures are "unadjusted" and therefore do not take account of lags in reporting by various countries, double counting of certain Chinese exports, the costs of freight and insurance on Peking's imports, and other factors. If adjusted, the figure for 1956 should probably be about 940 million dollars instead of 1.05 billion dollars.

60. *Peking Review*, June 17, 1958.

61. See Shigeyoshi Takami, "Prospects for Trade with Continental China," *Contemporary Japan*, vol. 15, April 1958, pp. 208-223.

62. Text in NCNA, March 5, 1958, SCMP 1727, March 10, 1958.

63. NCNA, February 26, 1958, SCMP 1722, March 3, 1958.

64. *The Sino-Soviet Bloc Economic Offensive in the Far East*, Intelligence Report No. 7670, Department of State (Washington, D.C., February 1958), p. 9.

65. NCNA, June 28, 1957, SCMP 1563, July 5, 1957.

66. Same as Note 64, p. 15.

67. Parsons speech, cited in Note 18 above.

68. NCNA, November 4, 1956, SCMP 1406, November 8, 1956.

69. Agreement of December 18, 1952, NCNA, January 3, 1953, SCMP 484, January 4-5, 1953.

70. NCNA, October 3, 1957, SCMP 1626.

71. *New York Times,* November 23, 1958; and *Eastern World,* January 1959.

72. *Christian Science Monitor,* January 19, 1959.

73. Derived from data from U.S. Department of Commerce trade sheets.

74. These estimates are based on the fragmentary data available on deliveries of Chinese Communist aid.

75. Same sources as listed in Note 53 above.

76. This figure is based upon the sum of all known Chinese Communist foreign aid grants in this period, without regard to delivery periods.

77. November 23, 1953, Sino-Korean agreement, text in NCNA, November 23, 1953, SCMP 694, November 24, 1953.

78. July 7, 1955, Sino-Vietnamese agreement, text in NCNA, July 8, 1955, SCMP 1085, July 9-11, 1955.

79. August 26, 1956, Sino-Mongol agreement, see SCMP 1363, September 5, 1956.

80. Chou En-lai November 6, 1956, cable to Kadar, SCMP 1409, November 13, 1956.

81. Communiqué on Sino-Albanian agreement on December 7, 1954, NCNA, December 7, 1954, SCMP 943, December 8, 1954.

82. May 13, 1957, Sino-Hungarian loan agreement, text in NCNA, May 13, 1957, SCMP 1532, May 17, 1957.

83. September 27, 1958, Sino-Korean agreements, summarized in NCNA, September 27, 1958, SCMP 1865, October 1, 1958.

84. December 29, 1958, Sino-Mongolian agreement, summarized in NCNA, December 29, 1958, SCMP 1926, January 5, 1959.

85. February 18, 1959, Sino-Vietnamese agreement, summarized in NCNA, February 18, 1959, SCMP 1959, February 24, 1959.

86. *New York Times,* August 28, 1956.

87. June 22, 1956, Sino-Cambodian agreement, text in NCNA, June 22, 1956, SCMP 1318, June 25, 1956.

88. October 7, 1956, Sino-Nepalese agreement, text in NCNA, November 3, 1956, SCMP 1407, November 8, 1956.

89. November 10, 1956, Chou En-lai message to Abdel Nasser, text in NCNA, November 12, 1956, SCMP, November 15, 1956.

90. September 19, 1957, Sino-Ceylonese agreement, communiqué text in NCNA, September 20, 1957, SCMP 1617, September 25, 1957.

91. NCNA, November 4, 1956, SCMP 1406, November 6, 1956.

92. NCNA, March 25, 1958, SCMP 1742, March 31, 1958; and NCNA, April 17, 1958, SCMP, April 24, 1958.

93. *The Communist Economic Threat*, p. 21.

94. NCNA, January 9, 1958, SCMP 1690, January 14, 1958.

95. January 12, 1958, Sino-Yemeni agreement, text in NCNA, January 13, 1958, SCMP 1692, January 16, 1958.

96. September 17, 1958, Sino-Ceylonese exchange of notes, described in NCNA, September 22, 1958, SCMP 1861, September 25, 1958.

97. Total United States foreign aid is currently under one per cent of the United States' gross national product; United States foreign aid for "economic growth"—that is, strictly economic aid—is less than one-third of one per cent of gross national product. (See Eisenhower's message to Congress, March 13, 1959, *New York Times*, March 14, 1959.) Current Chinese Communist foreign economic aid may be in the vicinity of one-half of one per cent of China's gross national product.

Chapter 10. Communist China's Foreign Policy: Japan and Korea

1. Text in *Sino-Soviet Treaty and Agreements* (Peking: Foreign Languages Press, 1951).

2. See, for example, Peking *People's Daily* editorials of July 7 and September 3, 1950.

3. For an example of Peking's protests, see Chou En-lai's article entitled "A Great Year of Sino-Soviet Friendship and Alliance," reprinted in *People's China*, March 1, 1951, in which he asserted that the Western move toward a treaty with Japan "violates all international agreements and overthrows the foundations of a common peace treaty with Japan."

4. Article by Premier Yoshida in *Foreign Affairs*, vol. 29, January 1951, p. 179.

5. See Richard P. Stebbins, *The United States in World Affairs, 1951* (New York: Harper, for the Council on Foreign Relations, 1952), pp. 186 ff.

6. Same, p. 189.

7. Texts of Yoshida and Dulles letters in *The Department of State Bulletin*, vol. 26, no. 657, January 28, 1952, p. 120.

8. Text in *People's China*, June 19, 1952. For a discussion of this agreement, see Hsin Ying, *The Foreign Trade of China*, Communist China Problem Research Series (Hong Kong: Union Research Institute, 1954), pp. 116 ff.

9. One of the main subjects for discussion at the conference

was, "The opposing of the remilitarization of Japan and the opposing of the use of Japan as a base for aggression, in order to eliminate the serious threat to peace in the Asian and Pacific Regions." (Quotation from "Declaration of the Preparatory Conference for a Peace Conference of the Asian and Pacific Regions," *People's China*, June 16, 1952.) The resolutions at the end of the conference called for the end of Japanese "remilitarization" and the withdrawal of all foreign troops and military bases from Japan. (NCNA, October 12, 1952, SCMP 433, October 14-15, 1952.)

10. See *People's China*, December 16, 1952.

11. See NCNA, January 7, 1953, SCMP 487, January 8, 1953; and NCNA, January 8, 1953, SCMP, January 9, 1953.

12. The first important Japanese trade promotion organizations were established in 1952. The Dietmen's League contained about one-half the members of the Diet by late 1958. See Kumaichi Yamamoto, "Trade Problems with China," *Contemporary Japan*, vol. 15, September 1958, pp. 363-398.

13. *Nippon Times*, August 2, 1953.

14. Chou En-lai to Ikuo Oyama, Chairman of Japanese National Peace Committee, NCNA, Peking, October 9, 1953, SCMP 666, October 10-13, 1953.

15. NCNA, October 30, 1953, SCMP 680, October 31-November 2, 1953.

16. The propaganda line of this delegation was a mild one, stressing the desirability of establishing diplomatic relations on the basis of peaceful coexistence; see NCNA, November 8, 1954.

17. See *Ta Kung Pao* editorial of November 5, 1954, SCMP 928, November 16, 1954. This editorial states: "We are willing to establish normal diplomatic relations with Japan through any legitimate Japanese government." However, a few days later Kuo Mo-jo gave as one of the reasons why reestablishment of Sino-Japanese relations was not then possible the fact that the Japanese had signed a treaty with the Chinese Nationalists; see NCNA, Peking, November 20, 1954.

18. For text of October 12, 1954, Sino-Soviet joint declaration on Japan, see SCMP 906, October 12, 1954.

19. For the Chinese reactions to these moves, and their attitudes toward Hatoyama and Shigemitsu, see NCNA, Peking, December 18, 1954, SCMP 952, December 21, 1954; Peking *People's Daily* editorial, December 30, 1954, SCMP 958, December 31, 1954; and NCNA, Peking, December 18, 1954, SCMP 952, December 21, 1954.

20. George McT. Kahin, *The Asian-African Conference* (Ithaca, N.Y.: Cornell University Press, 1956), p. 28.

21. See NCNA, April 2, 1955, SCMP 1021, April 2-4, 1955, for a statement of Peking's objectives. See NCNA, May 4, 1955, SCMP 1041, May 5, 1955, for the text of agreement.

22. For a summary of agreement, see NCNA, April 15, 1955, SCMP 1029, April 16-18, 1955.

23. NCNA, February 11, 1956, SCMP 1230, February 17, 1956.

24. NCNA, August 16, 1955, SCMP 1111, August 17, 1955. See also NCNA, February 11, 1956, SCMP 1230, February 17, 1956.

25. NCNA, August 17, 1955, SCMP 1112, August 18, 1955.

26. Chou En-lai speech, "The Present International Situation, China's Foreign Policy, and the Question of the Liberation of Taiwan," June 28, 1956, to National People's Congress, *Current Background*, No. 395, July 5, 1956. For a list of major Japanese groups visiting Communist China during 1954-1957, see Leng Shao Chuan, *Japan and Communist China* (Tokyo: Doshisha University Press, 1958), pp. 22-23.

27. Incomplete reports on these interviews are in SCMP 1151, October 15-17, 1955.

28. NCNA, December 4, 1955, SCMP 1183, December 7, 1955.

29. NCNA, June 21, 1956, SCMP 1317, June 26, 1956.

30. NCNA, May 8, 1956, SCMP 1267, May 11, 1956.

31. NCNA, May 26, 1956, SCMP 1299, May 31, 1956.

32. Leng, cited in Note 26 above, p. 21.

33. For the Chinese reaction, see NCNA, November 5, 1956, SCMP 1407, November 8, 1956.

34. NCNA, October 15, 1956, SCMP 1392, October 18, 1956.

35. NCNA, October 8, 1956, SCMP 1388, October 11, 1956.

36. For a useful summary of major developments in Sino-Japanese relations during 1957-1958, see Akira Doi, "Two Years' Exchanges with China," *Japan Quarterly*, vol. 5, October-December 1958, pp. 435-450.

37. Text of April 22, 1957, joint statement, in NCNA, April 22, 1957, SCMP 1516, April 25, 1957.

38. See Peking *People's Daily* editorial, July 30, 1957, released early, in NCNA, July 29, 1957, SCMP 1582, August 1, 1957.

39. NCNA, July 29, 1957, SCMP 1582, August 1, 1957.

40. NCNA, August 2, 1957, SCMP 1586, August 8, 1957.

41. NCNA, February 26, 1958, SCMP 1722, March 3, 1958.

42. Text in NCNA, March 5, 1958, SCMP 1727, March 10, 1958.

43. See the memorandum on Arita's talks with Chou En-lai

and others, which the Chinese Communists publicized, in NCNA, September 2, 1957, SCMP 1604, September 5, 1957.

44. Akira Doi, cited in Note 36 above, p. 448.

45. NCNA, May 9, 1958, SCMP 1772, May 15, 1958.

46. Peking *People's Daily* editorial, June 25, 1958, SCMP 1801, June 21, 1958.

47. Peking *People's Daily* editorial, July 7, 1958, SCMP 1807, July 9, 1958.

48. Peking *People's Daily*, September 16, 1958, SCMP 1856, September 18, 1958.

49. Text of Ch'en Yi statement, in NCNA, November 19, 1958.

50. See *New York Times*, May 9, 1959.

51. Text of the joint statement between Chang Hsi-jo, president of the Chinese People's Institute of Foreign Affairs, and Inejiro Asanuma, leader of the Socialist party delegation, in NCNA, March 17, 1959.

52. See Kumaichi Yamamoto, cited in Note 12 above. Wilbur cited in Note 54 below, pp. 233-234, and Leng, cited, pp. 119-120, give the results of other opinion polls.

53. Leng, cited in Note 26 above, pp. 106 ff., has a good discussion of Japanese attitudes toward China.

54. C. Martin Wilbur, chapter on "Japan and the Rise of Communist China," in Hugh Borton and others, *Japan between East and West* (New York: Harper, for the Council on Foreign Relations, 1957), p. 228.

55. Wilbur, same, p. 231.

56. Kishi's New Year's message, 1958, *Asahi*, January 1, 1958, quoted by Paul F. Langer in "Japan and the West," *Current History*, vol. 34, April 1958, pp. 208-213.

57. Treaty of Portsmouth, cited in Harold M. Vinacke, *A History of the Far East in Modern Times* (New York: Crofts, 1945), p. 183.

Chapter 11. Communist China and South and Southeast Asia

1. The term "nonalignment" is preferred to "neutralism" by a majority of the "neutralist" leaders in South and Southeast Asia, and it will generally be used in the discussion which follows. In the minds of these leaders, "neutralism" has undertones of passivity and ideological or moral "neutrality" which they disclaim, whereas "nonalignment," in their view, is a less emotionally charged and more factual description of their policies of avoidance of military and political alliances. When the term

"neutralism" is used in the text that follows, its sense will generally be the same as that of the term "nonalignment." However, "neutralism" in South and Southeast Asia is a complex phenomenon and is inadequately described by any simple label; see discussion on pp. 299 ff.

2. Chou En-lai's March 5, 1957, "Report on Visit to 11 Countries in Asia and Europe," made to the National Committee of the People's Political Consultative Conference on March 5, 1957 (*Current Background*, No. 439, March 8, 1957), is one of the clearest expressions of Peking's tactical approach to South and Southeast Asia during this period, and the following fragmentary quotations of remarks he made about different countries illustrate the changes in Peking's tactics as compared with 1949. Cambodia: "Kinship has existed since ancient times between the peoples of Cambodia and China.... We are pleased to find that the estrangement between our two countries caused by colonial rule has been removed with our respective attainment of independence and that better relations than ever before have now been established between our two kinsman countries." India: "There is much we Chinese people can learn from our Indian friends.... The enthusiastic welcome given us by the Indian people defies description.... Wherever we went we heard the hearty cheer: 'Hindi Chini Bhai Bhai' (Indians and Chinese are brothers).... Naturally China and India do not hold, nor can they hold identical views on all questions.... But, just as Prime Minister Nehru said during our visit to India, 'When we disagree in some matters, it is friendly disagreement, and it does not affect our friendship and cooperation.' ... These talks will further help our two countries ... to play their roles in the common cause of safeguarding world peace and promoting international cooperation...." Burma: "We saw the beautiful land of our close neighbor.... The Burmese people who cherish a profound friendship toward the Chinese people gave us a warm welcome everywhere we went, addressing us as 'Baobo' [paukpaw] which means brothers.... [We held a meeting in Mangshih, in Yunnan, China, which] was a vivid expression of the brotherly feelings that had developed between our two peoples across the centuries...." Pakistan: "Pakistan is a young republic, but has a long history and a rich and fine culture. Friendly contacts between the peoples of Pakistan and China go back to the remote past.... As everybody knows, we differ on certain questions.... Nevertheless, we expressed a common desire for promoting the course of world peace and for further developing the existing

friendly relations between China and Pakistan." Nepal: "Nepal is known to all Chinese people as an ancient country, the birthplace of Buddhism 2,500 years ago. Although the world's highest mountains, the Himalayas, separate our two countries, it has not been able to prevent the friendly exchanges between our two countries since the earliest days.... The Nepalese people warmly welcomed us like brothers.... We reaffirmed the desire of our two countries to further the friendship between China and Nepal, to strengthen the solidarity of the Asian and African countries and to promote world peace...." Ceylon: "In the past few years, rice, rubber trade between our two countries has had a very favorable influence upon the economics of our two countries, and this has made a deep impression on our two peoples.... We all felt like old friends.... [We saw for ourselves] this rich and beautiful island, which is worthy of its name—the Pearl of the Indian Ocean.... [The Ceylonese] are friends worthy of our respect and admiration."

3. For details on Peking's establishment of diplomatic relations with countries in this region, see "Diplomatic Relations of Communist China," *Current Background,* No. 440, March 12, 1957.

4. For a perceptive analysis of neutralism, see William Henderson, "The Roots of Neutralism in Southern Asia," *International Journal,* vol. 13, Winter 1957-1958, pp. 30-40.

5. "Southeast Asia: Critical Area in a Divided World," *Background,* June 1955, Department of State Publication 5841 (Washington, D.C., June 1955), p. 4.

6. The history of Sino-Vietnamese relations is well summarized in Harold C. Hinton, *China's Relations with Burma and Vietnam* (New York: Institute of Pacific Relations, 1958). See also Bernard B. Fall, *The Viet-Minh Regime* (New York: Institute of Pacific Relations, 1956).

7. Communist China recognized the Communist regime on January 16, 1950; the Soviet Union followed suit on January 30, 1950. Regarding Chinese military aid to the Vietminh, see Hinton, cited in Note 6 above, p. 18; and Richard P. Stebbins, *The United States in World Affairs, 1954* (New York: Harper, for the Council on Foreign Relations, 1956), p. 217.

8. On March 7, 1958, Premier Pham Van Dong sent a letter to South Vietnam urging North-South discussion on troop reductions and trade. Although there had been earlier overtures of a similar sort, this appeared to mark a major campaign to open up contacts with the South—at approximately the same time as the

adoption of a similar approach by North Korea, also with Chinese backing. On December 22, 1958, Pham Van Dong sent a note to Premier Ngo Dinh Diem in South Vietnam proposing the establishment of "normal" relations between the two regimes. In early 1959, however, after numerous efforts along this line had failed, the North Vietnamese, with Chinese backing, began to adopt a tougher and more threatening line both toward South Vietnam and toward neighboring Laos and Thailand.

9. See, for example, column by "The Observer," in *China Digest,* September 21, 1949, which labels Nehru—together with Quirino, Hatta, Bao Dai, U Nu, Phibul, Rhee, and Chiang—as "all dregs of mankind."

10. "Sino-Indian Communications Regarding Tibet, October-November 1950," *Current Background,* No. 31, November 27, 1950. See also C. H. Alexandrowicz, "India and the Tibetan Tragedy," *Foreign Affairs,* vol. 31, April 1953, pp. 495-500.

11. Chou En-lai December 14, 1952, cable to Lester B. Pearson, President of the General Assembly, NCNA, December 14, 1952, SCMP 473, December 16, 1952.

12. Phillips Talbot and S. L. Poplai, *India and America* (New York: Harper, for the Council on Foreign Relations, 1958), p. 98.

13. When the "Bandung spirit" was at its peak, Indian public opinion was almost overwhelmingly favorable to Communist China and critical of American policy toward China. In the *Christian Science Monitor,* March 10, 1954, for example, the *Monitor*'s correspondent in India stated his opinion that: "It is no understatement to say today that most Indians admire the new China, or what they believe the new China to be, and this mental neighborhood is fraught with greater potential for Asia and the world than the two countries' physical juxtaposition." Extravagant assessments of the significance of Sino-Indian friendship were widely published. The following statement can be taken as an example: China and India "together are acting as the midwives of the new trend in history." (K. P. Gosh, "Sino-Indian Relations," *Eastern World,* June 1956.) Even pro-Western Indian opinion tended to blame the United States rather than Communist China for the tensions in Asia. See, as an example, an article entitled "Mao, Moscow and the Middle East," in *The Eastern Economist,* August 8, 1958. "The West's irrational fear of Communist China has apparently compelled the latter to seek security only in the unity and solidarity of the Communist bloc," it asserted. "Had the international tension been less severe and had the West been more realistic in its dealings with Communist

China, the latter would not have been so hostile to or bitter against the West or to Yugoslavia's concept of 'independent roads to Socialism.' The root cause of China's devotion to Marxism-Leninism and its tirade against 'revisionism' lies in the West's unmitigated hostility toward it. . . . Even now it is perhaps not too late to recognize the realities of the situation."

14. As early as 1950 Prime Minister Nehru, after the Chinese Communist invasion of Tibet, took pains to make clear to the world that: "The McMahon line is our boundary, map or no map. We will not allow anybody to come across that boundary." Quoted in Mark C. Feer, "India's Himalayan Frontier," *Far Eastern Survey*, vol. 22, October 1953, pp. 137-141.

15. See, for example, *The Hindu Weekly*, September 8, 1958, and *The Times* (London), January 1, 1955.

16. Talbot and Poplai, cited in Note 12 above, p. 114.

17. A good outline summary of Sino-Nepalese relations, both historical and contemporary, is contained in Werner Levi, "Nepal in World Politics," *Pacific Affairs*, vol. 30, September 1957, pp. 236-240. See also "The Himalayan Border," *Atlantic Monthly*, vol. 194, September 1954, pp. 10, 12-14.

18. Levi, cited in Note 17 above, p. 243.

19. Text of August 1, 1955, joint Sino-Nepalese communiqué, in NCNA, August 1, 1955, SCMP 1100, July 30-August 2, 1955.

20. Text of September 20, 1956, Sino-Nepalese agreement in NCNA, September 24, 1956, SCMP 1378, September 27, 1956.

21. U Kyaw Nyein, one of Burma's leading political figures, stated in an interview on March 30, 1951: "Small nations always mistrust bigger ones, especially those close by. For years past, every Burman has mistrusted China, whether under Mao or Chiang. They also mistrust India; for that matter they also mistrust Soviet Russia and even America. We don't consider China a menace, but we accept a possibility of China one day invading us. We are not alone in this concern. Our neighbors will also be perturbed as our fate may likely be theirs. We are entering into closer relations with India, Pakistan, Indonesia, and are trying to find a formula for peaceful coexistence in this part of our world. We don't want anything that will provoke China, but if she does invade, I am confident that the national spirit of our people will stand firm against her. We don't want Communist Russia or Communist China, but being a small nation, we must find ways and means of avoiding embroilment in power blocs." Quoted in Frank W. Trager, "Burma's Foreign Policy, 1948-56," *The Journal of Asian Studies*, vol. 16, November 1956, p. 93.

22. Speech by Prime Minister U Nu on December 11, 1949, provided to the author by Frank W. Trager.

23. Hinton, cited in Note 6 above, p. 32.

24. Art. III of July 24, 1886, Sino-Burmese treaty, quoted by Hinton, same, p. 34.

25. For good general background on the border problem, see W. Stark Toller, "The Undefined China-Burma Frontier," *Eastern World*, October-November 1948, pp. 12-14.

26. Victor Purcell, *The Chinese in Southeast Asia* (London: Oxford University Press, 1952), pp. 98-101.

27. Text of December 12, 1954, communiqué on Sino-Burmese talks, in NCNA, December 12, 1954, SCMP 946, December 11-13, 1954.

28. Hinton, cited in Note 6 above, p. 39.

29. See Richard P. Stebbins, *The United States in World Affairs, 1953* (New York: Harper, for the Council on Foreign Relations, 1955), pp. 280-282.

30. See Hinton, cited in Note 6 above, pp. 40-44.

31. Detailed analyses of the border problem in recent years are contained in Richard J. Kozicki, "The Sino-Burmese Frontier Problem," *Far Eastern Survey*, vol. 26, March 1957, pp. 33-38, and Hugh Tinker, "Burma's Northeast Borderland Problems," *Pacific Affairs*, vol. 29, December 1956, pp. 324-346.

32. U Nu December 10, 1954, speech in Peking, NCNA, December 10, 1954, SCMP 946, December 11-13, 1954. In this speech, made during the first Quemoy crisis, U Nu praised the United States and argued that a Sino-American understanding was possible. In dealings with the United States he took a similar line, urging attempts to relax tensions.

33. See, for example, Chou En-lai December 12, 1957, statement, made during an interview: "The struggle of the Indonesian people for the recovery of West Irian is a just struggle, and a just struggle is bound to triumph." NCNA, December 13, 1957, SCMP 1674, December 18, 1957.

34. The Chinese Communist government in an official statement, made on May 15, 1958, asserted that the Chinese government and people "fully support" the Indonesian government and are "prepared to give further assistance" on request. Text of statement in *Peking Review*, May 20, 1958.

35. Prince Norodom Sihanouk, "Cambodia Neutral: The Dictate of Necessity," *Foreign Affairs*, vol. 36, July 1958, pp. 582-586.

36. George McT. Kahin, *The Asian-African Conference* (Ithaca, N.Y.: Cornell University Press, 1956), p. 26.

37. Russell H. Fifield, *The Diplomacy of Southeast Asia 1945-1958* (New York: Harper, 1958), p. 385.

38. Text of August 24, 1958, joint Sino-Cambodian statement, in NCNA, August 24, 1958, SCMP 1841, August 27, 1958.

39. Kahin, cited in Note 36 above, p. 27.

40. Text of August 25, 1956, Sino-Laotian joint statement, NCNA, August 25, 1956, SCMP 1360, August 29, 1956.

41. *The Times of Viet Nam*, September 8, 1956, quoted in Fifield, cited in Note 37 above, p. 363.

42. See Albert Ravenholt, "Red China Beckons Its Neighbors," AUFS Report AR-1-59, Manila, January 28, 1959.

43. See Edwin F. Stanton, "Spotlight on Thailand," *Foreign Affairs*, vol. 33, October 1954, pp. 72 ff.

44. *New York Times*, June 3, 1956.

45. Tengku Abdul Rahman first stated this position on August 23, 1957, before independence, but he subsequently repeated it on several occasions, and his successor has taken the same line. A *New York Times* dispatch of May 11, 1959, states: "On the subject of recognition of Communist China, Dato Abdul Razak bin Hussein, new Prime Minister, said it would be unthinkable as long as any Red terrorists remained in the Malayan jungles."

Chapter 12. The Sino-Soviet Alliance

1. Ch'en Po-ta, "Stalin and the Chinese Revolution," *Current Background*, No. 181, May 10, 1952. In this article, Ch'en states: "It was a great misfortune for our Party that the opportunists, in the interests of disseminating their own erroneous concepts and proposals, either intentionally or unintentionally kept back Stalin's works on China. But, despite this situation, Comrade Mao Tse-tung has been able to reach the same conclusions as Stalin on many fundamental problems through his own independent thinking based on the fundamental revolutionary source of Marx, Engels, Lenin and Stalin. . . . It was during the anti-Japanese War that Comrade Mao Tse-tung had an opportunity to read Stalin's works extensively."

2. Ambassador Patrick J. Hurley's report of April 17, 1945, quoting Molotov, in *United States Relations with China* (Department of State White Paper), Department of State Publication 3573 (Washington, D.C., August 1949), p. 94. See also White Paper, p. 72.

3. Same, text on p. 13.

4. Same, text on p. 585.

NOTES

5. Vladimir Dedijer, *Tito* (New York: Simon & Schuster, 1958), p. 322.

6. White Paper, cited in Note 2 above, pp. 145 ff.

7. Liu Shao-ch'i, *Internationalism and Nationalism* (Peking: Foreign Languages Press, 1949), p. 11.

8. Mao Tse-tung, *On People's Democratic Dictatorship* (Peking: English Language Service, New China News Agency, 1949), p. 4.

9. Same, p. 9.

10. A good summary of official Russian contacts with China from 1949 on is in Howard L. Boorman, Alexander Eckstein, Philip E. Mosely, and Benjamin Schwartz, *Moscow-Peking Axis, Strengths and Strains* (New York: Harper, for the Council on Foreign Relations, 1957), pp. 4 ff.

11. Text in *Sino-Soviet Treaty and Agreements* (Peking: Foreign Languages Press, 1951), pp. 5-8. Text of the treaty and other early Sino-Soviet agreements mentioned below are also in *Current Background*, No. 62, March 5, 1951.

12. Text of Sino-Soviet communiqué of September 15, 1952, NCNA, September 16, 1952, SCMP 417, September 17, 1952.

13. Texts of October 12, 1954, agreements, NCNA, October 12, 1954, SCMP 906, October 12, 1954.

14. *New York Times*, June 4, 1956.

15. Khrushchev, September 30, 1954, speech, NCNA, September 30, 1954, SCMP 902, October 6, 1954.

16. Texts of Sino-Soviet communiqués and declarations of October 12, 1954, NCNA, October 12, 1954, SCMP 906, October 12, 1954.

17. Text of Sino-Soviet communiqué of April 7, 1956, NCNA, April 7, 1956, SCMP 1265, April 11, 1956.

18. See Robert C. Herber, "Mao and Polycentric Communism," *Orbis*, vol. 2, Summer 1958, pp. 175-193.

19. A perceptive discussion of developments during this period is contained in Allen S. Whiting, "Contradictions in the Moscow-Peking Axis," *The Journal of Politics*, vol. 20, February 1958, pp. 127-161.

20. Text of Peking *People's Daily* editorial, April 5, 1956, *Current Background*, No. 403, July 25, 1956.

21. See article, "Several Questions on the Current Movement in International Communism," in *Chung Kuo Ch'ing Nien*, December 1, 1956.

22. Text of Peking *People's Daily*, December 29, 1956, article,

"More on the Historical Experience of the Dictatorship of the Proletariat," *Current Background*, No. 433, January 2, 1957.

23. Shu Wei-k'ung, "The Gradual Tempo of China's Transitional Period," *Hsin Hua Yueh Pao*, October 1955, quoted by Benjamin Schwartz, in Boorman and others, cited in Note 10 above, p. 131.

24. Same, p. 138.

25. Text of Mikoyan's September 17, 1956, speech, *Current Digest of the Soviet Press*, vol. 8, October 31, 1956, pp. 6 ff.

26. *New York Times*, October 16, 1956.

27. *New York Times*, January 11, 1957.

28. Text in *Current Digest of the Soviet Press*, vol. 8, November 14, 1956, pp. 10 ff.

29. "International Significance of the Soviet-Polish Talks," NCNA, November 21, 1956, SCMP 1418, November 27, 1956.

30. See Note 22 above. *Current Background*, No. 433, January 2, 1957.

31. *New York Times*, January 11 and 12, 1957.

32. *New York Times*, January 19, 1957.

33. Mao's speech was made on February 27, 1957, but was not released to the public until June 18, 1957. Text in NCNA, June 18, 1957, *Current Background*, No. 458, June 20, 1957.

34. See Note 20 above. *Current Background*, No. 403, July 25, 1956.

35. See Note 22 above. *Current Background*, No. 433, January 2, 1957.

36. See Note 33 above. *Current Background*, No. 458, June 20, 1957.

37. See Whiting, cited in Note 19 above.

38. Text of Chou En-lai March 5, 1957, speech, *Current Background*, No. 439, March 8, 1957.

39. This and following quotation referring to Hungary are from Chou En-lai speech, same.

40. Mao Tse-tung, November 6, 1957, speech, NCNA, November 6, 1957, *Current Background*, No. 480, November 13, 1957.

41. Mao Tse-tung speech to Chinese students in Moscow on November 17, 1957, summarized in NCNA, November 18, 1957, SCMP 1656, November 21, 1957.

42. Declaration of Twelve Communist and Workers' Parties, Moscow, November 22, 1957, text in *Current Digest of the Soviet Press*, vol. 9, January 1, 1958, pp. 3 ff.

43. The "general laws" listed in the Moscow declaration of November 1957 were: "Leadership of the masses of the working

people by the working class, the core of which is the Marxist-Leninist party, in bringing about a proletarian revolution in one form or another and establishing one form or another of the dictatorship of the proletariat; the alliance of the working class with the bulk of the peasantry and other strata of the working people; the abolition of capitalist ownership and the establishment of public ownership of the basic means of production; gradual Socialist reorganization of agriculture; planned development of the national economy with the aim of building socialism and communism, raising the working people's standard of living; the accomplishment of a Socialist revolution in the sphere of ideology and culture and the creation of a numerous intelligentsia devoted to the working class, the working people and the cause of socialism; the elimination of national oppression and the establishment of equality and fraternal friendship among the people; defense of the achievements of socialism against encroachments by external and internal enemies; solidarity of the working class of a given country with the working class of other countries—proletarian internationalism."

44. Ebert statement in *Neues Deutschland,* November 30, 1957, East Berlin; see Richard Lowenthal, "Shifts and Rifts in the Russo-Chinese Alliance," *Problems of Communism,* vol. 8, January-February 1959, pp. 14 ff.

45. *New York Times,* June 15, 1958; and *New York Times,* July 15, 1958.

46. Text in NCNA, May 27, 1958, SCMP 1782, June 2, 1958.

47. Mao Tse-tung, November 18, 1957, speech, in Moscow, quoted in "Mao Tse-tung on Imperialists and Reactionaries," *Current Background,* No. 534, November 12, 1958.

48. Text in NCNA, May 4, 1958, SCMP 1767, May 8, 1958.

49. See Note 22 above. *Current Background,* No. 433, January 2, 1957.

50. See Note 33 above. *Current Background,* No. 458, June 20, 1957.

51. See Note 40 above. *Current Background,* No. 480, November 13, 1957.

52. See *Die Welt,* May 10, 1958, and NCNA, May 23, 1958.

53. John L. Steele, *Life,* July 13, 1959.

54. Text in *New York Times,* August 4, 1958.

55. Khrushchev letter to President Eisenhower, text in *New York Times,* August 6, 1958.

56. See Herbert Ritvo, "Sino-Soviet Relations and the Summit,"

Problems of Communism, vol. 7, September-October 1958, pp. 47 ff.

57. Khrushchev message of September 7, 1958, to President Eisenhower, text in *New York Times,* September 9, 1958.

58. Text in *Peking Review,* September 16, 1958.

59. Senator Hubert H. Humphrey, "My Marathon Talk with Russia's Boss," *Life,* January 12, 1959.

60. December 10, 1958, Party Resolution on Questions Concerning People's Communes, in NCNA, December 18, 1958, *Current Background,* No. 542, December 29, 1958.

61. See Peking *People's Daily* editorial of February 5, 1959, SCMP 1952, February 12, 1959, and editorial of February 8, 1959, SCMP 1953, February 13, 1959. See also *Hung Ch'i* (*Red Flag*) article of February 16, 1959, "A Clarion Call for the Advance to Communism," reprinted in *Peking Review,* February 24, 1959, and Richard Lowenthal, "Khrushchev's 'Flexible Communism,'" *Commentary,* vol. 27, April 1959, pp. 277-284.

62. Edgar Snow, *Red Star over China* (New York: Random House, 1944), p. 96.

63. Gunther Stein, *The Challenge of Red China* (New York: Whittlesey House, 1945), pp. 442-443.

64. See John E. Tashjean, "Where China Meets Russia: An Analysis of Dr. Starlinger's Theory," Central Asian Collectanea No. 2 (Washington, D.C.: Central Asian Collectanea, 1958).

65. See, for example, *New York Times,* May 11, 1958, which reports that the Poles believed the Chinese were intimately involved in the power struggle then in progress in the U.S.S.R.

Chapter 13. Taiwan and the Nationalist Regime

1. Chang Chi-yun, *An Outline History of Taiwan* (Taipei: China Culture Publishing Foundation, 1953), p. 2.

2. Same, p. 8.

3. *China Handbook 1950* (New York: Rockport Press, Inc., 1951), p. 34. (Chang, cited, p. 12, gives 1886 as the year in which Taiwan was made a province.)

4. James W. Davidson, *The Island of Formosa, Past and Present* (London: The MacMillan Co., 1903), excerpts mimeographed by the American Embassy, Taipei, p. 273.

5. See George W. Barclay, *Colonial Development and Population in Taiwan* (Princeton: Princeton University Press, 1954), for a detailed study of Taiwan's population growth.

6. Detailed production data for the Japanese period from 1936

on are contained in *Economic Data Book Vol. II, Taiwan Monthly Production Data, Base Book for Years 1936-1953 Inclusive,* mimeographed (Taipei: Office of Assistant Director for Industry, FOA Mission to China, January 1954).

7. Text in *United States Relations with China* (hereafter cited as White Paper), Department of State Publication 3573 (Washington, D.C., August 1949), p. 519.

8. Joseph W. Ballantine, *Formosa, A Problem for United States Foreign Policy* (Washington, D.C.: The Brookings Institution, 1952), p. 59.

9. See "Memorandum on the Situation in Taiwan," submitted by U.S. Ambassador Stuart to President Chiang K'ai-shek on April 8, 1947, White Paper, cited in Note 7 above, pp. 923-938; and G. H. Kerr, "Formosa's Return to China," *Far Eastern Survey,* vol. 16, October 15, 1947, pp. 205-208; and "Formosa: the March Massacres," *Far Eastern Survey,* vol. 16, November 5, 1947, pp. 224-226.

10. Ballantine, cited in Note 8 above, p. 63.

11. Same, p. 64 (however, *China Handbook 1950,* p. 33, states that it became a province on October 25, 1945).

12. Text of President Truman's January 5, 1950, statement, in *The Department of State Bulletin,* vol. 22, no. 550, January 16, 1950, p. 79.

13. Text of President Truman's June 27, 1950, statement, in *The Department of State Bulletin,* vol. 23, no. 574, July 3, 1950, pp. 5-6.

14. The analysis which follows is based in large part on the author's own observations on Taiwan during 1949, 1952, and 1954. See A. D. Barnett, "Tension off the China Coast," AUFS Report ADP-11-54, Taipei, Taiwan, October 1, 1954; "Formosa: Political Potpourri," AUFS Report ADB-12-54, Hong Kong, October 8, 1954; and "The Economy of Formosa: Progress on a Treadmill," AUFS Report ADB-13-54, Hong Kong, October 15, 1954.

15. The army is also a key element in the political situation on Taiwan. See George Taylor, *Formosa* (Cambridge: Center for International Studies, Massachusetts Institute of Technology, July 7, 1954), p. 3.

16. *New York Times,* December 24, 1958.

17. See Richard L. Walker, "Taiwan's Development as Free China," *The Annals,* vol. 321, January 1959, pp. 122-135.

18. See Albert Ravenholt, "Formosa Today," *Foreign Affairs,* vol. 30, July 1952, pp. 612-624.

19. See Allen S. Whiting, "The United States and Taiwan," in

The United States and the Far East (New York: The American Assembly, Columbia University, December 1956), especially pp. 185-187.

20. See NCNA, December 25, 1957, SCMP 1693, January 17, 1958.

21. The history and aims of this movement are summarized in *Formosa Appeal!* and *Key to the Formosa Impasse,* mimeographed by the "Formosa Independence League," no place of publication given other than "U.S.A.," dated April 1, 1956.

22. For one Taiwanese viewpoint, see Li Thian-hok, "The China Impasse," *Foreign Affairs,* vol. 36, April 1958, pp. 437-448.

23. For recent estimates of Taiwanese political views, see Denis Warner, "What Are the Prospects for an Independent Formosa?," *The New Republic,* vol. 139, November 3, 1958, pp. 12-16; and Michael Lindsay, "Formosa's Future," *The New Republic,* vol. 139, October 6, 1958, pp. 12-16. Warner states his belief that, although there is sentiment favoring independence on Taiwan, the "fact is that the Formosans after years of subservience have no idea what they want." Lindsay believes the independence movement has become weaker rather than stronger in recent years, and he points out that "what people want does not mean much unless one knows how far they would go to get it."

24. For a general description and statistical data on economic plans and programs on Taiwan, see *The Industrial Program under the Four Year Economic Development Plan* (Taipei: Industrial Development Commission, ESB, Executive Yuan, Republic of China, June 30, 1954); and *Four-Year Plan for Economic Development of Taiwan—Agricultural Section* (Taipei: Economic Stabilization Board, Executive Yuan, January 1954; translated and mimeographed version, August 1954). General surveys of socio-economic conditions on Taiwan are summarized in Arthur F. Raper, *Rural Taiwan—Problem and Promise* (Taipei: Joint Commission on Rural Reconstruction, July 1953); and Arthur F. Raper, Chuan Han-sheng, and Chen Shao-hsing, *Urban and Industrial Taiwan—Crowded and Resourceful* (Taipei: Mutual Security Mission to China and National Taiwan University, September 1954).

25. *Chinese-American Joint Commission on Rural Reconstruction—General Report VII, 1957* (hereafter *JCRR Report 1957*) (Taipei, 1957), p. 101.

26. See *JCRR* (Washington, D.C.: Joint Commission on Rural Reconstruction, IOPA-33-258, January 1958); and T. H. Shen,

Agricultural and Land Reform Programs in Free China (Taipei: General Information Bureau, 1954).

27. 1957 statistics here and below are from table in Walker, cited in Note 17 above, p. 126.

28. Ralph N. Clough, "United States China Policy," *The Annals*, vol. 321, January 1959, p. 24.

29. Same.

30. See table in section on Taiwan in *ECAFE Bulletin*, September 1958.

31. *JCRR Report 1957*, cited in Note 25, p. 2.

32. Computed from data in table (see Note 30 above) in *ECAFE Bulletin*, September 1958.

33. *Operations Report* (Washington, D.C.: International Cooperation Administration, June 30, 1958), p. 26.

34. Same, p. 72.

35. Same.

36. Clough, cited in Note 28 above, p. 24.

37. Quoted in Warner, cited in Note 23 above, p. 15.

38. Statement by Su Yu, then commander of the Third Field Army, *People's China*, February 16, 1950.

39. Chou En-lai, "Report on Foreign Affairs" to the Central People's Government Council, August 11, 1954, text in *Current Background*, No. 288, August 16, 1954.

40. George McT. Kahin, *The Asian-African Conference* (Ithaca, N.Y.: Cornell University Press, 1956), pp. 28-29.

41. Chou En-lai, July 30, 1955, speech on "Foreign Policy" to the National People's Congress, *Current Background*, No. 342, August 3, 1955.

42. Chou En-lai, June 28, 1956, speech on "The Present International Situation, China's Foreign Policy, and the Question of the Liberation of Taiwan," to the National People's Congress, *Current Background*, No. 395, July 5, 1956.

43. In Phnom Penh on November 26, 1956, Chou En-lai reportedly expressed the hope that some day he would welcome his "old friend" Chiang K'ai-shek back to the mainland. See *New York Times*, October 6, 1958; and Richard P. Stebbins, *The United States in World Affairs, 1956* (New York: Harper, for the Council on Foreign Relations, 1957), p. 380.

44. Chou En-lai, March 5, 1957, speech to the National Committee of the People's Political Consultative Conference, *Current Background*, No. 439, March 8, 1957.

45. P'eng Teh-huai (Minister of National Defense), October 25,

1958, message to the Nationalists on Taiwan, NCNA, October 25, 1958, SCMP 1884, October 29, 1958.

46. See *New York Times,* November 23, 1958.

47. Ballantine, cited in Note 8 above, p. 117.

48. See Note 13 above.

49. See Ely Maurer, "Legal Problems Regarding Formosa and the Offshore Islands," *The Department of State Bulletin,* vol. 39, no. 1017, December 22, 1955, pp. 1005-1011.

50. Art. VI of treaty, text in Peter V. Curl, ed., *Documents on American Foreign Relations, 1954* (New York: Harper, for the Council on Foreign Relations, 1955).

51. Public Law 4, 84th Congress, 1st Session, text in Paul E. Zinner, ed., *Documents on American Foreign Relations, 1955* (New York: Harper, for the Council on Foreign Relations, 1956).

52. Text of these notes in Curl, cited in Note 50 above.

53. President Eisenhower's September 11, 1958, speech, text in *New York Times,* September 12, 1958.

54. Secretary Dulles' September 30, 1958, press conference, text in *New York Times,* October 1, 1958.

55. *New York Times,* October 3, 1958.

56. President Chiang's October 10, 1958, message to the armed forces and civilian population of Nationalist China, text in *New York Times,* October 10, 1958.

57. Secretary Dulles' October 14, 1958, press conference, text in *New York Times,* October 15, 1958.

58. Chiang-Dulles, October 23, 1958, joint communiqué, text in *New York Times,* October 24, 1958.

59. The legal situation regarding the waters in this area is highly ambiguous. If the baseline method of determining international waters is used, possibly even a three-mile territorial water claim would include at least part of the waters in the Quemoy area. On September 4, 1958, Peking claimed a 12-mile limit (see *New York Times,* September 5, 1958), but the United States and many other maritime powers have refused to accept this claim.

60. Clough, cited in Note 28 above, p. 23.

61. President Eisenhower, January 24, 1955, statement, text in Senate Report No. 13, "Report of the Committee on Foreign Relations and the Committee on Armed Services on S. J. Res. 28," 84th Congress, 1st Session.

62. Dean Acheson, September 6, 1958, statement, text in *New York Times,* September 7, 1958.

63. *Renunciation of Force, U.S. and Chinese Communist Posi-*

tions, Department of State Publication 6280 (Washington, D.C., February 1956), p. 5.

64. See Stewart Alsop, "The Story behind Quemoy: How We Drifted Close to War," *Saturday Evening Post,* vol. 231, December 13, 1958, pp. 26-27, 86-88.

65. *New York Times,* September 29, 1958.

Chapter 14. The Policy of Nonrecognition

1. Widely opposing views on this question are illustrated by: Eustace Seligman and Richard L. Walker, "Should the United States Change Its China Policy?," *Headline Series* No. 129, Foreign Policy Association, New York, May-June 1958; Quincy Wright, "Non-Recognition of China and International Tensions," *Current History,* vol. 34, March 1958, pp. 152-157; and George E. Taylor, "Why We Do Not Recognize Red China," *Atlantic Monthly,* vol. 202, August 1958, pp. 40-42.

2. John Foster Dulles, *Our Policies toward China,* Department of State Press Release, Public Service Division, Series S-No. 58 (Washington, D.C.: Department of State, June 28, 1957).

3. *Department of State Press Release No. 459,* August 11, 1958.

4. In the following discussion, quotations citing Mr. Dulles are drawn from his June 28, 1957, speech; all others attributed to the Department of State are from the August 11, 1958, memorandum, unless otherwise noted.

5. See Arthur H. Dean, "Note on Diplomatic Recognition of Governments," *The United States and the Far East* (New York: The American Assembly, Columbia University, 1956), pp. 212-218.

6. See, for example, the Department of State's Press Release of January 29, 1957, in *The Department of State Bulletin,* vol. 36, no. 921, February 18, 1957, pp. 261-263, and the United Nations Command Statement of May 31, 1956, in *The Department of State Bulletin,* vol. 34, no. 885, June 4, 1956, pp. 967-970. See also *Soviet Political Treaties and Violations,* U.S. Senate Subcommittee to Investigate the Administration of the Internal Security Act, Staff Study, 84th Congress, 2nd Session, Senate Document 125, Government Printing Office, Washington, D.C., 1956.

7. See Walter S. Robertson, "Meeting the Threat of Communism in the Far East," *The Department of State Bulletin,* vol. 36, no. 922, February 25, 1957, pp. 295-299. In his speech Robertson asserts: "By every standard of national and inter-

national conduct, Red China under its present regime is an outlaw nation."

8. See, for example, Ernest A. Gross, "Some Illusions of Our Asian Policy," *Far Eastern Survey*, vol. 26, December 1957, pp. 177-183, esp. pp. 178-179: "It seems to me that a continuous diplomatic channel open between the United States and Communist China at all requisite levels would serve our national interest more effectively than the sporadic, behind-the-barn type of negotiation which has been taking place in Geneva for more than two years between Ambassadors. There we have, in effect, been 'negotiating' for a basis on which real negotiations might take place. It appears to many Asians to be a formula for avoiding negotiations."

9. See A. G. Mezerik, "Representation of China in the United Nations," *International Review Service*, vol. 3, September 1957, pp. 1-10 and ff.; and David Brook, *The UN and the China Dilemma* (New York: Vantage Press, 1956).

10. In 1950 Secretary of State Acheson, while affirming that the United States would continue opposing the seating of Communist China in the United Nations, emphasized that the United States would not use the veto and would "accept the decision of any organ of the United Nations made by the necessary majority." (Quoted in Richard P. Stebbins, *The United States in World Affairs, 1950*, New York: Harper, for the Council on Foreign Relations, 1951, p. 195.) In 1951 Acheson intimated that if the United States were in a minority on this issue in the Security Council, he would favor seeking a ruling on the matter from the International Court of Justice. (See Richard P. Stebbins, *The United States in World Affairs, 1951*, New York: Harper, for the Council on Foreign Relations, 1952, p. 119.) In 1953 Senator Knowland introduced two resolutions in the Senate calling for United States' withdrawal from the United Nations if Peking were seated; the Senate Appropriations Committee determined to recommend ending American financial contributions to the United Nations if Communist China were seated in the Security Council; and Dulles said the United States was "not prepared . . . to buy the unity of Korea at the price of a concession which would involve bringing Communist China into the United Nations and, above all, into the Security Council." (Richard P. Stebbins, *The United States in World Affairs, 1953*, New York: Harper, for the Council on Foreign Relations, 1955, pp. 70 and 239.) In 1954 Ambassador Lodge (on March 18, April 19, and May 25) and Secretary Dulles (on July 8) declared that the United States could and

would invoke the veto, "if necessary" to block the seating of Communist China in the Security Council. (Richard P. Stebbins, *The United States in World Affairs, 1954*, New York: Harper, for the Council on Foreign Relations, 1956, p. 26.)

11. A detailed breakdown of the voting is in *New York Times*, September 24, 1958.

12. Among certain American business and labor groups, particularly on the West Coast, there has been increased pressure to open up trade. See Harold S. Quigley, "Trade with Communist China," *Current History*, vol. 35, December 1958, pp. 353-357.

13. "It is to be understood," the Department of State said, "that the United States will not accord visas to Chinese bearing passports issued by the Chinese Communist regime." *Department of State Press Release*, No. 473, August 22, 1957.

14. *New York Times*, October 5, 1958.

Chapter 15. The Choices before the United States

1. John Foster Dulles, *Our Policies toward China*, Department of State Press Release No. 393, Public Services Division, Series S-No. 58 (Washington, D.C.: Department of State, June 28, 1957).

2. Walter P. McConaughy, "China in the Shadow of Communism," *The Department of State Bulletin*, vol. 30, no. 759, January 11, 1954, p. 42.

3. John Foster Dulles, statement made in his press conference on February 5, 1957, *The Department of State Bulletin*, vol. 36, no. 922, February 25, 1957, p. 305.

The phrase "quasi state of war" was used by Acting Secretary of State Christian Herter; see his statement of August 12, 1957, in *The Department of State Bulletin*, vol. 37, no. 949, September 2, 1957, p. 393.

Appendix

1. Captain Malcolm Kennedy, *A History of Communism in East Asia* (New York: Praeger, 1957), p. 348.

2. Rodger Swearingen and Paul F. Langer, *Red Flag in Japan* (Cambridge: Harvard University Press, 1952), pp. 77 ff.

3. Same, p. 134.

4. Cominform Journal, January 6, 1950.

5. NCNA, Peking, September 30, 1951, SCMP 186, October 1-2, 1951.

6. Cited by Paul F. Langer in Borton and others, *Japan be-*

546   COMMUNIST CHINA AND ASIA

tween East and West (New York: Harper, for the Council on Foreign Relations, 1957), p. 93.

7. *World Strength of the Communist Party Organizations* (Washington, D.C.: Bureau of Intelligence and Research, Department of State, January 1959), pp. 68-69. This publication, which is issued annually, has a brief current analysis of each Asian Communist party; it is the source of most current figures on party membership used in this chapter.

8. Devillers, *Histoire du Viet-Nam de 1940 à 1952* (Paris, 1952), p. 38, cited in Harold C. Hinton's *China's Relations with Burma and Vietnam* (New York: Institute of Pacific Relations, 1958), p. 11.

9. Virginia Thompson and Richard Adloff, *The Left Wing in Southeast Asia* (New York: Institute of Pacific Relations, Sloane, 1950), p. 24.

10. Same, p. 29.

11. Hinton, cited in Note 8 above, p. 18.

12. Bernard B. Fall, *The Viet-Minh Regime* (New York: Institute of Pacific Relations, 1956), p. 59.

13. See Ho Chi-minh remarks to Paul Mus cited in Hinton, cited above, p. 13.

14. *World Strength of the Communist Party Organizations*, January 1959, p. 63.

15. In early 1959 North Vietnam strongly protested to Thailand concerning arrests of Vietnamese in Thailand and the delay in negotiating about their return to Vietnam; Communist China gave North Vietnam strong propaganda support. See texts of letters exchanged between Pham Van Dong and Chou En-lai, *Peking Review*, February 16, 1959. See also Fall, cited above, p. 59.

16. *World Strength of the Communist Party Organizations*, January 1958, p. 60.

17. See *New York Times*, May 13 and 14, 1958; and *World Strength . . .* , cited above (both January 1958 issue, p. 60; and January 1959 issue, p. 62.)

18. See *New York Times*, May 18 and 19, 1959.

19. See *New York Times*, January 15, 17, 21, 1959.

20. Gene Z. Hanrahan, *The Communist Struggle in Malaya* (New York: Institute of Pacific Relations, 1954), pp. 7-8.

21. The wartime and postwar developments described here are concisely summarized in J. H. Brimmel, *A Short History of the Malayan Communist Party* (Singapore: Malaya Publishing House Ltd., 1956).

22. *World Strength of the Communist Party Organizations,* January 1959, p. 60.

23. Victor Purcell, *Malaya: Communist or Free?* (London: Gollancz, 1954), p. 69.

24. NCNA, August 1, 1958.

25. *The Economist,* August 2, 1958.

26. *New York Times,* May 12, 1959.

27. See A. D. Barnett, "Self-Rule and Unrest: Overseas Chinese in Singapore," AUFS Report ADB-8-55, Singapore, July 7, 1955; "Notes on Three Growing Forces among Singapore Chinese: Political Parties, Students and Workers," AUFS Report ADB-9-55, Singapore, July 11, 1955; and "A Chronology of Three Months of Unrest in Singapore," AUFS Report ADB-10-55, Singapore, July 15, 1955.

28. See article by "Singapore Correspondent," in *Eastern World,* March 1958, and *Commonwealth Survey,* January 7, 1958.

29. *New York Times,* May 31, 1959.

30. Thompson and Adloff, cited in Note 9 above, pp. 51-58.

31. *World Strength of the Communist Party Organizations,* January 1959, p. 61.

32. See Geoffrey Fairburn, "Aspects of Burma and Thailand," *The Australian Outlook,* vol. 12, September 1958, pp. 3-10.

33. See, for example, *New York Times,* October 21, 24, 26 and November 10, 1958.

34. Jesus Vargas and Tarciano Rizal, *Communism in Decline: The Huk Campaign* (Bangkok: Southeast Asia Treaty Organization, 1958), p. 3.

35. Kennedy, cited in Note 1 above, p. 474.

36. Vargas and Rizal, cited in Note 34 above, p. 22.

37. Musso had also spent a considerable period of time in China during his wanderings as a revolutionary exile.

38. Ruth Thomas McVey, *The Development of the Indonesian Communist Party and Its Relations with the Soviet Union and the Chinese People's Republic* (Cambridge: Center for International Studies, Massachusetts Institute of Technology, 1954), pp. 60-62.

39. Aidit's past contacts with the Chinese Communists are not wholly clear. McVey, same, p. 70, states that he "spent a considerable time in China in 1949." In 1955, however, Aidit, in an interview with the author, asserted that he had not been in China up to that time; see A. D. Barnett, "Echoes of Mao Tse-tung in Djakarta, An Interview with D. N. Aidit," AUFS Report ADB-6-55, Djakarta, May 21, 1955. Subsequently, in any case, he has definitely visited Communist China.

40. *World Strength of the Communist Party Organizations,* January 1949, p. 71.

41. Same.

42. *New York Times,* September 23, 1958.

43. Author's interviews with Western diplomatic sources in Djakarta, May 1955. See also, "Role of Bank of China in Financing Indonesian Transactions," *PRRI Bulletin,* April 1959 (published in PRRI—that is, rebel-territory), p. 18.

44. McVey, cited in Note 38 above, p. 67.

45. See Alex Josey, "The Political Significance of the Burma Worker's Party," *Pacific Affairs,* vol. 31, December 1958, pp. 372-379.

46. *World Strength of the Communist Party Organizations,* January 1959, p. 59.

47. See Frank N. Trager, "Political Divorce in Burma," *Foreign Affairs,* vol. 37, January 1959, pp. 317-327.

48. NCNA, March 7, 1958.

49. *New York Times,* March 8, 11, 12, 14, 1959.

50. Richard Butwell, "Communist Liaison in Southeast Asia," *United Asia* (Bombay), June 1954, p. 148; Hinton, cited in Note 8 above, pp. 42-45.

51. John H. Kautsky, *Moscow and the Communist Party of India* (New York: Wiley, 1956), p. 75.

52. Same, pp. 103-104.

53. Same, p. 137.

54. Following figures are from *World Strength of the Communist Party Organizations,* January 1958, p. 53; and January 1959, p. 55.

BIBLIOGRAPHIC NOTE

ALTHOUGH A CONSIDERABLE NUMBER of studies on Communist China have been published, there is an urgent need for more scholarly research on every aspect of the Peking regime. If one compares what has been written on contemporary China over the past decade with the research done on the Soviet Union during the same period, it is clear that there has been a serious lag in work on China.

Study of closed, totalitarian, Communist societies must depend heavily on careful research and analysis of material which the Communists themselves publish. There is a large amount of this material available in the United States, ready to be tapped by serious scholars, researchers, and journalists. For several years, major American libraries have been acquiring a wide range of Chinese Communist publications, both in Chinese and in English translation.

The translated material, most of which is prepared in or comes through Hong Kong, is extensive, and in the past few years most of the writing about Communist China by Westerners, whether journalists or scholars, has been based on it.

The Chinese Communists broadcast and distribute their daily New China News Agency (NCNA) releases in English. The Peking Foreign Languages Press publishes a few books and pamphlets in English. In addition, there are English-language editions of several Chinese Communist magazines, the most useful of which are *Peking Review* (successor to *People's China* and *China Digest*) and *China Reconstructs*.

The most extensive, valuable, and readily available materials in English are the mimeographed translation series produced by the American Consulate General in Hong Kong. These include: the *Survey of the China Mainland Press* (SCMP), generally 30 to 60 single-space pages daily, which includes the most important articles from Chinese Communist newspapers; *Extracts from China Mainland Magazines,* usually issued two to four times monthly, which carries articles of particular interest drawn from a wide range of mainland periodicals; and the *Current Back-*

ground series, of which almost 600 have been issued in the past nine years, consisting of valuable collections of articles or documents grouped according to subjects.

Hong Kong is also the source of other useful translated material and publications. The Union Research Institute publishes the *Union Research Series,* a twice-weekly translation service which generally covers materials not included in the Consulate General's various series and is particularly useful for its articles drawn from provincial and local papers. The Institute also publishes the "Communist China Problem Research Series," consisting of well-documented book-length research studies on special subjects. The Hong Kong weekly newsletter, *China News Analysis,* contains discerning analytical reports on developments on the mainland, based largely on Chinese Communist publications. The weekly *Far Eastern Economic Review,* also published in Hong Kong, presents many articles on Communist China, covering a broader range of subjects than its title implies.

Several competent general surveys of Communist China have been published in the United States in recent years. Among the most comprehensive recent ones are Peter S. H. Tang's *Communist China Today: Domestic and Foreign Policies* (New York: Praeger, 1957), xvi, 536 pp., and its supplement, *Volume 2, Documentary and Chronological Index* (New York: Praeger, 1958), vi, 137 pp., and Ygael Gluckstein's *Mao's China: Economic and Political Survey* (Boston: Beacon Press, 1957), 438 pp. Two earlier books are still useful. *The Prospects for Communist China* (Cambridge: Technology Press of the Massachusetts Institute of Technology, 1954, and New York: John Wiley, 1954), xx, 379 pp., by Walt W. Rostow and others, analyzes the basic character of the regime in its first years, and Richard L. Walker's *China under Communism: The First Five Years* (New Haven: Yale University Press, 1955), xv, 403 pp., gives a summary of major developments through 1954. A general review is found in the author's section on Communist China in *The United States and the Far East* (New York: American Assembly, Graduate School of Business, Columbia University, 1956), pp. 105-171, covering the years through 1956.

Some of the best material on Communist China, dealing with a broad range of subjects, is contained in several recent issues of scholarly journals and magazines, particularly two special issues of the *Annals of the American Academy of Political and Social Science;* the first, *Report on China* (vol. 277, September 1951), ix, 291 pp., was edited by H. Arthur Steiner; the second, edited by Howard L. Boorman, was entitled *Contemporary China and the*

Chinese (vol. 321, January 1959), x, 220 pp. Three other special issues of magazines deserve mention: "Communist China," *Current History* (vol. 32, January 1957), pp. 1-64; "Communist China in World Politics," *Journal of International Affairs* (vol. 11, Spring 1957), pp. 99-207; and "Communist China: A Special Report," *New Republic* (vol. 136, May 13, 1957), 47 pp.

A number of eyewitness reports on Communist China have been published by European or Asian correspondents; they vary greatly in objectivity and perceptiveness. Among the most competent are Robert Guillain's *600 Million Chinese* (New York: Criterion Books, 1957), 310 pp., and Francis R. Moraes' *Report on Mao's China* (New York: Macmillan, 1953), 212 pp.

Almost all the works mentioned above describe and analyze the political structure of the Chinese Communist regime. In addition, there are several studies dealing specifically with the Peking government. S. B. Thomas's *Government and Administration in Communist China* (New York: Institute of Pacific Relations, 2nd rev. ed., 1955), 196 pp., although now dated, is still helpful for its description of government in the first years of the regime. More current and useful information is contained in Harold C. Hinton's section on "China" in *Major Governments of Asia,* edited by George McT. Kahin (Ithaca: Cornell University Press, 1958), pp. 3-132. A careful analysis of Chinese Communist leadership is to be found in *Kuomintang and Chinese Communist Elites* (Stanford: Stanford University Press, 1952), vii, 130 pp., written by Robert C. North with the collaboration of Ithiel de Sola Pool. *China's Red Masters; Political Biographies of the Chinese Communist Leaders* (New York: Twayne Publishers, 1951), 264 pp., by Robert S. Elegant, contains biographies of a few top Chinese Communist leaders.

Of particular interest for their insights into techniques of political organization in China are: Walter E. Gourlay's *The Chinese Communist Cadre: Key to Political Control,* mimeographed (Cambridge: Russian Research Center, Harvard University, 1952), 122 pp. (also condensed in *Problems of Communism,* November 3, 1952, pp. 28-37); Chao Kuo-chün's *The Mass Organizations in Communist China,* mimeographed (Cambridge: Center for International Studies, Massachusetts Institute of Technology, November 1953), 157 pp.; and Herbert F. Schurmann's "Organization and Response in Communist China" (*Annals of the American Academy of Political and Social Science,* vol. 321, January 1959, pp. 51-61).

Because indoctrination plays such a large role in Communist China, Robert J. Lifton's "Thought Reform of Chinese Intellectuals: A Psychiatric Evaluation" (*Journal of Asian Studies*, vol. 16, November 1956, pp. 75-88) is of special interest as a psychiatrist's analysis of the techniques used. One of the first descriptions of indoctrination methods was in Edward Hunter's *Brainwashing in Red China: The Calculated Destruction of Men's Minds* (New York: Vanguard Press, 1951), 311 pp. The author has also attempted to analyze methods of indoctrination in China through study groups, in "Hsüeh Hsi—Weapon of Ideological Revolution in China" (American Universities Field Staff, AUFS Report ADB-3-54, Hong Kong, March 5, 1954), 14 pp. Detailed analyses of one of the many mass campaigns which have been of great importance in Communist China throughout the past decade are contained in "The Three-Anti and Five-Anti Movements in Communist China" (*Pacific Affairs*, vol. 26, March 1953, pp. 3-23), by Theodore Hsi-En Chen and W. H. C. Chen, and the author's series of reports on the "Five Anti Campaign" for the American Universities Field Staff (AUFS Reports, ADB-2 through 6-1952, Hong Kong, July 29 through August 6, 1952): "Nation-wide Campaign," 7 pp., "Campaign in Shanghai," 7 pp., "Position of the Bourgeoisie," 5 pp., "National Finance," 5 pp., and "Control over Private Enterprise," 8 pp.

Although before 1949 the study of economic problems was one of the most neglected fields of research relating to China, since Peking initiated its first Five Year Plan interest in the Chinese economy has steadily increased, and several competent economic studies have recently been published. The two most comprehensive and useful general studies are Li Choh-ming's *Economic Development of Communist China: An Appraisal of the First Five Years of Industrialization* (Berkeley: University of California Press, 1959), xvi, 284 pp., and Wu Yuan-li's *An Economic Survey of Communist China* (New York: Bookman Associates, 1956), x, 566 pp. Serious attempts have also been made to estimate the growth of Communist China's material income. Alexander Eckstein has concentrated his interest on the year 1952, attempting to provide a sound basis for judging later progress, and his preliminary results are reported in "Communist China's National Product in 1952," written with Y. C. Yin and Helen Yin (*The Review of Economics and Statistics*, vol. 40, no. 2, May 1958, pp. 127-139). The best study to date of Communist China's national income during the entire Five Year Plan period is: *China's Gross National Product and Social Accounts, 1950-1957* (Glencoe: The Free Press, 1958), 161 pp., by William W. Hollister. Ta-Chung Liu has made careful estimates which differ somewhat from Hollister's, in "Structural Changes in the Economy of the Chinese Mainland, 1933 to 1952-57" (*American Economic Review*, Papers and Proceedings, vol. 49, May 1959, pp. 84-93). Richard Moorsteen of The RAND Corporation has also done valuable research on the Chinese economy; his article on "Economic Prospects for Communist China" (*World Politics*, vol. 11, January 1959, pp. 192-220) summarizes his basic findings.

Ronald Hsiu-yung Hsia's *Economic Planning in Communist China* (New York: Institute of Pacific Relations, 1955), vi, 89 pp., analyzes planning and economic organization in the initial phase of the first Plan period. Useful data on consumption and living standards are contained in Cheng Chu-yuan's *Income and Standard of Living in Mainland China* (Hong Kong: Union Research Institute, 1957), 2 vols., 166 pp. and 362 pp. Discerning comparisons of the development programs of China and India are contained in Wilfred Malenbaum's article on "India and China: Contrasts in Development Performance" (*American Economic Review*, vol. 49, June 1959, pp. 284-309), as well as in *Economic Development in India and Communist China* (U.S. Senate, Committee on Foreign Relations, Subcommittee on Technical Assistance Programs, Staff Study No. 6, 84th Congress, 2nd Session, Washington, D.C., Government Printing Office, June 2, 1956), v, 51 pp.

Anyone seriously interested in Chinese economic development must turn also to the most important original Chinese Communist reports, which provide the data on which almost all Western analysis is based. A few which are particularly useful should be mentioned here. They include: "Report on the Second Five-Year Plan," by Premier Chou En-lai, to the 8th National Congress on September 16, 1956 (*Current Background*, No. 413, October 5, 1956); "Proposals on the Second Five-Year Plan for the Development of the National Economy," adopted by the Party Congress on September 27, 1956 (*Current Background*, No. 413, October 5, 1956); "Report on the Work of the Government," by Chou En-lai to the National People's Congress on June 26, 1957 (*Current Background*, No. 463, July 2, 1957); "Final Accounts for 1956 and the 1957 State Budget," a report by Li Hsien-nien to the National People's Congress on July 29, 1957 (*Current Backgound*, No. 464, July 5, 1957); "Working of the National Economic Plan for 1956 and Draft National Economic Plan for 1957," a report by Po Yi-po to the National People's Congress on July 1, 1957 (*Current Background*, No. 465, July 9, 1957); "Communiqué on the Fulfillment of the National Economic Plan for 1956," issued by the

State Statistical Bureau on August 1, 1957 (*Current Background,* No. 474, August 12, 1957); "Principles for 1958 Economic Plan Outlined by Po Yi-po," a press summary of a report by Po to a cadre meeting on August 10, 1957 (SCMP 1602, September 3, 1957); "Draft Plan for the Development of the National Economy in 1958," a report by Po Yi-po to the National People's Congress on February 3, 1958 (*Current Background,* No. 494, February 19, 1958); "The Implementation of the State Budget for 1957 and the Draft State Budget for 1958," a report by Li Hsien-nien to the National People's Congress on February 1, 1958 (*Current Background,* No. 493, February 17, 1958); and "Communiqué on China's Economic Growth in 1958," issued by the State Statistical Bureau on April 14, 1959 (*Current Background,* No. 558, April 20, 1959).

Very little has been written on military affairs in Communist China, but there is useful background information in Lt. Colonel Robert B. Rigg's *Red China's Fighting Hordes: A Realistic Account of the Chinese Communist Army by a U.S. Army Officer...* (Harrisburg: Military Service Publishing Company, 1951), xiv, 378 pp., and in the article "China as a Military Power," by Hanson W. Baldwin (*Foreign Affairs,* vol. 30, October 1951, pp. 51-62). More recent data of a general sort can be found in current periodicals; articles of interest include: Robert B. Rigg's "Red Army in Retreat" (*Current History,* vol. 32, January 1957, pp. 1-6); Richard L. Walker's "The Chinese Red Army" (*The New Republic,* vol. 136, May 13, 1957, pp. 39-42); and Sin-ming Chiu's "The Chinese Communist Army in Transition" (*Far Eastern Survey,* vol. 27, November 1958, pp. 168-175). A stimulating discussion of the military problems which Communist China poses for SEATO is presented in *Collective Defence in South East Asia: The Manila Treaty and Its Implications* (London: Royal Institute of International Affairs, Oxford University Press, 1956), xiv, 197 pp.

The relationship of the Chinese Communist party to other Asian Communist parties is an extremely difficult subject to explore, but by laborious research a good deal of information can be pieced together. Several articles of more than ordinary interest deserve mention. Richard Butwell's "Communist Liaison in Southeast Asia" (*United Asia* [Bombay], vol. 6, June 1954, pp. 146-151) contains interesting data on the interrelations of various Communist parties. Shen-yu Dai's *Peking, Moscow, and the Communist Parties of Colonial Asia* (Cambridge: Center for International Studies, Massachusetts Institute of Technology, July 23, 1954), 167 pp., expounds the thesis that Communist China has become the dominant center for directing the movements in Southeast Asian countries. In "Communism in Southeast Asia" (*Yale Review*, vol. 45, March 1956, pp. 417-429) Harry J. Benda analyzes in enlightening fashion the basic social forces underlying the growth of communism.

The most comprehensive studies of Communist movements in Asia are *A History of Communism in East Asia* (New York: Praeger, 1957), ix, 556 pp., by Captain Malcolm D. Kennedy, and *The Left Wing in Southeast Asia* (New York: Institute of Pacific Relations, Sloane, 1950), xiv, 298 pp., by Virginia M. Thompson and Richard Adloff; both books throw much light on Communist China's relations with other Asian Communist parties. Another useful reference work, which annually publishes statistical data and brief analyses on Asian Communist parties, is *World Strength of the Communist Party Organizations* (Washington, D.C.: Bureau of Intelligence and Research, Department of State, 1959), 97 pp.

In addition to these general works, several detailed studies of Communist parties in individual countries contain data and analyses essential to an understanding of Chinese Communist activities in Asia. *Red Flag in Japan: International Communism in Action, 1919-1951* (Cambridge: Harvard University Press, 1952), xii, 276 pp., by A. Rodger Swearingen and Paul F. Langer, is an excellent study of the Communists in Japan with much material on their relations with the Chinese party. Ruth Thomas McVey's *The Development of the Indonesian Communist Party and Its Relations with the Soviet Union and the Chinese People's Republic* (Cambridge: Center for International Studies, Massachusetts Institute of Technology, July 16, 1954), 97 pp., focuses specifically on the external relations of the Indonesian Communists. John H. Kautsky's *Moscow and the Communist Party of India: A Study in the Post War Evolution of International Communist Strategy* (Cambridge: Technology Press of the Massachusetts Institute of Technology, 1956), xii, 220 pp., is particularly interesting for its analysis of the Chinese ideological impact on the Indian Communists. One of the most probing studies of what makes people become Communists is Lucian W. Pye's *Guerilla Communism in Malaya, Its Social and Political Meaning* (Princeton: Princeton University Press, 1956), 369 pp., based on interviews with surrendered Chinese members of the Malayan Communist party.

Chinese Communist propaganda activities are regularly summarized in United States government reports, but these are not generally available. Two broad surveys which are available are

Target: The World; Communist Propaganda Activities in 1955 (New York: Macmillan, 1956), xxiv, 362 pp., and *Year of Crisis: Communist Propaganda Activities in 1956* (New York: Macmillan, 1957), xix, 414 pp., both edited by Evron M. Kirkpatrick. Richard L. Walker in his writings has devoted considerable attention to Peking's propaganda and "people's diplomacy"; his *The Continuing Struggle: Communist China and the Free World* (New York: Athene Press, 1958), 155 pp., contains useful insights into this subject.

American interest in the Overseas Chinese has risen sharply in the past decade, and an increasing number of carefully researched books and articles, based on actual field work, have appeared. The most comprehensive general reference work is still Victor W. W. S. Purcell's *The Chinese in Southeast Asia* (London: Oxford University Press, 1951), xxxvii, 801 pp. Of the Americans studying the Overseas Chinese, G. William Skinner has done the most thorough and extensive field research. Starting with his *Report on the Chinese in Southeast Asia, December 1950*, mimeographed (Ithaca: Southeast Asia Program, Cornell University, 1951), v, 91 pp., he has written prolifically, and his two recent books, *Chinese Society in Thailand: An Analytical History* (Ithaca: Cornell University Press, 1957), xvii, 459 pp., and *Leadership and Power in the Chinese Community of Thailand* (Ithaca: Association for Asian Studies, Cornell University Press, 1958), xvii, 363 pp., are among the best studies of Chinese groups anywhere. The most recent general book on the Overseas Chinese is Robert S. Elegant's *The Dragon's Seed, Peking and the Overseas Chinese* (New York: St. Martin's Press, 1959), 319 pp.; although written in a journalistic style, it is based on solid field research.

Among other useful books and articles on the Chinese in individual Southeast Asian countries, special mention should be made of Robert C. Bone's *The Role of the Chinese in Indonesia* (Washington, D.C.: Foreign Service Institute Monograph Series, June 1951), 148 pp.; Donald E. Willmott's *The National Status of the Chinese in Indonesia,* Modern Indonesia Project, Interim Report Series (Ithaca: Southeast Asia Program, Cornell University, 1956), 88 pp.; T'ien Ju-k'ang's *The Chinese of Sarawak* (London: The London School of Economics and Political Science, Monographs on Social Anthropology, 1953), 88 pp.; Bernard F. Fall's "Vietnam's Chinese Problem" (*Far Eastern Survey*, vol. 27, May 1958, pp. 65-72), and Albert Ravenholt's "Chinese in the Philippines—An Alien Business and Middle Class" (AUFS Report AR-12-55, December 9, 1955), 24 pp.

BIBLIOGRAPHIC NOTE 557

The results of the author's own field observations and research on the Overseas Chinese are included in a series of reports for the American Universities Field Staff, including the following: "A Contest of Loyalties: Overseas Chinese in Thailand" (AUFS Report ADB-15-54, Hong Kong, December 15, 1954), 23 pp.; "A Choice of Nationality: Overseas Chinese in Indonesia" (AUFS Report ADB-7-55, Djakarta, May 28, 1955), 29 pp.; "Self-Rule and Unrest: Overseas Chinese in Singapore" (AUFS Report ADB-8-55, Singapore, July 7, 1955), 11 pp.; "Notes on Three Growing Forces among Singapore Chinese: Political Parties, Students, and Workers" (AUFS Report ADB-9-55, Singapore, July 11, 1955), 18 pp.; and "Problems of Communalism and Communism: Overseas Chinese in Malaya" (AUFS Report ADB-11-55, Kuala Lumpur, August 10, 1955), 21 pp.

Useful general sources on Peking's policies toward the Overseas Chinese include Lu Yu-sun's *Programs of Communist China for Overseas Chinese,* Communist China Problem Research Series (Hong Kong: Union Research Institute, June 1956), 82 pp., and Harold C. Hinton's *Communist China and the Overseas Chinese,* mimeographed (June 1955, unpublished), 26 pp.

The United States government has published a number of studies and reports in recent years dealing with Sino-Soviet economic policies; although they devote primary attention to the U.S.S.R., many of them contain material on Communist China as well. Of these, several are particularly useful sources, including *The Communist Economic Threat,* Department of State Publication 6777 (Washington, D.C.: Department of State, March 1959), 22 pp.; Part II in *The Sino-Soviet Economic Offensive in the Less Developed Countries,* Department of State Publication 6632, European and British Commonwealth Series, No. 51 (Washington, D.C.: Department of State, May 1958), vi, 111 pp.; *The Sino-Soviet Bloc Economic Offensive in the Far East,* Intelligence Report No. 7670, unclassified (Washington, D.C.: Department of State, February 1958), 23 pp.; and *Foreign Assistance Activities of the Communist Bloc and Their Implications for the United States,* Study No. 8, by the Council for Economic and Industry Research, Inc., prepared at the request of the Special Committee to Study the Foreign Aid Program, United States Senate, 85th Congress, 1st Session (Committee Print, Washington, D.C.: March 1957), xvii, 134 pp. An excellent general study of Soviet foreign economic policies has been made by Joseph S. Berliner in his *Soviet Economic Aid: The New Aid and Trade Policy in Under-*

developed Countries (New York: Praeger, for the Council on Foreign Relations, 1958), xv, 232 pp.

Among available studies focused specifically on Communist China's foreign economic relations are the author's *Communist Economic Strategy: The Rise of Mainland China* (Washington, D.C.: National Planning Association, 1959), 106 pp.; *Three Essays on the International Economics of Communist China* (Ann Arbor: University of Michigan Press, for the Center for Japanese Studies and the Department of Economics, 1959), v, 221 pp., edited by Charles F. Remer; Leng Shao Chuan's "Communist China's Economic Relations with Southeast Asia" (*Far Eastern Survey*, vol. 28, January 1959, pp. 1-11); and Hsin Ying's *The Foreign Trade of Communist China*, Communist China Problem Research Series (Hong Kong: Union Research Institute, March 1954), 161 pp.

Most books on China's foreign policy deal mainly with the pre-1949 period. Werner Levi's *Modern China's Foreign Policy* (Minneapolis: University of Minnesota Press, 1953), 399 pp., has a short section on the first years after 1949. His article on "Nepal in World Politics" (*Pacific Affairs*, vol. 30, September 1957, pp. 236-248) contains an interesting account of Sino-Nepalese relations. A number of books and articles have been written on Peking's relations with individual countries. Harold C. Hinton has written a small but fact-filled book on China's relations with two of its small neighbors: *China's Relations with Burma and Vietnam: A Brief Survey* (New York: Institute of Pacific Relations, 1958), viii, 64 pp. Among the most perceptive recent writings on Sino-Japanese relations are C. Martin Wilbur's "Japan and the Rise of Communist China," pp. 199-239 in *Japan between East and West* (New York: Harper, for the Council on Foreign Relations, 1957), by Hugh Borton and others, and Leng Shao Chuan's *Japan and Communist China* (Tokyo: Doshisha University Press, distributed by the Institute of Pacific Relations, 1958), 166 pp. *India and America: A Study of Their Relations* (New York: Harper, for the Council on Foreign Relations, 1958), xviii, 200 pp. by Phillips Talbot and Sundar Lal Poplai, has a good section on Indian-Chinese relations. A comprehensive general book on the foreign relations of Southeast Asian countries, containing information on the relations of each of these countries with Peking, is Russell H. Fifield's *The Diplomacy of Southeast Asia: 1945-1958* (New York: Harper, 1958), xv, 584 pp. And in "Communist China's Foreign Policy" (*Current History*, vol. 33, December 1957, pp. 321-368), several authors analyze Peking's general policy.

BIBLIOGRAPHIC NOTE   559

Although serious research in the United States on the history of the Chinese Communist party and its relations with the Russian Communists was begun only a few years ago, the literature on this subject is growing fairly rapidly, and several excellent historical works have already been published. Among the most useful are Benjamin I. Schwartz's *Chinese Communism and the Rise of Mao* (Cambridge: Harvard University Press, 1951, 258 pp.); *A Documentary History of Chinese Communism* (Cambridge: Harvard University Press, 1952), 552 pp., by Conrad Brandt, Benjamin I. Schwartz, and John K. Fairbank; and Robert C. North's *Moscow and Chinese Communists* (Stanford: Stanford University Press, 1953), ix, 306 pp.

Several detailed studies have been written on Soviet policies toward China during certain periods. The best of these include: Allen S. Whiting's *Soviet Policies in China, 1917-1924* (New York: Columbia University Press, 1954), x, 350 pp.; *Documents on Communism, Nationalism, and Soviet Advisers in China, 1918-1927: Papers Seized in the 1927 Peking Raid* (New York: Columbia University Press, 1956), xviii, 617 pp., edited by C. Martin Wilbur and Julie Lien-ying How; Charles B. McLane's *Soviet Policy and the Chinese Communist Party, 1931-1946* (New York: Columbia University Press, 1958), 310 pp.; and Conrad Brandt's *Stalin's Failure in China, 1924-1927* (Cambridge: Harvard University Press, 1958), xi, 226 pp. The best book on recent Sino-Soviet relations is *Moscow-Peking Axis: Strengths and Strains* (New York: Harper, for the Council on Foreign Relations, 1957) by Howard L. Boorman, Alexander Eckstein, Philip E. Mosely, and Benjamin I. Schwartz. Articles on Sino-Soviet relations appear frequently in a wide variety of publications; Allen S. Whiting's "Contradictions in the Moscow-Peking Axis" (*Journal of Politics,* vol. 20, February 1958, pp. 127-161) deserves special mention.

Among the best general books on contemporary Taiwan are: Joseph W. Ballantine's *Formosa, A Problem for United States Foreign Policy* (Washington, D.C.: Brookings Institution, 1952), 218 pp.; Fred W. Riggs's *Formosa under Chinese Nationalist Rule* (New York: Macmillan, for the American Institute of Pacific Relations, 1952), ix, 195 pp.; H. Maclear Bate's *Report from Formosa* (New York: Dutton, 1952), 290 pp.; and *Taiwan Today* by Han Lih-wu (Taipei: Hwa Kuo Publishing Co., 1951), 157 pp. The geography of Taiwan is described in detail in *Taiwan (Formosa), a Geographical Appreciation,* Foreign Geography Information Series No. 5 (Ottawa: Department of Mines and Technical Surveys, Geographical Branch, 1952), 60 pp. Allen S.

Whiting's "The United States and Taiwan" in *The United States and the Far East* (New York: The American Assembly, Graduate School of Business, Columbia University, December 1956, pp. 173-201), and Richard L. Walker's "Taiwan's Development as Free China" (*Annals of the American Academy of Political and Social Science,* vol. 321, January 1959, pp. 122-135) are both extremely informative.

INDEX

Academy of Sciences (Peking), 262, 264, 366
Acheson, Dean, 419
Afghanistan, 92, 102, 134, 233, 295
AFPFL, *see* Anti-Fascist People's Freedom League
Africa, 74, 90, 213, 235
Afro-Asian bloc in UN, 448
Afro-Asian solidarity, 149, 294, 373
Agrarian reform, 21-22, 40; *see also* Communes
Agriculture, 43, 47, 51-54, 58, 60
Aichi, 275
Aid, economic: Communist Chinese to Asia, 244-50, 296, 317, 377; Soviet Union to Communist China, 220, 226-31, 344, 346, 365-66, 376, 522; U.S. to Asia, 142, 252, 309, 384, 397-402, 417, 421, 423, 525
Aid, military: Soviet Union to Communist China, 220, 366, 375-76; U.S. to Asia, 138-39, 401-2
Aidit, D. N., 494-95, 547
Air Forces, 113, 124
Albania, 245
Aleutians, 124
Alimin, 493, 495
All-China Federation of Trade Unions, 262
All-China Returned Overseas Chinese Association, 190
Alliance Group, 203
Amoy, 175, 385
Amritsar Party Congress, 501
Amur province, 380
Amur River, 228
Andhra faction, 499-501
Annam, 79, 303
Anticolonialism, 323
Anti-Fascist People's Freedom League (AFPFL), 166, 496-98
Anti-Japanese People's Army, 491

Antipest campaigns, 52
"Antirightist" campaign, 30, 363
ANZUS, *see* Australia, New Zealand
Arita, Hachiro, 274
Asia, 5, 74, 96, 110-11, 158-65; and Communist China, 4-5, 19, 36-37, 63, 66-67, 78-79, 81, 88-90, 97-98, 100-1, 213, 234-44; Communist parties in, 150-69, 374, 476-501; and UN, 451; and U.S., 5, 63-64, 82-83, 101, 132-45, 170-71, 300-1, 443-44
Asian-African bloc in UN, 448
Asian-African Solidarity committees, 149, 294
Asian and Pacific Peace Conference, 97-98, 261
Asian Solidarity, 88, 103, 278, 298, 373
Asanuma, Inejiro, 272
Atomic energy, 49, 228
Atomic weapons, *see* Nuclear weapons
Australia, 122, 323

"Baba" Chinese, 180
Baghdad Pact, 134, 309
Baikal, Lake, 118
Bandaranaike, S. W. R. D., 317
Bandung Conference, 87-88, 103-4, 324, 332, 448; and Cambodia, 327; and Chou En-lai, 295, 309; and India, 313; and Japan, 267; and Laos, 327; and Overseas Chinese, 187; and Nepal, 312
"Bandung spirit," 89, 105, 109, 292-93, 297
Bangkok, 208
Bases: Japanese on Taiwan, 419; U.S. in Asia, 123, 132, 144, 418-19; U.S. in Japan, 137-38, 258, 278, 285, 480, 526
Belgium, 232
Berlin, 107, 349, 365, 371
Bhutan, 79, 310-11

561

562   COMMUNIST CHINA AND ASIA

Big Four, 99
Birth control, 54-55
"Blast furnaces," 61
Border issues, 107, 129, 318-20, 322
Borneo, 175-77
"Brain-washing," 20
British Borneo, 176
British Commonwealth, 170; see also Great Britain
Brunei, 175-76
Budapest, 355
Buddhism, 306, 316, 320-21
Bulganin, N. A., 220, 348
Bulgaria, 225
Burma, 90, 103, 121, 152, 167; and Communist China, 78-79, 92, 125, 129-31, 161-62, 166, 177, 232, 240, 243, 249, 295-96, 317-23, 331, 529; Communist party in, 151, 321-22, 495-98; and Nationalist China, 79, 135, 206; "neutralist," 134, 299; and Overseas Chinese, 174-76, 179, 188-89, 199, 205-6, 444; and Soviet Union, 240; and Thailand, 135; and U.S., 134, 142, 321-23, 333
Burmans, 303, 318
Burma Road, 319
Burma Workers' and Peasants' party, 497
Burma Workers' party, 497

Cabinet (State Council), Chinese Communist, 27
Cairo Declaration, 410
Calcutta, 90, 152, 163, 493, 496, 499
Cambodia, 99, 121-22, 299; and Communist China, 102, 125, 159, 233, 242-43, 245, 247-48, 295-96, 326-27, 331, 529; Communist party in, 482-83; "neutralist," 134; and North Vietnam, 482-83; and Overseas Chinese, 175-76, 179, 189, 199, 205-6; and South Vietnam, 135; and U.S., 134, 333
Canada, 446
Canton, 160
Cantonese, 175
Capital goods, 215, 218, 284
Central Committee, of Chinese Communist party, 14, 16-17, 33-34, 156, 190, 217; and communes, 22-23, 369-70
"Central Kingdom," 66-67

Ceylon, 103; and Communist China, 92, 102, 295-96, 316-17, 529; and Communist Chinese aid and trade, 97, 216, 232, 241, 243, 245, 248-50; "neutralist," 134, 299
Changchun railway, 228
Ch'en Ch'eng, 392, 397
Cheng Ch'eng-kung, 386
Ch'en Po-ta, quoted, 534
Ch'en Yi, 116, 275, 277, 389, quoted, 512
Chiang Ching-kuo, 392
Chiang K'ai-shek, 389, 412, 423-26, 480; and Asian nations, 135, 273, 307; and Chou En-lai, 406-7; and "liberation," 466; quoted, 405-6, 412; regime of, 342, 391-93; and Taiwan, 388, 410
Ch'in Dynasty, 28
Chin Peng, 486-87
China: and Japan, 2-3; and Soviet Union, 3; and Taiwan, 385-87; and UN, 446-47; and U.S., 3; and Vietnam, 303-4; and West, 2; see also China, Communist; China, Nationalist; Taiwan
China, Communist: and Afghanistan, 92, 233; and Africa, 235; and Albania, 245; and Annam, 79; and Asia, 4-5, 19, 36-37, 63, 66-67, 78-79, 81, 88-90, 97-98, 100-1, 147-71, 234-44; and atomic weapons, 110, 115-17, 258, 273, 309, 366; and Belgium, 232; and Bhutan, 79; and border issues, 36, 107, 129, 134, 374; and Bulgaria, 225; and Burma, 78-79, 125-31, 161-62, 232, 240, 243, 249, 295-96, 317-23, 495-98; and Cambodia, 102, 125, 233, 242-43, 245, 247-48, 259, 296, 326-27, 482-83; and Ceylon, 14-17, 97, 102, 232, 241, 243, 245, 248-50, 296, 316-17; communes in, 14, 19, 22-25, 32, 61; and Asian Communist parties, 150-69, 476-501; and Czechoslovakia, 222; and Denmark, 92, 233; disaffection in, 10-11, 29-34; and East Europe, 213, 377, 379; and East Germany, 222, 512; economic aspects of, 38-64, 212-54, 459; education in, 19; and Egypt, 102, 232, 239, 245, 248; and Finland, 92, 102, 233; and France, 232; at Geneva, 433, 435; and Germany,

INDEX 563

454-55; and Ghana, 102; and Great Britain, 92, 232-33, 241, 436, 454; heritage of, 67-68; and Hong Kong, 78-79, 239; and Hungary, 29, 225, 245, 361; and India, 78, 92, 97, 103, 107-9, 129, 161, 232, 235, 243, 292-93, 296, 301, 306-15, 374, 499-501, 531-32; and Indo-China, 98-100; and Indonesia, 92, 104, 108, 161, 232, 240, 249, 296, 323-25, 492-95; and Iraq, 102, 233; and Israel, 92; and Italy, 232; and Japan, 78-80, 97, 108, 111, 116, 160-61, 213, 225, 232-33, 235-38, 242-43, 250, 255-87, 454, 487-90, 526; and Korea, 78-79, 93, 159-60, 287-90, 476-77; and Korean War, 94, 97, 114-15, 435, 454; and Laos, 108, 159, 249, 292, 296, 327-29, 482-85; and Lebanon, 233; and Macao, 78-79; and Malaya, 102, 159, 162, 241, 243, 296, 332, 485-88; and Marxism, 15, 20, 26, 30, 68; and Middle East, 232, 235, 239; military in, 12-14, 27, 56, 78-79, 108-46; and minorities, 27-29; and Morocco, 102, 233; and Nepal, 79, 102, 233, 245, 248, 296; and Netherlands, 92, 102, 232; and North Korea, 78, 119, 125, 160, 225, 245-47, 291, 379; and Norway, 92, 102; and offshore islands, 113, 367, 414-16; and Okinawa, 79; and Outer Mongolia, 78-79, 245-47, 377-78; and Overseas Chinese, 175, 185-209; and Pakistan, 92, 102, 233, 239-40, 296, 315-16; and Philippines, 161-62, 232-33, 242, 296, 329-30, 491-92; and Poland, 222, 225, 354, 360, 435; police in, 19; political parties in, 18; population problem in, 54-55; purges in, 15; and Quemoy, 113; and Rumania, 225; and Ryukyu Islands, 79; and Singapore, 159, 241, 243, 332, 488-90; and South Asia, 291-301, 306-17; and Southeast Asia, 64, 98-99, 128-29, 242-44, 250, 291-333; and South Korea, 128; and South Vietnam, 242, 296, 329, 509; and Soviet Union, 12, 30, 47-48, 72, 78, 82, 87-90, 95, 105-7, 110-11, 114, 117-18, 212-13, 215, 219-31, 253-54, 258, 337-81, 460-61, 511; and Sudan, 102, 232; and Sweden, 92, 233; and Switzerland, 92, 232; and Syria, 102, 232; and Taiwan, 92, 98, 102-3, 113, 125-27, 367, 373, 401, 406-9, 418, 424; and Thailand, 159, 242-43, 296, 330-32, 490-91; and Tibet, 13, 28-29, 82, 92-93, 95, 100, 108, 125, 293, 295, 308; and Tunisia, 233; and United Arab Republic, 233; and United Kingdom, 102; and UN, 95, 410, 447-53, 544-45; and U.S., 4-9, 21, 72, 79-80, 82-86, 92-93, 97, 99, 102, 104, 110-11, 128-29, 131, 140, 214, 221, 231-33, 250-54, 305, 316, 430-45, 447-58, 510, 544-45; and Vietminh, 291, 304; and Vietnam, 78, 159, 304-6, 480-82; and West, 225; and West Germany, 232; and Yemen, 233, 249; and Yugoslavia, 102, 107, 354, 356, 360, 364

"China differential," 454

China, Nationalist, 11-12, 102, 121, 135, 160, 342-44, 367, 433, 466-67; and Burma, 79, 135, 319, 321; and Chiang regime, 391-93; economic aspects of, 39, 56; and India, 79, 307; and Indonesia, 324; and Japan, 237, 260, 263-64, 266, 269, 271, 275, 279, 340, 429; and Lebanon, 366; and offshore islands, 127, 414-16; and Outer Mongolia, 79; and Overseas Chinese, 135, 173, 182-83, 186, 193, 198-200, 205, 208; and Quemoy, 113; and Soviet Union, 341, 452-53; and Taiwan, 79, 384-429; and Thailand, 331; and Tibet, 79; and U.S., 1, 93, 103, 122-23, 138, 139, 384, 416-17, 439, 464; and recognition issue, 439, 442-43; and Vietnam, 304; *see also* Taiwan

China Pictorial, 148

Chinese Communist party: and armed forces, 12-14, 27, 115; and Asia, 150-69, 374, 476-501; and Chinese revolution, 3-4; congresses of, 17, 41, 353-54; early history of, 2-3; organization and power of, 13-17; and Overseas Chinese, 191; and Soviet Union, 150, 338-39, 362-65; in Thailand, 159

Chinese revolution, 3-4, 156

Ch'ing Dynasty, 182, 303, 386

Chins, 318

Chou En-lai, 33-34, 57, 65, 68, 100, 348, 360; at Bandung, 103-4, 327;

and Burma, 320, 529; and Cambodia, 529; and Ceylon, 317, 530; in Geneva, 99; and India, 309, 529; in Indonesia, 324; and Japan, 264-68, 270-73, 277-78, 525; and Korean truce, 347; in Moscow, 346, 358; and Nepal, 312, 530; and Overseas Chinese, 187; and Pakistan, 529; quoted, 79, 94, 100-1, 185-86, 188-89, 510; and Southeast Asia, 295, 373, 529-30; and Taiwan, 102; and UN, 94; and U.S., 93-94, 406-8

Chu Jung-fu, quoted, 518

Churchill, Winston, 388

Citizenship issue, 183, 187-88, 194-95, 204, 207-8; *see also* Overseas Chinese

"Colombo Powers," 103, 317

Colonial and underdeveloped areas, 74

Colonialism, Western, in Southeast Asia, 297-98

Colonial problems, in Communist China, 27-29

Cominform, 96, 152, 165, 364, 500

Comintern, 150-51, 338, 340, 476, 481, 485, 491

"Committee for the Settlement of the February 28th Incident," 389

Committee of One Million against the Admission of Communist China to the UN, 469

Common Program, 91, 185, 190

Communes, 14, 19, 22-25, 32, 61; *see also* Communization program

Communications media, in Communist China, 19

Communist party: in Burma, 151, 321-22, 495-98; in Cambodia, 482-83; in India, 161-62, 313-14, 499-501; in Indo-China, 160; in Indonesia, 161, 324, 492-95; in Japan, 160, 166, 257-59, 263, 279, 478-81, 485; in Korea, 159-60, 162, 476-77; in Laos, 159, 163, 482-85; in Malaya, 151, 159, 162, 203, 332, 458-88; in North Vietnam, 160; in Singapore, 488-90; in Soviet Union, 15-16, 151-52, 157-65, 362; in Thailand, 151, 159, 490-91; in Vietnam, 159, 162, 480-82; *see also* Chinese Communist party

Communist Party of Burma, 161, 496-98; *see also* Communist party, in Burma

Communist Party of Thailand, 159, 490; *see also* Communist party, in Thailand

Communization program, 313, 369-71; *see also* Communes

"Competitive coexistence," 96, 105, 108-9, 125-26, 212, 243, 250, 292, 295-96, 320, 371

Control Yuan, 183

Conference of Asian and African Countries, *see* Bandung Conference

Conference of Asian and Australasian Trade Unions, 152

Conference of Asian Countries (New Delhi), 103

Congress, U.S., 103, 123, 469

Congresses: Seventh, of Chinese Communist party, 17, Eighth, 17, 41, 353-54; Second, of Indian Communist party, 152; Seventh, of Japanese Communist party, 480; Nineteenth, of Communist party of Soviet Union, 96, 346, Twentieth, 96, 106, 157-58, 349-51, 353, Twenty-first, 370

Congress party, Indian, 500

Conscription, 112

Constitution, Chinese Communist provisional, 91

Consumer goods, 49-51, 215, 218

"Contradictions" in Socialist states, 30, 358-60

Corruption, 18

"Counterrevolutionaries, campaign against," 21

Courts, 19

Cuba, 452

Cyrankiewicz, Jozef, 360

Czechoslovakia, 222

Dairen, 341, 345

Dalai Lama, 28, 293, 314-16

Declaration of Twelve Communist and Workers' Parties, 158, 362

Dedijer, Vladimir, 342

Denmark, 92, 233

De-Stalinization, 349-51

Dienbienphu, 99

Diet, Japanese, 259-61, 263-65, 268-69, 271, 281-82, 480

Dietmen's League for the Promotion of Sino-Japanese Trade, 263-64, 278

Disarmament, 145-46, 441

Djarkarta, 108, 165, 493

INDEX

Dulles, John Foster, 412-13, 430-31, 439, 447, 453-55, 469; in Japan, 260; quoted, 467
Dutch, 183, 323, 386, 492-93; *see also* Netherlands
Dutch New Guinea, 323

Eastern Europe, 351-55, 363, 369, 377, 379; *see also* Satellites, East European
East Germany, 222-23, 362, 512
East Indies, 183
"East wind," doctrine of Mao, 106-7, 364
Ebert, Friedrich, 362
"Economic Problems of Socialism in the U.S.S.R.," 96, 157
Economist party, 490-91
Economy, of Communist China, 21-25, 38-64, 212-54, 282-84, 459; "great leap forward," 31, 33; and Overseas Chinese, 177-79, 193-94; and Soviet Union, 219-31, 376-77
Economy, of Taiwan, 387-88, 397-99
Education, 19
Egypt, 102, 232, 239, 245, 248
Eisenhower, Dwight D., 412, 414, 466, quoted, 418
Embargo, U. S. on Communist China, 233, 253, 453-55
Endo, Saburo, 270
Exchange rate, dollar-yüan, dollar-ruble, 504
Exchanges of persons, 149; *see also* People's diplomacy
"Ex-Comrades Associations," 486
Expansionism, in China, 66-67
Exports, 216-19, 234, 243

Factories, small, 59
Far Eastern Bureau, Comintern, 150, 476, 485
Farming, in China, 39, 55
Fifth U.S. Air Force, 124
Finance and banking controls, 56
Finland, 92, 102, 233
"Five Anti" campaign, 21-22, 40
"Five principles," 358; *see also* "Peaceful coexistence"
Five Year Plan, First, 41-46, 49-50, 55-56, 58, 97, 220, 346; and agriculture, 52; and foreign aid, 244-45; growth during, 62, 214; and Soviet Union, 48, 227, 229; and trade, 215, 218, 223, 235
Five Year Plan, Second, 41-42, 46, 58, 228, 231, 245; and Soviet Union, 220, 226
Fisheries, 270, 275
Foochow, 385
Food shortages, 62
Foreign Languages Press (Peking), 148
Foreign policy, Chinese Communist, 71, 77-83, 87-109, 187-89, 255-87, 295-333, 373; U.S., 35-37, 64, 83-86, 139-45, 209-10, 250-54, 333-36, 381-83, 409-17, 427-75
Formosa, 123, 385; *see also* Taiwan
Formosan Democratic Independence party, 396
Four-Year Plan, Taiwan, 398
France, 121-22, 232, 248, 319, 331; and Indo-China, 98, 136; and Vietnam, 303-4, 481
Free China, 408
Free Kmer movement, 483
Free Lao movement, 483
Free Thai movement, 330
Fukien, 114, 174, 186, 385-86

Gandhian tradition, 298
Gawlun, 322
General Assembly, 367, 410, 451, 452; *see also* United Nations
General Assembly of the International Astronomical Union, 457
General Council of Japanese Labor Unions, 262
General Labor Union, 486
"General Line of the State," 41, 46-47
Geneva Conference, 79, 88, 99-100, 102, 295; and Communist China, 433; and India, 309; and Japan, 267; and U.S., 424, 435; and Vietnam, 304-5
"Geneva Spirit," 105
Germany, 255, 371, 454
Ghana, 102
Ghosh, Ajoy, 500
Goa, 309
Gomulka, Wladyslaw, 354, 358, 362
Great Britain, 121-22, 248, 331, 341, 427; and Burma, 318-19, 496; and Communist China, 92, 232-33, 241, 254, 454; and Hong Kong, 202; and India, 310-12; and Malaya, 134, 302, 332, 485-86, 488; and Overseas Chi-

nese, 201; and Singapore, 489; and U.S., 436, 446, 452
"Great leap forward," 31, 33, 42, 46, 58-62
Great-power status, for Communist China, 6, 65-66, 460
Gross, Ernest A., quoted, 544
Gross national product, 45-46
Guam, 123-24
Guerrillas, 12-13, 130, 163, 198, 330, 339, 491
"Guided democracy," 325
Guinea, 102

Hailams, 175
Hainan Island, 175
Hakkas, 175, 385
Han Chinese, 27-28, 378
Han Dynasty, 28, 287
"Hard" tactics, 105-8, 157, 361-65
Harriman, Averell, 117
Hatoyama, Ichiro, 265-67
Helsinki, 268
Herter, Christian A., 425
Himalayan frontier area, 310-15
Hinayana Buddhism, 298
Ho Chi-minh, 160, 480-82
Ho Hsiang-ning, 189, 191, quoted, 196-97
Hokkiens, 175, 385
Hollister, William W., 45
Hong Kong, 79, 160, 481, 485; and Communist China, 78, 239, 408; and Overseas Chinese, 193, 200-2, 210; and Taiwan, 395, 401
Hpimaw, 322
Hsiang (township), 22-23
Hsüeh hsi (study group), 20
Hukbalahap, 133, 161, 491-92
Humphrey, Hubert H., Jr., 370-71
"Hundred flowers," 36, 313, 363
Hungary, 356, 359; and Communist China, 29, 106, 225, 245, 354-55; revolt in, 31-32, 88-89, 313, 349, 466
Hurley, Patrick J., 340
Hu Shih, 395
Hyderabad, 499

Ideology, Chinese Communists and, 20, 24, 67-76, 368-71
Ili region, 379
"Imperialist camp," 72-75
Import policy, 215-16
Inchon, 94
Income: national, 44-45; personal, 51
India, 103, 120-21, 137, 302, 317, 325; and Asia, 145, 170; and border crisis, 36, 107, 129, 134, 374; and Cambodia, 327; and Communist China, 78, 92, 97, 100, 103, 108-9, 292-93, 296, 301, 307, 529, 531-32; trade with, 232, 235, 243; Communist party in, 161-62, 313-14, 499-501; economic aspects of, 38, 45, 64, 459; and Japan, 307; and Korean truce, 347; and Nationalist China, 79; "neutralist," 134, 299; and Overseas Chinese, 188-89; and Pakistan, 134; and SEATO, 136, 322; and Tibet, 28, 295; and UN, 446, 453; and U.S., 134, 141, 309, 443, 446, 531-32
Indians, in Singapore, 176
Indo-China, 90, 98, 102, 136, 151-52, 301; and Communist China, 98-100; Communist party in, 160; crisis in, 6, 88; and Geneva, 295; *see also* Vietnam
Indo-China War, 122, 483
Indonesia: Communist China and, 92, 104, 108, 232, 240, 296, 323-25; Communist party in, 161, 324, 492-95; and U.S., 134, 142, 323-25
Industry, 40-43, 48-51, 60-61, 214
Inflation, 40, 56-57
Inner Mongolia, 11, 27, 49, 342, 378-79
Intercontinental Ballistic Missile, 106, 363; *see also* Missiles
International Cooperation Administration, 401
International Economic Conference, 95, 97
International Trade Promotion Association, 265-66
Investment program, 42-43, 57
Iraq, 102, 107-8, 233, 365, 371
Irrawaddy-Salween watershed, 322
Irrigation works, 60
Iselin, Colonel, 319
Ishibashi, Tanzan, 278
Islam, 180
Israel, 92
Italy, 232

Jao Shu-shih, 16, 26, 33
Japan, 90, 120, 235, 256, 301, 397; and Asia, 145, 170, 297; and China, 2-3,

67; and Communist China, 38, 78-80, 108, 111, 116, 160-61, 250, 255-87, 340, 526; trade with, 97, 213, 221, 225, 232-38, 242-43, 261-64, 454; Communist party in, 160, 166, 257-59, 263, 279, 478-81, 485; economic aspects of, 45, 64; and India, 307; and Korea, 135, 256, 287; and Manchuria, 39; military in, 110, 120; and Nationalist China, 237, 260-61, 263-64, 266, 269, 275, 279, 429; and Soviet Union, 269, 341, 371; and Taiwan, 387-88, 390, 397, 401, 410; and UN, 269, 372; and U.S., 93, 108, 122-23, 133-34, 137-38, 141, 252-53, 255-56, 258, 260, 263-65, 267, 273, 277, 280-82, 285-87; and World War II, 5

Japan-China Cinema Society, 278
Japan-China Cultural Exchange Association, 278
Japan-China Fisheries Association, 262
Japan-China Fishery Problems Council, 265
Japan-China Friendship Association, 262, 277-78
Japan-China Music and Dancing Society, 278
Japan-China Translations Society, 278
Japan Council of Science, 262
"Japanese Emancipation League," 160, 478
Japanese League for the Protection of the Constitution, 269, 278
Japanese National Council for the Repatriation of Japanese Nationals Overseas, 262
"Japanese Peasants' and Workers' School," 160, 478
Japan International Trade Promotion Association, 278
Japan Peace Liaison Committee, 262, 278
Java, 162, 301, 324, 494
Jefferson, Thomas, 434
Joint Committee on Rural Reconstruction, 398
Joint Resolution of the Defense of Taiwan, 123
"Joint state-private enterprises," 47
Joshi, P. C., 499
Journalists, U.S., in Communist China, 7, 456-57

Kachins, 130, 167, 318, 321
Kadar, Janos, 245, 358
Kalimpong, 314
Kangkang, 322
Kao Kang, 16, 26, 33, 344
Karen revolt, 318-19, 496
Kashmir, 121, 134, 309, 311, 316
Katmandu, 312
Katsumata, Seichi, 271
Kazakhs, 379
Kerala, 162, 164, 500-1
Khrushchev, N. S., 82, 157, 354, 367-68, 373; on communes, 370; and Communist China, 118, 220, 226, 231, 380; on "contradictions," 360; in Peking, 107, 116-17, 348, 366, 368; quoted, 111, 211, 511; and Stalin, 29, 106, 347, 349-51, 363; to U.S., 293, 368, 374
Kiangsi, 339
Kim, Il-Sung, 159, 476
Kinmen, 385; *see also* Quemoy
Kishi, Nobusuke, 108, 237-38, 272-77, 279, quoted, 281
Kmer Issarak Front, 483
Korea, 90, 95, 128, 303, 320, 441; and Communist China, 56, 78, 93, 287-90, 449; Communist party in, 159-60, 162, 476-77; and Japan, 287; and Russia, 287; and Soviet Union, 288-89, 371, 378; and UN, 288-90; and U.S., 93, 288-89; *see also* North Korea, South Korea
Korean War, 5-6, 88, 92-98, 128, 244, 258, 466; and Communist China, 36, 94, 101, 112, 114-15, 213, 219, 241, 454; and Hong Kong, 239; and Japan, 256, 263; and Overseas Chinese, 199; settlement of, 41, 99, 259-60, 406, 433, 435; and Soviet Union, 345, 347, 378; and Taiwan, 405, 410, 419; and UN, 79; and U.S., 122, 253, 308, 345, 390, 435; and Vietminh, 481
Korean Workers' party, 477
Kotelawala, Sir John, 316-17
Kowloon Peninsula, 202
Krishna Menon, V. K., 308
Kuhara, Fusanosuke, 268
Kuomintang, 2, 91, 338, 378, 391, 480-81; and Burma, 496; and France, 304; and Malaya, 485; and Overseas Chinese, 183, 207; on Taiwan, 393-95, 422

Kuo Mo-jo, 264, 269
Kuo yü, 180, 182
Kurile Islands, 341
Kwangsi, 304
Kwangtung, 174-75, 186
Kyaw Nyein-Ba Swe group, 497
Kyaw Nyein, U, quoted, 532

Labor party, British, 452
Labor party, Vietnamese, 481
Labor force, 61-62
Labor shortages, 57
Ladakh, 310-11, 314
Landlords, 52
Lao Dong (Labor) party, 159, 481-83
Lao Patriotic Front, 484
Laos, 99, 121-22, 164, 303, 305; and Cambodia, 326; and Communist China, 108, 249, 292-93, 296, 327-29; Communist party in, 159, 163, 482-85; and Overseas Chinese, 174-75, 177; "neutralist," 299; and North Vietnam, 160, 327-28, 482-84; revolt in, 36, 81, 107, 131, 134, 143, 168-69, 306; and UN, 130, 328; and U.S., 123, 134, 138, 202, 299, 327-28, 333
Lao Union party, 484
Latin America, 74, 451
League of Nations, 319
Lebanon, 107-8, 233, 365-66, 371
Lee Kuan-yew, 389
Legislative Yuan, 182
Lenin, Nikolai, 74, 150
Leninism, 68; *see also* Marxism-Leninism
"Let All Flowers Bloom Together," 29
Lhasa, 312
Liaison Bureau, 98
Liao, Thomas, 396-97
Liberal Democratic party, 280
Lien Viet, 481
Li Fu-ch'un, quoted, 227
Liuchow Peninsula, 114
Lin Piao, 117
Liu Shao-ch'i, 33-34, 154-57, 268, 270, 346; quoted, 73-74, 80, 90, 153, 343
Liu, T. C., 45
Loi Tek, 486
London, 269, 499
"Long March," 339
Lu Ting-yi, 156
Luzon, 301, 491

Macao, 78-79, 200
MacArthur, Douglas, 388, 410, 418
McMahon Line, 311, 532
Magsaysay, Ramón, 491-92
Malaka, Tan, 492
Malaya, 90, 121, 152, 170, 397, 485-86; and Communist China, 102, 168, 241, 243, 296, 329, 332; Communist party in, 151, 159, 162, 203, 332, 485-88; "neutralist," 299; and Overseas Chinese, 173, 175-76, 180-81, 197, 203-4, 208-9, 216, 330, 445; and UN, 98; and U.S., 134
Malayan Chinese Association, 203
Malayan People's Anti-British Army, 486
Malayan People's Anti-Japanese Army, 485-86
Malayan Races Liberation Army, 486
Malenkov, Georgi, 380
"Malthusian counterrevolution," 55-56; *see also* "Neo-Malthusianism"
Manchu Dynasty, 28, 303, 318, 386
Manchuria, 27, 95, 341, 345, 388; and Communist China, 11, 344; industry in, 39, 49; and Overseas Chinese, 174; and Soviet Union, 279, 342; railways in, 114, 228, 345-46
Mao Tse-tung, 27, 34-35, 38, 79, 339, 354, 362, 367, 392; ideology of, 15, 29, 30, 69-70, 73, 75-76, 156, 161, 352-53, 358-60, 365, 369, 475, 493-94, 499-500, 508; and Japan, 268-70, 478; in Moscow, 361, 363-64; quoted, 16, 67-68, 75-76, 90, 106-7, 343, 364, 378; and Soviet Union, 89, 231, 273, 344, 347; and Stalin, 93, 340, 351; strategy of, 65, 76-77; in Warsaw, 360-61
Maritime Provinces, Soviet, 78, 118, 380
Marxism-Leninism, 54, 279, 298, 350, 364, 496, 536-37; and Communist China, 15, 20, 26, 30, 68-69, 348, 357-58, 368-71; and Mao, 15, 156-57, 343, 352-53
"Mass line," 18
Matsu, 385
Matsumura, Kenzo, 278
May Day, Chinese, 165
Mendès-France, Pierre, 99

INDEX

Middle East, 74, 108, 232, 235, 239, 371, 373, 451
"Middle Kingdom," 173
Mikoyan, Anastas, 220, 226, 230, 348, 353
Military power, 110-46; of Communist China, 12-14, 24, 27, 56, 63, 108-9, 112, 114, 125-26, 459-60; of U.S., 119
"Min Yuen" units, 487
Ming Dynasty, 28, 318, 386
Minorities, in Communist China, 27-29
Missiles, 106, 110, 124, 363
"Mobile striking force," 128
Molotov, Vyacheslav, 340, 363, 380
"Mongolian People's Republic," 341
Mongols, 28, 95, 318
"Monroe Doctrine" for Asia, 66
Morocco, 102, 233
Moscow, 16, 82, 106-7, 150, 153; Chou in, 346, 358; economic conference in, 95, 97; Mao in, 361-62; *see also* Soviet Union
Mukden, 92
Murata, Shozo, 266
Muslims, 315
Musso, 493
Mutual Defense Treaty, 411
Mutual Economic Assistance Council, 224
Myitkyina, 319, 322

Nagasaki, 275
Nagy, Imre, 355
Nai Prasert Sapsunthorn, 167
Namboodiripad, E. M. S., 500
Namwan Assigned Tract, 319, 322
Nanchao Kingdom, 318
Nanyang General Labor Union, 485
Nasser, Gamal Abdel, 248
Nasution, Abdul Haris, 494
National Assembly, Chinese, 182; Thai, 491
National Council for Banning Atomic and Hydrogen Bombs, 278
National Council for the Restoration of Diplomatic Relations with China and the Soviet Union, 265, 268, 277-78
National Day, Chinese, 165, 191, 479
National Defense Agency, 496
Nationalism, in China, 67, 180, 182-83; in Southeast Asia, 183-85

Nationalist party, Chinese, *see* Kuomintang
Nationalist party, Laotian, 483-84
National People's Congress, 30, 190, 270
National United Front, 161, 322, 497-98
NATO, 122, 135, 452
Navy, Chinese Communist, 113
Naw Seng, 167, 321
Near East, 90
Nehru, Jawaharlal, 104, 168, 327, 500; and Communist China, 100, 295, 307-9; and Communist party, 313-14, 501; and Overseas Chinese, 188, 310
Neo Lao Hak Xat, 160, 163, 484-85
"Neo-Malthusianism," 54; *see also* "Malthusian counterrevolution"
Nepal, 167, 311-12; and Communist China, 79, 102, 233, 245, 248, 295-96, 313, 530; "neutralist," 134, 299
Netherlands, 92, 102, 232
Netherlands East Indies, 151
Neutralism, 101, 105, 133-34, 332-33, 528-29; and Burma, 317-18, 333; and Cambodia, 326-27; and Ceylon, 316-17; and Communist China, 73-74, 213, 247-50; and Japan, 279, 281; and Laos, 328; and Southeast Asia, 299-301; and U.S., 142; *see also* Nonaligned nations
New China News Agency, 148
New Delhi, 100, 103
Ne Win, 498
New Territories, 202
"New Villages," 487
New York Times, 117
New Zealand, 122
Ngo Dinh Diem, 305-6, 329, 482, 531
Nonaligned nations, 73-74, 84, 105, 299, 307, 324, 528; *see also* Neutralism
Nonrecognition, 430-58; *see also* Recognition issue
North Atlantic Treaty Organization (NATO), 122, 135, 452
Northeast Asia, 145, 285, 287
Northeast Frontier Agency, 310-11, 314
North Korea, 111, 131, 164; and Communist China, 78, 119, 125, 165, 225, 245-47
North Korean Workers' party, 477

North Vietnam, 100, 130, 174, 379, 546; and Cambodia, 326-27, 482-83; and Communist China, 78-79, 114, 160, 165, 225, 245-47, 291, 295; and Laos, 163, 293, 327-28, 482-84; military in, 111, 119, 121, 125, 131

Northwest China-Soviet Central Asia Railroad, 49

Northwest-Southwest China Railroad, 49

Norway, 92, 102

Nozaka, Sanzo, 160, 478-79

Nuclear weapons: Asia and, 137, 141; Communist China and, 110, 115-17, 258, 273, 309, 366; Soviet Union and, 345, 375-76; U.S. and, 124-25, 137, 141

Nu, U, 100, 295, 317-18, 320, 322, 497-98; quoted, 323

Occupation, of Japan, 478-79

Ochab, Edward, 354

October Revolution, 74, 156, 343, 348, 361; *see also* Russian Revolution

Offshore islands, 77-78, 102-3, 121, 127, 385; and Communist China, 113, 367, 414-16; crises, 6, 107, 112, 384, 410-13, 513; and Nationalist China, 414-16; and U.S., 411, 413-16, 419-21, 423-26, 468

Okinawa, 79, 123, 138, 258, 278, 281, 419

"On the Correct Handling of Contradictions among the People," 30

Organization of European Economic Cooperation, 235

Outer Mongolia, 78-79, 114, 228, 245-47, 269, 341, 345, 377-78

Overseas Chinese, 135, 151, 172-210, 241, 243, 514-17; assimilation of, 179-81, 203-9; and Burma, 321-22, 444; and Cambodia, 327; and Communist China, 187-94; dialects of, 175; and Hong Kong, 200-2; and India, 310; and Indonesia, 104, 325, 444, 495, 517; and Malaya, 159, 332, 445; and Nationalist China, 182, 198-200, 400, 423; and Philippines, 161, 492; and Singapore, 444-45; and Southeast Asia, 296, 444-45; and Thailand, 159, 330-31, 444-45, 490; and U.S., 209-10, 440, 444-45

Overseas Chinese Affairs Commission, 189-90

Pacific Ocean, 123
Pagan Dynasty, 318
Pak, Heung-Yeung, 477
Pakistan, 103, 120-22, 136, 299, 317; and Communist China, 92, 102, 135, 233, 239-40, 295-96, 315-16, 529; and U.S., 134, 309, 333
Panmunjom, 435
Panikkar, K. M., 94, 116
Pan-Pacific Trade Union Secretariat, 151
Parliament, Indonesian, 493
Parties, political, in Communist China, 18
Pathet Lao, 130, 160, 163, 169, 293, 306; and Communist China, 130, 249, 327-28; and North Vietnam, 130, 166
Pathet Lao United Front, 483-85
Peace committees, 149
Peace conferences, 97-98, 268
"Peaceful coexistence," 74, 81-82, 87-88, 108, 126, 132, 168, 209, 213; and Communist China, 36; "five principles," 100-1, 196, 294-96, 306, 324; and Hungary, 355; and India, 309; *see also* "Five principles"
Peace Treaty, Japanese, 258-60, 265, 268, 309, 345, 427
Peasants, Chinese Communist, 32, 51, 59-60
Peking, 92, 165, 189, 262, 265, 322, 327-28, 330; conferences in, 89-91, 97, 152; Khrushchev in, 107, 116-17, 348, 366, 368
P'eng Teh-huai, quoted, 117-18, 408
Penghus, 385; *see also* Pescadores
People's Action party, 162, 203, 489
People's China, 148
"People's Committees," 486
People's Comrades party, 497
People's Daily, 262, 364, 370, quoted, 276
"People's Democracies," 72
"People's diplomacy," 97-98, 103, 148-50, 257, 261-63, 265, 308; and Japan, 268-69; and Southeast Asia, 296, 320
"People's Group," 483
People's Liberation Army, 12, 95, 111, 491
People's Volunteer Organization, 496

INDEX

"Peranakan," 180
Pescadores, 77-79, 103, 127, 385, 410-11; and China, 386, 410; defense of, 123, 409, 412; and Japan, 260, 387-88
Pham Van Dong, 530-31
Phibul Songgram, 167, 331, 490-91
Philippines, 120-21, 124, 136, 302, 419; and Communist China, 90, 204-5, 242, 296, 329-30, 332-33; Communist party in, 161-62, 166, 491-92; and Japan, 135; and neutrality, 299; Overseas Chinese, 175-77, 179, 187, 189, 199; and U.S., 122-23, 133, 137, 329-30, 333
Phong Saly, 483
Poland, 222-23, 225, 358, 360, 456; crisis in, 89, 349, 351, 354
Police, Communist Chinese, 19
Politburo: Chinese, 14, 16-17, 33, 350, 356, 358; Indian, 499
Population problem, 54-55, 380
Port Arthur, 79, 341, 345-46, 348
Portugal, 386
Potsdam Conference, 304, 388, 410
Power, balance of in Asia, 110-46
Poznan, 349
Pracheachon party, 483
Prasert Sapsunthorn, Nai, 167
Pravda, 156, 359
Press, Communist Chinese, quoted, 65
Pridi Phanomyong, 167, 330
Prisoner-of-war issue: Japanese, 262, 264, 267, 270, 478; Korean, 308
Proletarian party, 167, 490
Propaganda, Communist, *see* Subversion
Provincial Council, 395

Quemoy, 385, 412-14; crises over, 36, 113, 124, 201, 367, 415
Quirino, Elpidio, 491
Quotas, export, 217

Race prejudice, 298
"Radio Free Japan," 95, 160, 261, 332, 479
Rahman, Tungku Abdul, 488
Railways, 49, 114, 118, 228, 348, 377; in Manchuria, 341, 345-46
Ranadive, B. T., 499-500
Rangoon, 100, 165, 320; *see also* Burma
Rao, Rajeshwar, 499-500
Recognition of Communist China: issue in Japan, 256-57, 259-60, 279, 282; action by other governments, 91-92; question of in U.S., 323, 334, 431-45; *see also* Nonrecognition
"Rectification" campaign, 15-16, 30-31, 115
Red Cross, 270; Chinese, 262, 264; Japanese, 262, 264, 278
"Red Flag" Communists, 161, 496
Red River Valley, 301
Regionalism, in Communist China, 26-27
Republic of China, *see* China, Nationalist
"Resist-America Aid-Korea" campaign, 21
Returned Overseas Chinese Associations, 190
Revolutions and insurrections, Communist, 10, 152
Revisionism, 366-67
Rhee, Syngman, 90, 135, 288-89, 329, 466
Robertson, Walter S., 469, quoted, 513-14
Roces, Jesus Marcos, 330
Roosevelt, Franklin D., 388
Rumania, 225
Russia, 287; *see also* Soviet Union
Russian Revolution, 2, 106, 147; *see also* October Revolution
Russo-Japanese War, 5, 287
Ryukyu Islands, 79

Saipan, 144
Sajap Kiri, 493
Sakhalin, 341
Sam Neua, 483
Sananikone, Phoui, 328, 484
San Francisco Conference, 259, 268, 427
San Marino, 500
Sarawak, 175-76
Sardjono, 493
Sarit Thanarat, 208, 331, 491
Sastroamidjojo, Ali, 324
Satellite, earth, 106; *see also* Sputnik
Satellites, East European, 106, 213, 223; *see also* East Europe
Scandinavia, 170
SEATO, *see* Southeast Asia Collective Defense Treaty
Security Council, 328, 366-67, 450-53
Senate, Chinese, 182

Seventh U.S. Fleet, 93, 124, 390, 405, 416
Seven-Year Plan, 370
Shanghai, 38-39, 150, 476, 485
Shan States, 318-19, 321
Shantung Peninsula, 114
Shensi, 339
Shigemitsu, Mamoru, 265-66
Shimonoseki, Treaty of, 387
Siam, 90, 303; *see also* Thailand
Siberia, 114, 380
Sihanouk, Norodom, 206, 327, 483, quoted, 326
Sikkim, 311, 314
Singapore, 159, 162, 241, 243, 332; and Overseas Chinese, 173, 175-76, 180-81, 193, 197, 203, 208-9, 330, 444-45; Communist party in, 488-90
Singh, K. I., 167
Sinkiang, 11, 27, 228, 344-45, 379; and railroad, 49, 114, 348
Sino-Japanese Trade Promotion Council, 262-63
Sino-Japanese War, 182, 255, 287, 319, 340, 387, 485
Sino-Soviet Treaty of Friendship, Alliance, and Mutual Assistance, 89, 117-18, 337-83
Sino-Soviet Scientific and Technical Cooperation Commission, 227-28
Sipsongpanna, 330
Sjarifuddin, 493
Social Democratic party, on Taiwan, 393
Socialists, 72-75, 150, 275-76, 298-99; in Japan, 168, 237, 263, 271-72, 274, 277, 279-81
Social revolution in China, 21-25
"Socialization" program, 41-42, 46-47
Society for Research on Contemporary China, 278
Soe, Thakin, 496-97
"Soft" tactics, 105, 157
Souphanouvong, Prince, 484
South Asia, 108, 291-301, 306-17, 333-36, 529-30
South China, 27
South China Sea, 330
Southeast Asia, 81, 135-37, 145, 273, 301-2; and Communist China, 98-99, 128-29, 242-44, 250, 276, 285, 291-333, 371, 481; and Chinese Communist party, 151, 373, 485-86; and Overseas Chinese, 172-209, 444-45
Southeast Asian Collective Defense Treaty, 102, 122, 135-36, 170; and Burma, 322; and Cambodia, 327; and India, 136, 322; and Indonesia, 325; and Malaya, 332; and Pakistan, 134, 315; and Philippines, 330; and Thailand, 331; and U.S., 142
Southeast Asia Youth Conference, 152
South Korea, 128, 135, 443, 445; military in, 119, 121, 141, 404; and U.S., 122-23, 131, 133, 138-39, 256, 329, 443
"South Seas Communist party," 151
South Vietnam, 122, 135, 199, 204-5, 327; and Communist China, 221, 242, 296, 329, 509; military in, 119, 121-22; and neutrality, 299; and U.S., 123, 133, 138, 329, 333, 439, 443
Southwest China, 92
Souvanna Phouma, Prince, 328, 484
Soviet Academy of Science, 156
Soviet Russia in China—A Summing Up at Seventy (Chiang), 405
Soviet Union, 28-29, 35, 68, 74, 82, 89, 97, 105, 116, 145; and Asia, 5, 147-48; and Burma, 240, 498; and China, 3; and Communist China, 12, 30, 47-48, 72, 82, 87-90, 95, 105-7, 110-11, 114, 117-18, 150, 212-13, 215, 219-31, 253-54, 258, 337-81, 415, 436, 460-61, 511; Communist party in, 15-16, 151-52, 157-65, 362; and "competitive coexistence," 105, 212; and East Europe, 377; economic aspects of, 41, 95-96, 250, 454-55; and Hungary, 29, 354-55; and India, 161, 374, 499-500; and Indonesia, 161, 325, 492-93; and Inner Mongolia, 342; and Japan, 160-61, 258, 263-69, 272, 478-80; and Korea, 159-60, 288-89, 378, 476-77; and Manchuria, 39, 342; and Middle East, 373; and Nationalist China, 338, 341, 373, 452-53; and Outer Mongolia, 377-38; and Poland, 354, 356; and Potsdam, 388; and UN, 446; and U.S., 293, 340, 361-62, 368, 374, 382-83, 456, 465; and Vietnam, 304, 379, 480-82; at Yalta, 341; and Yugoslavia, 158, 337, 380
Spain, 235, 386

INDEX

Spratly and Paracel Island groups, 78
"Sputnik" (commune), 22
Sputnik, 106-7, 363
Stalin, Joseph, 29, 96, 106, 338, 341; and Communist China, 93, 340, 342, 344-45, 352, 368; death of, 220, 347; on economy, 38-39, 157; and Khrushchev, 349, 380
Standing Committee of People's Congress, 34
"State capitalism," 47
State Council, 17, 34, 190, 217
State Department, U.S., 430-31, 433, 435, 439-41, 456-57, 467, 545
State Planning Commission, 227
"Straits Chinese," 180
Strategic Air Force, 124
Strategic Army Corps, 143
Subversion, Communist, 147-71, 282, 296, 445, 460
Sudan, 102, 233
Suez invasion, 248, 355
Sukarno, President, 323-24, 494
Sumatra, 177
Summit Conference, 367
Sung Dynasty, 318
Sun Li-jen, 395, 404
Sun Yat-sen, 182, 186, 378, 393
Suzuki, Yoshio, 271, 274
Swatow, 175
Sweden, 92, 233
Switzerland, 92, 232, 328
Syria, 102, 232

Tachen Islands, 103, 407
Tactical Air Force, 124
Tagore, Rabindranath, 307
Taiwan, 77-79, 385-89, 394-401, 417-18; and China, 95; and Communist China, 6, 79, 92, 98, 102-3, 113, 125-27, 367, 401, 406-9, 418, 464; crisis, 88, 371; defense of, 409, 412, 420, 426-27; and Hong Kong, 401; and India, 309; and Japan, 260, 273, 287-88, 397, 401; and Nationalist China, 79, 121, 141, 384-429; and Overseas Chinese, 193, 200, 210, 400, 423; and Philippines, 419; revolt on, 389; and Soviet Union, 348, 373; and UN, 397, 410, 427-28; and U.S., 8, 33, 93, 121-27, 133, 309, 373, 397, 401-9, 418-29, 437-38, 443, 464, 468

"Taiwan Democratic Self-Government League," 396
Taiwanese, 385, 396-97, 422
Taiwan Strait, 93, 124, 365, 367, 406, 413, 424, 542
T'ang Dynasty, 28, 318
Tan Ling Djie, 495
Taruc, Luis, 491
Taxation, 56
Technical assistance: Communist Chinese to Asia, 246-47; Soviet to Communist China, 227
Telengana District, 499-500
Teochius, 175
Thai Autonomous Area, 330
Thailand, 64, 121-22, 299, 481, 546; and Cambodia, 135, 327; and Communist China, 159, 242, 243, 296, 329, 330 32; Communist party in, 151, 159, 490-91; and Nationalist China, 321, 331; and Overseas Chinese, 135, 174-76, 179, 184, 187, 189, 197, 199, 207, 209, 444-45; and SEATO, 122, 135-36, 170; and U.S., 123, 133, 138, 331-33
Thais, 130, 167, 303
Thakin Soe, 496-97
Than Tun, 496-97
Thep Chotinuchit, 491
"Third Force," 201
Thirteenth Air Force, 124
Thirty-eighth Parallel, 79, 94, 288, 308
"Three Anti" campaign, 21-22, 40
"Three People's Principles," 393
Tibet, 27-29, 79, 114, 134, 167; and Communist China, 11, 13, 77-78, 82, 92-93, 95, 100, 108, 125, 293, 295, 308, 310-15; revolt in, 31, 292, 325, 501
Tinian, 144
Tito, Josip Broz, 342, 349, 355, 368; and Communist China, 117, 313, 361
Togliatti, Palmiro, 349
Tokuda, Kyuichi, 160, 478-79
Tokyo, 396-97
Tongking, 303
Trade, Communist Chinese, 97, 211-44, 471-72, 518-19, 523; with Burma, 320; with Cambodia, 327; with Ceylon, 316; with Japan, 108, 257, 259, 261-64, 270-71, 273-74, 276, 279-80, 283-84; and Overseas Chinese, 178, 197; with Pakistan, 315; with Southeast Asia, 296; and U.S., 252, 453-55

Trade, Communist with West, 95-96, 454-55
Trade Union Conference of Asian and Australasian Countries, 89-91, 97
Trade Union Liaison Bureau for Asia and Australasia, 91, 165
Trans-Siberian Railroad, 49
Treaty of Commerce and Navigation, 225
Trotsky, Leon, 338
Truman, Harry S., 93, 389-90, 410
Truong Chinh, 482
Tsedenbal, Premier, 377
Tunisia, 233
Turk-Sib (Turkestan-Siberia) Railroad, 114
Turkey, 235
"Two Chinas" policy, 266, 279, 317, 407, 427-28, 452-53

Uighurs, 28, 379
Underdeveloped countries, 88, 211-12, 295
U.S.S.R., *see* Soviet Union
United Arab Republic, 233
United Front, 70-72, 162, 190
United Kingdom, 102, 122; *see also* Great Britain
United Nations, 98, 144, 170, 446-47, 474; and Ceylon, 232; and Communist China, 94-95, 315, 323, 325, 334, 544-45; and Hong Kong, 202; and India, 308-9; and Japan, 269, 372; and Korea, 93, 288-90, 449; and Korean War, 79, 454; and Laos, 130, 328; and Lebanon, 366-67; and Malaya, 98; and Nationalist China, 93, 321, 390, 397, 410, 427-28; and Outer Mongolia, 269; and U.S., 447-53, 468; and Vietnam, 98
United People's Liberation Front, 479
United States, 7, 125, 142, 212, 250, 435; and Afghanistan, 134; and Asia, 5, 63-64, 82-83, 101, 132-45, 170-71, 300-1, 434-44; and Australia, 122; and Burma, 134, 142, 321-23, 333; and Cambodia, 134, 333; and Canada, 446; and Ceylon, 134; and China, 3; and Communist China, 4-9, 21, 72, 79-80, 82-86, 92-93, 97, 99, 102, 104, 110-11, 128-29, 131, 140, 214, 221, 231-33, 250-54, 305, 316, 430-45, 447-58, 510, 544-45; and Great Britain, 436, 446, 452; and Hong Kong, 202; and Hungary, 466; and India, 134, 141, 309, 443, 446, 531-32; and Indo-China, 98, 122; and Indonesia, 134, 142, 323-25; and Japan, 93, 108, 122-23, 133-34, 137-38, 141, 252-53, 255-56, 258, 260, 263, 265, 267, 273, 277, 280-82, 285-87; and Korea, 93, 288-89; and Korean War, 122, 253, 308, 345, 390, 435; and Laos, 123, 134, 138, 202, 299, 327-28, 333; and Malaya, 134; and military in Asia, 119, 122-25; and Nationalist China, 1, 93, 103, 122-23, 138, 139, 384, 416-17, 439, 464; and Nepal, 134; and New Zealand, 122; and Offshore Islands crises, 411, 413-16, 419-21, 423-26, 468; and Pakistan, 134, 309, 333; and Philippines, 122-23, 133, 329-30, 333; and Poland, 435, 456; and Southeast Asia, 298; and South Korea, 122-23, 131, 133, 138-39, 256, 329, 443; and South Vietnam, 123, 133, 138, 329, 333, 439, 443; and Soviet Union, 293, 340, 361-62, 368, 374, 382-83, 456; and Taiwan, 8, 33, 93, 121-27, 133, 373, 397, 401-9, 418-29, 437-38, 443, 464, 468; and Thailand, 123, 133, 138, 331-33; and UN, 447-53, 468; and Vietnam, 305; at Yalta, 341; and Yugoslavia, 456
U.S. Military Assistance Advisory Group on Taiwan, 403
Urban population, 55
Uttar Pradesh, 311

Vietminh, 98-99, 125, 330, 481-83; and Communist China, 291, 304, 495
Vietnam, 56, 90, 128, 406, 441; and China, 303-6; and Communist China, 78, 159, 304; Communist party in, 159, 162, 480-82; and Geneva, 99; and Overseas Chinese, 175-77, 179; and Thailand, 330; and UN, 98; and West, 320; *see also* North Vietnam, South Vietnam
Vietnamese Nationalist party, 304, 481
Vietnam Independence League, 481; *see also* Vietminh
Vietnam Revolutionary Youth Association, 160, 480
Vo Nguyen Giap, 482

INDEX

Wa States, 319, 322
Wan Waithayakon, Prince, quoted, 331-32
Wang Yen-shu, 495
Ward, Angus, 92
Warlordism, 11
Warsaw, 354, 361, 424, 434
Warsaw Pact, 117-18, 355
Water conservation, 52
West, the, 2, 96, 105, 320, 326; and Southeast Asia, 294, 328; and Soviet Union, 250, 371; and trade with Communist China, 225, 231-44
West Bengal, 500-1
West Europe, 110
West Germany, 232
West Irian, 323-24
"White Band PVO," 496-97
"White Flag" Communists, 161, 496
Wilbur, C. Martin, 280
Workers' parties, 362
"Workers' party" (Korea), 159, 477
World Federation of Trade Unions, 90, 152
World Peace Council, 95
World War II, 1, 5, 121, 160, 339-40; and Burma, 319; and Communist parties in Asia, 150-51, 476, 481, 493; and Indo-China, 304; and Japan, 120, 255, 285, 419; and Korea, 288; and Overseas Chinese, 174, 178, 180, 198; and Southeast Asia, 297; and Taiwan, 388, 410; and Thailand, 123
Wu Hsiu-ch'uan, 94
Wu, K. C., 391, 395

Yalta Conference, 341
Yalu River, 246, 345
Yeh Chi-chuang, 217
Yemen, 102, 233, 249
Yenan, 478
"Yenan Independence Alliance," 159, 476-77
Yoshida, Shigeru, 258-61, 263-65, 271
Young China party, 393
Young Communist League, 14, 115
Yüan (Taiwan), 395
Yüan Dynasty, 28, 386
Yüeh, 303
Yugoslavia, 358, 362-64, 456; and Communist China, 102, 107, 354, 356; and Soviet Union, 158, 337, 342, 349-50, 364, 380
Yunnan, 304, 498

Zhdanov, Andrei, 152-53, 156
Zhukov, Georgi, 363

A. DOAK BARNETT, a graduate of Yale University, wartime officer in the United States Marine Corps, and former member of the State Department, has written extensively on China for the Institute of Current World Affairs, the Chicago *Daily News* Foreign Service, and the American Universities Field Staff. He has contributed many articles to leading periodicals and is also the author of *Communist Economic Strategy: The Rise of Mainland China*. In the preparation of *Communist China and Asia* he had the advice of an expert study group at the Council on Foreign Relations. Mr. Barnett is now on the staff of the Ford Foundation.

THE TEXT of this book has been set in a type face called BASKERVILLE. The face is a facsimile reproduction of types cast from molds made for John Baskerville (1706–1775) from his designs.

VINTAGE WORKS OF SCIENCE AND PSYCHOLOGY

V-129	Beveridge, W. I. B.	THE ART OF SCIENTIFIC INVESTIGATION
V-11	Brill, A. A., M.D.	LECTURES ON PSYCHOANALYTIC PSYCHIATRY
V-168	Bronowski, J.	THE COMMON SENSE OF SCIENCE
V-169	Brown, Norman O.	LIFE AGAINST DEATH
V-160	Buchheim, Robert W. (ed.)	THE SPACE HANDBOOK
V-172	Chadwick, John	THE DECIPHERMENT OF LINEAR B
V-156	Dunbar, Flanders, M.D.	YOUR CHILD'S MIND AND BODY
V-157	Eiseley, Loren	THE IMMENSE JOURNEY
V-132	Freud, Sigmund	LEONARDO DA VINCI: *A Study in Psychosexuality*
V-14	Freud, Sigmund	MOSES AND MONOTHEISM
V-124	Freud, Sigmund	TOTEM AND TABOO
V-195	Groddeck, Georg	THE BOOK OF THE IT
V-150	Hooper, Alfred	MAKERS OF MATHEMATICS
V-74	Köhler, Wolfgang	THE MENTALITY OF APES
V-151	Kuhn, Herbert	ON THE TRACK OF PREHISTORIC MAN
V-164	Kuhn, Thomas S.	THE COPERNICAN REVOLUTION
V-105	Leslie, Charles (ed.)	ANTHROPOLOGY OF FOLK RELIGION (*A Vintage Original*)
V-76	Linton, Ralph	THE TREE OF CULTURE
V-70	Rank, Otto	THE MYTH OF THE BIRTH OF THE HERO *and Other Essays*
V-99	Redlich, Fritz, M.D. and Bingham, June	THE INSIDE STORY: *Psychiatry and Everyday Life*
V-109	Thruelsen and Kobler (eds.)	ADVENTURES OF THE MIND

A free catalogue of VINTAGE BOOKS will be sent to you at your request. Write to *Vintage Books, Inc.*, 457 Madison Avenue, New York 22, New York.

VINTAGE POLITICAL SCIENCE AND SOCIAL CRITICISM

V-198	Bardolph, Richard	THE NEGRO VANGUARD
V-185	Barnett, A. Doak	COMMUNIST CHINA AND ASIA
V-87	Barzun, Jacques	GOD'S COUNTRY AND MINE
V-705	Bauer, Inkeles, and Kluckhohn	HOW THE SOVIET SYSTEM WORKS
V-42	Beard, Charles A.	THE ECONOMIC BASIS OF POLITICS *and Related Writings*
V-60	Becker, Carl L.	DECLARATION OF INDEPENDENCE
V-17	Becker, Carl L.	FREEDOM AND RESPONSIBILITY IN THE AMERICAN WAY OF LIFE
V-199	Berman, H. J. (ed.)	TALKS ON AMERICAN LAW
V-44	Brinton, Crane	THE ANATOMY OF REVOLUTION
V-37	Brogan, D. W.	THE AMERICAN CHARACTER
V-196	Bryson, L., *et al.*	SOCIAL CHANGE IN LATIN AMERICA TODAY
V-30	Camus, Albert	THE REBEL
V-98	Cash, W. J.	THE MIND OF THE SOUTH
V-704	Deutscher, Isaac	STALIN: *A Political Biography*
V-707	Fischer, Louis	SOVIETS IN WORLD AFFAIRS
V-174	Goodman, Paul & Percival	COMMUNITAS
V-69	Hand, Learned	THE SPIRIT OF LIBERTY
V-95	Hofstadter, Richard	THE AGE OF REFORM
V-9	Hofstadter, Richard	THE AMERICAN POLITICAL TRADITION
V-201	Hughes, H. Stuart	CONSCIOUSNESS AND SOCIETY
V-104	Huxley, Aldous	BEYOND THE MEXIQUE BAY
V-193	Malraux, André	TEMPTATION OF THE WEST
V-726	Marcuse, Herbert	SOVIET MARXISM
V-102	Meyers, Marvin	THE JACKSONIAN PERSUASION
V-19	Milosz, Czeslaw	THE CAPTIVE MIND
V-101	Moos, Malcolm (ed.)	H. L. MENCKEN ON POLITICS: *A Carnival of Buncombe*
V-192	Morgenstern, O.	QUESTION OF NATIONAL DEFENSE
V-703	Mosely, Philip E.	THE KREMLIN AND WORLD POLITICS
V-128	Plato	THE REPUBLIC
V-719	Reed, John	TEN DAYS THAT SHOOK THE WORLD
V-179	Stebbins, Richard P.	U. S. IN WORLD AFFAIRS, 1959
V-204	Stebbins, Richard P.	U. S. IN WORLD AFFAIRS, 1960
V-206	Wallerstein, Emanuel	AFRICA: THE POLITICS OF INDEPENDENCE
V-145	Warren, Robert Penn	SEGREGATION
V-729	Weidlé, W.	RUSSIA: ABSENT & PRESENT